Department of Economic and Social Affairs
Population Division

ST/ESA/SER.A/155

TOO YOUNG TO DIE:
GENES OR GENDER?

United Nations
New York, 1998

NOTE

The designations employed and the presentation of the material in the present publication do not imply the expression of any opinion whatsoever on the part of the Secretariat of the United Nations concerning the legal status of any country, territory, city or area or of its authorities, or concerning the delimitation of its frontiers or boundaries.

The designations "developed" and "developing" economies are intended for statistical convenience and do not necessarily express a judgement about the stage reached by a particular country or area in the development process.

The term "country" as used in the text and tables refers, as appropriate, to territories or areas.

The views expressed in the papers are those of the individual authors and do not imply the expression of any opinion on the part of the United Nations Secretariat.

Papers have been edited and consolidated in accordance with United Nations practice and requirements.

ST/ESA/SER.A/155

United Nations publication
Sales No. E.98.XIII.13

ISBN 92-1-151325-1

PREFACE

The plight of the girl child is a significant research and policy issue. The *World Declaration on the Survival, Protection and Development of Children* adopted at the World Summit for Children in 1990 and *the Programme of Action* adopted at the International Conference on Population and Development (ICPD) in 1994 both call for efforts to eliminate all forms of discrimination against the girl child. In particular, the ICPD *Programme of Action* calls for the elimination of excess mortality of girls where it exists, and for special education and public information efforts to promote equal treatment of girls and boys with respect to nutrition and health care. In response to those concerns and the need to identify measures aimed at eliminating the pattern of excess and preventable mortality among young girls, the Population Division of the Department for Economic and Social Affairs of the United Nations Secretariat has undertaken a study of the sex differentials in infant, child and under-five mortality and the specific mechanisms that may lead to excess female mortality in childhood.

The results of the Population Division's study consists of 10 chapters that explore a broad range of mechanisms, ranging from the biological to the social and economic, that influence sex differentials in childhood mortality. The mechanisms considered affect mortality differentials either directly, as in the case of the nutritional status of boys and girls or the differential use of health care by sex of child, or indirectly, as in the case of maternal education and decisions regarding the intra-household allocation of resources. The study also provides a historical account of the evolution of the sex differentials in childhood mortality in today's developed countries during the nineteenth and early twentieth centuries. Another major contribution is its measurement and analysis of the levels and trends of infant, child and under-five mortality for boys and girls during the 1970s and 1980s. Such analysis allows the identification of the countries and regions in which girls have a survival disadvantage compared to boys, and permits an objective assessment of the magnitude and extent of excess female mortality in childhood.

The United Nations wishes to accord recognition and appreciation to the experts who prepared the papers presented in the present volume. Acknowledgement is also due to Mr. Kenneth Hill, Department of Population Dynamics, School of Hygiene and Public Health, Johns Hopkins University, who assisted in the evaluation of the estimates of mortality by sex that are presented, and to Mr. John Cleland, Centre for Population Studies, London School of Hygiene and Tropical Medicine, who served as scientific editor. Lastly, the financial contributions of the United Nations Population Fund and the United Nations Children's Fund to this project are gratefully acknowledged.

CONTENTS

FIGURES

Annex Tables

Explanatory notes

Symbol of United Nations documents are composed of capital letters combined with figures.

The following symbols have been used in the tables throughout the present publication:

Two dots (..) indicate that data are not available or are not reported separately.
An em dash (—) indicates that the amount is nil or negligible.
A hyphen (-) indicates that the item is not applicable.
A minus sign (-) before a number indicates a decrease.
A point (.) is used to indicate decimals.
A slash (/) indicates a crop year or financial year, e.g., 1988/1989.
Use of a hyphen (-) between dates representing years (e.g., 1985-1989), signifies the full period involved, including the beginning and end years.

Details and percentages in table do not necessarily add to totals because of rounding.

Reference to "dollars" ($) indicates United States dollars, unless otherwise stated.

The term "billion" signifies a thousand million.

The following abbreviations have been used:

ACC/SCN	United Nations Administrative Committee on Coordination/Subcommittee on Nutrition
ARI	Acute respiratory infection
CDC	Centers for Disease Control
DALY	Disability adjusted life-year
DHS	Demographic and Health Surveys
DPT	diphtheria, pertussis and tetanus vaccine
EPI	Expanded Programme on Immunization
ENDEF	Estudo Nacional da Despesa Familiar
FAO	Food and Agriculture Organization of the United Nations
FSH	Follicle-stimulating hormone
HIV	human immunodeficiency virus
ICRISAT	International Crops Research Institute for the Semi Arid Tropics
IMR	Infant mortality rate
INED	Institut national d'études démographiques
IUSSP	International Union for the Scientific Study of Population
MM	Mild-to-moderate malnutrition
MUAC	Mid-upper arm circumference
NCHS	National Centre for Health Statistics
NFHS	National Family Health Survey of India
OMIM - TM	On-line Mendelian Inheritance in Man
ORS	Oral rehydration solution
PAR	Population adjusted risk

SD	Standard deviation
SSS	Sugar-salt solution
SUSENAS	Indonesian Socio-economic Survey
TFR	Total fertility rate
UNICEF	United Nations Children's Fund
USAID	United States Agency for International Development
WFS	World Fertility Survey
WHO	World Health Organization

THE EXTENT AND CAUSES OF FEMALE DISADVANTAGE IN MORTALITY: AN OVERVIEW

Although major improvements in child survival have been achieved in developing countries over the past two decades, deaths to children under age 5 still account for 23 per cent of all deaths in those countries. Approximately one child in 20 dies before reaching school age, and in many countries that proportion is well over one in five. The plight of female children has attracted particular attention. In most low-income countries, girls lag well behind boys in primary and secondary school enrolment. As adults, they experience severe disadvantage in labour markets and in control over resources. There are justifiable concerns that such disparities between the sexes extend to life itself. At the 1994 International Conference on Population and Development, special emphasis was placed on the need to improve the health, welfare and survival of the girl child.

The central purpose of the present volume is to provide a scientific assessment of the health and survival of girls relative to boys so that future policies and programmes can be based on a correct understanding of the situation. The volume begins with a broad analysis of historical trends in sex-specific mortality in today's developed countries, but its main focus is on childhood mortality in developing countries since 1970. The central questions addressed in the volume are simple and stark. In what regions and countries are girls disadvantaged relative to boys in terms of health and survival? Has the magnitude of such disadvantage changed over the last 25 years? What behavioural mechanisms are involved? And what are the motives underlying the disadvantage? As will become apparent, some of those key questions can be answered with reasonable confidence. Others, however, still require further study before firm conclusions can be reached.

The relative survival of males and females has intrigued commentators for centuries, and has been a major preoccupation of modern epidemiology and demography. The present volume builds upon a considerable body of earlier scientific studies, most recently studies by Tabutin and Willems (1995) and by Hill and Upchurch (1995). Its unique contribution stems partly from the amount of relevant information that has been assembled. Estimates of sex differences in under-five mortality have been made for 82 out of a total of 100 developing counties with a population in excess of one million in 1990. Those 82 countries contain over 90 per cent of the population of the developing world. That central material is complemented by data on the nutritional status of boys and girls from 41 developing country surveys, and by chapters that address the mechanisms and motives that underlie female-male differences in health and survival.

A. TOWARDS A DEFINITION OF FEMALE MORTALITY DISADVANTAGE

The identification of female disadvantage in terms of health and survival has to take into account genetic differences between the sexes. Sex differences in mortality that arise from innate genetic factors need to be distinguished as clearly as possible from differences that reflect behavioural and environmental factors, such as child-care practices. The distinction is necessary because the latter factors, unlike the former, may reflect gender bias and are more amenable to corrective action. The term "female disadvantage" is used here to denote mortality or morbidity in females that arises from differences between the sexes in behavioural factors, which may reflect deliberate discrimination by adults in favour of males or other considerations that have little to do with any conscious bias.

Female disadvantage may be masked by biological factors that tend to favour girls. Thus, as noted in Hill and Upchurch (1995), the occurrence of higher childhood mortality in girls than in boys may be too stringent a criterion of female disadvantage. The fact that expectations of life in most societies are longer for women than for men is sometimes erroneously interpreted to signify that men are generally more vulnerable to disease than women. The evidence reviewed in chapters II and III emphasizes the diversity and complexity of the genetic influences on male-female differences in mortality, as well as their interaction with environmental factors.

The picture that emerges from the present review is that males do indeed suffer a considerable genetic disadvantage at very young ages. Although little is reliably known about sex differences in foetal mortality in the first month or so following conception, males have higher mortality than females in the third to the fifth month of gestational age. That sex difference attenuates in the third trimester but re-emerges strongly after birth. Males are invariably more likely to die from perinatal causes than females, probably due to the greater incidence of prematurity in males and the fact that their lungs are less well developed. That greater susceptibility of males compared with females extends to infectious disease mortality during infancy, probably because the male immune system is weaker than that of females.

Between ages 1 and 5, evidence of genetic disadvantage in boys is inconclusive. The evidence presented in chapter III below suggests that the risks of dying from respiratory infections are probably similar for both sexes, although the risks vary for deaths due to diarrhoeal diseases. Measles mortality, however, tends to be higher among girls than among boys. Indeed, the only common cause of childhood death that is nearly always more common among one sex than the other is accidents and violence. Using data for 18 middle-income developing countries, Taket (1986) has shown that mortality risks due to accidents are on average 34 per cent higher among young boys than among young girls. The vulnerability of boys probably stems from their greater physical activity, aggression and risk-taking propensities. Some studies have pointed to a genetic origin for that difference between the sexes: higher prenatal levels of testosterone may predispose boys to physical activity and aggression. Any such genetic predisposition is reinforced by widespread differences in the socialization of boys and girls.

The genetic evidence serves to demonstrate the difficulty of reaching an objective definition of female disadvantage or excess female mortality. Expected male-female mortality ratios depend on the level, age structure and cause-of-death structure of mortality. As risks of death from communicable diseases recede, the genetic vulnerability of males in the early weeks of life becomes an increasingly important determinant of sex differences in mortality. At the same time, the contribution of accidents and violence to total mortality tends to increase, and that factor also acts to elevate mortality risks among boys relative to girls. The review contained

in chapter III below also implies that the importance of specific types of infectious diseases may have to be taken into account in any attempt to define a standard by which to identify excess female mortality.

One approach to the problem is that adopted by Hill and Upchurch (1995). They use life-tables covering the period 1920-1964 for four north-western European countries and New Zealand to derive standard or expected mortality sex ratios in infancy and early childhood. Those countries are selected because the data are of high quality and span a wide range of mortality levels. The latter feature allows the authors to calculate expected mortality sex ratios for different overall levels of under-five mortality. A further reason for selecting those countries is the authors' assumption that any discrimination against girls is small and stable over time.

The information and analysis contained in chapter I permits an assessment of the validity of using the historical record of today's developed countries as a yardstick to evaluate sex-specific mortality in developing countries. The main analysis is based on 201 life-tables covering the period 1700-1930 for 24 countries, most of which are in Europe.

One of the important lessons to emerge from chapter I is the fact that in many of those countries, girls experienced higher mortality than boys between the ages of 5 and 14 years (see figure 2). Clearly, excess female mortality, however defined, is not unique to developing regions. Furthermore, the data presented in chapter I demonstrate that the mortality of females at ages 5-14 relative to boys worsened in many countries during the nineteenth century. Sharp differentials in death rates due to tuberculosis and other infectious diseases appear to be the main contributor to higher female than male mortality at those ages.

More relevant to the main focus of the present volume is the historical evidence concerning sex differentials in infant and early child mortality. The detailed country-specific data are contained in annex table A.1, and are summarized in figures 1 and 2. Male-to-female ratios of infant mortality lie within the range of 110 to 122 deaths in males per 100 deaths in females, with very few exceptions, during the period 1800-1900. Thereafter, there is a clear upward drift in the ratios towards 130. As expected, sex ratios in child mortality are closer to unity. During the nineteenth century, they typically range from 98-108. A small excess male mortality between ages one and four is widespread but not universal.

The analysis in chapter I provides a valuable historical perspective to the later chapters, which focus on developing country data for the 1970s and 1980s. The results suggest, for instance, that male-to-female ratios of infant mortality that fall appreciably below 110 are sufficiently unusual to arouse suspicions that females may be disadvantaged. Similarly, for child mortality, ratios that are appreciably below 100 constitute *prima facie* evidence of female disadvantage. For several reasons, however, the experience of European and other now developed countries in the nineteenth century cannot be used with confidence as a yardstick by which to identify and quantify female disadvantage in today's developing countries. Those reasons include: (a) the variability in mortality sex ratios both between and within the countries studied; (b) differences in the disease environment (malaria, for instance, is a major cause of childhood death in Africa but had been eliminated from much of Europe by the nineteenth century); (c) huge differences between the nineteenth and late twentieth centuries in the efficacy of both preventive and curative medical practices; and lastly (d) the untenability of the assumption that discrimination against girls was of minor importance in Europe and was stable over time.

Accordingly, a pragmatic approach to the measurement of female disadvantage is adopted in the present volume. Rather than impose an unsatisfactory numerical standard, the relationship between the health and survival of females and males will be described with an emphasis on a search for regional patterns and for consistency between the different strands of evidence. As will become apparent, such an approach succeeds in identifying those countries and regions where there is good reason to believe that girls are disadvantaged compared to boys.

B. SEX DIFFERENCES IN MORTALITY

The key results concerning male-female differences in mortality are contained in chapter IV. As mentioned earlier, relevant estimates were obtained for 82 developing countries with a population in excess of 1 million in 1990. Table 28 further specifies the geographical coverage of the mortality analysis within three major areas and 12 regions. In Latin America and the Carib-

bean, coverage is total. In Asia, estimates were obtained for only 25 out of 41 countries in the region, but those 25 cases contain 94 per cent of Asia's population (excluding Japan). For Africa, data were assembled for 34 of the 44 countries with a population of over 1 million, representing 77 per cent of Africa's total population. Thus, the results and conclusions presented in chapter IV are based not only on the experience of a large number of countries but also on a reasonable cross-section of countries from all major regions. That representativity is an important achievement because hitherto a disproportionately large number of published studies on sex differentials in mortality have covered only a single region, South-central Asia.

The accuracy of the data gathered is a crucial concern and is fully discussed in chapter IV. Considerable efforts were made to exploit all information sources for specific countries. Averaging procedures were used when two independent sources were available for the same time period, and consistency was enforced between indirect estimates of under-five mortality and direct estimates of the components of under-five mortality. Despite those steps to obtain the best possible estimates of sex differences in infant and child mortality, biases undoubtedly remain, and a degree of uncertainty surrounds any specific mortality sex ratio.

The uncertainty stemming from possible errors in measurement is reinforced by considerations of sampling precision. Many of the estimates presented in chapter IV are based, in part, on sample surveys of 5,000-10,000 households. Estimates of sex-specific mortality, even when based on the experience of all children born in the preceding 10 years, have large standard errors and correspondingly wide confidence intervals. It was impossible for the estimates presented in chapter IV to conduct formal tests to establish whether observed differences between male and female mortality were statistically significant because many of the estimates were derived from a combination of different data sources. However, for the estimates presented in chapter VIII it was feasible to test for statistical significance because the mortality data used in that chapter were derived from a single source, namely, enquiries conducted by the Demographic and Health Survey programme. The relevant data for 27 surveys may be found in table 62. Despite the wide variation in male-to-female mortality ratios, which ranged from 53-120, only one difference was found to be statistically significant at the 5 per cent level using the Cox-Mantel test. The implications are clear: the analysis of sex differentials in mortality should concentrate not on isolated results for specific countries (which may have arisen by chance) but on more pervasive patterns within regions. Furthermore, it is important to link the evidence on mortality with other forms of evidence concerning nutritional status, immunization and health-care practices in order to build a coherent and convincing analysis.

Both the historical analysis in chapter I and the review of biological evidence in chapters II and III lead to an expectation that mortality in infancy will be higher in boys than girls because of greater male vulnerability to most causes of infant death. Specifically, excess male mortality at those young ages is expected to lie in the range of 10-30 per cent, depending on the relative contributions of perinatal causes (to which boys are particularly vulnerable) and infectious diseases in the post-neonatal period (to which boys are probably relatively less vulnerable).

For all 82 countries, the median sex ratio of infant mortality is 118 male deaths per 100 female deaths. The median ratio is highest in Latin America and in Eastern and South-eastern Asia (at 123); intermediate in sub-Saharan Africa (116) and Northern Africa and Western Asia (111); and lowest in South-central Asia (108). Those summary figures suggest that the search for female disadvantage in infancy should focus initially on South-central Asia, and to a lesser extent on Northern Africa and Western Asia. Country-specific details are contained in table 29. It is immediately clear that the regional averages conceal considerable intraregional variation. In South-central Asia, unexpectedly low ratios are confined to Afghanistan, Bhutan, India and Nepal. In all those countries, the number of male deaths per 100 female deaths is below 110. Conversely, the ratios for Bangladesh, Pakistan and Sri Lanka are above 110, and are thus broadly consistent with the European experience of the nineteenth century and other developing regions in the past two decades.

There is similar variability in Northern Africa and Western Asia. Of the 14 countries with relevant estimates, only five (Algeria, Egypt, Jordan, the Libyan Arab Jamahirya and Syria) record ratios that are consistently below 110 male deaths per 100 female deaths. In a further two countries (Tunisia and Turkey), the estimated ratio for the 1970s is below 110 but that for the more recent decade is higher.

Do the summary figures for the other regions mask country-specific results that may imply a relative female disadvantage in infancy? In Latin America, the verdict is negative. Out of 42 estimates for the 1970s and 1980s, only two ratios (Colombia in the 1980s and Paraguay in the 1970s) fall below 110, and in both of those countries a second estimate for a different decade is higher. In sub-Saharan Africa, a total of 40 estimates is available. In four cases, the number of male deaths per 100 female deaths is fractionally below 110, with ratios of 108 or 109. Only in Madagascar (100), the Niger (102) and Nigeria in the 1980s (105) are lower ratios recorded. It is entirely possible that female infants in those three countries experience some disadvantage relative to males, but the results might equally well reflect errors in the data. On balance, there is little convincing evidence of female disadvantage in that region during infancy. In the fifth region, Eastern and South-eastern Asia, there is one clear and very important exception to the predominant pattern of high male to female ratios: China, where the ratio is estimated to be 106 for the 1980s. The importance of that result stems from the huge population size of China.

To sum up, examination of the sex ratios of infant mortality has identified certain countries in South-central Asia and in Northern Africa and Western Asia where there are unexpectedly large numbers of deaths of girls relative to boys. Outside of those two regions, the occurrence of similarly high relative death rates among female infants is rare and evidence of female disadvantage is correspondingly unconvincing. China appears to be a potentially important exception.

Death rates in the early childhood years of one to five are a more sensitive test of female disadvantage than infant mortality rates. At those ages, exogenous rather than genetic causes of death predominate. Thus, any inequalities in the treatment of sons and daughters are less likely to be masked by genetic factors, though interpretation is still complicated by the greater susceptibility of boys than of girls to death from accidents and violence.

For all 82 countries considered together, the analysis in chapter IV shows that risks of death between the ages of one and five years are similar for males and females. The median ratio is 100 male deaths per 100 female deaths. Once again, South-central Asia and to a lesser extent Northern Africa and Western Asia stand out as regions with unexpectedly high female mortality relative to male mortality. In South-central Asia, a total of 12 estimates is available. In all cases, the mortality of girls exceeds that of boys. The median value of the mortality sex ratio is 86. The most pronounced excess female mortality is found in Bangladesh, India and Nepal in the 1980s. In those three countries, girls are 20 to 30 per cent more likely to die in the childhood years than boys. In India and Nepal, evidence of unexpectedly high risks of death was also found in female infants, which further reinforces the case for female disadvantage.

In Northern Africa and Western Asia, 24 estimates are available. In 15 cases, female mortality is higher than male mortality. The median value is 93 male deaths per 100 females deaths. Excess female mortality appears to be most severe (15 per cent or more) in Egypt, Oman, the Syrian Arab Republic and Yemen. In the case of Oman and the Syrian Arab Republic, however, the estimates date from the 1970s and more recent data are unavailable. It should be noted that Egypt and the Syrian Arab Republic are among the countries in that region with evidence of female disadvantage in infancy.

The pattern of results for the other major developing regions is broadly uniform. In all three regions, the median value of childhood mortality sex ratio is very close to 100. In both sub-Saharan Africa and Latin America, the number of estimates indicating higher mortality for males is slightly greater than the number showing higher mortality for females. In East and South-eastern Asia, those numbers are equal. In all three regions, the countries experiencing higher female child mortality than that among males fail to display clear-cut geographical patterns, although in Latin America and Africa they tend to cluster in Central America (including Mexico) and in Western and Central Africa. However, in most of those countries, the female disadvantage in childhood is small, amounting to less than a 10 per cent difference between the death rates of girls and boys between the ages of one and five. Countries for which excess female child mortality is 10 per cent or higher include, in sub-Saharan Africa, Cameroon in the 1980s, Burundi, Namibia, the Niger and Togo. In Latin America, they include Paraguay in the 1980s, Guatemala, the Dominican Republic in the 1980s and Haiti in the 1970s. In East and South-eastern Asia, the only countries that record marked excess female mortality in childhood are China and the Philippines in the 1970s. Although those data suggest that there are countries in all regions where girls are at a

disadvantage with respect to boys in terms of mortality risks, it is important to assess the strength of the available evidence. In four of the countries identified above (Cameroon, the Dominican Republic, Haiti and the Philippines), estimates for a different decade are available and they are all relatively close to 100. Though sex differentials do not necessarily remain constant, that inconsistency nevertheless argues for a cautious interpretation. Furthermore, in none of those four countries was there evidence of higher than expected infant mortality among girls. For Paraguay and Guatemala, estimates are also available for both the 1970s and the 1980s. In Guatemala, both estimates show consistently high excess female mortality in childhood, though no corresponding evidence of female disadvantage in infancy. In Paraguay, interpretation is complicated by erratic changes in mortality sex ratios, which probably reflect data errors. It would be unwise, therefore, to place much interpretative weight on the above-mentioned figures. In the remaining six countries, only one estimate is available. In both China and the Niger, evidence of excess female mortality in childhood is buttressed by unusually high female mortality in infancy relative to male mortality. That leaves three African countries (Burundi, Namibia, and Togo), where there is no corresponding evidence of female disadvantage in infancy. Thus, the evidence of excess female mortality in childhood outside of the two regions where it is prevalent (South-central Asia and Northern Africa and Western Asia) is most convincing for China, the Niger and Guatemala, and suggestive, though less convincing, for Burundi, Namibia and Togo. That is, although child mortality among girls is higher than that among boys in nearly half of the countries in Africa, Latin America and Eastern and South-eastern Asia, the differences in most cases are small and cannot be given much weight, except for the cases singled out above.

C. TRENDS IN SEX-SPECIFIC MORTALITY

Estimates of sex-specific mortality for both the 1970s and the 1980s are available for a total of 52 countries. Though a decade is a short period in which to expect appreciable changes in the relative survival of males and females, large declines in overall under-five mortality rates were recorded in many developing countries during that period. Those gains in child survival may have favoured one sex more than the other, so that shifts in ratios of male to female mortality might be anticipated.

5

For all 52 countries, the overall picture changes little between the 1970s and the 1980s. The median ratio of male to female deaths in infancy increased marginally from 118 to 119, as did the median ratio in childhood from 100 to 101. Disaggregation of those trends by region shows that male-to-female ratios in infant mortality increased in all regions except for East and South-eastern Asia. Thus, the gap between male and female infant mortality appears to be widening gradually.

The results in the childhood years of one to five are more interesting. In the countries of Northern Africa and Western Asia for which relevant estimates are available, the results suggest an improvement in the relative survival of females. The median ratio rose from 93 in the 1970s to 101 in the 1980s, implying that a 7 per cent excess female mortality in the earlier period disappeared in the 1980s. Out of the 10 countries in that region, seven experienced a relative improvement for females. In one, no change was observed and in two cases a relative deterioration was recorded. Those figures constitute powerful evidence that the survival of girls increased slightly more than that of boys between the 1970s and 1980s in Northern Africa and Western Asia. Evidence from other analyses suggest that that trend marks a continuation of a longstanding relative improvement in the health and welfare of girls.

Trends in South-central Asia appear to have moved in a different direction. Among the five countries of that region for which relevant data are available, an 11 per cent excess female mortality in the 1970s deepened into a 22 per cent excess in the 1980s. That relative deterioration of female survival appears to have a long history, stretching back to the early part of the twentieth century. Examination of results for individual countries, however, reveals considerable variation. In Pakistan and Sri Lanka, the relative survival chances of girls in childhood appear to have improved between the 1970s and the 1980s. In Bangladesh, India and Nepal, the relative survival chances of girls worsened. The result for India is particularly striking and important because of its large population. In the 1970s, excess female mortality in childhood was estimated at 11 per cent, but by the 1980s, the excess had grown to 28 per cent.

The data for Latin America and the Caribbean also provide grounds for concern that childhood survival trends may have favoured boys more than girls. Information for 18 countries is available. In nine countries,

the male-to-female childhood mortality ratio declined, compared with seven countries where it increased. In the 1970s, the median value showed a 6 per cent survival advantage for females. By the 1980s, that advantage had been reduced to 3 per cent.

That evidence for Latin America of a slight but pervasive relative deterioration in childhood survival chances for girls is particularly surprising in view of the low levels of overall childhood mortality in the 1980s. For those 18 countries, the mean level of childhood mortality (q_1) dropped from 28.3 per 1,000 in the 1980s to 13.6 per 1,000 in the 1980s, a 50 per cent decline. The expectation, based on the historical experience of developed countries, is for an increase in the male-female mortality difference because of a growing contribution of deaths due to accidents and violence to total deaths. Boys, it will be recalled, are more vulnerable to deaths due to those causes.

In sub-Saharan Africa, mortality in childhood remains much higher than in Latin America and the gains recorded between the 1970s and the 1980s were more modest. Moreover, many countries in that region suffered severely from the global recession of the 1980s. Falling household incomes may have led to attitudes that have favoured boys over girls, particularly with regard to the use of expensive curative health care. Trend data for 12 countries in sub-Saharan Africa permit an assessment of that proposition. In seven of those countries, the ratio of male to female probabilities of dying rose, and the median value changed from 101 to 104 male deaths per 100 female deaths. Thus, on average, in sub-Saharan Africa gains in survival for females appear to have outpaced those for males by a small margin.

In conclusion, the information provided in chapter IV about trends in male-to-female mortality ratios reveals a complex situation. Between the 1970s and 1980s, the situation of girls during the childhood years has improved appreciably in Northern Africa and Western Asia. Many countries of that region have also achieved large increases in school enrolments for girls. In sub-Saharan Africa, a marginal improvement in the relative survival of girls may have occurred, but in Latin America the trend has been in the opposite direction. Lastly, the evidence for several South-central Asian countries indicates that the survival chances of girls in childhood have actually worsened compared with those of boys.

D. SEX DIFFERENCES IN HEALTH STATUS

Of the myriad of possible indicators of health status in young children, it is widely accepted that simple measures of height and weight in relation to each other and to a child's chronological age provide the most useful overall assessment. That usefulness stems from the fact the anthropometric or nutritional indicators derived from weight and height reflect the combined effects of past and recent diet, morbidity and childcare. The relative contribution of those three factors to impaired nutritional status varies, but it is well established that they operate synergistically. Thus, infections affect the body's ability to absorb, transport, store and utilize nutrients, and that reduced ability erodes the body's capacity to resist and respond to infection. Preventive and curative health care affects health status because of its influence on the incidence, duration and severity of illness. To a large extent, death and malnutrition have common causes, and death represents the visible tip of the malnutrition iceberg.

The nutritional status of young boys and girls provides the central theme of two chapters. Chapter V presents a review of the causes and consequences of malnutrition, while chapter VI undertakes an empirical analysis of sex difference in nutritional status, drawing on data from recent surveys in developing countries.

The review of prospective studies in chapter V shows that mortality increases steeply as nutritional status (weight-for-age) deteriorates. Specifically, it increases on average at a compounded rate of 5.9 per cent for each percentage point decline in weight-for-age. Relative to the risks in well-nourished children, the risks of death for children with severe, moderate and mild malnutrition are 8.4, 4.6 and 2.4 times greater, respectively. Remarkably, the power of malnutrition to predict subsequent mortality appears to be similar in settings that have different disease environments, cultures and absolute levels of mortality.

The discussion in chapter V provides an ideal introduction to chapter VI, which presents nationally representative data on nutritional status for 35 countries, collected between 1986 and 1994 in 41 surveys in the Demographic and Health Surveys programme. Three indicators of nutritional status have been calculated: height-for-age, weight-for-age and weight-for-height. Low height-for-age—or stunting—reflects relatively long-term or chronic undernutrition. Low weight-for-height—or wasting—reflects the effects of recent morbidity or deficient food intake. Low weight-for-age is a composite indicator that may reflect stunting, wasting or both. An International Reference Population is used to classify the percentage of children who are suffering from each of those three dimensions of undernutrition.

The key results cover children aged from 3-35 months of age, though results from a subset of surveys are also available for all children under the age of five. The impression gained from all 41 surveys taken as a whole is that sex differences in nutritional status are generally very small in magnitude, and in most cases are within the bounds of sampling fluctuation. The median percentage of boys classified as stunted is 30.0, compared to 28.7 for girls. For wasting, the corresponding values are 5.5 and 4.1, and for low weight-for-age, 25.5 and 23.2. Inspection of individual estimates indicates that in the majority of populations, girls are slightly less likely than boys to suffer undernutrition. Thus, stunting is less common among girls than boys according to 35 out of the 41 surveys considered. The results for wasting favour females in 34 surveys, and those for low weight-for-age favour females in 30 surveys.

When the data are disaggregated by age, the same pattern is repeated for infants and for children aged one year (see figures 33, 34 and 35). However, among older children, the nutritional advantage of girls largely disappears. Among children aged 24-35 months and 36-59 months, girls are slightly more likely than boys to be underweight-for-age. With regard to stunting, levels in girls exceed those among boys at ages 24-35 months in 24 out of 41 surveys, though in the older age group the advantage of girls is reasserted. A plausible interpretation of those age differences in the relative nutritional status of boys and girls may be given. At ages below two years, the genetic vulnerability of boys to infection reduces their nutritional status relative to girls. Above the age of two years, that genetic difference is no longer relevant and the advantage of girls disappears, or in many countries is reversed.

Two countries from South-central Asia are included in the analysis: Pakistan and Sri Lanka. Girls in Pakistan record better nutritional status than boys. However, in Sri Lanka, girls are slightly more likely than boys to be stunted and underweight-for-age. Relevant information on nutritional status is also available from enquiries conducted under the auspices of the United Nations Children's Fund (UNICEF) (UNICEF, 1993). They show that even in countries where there is strong evidence of female disadvantage in mortality, the nutritional status of boys and girls is similar. For instance, the prevalence of low weight-for-age is 1-6 per cent higher among girls than boys in China but 1-9 per cent lower among girls than boys in India.

The fact that in all major developing regions the nutritional status of girls is little different from that of boys strongly suggests that systematic neglect of girls in terms of diet and domestic care is uncommon. The finding has major implications for an understanding of the mechanisms that are responsible for excess female mortality, which—as has already been shown—is widespread in South-central Asia and Northern Africa and Western Asia.

E. MECHANISMS

While the earlier chapters in the present volume lay out the descriptive evidence concerning the relative survival and health of young girls and boys in developing countries, the later chapters address the mechanisms and motives that underlie those sex differences. Following the well- known framework of Mosely and Chen (1974) and the diagrams provided in chapter V, the biomedical and behavioural mechanisms that may affect differentially the survival of the two sexes can be categorized. The first such category concerns exposure to infection or other life-threatening hazards. Daughters and sons may experience differential exposure to risk if their activities differ or are supervised in different ways, or if different standards of hygiene are imposed on them. The second category concerns resistance to infection. As already discussed, biological or genetic differences between males and females are a crucial consideration here, particularly in the early months of life. Nutritional status, itself determined by the synergistic effects of diet and morbidity, is a key influence on resistance. Of equal relevance is vaccination against infectious diseases. A third block of factors may be termed response to illness or personal illness control. Included here are both the domestic response to symptoms of distress in children and resort to health services. A final category of mechanisms—maternal factors—is identified by Mosely and Chen. They include the nutritional status of the mother, her age at the birth of successive children and other characteristics of family formation, such as spacing between successive births. Most of those factors are not of prime interest to the topic of sex differences in

mortality because many maternal characteristics will be the same for sons and daughters. However, birth spacing may differ by sex for reasons that are discussed later.

No attempt is made in the present volume to measure possible sex differentials in exposure to infection or other hazards. Indeed, the measurement of such exposure in large representative samples would be impossibly difficult because it would require detailed observations coupled with biomedical assessment of pathogenic risk in different micro-environments. In many if not all societies, there is probably no great difference between young girls and boys in terms of their exposure to infection, except for a difference disadvantaging boys in exposure to fatal accidents and violence.

Two dimensions of resistance to infection are explored. The first is nutritional status, which are considered in chapters V and VI. The conclusions are clearcut. In most developing countries, girls have similar levels of undernutrition to boys, and that generalization holds true even in settings where childhood death rates are markedly higher for girls than boys. That result implies but does not prove that the diets and domestic welfare of girls and boys do not differ radically. An alternative interpretation is that a greater susceptibility in males to infection is largely offset by superior nutritional intake.

A second dimension of resistance to infections is examined in chapter VII, which analyses data on immunization collected for children aged under five years in 44 national surveys conducted by the Demographic and Health Surveys programme between 1986 and 1994, together with the 1992-1993 National Family Health Survey of India. Results for India are presented at the national level and for northern and southern states of India separately. The rationale for that subnational breakdown is evidence that women have higher status and autonomy in the southern states than in the northern ones.

Differentials by sex in the probability of receiving any vaccination or in the probability of receiving the full series of doses of recommended vaccines are small in most parts of the world, and do not clearly favour either sex. Results are available for only three countries in South-central Asia, but they prove to be a striking exception to the general picture of equality between the sexes. In Bangladesh, northern India (but not southern India) and Pakistan, boys are significantly more likely

8

than girls to have received any vaccination and to have received a measles vaccination. The result for measles is particularly important because of evidence that vaccination against that disease exerts a powerful influence on survival. Among children who were given any vaccination, the proportion fully vaccinated was also higher for boys than girls in northern India and Pakistan but not in Bangladesh. Those results are entirely consistent with evidence of severe excess female mortality in childhood in Bangladesh and India. In Pakistan, data for the 1970s indicated a 19 per cent female excess, which shrank to a 10 per cent excess in the 1980s.

Can differential immunization coverage also help to explain the slight female mortality disadvantage in Northern Africa and Western Asia? Results are available for six countries. In Jordan and Morocco, there is little or no difference in immunization coverage between the sexes. In Egypt and the Sudan, there is a very slight male advantage, which becomes more apparent in Tunisia and Yemen. Thus, the proposition that excess female mortality in that region reflects differential treatment of boys and girls in that aspect of preventive care receives only weak support.

Sex differences in morbidity may reflect variability in exposure or resistance, and are thus not amenable to simple interpretation. Most small studies have found higher morbidity in boys than girls, and that impression is confirmed in tables 51, 52 and 53. The data in those tables are derived from subsets of the same 44 national surveys that furnished the immunization results. They are presented as a background to the analysis of treatment, but are also of interest in their own right. The information was gathered by questioning mothers about the occurrence of specified symptoms in surviving children under the age of five during the two weeks prior to interview, but no attempt was made to measure severity. To the extent that mothers are more sensitive to signs of illness of sons rather than daughters or vice versa, their morbidity reports will give a biased indication of genuine sex differences in the occurrence of recent illness.

Bearing in mind that caveat, the results suggest that the prevalence of morbidity is slightly higher among boys than girls. That difference is most marked for the symptoms of diarrhoeal diseases. In 38 of the 44 surveys, symptoms were more likely to be reported for sons than for daughters, and in 13 surveys, the difference was statistically significant. In the case of fever and

symptoms of respiratory infection, the results again show higher morbidity in males, though the male-female contrasts tend to be smaller and less consistent in direction across surveys than for diarrhoeal morbidity.

When attention is focused on countries with excess female mortality in childhood, the same pattern emerges. In northern India, all three symptom types are more likely to be reported for sons than for daughters. Despite genuine concerns about gender biases in reporting, it nevertheless seems most improbable that differential exposure or resistance to common infectious diseases (except perhaps for the immunizable diseases) is relevant to an understanding of excess female mortality. To the contrary, the morbidity information for South-central Asia and for Northern Africa and Western Asia implies that, all other factors being equal, mortality should be higher among males rather than lower.

In settings where morbidity from infections that account for the majority of deaths in childhood is higher among boys than girls and yet girls are more likely to die, the explanation for excess female mortality must stem from differences in case-fatality. As discussed above, case-fatality is determined largely by nutritional status, but it has already been shown that boys and girls differ little in that regard. The other major determinant of case-fatality is curative care, both within the home and from specialist health providers.

Several small-scale studies have shown large sex differences in the treatment of sick children. Chapter VII undertakes a systematic examination of that topic, using data from 44 Demographic and Health Survey enquiries. Among children for whom symptoms of diarrhoeal disease, fever and respiratory infections were reported in the two weeks preceding interview, information was collected on receipt of any treatment, the source of treatment and the nature of treatments. The latter two items permit a crude classification between more and less effective treatment. That information is used in chapter VII to compare the proportions of boys and girls who receive any treatment, and among those treated, the proportions for whom more effective care was sought. The detailed results are shown in tables 51, 52 and 53.

Considering all surveys together, there is little evidence of widespread or pronounced disparities in the curative health care of boys and girls. The median number of boys who received treatment of any sort per 100 girls treated is 102 for diarrhoea, and 101 for both

9

fever and respiratory infections. Among children treated in any way, the corresponding numbers of boys per 100 girls who were taken to a modern health facility or provider are 98, 104 and 101. Analysis of the nature of treatment yields a similar overall impression. For instance, among children who were treated in any way for diarrhoea, 104 boys per 100 girls received oral rehydration solution (ORS) packets. For fever, the corresponding ratio is 101 for receipt of antimalarials or antibiotics and, for symptoms of respiratory infections, again 101 boys per 100 girls among those treated were given antibiotics.

Those findings have limitations, as noted in chapter VII. There is no information on severity of illness episodes or on the speed with which expert advice and treatment were sought, nor on compliance with medical advice. Nevertheless, they strongly suggest that in many developing countries, there is little or no bias in favour of sons over daughters in the treatment of common childhood illnesses.

Regional patterns are shown in figures 40, 41 and 42. For sub-Saharan Africa, the general impression of near-equality holds. The number of surveys showing a male advantage in treatment is balanced by the number showing the opposite. Of the 23 statistically significant sex differences in the various indicators of treatment, 13 show a divergence favouring boys and 10 a difference favouring girls. That result is consistent with the evidence concerning mortality, nutritional status and immunization coverage.

In the earlier mortality analysis, the Niger was singled out as the only country in sub-Saharan Africa with convincing evidence of a female disadvantage, while in Burundi, Namibia and Togo the evidence of such a disadvantage was found but was less strong. The information on curative health care lends considerable support to the conclusion of female disadvantage in the Niger . That country is one of only five where boys are more likely than girls to be treated for all three symptoms. Moreover, two of those differences are statistically significant. The information on quality of treatment points in the same direction, particularly with regard to fever and symptoms of respiratory infections. Sex differences in curative care thus appear to provide at least a partial explanation for excess female mortality in that country. Togo is also one of the few countries where treatment probabilities are higher among boys for all three symptoms. The differences are small and not statistically significant, and are not corroborated by results on effective therapy. Nevertheless, they support the conclusion of female mortality disadvantage in Togo. In the other two countries, Burundi and Namibia, the information in chapter VII lends no support to the earlier impression of a female mortality disadvantage.

For Latin America and the Caribbean, data from nine surveys in eight countries are available. Although there is little difference between the sexes in the probability of receiving any type of treatment, there is a distinct tilt in favour of boys with regard to the probable quality of treatment. There are five statistically significant differences relating to type of facility or practitioner visited and the therapy given to the child, all of which show a male advantage. Here, then, is one plausible explanation for the earlier finding that the survival of boys improved more rapidly between the 1970s and the 1980s than that of girls.

Guatemala was identified earlier as the country in that region with the most convincing evidence of excess female mortality. The results relating to curative care of diarrhoeal disease show that girls are more likely to receive any treatment but among children treated are less likely than boys to be taken to a modern health facility or to be given ORS. None of those differences is statistically significant. Thus, those data do not provide further support for the existence of a marked female disadvantage in that country.

In Northern Africa and Western Asia, only six countries are represented, though in a couple of cases two surveys have been conducted, giving a total of eight sets of results. Information on fever morbidity and its treatment, however, was obtained in only two surveys. Sex differentials in receipt of any treatment exhibit an unmistakable bias in favour of boys. Of the five statistically significant differences, all are in the direction of higher treatment probabilities for boys than girls. In terms of the likely effectiveness of treatment, a bias towards males is less evident. Although the only two significant differences favour boys, the number of surveys showing higher levels of effective treatment among boys is balanced by the number showing the opposite. Thus, for Northern Africa and Western Asia, the data on curative care by sex provide only a weak confirmation of the existence of female mortality disadvantage.

Special interest is attached to the results in South-central Asia because of evidence of high excess female mortality and consistent sex differences in immunization coverage. Results relating to curative care are available for only four countries (Bangladesh, India, Pakistan and Sri Lanka). In Sri Lanka, information for only one morbid condition (diarrhoea) was obtained, and the results show a slight but not significant male advantage. In Bangladesh, information is available for two types of morbidity. Among children with reported symptoms of diarrhoeal disease, there is a slight female advantage in receipt of any treatment and in resort to a modern health facility or practitioners. However, among those treated, boys are significantly more likely to be given ORS than girls. With regard to children with symptoms of respiratory infection, levels of treatment are significantly higher for boys than girls, and boys are also more likely to be taken to a health facility. Those results may be taken as evidence of a bias towards boys in terms of curative health care, though in view of the very high excess female mortality in Bangladesh, the differences in receipt of health care are not as clear-cut as might have been expected. In Pakistan, sex differences in the indicators of curative health care are small and do not clearly favour either sex.

As with the analysis of immunization coverage, results for India are presented at the national level and separately for northern and southern states. The results for the northern states show a clear bias in favour of boys, who are significantly more likely than girls to receive treatment for all three morbid conditions. Furthermore, among those treated in any way, boys are significantly more likely to be taken to a health facility or practitioner for two of the three conditions. Those results, taken together with the immunization data, constitute unambiguous evidence of a bias that favours sons over daughters.

In southern India, excess female mortality in childhood is less severe than in the northern states. For instance, the results of the 1992-1993 National Family Health Survey show an excess of 33 per cent for the northern states, compared with 18 per cent for the southern states. Nevertheless, the disparity in the south is considerable when assessed against the experience of countries of other regions. The data on curative health care support that perspective. Boys are more likely to receive any treatment for all three symptom categories, though differences are less marked than in the northern states and none is statistically significant. Perhaps more

striking is the evidence that boys receive more effective treatment than girls. They are, for instance, significantly more likely to be taken to a modern health facility or practitioner for two of the three morbid conditions considered.

In conclusion, the results on sex differences in curative health care suggest that that factor is a major mechanism underlying excess female mortality. In South-central Asia, where there is evidence of severe excess female mortality, curative health care clearly favours boys over girls. In Northern Africa and Western Asia, where excess female mortality is modest and has diminished over time, the evidence on curative health care also shows a slight bias in favour of boys. A similar slight bias is apparent in Latin America, which offers a possible explanation for the unexpected trends in sex-specific mortality between the 1970s and the 1980s. In sub-Saharan Africa, boys and girls in most countries generally receive similar curative health care, and that equality is consistent with the mortality data.

In chapter IX, an investigation is undertaken of a very different mechanism that may contribute to a female disadvantage in survival. The central hypothesis is that in societies preferring sons, the birth of a daughter will be followed more swiftly by another birth than in the case of the birth of a son. That sequence is plausible because parents in such societies, having delivered a daughter, may be eager to have another child relatively soon in the hope that the additional child will be a son. Conversely, parents to whom a son has been born may be more likely to discontinue childbearing altogether or to delay the next birth. Such a pattern of family formation may disadvantage girls because children who experience a short interval to the birth of a younger sibling are known to be at higher risk of death than other children.

The possible contribution of that factor to excess female mortality is assessed for three countries that are characterized by evidence of a preference for sons: Bangladesh, Egypt and the Republic of Korea. In all three countries, the authors demonstrate that family formation patterns are influenced by the sex of a child. Daughters are more likely than sons to be followed by another birth within five years. The second part of the analysis shows that in Egypt, 5 per cent of the overall excess female mortality in childhood can be attributed to the greater probability that the birth of girls be followed by a short birth interval. In Bangladesh, the contribution of short birth intervals to excess female mortality was less than in Egypt, probably because birth intervals in general are longer than in Egypt. Lastly, the analysis for the Republic of Korea shows that short birth intervals following the birth of girls account for much of the higher than expected level of under-five mortality among girls.

The overall conclusion is that birth spacing patterns probably contribute to excess female mortality in countries where parents tend to desire sons more than daughters. However, that pathway of influence probably cannot account for more than a small fraction of the overall female mortality disadvantage in most countries. Nevertheless, the findings do suggest that the claims of deliberate discrimination against girls based on parity-specific probabilities of dying need to be reviewed, taking into account family formation patterns and birth intervals.

F. MOTIVES

The topic of the motives or considerations that underlie sex differences in childhood mortality is discussed in chapter X. A neo-classical economic framework is used, in which the distinction is made between unequal treatment of boys and girls that reflects preferences favouring one sex over the other and unequal treatment that stems from the pursuit of other goals, such as maximizing the productivity of the household. The former represents gender discrimination; the latter reflects rational choices that household decision takers perceive to be in their own interests. Thus, sex differentials in food allocation or in curative health care may arise from the perception that future income flows from sons are likely to be greater than those of daughters. Such behaviour by parents or other adults implies a stronger concern for productivity than equity but nevertheless needs to be distinguished from more innate gender-specific preferences or biases that imply a greater concern for the welfare of children of one sex than for the other.

The discussion in chapter X serves as a warning against cavalier and oversimplified interpretations of excess female mortality in terms of gender discrimination. It also emphasizes the extreme complexity of identifying the forces that underlie unequal treatment of sons and daughters. To date, very few empirical studies have collected sufficient empirical data or have used

sufficiently refined modelling techniques to permit confident conclusions about the origins of sex differentials in health or survival. To some commentators, the distinctions made in chapter X may seem unimportant. Unequal treatment of boys and girls, as for instance in resort to preventive and curative health services, is deplorable whatever the motives of household decision takers. However, the design of appropriate policies depends on a correct identification of underlying motives. If greater parental investment in sons, particularly in times of financial hardship, stems from a perception that greater returns will accrue than would accrue from investment in daughters, then the situation may be resistant to change until greater gender equality in labour markets and control over resources is achieved.

Those considerations have particular force in South-central Asia, where unequal treatment of boys and girls is most marked and widespread. In many countries of that region, dowry systems prevail and daughters retain little contact with their natal homes after marriage. Conversely, sons retain greater contact with parents after marriage and assume prime responsibility for old-age support. It is entirely plausible to argue that those features of socio-economic organization in parts of South-central Asia are primarily responsible for unequal investments in boys and girls, which in turn lead to excess female mortality.

One possibility raised in chapter X is that parental resource allocations may vary with the characteristics of individual children. A closely related idea is examined in chapter IX. In that chapter, the survival of sons and daughters according to sex composition of older siblings is analysed. A particular interest attaches to the relative survival of girls who have older sisters and those who do not, because previous studies have suggested that second or higher order daughters fare worse than first order daughters. One interpretation of that pattern is that parents, even in son-preferring societies, want one daughter but no more. Thus, girls who have an older sister may be particularly undervalued and may suffer from conscious or subconscious neglect.

In chapter IX, the results for Egypt support the results of earlier studies. Girls with older sisters are more likely to die than girls with older brothers but no sisters. However, the results for Bangladesh differ. According to the analysis for that country, girls with older brothers suffer higher mortality than girls with older sisters only. The authors hypothesize that the extreme poverty of many Bangladeshi households may act against the interests of daughters who have brothers. Limited resources are allocated disproportionately to sons. Daughters who have no brothers do not face such competition.

Chapter VIII also contains information relevant to the discussion of motives that underlie excess female mortality. The authors single out one household characteristic—the education of the mother—and assess whether it mediates sex differences in mortality, nutritional status or health care. Mother's education is selected because of its powerful effect on overall child survival, and because maternal characteristics are likely to be of particular importance to the welfare of children since mothers are typically the prime carers of children. The general expectation is that any unequal treatment of boys and girls will be greater among families with an uneducated than with a more educated mother. Some slight confirmation is found. The nutritional advantage of girls is slightly greater in the group with an educated mother. And in some countries, a male advantage in terms of curative health care is found for children with an uneducated mother but not among those whose mother is better educated.

G. Conclusions

At the outset of the present overview, a number of key questions were posed. The search for answers provided the underlying purpose of the volume and a framework for its scope and contents. One of the key questions was: *"In what regions and countries are girls disadvantaged relative to boys in terms of health and survival?"* The massive amount of evidence presented in the following nine chapters permits a relatively clear answer. It has emerged that girls are most severely disadvantaged in South-central Asia. Among the larger countries of that region, the situation of girls relative to boys was found to be worst in Bangladesh, India (particularly in the northern states) and Nepal. In the 1980s, girls were about 25 per cent more likely to die between the ages of one and five than boys. In Pakistan, there was also consistent evidence of female disadvantage, though its magnitude may be less than in the other three countries.

Northern Africa and Western Asia is the only other subregion for which evidence of a widespread female mortality disadvantage was found. That situation is less severe than in South-central Asia, however, and is more variable between different countries. Moreover, recent trends have favoured girls and thereby reduced the disparities by sex in childhood survival rates.

Outside of those two regions, evidence of female disadvantage is much less clear-cut. In sub-Saharan Africa, there are few convincing signs that girls fare less well than boys in terms of health and survival. The Niger and to a lesser extent Togo appear to be exceptions to that generalization. The conclusion for Latin America and the Caribbean is similar to that for sub-Saharan Africa, though there are worrying signs that girls have benefited less than boys from recent improvements in child survival. In Eastern and South-eastern Asia, relevant evidence is less abundant than for other subregions, but again there is no convincing evidence of widespread female disadvantage. China is a crucially important exception. In that vast country, the gap between male and female infant mortality rates is suspiciously narrow, and although overall childhood mortality is very low, girls are more likely to die than boys between the ages of one and five.

Perhaps the most important conclusion that may be drawn from the present volume is that discrimination against girls in ways that affect their health and survival is by no means universal in developing countries. To the contrary, it exists in only a small minority of developing countries, most of which are located in South-central Asia, and to a lesser extent in Northern Africa and Western Asia. However, that geographical concentration should not be allowed to conceal the fact that in terms of the size of population affected, the problem of female disadvantage is very significant: the countries of South-central Asia and China contain half of the world's population. One interpretation of the data reviewed in the present volume is that 50 per cent of humanity lives in countries where gender inequality results in excess or surplus mortality of girls.

It is also possible to express in a very crude fashion the implications of gender inequality in terms of the number of deaths to under-five girls. In the absence of the severe disadvantages that girls face in South-central Asia and China, the conservative assumption can be made that girls would be 10 per cent less likely than boys to die in infancy and equally likely to die between the ages of one and five. Those expected ratios can then be applied to the observed level of male mortality and the numbers of births in the larger countries of South-central Asia and China to give an estimate of the expected numbers of female deaths in the absence of severe gender inequality. That hypothetical estimate can be subtracted from the observed number of female deaths to give the number of girls who die each year under the age of five because of some form of gender inequality.

Those calculations suggest that about 250,000 girls die each year in South-central Asia and China because they experience some disadvantage relative to boys. By far the biggest contribution to that total comes from India, because that country has a large population, high overall childhood mortality and a particularly pronounced degree of excess female mortality.

That figure of 250,000 excess deaths gives some idea of the global scale of the problem. The gravity of the situation is further emphasized by the analysis of trends. The second central question posed at the start of the present overview was: *"Has the magnitude of female disadvantage changed over the last 25 years?"* The single most disturbing result of the present enquiry is the conclusion that the survival of girls relative to boys has worsened in those countries of South-central Asia where female disadvantage was initially most severe. For instance, in India, an 11 per cent excess female mortality between ages one and five found in the 1970s has deepened to a 28 per cent excess in the 1980s. The corresponding figures are 15 and 24 per cent for Bangladesh and 8 and 22 per cent for Nepal. Though overall childhood mortality continues to decline in those countries, the relative plight of girls has become worse.

There are also signs in Latin America and the Caribbean that the huge gains in child survival between the 1970s and 1980s have benefited boys rather more than girls. In the 1970s, girls were about 6 per cent less likely to die in childhood than boys. By the 1980s, that difference had narrowed to 3 per cent. That trend is particularly unexpected because it runs counter to the experience of the developed countries. In those countries, big declines in childhood mortality were associated with a widening gap in the relative survival of boys and girls, partly because of the growing contribution of violent and accidental causes of death to which boys are particularly susceptible.

The last key issue addressed in the present volume concerns the mechanisms and motives that underlie female disadvantage. The data on nutritional status reveal little systematic difference between boys and girls.

Even in countries with clear evidence of a female mortality disadvantage, the physical growth of girls - their height for age, weight for height or weight for age - matches that of boys, which strongly suggests that discrimination against daughters in terms of diet and day-to-day care is uncommon. However, that implied equality between the sexes is not maintained with regard to health care use outside the home. In South-central Asia, there is evidence of a clear bias in favour of boys in terms of curative health care. Sick sons are more likely to be treated and to receive effective treatment than sick daughters. That statement applies most strongly to the northern states of India, where boys are also more likely to be immunized. In Bangladesh and Pakistan, immunization coverage also favours boys, though the male advantage in curative care is less pronounced in Bangladesh than in northern India and is not evident in Pakistan.

South-central Asia is not the only subregion where there is discrimination that favours boys over girls in resort to health care. Both in Latin America and the Caribbean and in Northern Africa and Western Asia, there is evidence of a slight bias in favour of boys in curative care, though not in immunization, and findings are consistent with the data on trends in male-female differences in mortality for those two regions. In conclusion, the analysis contained in the present volume suggests that differential health care is the major mechanism responsible for female disadvantage in survival.

Why do parents in some countries favour sons over daughters when deciding whether or not to seek treatment for a sick child? Only limited progress has been made in the present volume towards a confident answer to that question. One plausible interpretation concerns the economic value of sons and daughters. Curative health care nearly always involves expense, and in societies where sons are perceived to be more important than daughters for the medium or long-term economic welfare of the household or family unit, there may be a greater willingness to incur health costs for sons than for daughters. In the stark language of neo-classical economics, parents, under that scenario, are merely behaving rationally by following the best interests of their family group.

That line of interpretation becomes immensely plausible when the contrast is made between sub-Saharan Africa, where there appears to be little or no female mortality disadvantage, and South-central Asia where it is most severe. In much of sub-Saharan Africa, women are economically active and daughters are valued for their bride wealth. In much of South-central Asia, by contrast, women's economic contribution is more likely to be restricted to the domestic domain and daughters are expensive because of the dowry system. To the extent that excess female mortality in childhood is a reflection of those wider economic and social realities, the obvious long-term policy prescription is to press ahead with reforms that will give greater educational, employment and financial opportunities to women.

The above interpretation and its attendant policy implications, however, are almost certainly oversimplified. They do not account adequately for the persistence of a gender bias in such countries as China and the Republic of Korea. China has experienced four decades of reform that have given women wide access to education and employment. In the Republic of Korea, a growing economy has led to rapid increases in female employment, accompanied by postponement of marriage. Yet in both countries, sex-selective abortion and higher than expected female mortality testify to the persistence of son preference. It appears that the greater social or cultural value attached to sons has not been eroded by macroeconomic changes that have favoured women.

Regardless of the origins of female disadvantage, the findings of the present study have highlighted the importance of providing preventive and curative care of reasonable quality and affordability. The policy shift towards greater cost recovery and reliance on the private sector in some countries is of concern because poor families may be less willing to spend money on daughters than on sons. That danger is particularly acute in South-central Asia. At the same time, any acceleration of the trend towards smaller family sizes should be of special benefit to girls. There is growing evidence to support the common sense expectation that parents of small families are able to spend more on the health and education of each child than are parents of large families. When competition for scarce family resources is severe, it is probable that daughters will suffer more than sons.

The present report has focused on inequalities between boys and girls, but even in regions where excess female mortality in childhood does not exist, such as in sub-Saharan Africa, the fact that mortality among children remains extremely high should not be overlooked. Improvements in child survival should remain a key priority in development policies. Policy and programme interventions that target morbidity and mortality of both boys and girls should continue to receive priority, as well as information and education that emphasize the importance of equal treatment for boys and girls.

REFERENCES

Hill, Kenneth, and Dawn M. Upchurch (1995). Gender differences in child health: evidence from the Demographic and Health Surveys. *Population and Development Review* (New York), vol. 21, No. 1 (March), pp. 127-151.

Mosley, W. H., and L. C. Chen (1984). An analystical framework for the study of child survival in developing countries. *Population and Development Review* (New York), vol. 10, Supplement, pp. 25-45.

Tabutin, Dominique, and Michel Willems (1995). Excess female child mortality in the developing world during the 1970s and 1980s. *Population Bulletin of the United Nations* (New York), No. 39, pp. 45-78.

Taket, A. (1986). Accident mortality in children, adolescents and young adults. *World Health Statistics Quarterly* (Geneva), vol. 39, No. 3, pp. 232-256.

United Nations Children's Fund (1993). *Child Malnutrition: Progress Toward the World Summit for Children Goal.* New York.

I. DIFFERENTIAL MORTALITY BY SEX FROM BIRTH TO ADOLESCENCE: THE HISTORICAL EXPERIENCE OF THE WEST (1750-1930)

Dominique Tabutin* and Michel Willems*

From the eighteenth to the mid-twentieth century, Europe and North America experienced a health revolution and a decline in mortality unprecedented in human history. The expectation of life at birth in Europe increased from an average of 35 years in 1800 to approximately 60 years in 1930. Mortality in childhood and during adolescence, which varied considerably by region and country,[1] declined markedly, especially after 1860. In Western Europe, infant mortality decreased from 180 deaths per 1,000 births in 1845 to 119 deaths per 1,000 by the end of the century, and reached 30 deaths per 1,000 in 1950. In France, the probability of dying between exact ages 1 and 5 dropped from 140 deaths per 1,000 in 1830 to only 31 per 1,000 a century later. In England and Wales, the probability of dying between exact ages 0 and 5 was reduced from 260 deaths per 1,000 in 1840 to 90 per 1,000 in 1930. The decline in mortality between exact ages 5 and 20 occurred almost as rapidly.[2] However, these advances in survival varied in timing and rapidity between countries, as did the reductions of mortality among males and females.

Over the last 200 years in Europe and North America, women have always had a higher expectation of life than men, the difference between the two varying between 1 and 3 years early in the nineteenth century, between 2 and 4 years early in the twentieth century, and between 3 and 5 years towards 1940. Because male mortality has declined more slowly than female mortality, the overall advantage experienced by women has increased steadily and continues to do so.[3] However, despite those overall trends and contrary to widespread assumption, the nineteenth century was characterized by excess female mortality during childhood and adolescence, or more specifically between ages 3 and 19. Such excess female mortality peaked during the second part of the nineteenth century before beginning to decline and finally disappearing towards 1940. Only in the 1970s did studies documenting the prevalence of excess female mortality in Europe among children and adolescents begin to appear. The present paper presents a review of what is known to date and an analysis of recently available data.

A. DATA AND METHODS

In the present section, the discussion will focus on three topics: the age range that should be the focus for the historical analysis of excess female mortality in today's developed countries; the sources of data used; and the measurement of differences in mortality between males and females.

The historical pattern of sex differentials in mortality in today's industrialized countries differs considerably from that characterizing developing countries today. In developing countries, excess female mortality tends to occur mostly over the age range 1-4, starting sometimes within the first year of life and disappearing generally towards ages 8 or 9.[4] In Europe, a century or so ago, excess female mortality tended to emerge at older ages (towards ages 3 or 4 years), became more apparent over the age range 5-9, and widened further from 10-14 years before giving way to excess male mortality at older ages. Consequently, historical assessment of excess female mortality requires that the full age range from 0-14 years be considered, with separate analysis of each age segment.

The review presented here will span the period 1600-1930, though special attention will be given to the nineteenth and early twentieth centuries, for which data are more widely available. More recent periods will not be considered because by 1930 excess female mortality had practically disappeared in most developed countries.

The data used have been gathered through an exhaustive search for mortality data by age and sex for the periods of interest. They were obtained from a review of the literature, by consulting historical sources of demo-

---

*Institut de Demographie, Université Catholique de Louvain, Belgium.

graphic statistics, and by contacting specialists in historical demography, statistical offices and research centres in each of the countries considered.

The study countries comprise the whole of Europe, including Russia, Canada and the United States of America, Australia, New Zealand and Japan. Data on a total of 24 countries were obtained, though the information is richer for some countries than for others. In particular, France and Northern European countries (Denmark, Finland, Norway and Sweden) have nearly complete national series dating as far back as 1750. For the seventeenth and eighteenth centuries, data were drawn mostly from studies on historical demography and tend to refer only to mortality at younger ages. For the period 1800 to 1930, the data consist mostly of national life-tables produced during the 1970s and 1980s but that go back, in a number of cases, to the mid-nineteenth century. Annex table A.1 displays the probabilities of dying by sex and age group available for various countries over the period 1740-1930. It also indicates the sources used in each case.

Whereas time series data of good quality[5] are available at the national level for most of the countries considered, that is not the case regarding data at the local or regional level: few countries have long time series of life-tables by province or department. In Belgium, for instance, one has at most mortality rates by age, sex and region for one or two points in time (1890 and 1910). In addition, there are considerable lacunae regarding information on cause of death during the nineteenth century, even at the national level. Although data on cause of death are often available (especially through the civil registration system), they are unreliable and tend to vary by sex and over time, reflecting changes in diagnostic practices. The proportion of deaths with cause unknown or poorly reported is generally high. Consequently, the use of those data for analytical purposes is limited.

The central aim of the present study is to analyse differences in mortality between males and females. At least three measures of such differences are possible.[6] Let q_m and q_f be the probability of dying for males and females, respectively, within a given age range $[x,y)$. Then, the relative difference between the sexes can be calculated as:

$$(q_m - q_f)/q_m \qquad (1)$$

a measure that, though rarely used in practice, indicates the relative excess or deficit of deaths among women with respect to those among 1,000 men surviving to exact age x. A second possible measure, which is also rarely used, is the absolute difference between the sexes:

$$q_m - q_f \qquad (2)$$

which indicates the excess (or deficit) in the absolute number of deaths of men with respect to that of women among 1,000 persons surviving to exact age x. Lastly, one can use the ratio of the male to female probability of dying, namely,

$$q_m/q_f \qquad (3)$$

which is the indicator most commonly used in the literature. That ratio is generally expressed as a percentage of male mortality over female mortality by age group. When it is greater than 100, it indicates the existence of excess male mortality; values below 100 indicate excess female mortality. The ratio as presented in the third measure described above will be used in the present paper as an indicator of sex differentials in mortality.

Although the ratio of male to female mortality measures the relative intensity of the excess or deficit in male mortality, it does not indicate its absolute size as does the difference presented in the second measure. Figure 1 illustrates a comparison of the second and third measures, as applied to estimates of mortality in Belgium by sex over the age range 0-80 during 1899-1901. Although the general differentials illustrated by the two indices are the same, each index conveys a different image of excess mortality among persons of one sex with respect to those of the other. Between ages 5 and 44, when mortality reaches its lowest levels, the ratios amplify existing differences, whereas above age 50, the ratios are attenuated and the absolute differences as represented by the second measure grow.

The type of basic data available vary according to the country considered, being presented variously as mortality rates, probabilities of dying, complete life-tables or reported numbers of deaths by age and sex, together with the population to which they correspond. To facilitate comparisons, all types of data have been converted to ratios of the probability of dying by sex, as indicated in the third measure, expressed as percentages.

Figure 1. **Absolute differences of probabilities of dying between males and females and male to female ratios of those probabilities, Belgium, 1899-1901**

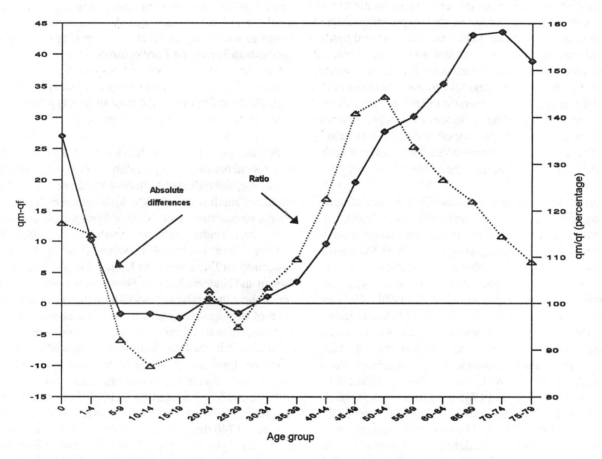

Source: M. Willems, *Réalité et diversité de la surmortalité féminine dans le monde et dans l'histoire* (Louvain-la-Neuve, Institute de demographie, 1993), Master's thesis.

B. PAST ASSESSMENTS OF SEX DIFFERENTIALS IN MORTALITY

During the seventeenth and eighteenth centuries, scientists in Europe were very concerned about the high levels of mortality that prevailed, especially among young children. The probability of dying before age 20 was about 50 per cent, and the expectation of life at birth fluctuated around 30 years. The first quantitative demography studies date from that period, including Graunt's estimation of a life-table in 1662. New ideas emerged from such concerns. As Hecht (1980, p. 33) notes:

"The attitude towards death and towards the death of a child changed drastically towards the middle of the eighteenth century, and that evolution was not independent, as we have said, from the historical, economic and demographic changes taking place. As the disappearance of a child began to be felt deeply, the treatises on child care, paediatrics and education multiplied. Physicians gained power over nursemaids and midwives, and scientific rationality replaced traditional methods in the care of infants. The couple adopted a new attitude towards their children, and the mother wished to know how to take better care of her child."

19

The quantitative scientists of the time[7] tried to estimate child mortality levels, the expectation of life and the mean length of life. They also considered variations of mortality among the young according to climate, region, social group and sex. In general, they deplored the existence of excess male mortality. Explanations for that excess included biological advantages (physiological differences between the sexes), sociocultural practices (the intemperance of men) and, more often, reasons of natural or divine order. Thus, according to Wargentin in 1766,[8] women were less likely to die because of a natural law that was in operation from an early age to the end of life. According to Deparcieux in 1746, excess male mortality was a happy initiative of God to reestablish the equilibrium between the two sexes whose numbers are unequal at the time of birth.[9]

During the eighteenth century, each statistician-demographer increased the understanding of mortality variations, adding precision to the ages where excess male mortality was strongest (generally high from birth to adolescence but reduced during the child-bearing ages when the mortality risks for women increased) and providing further explanations. In 1778, Moheau proposed a more sociocultural approach to the issue, suggesting that men, because of their activities and mode of life, are in general exposed to higher risks of death than women. Almost no author of the eighteenth century wrote about excess female mortality except Süssmilch, who, when considering in 1765 the critical ages at which life is particularly at risk, mentioned puberty, especially for the female sex.[10] As will be shown, adolescence was precisely the period of life during which excess female mortality was most difficult to combat, having existed since the eighteenth century and surviving well into the twentieth.

With the expansion of civil registration and the improvement of analytical methods during the nineteenth century, evidence of the existence of excess female mortality at certain ages, especially among the young, increased. In Belgium, for instance, statistician-demographers, such as Quetelet and Smits in 1832, Cauderlier in 1900 and Leclerc in 1906, documented that girls and young women between ages 3 and 19 were more likely to die than their male counterparts. They did not, however, explain why that excess female mortality existed. At the time, the main concern was differential mortality by socio-economic group and by urban-rural residence. In addition, the excess mortality of girls and young women was not necessarily considered an anom-

aly. Indeed, it was a common belief at the end of the nineteenth century that the physiology of women was less resilient than that of men. It was the excess mortality of male children under age three that captured the attention of researchers and was described as "a remarkable event" or even "an unnatural outcome". It was not until the 1970s that such mortality differentials by sex began to attract the attention of researchers in terms of both quantification and explanation.

C. FINDINGS RELATIVE TO THE SEVENTEENTH AND EIGHTEENTH CENTURIES

For the period 1600-1800, when civil registration systems did not exist and population censuses were still not in use, the only data available are those reported in studies of small populations, which are generally based on the reconstruction of families from parish registers. Many such studies, relating mostly to the eighteenth century, were published between 1960 and 1980, especially in France and the United Kingdom of Great Britain and Northern Ireland. However, according to the researchers themselves,[11] mortality is the most difficult type of demographic event to measure because of the underregistration of deaths and the confounding effect of migration.[12] In the latter half of the eighteenth century, evidence from small studies are complemented by national-level data in a few countries. Denmark, starting in 1780, and Sweden, starting in 1750, have data based on civil registration and censuses, whereas France has data from 1740 that were derived from a national survey of parish registers carried out by the *Institut national d'études démographiques* (INED).

During the period 1750-1800, France, Denmark and Sweden experienced very high mortality levels during childhood and adolescence, though there were marked differences between Denmark and Sweden (with a $_5q_0$ of 350 deaths per 1,000 towards 1785) and France (with a corresponding figure of 450 per 1,000) (table 1). In all three countries, there was also a clear excess male mortality during the first year of life (of the order of 10-15 per cent), which remained largely unchanged until 1930. In contrast, there was considerable variation beyond age 1. In Sweden, excess male mortality prevailed at all ages; in Denmark, excess female mortality was noticeable over the age range 1-9, and excess male mortality was minor for the 10-19 age group. In France, excess female mortality was also noticeable, though it varied by age according to the period considered.

TABLE 1. PROBABILITIES OF DYING (PER 1,000) FOR BOTH SEXES COMBINED AND MALE TO
FEMALE RATIOS OF THOSE PROBABILITIES IN THE NATIONAL LIFE-TABLES OF
DENMARK, FRANCE AND SWEDEN, EIGHTEENTH CENTURY

Country Period	Probabilities of dying Both sexes					Male to female ratio (percentage)				
	$_1q_0$	$_4q_1$	$_5q_5$	$_5q_{10}$	$_5q_{15}$	0 year	1-4 years	5-9 years	10-14 years	15-19 years
Denmark										
1780-1784	198	167	45	--- 58 ---		113	98	94	--- 124 ---	
1785-1789	215	192	50	--- 71 ---		112	97	92	--- 105 ---	
1790-1794	171	128	36	--- 60 ---		114	100	97	--- 105 ---	
1795-1799	178	137	38	--- 52 ---		114	99	96	--- 104 ---	
France										
1740-1749	296	253	108	49	50	115	100	107	104	122
1750-1759	277	239	86	38	39	111	97	96	113	93
1760-1769	281	245	84	41	36	120	101	91	105	108
1770-1779	273	235	82	45	35	115	103	94	119	115
1780-1789	278	238	90	37	38	110	96	102	97	85
1790-1799	254	218	72	33	39	117	104	103	97	-
Sweden										
1751-1760	204	143	61	31	31	110	104	107	103	107
1761-1770	216	146	64	32	32	110	103	104	113	113
1771-1780	202	170	76	43	40	110	104	110	117	104
1781-1790	199	157	67	38	37	110	104	108	111	111
1791-1800	195	130	51	25	27	112	105	107	105	113

Sources: Y. Blayo, "La mortalité en France de 1740 à 1829", in *Population*, vol. 30, pp. 123-142 (Paris, 1975); J. Houdaille, "La mortalité des enfants en Europe avant le XIXe siècle", in *La mortalité des enfants dans le monde et dans l'histoire*, P. M. Boulanger and Dominique J. Tabutin, eds. (Liège, Belgium, Ordina Editions, 1980); Sweden, National Central Bureau of Statistics, *Historical Statistics of Sweden*, part 1, *Population, 1720-1967* (Stockholm, 1969); O. Andersen, "The decline in Danish mortality before 1850 and its economic and social background", in *Pre-Industrial Population Change*, T. Bengtsson and others, eds. (Stockholm, Almquist and Wiksell, 1984).

Between 1740 and 1780, it was mostly evident for the age group 1-9; after 1780, it appeared also at ages 10-14 and 15-19, where it tended to become accentuated over the next century. During the pre-industrial period, which was characterized by important mortality reductions, there were no major changes in the sex differentials in mortality, at least at the national level.

Studies of specific subpopulations for the period 1600-1800 confirm that male children were subject to higher mortality risks than female children before age one (table 2). Excess male mortality was also noticeable over the age range 1-4 but not as consistently. In contrast, excess female mortality was evident in the majority of cases over age groups 5-9 and 10-14, and became more accentuated for age group 15-19. Although most studies refer to rural populations, some refer to other populations living in diverse economic and cultural contexts.

For instance, in Geneva the situation of adolescents and young women appears to have deteriorated relative to males between 1600 and 1800 (table 2). Perrenoud (1981) attributes such deterioration to the incorporation of women into the industrial labour force during the eighteenth century (as watch makers or workers in the textile industry, for instance) under conditions of work that were particularly difficult. Another relevant factor was the declining standard of living among the working class since inequality was pronounced and mortality varied according to social class. There was, for instance, a difference of 13 years between the life expectancy of a bourgeois (44 years) and that of an unskilled worker (31 years). Furthermore, in the age group 5-19, mortality differences between the social classes were more marked among women than among men (table 3). Among members of the working class, young women were subject to higher mortality risks than young men, but the reverse was true among the bourgeoisie and

TABLE 2. MALE TO FEMALE RATIOS OF THE PROBABILITIES OF DYING BY AGE GROUP ACCORDING TO LOCAL OR REGIONAL STUDIES, SEVENTEENTH AND EIGHTEENTH CENTURIES
(Percentage)

Region, country and years	Under 1 year	1-4 years	5-9 years	10-14 years	15-19 years	$_{10}q_0$
12 English parishes[a]						
1600-1649	115	109	113	-	-	251
1650-1699	116	94	84	-	-	265
1700-1749	113	102	86	-	-	277
Rural parish Cartmel[b] (United Kingdom)						
1600-1750	110	----------- 93 -----------			-	212
City of Geneva (Switzerland)[c]						
1625-1799	118	102	123	118	101	522
1700-1796	125	106	109	85	79	435
Duché de Brabant (Belgium)[d]						
1650-1699	121	122	110	-	-	375
1700-1796	122	100	107	-	-	367
Brittany and Anjou (France)[e]						
1740-1769	127	96	94	-	-	466
1770-1799	125	95	88	-	-	436
Rural Parisian basin[f](France)						
1671-1720	111	94	91	76	76	484
Rural Bas-Quercy (France)[g]						
1751-1771	102	105	79	-	-	-
1793-1815	124	96	75	95	-	-
Two regions of Germany[h], 1740-1800						
Herrenberg	119	107	92	113	98	417
Ortenau	120	101	98	96	71	376
Quebec (Canada)[i]						
1640-1729	109	100	83	133	71	206

Sources: [a]E.A. Wrigley and R.S. Schofield, The Population History of England, 1541-1871: A Reconstruction (Cambridge, United Kingdom, Cambridge University Press, 1989); [b]R. Finlay, "Differential child mortality in pre-industrial England: the example of Cartmel, Cumbria, 1600-1750", Annales de démographie historique, vol. 18, pp. 67-80 (Paris, 1981); [c]A. Perrenoud, "Surmortalité féminine et condition de la femme (XVII-XIXe siècles): une vérification empirique", Annales de démographie historique, vol. 18, pp. 89-105 (Paris, 1981); [d]C. Bruneel, La mortalité dans les campagnes: le duché de Brabant aux XVIIe et XVIIIe siècles (Louvain-la-Neuve, Belgium, Editions Nauwelaerts,1977); [e]Y. Blayo and L. Henry, "Données démographiques sur la Bretagne et l'Anjou de 1740 à 1829, Annales de démographie historique, vol. 3, pp. 91-171 (Paris, 1967); [f]J. Dupaquier, La population rurale du Bassin Parisien à l'époque de Louis XIV (Paris, Editions de l'école des hautes études en sciences sociales, 1979); [g]J. C. Sangoi, Démographie paysanne en Bas-Quercy, 1751-1872 (Paris, Editions du CNRS, 1985); [h]A. Imhof, Life Expectancies in Germany from the Seventeenth to the Nineteenth centuries (Weinheim, Germany: Acta Humaniora, 1980; in German); [i]H.Charbonneau, Vie et mort de nos ancêtres (Montreal, 1975).

TABLE 3. MALE AND FEMALE PROBABILITIES OF DYING[a]
(per 1,000), MALE TO FEMALE RATIOS OF THE PROBABILITY
OF DYING FOR AGE GROUP 5-19 AND EXPECTATIONS OF
LIFE ACCORDING TO SOCIAL GROUP, GENEVA
(1725-1790 COHORTS)

Social group	Male	Female	Male/female ratio (percentage)	e_0 Both[b]
High and middle bourgeoisie	143	124	115	43.6
Artisans and skilled workers	179	166	108	34.5
Unskilled workers ...	180	193	*93*	31.4
Ratio of unskilled workers to bourgeoisie	1.26	1.56	-	0.72

Source: A. Perrenoud, "Surmortalité féminine et condition de la femme (XVII-XIXe siècles): une vérification empirique", *Annales de démographie historique*, vol. 18, pp. 89-105 (Paris, 1981).

NOTE: We have taken the mean of the expectations of life by sex and regrouped the probabilities of dying over age groups 5-9 and 10-19.

[a]Probability of dying for age group 5-19 obtained by grouping probabilities of dying over age group 5-9 and 10-19.

[b]Life expectancy for both sexes (e_0 both sexes) taken as the mean of the expectation of life by sex.

among the class of tradesmen and craftsmen. According to Perrenoud, these findings suggest that industrial work may have damaged the health of young workers during the eighteenth century, especially that of young women in urban areas or in areas where female industrial employment was high. A century earlier, before the industrial revolution, there seemed to be no excess female mortality among the poor in either Geneva or London.[13]

In summary, there have been marked differences in the mortality of young men and women since the eighteenth century: although excess male mortality was generally present before the age of one, excess female mortality appeared occasionally in the age group 1-4, became more common by ages 5-14 and more common still at ages 15-19. The differences in mortality by sex became more marked during the nineteenth century, as will be documented below.

D. SEX DIFFERENTIALS IN CHILDHOOD AND ADOLESCENT MORTALITY BETWEEN 1800 AND 1930

The establishment of civil registration systems and the generalized use of censuses permit the study of sex differentials in mortality for a large number of countries or areas in the nineteenth century. Thus, 201 life-tables or mortality rates by age and sex for 24 countries or areas could be assembled. In the cases with the best documentation, a series of estimates covering a long period are available, as in the cases of Denmark, England and Wales, France and Sweden. For the last two countries, data are available for the period 1740-1930, so that the 201 estimates considered cover part of the eighteenth century. For some countries, such as Greece or Spain, the data available refer only to one point in time and are relatively recent. The countries or areas considered can be grouped into five regional sets: Northern Europe, comprising Denmark, Finland, Norway and Sweden; Western Europe, including Austria, Belgium, England and Wales, France, Ireland, the Netherlands and Switzerland; Southern Europe, which comprises Greece, Italy, Portugal and Spain; Eastern Europe, including the Czech Provinces of Bohemia, Moravia and Silesia, Hungary, and the European part of Russia; and lastly, the overseas countries of European settlement, Australia, Canada, New Zealand and the United States. Japan stands alone and may be considered the sixth set.

The 201 life-table estimates available are presented in annex table A.1, and are distributed in the following manner according to different criteria:

According to time period	1700-1799	10
	1800-1849	21
	1850-1899	79
	1900-1930	91
According to region	Northern Europe	45
	Western Europe	89
	Southern Europe	10
	Eastern Europe	15
	Overseas countries of European settlement	36
	Japan	6

Three age groups were selected for analysis: less than 1 year, 1-4 years and 5-14 years. Thus, three different ratios of male to female probabilities of dying were calculated. For some countries, the data do not permit the calculation of infant mortality (that is, mortality under age 1). Accordingly, the number of ratios regarding infant mortality is only 188 rather than the 201 potentially available. In the case of mortality for age group 1-4, the mortality ratios could be calculated only in 192 cases. The set of ratios for age group 5-14 is the most complete, covering 199 cases.[14]

1. *Sex differentials in infant mortality*

The data available confirm the general finding that male mortality between 1800 and 1930 was higher than female mortality under age 1 (figure 2). In most cases, the female advantage since 1800 was above 10 per cent, and except perhaps in Southern Europe and Japan, it showed a tendency to increase over time as overall infant mortality levels declined. Thus, by the twentieth century the female advantage was generally above 20 per cent. Around 1930, the variation in excess male mortality under age 1 was large, with the ratios of male to female mortality ranging from 113 in Japan to 130 in the Netherlands. Such variation was related to an equally wide span of infant mortality levels, ranging from 63 deaths per 1,000 births in the Netherlands to 140 deaths per 1,000 in Japan.

There are remarkable similarities between the evolution of sex differentials in infant mortality in Northern and Western Europe. The experiences of countries in those regions tend to fall between those of England and Wales or Sweden, on the one hand, and Finland on the other. The overseas countries of European settlement and Japan show greater diversity, with Australia, New Zealand and the United States experiencing relatively high levels of excess male mortality under age one. Canada, in contrast, experienced a slower rise in excess male mortality. Between 1885 and 1928, Japan experienced the lowest excess male mortality among infants.

The case of Greece in 1928, where the ratio of male to female mortality under age 1 was 101.4, is atypical and suggests that the data may not be reliable, although there is also the possibility that there might have been a certain excess female mortality at a very early age. However, the weak sex differential in child mortality observed does not justify that conclusion (the male to female ratio for age group 1-4 was only 99.1).

2. *Sex differentials in child mortality*

Among children aged 1-4, the female advantage in terms of lower mortality was not as consistently strong as it was among infants. Excess female mortality was evident in some populations including Canada, France, Italy and Japan (figure 2). Although the ratio of the male to female probability of dying at ages 1-4 tended to increase over the period 1800-1990, trends were less regular than in the case of infant mortality. In Northern Europe, for instance, that ratio declined from a relatively high level in the early 1800s to a value close to 100 by the second half of the nineteenth century before rising again during the early twentieth century. In Western Europe and in France in particular, male excess mortality did not become firmly established until after 1870, whereas before that date there was near parity in the risks of dying among males and females. The experience of Canada was similar. Such trends suggest that excess female mortality appeared earlier in that region in terms of both time and age. It is worth noting that in today's developing countries, excess female mortality is most marked in the age group 1-4 (Tabutin and Willems, 1993).

3. *Sex differentials in mortality over age group 5-14*

Between 1800 and 1930, excess female mortality was generally evident among persons aged 5-14. Almost two thirds of the estimates available indicate its existence (figure 2). Only a few countries failed to exhibit excess female mortality during late childhood and early adolescence; they included Australia, New Zealand and the United States. In contrast to the patterns exhibited by European countries, Australia and New Zealand were characterized by relatively low overall mortality at ages 5-14. In the United States, although mortality levels were closer to those of France or Sweden, male mortality was higher.

Among the trends that can be assessed because of the existence of long time series, three patterns can be distinguished. In Western Europe, excess female mortality over age group 5-14 was marked at the beginning of the nineteenth century, and remained high during most of the century before it began a slow decline and virtually disappeared by 1920. That was the trend experienced by Austria, Belgium, England and Wales and France, although in France, excess female mortality over that age range was still noticeable in the late 1920s. Eastern Europe seemed to experience a similar trend, at least as suggested by the series for the Czech provinces mentioned above. In contrast, Northern Europe experienced a much later appearance of excess female mortality (after 1870, except in the case of Denmark), which remained evident until its disappearance during the 1920s. Lastly, in Canada, the excess female mortality revealed by early estimates (those dating from 1831) declined continuously until it disappeared early in the twentieth century (in 1911 and 1921, respectively).

Figure 2. Male to female ratios of the probability of dying, 1800-1980

Under 1 year

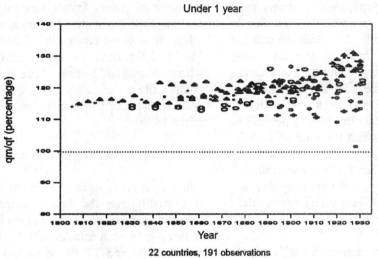

22 countries, 191 observations

1-4 years

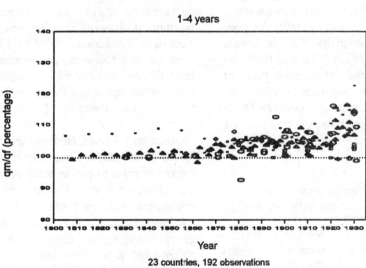

23 countries, 192 observations

5-14 years

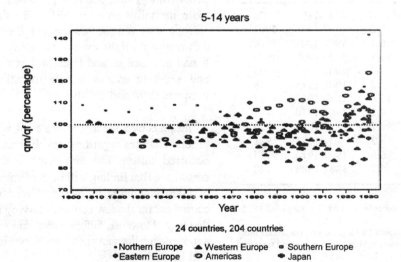

24 countries, 204 countries

• Northern Europe ▲ Western Europe ▫ Southern Europe
● Eastern Europe ⊙ Americas ◆ Japan

Source: Annex table A.1.

25

The countries of European settlement (Australia, New Zealand and the United States), where excess male mortality prevailed, and Japan, where excess female mortality was noticeable, both fall outside the patterns of change described above. In Japan, mortality levels were higher than those prevalent in Northern or Western European countries, and excess female mortality was most evident between 1885 and 1928 . In addition, although mortality in Japan declined by 35 per cent in 40 years, that fall did not affect the ratio of male to female mortality over the age group 5-14. In contrast, in the other non-European countries, the late nineteenth and early twentieth centuries witnessed a more rapid reduction of mortality among girls and young women than among their male counterparts.

Information for the 12 populations having compete data between 1875 and 1930 can be used to characterize further the extent of excess female mortality for ages 5-14 years . The maximum intensity of excess female mortality, measured in terms of the difference from 100 of the ratio of the male to the female probability of dying, varied considerably, ranging from 4-19 per cent. The timing of the peak intensity ranged between 1831-1917 (table 4). However, for most of the countries considered, the peaks tended to occur towards the turn

TABLE 4. SELECTED CHARACTERISTICS OF EXCESS FEMALE MORTALITY OVER AGE GROUP 5-14 AT THE NATIONAL LEVEL, 1820 TO 1930

Country or area[a]	Maximum intensity[b] (percentage)	Period of maximum intensity	Date of disappear-ance
Austria	12.4	1889-1892	1928
Canada	10.2	1831	1901
Czech regions	16.4	1900-1901	1930
Denmark	12.8	1885-1895	1923
England and Wales . .	3.6	1903-1908	1923
Finland	11.2	1908-1913	1928
France	11.6	1887-1917	1937
Ireland	19.2	1901-1910	..
Netherlands	4.7	1888-1893	1925
Quebec (Canada)	8.2	1851	1921
Sweden	6.6	1901-1910	1935
Switzerland	5.7	1881-1888	1920

Source: Annex table A.1.

[a]Includes countries for which a series is available for the period 1875-1930.

[b]Measured as the difference between 100 and the male to female ratio of the probabilities of dying in percentage terms (for instance, Denmark, with a ratio of 87.2, had an index of 12.8 per cent in 1890).

of the century (between 1885 and 1905). The disappearance of excess female mortality tended to occur towards the 1920s in most countries, except for Canada, where it occurred very early. Sweden, with a ratio of 99.7 in 1925, does not really constitute an exception, whereas France and Ireland, whose mortality levels were comparable to those of Sweden, experienced the disappearance of excess female mortality only towards the end of the 1930s.

4. Regional overview

In order to give a regional overview of sex differentials in mortality over the three relevant age groups, the means of the ratios of the male to the female probability of dying have been calculated by region for three dates (1860, 1900 and 1930), as shown in table 5. For mortality under age one, an increase in excess male mortality is observed in all regions, although it is more marked in Northern and Western Europe, and in North America and Oceania, where excess male mortality ranged between 24 and 28 per cent towards 1930. By that date, the equivalent figure for Eastern and Southern Europe and for Japan was 12-13 per cent.

Over ages 1-4 years, Northern and Western Europe, as well as North America and Oceania again experienced a marked increase in excess male mortality between 1860 and 1930, whereas in Eastern Europe and Japan there was almost no change between 1900 and 1930, the only two periods for which data are available. For the age group 5-14, excess female mortality became more accentuated in Northern and Western Europe over the period 1860-1900, before it gave way to a slight excess male mortality around 1930. By that date, Eastern Europe was unique among the European regions in exhibiting a slight excess mortality among girls and female adolescents, and Japan still experienced a marked and growing excess female mortality at ages 1-14 between 1900 and 1930.

Thus, it is over the age group 5-14 years that the most crucial changes regarding sex differentials in mortality occurred during the nineteenth and early twentieth centuries. That finding will be confirmed by the analysis of differential mortality by single year of age that can be carried out for the few countries having data classified in that way. However, before undertaking such an analysis, a more detailed review of trends between 1850 and 1930 will be undertaken.

TABLE 5. MALE TO FEMALE RATIOS OF THE PROBABILITIES OF DYING,
BY MAJOR REGION, 1860, 1900 AND 1930

(*Percentage*)

Region	Circa 1860			Circa 1900			Circa 1930		
	Under 1 year	1-4 years	5-14 years	Under 1 year	1-4 years	5-14 years	Under 1 year	1-4 years	5-14 years
Europe									
Eastern Europe	-	-	-	120	101	91	112	102	98
Northern Europe	117	104	101	121	105	92	126	112	106
Southern Europe	-	-	-	-	-	-	112	102	101
Western Europe	120	102	96	119	105	91	128	114	104
Japan	-	-	-	111	100	89	113	99	84
Northern America/Oceania	113	100	95	118	104	99	124	109	115
Total	116	102	97	120	104	92	119	107	104

Source: Annex table A.1; unweighted arithmetical means; number of countries: 8 in 1860, 15 in 1900 and 19 in 1930.

5. *Trends in sex differentials in mortality between 1850 and 1930*

Five countries have data that permit the study of the evolution of sex differentials in mortality over nearly a century: Denmark and Sweden in Northern Europe; England and Wales, and France in Western Europe; and Canada.[15] Under age 1, the trends experienced by all five countries are very similar: excess male mortality, already evident in 1850, increased almost monotonically until 1930 (figure 3). The experience of Canada, where the ratio of male to female infant mortality rose from 114 to 122 over the period, and that of England and Wales, where the ratio changed from 122 to 130 over the same period, generally set the bounds within which the experiences of other countries are circumscribed.

For age group 1-4 years, excess male mortality remained the norm, with only a few departures (figure 3). In Canada, Denmark, and England and Wales, the trend towards of a greater affirmation of a female advantage occurred smoothly. France followed a similar pattern, but with greater irregularities, with mortality among female children being higher than male mortality around 1860. In England and Wales and in Sweden, a reduction of the female advantage, which was large around 1850, preceded its later increase (mostly after 1910).

There is considerable variation in the trends followed for the age group 5-14, though most indicate the persistence of excess female mortality between 1850 and 1930 period (figure 3). Canada illustrates the case of a progressive and early disappearance (around 1900) of excess mortality among older female children and young adolescents. In Denmark, excess female mortality increased between 1860 and 1890, before diminishing and eventually disappearing towards 1920. England and Wales, as well as Sweden, had no excess female mortality around 1850 but experienced a relatively deteriorating situation for female children aged 5-14 as the century advanced, and did not experience the disappearance of excess female mortality until the 1920s. In France, excess female mortality among those aged 5-14 was prevalent over the full 1850-1930 period, and an increase was noticeable between 1872 and 1887 and again between 1900 and 1917, when a decreasing trend set in (figure 3 and annex table A.1).

6. *The evolution of sex differentials in mortality by single year of age*

Only a few countries have complete life-tables allowing the analysis of sex differentials by single year of age. The cases of France and Switzerland will be considered here,[16] focusing on the age range 0-19 years. Data for France allow the identification of the range of ages over which excess female mortality prevailed, the measurement of the magnitude of such excess, and the identification of those ages that were more resistant to change. As early as the 1820s, excess female mortality was evident over the age range 9-18 years. By 1875-1879, it had become more accentuated, being apparent over most of the range 3-18 years and being particularly marked between ages 12 and 17 (figure 4).[17] That pattern remained almost constant until 1920-1924. Those changes occurred against a background of substantial improvements in survival; the expectation of life at birth among women rose from 38 to 56 years between 1827 and 1922.

Figure 3. Evolution of the male to female ratios of the probability of dying by age, 1850-1930, selected countries

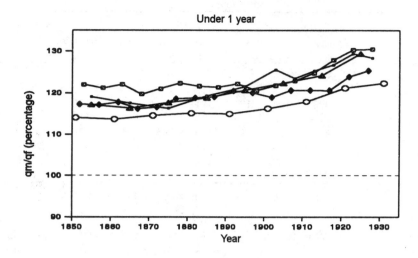

Under 1 year

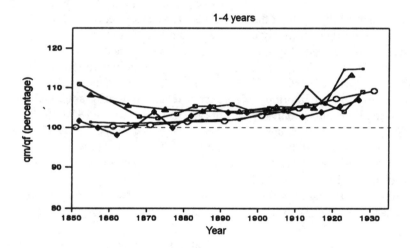

1-4 years

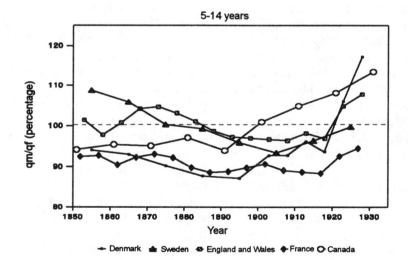

5-14 years

—•— Denmark ▲ Sweden ⊕ England and Wales ◆ France ○ Canada

Source: Annex table A.1.

28

Figure 4. Evolution by single year of age (0-20) of the male to female ratios of the probability of dying, France and Switzerland

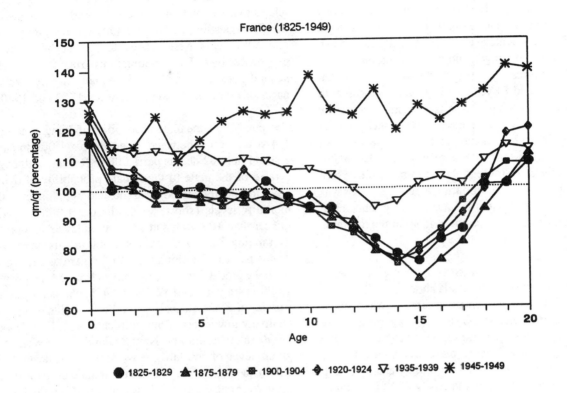

France (1825-1949)

● 1825-1829 ▲ 1875-1879 ⊞ 1900-1904 ◆ 1920-1924 ▽ 1935-1939 ✳ 1945-1949

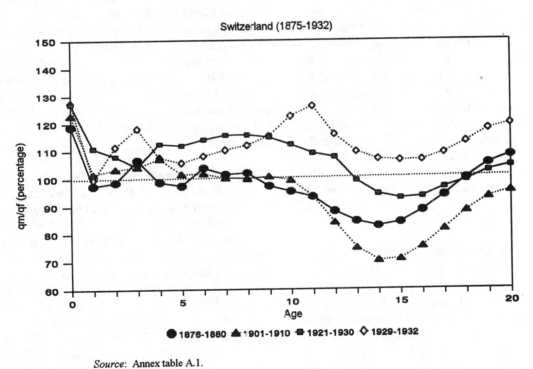

Switzerland (1875-1932)

● 1876-1880 ▲ 1901-1910 ⊞ 1921-1930 ◇ 1929-1932

Source: Annex table A.1.

In France, the maximum level of excess female mortality varied between 25 and 30 per cent, observed mostly among young women aged 14, 15 and 16 years (figure 4). Before age 10, the female disadvantage rarely surpassed 5 per cent. The life-table corresponding to the period 1935-1939, with an expectation of life for women of 60.7 years, no longer showed any excess female mortality by five-year age groups, but still indicated that women aged 13 and 14 years had a small handicap with respect to their male counterparts in terms of mortality risks. Those ages, characterized by the onset of menarche, were the most resistant to the disappearance of excess female mortality. Figure 4 shows that major changes in the sex differentials in mortality took place between 1920 and 1935, initiating a new trend that was maintained or accentuated in later years, so that a clear excess in male mortality became evident in the life-table corresponding to 1945-1949.

In the case of Switzerland, similar conclusions can be reached, although the time series is shorter (1875-1932). In 1876-1880, excess female mortality was almost general over the age range 1-18, being particularly marked for ages 11-17 (figure 4). Differentials over the latter age range became even more accentuated for the period 1901-1910, when excess mortality among young women reached a maximum intensity of 30 per cent at ages 14 and 15. By 1921-1930, however, excess female mortality had largely disappeared, giving way to excess male mortality over most young ages except between 14 and 17 years, which again proved to be resistant to the disappearance of excess female mortality. During the period 1929-1932, excess male mortality became generalized, and the graph of the ratio of the male to the female probability of dying is similar to that for France during the quinquennium 1945-1949. Interestingly, excess female mortality disappeared in Switzerland somewhat earlier (before 1930) than in France, at a time when the expectation of life at birth among women had reached 62 years.

E. INTERRELATIONS BETWEEN SEX DIFFERENTIALS IN MORTALITY AND THE LEVEL OF MORTALITY

Between 1850 and 1930, mortality risks by age in the currently developed countries evolved from a situation in which girls and young women experienced excess mortality at various ages towards a situation where excess male mortality was the rule. It is worth inquiring whether, at a given point in time, sex differentials in mortality were related to the mortality level experienced by the population, and whether over time the disappearance of excess female mortality at young ages was related to the reduction of overall mortality. To answer the first question, sex differentials for age groups 1-4 and 5-14 years were related to the mortality levels experienced by different populations around 1900. The second question is addressed by analysing the experiences of France and Sweden between 1750 and 1930.

Around 1900, the male probability of dying over ages 1-4 years varied between 26 deaths per 1,000 in New Zealand and 202 deaths per 1,000 in Russia. Although a ratio of the male to the female probability of dying close to 100 appears to be associated with higher child mortality levels (above 80 deaths per 1,000), a ratio greater than 105 occurs at very varied levels of mortality, ranging from 32 deaths per 1,000 in Austria to 100 deaths per 1,000 in Finland. With regard to age group 5-14, the probability of dying ranges from 14 deaths per 1,000 in England and Wales to 84 deaths per 1,000 in Russia, and excess male mortality is evident only at relatively low levels of mortality: around 20 deaths per 1,000 in Australia and New Zealand. However, at a given level of mortality (say, around 37 deaths per 1,000), the ratio of the male to the female probability of dying over age group 5-14 varied from 84 in the Czech provinces mentioned above to 101 in Canada. Furthermore, near parity between male and female mortality can be observed in the United States, whose probability of dying over age group 5-14 was 37 deaths per 1,000 around 1900, and in Russia, where that probability amounted to 84 deaths per 1,000. Consequently, it appears that the overall level of mortality is not a good predictor of the sex differentials in mortality prevalent at young ages.

From a time series perspective, however, the conclusion may be different. In France and Sweden, mortality at the younger ages declined markedly, dropping from over 100 deaths per 1,000 in 1755 to below 20 per 1,000 in 1930 for children aged 5-14. As figure 5 shows, for the age group 1-4 years there appears to be a negative relation between the ratio of the male to the female probability of dying and the level of male mortality, but it is weak, and in the case of Sweden a ratio of nearly 105 is associated with male probabilities of dying ranging from 30 to 140 deaths per 1,000. Excess male mortality only seems to become established (ratio over 110) at mortality levels below 40 deaths per 1,000 for age group 1-4.

The situation is more complex regarding age group 5-14, because the relation between the ratio of the male to the female probability of dying and the level of mortality appears to be curvilinear (figure 5). During an early period, when the probability of dying over age group 5-14 declined from 160 to 35 deaths per 1,000 in France and from 120 to 35 deaths per 1,000 in Sweden, the relation between the two appears to be positive since a reduction of the probability of dying is associated with a reduction of the male to female mortality ratio. Consequently, there is an accentuation in France and the appearance in Sweden of excess female mortality. Later on, however, the relation reverses itself and the male to female mortality ratio increases as mortality over age group 5-14 continues to decline. Furthermore, although the trends experienced by France and Sweden display similar shapes, their levels differ. Thus, France consistently presents a more marked excess female mortality at a mortality level equivalent to that of Sweden. In conclusion, it appears that the relation between level of mortality and excess female mortality is variable, even if the trends followed by different countries with respect to mortality differentials for age group 5-14 have many similarities.

To sum up, male children under age one have invariably been subject to higher mortality risks than their female counterparts in the countries currently considered as developed. For age group 1-4, sex differentials in mortality have tended to be weak and indicate that female children have generally been subject to lower mortality risks than male children, an advantage that became accentuated during the twentieth century. However, when single years of age are considered, excess female mortality is detected even among children aged three in France towards 1875 or among those aged one in Switzerland at about the same time. Such excess female mortality was considerably more prevalent between ages 5 and 15, with ages 13-16 being the most likely to show such excess and the most resistant to change. The excess mortality of young adolescent women disappeared only after 1930.

For none of the age groups considered is there at any point in time a clear relation between the level of age-specific mortality and the intensity or direction of the sex differentials in mortality at young ages. It is not until mortality becomes relatively low (around 40 deaths per 1,000 in age group 1-4 or 35 deaths per 1,000 in age group 5-14) that excess male mortality becomes the rule. Yet excess female mortality at young ages has had only a small impact on the evolution of sex differentials in the expectation of life at birth between 1825 and 1940, as will be discussed below.

F. REGIONAL AND SPATIAL DIFFERENCES IN MORTALITY BY SEX: THE CASE OF BELGIUM

Already before 1800, there was a distinct geographical distribution of deaths. Numerous studies of the demographic characteristics of population groups between 1600 and 1800 show that local differences, between neighbouring parishes or between cities and the countryside, were marked, depending on ecological conditions, such as access to clean water, or on the incidence of epidemics. As Blum (1990) notes, one cannot deny the importance of differences between localities; but such studies, since they are mostly devoted to a single site, do not provide a comprehensive view, and lacking reliable bases for comparison, simply catalogue differences between localities. For most of the period 1800-1930, data allowing the comparative study of mortality by age between a country's regions or geographical habitats are lacking. Only infant mortality is slightly better documented at the local level.[18] Furthermore, data by sex are not always available.

Although important differences in the mortality of the young by region have been known to exist, regional variations in sex differentials in mortality have not been systematically studied, nor has their relation with type of habitat, level of mortality at the local level or other sociocultural characteristics of localities been explored. Such analysis is crucial to understanding why certain types of sex differentials in mortality arise and how they evolve over time. Using data from studies of selected countries, the regional variation in sex differentials in mortality over age groups 0-14 or 0-19 years can be explored.

Using data for the period 1890 and 1910, it is possible to study trends in sex differentials in child and adolescent mortality at the regional level in Belgium, an area of research pioneered by Eggerickx and Tabutin (1994) and Devos (1994). During that period, mortality declined by 28 per cent among those aged 0-4 years and by 32 per cent among those aged 5-19 (table 6). Probabilities of dying under age 1 and over age groups 1-4 and 5-19 years have been calculated for 1890 and 1910 for each of the 41 municipalities, 9 provinces and 2 major regions that constitute Belgium, as well as according to

Figure 5. Comparison of male mortality levels and male to female ratios
of the probability of dying in France and in Sweden, 1750-1930

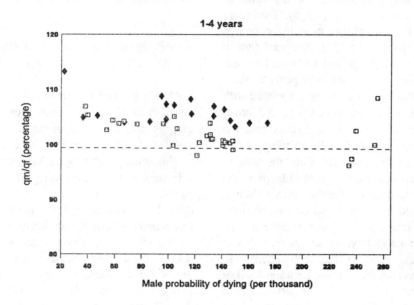

1-4 years

qm/qf (percentage)

Male probability of dying (per thousand)

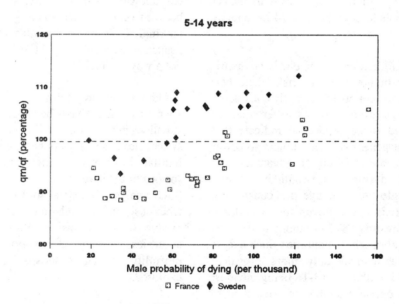

5-14 years

qm/qf (percentage)

Male probability of dying (per thousand)

□ France ◆ Sweden

Source: Annex table A.1.

the size of communes (from less than 5,000 inhabitants to more than 100,000) and the economic specialization of each municipality (mining, textile industry, rural, tertiary urban and mixed). Such estimates permit the analysis of geographical variations in mortality by sex and their linkage to the sociocultural and economic context.

Between 1890 and 1910, the pattern of sex differentials in mortality changed markedly (table 7). Thus, excess male mortality of children under age 1 increased. Excess female mortality evident among children aged 1-4 in 1890 in the two largest cities of the country (Brussels and Ghent), in rural areas and in about 15 municipalities (not shown) diminished noticeably; it

32

TABLE 6. PROBABILITY OF DYING (PER 1,000) FOR BOTH SEXES COMBINED, BY AGE GROUP, ACCORDING TO TYPE OF HABITAT AND ECONOMIC STRUCTURE, BELGIUM, 1890 AND 1910

Type of habitat	$_5q_0$			$_{15}q_5$		
	1890	1910	Change (percentage)	1890	1910	Change (percentage)
Large cities						
Antwerp	334	236	-29	58	40	-31
Brussels	344	254	-26	66	50	-24
Ghent	384	289	-25	68	42	-38
Liège	272	196	-28	60	43	-28
The regions						
Wallonia	189	144	-24	60	41	-32
Flanders	272	221	-19	62	42	-32
Type of district						
Mining	229	156	-32	63	39	-38
Textiles-garments	298	238	-20	64	41	-36
Rural	203	163	-20	58	40	-31
Tertiary-urban	302	207	-31	63	42	-33
Other (mixed)	239	198	-17	62	42	-32
Total	258	186	-28	61	42	-32

Sources: T. Eggerickx and D. Tabutin, "La surmortalité des filles vers 1890 en Belgique: une approche régionale", *Population*, vol. 49, No. 3 (May-June) (Paris, 1994); and I. Devos, *La surmortalité des filles en Belgique de 1890 à 1910: une analyse régionale* (Louvain-la-Neuve, Belgium, Institut de démographie, 1994), Master's thesis; for districts, the classification relates to 41 administrative units according to dominant type of production in each.

disappeared almost entirely in the large cities and in rural areas but persisted in nine municipalities. Yet the most important changes occurred over the age group 5-19 years. In 1890, excess female mortality in that age group was almost universal (present in 39 of the 41 municipalities constituting Belgium) and high (averaging 16 per cent). It showed considerable variability by region, being especially marked in rural areas where mortality levels were low and in regions characterized by textile and tertiary industries. By 1910, excess female mortality among those aged 5-19 had declined almost everywhere. It had been replaced in all large cities, except Brussels, by relatively high excess male mortality. It was also gone from mining regions, and even from rural areas and those dedicated to tertiary activities. Yet it persisted in municipalities where the textile and the garment industry predominated, especially in Flanders. Those industries were characterized by the very poor conditions in which a largely female labour force toiled. The excess female mortality of young women also persisted in 10 or so municipalities in which a mixed economy still prevailed.

All over the country, the reductions in mortality registered between 1890 and 1910 were greater among girls and young women than among their male counterparts (table 8), especially in regions with a completely urban or a completely rural economy. In regions with a mixed economy, the difference in mortality gains over the age range 5-19 was smaller. As result, by 1910 there was a relative homogeneity in the mortality of males by region, whereas sharp inequalities in mortality existed among females. Yet there was no clear relation between the level of excess female mortality over the age group 5-19 years and the overall levels of mortality in each of the 41 municipalities constituting Belgium (figure 6). Thus, the same level of excess female morality prevailed for mortality levels ranging from 50-70 deaths per 1,000. Furthermore, at a given mortality level (60 per 1,000, for instance), excess female mortality at the regional level ranged from 5-30 per cent.

The ratio of the male to the female probability of dying varied among Belgian municipalities partly as a result of excess female mortality and partly because of

TABLE 7. MALE TO FEMALE RATIOS OF THE PROBABILITY OF DYING, BY AGE GROUP,
REGION AND TYPE OF DISTRICT, BELGIUM, 1890 AND 1910
(*Percentage*)

Region and type of habitat	$_1q_0$		$_4q_1$		$_{15}q_5$	
	1890	1910	1890	1910	1890	1910
Large cities						
Antwerp	116	130	101	107	92	126
Brussels	119	121	97	112	84	98
Ghent	122	118	99	107	103	119
Liège	126	115	107	105	85	117
Type of district						
Mining	125	121	109	116	91	108
Textiles-garments	124	118	102	102	87	93
Rural	116	121	94	105	81	101
Tertiary-urban	117	120	105	105	86	103
Other (mixed)	118	121	102	106	85	93
Regions						
Wallonia	120	128	100	105	84	100
Flanders	118	119	102	105	85	94
Total	121	123	101	105	84	97

Sources: T. Eggerickx and D. Tabutin, "La surmortalité des filles vers 1890 en Belgique: une approche régionale", *Population*, vol. 49, No. 3 (May-June) (Paris, 1994); and I. Devos, *La surmortalité des filles en Belgique de 1890 à 1910: une analyse régionale* (Louvain-la-Neuve, Belgium, Institut de démographie, 1994), Master's thesis; for districts, the classification relates to 41 administrative units according to dominant type of production in each.

TABLE 8. PROBABILITY OF DYING (PER 1,000) OVER AGE GROUP 5-19 BY SEX,
REGION AND TYPE OF DISTRICT, BELGIUM, 1890 AND 1910

Type of district and region	Male			Female		
	1890	1910	Change (percentage)	1890	1910	Change (percentage)
Districts						
Mining	60	41	-32	66	38	-42
Textiles	60	40	-33	69	43	-38
Rural	52	42	-19	64	41	-36
Tertiary-urban	59	40	-32	68	39	-43
Mixed	57	41	-28	67	44	-34
Four largest cities	59	47	-20	65	40	-37
Flanders	58	42	-27	68	43	-37
Wallonia	57	41	-28	65	41	-37
Total	58	41	-28	67	42	-37

Sources: T. Eggerickx and D. Tabutin, "La surmortalité des filles vers 1890 en Belgique: une approche régionale", *Population*, vol. 49, No. 3 (May-June) (Paris, 1994); and I. Devos, *La surmortalité des filles en Belgique de 1890 à 1910: une analyse régionale* (Louvain-la-Neuve, Belgium, Institut de démographie, 1994), Master's thesis; for districts, the classification relates to 41 administrative units according to dominant type of production in each.

Figure 6. Probabilities of dying over age group 5-19 for both sexes compared with male to female ratios of those probabilities in 41 districts in Belgium, 1890

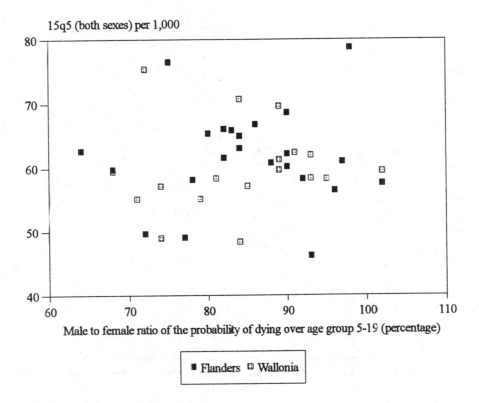

15q5 (both sexes) per 1,000

Male to female ratio of the probability of dying over age group 5-19 (percentage)

■ Flanders ⊡ Wallonia

Source: Annex table A.1.

variations in excess male mortality. Figure 7 displays the relation of the male to the female probability of dying in 1890 for each of the 41 municipalities constituting Belgium; the lines indicating different levels of excess female mortality confirm that excess female mortality was largely independent of the level of mortality prevalent in each municipality, especially when excess female mortality was high. There was considerable diversity in the situations observed. In some cases, diversity arose from variations in male mortality (especially in the case of regions within Wallonia) and in others it was related to variations in female mortality (as in the case of regions within Flanders).

The role of the system of production and the type of economic activities performed by children and young persons of each sex is an important correlate of the spatial variation of mortality over age group 5-19 years by sex. In 1890, the higher excess female mortality prevalent in rural areas was not caused by female mortality that was higher than in other areas but rather

by the fact that mortality among boys and young men was lower in rural areas than in cities. However, in Flanders and other zones where textile production was common, excess female mortality was directly associated with poor conditions of work under which girls and young women toiled.

Regression analysis of the relation between sex differentials in mortality and certain independent variables, such as female and male educational attainment or differential literacy levels between the sexes, yielded no significant results, partly because the municipality is too heterogeneous as a unit of analysis to be a good basis for the measurement of the effects of relevant independent variables. The use of smaller and more homogeneous units (defined in terms of economic activity, for instance) has yielded better though still far from definite results. In particular, the spatial analysis of sex differentials in mortality under age 20 in Belgium towards the end of the nineteenth century suggests that such differentials are associated both with changes in values and attitudes,

**Figure 7. Probability of dying over age group 5-19
in the 41 districts of Belgium, 1890**

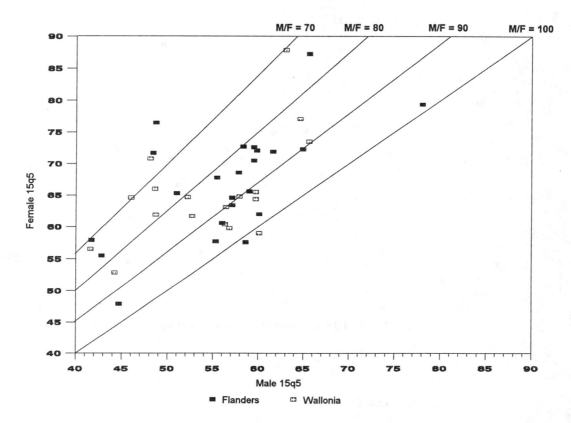

Source: T. Eggerickx and D. Tabutin, "La surmortalité des filles vers 1890 en Belgique: une approche régionale", in *Population*, vol. 49, No. 3 (May-June), pp. 657-684 (Paris, France, 1994).
NOTE: M/F is the ratio of the male to the female probability of dying over age group 5-19.

especially regarding the treatment of young infants, and with the type of economic activity of children aged 7 or over. Naturally, such economic activity was determined by the structure of production at the local level, the type of urbanization taking place, and the social relations between the sexes, which are themselves related to the process of production and urbanization.

In conclusion, whether at the national, regional or local level, there were important sex differentials in mortality and morbidity during the nineteenth century. Beyond age 1 and until the end of adolescence, girls and young women were subject to higher mortality risks than boys or young men. Overall, such a state of affairs lasted until the 1930s, when infectious and parasitic diseases began losing ground as major causes of death in the countries that are today considered developed.

G. THE CAUSES OF DEATH LEADING TO EXCESS FEMALE MORTALITY

Excess female mortality, not only in childhood and during adolescence but also at other ages, was closely linked with higher female mortality caused by infectious and parasitic diseases (Tabutin, 1978; Henry, 1987; Pinnelli and Mancini, 1991). However, most studies refer only to specific countries or to specific periods rather than being comparative; in addition, few focus on children and youth.

A major problem is the lack of comparable data for a long period. Only a minority of countries have data that permit the estimation of the probability of dying by age, sex and cause of death during the nineteenth and early twentieth centuries. A few, such as England, Italy and

New Zealand, have five or six sets of data relating to the period 1860-1930. About 10 additional countries have one or two sets only (Preston, Keyfitz and Schoen, 1972). Most, especially Eastern European countries, lack any information whatsoever.

The reliability of cause of death data is a key concern in several countries where it was not necessary to have a death certificate issued by a physician before register-ing a death.[19] Consequently, the cause of death was established from the reports made by close relatives, and recorded—possibly after reinterpretation—by the officer in charge of death registration. There were, therefore, high proportions of deaths whose cause was poorly reported or unknown, especially among young children. In other cases, causes that carried some stigma, such as tuberculosis, were wilfully misreported (Biraben, 1988).

The proportion of causes reported as "other and unknown" was high among the young. Thus, in most countries with available data, about 20 per cent of deaths to persons aged 1-9 were in that category around 1900 (table 9), though that proportion reached 30 per cent in New Zealand and nearly 50 per cent in Japan. In Belgium, the proportion of deaths with cause unknown was 24 per cent in 1890 among those aged 7-21 but only 5 per cent among persons of all ages. Such variations pose serious problems in the use and interpretation of cause-of-death data for a comparative study. However,

TABLE 9. PERCENTAGE OF DEATHS OF PERSONS AGED 1-9 WHOSE CAUSE IS "OTHER OR UNKNOWN", BY SEX IN SELECTED COUNTRIES, CIRCA 1900

Country or area	Year	Male	Female
England and Wales	1871	22.7	21.3
	1891	20.6	19.6
	1911	12.7	12.0
Japan	1899	47.8	40.7
	1908	49.0	41.6
Italy	1881	22.1	21.8
	1910	22.4	22.1
New Zealand	1901	30.0	27.4
Sweden	1911	21.7	21.5
United States	1900	21.2	20.7

Source: S. Preston, N. Keyfitz and R. Schoen, *Causes of Death, Life-Tables for National Populations* (New York, Seminar Press, 1972).

to the extent that poor reporting affects both sexes similarly, it should not affect an analysis of sex differen-tials in mortality by cause. The evidence suggests that the proportion of deaths reported as unknown is only slightly higher among girls and young women than among their male counterparts. One must also assume, however, that among the deaths whose cause is reported, the quality of reporting is similar for both sexes. The last problem is random variations associated with small numbers of events, especially in the case of rare causes of death.

1. *The general burden of infectious and parasitic diseases*

Infectious and parasitic diseases were still the major cause of death during the nineteenth and early twentieth centuries. Such diseases include tuberculosis, typhus, typhoid, scarlet fever, measles and whooping cough, whose importance varied from one country to another and from region to region, although their relative contri-bution to mortality was high everywhere, accounting for between 30 and 40 per cent of all deaths towards 1880. Their contribution was even greater when mortality over age group 1-4 or 5-19 only is considered. In England and Wales in 1860, more than half of the deaths of children aged 1-4 and over two thirds of those occurring to persons aged 5-24 were caused by infectious diseases. Some diseases were especially prevalent among children of certain ages. Scarlet fever, for instance, predominated among those aged 1-14 years; measles among children under 5; tuberculosis among children aged 1-5, but more especially among those aged 5-24; and whooping cough among the very young.

Mortality due to infectious and parasitic diseases declined considerably between 1860 and 1930, a period that constitutes the critical phase of the epidemiological and public health transition experienced by the Western world (Caselli, 1993; Vallin, 1989). As table 10 shows, there was a progressive decline at all ages of the share of deaths attributed to infectious and parasitic diseases in England. Trends in the probability of dying were even more striking: from 1860-1921, the probability of dying declined from 36 to 10 per 1,000 for age group 1-4, and from 7 to 2 per 1,000 for age group 5-14. In Italy, mortality rates due to infectious diseases declined from 29 per 1,000 in 1881 to 4.3 per 1,000 in 1921 among those aged 1-4 (Pinnelli and Mancini, 1991). In the age group 0-14 years, there was an increase in the relative importance of respiratory diseases (bronchitis and

TABLE 10. PERCENTAGE OF DEATHS CAUSED BY INFECTIOUS
DISEASES AMONG ALL DEATHS, BY AGE, ENGLAND
AND WALES, SELECTED DATES

Age group	1848-1872	1901-1910	1939
Under 1	18	12	6
1-4	55	44	36
5-14	65	49	35
15-24	65	47	42
25-44	50	36	28
45-64	22	14	9
All ages	33	19	9

Source: D. Tabutin, "La surmortalité féminine en Europe avant 1940", *Population*, vol. 33, No. 1 (January-February), pp. 121-147 (Paris, 1978).

pneumonia), diseases of the digestive system (diarrhoea and enteritis) and accidents and violence.

2. *Mortality by sex and cause under age one*

Excess male mortality under age 1 is a constant throughout Western history for all causes of death, and appears therefore to have a biological explanation (see chapter III below). Table 11 shows data for six different countries over the period 1880-1930. Excess male mortality varies considerably from one country to another, being higher in England and New Zealand than in Italy or Japan. In addition, there is also considerable variation by cause of death. Generally, excess male mortality is particularly high when death is caused by pneumonia, colds or bronchitis (varying from 20-30 per cent) and lower when infectious or parasitic diseases are involved (varying from 7-12 per cent). Between 1890 and 1930, excess male mortality increased slightly, in particular for the diseases most common among infants, whose share of overall mortality increased steadily.

Table 12 shows the evolution of mortality by sex for the six most important causes of death in Italy between 1881 and 1921. In every case, there is excess male mortality, which is especially marked in relation to diseases of perinatal origin and those of the respiratory system (bronchitis, pneumonia and colds); the excess ranges from 13-21 per cent. Excess male mortality is again lower when infectious and parasitic diseases are involved and also in relation to gastrointestinal diseases. The distribution of deaths by cause changes markedly between 1881 and 1921, with a dramatic decrease of infectious diseases and diseases of perinatal origin, and an increase of diseases associated with malnutrition.

However, for each cause of death there is a slight increase in the excess mortality experienced by male infants over the 40-year period considered.

Thus, during the first year of life excess male mortality appears to be biologically determined ,[20] with male children being subject to considerably higher risks of dying than female children, be it from diseases of endogenous or exogenous origin. But even at that age, the female advantage is weaker in relation to diseases of infectious or nutritional origin than for other categories.

3. *A decline in the female advantage: mortality by cause at ages 1-4*

Over age group 1-4, girls maintain on average a certain advantage over boys, but it is typically no higher than 2-4 per cent for all causes of death taken together. When attention is restricted to tuberculosis and other infectious and parasitic diseases, which at those ages accounted for 40-60 per cent of all mortality boys died slightly more often than girls in the majority of countries (table 13). However, excess female mortality from those causes was evident in certain countries. That is the case of Norway in 1910 and 1930, Sweden in 1930, and Japan in 1940 or even in 1951, when excess female mortality had disappeared in every other developed country. For other countries, excess male mortality from those causes increased only slightly between 1880 and 1930.

In England and Wales, where reliable data on mortality by age and cause of death for the period 1860-1947 are available thanks to the work of Logan (1950), excess male mortality since 1860 was high for deaths associated with accidents, which accounted for 3 per cent of all deaths, and slight for deaths associated with respiratory diseases and those of the digestive system, which accounted for 23 per cent of all deaths. In contrast, there were almost equal mortality risks for male and female children in relation to mortality caused by infectious and parasitic diseases (table 14). Such equality was largely maintained until 1930, when the importance of infectious and parasitic diseases declined (passing from 54 per cent of all deaths in 1860 to 33 per cent in 1935) an excess male mortality increased rapidly for all other causes. In Italy, mortality differentials by sex were also weakest for infectious and parasitic diseases, but excess male mortality from those causes increased from 1900 (Pinnelli and Mancini, 1991).

Country or area	Year	Infectious and parasitic diseases	Pneumonia, colds and bronchitis	Childhood diseases	Diarrhoea enteritis	All diseases[a]	$_1q_0$ Male (percentage)
England and Wales	1891	112 (18)	135 (29)	127 (38)	126 (12)	128	177
	1931	110 (11)	134 (29)	136 (49)	149 (10)	134	75
Japan	1899	109 (10)	112 (31)	111 (32)	114 (18)	115	168
	1940	105 (8)	118 (28)	118 (43)	112 (19)	117	96
Italy.................	1891	110 (14)	131 (6)	113 (45)	109 (33)	113	201
	1931	110 (6)	123 (25)	116 (28)	107 (40)	114	112
New Zealand	1881	107 (19)	160 (18)	111 (36)	124 (25)	126	99
	1911	160 (6)	145 (14)	125 (54)	117 (19)	128	64
Norway..............	1910	118 (16)	107 (24)	122 (37)	117 (20)	123	75
United States	1900	113 (11)	125 (21)	132 (31)	116 (33)	123	162

Source: S. Preston, N. Keyfitz and R. Schoen, *Causes of Death, Life-Tables for National Populations* (New York, Seminar Press, 1972)

NOTE: Figures between parentheses ( ) indicate percentage of male deaths caused by each group of diseases among all male deaths occurring before age one whose cause is declared.

[a] These four groups represent 70 to 85 per cent of the total causes of death; to that total must be added all deaths from "unknown causes" (which account for 10 to 20 per cent of all deaths) and other less important causes (cardiovascular disease, accidents, neoplasms).

TABLE 12. PROBABILITY OF DYING (PER 1,000) BEFORE AGE 1, BY CAUSE FOR MALES, AND
MALE TO FEMALE RATIOS OF THOSE PROBABILITIES, ITALY, 1891, 1901 AND 1921

Cause of death	Male $_1q_0$			Male to female ratio (percentage)		
	1891	1901	1921	1881	1901	1921
Tuberculosis (respiratory)	0.9	0.4	0.4	118	-	-
Other infectious and parasitic diseases	31.4	10.0	5.4	104	104	107
Cardiovascular diseases	2.7	0.7	0.7	108	-	-
Bronchitis, pneumonia, colds	25.9	34.1	24.6	113	120	121
Diarrhoea, gastritis, enteritis	31.1	45.3	49.7	102	105	108
Congenital diseases	59.2	49.4	29.6	118	102	110
Accidents and violent deaths	4.1	0.3	0.2	144	-	-
Other causes and cause unknown	46.2	33.6	26.7	109	112	116
All causes	201.5	173.8	137.3	110	110	112

Source: A. Pinnelli and P. Mancini, "Différences de mortalité par sexe de la naissance à la puberté en Italie: un siècle d'évolution", *Population*, vol. 46, No. 6 (November-December), pp. 1651-1676 (Paris, 1991).

NOTE: A hyphen (-) indicates that the probabilities of dying by sex were too low to calculate male to female ratios.

Among infectious and parasitic diseases, whooping cough was particularly deadly for girls aged 1-4: between 1860 and 1947, their excess mortality due to whooping cough increased even in England and Wales, rising from 26 to 36 per cent (table 14). The same trend was observed in Belgium (Poulain and Tabutin, 1980): between ages 1 and 6, excess female mortality because of whooping cough remained at about 13 per cent between 1880 and 1925, whereas excess male mortality increased slowly for scarlet fever, diphtheria, respiratory

39

TABLE 13. MALE TO FEMALE RATIOS OF THE PROBABILITY OF DYING DUE TO PULMONARY
TUBERCULOSIS OR INFECTIOUS AND PARASITIC DISEASES, BY AGE GROUP

(Percentage)

Country or area	Year	Male to female probability ratio			Percentage of deaths[a]	$_{14}q_1$ Male
		1-4 years	5-9 years	10-14 years		
Australia	1911	106	96	99	39	14
	1933	93	90	76	29	7
	1940	120	87	93	25	5
Denmark	1921	125	*99*	*68*	52	17
England and Wales	1871	97	103	80	68	92
	1891	101	89	70	54	58
	1911	101	93	74	51	41
	1931	104	104	76	43	18
	1940	105	103	82	32	11
Greece	1928	100	*93*	*71*	58	54
Italy	1881	100	86	74	64	142
	1901	103	88	59	32	41
	1921	105	92	66	25	26
Japan	1899	127	96	65	35	28
	1908	102	78	47	28	23
	1940	97	90	61	33	26
	1951	93	86	77	37	15
Norway	1910	94	88	72	53	25
	1930	92	91	84	42	11
Spain	1930	103	*97*	*66*	32	19
Sweden	1911	105	83	77	58	31
	1930	92	91	84	42	11
United States	1900	104	92	68	44	40
	1930	107	109	89	32	11

Source: S. Preston, N. Keyfitz and R. Schoen, *Causes of Death, Life-Tables for National Populations* (New York, Seminar Press, 1972).

[a] Percentage of deaths by tuberculosis and infectious and parasitic diseases among all deaths with a declared cause among persons aged 1-14.

diseases and diarrhoea. Whooping cough was not a major killer over the age group 1-4: at the end of the nineteenth century, it accounted for 7 per cent of all deaths in England and 11 per cent of all deaths in Belgium. Children died more often from tuberculosis, but whooping cough was a disease whose inflammatory complications were frequent and severe, necessitating careful management.

4. Causes of death over the most dangerous age range for females: 5-14 years

All over the Western world, as well as in the overseas countries of European settlement and in Japan, infectious and parasitic diseases killed more girls than boys age 5-14 years during the nineteenth century (table 13). Around 1890, excess female mortality at ages 5-9 years

TABLE 14. RATIOS OF MALE TO FEMALE MORTALITY RATES, BY AGE GROUP
AND CAUSE OF DEATH, ENGLAND AND WALES, 1848-1947

(Percentage)

Cause of death	1848-1872		1901-1910		1921		1947	
A. *1-4 years*								
Infectious and parasitic diseases	100	(54)	98	(43)	100	(35)	103	(33)
Of which								
German measles	101	(8)	104	(13)	118	(6)	105	(5)
Scarlet fever	105	(20)	105	(4)	109	(2)	-	-
Whooping cough	74	(6)	73	(7)	71	(6)	64	(1)
Tuberculosis	115	(12)	111	(11)	117	(10)	113	(15)
Respiratory diseases Bronchitis and pneumonia	103	(17)	108	(28)	113	(34)	122	(20)
Digestive illnesses Diarrhoea and enteritis	101	(6)	107	(10)	113	(12)	161	(9)
Accidents and violent deaths	140	(3)	127	(4)	141	(6)	158	(15)
Other causes	105	(20)	113	(15)	112	(13)	122	(23)
All causes	103	(100)	105	(100)	109	(100)	122	(100)
All causes except infectious diseases	106	(46)	110	(57)	112	(65)	134	(67)
All causes except accidents violent deaths	102	(97)	104	(96)	108	(94)	117	(85)
B. *5-14 years*								
Infectious and parasitic diseases	91	(62)	84	(45)	84	(39)	99	(24)
Of which:								
German measles	89	(2)	86	(3)	-	-	-	-
Scarlet fever	96	(24)	98	(6)	85	(3)	-	-
Whooping cough	63	(1)	61	(1)	-	-	-	-
Tuberculosis	87	(16)	78	(20)	78	(17)	85	(13)
Respiratory diseases Bronchitis and pneumonia	96	(6)	103	(9)	108	(12)	-	-
Digestive diseases Diarrhoea and enteritis	106	(4)	105	(8)	107	(10)	121	(7)
Accidents and violent deaths	259	(10)	191	(10)	235	(12)	264	(33)
Other causes	108	(18)	97	(28)	100	(27)	116	(35)

41

TABLE 14 (*continued*)

Cause of death	1848-1872		1901-1910		1921		1947	
All causes	101	(100)	*97*	(100)	101	(100)	133	(100)
All causes except infectious diseases	125	(40)	110	(55)	117	(60)	150	(76)
All causes except accidents and violent deaths	*95*	(90)	*91*	(89)	*93*	(87)	107	(68)

Source: W. P. D. Logan, "Mortality in England and Wales from 1848 to 1947", *Population Studies*, vol. 4, No. 2, pp. 132-180 (Cambridge, United Kingdom, and New York, 1950).

NOTE: Data between parentheses ( ) represent the percentage of male deaths by a certain cause among all male deaths. A hyphen (-) indicates that the mortality rates were less than 0.2 ‰.

Male mortality rates for age group 1-4 were 36.4 ‰, 18.9 ‰, 10.9 ‰ and 2.4 ‰, respectively, for each of the four dates.

Male mortality rates for age group 5-14 were 6.7 ‰, 2.8 ‰, 2.3 ‰ and 0.9 ‰, respectively.

was of the order of 10 per cent, and could reach 25 or 30 per cent for the age group 10-14. The contribution to mortality of infectious diseases was very high around 1890 (accounting often for 60 per cent of all deaths) but declined steadily during the early twentieth century to reach 30 to 40 per cent towards 1930. However, in 1930 girls and young women were still disadvantaged, experiencing a slight excess mortality at ages 5-9 but a consistently high excess mortality at ages 10-14 (of the order of 30-35 per cent). In fact, excess female mortality because of infectious diseases at ages 5-14 remained evident until 1940 and even until 1951 in Japan, a country where infectious diseases remained common. Thus, even during the period 1880-1930, when a major epidemiological transition was taking place, that change did not reduce the mortality disparities between the sexes associated with the incidence of infectious diseases over ages 5-14. Indeed, excess female mortality at those ages disappeared only when infectious diseases were no longer a major cause of death.

Data for England and Wales confirm the obduracy of excess female mortality at ages 5-14 (table 14). In 1921, the excess female mortality associated with infectious diseases was even higher than in 1860, and it was still evident in 1947, even though the share of deaths due to those diseases had dropped radically. Whooping cough, which rarely caused death beyond age 5, scarlet fever and above all measles and tuberculosis remained the banes of girls and young women. Between 1860 and 1940, the relative importance of digestive and respiratory diseases increased, together with that of accidents and violent deaths, all of which were characterized by an increasing excess of male mortality, especially in the case of accidents. In 1921, the ratio of the male to the female probability of dying by all causes

combined was 101, but if infectious diseases were eliminated it would have increased to 117. In contrast, if accidents were excluded, the ratio would have declined to 93 (table 14).

In Italy, a marked excess female mortality was present at ages 5-9 (table 15) and 10-14 (not shown) until 1910, with a mean of 10 per cent that increased to 40 per cent for deaths due to pulmonary tuberculosis, 15 per cent for bronchitis and pneumonia (a level that rose even further from 1890-1910), and 15 per cent for diarrhoea and enteritis. Because of accidents and tumours mortality was higher among males. Until 1940, excess female mortality was clearly associated with specific causes of death.

For a wider age span, 7-20 years, which includes many working women, the data for Belgium show that excess female mortality increased from 1890-1910 as industry expanded (table 16). Over those 20 years, mortality for both sexes combined and all causes declined by nearly 35 per cent, while mortality due to infectious and parasitic diseases dropped by 47 per cent. For infectious and parasitic diseases, excess female mortality over the age range 7-20 increased from 19 to 27 per cent (table 16). For respiratory diseases, the transition was from excess male mortality in 1890 to excess female mortality 20 years later. Only for diseases of the digestive system did excess female mortality disappear.

5. Tuberculosis, a disease typical of girls and young women

Tuberculosis was not a new disease in the nineteenth century but during that period it became a major cause of death. Being particularly hazardous because of its

TABLE 15. MORTALITY RATES (PER 1,000), BY SEX AND CAUSE OF
DEATH FOR AGE GROUP 5-9, ITALY, 1881-1940

Cause of death	Sex	1881	1891	1901	1910	1921	1931	1940
Pulmonary tuberculosis	Male	5.5	1.7	2.2	1.7	1.4	0.5	0.4
	Female	9.5	3.0	3.5	2.8	2.0	0.7	0.4
	Ratio	58	57	63	61	64	71	100
Other infectious and parasitic diseases	Male	59.6	37.3	18.9	14.5	12.0	7.4	5.3
	Female	65.9	43.3	20.4	15.5	12.6	7.8	5.9
	Ratio	90	86	93	94	95	95	90
Bronchitis, pneumonia, colds	Male	9.2	5.5	8.1	7.3	6.1	3.7	3.8
	Female	9.0	5.9	9.5	9.1	6.9	4.0	3.9
	Ratio	102	93	85	80	88	93	98
Diarrhoea, gastritis, enteritis	Male	9.2	6.3	6.5	6.2	5.5	1.3	0.9
	Female	11.5	7.8	7.4	7.6	5.9	1.5	0.9
	Ratio	80	81	87	82	93	87	100
Accidents and violent deaths	Male	5.3	2.5	2.6	2.5	2.6	2.2	2.4
	Female	1.4	2.3	2.6	2.2	1.6	1.1	1.1
	Ratio	378	109	100	114	163	200	218
Neoplasms and cardiovascular diseases	Male	4.6	2.5	2.1	2.3	2.1	1.4	2.0
	Female	4.4	2.5	2.3	2.0	2.0	1.2	1.7
	Ratio	105	100	91	115	105	116	117
Other causes or cause unknown	Male	22.9	27.1	16.7	14.1	11.8	5.4	6.3
	Female	21.4	28.0	17.5	14.0	10.7	5.2	5.1
	Ratio	107	97	95	101	110	104	123
All causes	Male	116.3	82.9	57.1	48.6	41.5	21.9	21.1
	Female	123.1	92.8	63.2	53.2	41.7	21.5	19.0
	Ratio	94	89	90	91	99	102	111

Source: A. Pinnelli and P. Mancini, "Différences de mortalité par sexe de la naissance à la puberté en Italie: un siècle d'évolution", *Population*, vol. 46, No. 6 (November-December), pp. 1651-1676 (Paris, 1991).
NOTE: Male to female ratios are presented as percentages.

TABLE 16. MORTALITY RATES (PER 1,000) OVER AGE GROUP 7-20,
BY CAUSE OF DEATH, BELGIUM, 1890 AND 1910

	Mortality rates (per 1,000)				Male to female ratio (percentage)	
	1890		1910			
Cause of death	Male	Female	Male	Female	1890	1910
Infectious diseases	18.4	22.8	9.2	12.6	*81*	*73*
Small pox, diphtheria	2.1	2.4	0.6	0.7	*88*	*86*
German measles, scarlet fever, whooping cough	1.1	1.4	1.0	1.1	*78*	*91*
Tuberculosis and other respiratory ailments	11.2	14.7	6.4	9.5	*76*	*67*
Typhoid, cholera, dysentery	4.0	4.3	1.2	1.3	*93*	*92*
Respiratory diseases	6.1	5.1	3.7	3.9	120	*95*
Digestive diseases	0.7	0.8	1.0	0.8	*88*	125
Other diseases	1.3	1.9	4.9	5.9	*68*	*83*
Unstated or uncertain causes	9.3	9.3	3.7	3.5	100	106
Total	35.8	39.9	22.5	26.7	*90*	*85*

Source: I. Devos, "La surmortalité des filles en Belgique de 1890 à 1910: une analyse régionale" (Louvain-la-Neuve, Belgium, Institut de démographie, 1994), Master's thesis.

43

contagious character, it became associated with various myths and fears.[21] Tuberculosis was considered a shameful disease, attributed to heredity, to alcoholism, to the conditions of life, housing and work, and even to urbanization and industrialization.[22] The incidence of tuberculosis increased considerably during the nineteenth century, reaching a peak between 1880 and 1890 and declining thereafter, although there were certain epidemic episodes when the conditions of life changed markedly, especially as a consequence of war (Puranen, 1989; Mercer, 1990). Mortality due to tuberculosis varied by age, with high rates below age 1, declining over ages 1-9, and high rates thereafter, reaching a maximum between ages 20 and 30. Among women, the disease tended to be more common over the teenage years and early in the child-bearing period (Puranen, 1989).

Towards the end of the nineteenth century, tuberculosis was no longer the main cause of death over such an extended age range; however, from birth to puberty its importance increased. Thus, between 2 and 4 per cent of deaths under age 1, from 5 to 10 per cent of deaths in age group 1-4, and between 10 and 20 per cent of deaths in age group 10-14 were due to tuberculosis. In addition, the share of deaths caused by tuberculosis varied by sex. For instance, around 1905 in England and Wales, deaths from tuberculosis in all its forms accounted for 19 per cent of all deaths among male children aged 5-14 and for 24 per cent of those among females in the same age group.

Indeed, tuberculosis afflicted more girls and young women than their male counterparts, at least between 1870 and 1950, when its incidence in developed countries virtually disappeared. Table 17 shows examples of mortality rates due to tuberculosis over age groups 0-4 and 5-19. In general, below age 5 but especially during the first year of life, there was an excess mortality of male children due to tuberculosis, as there was in relation to other infectious and parasitic diseases. However, there are cases, such as that of Italy (tables 17 and 18) and England and Wales, where mortality associated with tuberculosis was higher among girls than among boys starting at ages 1 or 2. At very early ages, masculine frailty in relation to respiratory diseases was confirmed in most cases.

Excess female mortality due to tuberculosis was almost universal above age 5, increasing rapidly from ages 5-9 to 10-14, where it reached a peak (e.g., the case

of Italy in table 18). Almost everywhere in the Western world, girls and young women aged 5-19 years had at least a 29 per cent higher probability of dying from tuberculosis than their male counterparts (table 17). When data for the different age groups are available, as in the case of Italy (table 18), the differentials between the sexes show an increase with age until puberty, so that excess female mortality because of tuberculosis rises from a level of 30-40 per cent at ages 5-9 to 60 or even 70 per cent at ages 10-14 (before 1940). Furthermore, until 1940 the declining trend in the incidence of tuberculosis in the population as a whole was not accompanied by a parallel decline in the excess female mortality associated with the disease, as was observed in the case of other infectious diseases, where excess male mortality appeared early on during the transition process. There may even have been an increase in excess female mortality due to tuberculosis, especially over ages 10-14. Thus the ratios of the male to the female probability of dying because of tuberculosis over age group 5-19 for four countries were lower in 1930 than around the end of the nineteenth century (table 17), but those referring to age group 10-14 in Italy declined from 1880-1900 and then remained almost unchanged until 1940 (table 18). In England and Wales, as well as in France and probably in other countries, it is only when mortality due to tuberculosis had almost disappeared towards 1947 that excess male mortality associated with that disease began to prevail. That reversal occurred considerably later than for other infectious diseases.

H. A REVIEW OF THE FINDINGS PRESENTED AND CAUSAL HYPOTHESIS

A summary of the findings presented so far is useful before hypotheses about the causes and determinants of the trends observed are discussed. In general, in nineteenth century Europe, excess male mortality under age 1 was high, ranging between 10 and 25 per cent according to country. In most cases, excess male mortality was lower over age group 1-4 and it was even non-existent in certain countries. In contrast, over age group 5-14, excess female mortality prevailed almost everywhere.

The existence of excess female mortality among children and young women is not confined to the nineteenth century. In fact, it can be traced as far back as the seventeenth and eighteenth centuries in such countries as Denmark or France. Evidence of its existence is also present in studies of rural villages and of such cities as

TABLE 17. RATIO OF MALE TO FEMALE MORTALITY RATES (PER 1,000) CAUSED BY
PULMONARY TUBERCULOSIS OVER AGE GROUPS 0-4 AND 5-19

Country or area	Year	0-4 Male	0-4 Female	0-4 Male to female (percentage)	5-19 Male	5-19 Female	5-19 Male to female (percentage)
England and Wales	1871	3.3	3.3	100	13.5	18.9	71
	1931	0.5	0.4	125	3.6	5.8	62
Italy........................	1881	4.8	5.0	96	13.7	22.6	61
	1921	1.4	1.3	108	5.5	10.7	51
Japan	1908	1.9	1.7	112	12.5	23.2	54
Sweden.....................	1911	2.0	1.7	118	10.0	15.8	63
	1930	0.6	0.6	120	6.3	9.8	64
United States	1900	2.6	2.3	113	6.6	10.7	62
	1930	0.5	0.4	125	2.1	4.0	53

Source: S. Preston, N. Keyfitz and R. Schoen, *Causes of Death, Life-Tables for National Populations* (New York, Seminar Press, 1972).

TABLE 18. MORTALITY RATES (PER 10,000) CAUSED BY PULMONARY TUBERCULOSIS FOR MALES,
BY AGE GROUP, AND MALE TO FEMALE RATIOS, ITALY, 1881-1951

Year	Rates 1-4 years	Rates 5-9 years	Rates 10-14 years	Male to female ratios (percentage) 1-4 years	Male to female ratios (percentage) 5-9 years	Male to female ratios (percentage) 10-14 years
1881	14.20	5.48	5.06	94	58	53
1891	3.39	1.75	3.56	99	59	41
1901	4.36	2.21	2.88	97	64	28
1910	4.13	1.74	2.00	106	62	33
1921	2.89	1.44	1.50	104	72	34
1931	1.61	0.46	0.98	118	67	37
1940	1.06	0.37	0.51	116	84	32
1951	0.68	0.18	0.21	102	120	54

Source: A. Pinnelli and P. Mancini, "Différences de mortalité par sexe de la naissance à la puberté en Italie: un siècle d'évolution", *Population*, vol. 46, No. 6 (November-December), pp. 1651-1676 (Paris, 1991).

Geneva. It is therefore a well established feature that became more marked during the nineteenth century, when excess female mortality appeared even in Sweden, a country that until 1870 had been exempt from it.

For almost half a century (1840-1890), excess female mortality was evident over an extended age range (from age 3-19 in France, for instance), which included ages characterized by activities as diverse as school attendance and factory work. Excess female mortality was particularly marked over age group 10-14 (where it ranged from 20-40 per cent) and especially at the age of

puberty, that is, at ages 13-15; at those ages, excess female mortality persisted until in the early 1930s, and in some cases even after the Second World War.

In general, there was no significant relation between the level of mortality prevailing over a period and the magnitude of excess female mortality in childhood. However, the distribution of deaths by cause did matter, since sex differentials by cause of death varied considerably. Before age 1, excess male mortality prevailed for all causes, especially for the typical diseases of the very young, including those of endogenous origin. Beyond age 1 and particularly over age group 5-19, infectious and parasitic diseases, which accounted for between 40 and 60 per cent of all deaths at those ages, were associated with excess female mortality, especially in the case of tuberculosis. At ages 10-14, such excess female mortality varied between 30 and 50 per cent around the turn of the century.

The share of infectious diseases as a cause of death declined between 1890 and 1930, whereas that of accidents and violence, which tended to affect males more, increased. Although overall excess female mortality for all causes of death combined disappeared towards 1935, that associated with certain infectious diseases was still evident in the 1950s, at a time where effective treatments were already available. Such excess female mortality disappeared only with the eradication of the diseases that caused it.

In conclusion, with only a few exceptions, such as Sweden,[23] the excess mortality of girls, female adolescents and young women prevailed over at least three and a half centuries (1600-1930) in countries that are today considered developed.[24] Such excess female mortality probably increased during the nineteenth century and disappeared only about 60 years ago. Its disappearance has led to the current marked excess male mortality beyond age 5. Before 1930, excess female mortality, though universal, displayed different patterns and intensity by age, country, region and social class. The causes of its prevalence, therefore, cannot be simple or uniform.

1. *Hypotheses about the causes of excess female mortality*

Several studies have already been devoted to disentangling the origin of sex differentials in mortality (e.g., Lopez and Ruzicka, 1983; Waldron, 1983, 1985, 1987; and the present volume). It has become an established approach to distinguish biological factors from behavioural or environmental factors deriving from the different roles and status that men and women have in society. Biology and genetics appear to be unfavourable to men, since male children seem to be more vulnerable and less resistant to various diseases, though there are important exceptions to that generalization, as noted in chapter III below. Sociocultural factors, in contrast, are more likely to be unfavourable to females because of overt or covert discrimination against females in relation to access to health care, nutrition, housing and so on.

It is useful to distinguish between biological differences, environmental factors (work, nutrition, education) and cultural factors (the status of women in society and within the family), as proposed by Arriaga and Way (1987) or Wall (1981). However, there is agreement regarding the extreme difficulty of measuring separately the effects of each factor in determining sex differentials in mortality, since biological and sociocultural factors interact in numerous ways. As Vallin (1988) has noted, sex divides the population into two distinct groups according to the biological difference introduced by the presence or absence of a Y chromosome. Since sex in those terms is an immutable characteristic of each individual, it cannot involve a selection effect. However, sex does not provide a firm biological reference or a theoretical norm with respect to which one can measure deviation, since biological sex is itself the basis for sociocultural differences that cannot always be distinguished from biological factors (Vallin, 1988). Thus, in some cases the effects of sociocultural and environmental factors may reinforce and in others may run counter to biological factors. Despite that complexity there is agreement on the existence of a biological advantage in favour of females, whose influence, though certain, is modest and varies according to age and type of habitat.[25]

According to the sociologist Chenu (1988), it is impossible to exclude the influences of social factors, including social constructions of gender, from analysis of the human condition. There is no theory or explanation of sex differentials in mortality that integrates biological, social and economic factors. As Johansson (1991) rightly notes, there is a lack of historical perspective and of well-documented microlevel studies. Thus, there has been a tendency to emphasize the existence of excess male mortality, forgetting that at certain ages excess female mortality tended to prevail (Tabutin, 1978).

Furthermore, the explanatory perspective must be expanded so that the focus is not merely mortality but the more encompassing concept of health. For both girls and boys, death is but one of the possible outcomes of a complex process of illness (Tabutin, 1995). Consequently, just as the analysis of changes in mortality levels requires consideration of the diseases that lead to death, a study of the causes of the sex differentials in mortality requires an analysis of morbidity and the disease process by sex.

Two elements must be taken into account when considering explanations for the sex differentials in mortality at a particular age and in a given historical context: (a) the risk of exposure to disease, that is, the type and intensity of contacts with micro-organisms, parasites or toxins that cause disease and that have various modes of transmission, which are linked to housing conditions, type of work, personal cleanliness, sexual behaviour and so on; and (b) the individual's resistance to disease, which may be genetically determined, dependent on nutritional status (all other things being equal, a better nourished person is better able to resist a microbial infection), or related to specific behaviours (use of the health system, for instance).

Following such an approach, Johansson (1991) notes that "the average woman, who is usually socialized to lead a gender-specific lifestyle which is different from the average man's, will either be exposed to life-threatening hazards equally, more or less often than men. If exposure levels were the same for both sexes, it could still happen that the average woman could be more, less or equally resistant to disease than the average man. If resistance levels were the same for both sexes, it would still be possible for the average women to be more, less or equally exposed than the average man. Those three logical possibilities (higher than, equal to or lower than), when applied to exposure and resistance, produce nine empirically possible biological "stories" about why males or females die at higher rates in any one place and time. There is no biological basis for assuming that any one of those stories will always be true, irrespective of the cultural and biological context in which it must be told. In fact, there is no biological reason to assume that they could not all have been true in different times and places. That makes the study of differential mortality intrinsically historical."

Ultimately, complex theories of differential mortality between the sexes work backwards from sets of age-specific death rates, which are initially explained in terms of differential patterns of exposure and resistance within a specified disease environment. Differences in exposure and resistance are interpreted as a result of cultural norms regarding conduct or welfare (including both positive and negative rights), except where behavioural differences can be explicitly linked to inborn genetic differences that are physiologically expressed (for example, through pregnancy and childbirth) in the same way irrespective of time and place.

Let us address the three major questions raised by the analysis carried out so far. Why is it that excess female mortality over the age group 5-19 persisted for over three centuries? Why did such excess increase during the nineteenth century? And why did it disappear?

2. Excess female mortality under age 20: a general problem linked to the status of women

According to current knowledge, biological factors are favourable in the early years of life to female children and unfavourable to male children in relation to most though not all infectious and parasitic diseases that were important causes of death in the past (see Waldron, 1985, and the present volume). Biologically, males are more vulnerable and females are more vigorous and resistant. That "biological order" was evident in the past up to ages three or four, below which boys were subject to greater mortality risks than girls in almost every one of the currently developed countries. However, beyond the first years of life, the environment gained ground over biology, since only differential behaviour or treatment of children by sex within the family and in society at large can explain the excess mortality to which female children and young women were subject.

From 1600-1900, most of the societies considered in the present chapter kept women in a subordinate position, subject to physical stress (enduring multiple pregnancies and working both outside and inside the home) and largely without access to education. The birth of a boy was a source of joy, that of a girl was no more than a minor compensation. Thus, in nineteenth century France a farmer whose only offspring were daughters was likely to declare that he had no children and one whose wife had just given birth to a daughter might say, as is said even today, that she had a false delivery (Legouvé, 1849). Discrimination against girls was such that it led to higher morbidity and earlier mortality among girls than among boys up to ages 15 or 20. According to Shorter (1984), the sentimentalization of the relationship between men and women, which occurred towards the end of the nineteenth century, was responsible for the emergence of female liberation and the improvement of their status.

3. The nineteenth century and its impact on women

Excess female mortality below age 20 is evident throughout the nineteenth century, often showing an increasing trend or, as in Sweden, appearing in countries where it had not existed before. As industrialization and urbanization expanded, there was a diversification of ideology, social movements appeared, individualism asserted itself, religion lost ground and capitalism took root. During the "century of revolutions", the status of women showed little improvement in a number of European countries.

During the nineteenth century, girls and women were recruited in large numbers to work in industry under conditions detrimental to their health. Women were largely denied access to expanding educational opportunities and the dominant ideology of the time was anti-feminist.[26] Thus, whether women lived in urban or rural areas, whether they worked in a factory or at home, whether they belonged to the bourgeoisie or to the proletariat, the nineteenth century only accorded them a secondary role characterized by submission and dependence (Tabutin, 1978). It is not surprising, therefore, that in a context in which the majority of the population lived in poverty (subject to poor housing and working conditions, poor hygiene, high levels of prostitution etc.), the unfavourable condition of women had a major negative impact on their survival.

It is important, however, to determine more precisely through which mechanisms the low status of women was translated into high female mortality. Which factors were susceptible to the deliberate or even unintended neglect of parents towards their daughters? Why, when overall mortality began to decline, was the progress made by girls and young women aged 5-14 less rapid than that made by their male counterparts?

4. The mechanisms involved in sex discrimination

Up to age 15, discrimination against girls and young women, stemming from conscious or subconscious behaviour on the part of their parents and other family members, might be exercised through five major channels: nutrition; housing conditions and hygiene; access to education; access to the health system; and the conditions of work. The effect of each will vary according to age, culture and local custom, and also according to the dominant system of production.

Nutrition. The essential role that nutrition plays in determining the health of individuals is well known, especially in terms of the relation between nutritional status and resistance to viral or bacterial infections (see chap. V below). A well nourished individual has a better capacity to resist the onslaught of such infections as pulmonary tuberculosis than someone who is malnourished either because of low calorie intake or because of lack of vital nutrients (Puranen, 1989). There is much historical evidence to support the fact that girls and women were not as well nourished as boys or men (Shorter, 1984). In fact, girls were often trained from an early age to "sacrifice themselves" for the benefit of boys. The existence of discriminatory practices between the sexes in the realm of nutrition was very likely in contexts where extreme poverty reigned and the family depended on a subsistence economy, a situation that prevailed in most rural societies during the nineteenth century. However, the extent of such discrimination in other contexts is not clear. It seems, for instance, that discriminatory practices affecting the nutritional status of girls and women were not generally present in England, where early in the twentieth century boys were more likely to be malnourished than girls (Wall, 1981), or in the United States (Courtwright, 1990).

Housing conditions and hygiene. Even early in life, boys and girls had different roles and tasks within the family. Simplifying considerably, it can be said that girls were devoted to activities within the home, whereas boys were expected to undertake activities outside the home. Given the poor housing conditions of the period, which were characterized by lack of ventilation, excess humidity, lack of running water and waste disposal facilities and a large number of persons per room, female children may have been subject to greater risks of infection than male children. In addition, girls and women were more likely to take care of the sick. As Aaby (1989 and 1992) notes, the number of persons per room is an important factor in the transmission of such diseases as measles or whooping cough: their gravity and therefore their lethality depend, it seems, on the dose of virus absorbed. That dose would be greater in constrained environments lacking ventilation. Similarly, housing conditions and personal hygiene are important factors in the transmission of tuberculosis: the bacillum may survive long periods in dirt or debris, in both rural and urban areas. According to surveys of English schools towards the end of the nineteenth century, personal hygiene appeared to be better among boys than among girls (Wall, 1981).

Access to health care and schooling. There is little information on this topic, but as is common today in developing countries, sick girls were taken to hospital or to a physician less often than boys, especially in cases where health services were costly and distant (as was often the case in rural areas). Furthermore, until the introduction of mandatory education,[27] girls were less likely to attend school than boys or to stay in school as long as boys, except perhaps in industrial regions where boys started working very early in life. Yet school attendance had a important role to play in fostering personal hygiene and raising consciousness about health problems. Equality in terms of schooling took some time to be achieved.

The conditions of work. Excess female mortality under age 20, as the present paper has shown, was not restricted to the nineteenth century. It appears to have been a characteristic of rural societies before 1800, and it is in those societies that it lasted the longest over ages 1-4, when children did not participate in either educational or productive activities, and over ages 5-14, when sociocultural and economic segregation by sex becomes marked.

The city, centre of new ideas regarding the family, fertility and the value of children, contributed to reduce the culturally based inequalities between the sexes, but industrialization created other links with the conditions of work. Until the end of the nineteenth century, industrialization depended heavily on the work of children and adolescents. Those segments of the population constituted a cheap and docile labour force, whose economic activity was essential to household survival. Young boys worked in mines, coal pits and metalworks, whereas young girls, being more dexterous and cheaper, were concentrated in the textile industry, lacemaking and domestic work in both urban and rural areas. Thus, in Belgium towards 1896, the coal pits of Wallonia employed 18 per cent of males and 5 per cent of females under age 21, whereas the textile industry of Flanders employed 13 and 33 per cent, respectively, of young males and females under age 21. Excess female mortality over ages 5-14 was general, but its magnitude varied according to the type of industry involved, and thus according to the relative risks to which members of each sex were subject (Eggerickx and Tabutin, 1994). Factory work and domestic service conspired to increase the risks that girls and young women had of becoming sick and dying by reducing their resistance to disease. As a 1890 report of a Belgian medical commission stated, a healthy status among female factory workers was the exception and illness was a common state.

Consequently, during the nineteenth century young women were not able to make up for the handicaps that they had accumulated over past centuries. However, the mechanisms of discrimination by sex became more diversified as urbanization and industrialization expanded and gained in complexity with modernization, especially through the provision of schooling and better health services. Although real progress in reducing mortality among the young was made, sex differentials unfavourable to females persisted well into the twentieth century.

5. *The disappearance of excess female mortality*

The reduction of excess female mortality under age 20 and its final disappearance towards 1930 or 1940 is attributable to three major developments. First, a rapid and irreversible reduction of the incidence of infectious and parasitic diseases occurred, accompanied by an increasing incidence of causes of death that disadvantaged males , such as accidents and violence. Second, social progress favoured females: schooling became universal; the health system expanded; there was increasing regulation of work in terms of minimum age and maximum hours of work; and legal protection of women and children was established. France, for instance, adopted policies protecting children between 1870 and 1940 (Rollet, 1990). Third, the modern family and a different vision of women and childhood emerged, which was accompanied by a decline in fertility and changing aspirations.

Those three changes occurred simultaneously and are linked. As a result, the twentieth century witnessed the transformation of countries that are defined today as developed from rural and patriarchal societies into urban and more egalitarian societies. The recent disappearance of excess female mortality at young ages indicates that the most obvious discrimination against women has also disappeared. There remain, however, many modes of covert discrimination that although less blatant still have pernicious effects and must be combated.

[1]Infant mortality, for instance, ranged from 100 deaths per 1,000 live births in Norway to 260 deaths per 1,000 births in Russia in 1880. At that time, infant mortality averaged 100 deaths per 1,000 in Northern Europe, 162 in Western Europe, 194 in Southern Europe and 242 in Eastern Europe (Poulain and Tabutin, 1980).

[2]See Poulain and Tabutin (1980) for a review of the changes in under-five mortality that took place between the nineteenth century and 1970; Houdaille (1980) for a review of mortality trends over the seventeenth and eighteenth centuries; the special volume of *Annales de démographie historique* (Société de démographique historique,1989) on the decline of mortality; the work of the Committee on Historical Demography of the International Union for the Scientific Study of Population (IUSSP) (Schofield and others, eds., 1991); and Chesnais (1986).

[3]See, for instance, Vallin (1989) on the long-term changes of age and sex-specific mortality in Europe.

[4]This does not exclude the possibility of the existence of excess female mortality during the childbearing ages. For a review of excess female child mortality in developing countries, see Tabutin and Willems (1993); for an analysis of the phenomenon in Northern Africa since 1965, see Tabutin (1992).

[5]Analysis of data quality is beyond the scope of the present paper; note, however, that only the most recent life-tables or mortality rates by age calculated with the greatest rigour were used in the analysis, and that those that lacked internal coherence were rejected.

[6]For an in-depth discussion of the possible measures of sex differentials in mortality, especially excess female mortality, see Willems (1993), chap. 2.

[7]Examples of such scientists during the seventeenth and eighteenth centuries include J. Graunt, W. Petty and E. Halley in England; W. Kersseboom and N. Struyck in the Netherlands; G. Buffon, J. L. Muret, J. B. Moheau and A. Deparcieux in France; J. P. Süssmilch in Germany; P. Wargentin in Sweden; and D. Bernoulli in Switzerland.

[8]Cited by Hecht (1980), p. 62.

[9]Other examples can be found in Behar (1976) and Willems (1993).

[10]Two centuries later, Simone de Beauvoir emphasized that the period of puberty is one of very high risk for women.

[11]See Houdaille (1980) for a critical analysis of these sources of child mortality estimates.

[12]In addition, because of the small numbers considered many studies do not report deaths by sex or present only data relative to adult mortality.

[13]See the study by Finlay (1981) on sex differentials in mortality in London between rich and poor parishes from 1580 to 1650.

[14]In the cases of the Netherlands and Norway, series of national mortality estimates based on reported deaths and population counts that are richer than those used in the present study have recently become available; they could not, however, be integrated into the present study.

[15]The city of Quebec also has detailed data, but its demographic trends are similar to that of Canada as a whole and therefore will not be considered separately here.

[16]Such data are also available for Austria and Belgium, both of which have experienced similar trends.

[17]Mortality during the nineteenth century is still rarely the subject of analysis. Methodological problems (underestimation of deaths, quality of age reporting etc.) are numerous, but in a number of countries civil registration and census data can be classified by province, locality, region or type of habitat, especially after the period 1860 to 1870.

[18]The attenuation of excess female mortality from age 15 or 16 onwards and its disappearance by age 20 in both France and Switzerland reflects the fact that male mortality rises faster than female mortality from ages 15 and 16.

[19]In Belgium, for instance, physician certification began to be required only in 1954.

[20]The only possible exception comprises deaths due to tumours, which in any case account for a very low proportion of all deaths under age one, as seen in the data for Italy.

[21]See, for instance, the chapters on tuberculosis in Bardet and others (1988).

[22]There are several forms of tuberculosis. The pulmonary form was the most common, accounting for 80 or 90 per cent of all cases. It may be transmitted directed through expectorant or indirectly by the presence of bacteria in milk, dirt etc.

[23]There may be other exceptions; however, only Denmark, France and Sweden have national life-tables for the eighteenth century.

[24]There are no reliable data for earlier periods. Although some figures are proposed here and there, they must be interpreted with caution.

[25]Using data for pre-industrial Europe, Pressat (1973) tried to measure the biological female advantage. He concluded that there were two extra years of expectation of life, though he himself recognized that such a difference was determined by both biological and environmental factors.

[26]In his work *La pornocratie ou les femmes* (1865), Proudhon writes that one cannot compare the faculties of men and women, whether in the realm of economics or industry, in that of philosophy or literature, or in that of law. The only role of a woman is to be at the service of her husband and to have children. Proudhon thus arrives at his famous "scientific" calculation that a woman is equivalent to 8/27 of a man.

[27]Mostly dating from the end of the nineteenth century, except in Russia and Belgium, where mandatory education was introduced in 1914.

REFERENCES

Aaby, Peter (1989). La promiscuité, un facteur déterminant de la mortalité par rougeole. In *Mortalité et société en Afrique*, Gules-Pison, Etienne Van de Walle and Mpembele Sala Diakanda, eds. INED Travaux et documents, Cahier No. 124. Paris: Presses universitaires de France.

_____ (1992). Lessons from the past: third world evidence and the reinterpretation of developed world mortality decline. *Health Transition Review* (Canberra, Australia), vol. 2, Supplementary issue, pp. 155-183.

Andersen, Otto (1984). The decline in Danish mortality before 1850 and its economic and social background. In *Pre-Industrial Population Change*, T. Bengtsson and others, eds. Stockholm, Sweden: Almquist and Wiksell International.

André, Robert J., and J. Pereira-Roque (1974). *La démographie de la Belgique au XIXe siècle*. Brussels: Editions de l'Université de Bruxelles.

Armengaud, A. (1973). L'attitude de la société à l'égard de l'enfant au XIXe siècle. *Annales de démographie historique* (Paris), vol. 10, pp. 310 and 311.

Arriaga, Eduardo, and Peter Way (1987). Determinants of excess female mortality. *Population Bulletin of the United Nations* (New York), Nos. 21 and 22. United Nations publication, Sales No. E.87.XIII.5, pp. 45-54.

Bardet, Jean-Pierre, and others, eds. (1988). *Peurs et terreurs face à la contagion*. Paris: Fayard.

Behar, L. (1976). Des tables de mortalité aux XVIIe et XVIIIe siècles. *Annales de démographie historique* (Paris), vol. 13, pp. 173-200.

Berin, B., George Stolnitz and A. Tenenbein (1989). Mortality trends of males and females over the ages. *Transactions* (Itasca, Minnesota), vol. 41, pp. 1-19.

Biraben, Jean-Noël (1988). La tuberculose et la dissimulation des causes de décès. In *Peurs et terreurs face à la contagion*, J. P. Bardet and others, eds. Paris: Fayard.

Blayo, Yves (1975). La mortalité en France de 1740 à 1829. *Population* (Paris), vol. 30, pp. 123-142.

_____, and Louis Henry (1967). Données démographiques sur la Bretagne et l'Anjou de 1740 à 1829. *Annales de démographie historique* (Paris), vol. 3, pp. 91-171.

Blum, Alain Gilles (1990). Mortalité différentielle du XVIIe au XIXe siècle, espace et société. *Annales de démographie historique* (Paris), vol. 27, pp. 13-22.

Boulanger, P. M., and Dominique J. Tabutin, eds. (1980). *La mortalité des enfants dans le monde et dans l'histoire*. Liège, Belgium: Ordina Editions.

Bourbeau, Robert, and Jacques Légaré (1982). *Evolution de la mortalité au Canada et au Québec 1831-1931*. Montreal: Presses de l'Université de Montréal.

Bruneel, C. (1977). *La mortalité dans les campagnes : le duché de Brabant aux XVIIe et XVIIIe siècles*. Louvain, Belgium: Editions Nauwelaerts.

Caselli, Graziella (1993). L'évolution à long terme de la mortalité en Europe. In *European Population, vol. II, Demographic Dynamics*, A. Blum and J. L. Rallu, eds. Paris: Editions John Libbey Eurotext/ INED.

_____, and Viviana Egidi (1991). A new insight into morbidity and mortality transition in Italy. *Genus* (Rome), Nos. 3 and 4, pp. 1-29.

Charbonneau, Hubert (1975). *Vie et mort de nos ancêtres*. Montreal: Les Presses de l'Université de Montréal.

Chenu, A. (1988). Sexe et mortalité en France, 1906-1980. *Revue française de sociologie* (Paris), vol. 29, No. 2, pp. 293-324.

Chesnais, Jean-Claude (1986). *La transition démographique, étapes, formes, implications économiques*. INED Travaux et documents, Cahier No. 113. Paris.

Courtwright, D. (1990). The neglect of female children and childhood sex ratios in nineteenth-century America: a review of the evidence. *Journal of Family History* (Greenwich, Connecticut), vol. 15, No. 3, pp. 313-323.

Del Panta, L. (1992). Infant and child mortality in Italy, eighteenth to twentieth centuries: long-term trends and territorial differences. Paper presented at an IUSSP seminar on infant and child mortality in the past. Montreal, 7-9 October.

Devos, I. (1994). La surmortalité des filles en Belgique de 1890 à 1910: une analyse régionale. Louvain-la-Neuve, Belgium: Institut de démographie. Master's thesis.

Dupaquier, Jacques A. (1979). *La population rurale du Bassin Parisien à l'époque de Louis XIV*. Paris: Editions de l'école des hautes études en sciences sociales.

Eggerickx, Thierry, and M. Debuisson (1990). La surmortalité urbaine: le cas de la Wallonie et de Bruxelles à la fin du 19e siècle (1889-1892). *Annales de démographie historique* (Paris), vol. 27, pp. 23-41.

_____, and Dominique Tabutin (1994). La surmortalité des filles vers 1890 en Belgique: une approche régionale. *Population* (Paris), vol. 49, No. 3 (May-June), pp. 657-684.

Faber, J., and A. H. Wade (1983). *Life-tables for the United States: 1900-2050*. Actuarial Study, No. 89. Washington, D.C.: United States Department of Health and Human Services.

Finlay, R. (1981). Differential child mortality in pre-industrial England: the example of Cartmel, Cumbria, 1600-1750. *Annales de démographie historique* (Paris), vol. 18, pp. 67-80.

Gini, C., and L. Galvini (1931). Tavole di mortalita della populazione italiana. *Annali di Statistica* (Rome), Serie VI, vol. VIII, pp. 321-378.

Hammel, E., S. Johansson and C. Ginsberg (1983). The value of children during industrialization: sex ratios in childhood in 19th century America. *Journal of Family History* (Greenwich, Connecticut), vol. 8, pp. 346-366.

Hecht, J. (1980). L'évaluation de la mortalité aux jeunes âges dans la littérature économique et démographique de l'ancien régime. In *La mortalité des enfants dans le monde et dans l'histoire*, P. M. Boulanger and Dominique Tabutin, eds. Liège, Belgium: Ordina Editions.

Henry, L. (1987). Mortalité des hommes et des femmes dans le passé. *Annales de démographie historique* (Paris), vol. 24, pp. 87-118.

Houdaille, J. (1980). La mortalité des enfants en Europe avant le XIXe siècle. In *La mortalité des enfants dans le monde et dans l'histoire*, P. M. Boulanger and Dominique Tabutin, eds. Liège, Belgium: Ordina Editions.

Imhof, A. (1990). Life Expectancies in Germany from the Seventeenth to the Nineteenth Centuries. Weinheim, Deutschland: Acta Humaniora. In German.

Ireland, Central Statistics Office (1930). *Annual Report*. Cork.

Japan, Ministry of Health and Welfare, Statistics and Information Department (1987). *The Sixteenth Life-tables*. Tokyo.

Johansson, S. R. (1984). Deferred infanticide: excess female mortality during childhood. In *Infanticide*, G. Hausfater and S. Blaffer Hardy, eds. Chicago: Atherton, Aldine.

_____ (1991). Welfare, mortality and gender: continuity and change in explanations for male/female mortality differences over three centuries. *Continuity and Change* (Cambridge, United Kingdom), vol. 6, No. 2, pp. 135-177.

Kane, P. (1991). *Women's Health, From Womb to Tomb*. London: St. Martin's Press.

Legouvé (E. (1849). *Histoire morale des femmes*. Paris.

Logan, W. P. D. (1950). Mortality in England and Wales from 1848 to 1947. *Population Studies* (Cambridge, United Kingdom and New York), vol. 4, No. 2, pp. 132-180.

Lopez, Alan D. (1983). The sex mortality differential in developed countries. In *Sex Differentials in Mortality, Trends, Determinants and Consequences*, A. Lopez and L. Ruzicka, eds. Canberra: Australian National University.

_____, and Lado T. Ruzicka, eds. (1983). *Sex Differentials in Mortality, Trends, Determinants and Consequences*. Miscellaneous Series, No. 4. Canberra: Australian National University.

Masuy-Stroobant, Godelieve (1983). *Les déterminants de la mortalité infantile, La Belgique d'hier et d'aujourd'hui*. Louvain-la-Neuve, Belgium: CIACO-Editeur.

Mercer, A. (1990). *Disease Mortality and Population in Transition*. Leicester, United Kingdom: Leicester University Press.

Mesle, France, and Jacques Vallin (1989). Reconstitution des tables annuelles de mortalité pour la France au XIXe siècle. *Population* (Paris), vol. 44, No. 6, pp. 1122-1158.

Netherlands, Centraal Bureau voor de Statistiek (1975). *Generatie- sterftetafels voor Nederland, 1871-1973*. The Hague.

Osterreichischen Statistischen Zentralamt (1960). *Entwicklung der Sterblichkeit in der Republik Osterreich*. Vienna.

_____ (1979). *Geschichte und Ergebnisse der Zentralen amtlichen Statistik in Osterreich, 1829-1879*. Vienna.

Perrenoud, Alfred (1981). Surmortalité féminine et condition de la femme (XVII-XIXe siècles): une vérification empirique. *Annales de démographie historique* (Paris), vol. 18, pp. 89-105.

Petrioli, L. (1968). Evoluzione della mortalita per cause in Italia dal 1899 al 1962, con prevision fino al 1980. *Rivista Italiana di Economia Demografia e Statistica* (Rome), vol. XXII, No. 1. Special issue.

Piettre, M. (1974). *La condition féminine à travers les âges*. Verviers, Belgium: Marabout Université.

Pinnelli, Antonella, and Paola Mancini (1991). Différences de mortalité par sexe de la naissance à la puberté en Italie: un siècle d'évolution. *Population* (Paris), vol. 46, No. 6 (November-December), pp. 1651-1676.

Pitkanen, Kari J., and James H. Mielke (1993). Age and sex differentials in mortality during two nineteenth century population crises. *European Journal of Population* (Amsterdam), vol. 1, No. 9, pp. 1-32.

Pool, Ian (1983). Changing patterns of sex differentials in survival: an examination of data for Maoris and non-Maoris in New-Zealand. In *Sex Differentials in Mortality, Trends, Determinants and Consequences*, Alan D. Lopez and Lado Ruzicka, eds. Canberra: Australian National University.

Poulain, Michel, and Dominique Tabutin (1980). La mortalité aux jeunes âges en Europe et en Amérique du Nord du XIXe à nos jours. In *La mortalité des enfants dans le mondeet dans l'histoire*, P. M. Boulanger and D. Tabutin, eds. Liège, Belgium: Ordina Editions.

Pressat, Roland (1973). Surmortalité biologique et surmortalité sociale. *Revue française de sociologie* (Paris), vol. XIV, Special issue, pp. 103-110.

Preston, Samuel, Nathan Keyfitz and Robert Schoen (1972). *Causes of Death: Life-Tables for National Populations*. New York: Seminar Press Limited.

Puranen, B. (1989). La tuberculose et le déclin de la mortalité en Suède. *Annales de démographie historique* (Paris), vol. 26, pp. 79-100.

Rollet, C. (1975). *La mortalité infantile en France au XIXe siècle, importance du mode d'alimentation*. Communication au colloque national du CNRS. Paris: Presses universitaires de France.

_____ (1990). *La politique à l'égard de la petite enfance sous la IIIe République*. INED Travaux et documents, Cahier No. 127. Paris: Presses universitaires de France.

Sangoi, J. C. (1985). *Démographie paysanne en Bas-Quercy, 1751-1872*. Paris: Editions du CNRS.

Schofield, R., D. Reher and A. Bideau, eds. (1991). *The Decline of Mortality in Europe*. Oxford: Clarendon Press.

Shorter, E. (1984). *Le corps des femmes*. Paris: Le Seuil.

Société de démographie historique (1989). Le déclin de la mortalité. *Annales de démographie historique* (Paris), vol. 26, pp. 7-195.

_____ (1990). Démographie des villes et des campagnes. *Annales de démographie historique* (Paris), vol. 27, pp. 7-151.

Srb, V., and M. Kucera (1959). *Vyvoj objvatelstva ceskyck zeni XIX. stoleti*. In Statistika a demografie. Prague: Czechoslovak Academy of Sciences Press.

Strömmer, A. (1969). *The Demographic Transition in Finland*. Tornio, Finland.

Sweden, National Central Bureau of Statistics (1969). *Historical Statistics of Sweden*, part 1, *Population, 1720-1967*. Stockholm.

Switzerland, Bureau fédéral de statistique (1935). *Tables de mortalité de la population suisse, 1876-1932*. Contributions à la statistique suisse, 4e fascicule. Berne.

Tabutin, D. (1978). La surmortalité féminine en Europe avant 1940. *Population* (Paris), vol. 33, No. 1 (January-February), pp. 121-147.

_____ (1992). Excess female mortality in Northern Africa since 1965: a description. *Population: An English Selection* (Paris), No. 4, pp. 187-208.

_____ (1995). Transitions et théories de mortalité. In *Sociologie de la population*, Hubert Gerard and V. Piché, eds. Montréal: Presses de l'Université de Montréal-AUPELF-UREF.

_____, and M. Willems (1993). La surmortalité des petites filles dans le Sud des années 1970 aux années 1980. Editions Academia, Working Paper No. 173. Louvain-la-Neuve, Belgium: Institut de démographie.

Takahashi, Shinichi (1993). An attempt to estimate vital statistics in Meiji period based on Honseki population date. *Kokumin Keizai Zasshi* (Kobe, Japan), vol. 163, No. 5, pp. 39-58.

Tugault, Y. (1973). *La mesure de la mobilité*. INED Travaux et documents, Cahier No. 67. Paris: Presses universitaires de France.

United Kingdom of Great Britain and Northern Ireland, Office of Population Censures and Surveys (1992). *Mortality Statistics, 1841-1990*. Series DH1, No. 25. London.

United Nations (1983a). *Levels and Trends of Mortality since 1950*. Sales No. 81.XIII.3. New York.

_____ (1983b). Patterns of sex differentials in mortality in less developed countries. In *Sex Differentials in Mortality, Trends, Determinants and Consequences*, Alan Lopez and Lado Ruzicka, eds. Canberra: Australian National University.

_____ (1988). Sex differentials in survivorship in the developing world: levels, regional patterns and demographic determinants. *Population Bulletin of the United Nations* (United Nations publication, Sales No. E.88.XIII.6), No. 25, pp. 51-64.

Former USSR, Département de l'economie et des statistiques du Gosplan (1930). *Mortalité et durée de la vie de la population de l'URSS, tables de mortalité*. Moscow.

Vallin, J. (1988). *Evolution sociale et baisse de la mortalité, conquête ou reconquête d'un avantage féminin*. INED Dossiers et recherches, No. 17. Paris: Institut national d'études démographiques.

_____ (1989). La mortalité en Europe de 1720 à 1914: tendances à long terme et changements de structure par sexe et âge. *Annales de démographie historique* (Paris), vol. 26, pp. 31-54.

Veys, D. (1983). *Cohort Survival in Belgium in the Past 150 Years*. Leuven, Belgium: Sociological Research Institute.

Waldron, Ingrid (1983). Sex differences in human mortality: the role of genetic factors. *Social Science and Medicine* (Elmsford, New York), vol. 17, No. 6.

_____ (1983). The role of genetic and biological factors in sex differences in mortality. In *Sex Differentials in Mortality, Trends, Determinants and Consequences*, Alan Lopez and Lado T. Ruzicka, eds. Canberra: Australian National University.

_____ (1985). What do we know about causes of sex differences in mortality? A review of the literature. *Population Bulletin of the United Nations* (Sales No. E.85.XIII.6), No. 18, pp. 67-87.

_____ (1987). Profils et causes de la surmortalité féminine chez les enfants dans les pays en développement. *Rapport trimestriel de statistiques sanitaires mondiales* (Geneva), vol. 40, No. 3, pp. 194-210.

Wall, R. (1981). Inferring differential neglect of females from mortality data. *Annales de démographie historique* (Paris), vol. 18, pp. 119-140.

Ware, H. (1986). La disparité entre les reculs de la mortalité et ses répercussions sur la condition et le rôle de la femme. In Nations-Unies, *Effet de l'évolution de la mortalité et des différentiels de mortalité*. Etudes démographiques, No. 95, pp. 256-285. New York.

Willems, M. (1993). *Réalité et diversité de la surmortalité féminine dans le monde et dans l'histoire*. Louvain-la-Neuve: Institut de démographie. Thèse de maîtrise.

Woods, R. I., P. A. Watterson and J. H. Woodward (1988). The causes of rapid infant mortality decline in England and Wales, 1861-1921, part 1. *Population Studies* (London), vol. 42, No. 3 (November), pp. 343-366.

_____, N. Williams and C. Galley (1993). Infant mortality in England: 1550-1950. In *The Decline of Mortality in Europe, 1800-1950: Four National Case Studies*, C. Corsini and P. Viazzo, eds. New York: United Nations Children's Fund.

Wrigley, E. A., and R. S. S. Schofield (1989). *The Population History of England, 1541-1871: A Reconstruction*. Cambridge, United Kingdom: Cambridge University Press.

II. FACTORS DETERMINING THE SEX RATIO AT BIRTH

Ingrid Waldron*

There are more male than female live births in human populations throughout the world, although the extent of the male excess varies between groups. That observation implies that more males are conceived and/or fewer males die between conception and birth. It has been widely argued that males have higher mortality risk than females *in utero,* and consequently it can be concluded that more males than females are conceived. However, evidence reviewed in the present chapter shows that sex differences in mortality risk are unknown for the early period of embryonic development when mortality risk is highest, and the sex ratio at conception is also unknown at present. After a methodological introduction (sect. A), the present chapter discusses three interrelated topics: the patterns and correlates of sex ratios at birth (sect. B); sex differences in mortality before birth (sect. C); and the sex ratio at conception (sect. D).

A. DEFINITIONS AND METHODOLOGICAL CAUTIONS

International classifications define a live birth as one in which the baby shows any signs of life once fully born (United Nations, 1988). One practical problem of measurement is that in a few countries, an infant that dies on the first day or before registration of the birth is not registered as a live birth. A late foetal death (or stillbirth) refers to the death before labour begins or during the birth process of a foetus of at least 28 weeks of gestational age. Gestational age is measured as the time from the beginning of the mother's last menstrual period. Gestational age at the time of birth as a measure of the developmental age at which a foetus dies is imprecise for several reasons, including poor recall of the date of last menstrual period, variable intervals between the time of the last menstrual period and the time of conception, and in many cases a delay of days or weeks between a foetal death and the subsequent birth (Simpson and Carson, 1993). A spontaneous abortion is the birth of a dead embryo or foetus before the twenty-eighth week of gestational age. The term "embryo" is

used until the eighth week of gestational age, and the term "foetus" is used from the ninth week of gestational age. Methodological problems in studying sex differences in spontaneous abortion and late foetal mortality risk include difficulties in identifying the sex of embryos and early foetuses; very limited data concerning spontaneous abortions; widespread underreporting of late foetal mortality; and inconsistencies in different studies and countries in the criteria used to distinguish between a spontaneous abortion and a late foetal death, or between a late foetal death and an early neonatal death (Howell and Blondel, 1994; United Nations, 1988; Waldron, 1983).

The sex ratio of live births is the number of male live births divided by the number of female live births, multiplied by 100. The sex ratio of total births is the comparable ratio for total births, i.e., live births plus late foetal deaths. Those ratios are closely similar if the risk of late foetal mortality is low. Many publications refer to the sex ratio at birth without distinguishing between live births and total births; in most cases, the number reported appears to refer to the sex ratio of live births. The sex ratio at birth is also referred to as the secondary sex ratio (Neel, 1990). The sex ratio at conception is referred to as the primary sex ratio. As will be discussed below, serious methodological problems arise in estimating the primary sex ratio.

All the above-mentioned sex ratios are subject to substantial chance fluctuation unless based on large numbers. For example, for an observed sex ratio at birth of 106, the 95 per cent confidence intervals are 93.6-120.0 for a sample of 1,000 births; 101.9-110.2 for a sample of 10,000 births; and 104.7-107.3 for a sample of 100,000 births (Chahnazarian, 1986).

B. SEX RATIOS AT BIRTH

1. *International and historical variation*

The present section summarizes evidence concerning sex ratios of live births and sex ratios of total births as

---

*Leidy Laboratory, Department of Biology, University of Pennsylvania.

derived from contemporary and historical international data. The evidence indicates that sex ratios at birth are influenced by ethnic differences, foetal mortality rates, fertility rates and social processes, such as sex-selective abortion.

In large developing countries with reliable data, the sex ratios of live births have varied between 103 and 106 in recent decades (table 19). For developing countries with reliable data for both live births and late foetal deaths, sex ratios for live births ranged from 103 in Mauritius to 108 in Singapore (table 20). In countries with good civil registration systems, rates of late foetal mortality are relatively low, and thus there is little difference between sex ratios for live births and sex ratios for total births. Mauritius and Cuba had somewhat higher late foetal mortality rates, with higher rates for males than for females; consequently, the sex ratios for total births were slightly greater than the sex ratios for live births. It is likely that late foetal mortality rates are still higher in many other developing countries lacking good civil registration systems, so that those countries may have a greater difference between the sex ratio of total births and the sex ratio of live births, as observed in historical data for developed countries (discussed further below). Most contemporary data for developed countries show sex ratios at birth between 104 and 107, with relatively little difference between sex ratios for live births and sex ratios for total births

TABLE 19. SEX RATIOS OF LIVE BIRTHS, SELECTED DEVELOPING COUNTRIES[a]

Country	1965-1970	1978-1982
Chile	103.8	104.3
Egypt	—	106.3
Guatemala	—	104.0
Sri Lanka	103.5	104.5
Tunisia	104.6	105.8
Venezuela	103.4	104.5

Sources: M. Schtickzelle, "Evolution du rapport de masculinité a la naissance dans quelques pays occidentaux", *Genus*, vol. 37, pp. 55-60 (Rome, 1981); and United Nations, *Demographic Yearbook*, *1986* (United Nations publication, Sales No. E/F.87.XIII.1).

[a]Including those developing countries with data concerning number of live births by sex for 1978-1982, with at least 100,000 births per year, at least 90 per cent complete reporting and births classified as alive at the time of birth, not later.

TABLE 20. SEX RATIOS OF LIVE BIRTHS, TOTAL BIRTHS AND LATE FOETAL MORTALITY RISK, SELECTED DEVELOPING COUNTRIES, 1980-1984[a]

Country	Sex ratio of live births	Sex ratio of total births	Late foetal mortality risk[b] Male	Female	Sex ratio
Chile	104.3	104.3	7.1	7.2	99
Cuba	106.3	106.5	12.6	10.5	120
Mauritius	103.3	103.6	22.9	20.2	114
Singapore	108.2	108.2	6.2	6.0	103

Source: United Nations, *Demographic Yearbook, 1986* (United Nations publication, Sales No. E/F.87.XIII.1).
[a]Including data for developing countries with at least 90 per cent complete reporting of live births and late foetal deaths and at least 1,000 late foetal deaths in 1980-1984 (or, for Cuba, 1981-1984).
[b]Late foetal deaths per 1,000 (live births plus late foetal deaths).

(Chahnazarian, 1986 and 1988; Johansson and Nygren, 1991; Schtickzelle, 1981; Ulizzi and Zonta, 1993).

Sex ratios of live births generally vary between about 103 and 107. One cause of the variation in sex ratios of live births may be ethnic differences. Blacks generally have lower sex ratios at birth, as shown both by data on sub-Saharan African countries and by data classified by race within countries (Chahnazarian, 1986 and 1988; Feitosa and Krieger, 1993; James, 1987a; MacGillivray, Davey and Lawley, 1986). However, it appears that not all black populations have low sex ratios at birth, since studies of local or regional samples with reliable data have shown high sex ratios for blacks in parts of Africa, as for instance in regions of Nigeria, where ratios of 106-107 have been recorded (Ayeni, 1975; Rehan, 1982).

Additional causes of variation in sex ratios of live births are suggested by the observation that countries with better health and lower fertility tend to have higher sex ratios of live births (Klasen, 1994; Mackey, 1993). For example, data for the 1970s and 1980s, excluding countries where a significant share of the population is African or of African descent, show average sex ratios of 104-108 and 105-106 for countries with life expectancies of 65 and 75 years, respectively (Klasen, 1994). Improved maternal health may be associated with lower late foetal mortality, particularly for males. Decreased foetal mortality for males contributes to higher sex ratios of live births. Fertility rates may also influence sex ratios at birth. Specifically, in low-fertility populations there are fewer high-order births and a higher proportion of low-order births; since low-order births have higher sex ratios at birth, low fertility may contribute to higher sex ratios at birth (Chahnazarian, 1988; James, 1987a; MacGillivray, Davey and Lawley, 1986; Martin, 1994). Based on those relations, it is reasonable to expect that the sex ratio of live births has increased, parallel with the historical trend towards better health and lower fertility.

The prediction that the sex ratio of live births will increase receives only weak empirical support. Historical data for developed countries and recent trend data for developing countries show variable trends in sex ratios at birth (Chahnazarian, 1986; Feitosa and Krieger, 1993; MacGillivray, Davey and Lawley, 1986; Schtickzelle, 1981; Ulizzi and Zonta, 1993). Some of the variation may reflect chance fluctuations and effects of improvements in civil registration systems. However, much of it cannot be attributed to methodological problems and represents genuine historical variation in sex ratios at birth. One factor that has contributed to the historical variation, at least in European countries, has been that sex ratios at birth tend to increase during and just after wars (Chahnazarian, 1986 and 1988; James, 1987a).

Although historical trends in sex ratios of live births have been highly variable, increases in sex ratios of live births have been observed during varying periods in some developed countries (Chahnazarian, 1986 and 1988; Johansson and Nygren, 1991; Schtickzelle, 1981). Also, data for a number of developing countries indicate an increase in the sex ratio of live births between the 1960s and early 1980s (table 19; MacGillivray, Davey and Lawley, 1986). In Tunisia, for example, the sex ratio of live births increased from 104.6 during the period 1965-1970 to 105.8 during 1978-1982.

Increasing sex ratios of live births have been due in part to trends in late foetal mortality rates. Historically, males generally have had a higher risk of late foetal mortality than females, so the sex ratio of live births has been lower than the sex ratio of total births (Chahnazarian, 1986; Schtickzelle, 1981; Waldron, 1983). Thus, the average sex ratio of live births in France between 1900 and 1940 was 104.5, while the average sex ratio of total births was 105.7 (Chahnazarian, 1986). As late foetal mortality rates decreased, the male disadvantage for late foetal mortality has generally declined as well and even disappeared

(Johansson and Nygren, 1991; Klasen, 1994; Schtickzelle, 1981; Ulizzi and Novelletto, 1984; Waldron, 1983). As a consequence, the difference between the sex ratio of live births and of total births has narrowed, and the sex ratio of live births has risen over some periods in certain developed countries (Chahnazarian, 1986 and 1988; Schtickzelle, 1981; Ulizzi and Zonta, 1993). In other cases, the sex ratios of live births and of total births have both increased (Chahnazarian, 1986; Schtickzelle, 1981). Historical declines in fertility, which have resulted in decreasing proportions of higher order births, have probably contributed to such trends. In summary, it seems that decreased late foetal mortality, particularly for males, and decreased fertility have both served to raise the sex ratios of live births over certain periods in some countries.

Recent increases in sex ratios at birth in China and the Republic of Korea have provoked special interest because of the very high sex ratios at birth that have been reported in those countries. In China, the sex ratio at birth increased from about 107 in the 1960s to 111-113 in the late 1980s, while in the Republic of Korea it increased from a range of 104-107 in the early 1980s to 114-117 in the late 1980s (Coale and Bannister, 1994; Lee and Choe, n.d.; Yi and others, 1993). Although ratios of first births have remained relatively stable during that period, sex ratios for higher order births have increased to very high levels. Specifically, in China in 1989 and the Republic of Korea in 1988, reported sex ratios of second births were 121 and 114, respectively, sex ratios of third births were 125 and 171, and sex ratios of fourth and higher order births were 132 and 199 (Yi and others, 1993). Those elevated sex ratios for higher order births in China and the Republic of Korea are in striking contrast to the lower sex ratios observed for similar births recorded in most populations (Chahnazarian, 1988; James, 1987a; MacGillivray, Davey and Lawley, 1986; Martin, 1994).

In both China and the Republic of Korea, strong son preference has been combined with a trend towards smaller family sizes. The desire for at least one son appears to make a major contribution to the high reported sex ratios at birth. That conclusion is supported by the observation that families which have daughters and no sons have very high reported sex ratios at birth. In China, for example, the reported sex ratios of third and fourth births were over 200 in families which had two or three daughters and no sons (Yi and others, 1993).

Several processes appear to contribute to those very high sex ratios at birth, although there is considerable controversy concerning their relative importance. In both China and the Republic of Korea, it appears that prenatal sex screening (using ultrasound, amniocentesis etc.) and sex-selective abortion have contributed to higher sex ratios at birth (Bae, n.d.; Coale and Bannister, 1994; Lee and Choe, n.d.; Yi and others, 1993). In addition, evidence for China indicates that some female births are not registered, so that the reported sex ratio at birth is greater than the actual one (Wen, 1993; Yi and others, 1993). Female babies may be raised by their birth families without being registered, may be registered later as "in-migrants", or may be given up for adoption, abandoned or killed (Coale and Bannister, 1994; Hull and Xingyan, 1993; Johansson and Nygren, 1991; Yi and others, 1993). Although the relative importance of the various contributing factors is controversial, there is general agreement that the high and rising sex ratios at birth in China and the Republic of Korea reflect social processes and not natural biological processes.

In summary, sex ratios of live births have generally ranged between 103 and 107. Several factors appear to contribute to relatively high sex ratios of live births, including ethnicity, reduced late foetal mortality (particularly for males) and reduced fertility. Recent increases of sex ratios at birth in China and the Republic of Korea appear to be due to additional processes, including sex-selective abortion and, in China, underreporting of female births.

2. Correlates of sex ratios at birth

The relations between many different factors and sex ratios at birth, primarily in developed countries, have been studied intensively. Many of the observed relations are of small magnitude or appear inconsistent in different studies (Bromwich, 1989; Chahnazarian, 1988; James, 1987a). The present section discusses several general hypotheses concerning factors influencing sex ratios at birth.

One hypothesis is that the developing male foetus may be more vulnerable than the female foetus to physiological stresses, such that various physiological stressors decrease the sex ratio of live births (Bromwich, 1989). There is some support for that hypothesis but the

findings are inconsistent, which suggests that stressors do not always reduce the sex ratio of live births. Evidence that physiological stressors may reduce the proportion of male births includes the findings that maternal cigarette smoking, excessive use of alcohol and use of amphetamines, opiates and other street drugs are each associated with lower sex ratios at birth (Bromwich, 1989; James, 1987a; Martin, 1985). In addition, poor maternal nutrition appears to retard foetal growth more for males than for females, and chronic malnutrition may decrease the sex ratio of live births (Mora and others, 1981; Williams and Gloster, 1992). However, evidence concerning that last link is inconsistent. Although analyses of recent trends in international data suggest an effect of malnutrition on the sex ratio at birth, earlier studies did not find evidence for that effect, perhaps due to shorter durations of maternal malnutrition (James, 1987a; Williams and Gloster, 1992).

Limited evidence suggests that the relations between maternal disease and sex ratios at birth may vary for different types of diseases (Bromwich, 1989; Chahnazarian, Blumberg and London, 1988; James, 1987a; McGregor and Leff, 1990). Those varied associations appear to reflect a variety of effects, including effects of the sex of a foetus on maternal risk of disease, effects of maternal disease on foetal mor-tality, and possibly the effects of disease on the sex ratio at conception. The physiological effects of a male foetus may increase the risk for certain pregnancy-related conditions, such as pre-eclampsia and eclampsia (Adinolfi, Polani and Crolla, 1985; Lopez-Llera, 1990). Certain types of infection (e.g., genital herpes) may alter reproductive tract physiology in ways that may decrease the proportion of males conceived or surviving to a live birth (McGregor and Leff, 1990). However, contrary to the hypothesis of selective male vulnerability, some types of infectious diseases may increase the proportion of male births. For example, one study found evidence that the sex ratio at birth was higher for mothers that had been exposed to measles at about the time of conception (Langaney and Pison, 1979), although a subsequent study failed to confirm that association (Robert-Lamblin and others, 1983). The sex ratio at birth appears to be higher if either parent is chronically infected with hepatitis B (Chahnazarian and others, 1988). The relations between paternal hepatitis infection status and sex ratio at birth suggest possible effects at the time of conception, not just differential survival *in utero*. There is also evidence that men that experience physiological stressors in their occupations may tend to father fewer sons (Bromwich, 1989), which again suggests possible effects on the sex ratio at conception, rather than on differential survival *in utero*.

James (1987a, 1987b and 1992) has presented evidence that the sex ratio at birth may depend upon hormone levels at the time of conception. Thus, the sex ratio at birth appears to be lower following medical use of hormones to induce ovulation (James, 1987a; Zarutskie and others, 1989). For babies conceived through "natural insemination", the sex ratio at birth appears to be lower if natural insemination occurred on the day of ovulation and higher if natural insemination occurred earlier or later in the cycle (Gray, 1991; Guerrero, 1974; Harlap, 1979; James, 1987a; Zarutskie and others, 1989; but see Martin, 1994). On the day of ovulation, women have high natural levels of the hormones that induce ovulation, and the effects of those hormones may contribute to low sex ratios for natural inseminations on that day. Curiously, the reverse pattern has been observed for conceptions following artificial insemination (Guerrero, 1974; James, 1987a). James (1987b and 1992) has proposed a speculative hormonal interpretation for that latter observation, and has developed a large number of predictions concerning relations between additional variables and sex ratios at birth. For example, he argues that for couples that have intercourse more often, conception occurs earlier in the woman's menstrual cycle, on average, and that is predicted to result in higher sex ratios at birth (James, 1987b). There are several problems with the factual and logical basis for that hypothesis (Martin, 1994). Nevertheless, some evidence suggests that sex ratios at birth may be higher when the frequency of intercourse is higher, for example, for births resulting from conceptions during the first few months of marriage (James, 1987b). Similarly, in several Micronesian populations with a high frequency of intercourse, sex ratios at birth appear to be high (e.g., 110-111) (Brewis, 1993).

Several hypotheses have been proposed with regard to a variety of immunological effects on sex ratios at birth, but attempts to test them have resulted in contradictory findings (Adinolfi and others, 1985; Astolfi and others, 1990; Ober, 1992; Wilkinson and others, 1989). One interesting exception concerns an X-linked gene that influences one type of blood group antigen. Evidence indicates that matings between fathers that have that antigen and mothers that do not have the antigen result in elevated sex ratios at birth, probably due to immunological effects that increase spontaneous abortion risk for females foetuses (Adinolfi, Polani and Crolla, 1985; Jackson, Mann and Schull, 1969). For matings of that type, about half of female embryos would be expected to inherit the X-linked gene for the blood antigen from their fathers, and maternal immune responses may increase mortality risk for those female embryos. Males do not inherit X-linked genes from their fathers. The net effect appears to be a high sex ratio at birth for that parental combination, which may occur in approximately 10 per cent of white and black couples.

Additional evidence suggests that sex ratios at birth are influenced by other genetic characteristics of parents, although the evidence is inconsistent (Chahnazarian, 1986 and 1988; James, 1987a and 1987b). It seems likely that genetic factors contribute to differences in sex ratios at birth between ethnic groups, such as the relatively low sex ratios at birth for the offspring of black fathers (Chahnazarian, 1988; James, 1987a).

As already mentioned, substantial evidence from developed countries and limited evidence from developing countries indicate that the sex ratio of live births is lower for higher order births (Chahnazarian, 1988; Feitosa and Krieger, 1993; James, 1987a; MacGillivray, Davey and Lawley, 1986; Martin, 1994). In addition, sex ratios of live births are generally lower for older fathers. Limited evidence indicates that those relations also apply to sex ratios of total births. Findings concerning the relation between sex ratios at birth and maternal age have been conflicting (Astolfi and Zei, 1987; Chahnazarian, 1988; Feitosa and Krieger, 1993; James, 1987a). No persuasive evidence was found for any of the hypotheses concerning possible reasons for sex ratios at birth to be related to birth order and paternal age (Chahnazarian, 1988; James, 1987a; Martin, 1994). One study found evidence that the sex ratio of live births may be lower for births with older maternal grandfathers (Astolfi and Zei, 1987). That effect is attributed to an accumulation of mutations in the sperm of older men, resulting in increased rates of X-linked recessive lethal mutations; those would not be expected to affect the survival chances of their daughters or their daughters' daughters, but might increase the embryonic and foetal mortality of their daughters' sons.

In summary, multiple factors appear to influence sex ratios at birth. For example, sex ratios at birth appear to be lower for births to mothers that smoke, births to black fathers and older fathers, higher order births and births following induced ovulation. It is unknown to what extent the factors that influence sex ratios at birth act through effects on sex ratios at conception or effects on sex differences in mortality before birth.

C. SEX DIFFERENCES IN RISK OF DEATH PRIOR TO BIRTH

It would be of considerable interest to determine sex differences in mortality throughout the period from conception to birth. Unfortunately, that is not possible because of serious methodological problems. In many cases, death of the conceptus occurs very early, even before the woman or her physician recognize that she is pregnant. For example, one very good study of healthy women used sensitive hormonal assays that could detect a pregnancy as early as a week after fertilization of an egg and found that 22 per cent of detected pregnancies ended before the pregnancy was clinically recognized; an additional 9 per cent of pregnancies ended in spontaneous abortion after the pregnancy was clinically recognized and before 28 weeks of gestational age (Wilcox and others, 1988). Other studies have also found evidence of high rates of loss before pregnancies have been clinically recognized, followed by spontaneous abortion rates of about 10 per cent for clinically recognized pregnancies (Simpson and Carson, 1993; Wilcox and others, 1988; World Health Organization, 1984). Thus, current evidence indicates that more than two thirds of prenatal mortality occurs before pregnancies are clinically recognized. The sex ratio for those very early deaths is unknown, because in those cases the conceptus is almost never available for sex identification.

1. *Spontaneous abortions*

Studies of sex differences in the risk of spontaneous abortion have investigated embryonic and foetal mortality from the time that the pregnancy is clinically recognized (typically about 6 weeks of gestational age) to 27 weeks of gestational age. Those studies have encountered substantial methodological problems. Anatomical identification of sex is impossible in the early stages of development and very difficult throughout the first trimester (Byrne and Warburton, 1987). Analysis of chromosomal make-up can identify sex, but many findings have been distorted by problems, such as contamination of samples with maternal tissue or a tendency

for sex chromatin analyses of spontaneous abortions to overestimate the proportion of males (Hassold, Quillen and Yamane, 1983; Waldron, 1983).

It is also important to recognize that a substantial portion of early spontaneous abortions involve conceptuses that are not normal males or females (i.e., not XY or XX). For example, current evidence indicates that approximately 5-10 per cent of spontaneous abortions are monosomy X (i. e., have a single X chromosome in each cell), about the same proportion are triploid (i.e., have three sets of chromosomes, including three sex chromosomes, either XXX or XXY), and approximately 1-5 per cent are tetraploid (Eiben and others, 1990; Neel, 1990; Simpson and Carson, 1993). Taken together, those chromosomal abnormalities have been observed in approximately 15-25 per cent of spontaneous abortions, compared to less than 2 per cent of a representative sample of embryos and less than 0.02 per cent of live births (Eiben and others, 1990; Neel, 1990; Simpson and Carson, 1993; Zhou and others, 1989). Thus, embryos with those types of sex chromosome abnormalities have a high risk of spontaneous abortion and they constitute a substantial fraction of all spontaneous abortions. The proportion of embryos which are neither XX nor XY is particularly high for spontaneous abortions at younger gestational ages.

Studies of sex differences in spontaneous abortion risk continue to yield conflicting results, even in those with very good methodology and chromosomally normal samples. For example, two such studies of chromosomally normal spontaneous abortions found sex ratios of 72 and 124 to 145, respectively (Eiben and others, 1990; Hassold, Quilllen and Yamane, 1983). Another excellent study found a sex ratio of 123 for chromosomally and anatomically normal spontaneous abortions (Byrne and Warburton, 1987). As sample sizes in those studies ranged from 350 to 1,000, chance fluctuation could account for some but probably not all of the differences in results. Another possible reason for the lower sex ratio in the first study might be the younger gestational age of the sample (primarily 8-13 weeks, compared with primarily 9-20 and 12-24 weeks in the other studies). However, that interpretation is not supported by analyses of the relations between sex ratio and gestational age within samples (Eiben and others, 1990; Byrne and Warburton, 1987).

In all of the three studies mentioned above, many of the spontaneous abortions had at least some chromosomal or anatomical abnormality (52, 50 and 19 per cent abnormal, respectively) (Eiben and others, 1990; Hassold and others, 1983; Byrne and Warburton, 1987). In each study, the sex ratio for spontaneous abortions with abnormalities was closer to 100 than the sex ratio for spontaneous abortions that were chromosomally or anatomically normal (sex ratios of 95 and 113 for autosomal trisomies and 92 for anatomical abnormalities).[1] Thus, abnormal embryos and foetuses have a high mortality risk that appears to be associated with a reduced sex difference in risk.

Sex differences in embryonic and foetal mortality can also be estimated on the basis of trends in the sex ratio of embryos and foetuses *in utero* at different gestational ages. Studies of sex ratios *in utero* have yielded conflicting results because of methodological problems and chance variation due to small sample sizes (Waldron, 1983). Results of studies with reliable methodology and large sample sizes (over 400) are summarized below. Nevertheless, those data must be interpreted with caution because all but one of the studies (Bartels, Hansmann and Eiben, 1990) were based on samples of induced abortions, which could be sex-biased if the decision to have an induced abortion is influenced by the sex of the foetus (for example, when there is the possibility of an X-linked disease that would affect sons and not daughters). In addition, comparisons between studies could be affected by differences in methods and samples.

The sex ratio of embryos and foetuses *in utero* appears to decrease as gestational age increases. For younger gestational ages, sex ratios have been estimated at 132 for approximately the seventh week of gestational age (Lee and Takano, 1970) and 116-117 for samples primarily 6-8 weeks and approximately 5-12 weeks gestational age (Bartels and others, 1990; Zhou and others, 1989). In contrast, for older gestational ages sex ratios have been estimated at 111 for approximately 10-26 weeks of gestational age (Kellokumpu-Lehtinen and Pelliniemi, 1984) and 106 for approximately 17-20 weeks of gestational age (Jakobovits, Jakobovits and Iffy, 1986). Those results suggest that there are more males than females by the second month of gestational age and that the sex ratio is reduced at older gestational ages. Trends observed within samples also suggest that sex ratios *in utero* decrease with increasing gestational age (Jakobovits and others, 1986; Kellokumpu-Lehtinen and Pelliniemi, 1984). Taken together, the findings suggest that between the second and fifth month of

gestational age males may have higher mortality risk than females. It is also of interest that for two of the three previously cited studies of spontaneous abortion, the sex ratio for chromosomally normal spontaneous abortions was higher than the sex ratio *in utero* for approximately the third, fourth and fifth months of gestational age; that pattern implies a higher risk of spontaneous abortions for males.

In summary, evidence concerning sex differences in risk of spontaneous abortion is conflicting but nevertheless suggests that, for chromosomally and anatomically normal foetuses, males may have higher mortality risk than females from about the third to the fifth month of gestational age. For chromosomally or anatomically abnormal foetuses, limited evidence suggests that sex differences in mortality risk are reduced or absent. For younger embryos, mortality risk is very high, and it is unknown what—if any—sex differences in mortality risk there may be during the first few months.

2. *Late foetal mortality*

Data for developing countries with adequate registration indicate that males have as high or higher late foetal (i.e., at least 28 weeks of gestational age) mortality than females (table 20). Similarly, a community study in Central Sudan found that males had a higher late foetal mortality risk than females (Taha and others, 1994). Hospital data also suggest higher male risk or no sex difference in risk. A study in Shanghai included only late foetal deaths before labour began and found no significant sex difference in risk (Zhang and Cai, 1992). A study of a very large sample of Latin American hospital births found a sex ratio of 113 for the combined risk of late foetal mortality and late spontaneous abortions (including all foetal deaths from about 20 weeks of gestational age) (Gadow and others, 1991).

Data for developed countries show that males had higher rates of late foetal mortality than females in the early and mid-twentieth century, but that sex difference decreased during the twentieth century (Chahnazarian, 1986 and 1988; Johansson and Nygren, 1991; Klasen, 1994; Little and Weinberg, 1993; Schtickzelle, 1981; Ulizzi and Novelletto, 1984; Waldron, 1983). No significant sex difference in late foetal mortality risk has been observed in recent data for a number of developed countries. In order to understand that attenuation of sex differences, it is useful to consider trends for specific categories of late foetal mortality. Evidence indicates that improved medical care and maternal health have been particularly effective in reducing the specific categories of late foetal mortality that were responsible for males' higher risk, and that factor has been a major cause of the decrease in sex differences (Waldron, 1983). Specifically, data for England and Scotland for an early period around 1940 and for more recent decades indicate that males have had higher rates of late foetal mortality due to difficult labour and birth injuries, and also to diseases and accidents of the mother (McKeown and Lowe, 1951; United Kingdom, Registrar General, 1976; United States Department of Health, Education and Welfare, 1966). Females have had higher late foetal mortality due to congenital malformations, in particular congenital malformations of the central nervous system. As obstetric care and maternal health have improved, the proportion of late foetal deaths due to difficult labour, birth injuries and diseases and accidents of the mother has been substantially reduced, while the proportion due to congenital malformations has increased. As the importance of the categories with a male excess has declined, the male excess for total late foetal mortality has declined and disappeared in many developed countries. Those observations illustrate how environmental factors, such as changes in medical technology, can influence sex differences in mortality risk, even prior to birth.

D. SEX RATIO AT CONCEPTION

The sex ratio at conception cannot be measured directly, at least not in humans at the present time. Several authors have attempted to estimate it indirectly from observed sex differences in live births, late foetal deaths and spontaneous abortions. Most authors have concluded that more males than females are conceived, since there are more male than female live births; males have as many or more late foetal deaths than females; and it appears that the risk of spontaneous abortions may also be higher for males than for females from about the third month of gestational age. Estimates of sex ratios at conception range as high as 170 but are generally lower, e.g., 115 based on more recent, methodologically superior data (Chahnazarian, 1988; Hassold, Quillen and Yamane, 1983). Other researchers have also argued that the sex ratio at conception is substantially greater than 100, based on evidence that there are more male than female embryos by the end of the second month of gestational age (Lee and Takano, 1970).

However, all those estimates must be considered highly speculative since no information is available concerning sex differences in mortality risk during the period of high mortality rates in the first few weeks after conception. Since the causes of death vary for different developmental stages, it is possible that females have higher mortality risk during the very early stages of development, even though males have higher mortality risk during later stages of development. For example, Gartler (1990) suggests that females may be at risk during early development due to problems related to inactivation of one X chromosome in each cell, a process that occurs only in females. At an even earlier stage of development, researchers have studied cell divisions during the first few days after an egg has been fertilized; in both cows and mice, those early cell divisions occur more rapidly in males than females, and limited evidence suggests the possibility of greater female vulnerability at that very early stage of development (Burgoyne, 1993; Yadav, King and Betteridge, 1993). Although those last observations are based on data for other mammals, they may be relevant for humans also (Burgoyne, 1993).

In summary, sex differences in mortality risk during early development are currently unknown. Consequently, it is impossible to extrapolate from data on live births, late foetal mortality and recognized spontaneous abortions to estimates of sex ratios at conception.

An alternative approach to estimating the sex ratio at conception has been to measure the relative numbers of X-bearing and Y-bearing sperm, which are responsible for the conception of females and males, respectively. Recent studies using excellent methods to identify X and Y chromosomes in large samples of sperm have found equal numbers of X- and Y-bearing sperm (Goldman and others, 1993; Han and others, 1993a and 1993b; Lobel, Pomponio and Mutter, 1993; Williams and others, 1993). Of course, it is possible that X- or Y-bearing sperm are favoured by the particular conditions encountered in the female reproductive tract or in the process of fertilization, so the sex ratio at conception may differ from the sex ratio of sperm. However, it is of interest that the sex ratio at birth following *in vitro* fertilization appears to be about the same as the sex ratio at birth following natural insemination (Friedler, Mashiach and Laufer, 1992). Also, there does not appear to be maternal immunological selection against Y- or X-bearing sperm (Adinolfi and others, 1985). In addition, equal numbers of X- and Y-bearing sperm have generally been found after a variety of manipulations, including requiring sperm to swim up from the bottom of a centrifuge tube or requiring human sperm to penetrate a hamster egg (Han and others, 1993a and 1993b; Lobel, Pomponio and Mutter, 1993), although some studies using the hamster egg method have observed a modest excess of X-bearing sperm (Martin and Rademaker, 1992). It appears that some laboratory procedures can select for X- or Y-bearing sperm but they are unrelated to conditions occurring during natural insemination (Johnson and others, 1993).

Taken together, current evidence concerning X- and Y-bearing sperm suggests that the sex ratio at conception may be about 100. However, that conclusion remains highly tentative since it is not known whether the conditions of natural insemination significantly alter the sex ratio observed in the studies of sperm samples.

In conclusion, it has been proven impossible thus far to estimate the sex ratio at conception or even to conclude whether more males or females are conceived. However, it appears that either more males are conceived or females have higher mortality than males during the very early stages of development, since evidence from chorionic villus testing and induced abortions indicates that there are already more males than females by the second month of development (Bartles, Hansmann and Eiben, 1990; Lee and Takano, 1970; Zhou and others, 1989).

E. CONCLUSIONS

In both developing and developed countries, more males than females are born. Sex ratios of live births usually vary between about 103 and 107. Higher sex ratios at birth have been reported in recent years in China and the Republic of Korea but they appear to be due to sex-selective abortion and underreporting of female births.

The sex ratio of live births is determined by the sex ratio at conception and sex differences in mortality between conception and birth. Relatively good information is available concerning sex differences in mortality risk in the later stages of pregnancy. However, information is increasingly incomplete and inconclusive for earlier stages in the process.

The risk of late foetal mortality has generally been higher for males than for females in developing countries and in historical data for developed countries. Recent data for several developed countries indicate that sex differences in late foetal mortality have decreased and even disappeared, as improvements in maternal health and obstetric care have reduced the causes of late foetal mortality that contribute to males' higher risk. Decreased rates and sex ratios for late foetal mortality have contributed to a trend towards higher sex ratios of live births in more developed countries.

Current evidence concerning sex differences in spontaneous abortion risk is limited and inconsistent. However, the evidence suggests that for chromosomally and anatomically normal embryos and foetuses, males may have higher mortality risk than females from about the third month of gestational age. For the substantial fraction of spontaneous abortions that have chromosomal or anatomic abnormalities, sex differences in risk of spontaneous abortion appear to be reduced or absent.

During the first few weeks after conception, mortality risk is very high, and it appears that more than two thirds of prenatal mortality occurs during that very early period. Unfortunately, no information is available concerning sex differences in mortality risk in that period. Because mortality risk at different stages of development is influenced by different developmental processes and causes of death, it cannot be assumed that the greater mortality risk for males at later stages of development also applies to the very early stages of development.

The sex ratio at conception has not been observed directly and cannot be inferred from available information. However, available evidence does indicate that there are already more male than female embryos by the second month after conception. That differences implies that more males are conceived and/or females have higher mortality risk during the first few weeks after conception.

Given the uncertainty concerning the basic processes that contribute to the excess of male over female births, it is not surprising that there has been only limited understanding of the processes by which various factors influence sex ratios at birth. For example, there is good evidence that sex ratios at birth are generally lower for higher order births, for older fathers, for mothers who smoke and for blacks, but it is not known whether those variables influence the sex ratio at conception or sex differences in mortality before birth, or both. In conclusion, much remains to be learned concerning the basic processes that contribute to the birth of more males than females and the factors that contribute to variation in sex ratios at birth.

NOTE

[1] An autosomal trisomy, with a third copy of one of the autosomal or non-sex chromosomes, is a very common type of chromosomal abnormality in samples of spontaneous abortions.

REFERENCES

Adinolfi, M., P. E. Polani and J. A. Crolla (1985). Is the sex ratio at birth affected by immune selection? *Experimental and Clinical Immunogenetics* (Basel), vol. 2, pp. 54-64

Astolfi, P., and others (1990). The effect of parental and maternal-fetal histocompatibility at MHC on sex ratio in offspring. *Tissue Antigens* (Copenhagen), vol. 35, pp. 172-177.

Astolfi, P., and G. Zei. (1987). Variation of the human secondary sex ratio and lethal recessive X-linked mutations. *Journal of Biosocial Science* (Cambridge, United Kingdom), vol. 19, pp. 283-294.

Ayeni, O. (1974). Sex ratio of live births in south-western Nigeria. *Annals of Human Biology* (London), vol. 2, No. 2, pp. 137-141.

Bartels, I., I. Hansmann and B. Eiben (1990). Excess of females in chromosomally normal spontaneous abortuses. *American Journal of Medical Genetics* (New York), vol. 35, pp. 297-298.

Bae, W.-O. (n.d.). Sex ratio at birth in Korea. Seoul, Republic of Korea: Korea Institute for Health and Social Affairs.

Brewis, A. A. (1993). Sex ratios at birth in a Micronesian atoll population. *Social Biology* (Madison, Wisconsin), vol. 40, Nos. 3 and 4, pp. 207-213.

Bromwich, P. (1989). The sex ratio, and ways of manipulating it. In *Progress in Obstetrics and Gynecology*, vol. 7, John Studd, ed. Edinburgh and New York: Churchill Livingstone.

Burgoyne, P. S. (1993). A Y-chromosomal effect on blastocyst cell number in mice. *Development* (Rome), vol. 117, pp. 341-345.

Byrne, J., and D. Warburton (1986). Male excess among anatomically normal fetuses in spontaneous abortions. *American Journal of Medical Genetics* (New York), vol. 26, pp. 605-611.

Chahnazarian, A. (1986). Determinants of the sex ratio at birth. Princeton, New Jersey: Princeton University, Department of Sociology and Program in Demography. Doctoral thesis.

_____ (1988). Determinants of the sex ratio at birth: review of recent literature. *Social Biology* (Madison, Wisconsin), vol. 35, Nos. 3 and 4, pp. 214-235.

_____, B. S. Blumberg and W. T. London (1988). Hepatitis B and the sex ratio at birth: a comparative analysis of four populations. *Journal of Biosocial Science* (Cambridge, United Kingdom), vol. 20, pp. 357-370.

Coale, Ansley J., and J. Banister (1994). Five decades of missing females in China. *Demography* (Washington, D.C.), vol. 31, pp. 459-479.

Eiben, B., and others (1990). Cytogenetic analysis of 750 spontaneous abortions with the direct-preparation method of chorionic villi and its implications for studying genetic causes of pregnancy wastage. *American Journal of Human Genetics* (Chicago), vol. 47.

Feitosa, M. F., and H. Krieger (1993). Some factors affecting the secondary sex ratio in a Latin American sample. *Human Biology* (Detroit), vol. 65, No. 2, pp. 273-278.

Friedler, S., S. Mashiach and N. Laufer (1992). Births in Israel resulting from in vitro fertilization/embryo transfer, 1982-1989. *Human Reproduction* (Oxford), vol. 7, No. 8, pp. 1159-1163.

Gadow, E. C., and others (1991). Stillbirth rate and associated risk factors among 869,750 Latin American hospital births, 1982-1986. *International Journal of Gynecology and Obstetrics* (Limerick, Ireland), vol. 35, pp. 209-214.

Gartler, S. M. (1990). The relevance of X-chromosome inactivation to gender differentials in longevity. In *Gender, Health and Longevity: Multidisciplinary Perspectives*, M. G. Ory and H. R. Warner, eds. New York: Springer.

Goldman, A. S. H., and others (1993). Analysis of the primary sex ratio, sex chromosome aneuploidy and diploidy in human sperm using dual-colour fluorescence in situ hybridization. *European Journal of Human Genetics* (Basel), vol. 1, pp. 325-334.

Gray, R. H. (1991). Natural family planing and sex selection: fact or fiction? *American Journal of Obstetrics and Gynecology* (St. Louis), vol. 165, pp. 1982-1984.

Guerrero, R. (1974). Association of the type and time of insemination within the menstrual cycle with the human sex ratio at birth. *New England Journal of Medicine* (Boston), vol. 291, No. 20, pp. 1056-1059.

Han, T. L., and others (1993a). Detection of X- and Y-bearing human spermatazoa after motile sperm isolation by swim-up. *Fertility and Sterility* (Birmingham, Alabama), vol. 60, No. 6, pp. 1046-1051.

Han, T. L., and others (1993b). Simultaneous detection of X- and Y-bearing human sperm by double fluorescence in situ hybridization. *Molecular Reproduction and Development*, vol. 34, pp. 308-313.

Harlap, S. (1979). Gender of infants conceived on different days of the menstrual cycle. *New England Journal of Medicine* (Boston), vol. 300, No. 26, pp. 1445-1448.

Hassold T., S. D. Quillen and J. A. Yamane (1983). Sex ratio in spontaneous abortions. *Annals of Human Genetics* (Cambridge, United Kingdom), vol. 47, pp. 39-47.

Howell, E. M., and B. Blondel (1994). International infant mortality rates: bias from reporting differences. *American Journal of Public Health* (Washington, D.C.), vol. 84, No. 5, pp. 850-852.

Hull, T. H., and W. Xingyan (1993). Rising sex ratios at birth in China: evidence from the 1990 population census. Briefing Paper, No. 31. Canberra: Australian National University, Australian Development Studies Network.

Jackson, C. E., J. D. Mann and W. J. Schull (1969). Xg[a] blood group system and the sex ratio in man. *Nature* (London), vol. 222, pp. 445-446.

Jakobovits, A. A., A. Jakobovits and L. Iffy (1986). Sex ratio of fetuses during the second trimester of gestation. *Acta Anatomica* (Basel), vol. 126, pp. 54-56.

James, W. H. (1987a). The human sex ratio, part: a review of the literature. *Human Biology* (Detroit), vol. 59, No. 5, pp. 721-752.

_____ (1987b). The human sex ratio, part 2, A hypothesis and a program of research. *Human Biology* (Detroit), vol. 59, No. 6, pp. 873-900.

_____ (1992). The hypothesized hormonal control of mammalian sex ratio at birth: a second update. *Journal of Theoretical Biology* (London), vol. 155, pp. 121-128.

Johansson, S., and O. Nygren (1991). The missing girls of China: a new demographic account. *Population and Development Review* (New York), vol. 17, No. 1, pp. 35-51.

Johnson, L. A., and others (1993). Gender preselection in humans? Flow cytometric separation of X and Y spermatozoa for the prevention of X-linked diseases. *Human Reproduction* (Oxford), vol. 8, No. 10, pp. 1733-1739.

Kellokumpu-Lehtinen, P., and L. J. Pelliniemi (1984). Sex ratio of human conceptuses. *Obstetrics and Gynecology* (New York), vol. 64, pp. 220-222.

Klasen, S. (1994). "Missing women" reconsidered. *World Development* (Boston and Oxford, United Kingdom), vol. 22, pp. 1061-1071.

Langaney, A., and G. Pison (1979). Rougeole et augmentation temporaire de la masculinité des naissances: coincidence ou causalité. *Compte rendu Academy Science* (Paris), Series D, vol. 289, pp. 1255-1258.

Lee, S., and K. Takano (1970). Sex ratio in human embryos obtained from induced abortion: histological examination of the gonad in 1,452 cases. *American Journal of Obstetrics and Gynecology* (St. Louis), vol. 108, pp. 1294-1296.

Lee, S. W., and M. K. Choe (n.d.). Child mortality by sex in the Republic of Korea. Unpublished manuscript.

Little, R. E., and C. R. Weinberg (1992). Risk factors for antepartum and intrapartum stillbirth. *American Journal of Epidemiology* (Baltimore), vol.137, No. 11, pp. 1177-1189.

Lobel, S. M., R. J. Pomponio and G. L. Mutter (1993). The sex ratio of normal and manipulated human sperm quantitated by the polymerase chain reaction. *Fertility and Sterility* (Birmingham, Alabama), vol. 59, No. 2, pp. 387-392.

Lopez-Llera, M. (1990). Eclampsia and fetal sex. *International Journal of Gynecology and Obstetrics* (Limerick, Ireland), vol. 33, pp. 211-213.

Luthra, R. (1994). A case of problematic diffusion: the use of sex determination techniques in India. *Knowledge: Creation, Diffusion, Utilization* (Thousand Oaks, California, and London), vol. 15, No. 3, pp. 259-272.

MacGillivray, I., D. A. Davey and C. Lawley. (1986). Sex ratio at birth in a Cape coloured population. *Social Science and Medicine* (Elmsford, New York), vol. 22, No. 9, pp. 929-930.

Mackey, W. C. (1993). Relationships between the human sex ratio and the woman's microenvironment. *Human Nature* (Hawthorne, New York), vol. 4, No. 2, pp. 175-198.

Martin, J. C. (1985). Perinatal psychoactive drug use: effects on gender, development and function in offspring. In *Nebraska Symposium on Motivation, 1984: Psychology and Gender*, Theo B. Sonderegger, ed. Lincoln, Nebraska: University of Nebraska Press.

Martin, J. F. (1994). Changing sex ratios: the history of Havasupai fertility and its implications for human sex ratio variations (with comments by other authors). *Current Anthropology* (Chicago), vol. 35, pp. 255-280.

Martin, R., and A. Rademaker (1992). A study of paternal age and sex ratio in sperm chromosome complements. *Human Heredity* (Basel), vol. 42, pp. 333-336.

McGregor, J. A., and M. Leff (1990). Does maternal genital herpes infection influence fetal gender? *American Journal of Obstetrics and Gynecology* (St. Louis), vol. 105, No. 4, pp. 1346-1347.

McKeown, T., and C. R. Lowe (1951). The sex ratio of stillbirths related to cause and duration of gestation. *Human Biology* (Detroit), vol. 23, pp. 41-60.

Minkoff, G., A. McCormack and R. H. Schwartz. (1985). Relationship of vaginitis to sex of conceptuses. *Obstetrics and Gynecology* (New York), vol. 86, pp. 239-245.

Mora, J. O., and others (1981). Sex-related effects of nutritional supplementation during pregnancy on fetal growth. *Early Human Development* (Limerick, Ireland), vol. 5, pp. 243-251.

Neel, J. V. (1990). Toward an explanation of the human sex ratio. In *Gender, Health and Longevity: Multidisciplinary Perspectives*, M. G. Ory and H. R. Warner, eds. New York: Springer.

Ober, C. (1992). The maternal-fetal relationship in human pregnancy: an immunogenetic perspective. *Experimental and Clinical Immunogenetics* (Basel), vol. 9, pp. 1-14.

Radvany, R. M., and others (1987). The human sex ratio: increase in first-born males to parents with shared HLA-DR antigens. *Tissue Antigens* (Copenhagen), vol. 29, pp. 34-42.

Rehan, N-E. (1982). Sex ratio of live-born Hausa infants. *British Journal of Obstetrics and Gynecology* (Oxford, United Kingdom), vol. 89, pp. 136-141.

Robert-Lamblin, J., and others (1983). Epidémies virales et rapports de masculinité des naissances. *Population* (Paris), vol. 38, pp. 152-165.

Schtickzelle, M. (1981). Evolution du rapport de masculinité a la naissance dans quelques pays occidentaux. *Genus* (Rome), vol. 37, pp. 35-60.

Simpson, J. L., and S. Carson (1993). Biological causes of foetal loss. In *Biomedical and Demographic Determinants of Reproduction*, R. Gray, ed. Oxford: Clarendon Press.

Taha, T. E., and others (1994). Levels and determinants of perinatal mortality in central Sudan. *International Journal of Gynecology and Obstetrics* (Limerick, Ireland), vol. 45, pp. 109-115.

Ulizzi, L., and L. A. Zonta (1993). Sex ratio and natural selection in humans: a comparative analysis of two Caucasian populations. *Annals of Human Genetics* (Cambridge, United Kingdom), vol. 57, pp. 211-219.

_____, and A. Novelletto (1984). Secular changes of the sex-ratio of stillbirths and early deaths in Italy: evidence for postponement of male specific risk. *Japanese Journal of Human Genetics* (Tokyo), vol. 29, pp. 139-145.

United Kingdom, Registrar General (1976). *The Registrar General's Statistical Review of England and Wales for 1973*. Part I, tables, medical. London: Her Majesty's Stationery Office.

United Nations (1988). *Demographic Yearbook, 1986*. Sales No. E/F.87.XIII.1.

United States Department of Health, Education and Welfare (1966). Infant and perinatal mortality in Scotland. *Vital and Health Statistics*, Series 3, No. 5. Hyattsville, Maryland.

Waldron, Ingrid (1983). Sex differences in human mortality: the role of genetic factors. *Social Science and Medicine* (Elmsford, New York), vol. 17, No. 6, pp. 321-333.

Wen, X. (1993). Effect of son preference and population policy on sex ratios at birth in two provinces of China. *Journal of Biosocial Science* (Cambridge, United Kingdom), vol. 25, pp. 509-521.

Wilcox, A. J., and others (1988). Incidence of early loss of pregnancy. *The New England Journal of Medicine* (Boston), vol. 319, No. 4, pp. 189-194.

Wilkinson, G. S., and others (1989). Perinatal mortality and sex ratios in Hawaii. *Ethology and Sociobiology* (New York), vol. 10, pp. 435-447.

Williams, B. J., and others (1993). Non-disjunction in human sperm. *Human Molecular Genetics* (Oxford), vol. 2, No. 11, pp. 1929-1936.

_____, and S. P. Gloster (1992). Human sex ratio as it relates to caloric availability. *Social Biology* (Madison, Wisconsin), vol. 39, pp. 285-291.

World Health Organization (1984). A prospective multicentre study of the ovulation method of natural family planning, part IV: the outcome of pregnancy. *Fertility and Sterility* (Birmingham, Alabama), vol. 41, No. 4, pp. 593-598.

Yadav, B. R., W. A. King and K. J. Betteridge (1993). Relationships between the completion of first cleavage and the chromosomal complement, sex and developmental rates of bovine embryos generated in vitro. *Molecular Reproduction and Development* (New York), vol. 36, No. 4, pp. 434-439.

Yi, Z., and others (1993). Causes and implications of the recent increase in the reported sex ratio at birth in China. *Population and Development Review* (New York), vol. 19, No. 2, pp. 283-302.

Zarutskie, P., and others (1989). The clinical relevance of sex selection techniques. *Fertility and Sterility* (Birmingham, Alabama), vol. 52, No. 6, pp. 891-905.

Zhang, J., and W. Cai (1992). Risk factors associated with antepartum fetal death. *Early Human Development* (Limerick, Ireland), vol. 28, pp. 193-200.

Zhou, X., and others (1989). Chromosome abnormalities in early pregnancy analysed by direct chromosome preparation of chorionic villi. *Human Genetics* (Berlin), vol. 83, pp. 277-279.

III. SEX DIFFERENCES IN INFANT AND EARLY CHILDHOOD MORTALITY: MAJOR CAUSES OF DEATH AND POSSIBLE BIOLOGICAL CAUSES

Ingrid Waldron*

Sex differences in mortality vary by age, even in the relatively narrow age range of 0-4 years. For infants, males have higher mortality than females in almost all countries or regions studied (Waldron, 1987; Makinson, 1994; Tabutin and Willems, 1993). The male disadvantage is particularly consistent for the neonatal period (first month after birth), during which higher male mortality is nearly universal. In contrast, during the post-neonatal period of infancy (from the second through the eleventh month after birth) sex differences are more variable, and in some developing countries females have higher mortality than males (Arnold, 1992; Bhatia, 1989; Fargues and Nassour, 1988; Tabutin and Willems, 1993). For young children (ages 1-4), sex differences in mortality are very variable; boys have higher mortality than girls in all developed countries and many developing countries, but in many other developing countries the reverse is true or there is very little sex difference in mortality (Waldron, 1987; Makinson, 1994; Tabutin and Willems, 1993; and chapter IV below). Thus, in developing countries the pattern of sex differences in mortality shifts from a consistent male excess in the neonatal period to variable sex differences in early childhood.

One reason that the pattern of sex differences in mortality differs between infancy and childhood is that the major causes of death differ for those two age groups (Waldron, 1987). For example, perinatal conditions make a major contribution to infant mortality, and consistently higher mortality for perinatal conditions among males is a major cause of their higher infant mortality. Infectious diseases make a major contribution to early childhood mortality in developing countries, and variable sex differences in infectious disease mortality are a major cause of variable sex differences in total mortality in early childhood.

Sex differences in infant and early childhood mortality are influenced by both environmental and biological factors (Makinson, 1994; Waldron, 1983 and 1987). For example, where girls have higher mortality than boys, one important cause appears to be sex discrimination resulting in less adequate nutrition and health care for females. In contrast, higher infant mortality among males appears to be due primarily to inherent biological disadvantages. Some authors have generalized the concept of an inherent biological disadvantage for males to apply to all age ranges and almost all causes of death. The evidence reviewed in the present chapter indicates that rather than a general biological disadvantage for males, there are multiple sex differences in biology, some of which increase mortality for males, while others increase mortality for females. The relative importance of specific sex differences in biology varies for different causes of death, different age groups and different environmental conditions.

Those issues are further investigated in the present chapter which summarizes recent evidence concerning two major questions. First, which causes of death contribute to sex differences in infant and early child mortality in developing countries? Second, what biological factors contribute to sex differences for each of the major causes of death? Biological factors are defined broadly to include: (*a*) direct genetic effects, such as X-linked diseases; (*b*) effects of sex hormones on anatomy, physiology and behaviour; and (*c*) physiological differences between males and females, which may be due primarily to genetic and hormonal effects but may also be influenced by environmental factors. Environmental factors are mentioned only briefly in the present chapter since they are discussed extensively in subsequent chapters of the present volume.

Section A of the present chapter provides brief comments concerning the validity of the cause of death data. Section B summarizes the basic sex differences in biology that are relevant for understanding sex differences in infant and child mortality. Each of the subsequent four sections discusses a major cause of death category that makes a significant contribution to sex

---

*Leidy Laboratory, Department of Biology, University of Pennsylvania.

differences in infant and/or early childhood mortality in developing countries: perinatal conditions (sect. C); congenital anomalies (sect. D); infectious diseases (sect. E); and accidents (sect. F). Data concerning sex differences in mortality and morbidity are from developing countries, except where explicitly noted. Data concerning sex differences in biology are taken from both developing and developed countries without explicitly noting the source, except in a few cases where there is reason to believe that socio-economic conditions or ethnic differences may influence a particular sex difference under discussion.

A. ASSESSMENT OF CAUSE-OF-DEATH DATA

Many developing countries lack accurate mortality data by cause of death. The cause-of-death data presented in the present chapter have been selected on the basis of two criteria: (*a*) to provide representative data for a broad range of geographical regions and mortality conditions; and (*b*) to provide data of as high quality as possible, including relatively complete coverage of deaths, reasonably accurate causes of death and adequate sample sizes.[1] Generalizations in the present chapter concerning sex differences for various causes of death are based on the data presented in the tables and previously published data, especially two previous compilations of data concerning sex differences in mortality by cause of death, one for infants and children in diverse developing countries (Waldron, 1987) and the other for young children in Latin American countries (Gomez, 1993).

The available data provide information concerning the principal cause of death. However, it should be mentioned that in developing countries, many infant and child deaths stem from the interacting effects of multiple causes (Bhatia, 1989; Fauveau, Koenig and Wojtyniak, 1991). For example, death is often due to the interacting effects of malnutrition and infection. Malnutrition increases susceptibility to infections, and repeated or chronic infections can increase malnutrition by causing diarrhoea, anorexia, increased metabolic rate etc. (Cunningham-Rundles, 1992; Fauveau, Koenig and Wojtyniak, 1991; Greenwood and Whittle, 1981). Because of those effects and for other reasons, one infectious disease can increase subsequent susceptibility to other infectious diseases (Leon and others, 1993;

Narain and others, 1989). Thus, the data concerning the principal cause of death provide important but incomplete information.

B. BIOLOGY OF SEX DIFFERENCES

It is well known that in females each cell contains a pair of X chromosomes, whereas in males each cell contains an X and a Y chromosome. The X and Y chromosomes have small matched regions that carry a number of shared genes, but for the most part the X and Y chromosomes carry very different genetic information.

The X chromosome is much larger than the Y chromosome, and carries many genes essential for immune function, blood clotting, the development and function of the nervous system and muscles, and other vital functions. Thus, a female, having two X chromosomes, has two copies of many genes that are essential for normal bodily development and function, while a male has only one copy of those X-linked genes. Consequently, a female that carries an X-linked recessive genetic defect is usually protected against disease by a normal gene on her other X chromosome, whereas a male that carries an X-linked recessive genetic defect will develop the associated disease.[2]

Although males are more vulnerable to X-linked genetic diseases, the contribution of those diseases to sex differences in mortality is limited because they are rare. For example, two of the most common fatal X-linked diseases are haemophilia A and Duchenne muscular dystrophy, each of which occurs in about 0.01-0.03 per cent of male live births (Sankaranarayanan, 1991; van Essen and others, 1992). Data for the United States of America suggest that haemophilia A probably increases infant and early childhood mortality among males by less than 0.2 per cent,[3] and Duchenne muscular dystrophy has even less effect in that age range since available evidence indicates that it is rarely fatal during infancy or early childhood (Emery, 1987; Mukoyama and others, 1987; OMIM-TM, 1994; van Essen and others, 1992). As discussed below, X-linked immunodeficiencies are also rare, and thus their effects on sex differences in total mortality are probably minor, although X-linked immunodeficiencies may make a modest contribution to higher infectious disease mortality for males in some countries.

The Y chromosome is much smaller than the X chromosome but it contains several unique genes, including the SRY gene, which plays a crucial role in the development of the testes, apparently by activating a cascade of genes that direct the gonads of males to develop into testes instead of ovaries (Moore and Grumbach, 1992). The SRY and other genes on the Y chromosome may influence aspects of development, possibly including the rate of cell division in early development (Pilgrim and Hutchinson, 1994); as discussed in a subsequent section, those effects may contribute to sex differences in mortality for specific causes of death.

In a male foetus, the testes secrete testosterone and other hormones, and those hormones control the development of male reproductive anatomy (Moore and Grumbach, 1992; Winter, Faiman and Reyes, 1981). It appears that male hormones also influence the development of other parts of the body, including the lungs, brain and immune system. Accordingly, the effects of male hormones may contribute to sex differences in mortality due to respiratory distress, accidents and infectious diseases. That topic is elaborated on below.

The gonads of males begin to develop into testes during the second month of prenatal development, and males have higher levels of testosterone than females from about the third month. Peak testosterone levels in male foetuses occur in about the fifth month of prenatal development (Winter, Faiman and Reyes, 1981). After birth, males generally have higher testosterone levels than females during the first few postnatal months (Corbier, Edwards and Roffi, 1992; Forest, de Peretti and Bertrand, 1977; Winter and others, 1976; Winter, Faiman and Reyes, 1981). However, beginning about the sixth month postnatal and throughout early childhood, testosterone levels are very low and similar in males and females (Forest, de Peretti and Bertrand, 1977; Meites, 1989; Winter and others, 1976; Winter, Faiman and Reyes, 1981).[4]

In summary, multiple X-linked and Y-linked genes appear to have a wide variety of effects on sex differences in mortality. Because males have only one X chromosome they are more vulnerable to X-linked recessive diseases, but those are not common causes of death. In males, the testes produce testosterone during prenatal development and the first few months after birth, and higher testosterone levels among males may have several adverse effects on survival during infancy and childhood.

C. PERINATAL CONDITIONS

The term "perinatal conditions" is the short name for the cause-of-death category designated "certain conditions originating in the perinatal period", which includes conditions arising during pregnancy and labour and conditions specific to the newborn. Perinatal conditions include birth trauma, intrauterine hypoxia and birth asphyxia (insufficient oxygen before or during birth), prematurity, respiratory distress syndrome and neonatal tetanus.

Males have had higher mortality than females for perinatal conditions in almost all countries or regions studied (tables 21 and 22; Waldron, 1987). Excess male mortality for perinatal conditions makes a major contribution to sex differences in neonatal mortality. Data available for Cuba and Chile indicate that over two thirds of the sex difference in neonatal mortality is due to higher mortality for perinatal conditions among males (table 23).

Available evidence indicates that in general, males have higher mortality than females for each major type of perinatal conditions. For example, limited data for developing countries indicate that males have higher mortality for hypoxia and birth asphyxia, birth trauma, prematurity and neonatal tetanus (tables 22 and 23; Alemu, 1993; Bhatia, 1989; Leroy and Garenne, 1989). More complete data for developed countries provide further evidence that males have higher mortality than females for each major category of perinatal conditions (table 24; Khoury and others, 1985). Because that sex difference is so consistent and because no plausible environmental cause has been identified, it is probable that inherent biological sex differences represent the main underlying cause.

Recent research has identified a few specific biological pathways. One factor appears to be that the lungs of male foetuses mature more slowly than the lungs of female foetuses. It appears that testosterone and other hormones produced by male foetuses delay the maturation of the lungs; in particular, there is delayed development of the lungs secretion of surfactant, a substance that is necessary for normal lung function (Catlin and

TABLE 21. SEX DIFFERENTIALS IN INFANT MORTALITY, BY CAUSE OF DEATH, CUBA, CHILE, ARGENTINA AND SRI LANKA

	Cuba, 1987-1989		Chile, 1987-1988		Argentina, 1987		Sri Lanka, 1986	
	Sex difference[a]	Sex ratio[b]	Sex difference	Sex ratio	Sex difference	Sex ratio	Sex difference	Sex ratio
Infectious and parasitic diseases .	23.3	1.22	33.5	1.35	27.9	1.17	6.4	1.04
Intestinal infectious diseases	18.9	1.39	14.5	1.36	18.4	1.25	-9.9	0.88
Septicaemia	0.6	1.02	10.9	1.28	19.0	1.32	15.0	1.41
Pneumonia	27.3	1.33	57.2	1.20	30.6	1.26	17.7	1.15
Meningitis	8.0	1.22	9.1	1.33	12.7	1.32	3.5	1.05
Nutritional deficiencies	—	—	—	—	15.0	1.30	6.2	1.17
Congenital anomalies	60.4	1.23	18.3	1.05	52.8	1.15	18.0	1.26
Spina bifida and hydrocephalus ..	—	—	-13.6	0.70	-9.1	0.79	—	—
Cong. anom. heart and circulat. ..	19.0	1.14	17.8	1.14	38.6	1.26	10.5	1.28
Perinatal conditions	205.2	1.48	162.6	1.30	352.2	1.29	299.1	1.25
Accidents and other violence	1.4	1.03	55.8	1.25	7.9	1.09	1.5	1.05
All causes	344.0	1.33	373.1	1.22	595.6	1.25	439.2	1.21
Total death rate (per 100,000 live births) (males and females) ...	1 207.9		1 870.4		2 660.8		2 333.8	

Source: World Health Organization, 1989-1992 World Health Statistics Annual (Geneva, 1989-1993).
NOTE: A dash (—) indicates less than 100 deaths recorded for that cause of death category.
[a]Male minus female death rates (infant deaths per 100,000 live births).
[b]Male/female death rates.

TABLE 22. SEX DIFFERENTIALS IN INFANT AND EARLY CHILD MORTALITY, BY CAUSE OF DEATH BAMAKO, MALI, AND MATLAB, BANGLADESH

	Infants		Young children			
	Bamako, 1980-1985		Bamako, 1980-1985		Matlab, 1986-1987	
	Sex difference[a]	Sex ratio	Sex difference	Sex ratio	Sex difference	Sex ratio
Intestinal infectious diseases	5	1.01	-23	0.86	-270	0.47
Measles	-277	0.77	-123	0.84	..	..
Malaria	-136	0.86	-59	0.83	..	..
Meningitis	51	1.22	8	1.28	..	..
Pneumonia	6	1.04	-3	0.93	—[b]	—
Nutritional deficiencies	29	1.12	-6	0.97	-450[c]	0.39
Prematurity	290	1.26	—	—	..	..
Accidents	..	..	..	..	-20	0.92
All causes	39	1.01	-183	0.91	-820	0.56
Total death rate (males and females)	7 099		1 852		1 460	

Sources: P. Fargues and O. Nassour, Douze ans de mortalité urbaine au Sahel-niveaux, tendances, saisons et causes de mortalité à Bamako, 1974-1985, Travaux et documents, Cahier No. 123 (Paris, Institut national d'études démographiques/Institut du Sahel, 1988); and V. Fauveau, M. A. Koenig and B. Wojtyniak, "Excess female deaths among rural Bangladeshi children: an examination of cause-specific mortality and morbidity", International Journal of Epidemiology (Oxford, 1991), vol. 20, No. 3, pp. 729-735.
NOTE: A dash (—) indicates less than 100 deaths recorded for that cause of death category.
[a]Death rates and sex differences in death rates are infant deaths per 100,000 live births, or deaths per 100,000 children per year for children ages 1-4.
[b]Acute lower respiratory infection.
[c]Severe malnutrition (primarily severe malnutrition with recurrent diarrhea).

TABLE 23. SEX DIFFERENTIALS IN INFANT MORTALITY, BY AGE AND CAUSE OF DEATH, CUBA AND CHILE[a]

	Neonatal								Post-neonatal			
	0-6 days				7-27 days				28-364 days			
	Cuba, 1987-1989		Chile, 1987-1988		Cuba, 1987-1989		Chile, 1987-1988		Cuba, 1987-1988		Chile, 1987-1989	
	Sex difference	Sex ratio	Sex difference	Sex ratio	Sex difference	Sex ratio	Sex difference	Sex ratio	Sex difference	Sex ratio	Sex difference	Sex ratio
Infectious and parasitic diseases	—	—	—	—	5.3	1.20	—	—	16.5	1.21	30.6	1.33
Intestinal infectious diseases	—	—	—	—	—	—	—	—	16.2	1.36	13.7	1.36
Meningitis	—	—	—	—	—	—	—	—	0.3	1.01	9.2	1.42
Pneumonia	11.7	1.90	9.8	1.52	4.8	1.16	3.1	1.11	11.5	1.29	44.9	1.19
Congenital anomalies	26.4	1.25	19.9	1.12	18.8	1.39	8.2	1.18	15.9	1.14	-9.3	0.94
Spinal bifida and hydrocephalus	—	—	—	—	—	—	—	—	—	—	-12.1	0.60
Cong. anom. heart and circulat.	10.9	1.23	12.8	1.34	7.8	1.29	4.7	1.21	0.5	1.01	0.9	1.01
Perinatal conditions[b]	184.2	1.49	143.3	1.32	15.0	1.33	10.0	1.12	—	—	10.0	1.51
Birth trauma	9.5	1.45	—	—	—	—	—	—	—	—	—	—
Hypoxia and birth asphyxia	149.3	1.57	87.8	1.46	9.5	1.45	2.2	1.10	—	—	—	—
Sudden infant death syndrome	—	—	—	—	—	—	—	—	—	—	10.0	1.37
Accidents[c]	—	—	—	—	—	—	0.4	1.02	3.4	1.10	51.6	1.33
All causes	226.3	1.45	182.1	1.28	55.1	1.34	24.4	1.13	65.9	1.18	170.7	1.20
Total death rates (males and females)	622.2		751.5		191.5		205.2		398.7		924.1	

Sources: World Health Organization, 1989-1992 World Health Statistics Annual (Geneva, 1989-1993).

Note: A dash (—) indicates less than 100 deaths recorded for that cause of death category.

[a] Death rates calculated as deaths on days 0-6 per 100,000 live births, deaths on days 7-27 per 100,000 infants who lived to 7 days of age, and deaths on days 28-364 per 100,000 infants who lived to 28 days.

[b] Certain conditions originating in the perinatal period.

[c] For Cuba, accident mortality data were not available for 1987, so accident mortality rates are for 1988-1989.

	United States whites (1988)		United States blacks (1988)		Japan (1990)	
	Sex difference[a]	Sex ratio	Sex difference	Sex ratio	Sex difference	Sex ratio
Congenital anomalies	22.2	1.11	18.2	1.09	5.9	1.04
Central nervous system and eye	-8.9	0.74	-6.4	0.77	-1.1	0.88
Heart	10.8	1.17	3.9	1.06	10.2	1.17
Other circulation	2.4	1.19	3.5	1.19	5.2	1.22
Respiratory system	12.2	1.56	11.8	1.45	-1.2	0.92
Due to chromosome anomalies	-7.9	0.72	0.2	1.01	-7.6	0.69
Perinatal conditions	96.3	1.31	192.7	1.22	38.3	1.31
Maternal complications	5.6	1.20	15.8	1.21	—	—
Complications of placenta etc.	5.1	1.29	1.7	1.04	—	—
Short gestation, birth weight	13.7	1.27	51.8	1.26	—	—
Birth trauma	0.5	1.11	—	—	4.7	1.34
Intrauterine hypoxia, birth asphyxia	4.9	1.33	1.8	1.05	3.0	1.31
Respiratory distress syndrome	30.8	1.56	30.2	1.24	5.8	1.34
Other respiratory cond. newborn	22.4	1.36	43.7	1.27	16.6	1.41
Perinatal infections	3.6	1.21	5.5	1.14	0.3	1.03
All causes	207.4	1.28	289.9	1.18	78.8	1.19
Total death rate (males and females)	851.1		1 762.0		459.7	

Sources: United States Department of Health and Human Services, *Vital Statistics of the United States, 1988*, vol. II, *Mortality* (Hyattsville, Maryland: National Center for Health Statistics, 1991); Japan, Ministry of Health and Welfare, *Vital Statistics, 1990: Japan* (Tokyo, Koseisho Daijinkanbo Tokei Johobu, 1992).

NOTE: A dash (—) indicates less than 100 deaths reported under that cause of death category.

[a]Death rates and differences in death rates are infant deaths per 100,000 live births.

others, 1990; Nielsen, 1992; Torday and Nielsen, 1987). Without adequate surfactant synthesis, premature babies are vulnerable to respiratory distress syndrome; as expected, male babies have higher rates of respiratory distress syndrome. Evidence for developed countries indicates that higher male mortality due to respiratory distress syndrome is one important cause of their overall higher infant mortality (table 24; Khoury and others, 1985). However, limited evidence suggests that the importance of that effect may vary in different ethnic groups. For example, research in Nigeria has found very low levels of respiratory distress syndrome, early maturation of foetal lungs and no delay in maturation of the lungs in males relative to females (Olowe and Akinkugbe, 1978; Torday and Nielsen, 1987).

Another disadvantage for male infants appears to be that males are more likely to be born at younger gestational ages, which contributes to a higher risk of mortality due to prematurity and other perinatal conditions (Golding, 1991; Hall and Carr-Hill, 1982; MacGillivray and Davey, 1985; McGregor and others, 1992; Seki and Kato, 1987; Kramer, 1987). It should be noted that any

male disadvantage due to birth at younger gestational ages is counteracted by a male advantage due to higher average birthweights (Hall and Carr-Hill, 1982; Karn and Penrose, 1951; Kramer, 1987; Shapiro, Schlesinger and Nesbitt, 1968; Waldron, 1983). Nevertheless, it is of interest to explore possible biological reasons why males may be born at younger gestational ages. Limited evidence suggests that one reason is that male foetuses may be less able than female foetuses to counteract the effects of infections of the maternal reproductive tract. Reproductive tract infections increase the risk of preterm labour, apparently in part because maternal defences against those infections include secretion of chemical messengers that may stimulate uterine contractions (Bry and others, 1994; McGregor and others, 1992). Foetuses produce another chemical messenger that may counteract that effect, and female foetuses appear to produce more of that protective chemical messenger, which may reduce their risk of premature birth (Bry and others, 1994).

In summary, in almost all available data males have higher mortality than females for perinatal conditions,

69

and it is probable that biological causes are primarily responsible for that consistent male excess. It appears that male infants have higher risk of mortality from perinatal conditions in part because males are more likely to be born at younger gestational ages, and for a given gestational age their lungs are less mature because of the effects of male hormones. As discussed in section E below on infectious diseases, higher male mortality for neonatal tetanus and other perinatal infections may be due to inherent sex differences in immune function, although the relevant sex differences in immune function have not yet been identified. Thus, current research suggests several potentially important biological causes of higher male mortality due to perinatal conditions. Additional causes remain to be identified in future research.

D. CONGENITAL ANOMALIES

Mortality due to congenital anomalies or congenital malformations has been higher for male infants than for female infants in almost all countries studied (table 21; Waldron, 1987). However, that difference makes only a modest contribution to higher infant mortality among males. Sex differences in congenital anomalies because of mortality vary, depending upon the type of congenital anomaly and the population considered. For example, males have higher infant mortality due to congenital anomalies of the heart and circulation, whereas females generally have higher infant mortality due to congenital anomalies of the central nervous system, such as spina bifida (table 21; Xiao and others, 1990). That pattern is observed in representative developed countries (table 24). The data for developed countries also show that for certain categories of congenital anomalies, a sex difference in mortality that is present in one population may be absent or even reversed in another population.

Sex differences in congenital anomalies of the central nervous system have been studied extensively, and that research has revealed unexpected specificity and complexity in the patterns and causes of sex differences in that category of congenital anomalies. Sex differences vary for different types of congenital anomalies of the central nervous system (Van Allen and others, 1993; Xiao and others, 1990). For example, females generally have higher rates than males for anencephaly (partial or complete absence of the cerebrum) and for spina bifida

in both developing and developed countries (Elwood and Little, 1992; Xiao and others, 1990). Within the category of spina bifida, females generally have higher risk for defects in the upper and middle spinal cord, but males generally have higher risk for defects restricted to the lower spinal cord. Evidence on that question is restricted to developed countries (Elwood and Little, 1992; Park and others, 1992; Seller, 1987).

The following hypothesis may explain why females have higher risk of anencephaly and spina bifida of the upper and middle spinal cord. The basic structure of the brain and upper part of the spinal cord begins to develop at a very early stage of embryonic development, somewhat before the lower spinal cord; cell division appears to be slower in females than in males in the very early stages of embryonic development, and some female embryos may have insufficient cells for the earliest stages of nervous system development to proceed correctly; that may explain why females may be more vulnerable to developmental errors in the formation of the brain and upper spinal cord (Hall, 1986; Pilgrim and Hutchison, 1994; Seller, 1987; Yadav, King and Betteridge, 1993). Multiple additional inherent sex differences in development are believed to contribute to sex differences in the risk of spina bifida, as well as other congenital anomalies of the central nervous system (Elwood and Little, 1992; Van Allen and others, 1993).

It appears that environmental factors may also influence sex differences in congenital anomalies of the central nervous system. For example, some data suggest that where anencephaly rates are higher, the proportion of female cases tends to be higher, apparently because environmental factors increase anencephaly rates more for females than for males (Elwood and Little, 1992; Van Allen and others, 1993).

In summary, sex differences in mortality due to congenital anomalies of the central nervous system vary, depending upon the specific congenital anomaly considered. It appears that multiple specific sex differences in development contribute to those variable sex differences in congenital anomalies of the central nervous system. Unfortunately, very little evidence is available concerning the causes of sex differences in the major categories of congenital anomalies with higher male mortality, but it seems likely that they too are caused by multiple sex differences in development.

E. INFECTIOUS DISEASES

The term "infectious diseases" is used in the present chapter to refer to all infectious and parasitic diseases, including intestinal and respiratory infections, measles, malaria, meningitis and neonatal tetanus. In contrast, tables 21, 23, and 25 are based on the International Classification of Diseases, Injuries and Causes of Death-9 (World Health Organization, 1989-1993). Under that system, the category "infectious and parasitic diseases" does not include several important infectious diseases, such as pneumonia (which is classified as a respiratory disease), meningitis (which is classified as a disease of the nervous system), and neonatal tetanus (which is classified as a perinatal condition)

Sex differences in infectious disease mortality vary depending upon the age group considered (tables 21-23 and 25; Bhatia, 1989; Gomez, 1993; Waldron, 1987). In infancy, males have higher infectious disease mortality than females in most countries or regions studied. In contrast, for young children sex differences in infectious disease mortality vary, and girls have higher mortality than boys in many countries or regions. For young children, that variation in sex differences in infectious disease mortality is a major cause of the variation in sex differences in total mortality; where girls have higher infectious disease mortality than boys, that factor has been a major cause of higher total female mortality (tables 22 and 25; Gomez, 1993; Waldron, 1987).

The relatively consistent male excess for infectious disease mortality in infancy suggests that inherent biological sex differences may be largely responsible. Conversely, a variety of evidence indicates that environmental influences probably make a substantial contribution to the variation in sex differences in infectious disease mortality in early childhood (Fauveau and others, 1991; Makinson, 1994; Narain and others, 1989; Waldron, 1987).

Subsection 1 below summarizes evidence concerning sex differences in mortality and morbidity for several major types of infectious disease for infants and young children in developing countries. It will be seen that for a given type of infectious disease, sex differences in mortality may differ between infants and young children, with higher male mortality more common in infancy and variable sex differences more common for young children. In addition, sex differences in mortality vary to some extent for different types of infectious disease. Subsection 1 also presents evidence concerning sex differences in morbidity and case-fatality rates for several types of infectious disease, and identifies some

TABLE 25. SEX DIFFERENTIALS IN EARLY CHILD MORTALITY, BY CAUSE OF DEATH,
ARGENTINA, CHILE, CUBA AND SRI LANKA

	Cuba, 1987-89		Chile, 1987-88		Argentina, 1987		Sri Lanka, 1986	
	Sex difference[a]	Sex ratio	Sex difference	Sex ratio	Sex difference	Sex ratio	Sex difference	Sex ratio
Infectious and parasitic diseases	-0.4	0.96	2.7	1.48	1.5	1.13	1.8	1.04
Intestinal infectious diseases	—	—	—	—	0.5	1.09	0.5	1.02
Pneumonia	1.4	1.33	3.3	1.27	0.7	1.10	-1.9	0.90
Nutritional deficiencies	—	—	—	—	-1.2	0.80	—	—
Accidents and other violence	11.5	1.70	14.1	1.60	7.9	1.42	0.7	1.04
All causes	14.8	1.22	23.5	1.32	12.9	1.13	-0.8	1.00
Total death rate (males and females)	74.6		84.7		90.2		178.5	

Sources: World Health Organization, *1989-1992 World Health Statistics Annual* (Geneva, 1989-1993).
NOTE: A dash (—) indicates less than 100 deaths reported for that cause of death category.
[a]Death rates and differences in death rates per 100,000 children per year for children ages 1-4.

of the environmental factors that may contribute to those differences. Discussion of possible biological causes of sex differences in infectious disease mortality is postponed to subsection 2, which summarizes evidence concerning sex differences in the immune system.

1. Sex differences for different types of infectious disease

One major category of infectious disease mortality in developing countries is intestinal infections or diarrhoeal diseases. Sex differences in mortality due to intestinal infections vary in different countries and age groups (tables 21-23 and 25; Bhatia, 1989; Gomez, 1993; Waldron, 1987). In infancy, mortality due to intestinal infections is usually higher for males than for females. In contrast, for young children, mortality due to intestinal infections is often higher for females than for males. Morbidity due to diarrhoeal diseases shows a different pattern of sex differences than mortality. Males and females tend to have similar rates of diarrhoeal disease morbidity, or males tend to have slightly higher rates, beginning at about six months of age (Arnold, 1992; Diame, N'diaye and Airey, 1990; Fauveau, Koenig and Wojtyniak, 1991; Kirkwood, 1991; Mock and others, 1993; El Samani, Willett and Ware, 1989). One possible reason that males may have higher rates of intestinal infections may be that as infants become mobile, males may be allowed greater freedom of movement than females, and consequently males may be exposed more to infection (Daime, N'diaye and Airey, 1990). Thus, girls generally do not have higher morbidity for intestinal infections but in some developing countries they do have higher mortality from those causes. That contrast suggests that, in some countries, an intestinal infection is more likely to be fatal for girls than for boys. That is confirmed by evidence from Matlab, Bangladesh, where it appears that there is little sex difference in morbidity for diarrhoeal diseases, but girls have higher case-fatality rates (Fauveau, Koenig and Wojtyniak, 1991). It appears that higher female case-fatality rates may be due in large part to a sex difference in curative medical care that favours boys. A similar sex difference in medical and home treatment for diarrhoea has been observed in a few other countries, although not in most countries studied (Arnold, 1992; McDivitt, Hornik and Carr, 1994; chapter VII below).

Another major category of infectious disease mortality in developing countries is lower respiratory infections, particularly pneumonia. In infancy, males usually have higher mortality due to pneumonia or respiratory infections; in contrast, sex differences in mortality in early childhood due to pneumonia or respiratory infections are variable, and in many populations, girls have as high or higher mortality than boys (tables 21-23 and 25; Bhatia, 1989; Gomez, 1993; Waldron, 1987). It appears that sex differences in the prevalence and treatment of respiratory infections are small and generally not significant, based on data for infants and young children combined for various African and Latin American countries (Arnold, 1992; chapter VII below).

In many developing countries, one major cause of neonatal mortality is neonatal tetanus resulting from infection through the cut umbilical cord or infection occurring during circumcision (Bhatia, 1989; Stanfield and Galazka, 1984). Males have higher mortality for neonatal tetanus than females in most regions studied, although no sex difference or slightly higher female mortality has been observed in a few cases (Alemu, 1993; Bhatia, 1989; Leroy and Garenne, 1989; Stanfield and Galazka, 1984). It is unclear whether sex differences in exposure make any significant contribution to sex differences in neonatal tetanus (Leroy and Garenne, 1989; Stanfield and Galazka, 1984).

In some developing countries, mortality due to human immunodeficiency virus (HIV) infection has become an increasingly important cause of infant and child mortality (Mulder and others, 1994; Ryder and others, 1989). No information on sex differences is available in most studies of HIV transmission from mother to child or studies of mortality risk for HIV-infected infants and children. Limited data suggest that males and females may have similar risks of vertical transmission of HIV (Mulder and others, 1994).

Measles is a major cause of child mortality in the developing world, resulting in deaths that are directly attributed to measles and additional deaths due to subsequent increased risk of infectious diseases, such as pneumonia and diarrhoeal diseases (Aaby, 1993; Bhatia, 1989; Bhuiya and others, 1987; Fargues and Nassour, 1988; Garenne, 1994; Narain and others, 1989). Measles infections suppress the immune system, which contributes to the increased risk of pneumonia and other infectious diseases during and after measles infections (Greenwood and Whittle, 1981; Leon and others, 1993).

Sex differences in measles mortality show a different pattern than most infectious diseases, with a general trend towards higher measles mortality for females (Garenne, 1994). For young children, a substantial female excess mortality has been observed primarily in the Arab States and other Moslem societies, but generally smaller and inconsistent sex differences have been observed in other countries (table 22; Aaby, 1993; Garenne, 1994). Where it occurs, excess female mortality from measles appears to be due to higher case-fatality rates, not higher risk of infection (Garenne, 1994; Narain and others, 1989). One proposed explanation is that, boys are more likely to be exposed to measles outside the home, particularly in Moslem societies, whereas girls are kept at home more and thus are more likely to be infected by a sibling; infection by a sibling may result in a more severe case of measles, on average, because the greater contact between siblings may result in a larger infecting dose of measles virus (Aaby, 1993; Fargues and Nassour, 1988). Thus, sex differences in behaviour and consequent sex differences in type of exposure may contribute to higher case-fatality rates for girls, although that factor is probably not the only cause (Bhuiya and others, 1987; Garenne, 1994). Other possible causes may be less adequate medical care for girls in some societies, and an inherent sex difference in susceptibility to measles-related mortality (Bhuiya and others, 1987; Fargues and Nassour, 1988; Garenne, 1994; Narain and others, 1989).

In summary, the direction and magnitude of sex differences in infectious disease mortality depend upon the age group, type of infectious disease and country. Higher male mortality is particularly common for neonatal tetanus, and for intestinal infections and pneumonia in infancy. Higher female mortality is most common for measles. It appears that environmental factors, such as sex differences in exposure to infection or sex differences in health care, contribute to sex differences in infectious disease mortality in some cases. For infants, the relatively consistent pattern of higher male mortality for most types of infectious diseases suggests that male infants may have inherent disadvantages in resistance to infectious diseases. Possible biological causes of sex differences in infectious disease mortality are discussed in subsection 2 below.

2. Sex differences in immune function

Sex differences in susceptibility to infectious disease mortality may be influenced by a wide variety of sex differences in physiology and anatomy, but primary research attention has been focused on the possible contributions of sex differences to immune function. It has frequently been proposed that males have weaker immune defences than females, with correspondingly greater vulnerability to a broad range of infectious diseases. However, the following review of the evidence for infants and children shows relatively weak and inconsistent support for that proposition.

Research findings concerning sex differences in immune function must be understood in the context of the considerable complexity and variability of the immune system. The body's defences against infection involve many different cell types, chemical messengers and protective molecules, such as antibodies. Those immune system components interact in complex ways, resulting in both beneficial and sometimes harmful or damaging effects. Levels of many immune system components are highly variable between individuals, and many change substantially during the early months and years after birth (Butterworth, McClellan and Allansmith, 1967; Cunningham-Rundles, 1993; Lau, Jones and Yeung, 1992; Roach and others, 1981). In early infancy when the immune system is immature, resistance to infection is provided in part by antibodies, other protective molecules and immune cells received from the mother across the placenta and in colostrum and breast milk. The maternal contribution is of decreasing importance as the baby's immune system matures and secretes increasing levels of many immune components. Given those complexities, it is not surprising that there is only limited understanding of possible inherent sex differences in immune function and their contributions to sex differences in infectious disease mortality.

The following paragraphs summarize the results of (a) studies on the effects of X-linked genes on immune function; (b) the effects of testosterone on immune function; and (c) sex differences in levels of various immune components. Although each type of research provides some evidence of biological contributions to sex differences in immune function, there appear to be inconsistencies between the proposed genetic and hormonal effects on immune function and the observed sex differences in immune components. In addition, the quantitative importance of the observed effects is uncertain.

Recent research has identified a number of X-linked genes that influence immune function, and defects in those X-linked genes can result in immunodeficiencies in males (Conley, 1992; OMIM-TM, 1994). X-linked immunodeficiencies are uncommon in females, because normal immune function is usually preserved by a normal gene on one of the two X chromosomes. Although X-linked immunodeficiencies contribute to greater male vulnerability to infectious diseases, the quantitative importance of that effect is uncertain. Each of the identified X-linked immunodeficiencies is rare, and data for developed countries suggest that the frequency of all types combined is perhaps 1-10 per 100,000 male births.[5] In environments with high rates of infectious diseases and poor medical care, most males with X-linked immunodeficiencies would be expected to die of an infectious disease by age 5, which suggests that X-linked immunodeficiencies might contribute roughly 0.5-10 infectious disease deaths per 100,000 males.[6] In comparison, the excess of male over female infectious disease mortality for infancy and early childhood is roughly 30-130 deaths per 100,000 in some developing countries.[7] Those estimates suggest that X-linked immunodeficiencies may make a minor to moderate contribution to excess male infectious disease mortality in some developing countries. That conclusion must be considered tentative, however, since the estimates are subject to considerable uncertainty and variability between countries.

Another possible cause of greater male vulnerability to infectious disease mortality is that testosterone may inhibit immune function (Schuurs and Verheul, 1990). Males have higher levels of testosterone during foetal development and the first few months after birth, which may contribute to decreased immune function and greater vulnerability to infectious disease for male infants. However, that hypothesis must be considered tentative at present since current research has identified very few sex differences in immune function in early infancy, and it is unclear whether the few observed sex differences would benefit males or females or have no significant effect on sex differences in infectious disease mortality in infancy (table 26).

Table 26 summarizes the available evidence concerning sex differences in the levels and function of various components of the immune system in infants and children. As mentioned above, the limited data available for infants do not provide clear evidence of sex differences in immune function. For children, sex differences in immune function vary depending upon the specific immune component considered. It appears that girls have higher levels of antibodies to rubella vaccine and Epstein-Barr virus, and higher levels of immunoglobulin

M (IgM). However, boys may have stronger responses in one test of immune cell responsiveness, and no sex differences have been found for many of the components involved in defences against infectious disease. Those generalizations are supported by evidence for both developed and developing countries (Biggar and others, 1981; Kafuko and others, 1972; Rowe and others, 1968; Lau, Jones and Yeung, 1992; Leon and others, 1993).

The most well-established sex difference in immune function is higher levels of the class of antibodies designated IgM in females than in males. The sex difference in IgM levels is not observed in early infancy but begins in the second half of infancy or the second year (figure 8). The magnitude of the sex difference is small compared to the substantial variation within each sex, and it is uncertain whether that modest difference in IgM levels has significant effects on resistance to infection (Berg and Johansson, 1969; Lau, Jones and Yeung, 1992; Rowe and others, 1968; Wiedermann and Wiedermannova, 1981). It seems very likely that the sex difference in IgM levels is due to inherent biological causes since it has been very consistently observed in many different populations and there does not appear to be a plausible environmental explanation. However, the biological mechanisms are unclear at present.

Earlier research had suggested that the X chromosome has one or more genes that increase IgM production, and those genes would be active on both X chromosomes in females but only on the single X chromosome in males, resulting in higher IgM levels for females (Waldron, 1983). However, that hypothesis is not supported by current genetic evidence (Conley, 1994; McGue and others, 1990).[8]

Another possible cause of lower levels of IgM among males are inhibitory effects of testosterone on immune function (Schuurs and Verheul, 1990). However, discrepancies between the age patterns of testosterone production and sex differences in IgM levels argue against that hypothesis. Males have relatively high levels of testosterone during foetal development and the first few months after birth, but there does not appear to be a significant sex difference in IgM levels during that period (figure 8; Butterworth, McClellan and Allansmith, 1967; Corbier, Edwards and Roffi, 1992; Lau, Jones and Yeung, 1992; Meites, 1989; Winter and others, 1976; Winter, Faiman and Reyes, 1981). In contrast, males have lower levels of IgM than females beginning in the second half of infancy or the second

TABLE 26. SUMMARY OF DATA ON SEX DIFFERENCES IN LEVELS OF IMMUNE
COMPONENTS IN INFANTS AND CHILDREN UP TO AGE 10

Immune component	Summary of evidence	References[a]
Immunoglobins (antibodies)		
IgA, IgD	No significant sex difference in infants or children	Berg and Johansson (1969) Butterworth and others (1967) Lau and others (1992) Rowe and others (1968) Stoop and others (1969) Wiedermann and Wiedermannova (1981)
IgE	Males had higher levels than females in umbilical cord blood, but no significant sex difference for young children	Berg and Johansson (1969) Kimpen and others (1989)
IgG	Sex differences small and inconsistent, but possibly after infancy girls slightly higher than boys	Berg and Johansson (1969) Butterworth and others (1967) Lau and others (1992) Rowe and others (1968) Stoop and others (1969) Wiedermann and Wiedermannova (1981)
IgM	Appears to be no sex difference in the first half of infancy; thereafter, girls higher than boys	Butterworth and others (1967) Lau and others (1992.)
Antibody against rubella in response to rubella vaccination	Girls higher than boys	Michaels and Rogers (1971) Spencer and others (1977)
Antibody against Epstein-Barr virus	Girls higher than boys	Biggar and others (1981) Kafuko and others (1972)
Immune system cells	Variable sex differences in young children approximately two years after measles vaccination; girls had higher levels of helper T-cells than boys after low titre measles vaccinations but not after high titre measles vaccinations; in one test, boys' immune cells had stronger responses than girls' immune cells; skin tests of delayed hypersensitivity response did not show significant sex differences	Leon and others (1993)
	In newborns, possible sex differences in proportions of different types, but unclear whether male or female pattern would optimize resistance to infection	Komlos and others (1989)
Complement (circulating proteins involved in defenses against infection)	Essentially no sex difference, ages 1-10; tests of sex differences in eight components for five age groups showed only three significant differences (females higher in two cases; males higher in one case)	Roach and others (1981)
Interleukin-1 receptor antagonist (chemical messenger which may reduce the toxic effect of the body's immune responses to infection)	Newborn females may have higher levels than males	Bry and others (1994)

[a]See keyed reference list for chap. III of the present publication.
[b]See fig. 8.

Figure 8. Sex ratios of blood levels of immunoglobulin M (IgM) in infants and children

Male/female IgM level

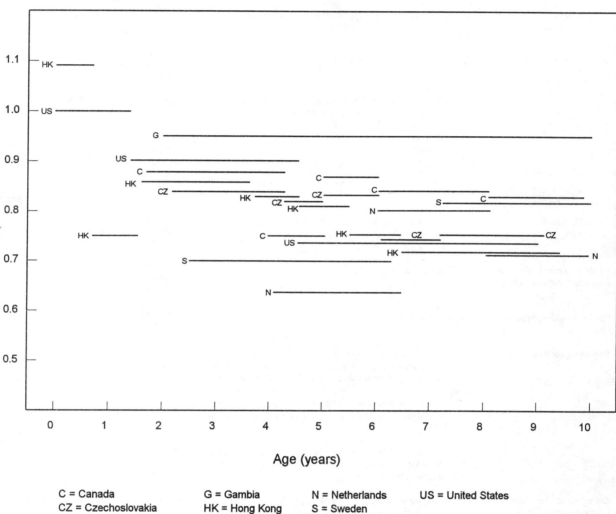

Age (years)

C = Canada   G = Gambia   N = Netherlands   US = United States
CZ = Czechoslovakia   HK = Hong Kong   S = Sweden

Sources: Canada: J. W. Gerrard, R. Dalgleish and L. K.-T. Tan, "Immunoglobin levels in white and Metis communities in Saskatchewan", *Clinical and Experimental Immunology,* vol. 29, pp. 447-456 (Oxford, 1977); former Czechoslovakia, D. Weidermann and D.Weidermannova, "The development of three major immunoglobulin serumlevels in healthy children between 2 and 16 years of age with regard to sex", *Physiologica Bohemoslovaca,* vol. 30, Fasc. 4, pp. 315-322 (London, 1981); the Gambia, D. S. Rowe and others, "Plasma immunoglobulin concentrations in a West African (Gambian) community and in a group of healthy British adults", *Clinical and Experimental Immunology,* vol. 3, pp. 63-79 (Oxford, 1968); Hong Kong, Y. L. Lau, B. M. Jones and C. Y. Yeung, "Biphasic rise of serum immunoglobulin s G and A and sex influence on serum immunoglobulin M in normal Chinese children", *Journal of Pediatric and Child Health,* vol. 28, pp. 240-243 (1992); Netherlands, J. W. Stoop and others, "Serum immunoglobulin levels in healthy children and adults ", *Clinical and Experimental Immunology,* vol. 4, pp. 101-112 (Oxford, 1969); Sweden, T. Berg and S. G. O. Johannson, "Immunoglobulin levels during childhood, with special regard to IgE", *Acta Pediatrica Scandinavia,* vol. 58, pp. 513-524; United States, M. Butterworth, B. McClellan and M. Allansmith, "Influence of sex on immunoglobulin levels", *Nature,* vol. 214, pp. 1224-1225 (London, 1967).

NOTE: Vertical alignment of each line shows sex ratio for IgM levels for one age group, and length of line indicates age range; all data for general population samples, often restricted to "healthy" infants and children, with at least 40 infants or children in each age group shown.

year, but by that age there is no significant sex difference in testosterone levels. Thus, the biological basis for sex differences in IgM levels remains unclear.

One additional point of interest is that sex differences in immune function may vary depending upon environmental exposures. One interesting example concerns measles vaccination, which appears to have long-term effects on immune function. It appears that girls are relatively disadvantaged by high titre measles vaccination; one type of immune advantage for girls is observed after low titre measles vaccination but is absent after high titre measles vaccination (table 26; Leon and others, 1993). In high mortality populations, girls tend to have higher survival probabilities than boys for several years after low titre measles vaccination but lower probabilities after high titre measles vaccination (Aaby and others, 1994; Holt and others, 1993). Those results suggest that sex differences in immune function and infectious disease mortality may be influenced by complex interactions between inherent sex differences in biology and environmental factors, such as the level of exposure to measles virus. In the future, it will be of interest to evaluate whether sex differences in immune function are influenced by additional environmental factors, such as nutrition.

In conclusion, several lines of evidence suggest that biological factors may contribute to greater vulnerability of male infants and children to infectious disease mortality, although evidence is incomplete and somewhat inconsistent. Among infants, males have had higher rates of infectious disease mortality than females for most types of infectious disease in most populations studied, and the consistency of that sex difference suggests that it may be due to inherent sex differences in immune function. X-linked immunodeficiencies contribute to higher susceptibility to infectious disease for some males, but those X-linked immunodeficiencies are rare, and they appear to make only a minor to moderate contribution to sex differences in infectious disease mortality. Males have higher levels of testosterone before birth and during the first few months after birth, and testosterone has varied inhibitory effects on the immune system. However, research has not identified specific components of the immune system that show a male disadvantage in early infancy. After early infancy, males do have lower levels of IgM. However, the biological basis of that sex difference is unclear, and it is not known how much effect the relatively modest sex difference in IgM levels has on susceptibility to infec-

tious disease mortality. For many components of the immune system, no sex difference has been observed, and in some cases sex differences are variable under different circumstances. In summary, the evidence suggests that males have inherently greater vulnerability to infectious disease mortality, but current research has not yet identified its specific biological basis.

F. ACCIDENTS AND OTHER VIOLENCE

In most countries, males have higher mortality from accidents and other violence at all ages, including infancy and early childhood (tables 21-23 and 25; Taket, 1986; Waldron, 1987). For young children, higher male mortality due to accidents and other violence is often the primary cause of higher total mortality for boys, particularly in countries with relatively low mortality due to infectious diseases (table 25; Gomez, 1993; Waldron, 1987).

The present section focuses on accident mortality, the largest category within accidents and other violence. Data concerning different types of accidents indicate that males have higher mortality than females from most types of accidents in most countries (Taket, 1986). For example, data for young children in 18 middle-income developing countries yield the following sex mortality ratios (male/female death rates): 1.86, fatal falls; 1.48, drownings; 1.43, accidental poisonings; 1.34, motor vehicle accidents; 1.14, accidental deaths from fire; and 1.34, total accidents (calculated from data in Taket, 1986).[9]

It appears that boys have more injuries than girls in large part because boys are more physically active and engage in more risky physical activities. Although the evidence comes primarily for developed countries, the behavioural difference probably applies in other settings (Eaton and Enns, 1986; Matheny and Fisher, 1984; Okasha and others, 1976; Rosen and Peterson, 1990). On average, boys are more involved in rough-and-tumble play, are more aggressive physically and are more frequently engage in antisocial or acting out behaviours, and those characteristics are also associated with higher risk of injury (Matheny and Fisher, 1984; Okasha and others, 1976; Rosen and Peterson, 1990; Whiting and Edwards, 1973).

Gender differences in activity level and rough-and-tumble play may be due in part to biological effects.

Specifically, studies of humans and non-human primates suggest that higher prenatal levels of testosterone may predispose males to high-energy physical activity and physical aggressiveness (Goy, Bercovitch and McBrair, 1988; Hines, 1982; Hines and Kaufman, 1994; Reinisch, Ziemba-Davis and Sanders, 1991). However, some studies have not shown evidence of those effects, and methodological problems necessitate caution in interpreting the evidence from the human studies (Hines, 1982; Hines and Kaufman, 1994; Waldron, 1983). One additional line of evidence is derived from studies of activity levels in human foetuses during the last trimester of pregnancy; those studies suggest that male foetuses may be more active than female foetuses, on average, and that difference may be due to effects of male hormones on activity levels (Eaton and Enns, 1986).

It appears that any biological predisposition to higher male activity levels and risk-taking is reinforced by widespread differences in the socialization of boys and girls. Evidence from both developed and developing countries indicates that boys have less adult supervision, in part because boys spend more time away from home, and that probably contributes to their higher rates of serious accidents (Rosen and Peterson, 1990; Weisner, 1979; Whiting and Edwards, 1973). In many developing countries, that gender difference arises in part because girls are required to take responsibility for domestic and child-care tasks near the home. Studies of parents in developed countries indicate that boys are encouraged more than girls to be physically active and adventurous (Rosen and Peterson, 1990; Waldron, 1983). Thus, recent evidence suggests that higher accident mortality for males may reflect the combined effects of biological factors (prenatal hormones) and environmental factors (culturally influenced differences in the socialization of boys and girls).

G. CONCLUSIONS

In developing countries, males have consistently higher mortality than females during the neonatal period. Sex differences in mortality are more variable during the post-neonatal period of infancy, and by early childhood, females have higher mortality than males in many developing countries. That shift from a consistent male excess to more variable sex differences in mortality is due in part to a shift with age in the major causes of death that contribute to total mortality.

In the neonatal period, perinatal conditions are a major component of total mortality, and excess male mortality from those conditions is a major reason that males have higher total mortality during that period. In addition, males generally have higher mortality for congenital anomalies, which makes an additional but modest contribution to higher male neonatal mortality.

During early childhood, infectious diseases and accidents are the biggest contributors to sex differences in mortality. Sex differences in infectious disease mortality are variable, which is a major cause of the variable sex differences in total mortality in early childhood. In contrast, boys have higher accident mortality than girls in almost all countries, which contributes to higher total mortality for boys, particularly in low-mortality countries in which infectious diseases play a less important role. Thus, for young children variation in sex differences in total mortality reflects both variable sex differences in infectious disease mortality and variation in the relative contributions of infectious diseases and accidents to total mortality.

Within the categories of perinatal conditions and accidents, the male disadvantage is quite consistent for various specific causes of death, for different age groups and under different environmental conditions. Within the categories of congenital anomalies and infectious diseases, sex differences are more variable. Males have higher mortality risk than females from many types of congenital anomalies, but females have higher mortality risk from congenital anomalies of the central nervous system. Sex differences in infectious disease mortality vary with age group, environmental conditions and specific type of infectious disease. In infancy, males generally have higher mortality than females from most types of infectious diseases, whereas for young children sex differences are more variable and appear to be influenced by environmental factors, such as discrimination against females. For measles, females have tended to have higher mortality than males. Those patterns of sex differences in mortality suggest that males may be inherently more vulnerable than females to perinatal conditions, accidents, most types of congenital anomalies and infectious diseases in infancy. In contrast, females may be inherently more vulnerable than males to congenital anomalies of the central nervous system and measles.

The biological factors that contribute to sex differences in various causes of death are diverse, and to date only poorly understood. Consistently higher male mortality for perinatal conditions is most likely due to inherent biological disadvantages. Biological disadvantages for males may include greater risk of birth at younger gestational ages, greater immaturity of males' lungs at a given gestational age, and other factors that have not yet been identified. It appears that the biological disadvantages for males are sufficient to outweigh one well-established male advantage—their higher birth-weights. The causes of sex differences in congenital anomalies mortality are poorly understood, but it appears that they are influenced by multiple sex differences in development, some of which favour females and others males.

It appears likely that inherent sex differences in biology contribute to sex differences in infectious disease mortality, although evidence is limited and inconsistent. Immune resistance among males may be reduced by X-linked genetic defects. However, recent evidence indicates that X-linked immunodeficiencies are relatively rare, and thus probably make only a minor to moderate contribution to sex differences in infectious disease mortality. Immune function among males may also be inhibited by exposure to testosterone during the prenatal period and early infancy. However, it is unclear which components of the immune system, if any, show a male disadvantage during early infancy. Among young children, girls have higher levels than boys for several components of the immune system, but many components show no sex difference and boys may have an advantage for at least one measure of immune cell responsiveness. Also, sex differences in immune function may vary depending upon environmental influences. Thus, the balance of evidence suggests that males may have inherent disadvantages in resistance to infectious diseases, but additional evidence will be required to evaluate the extent and nature of the male disadvantage in different age groups, for different types of infectious disease and under different environmental circumstances.

Concerning accidents, recent research suggests that prenatal exposure of male brains to higher testosterone levels may predispose males to higher activity levels and other behavioural characteristics that may contribute to higher accident mortality. Any hormonal contribution to sex differences in behaviour appears to be reinforced by differences in the socialization of males and females in most cultures.

The evidence reviewed in the present chapter under-scores the diversity and complexity of biological effects on sex differences in infant and child mortality. Rather than a general male vulnerability, as implied by some authors, there are multiple sex differences in biology that have variable effects on sex differences in mortality. Many of those sex differences in biology contribute to higher mortality risk for males, but others to contribute to higher risk for females.

Although the present chapter has been primarily concerned with biological factors, it is useful to point out that the contribution of environmental factors to sex differences in mortality also varies. For example, discrimination against females can increase their mortality risk, but some of the advantages or privileges granted to boys may increase their mortality risk. For instance, greater freedom to play may increase boys' risks of diarrhoeal infections and accidents.

Given the above-mentioned complexities, it cannot be assumed that higher male mortality is necessarily due to inherent male vulnerability, nor that higher female mortality is necessarily due to environmental disadvantages for females. The available evidence suggests that males have inherently greater vulnerability for mortality due to perinatal conditions and for total mortality in the neonatal period, but the assumption that males have a pervasive inherent disadvantage is incorrect for some types of congenital anomalies, and is of uncertain validity for infectious diseases and total mortality in early childhood. Thus, proper understanding of the causes of sex differences in mortality cannot be based on general assumptions concerning inherent male vulnerability or environmental disadvantages as the cause of higher female mortality. Instead, it is important to continue to investigate the specific biological and environmental factors contributing to sex differences in mortality, and to analyse how the various causal factors interact and vary in importance under different circumstances.

Similar conclusions have been reached in previous analyses that have included data for other age groups and have included historical and contemporary data for developed and developing countries (Johansson, 1991; Preston, 1976; Waldron, 1983, 1987). Those analyses support the conclusion that sex differences in mortality are influenced by the interacting effects of a variety of biological and sociocultural factors, and the relative importance of specific biological or sociocultural factors depends upon age, cause of death and environmental conditions.

NOTES

[1]For some countries in Latin America, civil registration systems provide cause of death data that are complete and accurate. The data for Argentina, Chile and Cuba have been rated very good and are presented in the present chapter (Vallin, D'Souza and Palloni, 1990; World Health Organization, 1989-1993); for those three countries, at least 90 per cent of deaths were registered, at least 90 per cent of registered deaths were medically certified, and less than 10 per cent of registered deaths for infants or young children were attributed to signs, symptoms and other ill-defined conditions. For Chile and Cuba, data for multiple years have been combined in order to include at least 1,000 deaths for each age group shown in the tables.

In order to provide cause-of-death information for other regions of the developing world, two types of data are presented. First, civil registration data are presented for Sri Lanka, although they are less reliable than the data presented for Latin American countries. Sri Lanka has relatively complete civil registration (over 90 per cent), but only 35 per cent of deaths were medically certified and 10 per cent of infant deaths and 23 per cent of early childhood deaths were due to signs, symptoms and other ill-defined conditions (World Health Organization, 1989-1993).

Since reasonably reliable cause-of-death data are not available from civil registration systems in high mortality regions, data are presented from special studies in two local areas. The International Centre for Diarrhoeal Disease Research, Bangladesh, provides very complete mortality data based on frequent field visits and continuous registration of vital events in Matlab, a rural region in Bangladesh. Cause of death data are derived from verbal autopsies based on information reported by family members; those cause of death data appear to be reasonably accurate for young children but appear to have major errors for infants (Bhatia, 1989; Vallin, D'Souza and Palloni, 1990). Consequently, for Matlab, only the early child mortality data are included in the tables and the text describes findings from a special in-depth study which provides some accurate cause-of-death data for infants (Bhatia, 1989; Fauveau, Koenig and Wojtyniak, 1991). It should be mentioned that the Matlab data in the tables are based on only 677 deaths for young children.

For Bamako, a town in Mali, the cause-of-death data are derived from local death registration (Fargues and Nassour, 1988). Those data are less complete than the other data shown but they appear to be the best cause-of-death data available for the high mortality region of sub-Saharan Africa. In Bamako, it is estimated that slightly over one half of the deaths of infants and young children were registered. Causes of death were based on hospital reports (60 per cent) or verbal autopsies of information provided by a family member. The data shown in the present chapter are based on over 5,000 deaths for each age group.

[2]During the early development of females, one of the X chromosomes in each cell is inactivated. It appears that in each cell, either X chromosome is inactivated at random and thereafter remains inactive in all daughter cells. Even though one X chromosome is inactive in each cell, females are protected against X-linked recessive genetic defects for two reasons. First, in some tissues in which the activity of a particular X-linked gene is required, there is selective elimination of the cells in which the X chromosome with the defective gene is active; consequently, in most of the cells in that tissue, the X chromosome with the normal gene is active (Conley, 1992). Second, in tissues in which that type of selective elimination does not occur, one half of the cells have the X chromosome with the normal gene active, and in many cases those cells can accomplish the necessary function.

[3]Haemophilia A is estimated to occur in 0.01-0.03 per cent of male live births, and that disease appears to have increased infant and child mortality by a factor of roughly 4-5 throughout the twentieth century in the United States of America (Jones and Ratnoff, 1991; Sankaranara-yanan, 1991); calculations based on those estimations indicate that haemophilia A has increased death rates for male infants and young boys in the general population by about 0.03-0.12 per cent.

[4]Available evidence suggests that little sex difference in levels of oestrogen and progesterone exists in foetuses, infants or young children, although some studies suggest that males may have higher levels of oestrogen and/or progesterone at birth and/or during early infancy (Simmons and others, 1994; Winter and others, 1976; Winter, Faiman and Reyes, 1981). Some additional sex differences in hormone levels have been observed; for example, females have higher levels of follicle-stimulating hormone during foetal development and infancy (Winters and others, 1976; Winter, Faiman and Reyes, 1981). However, since there appears to be no evidence that those other hormonal differences influence sex differences in infant or child mortality, they are not discussed here.

[5]The higher estimate has been calculated on the basis of rates of immunodeficiencies in male and female Swedish children, based on complete data, including relatively mild immunodeficiencies (Fasth, 1982). The lower estimate has been calculated on the basis of similar but less complete data for Japan (Hayakawa and others, 1981). Summing the rates of various identified X-linked immunodeficiency diseases also suggests estimates in that range for various developed countries (Conley, 1992; OMIM-TM, 1994).

[6]For the Swedish sample of immunodeficient children, recorded mortality due to infectious diseases was about 15 per cent, based on limited duration of follow-up in a country with relatively low exposure to infectious diseases and very good medical care (Fasth, 1982). Much higher mortality has been observed in historical and contemporary data for various X-linked immunodeficiencies (as high as 90-100 per cent by age 5 (OMIM-TM, 1994; Perry and others, 1980).

[7]Sum of the sex differences in mortality for all the infectious diseases shown for infants and young children for the countries in tables 21 and 25.

[8]One of the identified X-linked immunodeficiencies reduces levels of IgM (and does not reduce levels of several other classes of immunoglobu-lin); however, that factor is unlikely to account for the sex difference in IgM levels in the general population because that genetic defect is rare (probably less than 5 cases per 100,000 live-born males (Conley, 1992; Fasth, 1982; Perry and others, 1980)).

[9]For young children in those countries, boys had slightly lower total mortality than girls (sex ratio 0.95) despite their higher accident mortality (Taket, 1986).

REFERENCES

Aaby, P. (1993). Are men weaker or do their sisters talk too much (II). Paper presented at a meeting of the International Union for the Scientific Study of Population, on the teme "New approaches to anthropological demography", Barcelona, 10-13 November 1993.

_____, and others (1994). Sex-specific differences in mortality after high-titre measles immunization in rural Senegal. Bulletin of the World Health Organization (Geneva), vol. 72, No. 5, pp. 761-770.

Alemu, W. (1993). Neonatal tetanus mortality survey, North and South Omo administrative regions, Ethiopia. Ethiopian Medical Journal (Addis Ababa), vol. 31, No. 2 (April), pp. 99-107.

Arnold, F. (1992). Sex preference and its demographic and health implications. International Family Planning Perspectives (New York), vol. 18, No. 3 (September), pp. 93-101.

Berg, T., and S. G. O. Johansson (1969). Immunoglobulin levels during childhood, with special regard to IgE. Acta Pediatrica Scandinavia, vol. 58, pp. 513-524.

Bhatia, S. (1989). Patterns and causes of neonatal and postneonatal mortality in rural Bangladesh. Studies in Family Planning (New York), vol. 20, No. 3, pp. 136-146.

Bhuiya, A., and others (1987). Measles case fatality among the under-fives: a multi-variate analysis of risk factors in a rural area of Bangladesh. *Social Science and Medicine* (Elmsford, New York), vol. 24, No. 5, pp. 439-443.

Biggar, R. J., and others (1981). Malaria, sex, and place of residence as factors in antibody response to Epstein-Barr virus in Ghana, West Africa. *The Lancet* (Baltimore and London), 18 July, pp. 115-118.

Bry, K., and others (1994). Influence of fetal gender on the concentration of Interleukin-1 receptor antagonist in amniotic fluid and newborn urine. *Pediatric Research* (Baltimore), vol. 35, No. 1, pp. 130-134.

Butterworth, M., B. McClellan and M. Allansmith (1967). Influence of sex on immunoglobulin levels. *Nature* (London), vol. 214, pp. 1224-1225.

Catlin, E. A., and others (1990). Sex-specific fetal lung development and Mullerian Inhibiting Substance. *American Review of Respiratory Diseases* (New York), vol. 141, pp. 466-470.

Conley, Mary Ellen (1992). Molecular approaches to analysis of X-linked immunodeficiencies. *Annual Review of Immunology* (Palo Alto), vol. 10, pp. 215-238.

_____ (1994). Personal communication, 12 April.

Corbier, P., D. A. Edwards and J. Roffi (1992). The neonatal testosterone surge: a comparative study. *Archives internationales de physiologie, de biochimie et de biophysique* (Liège, Belgium), vol. 100, pp. 127-131.

Cunningham-Rundles, S., ed. (1993). *Nutrient Modulation of the Immune Response*. New York: Marcel Dekker, Inc.

Diame, E-H. M., S. N'diaye and P. Airey (1990). Diarrhoeal morbidity among young children: findings from the Demographic and Health Survey of Senegal, 1986. Demographic and Health Surveys Further Analysis Series, No. 10. In *Determinants of Health and Mortality in Africa*, A. G. Hill, ed. Columbia, Maryland: Institute for Research Development/Macro Systems, Inc..

Eaton, W. O., and L. R. Enns (1986). Sex differences in human motor activity level. *Psychological Bulletin* (Washington, D.C.), vol. 100, No. 1, pp. 19-28.

El Samani, F. Z., W. C. Willett, and J. H. Ware (1989). Predictors of simple diarrhoea in children under 5 years: a study of a Sudanese rural community. *Social Science and Medicine* (Elmsford, New York), vol. 29, No. 9, pp. 1065-1070.

Elwood, M., and J. Little (1992). Distribution by sex. In *Epidemiology and Control of Neural Tube Defects*, J. M. Elwood, J. Little and J. Harold Elwood, eds. Monographs in Epidemiology and Biostatistics, vol. 20. Oxford: Oxford University Press.

Emery, A. H. (1987). *Duchenne Muscular Dystrophy*. Oxford, United Kingdom: Oxford University Press.

Fargues, P., and O. Nassour (1988). *Douze ans de mortalite urbaine au Sahel- niveaux, tendances, saisons et causes de mortalité a Bamako 1974-1985*. Institut national d'études démographiques/Institut du Sahel, Travaux et documents, Cahier no. 123. Paris: Presses universitaires de France.

Fasth, A. (1982). Primary immunodeficiency disorders in Sweden: cases among children, 1974-1979. *Journal of Clinical Immunology* (New York), vol. 2, No. 2, pp. 86-92.

Fauveau, V., M. A. Koenig and B. Wojtyniak (1991). Excess female deaths among rural Bangladeshi children: an examination of cause-specific mortality and morbidity. *International Journal of Epidemiology* (Oxford), vol. 20, No. 3, pp. 729-735.

Forest, M. G., E. de Peretti and J. Bertrand (1977). Plasma androgens in infancy. In *Endocrinology: Proceedings of the Fifth International Congress of Endocrinology, 1976, Excerpta Medica*, V. H. T. James, ed. Amsterdam: Elsevier.

Garenne, M. (1994). Sex differences in measles mortality: a world review. *International Journal of Epidemiology* (Oxford), vol. 23, No. 3, pp. 632-642.

Gerrard, J. W., R. Dalgleish and L. K.-T. Tan (1977). Immunoglobulin levels in white and metis communities in Saskatchewan. *Clinical and Experimental Immunology* (Oxford), vol. 29, pp. 447-456.

Golding, J. (1991). The epidemiology of perinatal death. In *Reproductive and Perinatal Epidemiology*, M. Kiely, ed. Boca Raton, Florida: CRC Press.

Gomez, E. G. (1993). Sex discrimination and excess female mortality in childhood. In *Gender, Women, and Health*, E. G. Gomez, ed. Washington, D.C.: Pan American Health Organization.

Goy, R. W., F. B. Bercovitch and M. C. McBrair (1988). Behavioral masculinization is independent of genital masculinization in prenatally androgenized female rhesus macaques. *Hormones and Behavior* (San Diego), vol. 22, pp. 552-571.

Greenwood, B. M., and H. C. Whittle (1981). *Immunology of Medicine in the Tropics*. London: Edward Arnold.

Hall, J. G. (1986). Neural tube defects, sex ratios and X inactivation. *The Lancet* (Baltimore), vol. 2, No. 8519 (6 December), pp. 1334-1335.

Hall, M. H., and R. Carr-Hill (1982). Impact of sex ratio on onset and management of labor. *British Medical Journal* (London), vol. 285, pp. 401-403.

Hayakawa, H., and others (1981). Primary immunodeficiency syndrome in Japan. *Journal of Clinical Immunology* (New York), vol. 1, No. 1, pp. 31-39.

Hines, M. (1982). Prenatal gonadal hormones and sex differences in human behavior. *Psychological Bulletin* (Washington, D.C.), vol. 92, No. 1, pp. 56-80.

_____, and F. R. Kaufman (1994). Androgen and the development of human sex-typical behavior. *Child Development* (Chicago), vol. 65, pp. 1042-1053.

Holt, E. A., and others (1993). Differential mortality by measles vaccine titer and sex. *Journal of Infectious Diseases* (Chicago), vol. 168, pp. 1087-1096.

Japan, Ministry of Health and Welfare (1992). *Vital Statistics, 1990: Japan*. Tokyo: Koseisho Daijin Kanbo Tokei Johobu.

Johansson, S. R. (1991). Welfare, mortality and gender: continuity and change in explanations for male/female mortality differences over three centuries. *Continuity and Change* (Cambridge, United Kingdom), vol. 6, No. 2, pp. 135-177.

Jones, P. K., and O. D. Ratnoff (1991). The changing prognosis of classic hemophilia (Factor VIII "deficiency"). *Annals of Internal Medicine* (Philadelphia), vol. 114, pp. 641-648.

Kafuko, G. W., and others (1972). Epstein-Barr virus antibody levels in children from the West Nile district of Uganda. *The Lancet* (Baltimore and London), 1 April, pp. 706-709.

Karn, M. N., and L. S. Penrose (1951). Birthweight and gestation time in relation to maternal age, parity and infant survival. *Annals of Eugenics*, vol. 16, pp. 147-164.

Khoury, M. J., and others (1985). Factors affecting the sex differential in neonatal mortality: the role of respiratory distress syndrome. *American Journal of Obstetrics and Gynecology* (St. Louis), vol. 151, pp. 777-782.

Kimpen, J., and others (1989). Influence of sex and gestational age on cord blood IgE. *Acta Pediatrica Scandinavia* (Uppsala, Sweden), vol. 78, pp. 233-238.

Kirkwood, B. R. (1991). Diarrhea. In *Disease and Mortality in Sub-Saharan Africa*, R. G. Feachem and D. T. Jamison, eds. Oxford: Oxford University Press.

Komlos, L., and others (1989). Lymphocyte subpopulations in mother and newborn: correlation with sex of the newborn and number of pregnancies. *Gynecologic and Obstetric Investigation* (Basel), vol. 27, pp. 143-147.

Kramer, M. S. (1987). Determinants of low birth weight: methodological assessment and meta-analysis. *Bulletin of the World Health Organization* (Geneva), vol. 65, pp. 663-737.

Lau, Y. L., B. M. Jones and C. Y. Yeung (1992). Biphasic rise of serum immunoglobulins G and A and sex influence on serum immunoglobulin M in normal Chinese children. *Journal of Pediatric and Child Health*, vol. 28, pp. 240-243.

Leon, M. E., and others (1993). Immunologic parameters 2 years after high-titre measles immunization in Peruvian children. *Journal of Infectious Diseases* (Chicago), vol. 168, pp. 1097-1104.

Leroy, O., and M. Garenne (1989). La mortalité par tetanos néonatal: la situation à Niakhar au Senegal. In *Mortalité et sociétée en Afrique*, G. Pison, E. van de Walle and M. Sala-Diakanda, eds. Institut national d'études démographiques, Travaux et documents, Cahier, No. 124. Paris: Presses universitaires de France.

MacGillivray, I., and D. A. Davey (1985). The influence of fetal sex on rupture of the membranes and pre-term labour. *American Journal of Obstetrics and Gynecology* (St. Louis, Missouri), vol. 153, No. 7, pp. 814-815.

Makinson, C. (1994). Discrimination against the female child. *International Journal of Gynecology and Obstetrics* (Limerick, Ireland), vol. 46, pp. 119.

Matheny, A. P., and J. E. Fisher (1984). Behavioural perspectives on children's accidents. *Advances in Developmental and Behavioral Pediatrics* (London), vol. 5, pp. 221-264.

McDivitt, J. A., R. C. Hornik and C. D. Carr (1994). Quality of home use of oral rehydration solutions: results from seven Healthcom sites. *Social Science and Medicine* (Elmsford, New York), vol. 38, No. 9, pp. 1221-1234.

McGregor, J. A., and others (1992). Foetal gender differences in preterm birth: findings in a North American cohort. *American Journal of Perinatology* (New York), vol. 9, No. 1 (January), pp. 43-48.

McGue, M., and others (1990). Sex-linked determinants for IgM? *Human Heredity* (Basel), vol. 40, pp. 231-234.

Meites, S., ed. (1989). *Pediatric Clinical Chemistry*. Washington, D.C.: AACC Press.

Michaels, R. H., and K. D. Rogers (1971). A sex difference in immunologic responsiveness. *Pediatrics* (Elle Grove Village, Illinois), vol. 47, No. 1 (January), pp. 120-123.

Mock, N. B., and others (1993). Socio-economic, environmental, demographic and behavioural factors associated with occurrence of diarrhea in young children in the Republic of the Congo. *Social Science and Medicine* (Elmsford, New York), vol. 36, No. 6, pp. 807-816.

Moore, C. C., and M. Grumbach (1992). Sex determination and gonadogenesis: a transcription cascade of sex chromosome and autosome genes. *Seminars in Perinatology* (Philadelphia), vol. 16, No. 5, pp. 266-278.

Mukoyama, M., and others (1987). Life spans of Duchenne muscular dystrophy patients in the hospital care programme in Japan. *Journal of the Neurological Sciences* (Turin), vol. 81, pp. 155-158.

Mulder, D. W., and others (1994). Two-year HIV-1-associated mortality in a Ugandan rural population. *The Lancet* (Baltimore and London), vol. 343, pp. 1021-1023.

Narain, J. P., and others (1989). Epidemic measles in an isolated unvaccinated population, India. *International Journal of Epidemiology* (Oxford), vol. 18, No. 4, pp. 952-958.

Nielsen, H. C. (1992). Testosterone regulation of sex differences in fetal lung development. *Proceedings of Society for Experimental Biology and Medicine*, vol. 199, pp. 446-452.

Okasha, A., and others (1976). A psychosocial study of accidental poisoning in Egyptian children. *British Journal of Psychiatry* (United Kingdom), vol. 129, pp. 539-643.

Olowe, S. A., and A. Akinkugbe (1978). Amniotic fluid lecithin/sphingomyelin ratio: comparison beween an African and a North American community. *Pediatrics* (Elle Grove Village, Illinois), vol. 62, No. 1 (July), pp. 38-41.

On-line Mendelian Inheritance in Man (OMIM-TM) (1994). *On-line Mendelian Inheritance in Man* (MIM Numbers, 300300, 300400, 301000, 306400, 308230, 308240, 310200, 312060). Baltimore: Johns Hopkins University.

Park, C. H., and others (1992). Is there etiologic heterogeneity between upper and lower neural tube defects? *American Journal of Epidemiology* (Baltimore), vol. 136, No. 12, pp. 1493-1501.

Perry, G. S., and others (1980). The Wiskott-Aldrich syndrome in the United States and Canada. *Journal of Pediatrics* (London), vol. 97, No. 1, pp. 72-78.

Pilgrim, C., and J. B. Hutchinson (1994). Developmental regulation of sex differences in the brain: can the role of gonadal steroids be redefined? *Neuroscience* (Oxford), vol. 60, No. 4, pp. 843-855.

Preston, Samuel H. (1976). *Mortality Patterns in National Populations, with Special Reference to Recorded Causes of Death*. New York: Academic Press.

Reinisch, J. M., M. Ziemba-Davis and S. A. Sanders (1991). Hormonal contributions to sexually dimorphic behavioural development in humans. *Psychoneuroendocrinology* (Oxford), vol. 16, No. 1-3, pp. 213-278.

Roach, B., and others (1981). Influence of age and sex on serum complement components in children. *American Journal of Diseases of Children*, vol. 135, No. 10, pp. 918-920.

Rosen, B. N., and L. Peterson (1990). Gender differences in children's outdoor play injuries: a review and an integration. *Clinical Psychology Review* (Oxford), vol. 10, pp. 187-205.

Rowe, D. S., and others (1968). Plasma immunoglobulin concentrations in a West African (Gambian) community and in a group of healthy British adults. *Clinical and Experimental Immunology* (Oxford), vol. 3, pp. 63-79.

Ryder, R. W., and others (1989). Perinatal transmission of the human immunodeficiency virus type 1 to infants of seropositive women in Zaire. *New England Journal of Medicine* (Boston), vol. 320, No. 25 (22 June), pp. 1637-1642.

Sankaranarayanan, K. (1991). Ionizing radiation and genetic risks-I. Epidemiological, population genetic, biochemical and molecular aspects of Mendelian diseases. *Mutation Research* (Amsterdam), vol. 258, pp. 3-49.

Schuurs, A. H. W. M., and H. A. M. Verheul (1990). Effects of gender and sex steroids on the immune response. *Journal of Steroid Biochemistry and Molecular Biology* (Oxford), vol. 35, No. 2, pp. 157-172.

Seki, K., and K. Kato (1987). Increased boy-to-girl ratio in women with pre-term labour beginning with contractions. *American Journal of Obstetrics and Gynecology* (St. Louis), vol. 157, No. 1 (July), pp. 215-216.

Seller, M. J. (1987). Neural tube defects and sex ratios. *American Journal of Medical Genetics* (Chicago), vol. 26, pp. 699-707.

Shapiro, S., E. R. Schlesinger and R. E. L. Nesbitt, Jr. (1968). *Infant, Perinatal, Maternal and Childhood Mortality in the United States*. Cambridge: Harvard University Press.

Simmons, D., and others (1994). Sex differences in umbilical cord serum levels of inhibin, testosterone, oestradiol, dehydroepiandrosterone sulphate, and sex hormone-binding globulin in human term neonates. *Biology of the Neonate* (Basel), vol. 65, No. 5, pp. 287-294.

Spencer, M. J., and others (1977). Antibody responses following rubella immunization analysed by HLA and ABO types. *Immunogenetics* (Berlin), vol. 4, pp. 365-372.

Stanfield, P., and A. Galazka (1984). Neonatal tetanus in the world today. *Bulletin of the World Health Organization* (Geneva), vol. 62, No. 4, pp. 647-669.

Stoop, J. W., and others (1969). Serum immunoglobulin levels in healthy children and adults. *Clinical and Experimental Immunology* (Oxford), vol. 4, pp. 101-112.

Tabutin, D., and M. Willems (1993). La surmortalité des petites filles dans le sud et notamment en Afrique sub-Saharienne, des années 1970 aux années 1980. Paper for réseau interuniversitaire Africain pour le développement et les études de population, Abidjan, 4-7 August 1993.

Taket, A. (1986). Accident mortality in children, adolescents and young adults. *World Health Statistics Quarterly* (Geneva), vol. 39, No. 3, pp. 232-256.

Torday, J. S., and H. C. Nielsen (1987). The sex difference in foetal lung surfactant production. *Experimental Lung Research* (Bristol, Pennsylvania), vol. 12, pp. 1-19.

United States Department of Health and Human Services (1991). *Vital Statistics of the United States, 1988*, vol. II, *Mortality*. Hyattsville, Maryland: National Center for Health Statistics.

Vallin, J., S. D'Souza and A. Palloni, eds. (1990). *Measurement and Analysis of Mortality: New Approaches*. New York: Oxford University Press.

Van Allen, M. I., and others (1993). Evidence for multi-site closure of the neural tube in humans. *American Journal of Medical Genetics* (Chicago), vol. 47, pp. 723-743.

van Essen, A. J., and others (1992). Birth and population prevalence of Duchenne muscular dystrophy in the Netherlands. *Human Genetics* (Berlin), vol. 88, pp. 258-266.

Waldron, I. (1983). Sex differences in human mortality: the role of genetic factors. *Social Science and Medicine* (Elmsford, New York), vol 17., No. 6, pp. 321-333.

_____ (1987). Patterns and causes of excess female mortality among children in developing countries. *World Health Statistics Quarterly* (Geneva), vol. 40, No. 3, pp. 194-210.

Weisner, T. S. (1979). Some cross-cultural perspectives on becoming female. In *Becoming Female: Perspectives on Development*, C. Kopp and M. Kirkpatrick, eds. New York: Plenum Press.

Whiting, B., and C. P. Edwards (1973). A cross-cultural analysis of sex differences in the behaviour of children aged three through 11. *The Journal of Social Psychology* (Washington, D.C.), vol. 91, pp. 171-188.

Wiedermann, D., and D. Wiedermannova (1981). The development of three major immunoglobulin serum levels in healthy children between 2 and 16 years of age with regard to sex. *Physiologica Bohemoslovaca* (London), vol. 30, Fasc. 4, pp. 315-322.

Winter, J. S. D., C. Faiman and F. Reyes (1981). Sexual endocrinology of fetal and perinatal life. In *Mechanisms of Sex Differentiation in Animals and Man*, C. R. Austin and R. G. Edwards, eds. London: Academic Press.

Winter, J. S. D., and others (1976). Pituitary-gonadal relations in infancy, 2, Patterns of serum gonadal steroid concentrations in man from birth to two years of age. *Journal of Clinical Endocrinology and Metabolism* (Baltimore), vol. 42, pp. 679-686.

World Health Organization (1989-1993). *1989-1992 World Health Statistics Annual*. Geneva.

Xiao, K. Z., and others (1990). Central nervous system congenital malformations, especially neural tube defects, in 29 provinces, metropolitan cities and autonomous regions of China: Chinese birth defects monitoring programme. *International Journal of Epidemiology* (Oxford), vol. 19, No. 4, pp 978-982.

Yadav, B. R., W. A. King and K. J. Betteridge (1993). Relationships between the completion of first cleavage and the chromosomal complement, sex and developmental rates of bovine embryos generated in vitro. *Molecular Reproduction and Development* (New York), vol. 36, No. 4, pp. 434-439.

IV. LEVELS AND TRENDS OF SEX DIFFERENTIALS IN INFANT, CHILD AND UNDER-FIVE MORTALITY

*United Nations Secretariat**

Over the past two decades, mortality among children under the age of five has declined in most developing countries. Health and nutrition interventions, including immunization against infectious diseases, improved sanitation and access to clean water, as well as increased availability and use of health services, have all contributed to the decline. Those interventions mostly affect the incidence of infectious and parasitic diseases, the major causes of death under the age of five in developing countries. As the proportion of deaths caused by infectious and parasitic diseases declines, the proportion of deaths due to endogenous causes and to certain exogenous causes, such as accidents, increases. That change results in an increasing concentration of deaths in the first few months of life, thus changing the structure of mortality under the age of five.

In most populations, female infants (i.e., female children under the age of one) have lower mortality than their male counterparts, an outcome that is attributed to the biological and genetic advantages that females have over males. The female advantage may also operate beyond infancy, although at some point during early childhood environmental and behavioural as opposed to biological factors begin to exert a greater influence in determining sex differentials in mortality (see chapter II above). Because a large proportion of mortality under age five is concentrated in the first year of life, a period in which mortality due to endogenous causes prevails, if overall levels of under-five mortality are considered they generally tend to be lower for girls than for boys.

In some developing countries, the biological advantage that girls have over boys is far outweighed by other factors, such as discriminatory child-care practices favouring boys, that result in excess female mortality among children, particularly between the exact ages of one and five. The countries where excess female mortality has been documented and studied extensively form a

belt that starts with Northern Africa, passes through Western and South-central Asia, and extends to China and the Republic of Korea (D'Souza and Chen, 1980, for Bangladesh; Dyson, 1987, for India; Tabutin, 1992, for Northern African countries; Bucht and El-Badry, 1986 and Makinson, 1986 on Egypt; Choe, 1985 on the Republic of Korea; and Nadarajah, 1983 on Sri Lanka). Excess female child mortality in the countries covered by that belt has been attributed to discriminatory practices against girls in terms of nutrition and the provision of health care. Evidence shows that excess female mortality has persisted even in countries experiencing economic development, declining fertility, improvements in nutritional levels and health-care provision, and increases in female educational attainment.

Hitherto, information allowing the estimation of mortality separately for boys and girls has been sparse, except for countries in the regions mentioned above. One reason for the lack of information is that because in most countries sex differentials in under-five mortality generally favour girls, it is assumed that the sex differentials of its components, infant and child mortality, also favour girls. Therefore, very little effort has been made to tabulate or publish data allowing the estimation of infant and child mortality by sex.

More recently, a number of efforts have been made to document and analyse indicators of mortality by sex among children under the age of five for a large number of developing countries. Hill and Upchurch (1995), using results from the Demographic and Health Surveys for 35 countries, and Tabutin and Willems (1995), using those surveys as well as other data sources for 62 countries, find that excess female mortality between the exact ages of one and five (child mortality) is far more widespread than previously thought. According to Tabutin and Willems (1995), there is on average a 2 per cent excess female child mortality in sub-Saharan Africa, a 1 per cent excess in Latin America and the Caribbean, a 12 per cent excess in Eastern and Southern Asia, and a 5 per cent excess in Northern Africa and Western Asia.

---

*Population Division of the Department for Economic and Social Affairs.

In contrast, among children under the age of one excess male mortality prevails, ranging from 37 per cent on average in Eastern and Southern Asia to 3 per cent in Northern Africa and Western Asia. Both studies reveal that the prevalence of excess female mortality is only weakly related to the level of overall mortality. For a number of countries Tabutin and Willems were able to study the relationship between mortality decline and changes in the sex ratio of child mortality. They found that excess female mortality tends to decline as mortality decreases but the relation between the two is weak.

In the present chapter, a new set of estimates of infant, child and under-five mortality by sex is derived, and sex differentials in mortality relative to each of those indicators are presented. The estimated sex differentials are based on all available data allowing the estimation of infant and child mortality by sex for a country. The data and methods used to obtain estimates of infant, child and under-five mortality by sex are described in the section A below. Section B is devoted to the analysis of levels and trends of sex differentials in mortality in childhood; both the relation between sex differentials in mortality and mortality level, and changes in sex differentials over time are examined.

A. THE DATA

The most common indicators of mortality in childhood are: infant mortality (i.e., the probability of dying between exact ages 0 and 1 year, denoted by $_1q_0$); child mortality (the probability of dying between exact ages 1 and 5 years, denoted by $_4q_1$); and under-five mortality (the probability of dying between exact ages 0 and 5 years, denoted by $_5q_0$). Those three indicators are related to one another by the following equation:

$$_5q_0 = {_1q_0} + {_4q_1}(1 - {_1q_0}) \qquad (1)$$

Direct estimates (those that do not require the use of models for their derivation) of $_1q_0$, $_4q_1$ and $_5q_0$ are based either on data from a vital registration system or on survey questions posed to adult women about their childbearing histories. To estimate the probability of dying before age one ($_1q_0$) by sex from vital registration data one requires information on the number of male and female live births occurring over a given period, and the number of girls and boys dying before age one during the same period. The estimation of child mortality ($_4q_1$) requires information on the number of girls and boys

dying between the exact ages of one and five over a given period, plus the population aged one to four at the mid-point of the period, classified by sex. Data derived from the complete registration of births and deaths constitute the ideal basis for the estimation of mortality since they cover the full set of events of interest and permit the estimation of trends. Unfortunately, most developing countries either lack vital registration systems altogether or have systems whose completeness of registration is low enough so as to severely compromise the accuracy of the estimates derived from them. Therefore, vital registration was used to derive estimates of mortality in childhood by sex for only a few developing countries.

Direct estimates of mortality in childhood can also be obtained from demographic surveys that record birth histories relative to women in the childbearing ages. Those histories comprise the date of each live birth and the age at death of children who have died before the survey. Period-specific probabilities of dying calculated from birth histories are based on reported deaths and numbers of children of a particular age exposed to the risk of dying during a specific period, such as the 10 years preceding the survey. Almost all direct estimates based on survey data and presented in the present chapter are calculated in that manner.[1] Although the calculation of cohort-specific probabilities of dying is more straightforward than period measures, particularly when using birth history data, the cohort approach is not used in the present study because censoring prevents the calculation of mortality rates for the most recent cohort.

Estimates of mortality in childhood derived from birth histories may be affected by several problems related to the quality of the basic data, the most important of which are: (a) errors in the dating of events; (b) omission of events; and (c) sampling errors. The accuracy of survey-based estimates can be jeopardized by the existence of one or more of those errors in the basic data. For example, the estimated male to female ratio of infant mortality from the Cameroon Fertility Survey (1978) was 0.97 for 1968-1972 and 1.20 for 1973-1977, but with respect to child mortality the corresponding ratios were 1.06 and 0.92. That is, if taken at face value the estimated ratios would imply that the situation in Cameroon changed from one in which there was excess female mortality under age one and excess male mortality between ages 1 and 4 to a reverse situation in only five years. Since such changes are implausible it seems more likely that the estimated variations are the result of a combination of error patterns affecting the basic data.

Among the possible errors relative to the dating of events, a common one results from the tendency for ages at death to be rounded to one year (i.e., 12 months). When the deaths of children who die at ages of exactly 12 months and over are reported as occurring at exactly 12 months, the estimates of the probabilities of dying before age one and at age one and over will not be affected. However, if respondents tend to round up to 12 months the ages of children dying at 10 or 11 months then the probability of dying before age one (infant mortality) will be underestimated and that of dying between exact ages one and five (child mortality) will be overestimated. In an analysis of the data quality of the first round of Demographic and Health Surveys, Sullivan and others (1990) report that overall, there were 10 times as many deaths reported at age 12 months than at ages of 10, 11, 13 or 14 months, and that the problem was particularly severe in sub-Saharan Africa. However, sex differentials in infant and child mortality will not be seriously affected if the tendency to round up or down to 12 months is the same regarding male and female children.

The second problem, omission of events, has generally more serious consequences for the estimation of sex differentials in childhood mortality if omission tends to occur selectively by sex of the child. Thus, greater omission of deaths of girls than of boys will bias the male to female sex ratios of infant and child mortality upwards, whereas the opposite will occur if deaths of boys are more prone to omission. In phase one of the Demographic and Health Surveys (22 countries), underreporting of female children who died in the neonatal period was detected in the cases of Botswana and Sri Lanka. In Trinidad and Tobago, in contrast, the evidence suggested that male neonatal deaths had been underreported (Sullivan and others, 1990). Since most reports on the demographic surveys used to derive estimates of mortality in childhood by sex include an evaluation of data quality, information on the likely errors affecting the basic data was used in assessing the reliability of the estimates obtained.

Inevitably, when the basic data are derived from sample surveys sampling errors related to the probabilistic nature of the sample used will affect the estimates obtained. Sampling errors are inversely related to sample size, so that the larger the number of events

covered the smaller the degree of expected errors. With respect to the estimation of infant and child mortality, the number of events can be rather small, particularly if the estimates are calculated for short reference periods (i.e., less than five years in length), and consequently they may be subject to relatively large standard errors. Because deaths among children under age one are considerably more likely than those among children aged 1 to 4, estimates of infant mortality are expected to have lower standard errors than those of child mortality. Similarly, estimates of under-five mortality, which include the relatively numerous deaths of children under one, are expected to have lower standard errors than estimates of child mortality. In assessing the quality of estimates of mortality in childhood derived from 50 Demographic and Health Surveys, Curtis (1995) showed that in most cases the relative standard error of the estimated infant and under-five mortality for both sexes over a five-year period fell within the range 0.04 to 0.08, implying that the estimates obtained were likely to under or overestimate mortality by a minimum of 4 per cent and a maximum of 8 per cent. In the case of child mortality, the range for the relative standard error was 0.06 to 0.15, implying that the estimates obtained were likely to under or overestimate actual child mortality levels by a minimum of 6 per cent and a maximum of 15 per cent. No information was provided on the likely range of the standard errors applicable to estimates by sex, but it would almost surely be wider. Expanding the reference period of the estimates to 10 years would reduce the range of variation of the expected standard errors by increasing the number of events covered. That strategy was used to obtain the estimates from sample surveys presented in the present chapter. Thus, they all refer to the 10-year period preceding the survey. When the basic data were not available and only estimates referring to five-year periods had been published, an average of the two periods preceding the survey was used.

Data on the number of children ever born and the number surviving to women in the reproductive ages can be used to derive indirect estimates of mortality in childhood. The method used in the derivation of indirect estimates (also known as the Brass method) is described in detail in United Nations (1990). Since the questions needed to gather the basic data are straightforward a large number of censuses and surveys have collected the required data. The Brass method yields a variety of estimates of mortality in childhood that can be translated to a single indicator using model life-tables. Use of under-five mortality as that indicator is recommended because $_5q_0$ is robust to changes in the underlying mortality model. Unfortunately, infant mortality is not equally robust and can vary considerably according to the model selected. Consequently, indirect estimates do not provide a solid basis for the estimation of infant and child mortality separately, and their value for the estimation of sex differentials in those indicators is limited since the differentials obtained may in large part depend on the mortality models used rather than on actual differences between the mortality risks to which girls and boys are subject.

The estimation of sex differentials in infant and child mortality must therefore rely primarily on direct estimates of mortality in childhood by sex, even though the latter may suffer from biases that distort the true underlying differentials by sex. Problems related to the quality of the basic data are likely to be responsible for inconsistencies in the sex differentials of $_1q_0$ and $_4q_1$ detected either in relation to estimates yielded by a given survey or by different surveys referring to the same country. Accordingly, in order to exploit all information available and to maximize the reliability of the estimated sex differentials both *direct and indirect* estimates of under-five mortality by sex were used to adjust *direct* estimates of the components of under-five mortality, namely, infant and child mortality. The procedure followed to do that involved calculating the male to female ratio of under-five mortality for all estimates, whether direct or indirect, referring to a particular period. In practice, two periods were distinguished: pre-1980 and post-1980 (i.e., one period ending on 31 December 1979 and another starting on 1 January 1980). The resulting ratios for a given period were then averaged to obtain a best estimate of the sex differential of under-five mortality (denoted by BSDQ5). Then, focusing on the set of under-five mortality estimates for both sexes combined and relative to the relevant period, a best estimate (denoted by BQ5) was selected, taking account of the strengths and limitations of each of the under-five mortality estimates available. The average ratio BSDQ5 was then used to derive best estimates of male and female under-five mortality from BQ5.

To obtain the corresponding best estimates in terms of infant mortality, the male to female ratios of all *direct* estimates of infant mortality were calculated and averaged for a particular period, thus yielding a preliminary estimate of the sex differential in infant mortality, denoted by BSDQ1*. In order to maintain the consistency of that estimate with BSDQ5, an adjusted BSDQ5* was calculated by averaging all male to female ratios of under-five mortality estimates derived using only *direct* methods and referring to the relevant period. Then, BSDQ1* was multiplied by BSDQ5/BSDQ5* to yield BSDQ1, the best estimate of the sex differential in infant mortality for the period considered. As in the case of under-five mortality, a best estimate of infant mortality for both sexes, BQ1, was obtained by considering all the infant mortality estimates available for the relevant period and assessing their likely strengths and limitations. Then, final estimates of infant mortality by sex were obtained from BQ1 by using BSDQ1. Once best estimates of infant and under-five mortality by sex were obtained, estimates of child mortality were derived from them on the basis of equation (1) above.

That approach to the estimation of both the sex differentials in infant and under-five mortality and that of mortality levels by sex has the advantage of making use of all the information available and ensuring that there is consistency between the estimated levels of under-five and infant mortality. However, in a number of countries only one source of data was available for a period, generally yielding a single set of estimates of infant and under-five mortality and thus making averaging unnecessary. Given that in most of those cases the data source involved was generally a survey and that there was no corroborative evidence on the accuracy of the estimates obtained, less confidence can be placed on them than on estimates derived from a variety of sources that are fairly consistent among themselves.

In deriving the set of estimates presented in the present chapter, every effort was made to obtain data from each developing country with a population of one million or more in 1990. Table 27 shows a distribution of the sets of estimates analysed for the present study[2] in terms of type of source yielding each set of estimates, the type of estimates obtained and the area to which the estimates refer. In total, 254 sets of estimates were used, covering 88 countries: 37 in Africa; 23 in Latin America and the Caribbean; and 28 in Asia. It is important to note that most data sources yield mortality estimates for more than one point in time. Thus, vital registration may yield estimates referring to several years, and indirect estimates derived from survey or census data usually cover a span of at least 15 years. As table 27 shows, the type of estimates most commonly available were direct estimates derived from birth histories recorded by surveys (141 sets), whereas estimates derived from

TABLE 27. NUMBER OF ESTIMATES OF UNDER-FIVE MORTALITY,
BY TYPE OF ESTIMATE, MAJOR AREA AND NUMBER
OF COUNTRIES WITH ESTIMATES

	Region		
Type of estimate/source	Africa	Latin America	Asia
Civil registration	4	14	9
Direct estimate from survey	64	35	42
Indirect estimates	35	22	29
Number of countries with estimates	37	23	28

vital registration data accounted for only 27 of the sets used.

Table 28 shows the distribution by major area and region of countries having at least one million inhabitants in 1990, as well as the number of countries for which reliable estimates of mortality in childhood by sex could be derived. Out of the 108 countries with populations exceeding one million in 1990, acceptable estimates of infant and child mortality by sex for at least one period could be derived for 82 countries, accounting for 92 per cent of the population of developing countries with at least one million inhabitants in 1990. Among those 82 countries, 34 were in Africa, 25 in Asia, and 23 in Latin America and the Caribbean. In addition, for 52 countries it was possible to obtain reliable estimates of mortality in childhood by sex for more than one period, thus allowing an assessment of trends. It is important to note that the number of countries with reliable estimates differs somewhat from the number of countries having data allowing the estimation of mortality in childhood by sex presented in table 27. The difference stems from the fact that for some countries with data the estimates obtained were not judged to be reliable.

Table 29 displays the complete set of estimates of male and female infant, child and under-five mortality used in the present study, and the corresponding sex

TABLE 28. NUMBER OF COUNTRIES AND PERCENTAGE OF POPULATION COVERED IN STUDY

Region	Number of countries with population of more than 1 million in 1990	Population size in 1990 (thousands)	Number in study	Population in 1990 covered in study	Percentage of population covered	Number of countries with trend information
Eastern Africa	14	204 068	10	120 699	59	4
Middle Africa	7	70 014	3	16 685	24	2
Northern Africa	6	142 791	6	142 791	100	5
Southern Africa	4	41 483	4	41 483	100	0
Western Africa	13	178 901	11	169 147	95	6
SUBTOTAL	44	637 257	34	490 805	77	17
Eastern Asia (excluding Japan) ..	5	1 227 830	3	1 203 879	98	2
South-central Asia	13	1 243 098	7	1 133 756	91	5
South-eastern Asia	9	441 315	7	428 272	97	5
Western Asia	14	146 809	8	110 648	75	5
SUBTOTAL	41	3 059 052	25	2 876 555	94	17
Caribbean	6	31 327	6	31 327	100	5
Central America	7	112 868	7	112 868	100	4
South America	10	291 816	10	291 816	100	9
SUBTOTAL	23	436 011	23	436 011	100	18
TOTAL	108	4 132 320	82	3 803 371	92	52

Source: World Population Prospects: the 1994 Revision (United Nations publication, Sales No. E.95.XIII.16).

TABLE 29. ESTIMATES OF MALE, FEMALE AND BOTH SEXES INFANT, CHILD AND UNDER-FIVE MORTALITY, AND SEX
DIFFERENTIALS IN INFANT, CHILD AND UNDER-FIVE MORTALITY, BY COUNTRY AND DATE OF ESTIMATE

Country or area	Date	Infant mortality			Child mortality			Under-five mortality			Sex differentials (males per 100 females)		
		Male	Female	Both sexes	Male	Female	Both sexes	Male	Female	Both sexes	Infant mortality	Child mortality	Under-five mortality
Sub-Saharan Africa													
Eastern Africa													
Burundi	1982	126	100	113	74	96	85	190	186	188	126	77	102
Ethiopia	1974	..	..	..	..	..	..	226	204	215	..	..	111
	1982	..	..	..	..	..	..	231	168	200	..	..	138
Kenya	1973	96	86	91	66	59	63	155	140	148	112	112	111
	1985	65	56	61	36	35	35	99	89	94	116	103	111
Madagascar	1987	100	100	100	73	69	71	166	162	164	100	106	102
Malawi	1975	..	..	..	..	..	..	317	309	313	..	..	103
	1987	140	129	135	99	91	95	225	208	217	109	109	108
Mauritius	1975	57	45	51	16	17	17	72	62	67	127	94	116
	1985	27	21	24	4.3	3.9	4	31	25	28	129	110	124
Mozambique	1982	..	..	..	..	..	..	284	275	280	..	..	103
Rwanda	1973	140	123	132	108	102	105	233	213	223	114	106	109
	1987	142	119	131	111	93	102	238	201	220	119	119	118
Uganda	1983	113	104	109	86	75	81	190	172	181	109	115	110
United Rep. of Tanzania	1978	124	109	117	92	87	89	205	186	196	114	106	110
	1983	115	105	110	85	79	82	190	175	183	110	108	109
Zambia	1973	..	..	..	..	..	..	179	171	175	..	..	105
	1987	117	99	108	82	77	80	189	169	179	118	106	112
Middle Africa													
Cameroon	1973	126	116	121	92	96	94	207	200	204	109	96	104
	1985	97	85	91	57	69	63	148	147	148	114	83	101
Congo	1975	89	81	85	38	38	38	124	116	120	110	100	107
	1983	73	63	68	26	27	27	97	89	93	116	96	109
Central African Republic	1990	100	87	94	40	44	42	137	127	132	115	91	108
Zimbabwe	1975	..	..	..	..	..	..	127	113	120	..	..	112
	1985	63	49	56	29	30	30	90	77	84	129	97	117
Southern Africa													
Botswana	1982	60	43	52	17	17	17	76	60	68	140	100	127
Lesotho	1972	129	120	125	75	59	67	195	172	184	108	127	113
Namibia	1987	75	64	70	18	25	22	92	87	90	117	72	106
South Africa	1987	50	40	45	24	22	23	72	51	67	125	109	118
Western Africa													
Benin	1975	143	127	135	111	104	108	238	218	228	113	107	109
Burkina Faso	1985	128	111	120	71	79	75	190	182	186	115	90	104
Côte D'Ivoire	1975	145	117	131	73	72	72	207	181	194	124	101	114
	1985	89	75	82	40	34	37	126	106	116	119	118	119
Ghana	1975	113	92	103	75	73	74	179	158	169	123	103	113
	1985	108	92	100	70	70	70	170	156	163	117	100	109
Liberia	1970	187	168	178	109	105	107	276	256	266	111	104	108
	1980	174	137	156	90	92	91	248	217	233	127	98	114
Mali	1982	167	148	158	127	130	128	273	259	266	113	98	105
Mauritania	1975	114	104	109	64	66	65	170	164	167	110	97	104
	1983	95	76	86	59	57	58	149	129	139	125	104	116

TABLE 29 (continued)

Country or area	Date	Infant mortality			Child mortality			Under-five mortality			Sex differentials (males per 100 females)		
		Male	Female	Both sexes	Male	Female	Both sexes	Male	Female	Both sexes	Infant mortality	Child mortality	Under-five mortality
Niger	1987	193	189	191	148	171	159	313	328	320	102	87	95
Nigeria	1975	128	108	118	91	90	91	207	188	198	119	101	110
	1985	119	113	116	94	80	87	202	184	193	105	117	110
Senegal	1973	171	148	160	127	137	132	277	265	271	116	93	105
	1985	119	102	111	84	81	82	193	175	184	117	104	110
Togo	1983	109	94	102	65	80	72	167	167	167	116	81	100
Northern Africa and Western Asia													
Northern Africa													
Algeria	1975	113	109	111	62	67	64	168	168	168	104	93	100
	1985	84	81	83	32	34	33	113	113	113	104	94	100
Egypt	1975	139	139	139	70	90	80	200	217	208	100	78	92
	1985	93	89	91	38	46	42	127	131	129	104	83	97
Libya	1975	101	99	100	50	53	51	146	146	146	102	94	100
Morocco	1972	122	111	117	69	77	72	183	179	181	110	90	102
	1985	83	75	79	28	31	29	109	103	106	111	90	106
Tunisia	1975	101	95	98	45	48	47	141	139	140	106	94	101
	1983	66	60	63	25	25	25	89	83	86	110	100	107
Sudan	1973	109	91	100	69	71	70	170	156	163	120	97	109
	1985	81	69	75	48	45	46	125	111	118	117	107	113
Western Asia													
Israel	1975	24	20	22	4.3	3.9	4	28	24	26	120	110	117
	1985	13	11	12	2.1	2.0	2	15	13	14	118	105	115
Iraq	1973	86	77	82	38	34	36	121	109	115	112	112	111
	1980	..	..	..	..	..	..	97	87	92	..	..	111
Jordan	1970	76	81	78	33	34	34	106	112	109	94	97	95
	1985	39	41	40	10.5	10.3	10	49	51	50	95	102	96
Kuwait	1975	39	33	36	8.5	8.1	8	47	41	44	118	105	115
	1983	25	21	23	5.8	4.5	5	31	25	28	119	129	124
Oman	1978	78	66	72	29	40	34	105	103	104	118	73	102
Saudi Arabia	1980	..	..	..	..	..	..	89	76	83	..	..	117
Syria	1972	80	80	80	33	39	36	111	116	113	100	85	96
	1982	..	..	..	..	..	..	68	60	64	..	..	113
Turkey	1973	147	135	141	47	60	54	187	187	187	109	78	100
	1988	91	75	83	25	23	24	113	96	105	121	109	118
United Arab Emirates	1980	..	..	..	..	..	..	33	26	30	..	..	127
Yemen	1975	165	146	156	113	124	118	259	252	256	113	91	103
	1987	106	90	98	41	48	44	142	133	138	118	85	107
East and South-eastern Asia													
Eastern Asia													
China	1985	36	34	35	7.7	8.9	8	43	43	43	106	87	100
Hong Kong	1975	15	12	14	3.2	2.9	3	19	15	17	125	110	127
	1985	8.5	7.5	8	1.1	1.0	1	10	8	9	113	110	125
Republic of Korea	1973	38	32	35	9	9	9	47	41	44	119	100	115
	1983	14	12	13	2	2	2	16	14	15	117	100	114

TABLE 29 (*continued*)

Country or area	Date	Infant mortality			Child mortality			Under-five mortality			Sex differentials (males per 100 females)		
		Male	Female	Both sexes	Male	Female	Both sexes	Male	Female	Both sexes	Infant mortality	Child mortality	Under-five mortality
South-eastern Asia													
Indonesia	1970	120	91	106	87	68	77	196	153	175	132	128	128
	1987	78	64	71	44	43	43	118	104	111	122	102	113
Malaysia	1975	36	28	32	13	12	12	48	40	44	129	108	120
	1985	19	15	17	6.3	5.9	6	25	21	23	127	107	119
Myanmar	1982	99	77	88	46	35	41	140	109	125	129	131	128
Philippines	1973	63	54	59	19	22	20	81	75	78	117	86	108
	1988	56	42	49	15	16	16	70	57	64	133	94	123
Singapore	1975	17	12	15	1.9	2.2	2	19	15	17	142	86	127
	1985	10	8	9	1.0	1.0	1	11	9	10	125	100	122
Thailand	1972	110	90	100	68	72	70	170	155	163	122	94	110
	1985	40	33	37	8.9	7.7	8	49	41	45	121	116	120
Viet Nam	1985	40	34	37	15	16	16	55	49	52	118	94	112
South-central Asia													
Afghanistan	1978	215	203	209	128	130	129	315	306	311	106	98	103
Bangladesh.................	1970	158	132	145	101	119	110	243	235	239	120	85	103
	1985	126	106	116	61	80	70	179	177	178	119	76	101
Bhutan	1983	111	103	107	79	80	80	181	175	178	108	99	103
India	1977	116	124	120	72	81	76	179	195	187	94	89	92
	1985	99	97	98	41	57	49	137	148	142	102	72	93
Nepal	1970	157	151	154	87	95	91	231	231	231	104	92	100
	1985	110	104	107	46	59	53	151	158	154	106	78	96
Pakistan	1975	114	101	108	54	67	61	162	162	162	113	81	100
	1985	106	91	99	47	52	50	149	139	144	116	90	107
Sri Lanka	1975	51	41	46	21	23	22	71	63	67	124	91	113
	1985	29	21	25	7.0	7.3	7	36	28	32	138	96	129
Latin America and the Caribbean													
Caribbean													
Cuba......................	1975	31	25	28	6.4	5.9	6	37	30	34	124	108	123
	1985	17	13	15	2.2	1.9	2	19	15	17	131	116	127
Dominican Republic	1970	100	84	92	46	38	42	141	119	130	119	121	118
	1983	77	55	66	17	22	19	93	75	84	140	77	124
Haiti	1970	158	141	150	80	96	88	226	224	225	112	83	101
	1987	121	95	108	53	57	55	167	147	157	127	93	114
Jamaica	1970	53	43	48	16	15	16	69	57	63	123	107	121
Puerto Rico	1972	30	22	26	5.7	4.6	5	35	26	31	136	124	135
	1985	17	13	15	2.2	1.8	2	19	15	17	131	122	127
Trinidad and Tobago	1972	51	41	46	8.6	8.2	8	59	49	54	124	105	120
	1985	31	23	27	4.2	4.0	4	35	27	31	135	105	130
Central America													
Costa Rica	1972	56	44	50	15	16	16	71	59	65	127	94	120
	1985	20	16	18	3.3	2.8	3	23	18	21	125	118	128
El Salvador	1980	97	82	90	41	44	43	135	123	129	118	93	110
Guatemala	1975	113	97	105	49	56	53	156	148	152	116	88	105
	1985	86	70	78	31	36	34	114	104	109	123	86	110
Honduras	1978	92	70	81	34	36	35	123	103	113	131	94	119

91

TABLE 29 (*continued*)

Country or area	Date	Infant mortality			Child mortality			Under-five mortality			Sex differentials (males per 100 females)		
		Male	Female	Both sexes	Male	Female	Both sexes	Male	Female	Both sexes	Infant mortality	Child mortality	Under-five mortality
Mexico	1975	76	62	69	27	29	28	101	89	95	123	93	113
	1983	58	50	54	19	19	19	75	68	72	116	100	110
Nicaragua	1980	103	83	93	48	40	44	146	120	133	124	120	122
Panama	1975	44	34	39	16	15	16	59	48	54	129	107	123
	1985	22	18	20	4.0	4.1	4	26	22	24	122	98	118
South America													
Argentina	1970	63	53	58	13	13	13	75	65	70	119	100	115
	1985	31	25	28	3.1	3.1	3	34	28	31	124	100	121
Bolivia	1970	..	..	..	..	..	..	260	225	243	..	..	116
	1987	103	86	95	46	43	44	144	125	135	120	107	115
Brazil	1977	86	65	76	30	24	27	113	88	101	132	125	128
	1985	71	54	63	19	16	17	89	69	79	131	119	129
Chile	1972	73	62	68	17	15	16	90	76	83	118	113	118
	1985	21	17	19	2.2	1.8	2	23	19	21	124	122	121
Colombia	1972	72	58	65	38	29	39	107	95	101	124	131	113
	1983	35	33	34	15	12	13	49	44	47	106	125	111
Ecuador	1975	82	70	76	46	50	48	123	116	120	117	92	106
	1985	48	40	44	21	20	21	69	59	64	120	105	117
Paraguay	1975	54	52	53	21	15	18	73	66	70	104	140	111
	1985	42	36	39	8.2	10.6	9	50	46	48	117	77	109
Peru	1973	118	104	111	67	63	65	177	160	169	113	106	111
	1985	77	66	72	30	32	31	105	97	101	117	94	108
Uruguay	1975	52	42	47	7.7	6.9	7	59	49	54	124	116	120
	1985	31	25	28	4.3	3.9	4	35	28	32	124	110	125
Venezuela	1975	51	41	46	13.6	13.7	14	64	54	59	124	99	119
	1985	29	23	26	4.1	4.1	4	33	27	30	126	100	122

Sources: *United Nations database on mortality in childhood by sex: Africa, database POP/1B/DB/95/2; ibid., Latin America and the Caribbean, database POP/1B/DB/96/1; ibid., Asia, database POP/1B/DB/96/2.*

differentials expressed as the male to female ratio for each of the childhood mortality estimates presented. The countries with estimates available are listed by region in table 29. Given that some regions have only a small number of countries with estimates, in the subsequent analysis countries have been grouped into larger areas, namely: (*a*) sub-Saharan Africa; (*b*) Northern Africa and Western Asia; (*c*) Eastern and South-eastern Asia; (*d*) South-central Asia; and (*e*) Latin America and the Caribbean. The countries included in each of those areas are listed in table 29.

B. SEX DIFFERENTIALS IN MORTALITY

Sex differentials are usually measured on the basis of the ratio of the male to the female probability of dying multiplied by 100. Note that such a ratio reflects only the relative risks of dying to which male and female children are subject, while saying nothing about the magnitude of those risks. Thus, whereas China and India have sex differentials in child mortality of 87 and 72 male deaths per 100 female deaths, respectively, in 1985, in India children aged 1 to 4 experienced a probability of dying of 49 per 1,000, whereas in China children in the same age group were subject to considerably lower risks of death (8 deaths per 1,000). Consequently, the absolute difference in the risks of dying between male and female children aged 1 to 4 was considerably higher in India (16 deaths per 1,000) than in China (1.2 deaths per 1,000) in 1985, a fact that the sex differential as normally measured would not reflect.

When mortality under age five is low, sex differentials in child mortality become erratic since relatively small absolute differences between the male and female probabilities of dying between exact ages one and five often result in large sex differentials. For example, in Kuwait in 1985 male child mortality was 6 per 1,000 and that of females was 4, giving a sex differential of 150 male deaths per 100 female deaths. Another problem encountered was that rounding of male and female mortality probabilities of dying to single digits often gave a ratio of 100 at very low levels of child mortality. For example, in Hong Kong in 1975, male child mortality was 3.2 per 1,000 and that of females was 2.9 per 1,000. The sex differential using the rounded figures is 100 whereas that using male and female mortality to one decimal place was 110. In order to overcome those problems, male and female probabilities of dying are presented to one decimal place in those instances where the level of child mortality of both sexes was 10 or lower.

Given that most deaths under age five occur during the first year of life, sex differentials in infant mortality tend to be similar to those in under-five mortality. Therefore, when considering sex differentials during the first five years of life it is important to focus separately on the first and the subsequent four years of life. The fact that mortality under one year of age is more likely to be influenced by endogenous factors than by exogeneous ones and that child mortality (i.e., mortality between exact ages 1 and 5) is more sensitive to exogenous factors than to endogeneous factors also validates such distinction. Consequently, in what follows attention will mostly be focused on the sex differentials in infant and child mortality considered separately.

Two different approaches will be used to summarize the findings at the overall and regional levels. The first will rely on the characteristics of the distribution of countries according to their estimated sex differentials in mortality. Countries having estimates of the sex differentials for two different periods (before and after 1

January 1980) are assigned only one value by averaging the estimates obtained for each period. The shape of a distribution can be assessed on the basis of five different indicators: the median, as a measure of centrality; the upper and lower quartiles, as indicators of the range over which the central part of the distribution lies; and the extremes of the distribution, indicating its absolute range.[3] Those indicators of the shape of a distribution assign equal weight to each observation. When—as in the case of the sex differentials of mortality in childhood—the observations refer to the sex differentials estimated for different countries, the relative importance of each observation depends on the number of births that a country has in relation to the overall or regional total. Consequently, in order to take into account the relative importance of the different countries for which estimates are available it is useful to consider as well the regional and overall average of the sex differentials in mortality derived from weighted estimates of the mortality indicators. In particular, estimates of $_1q_0$ and $_5q_0$ by sex at the country level are weighted by the estimated number of births by sex for a given country over the relevant period, and are used to derive regional weighted averages of those measures. The corresponding values of $_4q_1$ by sex are then derived from the weighted averages of $_1q_0$ and $_5q_0$ on the basis of equation (1) above, and sex differentials at the regional level are calculated for each indicator. Those sex differentials will be referred to as the appropriately weighted average sex differentials, though—being ratios of the weighted averages of $_1q_0$, $_4q_1$ and $_5q_0$—they are not themselves weighted averages. Table 30 displays both the median of the distribution of the sex differentials in each mortality indicator ($_1q_0$, $_4q_1$ and $_5q_0$), and the appropriately weighted sex differentials for each major region and for all developing countries with estimates available. The equivalent measures of centrality are also provided for all developing countries with estimates available but excluding China and India so as to ascertain the impact that those large countries have on the overall average.

Table 30 shows that when the distribution of all the developing countries with estimates available is considered, the median of the sex differentials in infant mortality stands at 118 male deaths per 100 female deaths, whereas that for sex differentials in child mortality ($_4q_1$) stands at 100 male deaths per 100 female deaths. Figures 9 and 10 present a graphic display of the distribution of the sex differentials in infant and child mortality by region. The box plots shown in those figures indicate, for each distribution, the location of the median

TABLE 30. MEDIAN AND WEIGHTED AVERAGE SEX DIFFERENTIALS, BY REGIONAL GROUPS

	Median ratios			Weighted average ratios		
	1q0	4q1	5q0	1q0	4q1	5q0
Sub-Saharan Africa	116	101	109	113	103	109
Northern Africa and Western Asia	111	93	104	109	89	102
East and South-eastern Asia	123	104	117	115	98	110
South-central Asia	108	86	103	102	84	95
Latin America	123	105	119	124	101	117
All	118	100	110	108	91	102
All (excluding China and India)	..	..	..	117	97	109

Sources: Table 29; and *United Nations database on mortality in childhood by sex: Africa, database POP/1B/DB/95/2; ibid., Latin America and the Caribbean, database POP/1B/DB/96/1; ibid., Asia, database POP/1B/DB/96/2.*

Figure 9. Sex differentials in infant mortality, by region and total

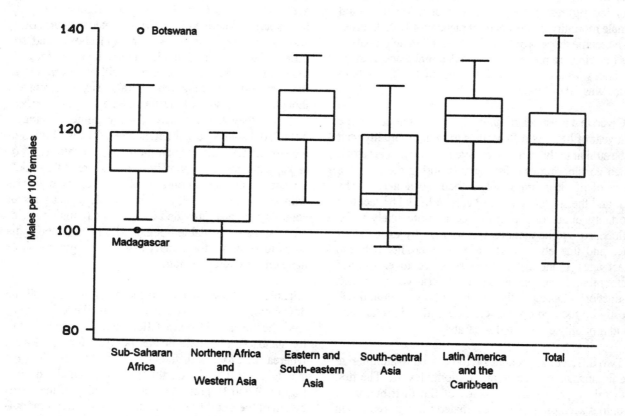

Source: Table 29.

94

Figure 10. Sex differentials in child mortality, by region and total

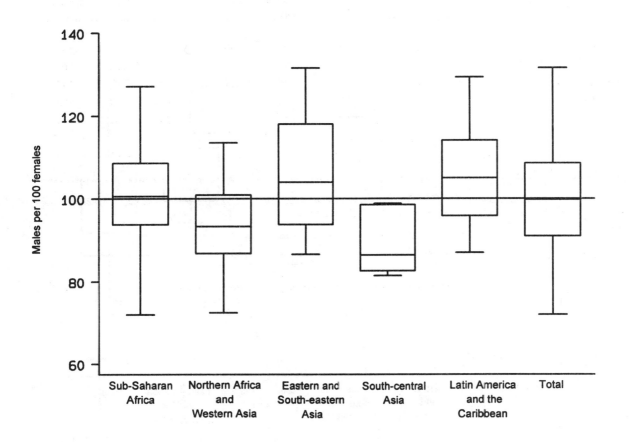

Source: Table 29.

(the horizontal line within the central box), the quartiles (the horizontal limits of the central box) and the extremes of the distribution (the ends of the vertical lines extending beyond the central box or the individual points just above or below them if outliers exist). It is clear from figure 9 that in the majority of the developing countries considered, male children are more likely to die in infancy (i.e., before one year of age) than female children. Indeed, in sub-Saharan Africa, Eastern and South-eastern Asia, and Latin America and the Caribbean, there is no case of a country in which female children are more likely to die in infancy than male children, and in only one country of Northern Africa and Western Asia (Jordan) and one country of South-central Asia (India) are female infants subject to higher proba-

bilities of dying than their male counterparts (see table 29). In contrast, as figure 10 shows, in half the countries covered by the present study female children aged 1 to 4 are more likely to die than their male counterparts; those countries include all countries in South-central Asia, nearly three-quarters in Northern Africa and Western Asia, a little less than half in sub-Saharan Africa, and somewhat less than half in Eastern and South-eastern Asia and Latin America.

As expected, the sex differentials relative to under-five mortality display regional patterns that are very similar to those detected with respect to infant mortality since most deaths under the age of five occur during the first year of life. As figure 11 shows, in most countries male

Figure 11. Sex differentials in under-five mortality, by region and total

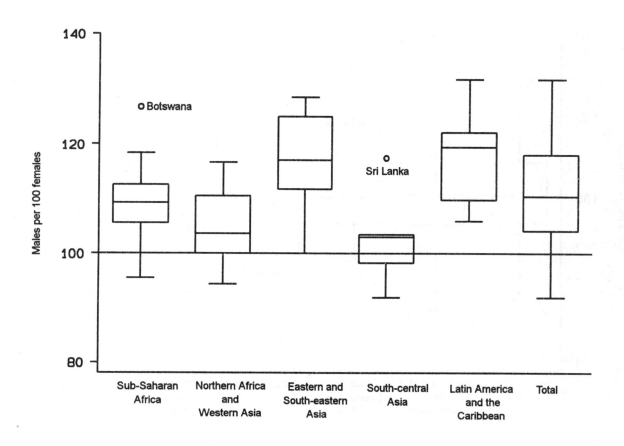

Source: Table 29.

children under the age of 5 are subject to higher risks of dying than female children. Notable exceptions include the Niger in sub-Saharan Africa, Egypt and Jordan in Northern Africa and Western Asia, and India and Nepal in South-central Asia.

A better assessment of the regional impact of existing sex differentials in child mortality can be obtained by considering the appropriately weighted sex differentials presented in table 27. For infant mortality, the overall average sex differential is smaller than the median of the distribution—108 versus 118 male per 100 female deaths—indicating that the weight of countries where female mortality is closer to male mortality levels is higher than that of countries where male mortality

surpasses female mortality by wide margins. With respect to child mortality, the average sex differential is again lower than the median—91 vs. 100 male deaths per 100 female deaths—indicating again that countries in which female mortality exceeds male mortality have higher weights than other countries. The same holds true for sex differentials in under-five mortality, whose appropriately weighted average is 102 male deaths per 100 female deaths as compared to a median value of 110. Because the average sex differentials for all developing countries is greatly influenced by the sex differentials in China and India—which together account for 53 per cent of the total number of births in the 82 countries under study—appropriately weighted averages were also calculated excluding those countries. As table 30 shows, the average sex differentials that exclude China and India differ little from the median values, indicating that among the remaining countries no single one exerts undue influence on the overall total.

At the regional level, the greatest differences between the median values and the appropriately weighted average sex differentials are found in Eastern and South-eastern Asia, in South-central Asia, and to a lesser extent in Northern Africa and Western Asia. In the two first regions, the major difference is between the median and the average sex differentials in infant mortality since China and India, respectively, exert a disproportionate influence. In Northern Africa and Western Asia, the major difference arises with respect to the median and the average sex differential in child mortality, and Egypt is probably the country exerting a major downward influence. In most cases, the median values are larger than the corresponding average sex differentials, suggesting that countries where sex differentials in mortality are lower have higher weights. In general, that set of estimates shows that countries where girls are subject to relatively high risks of dying in relation to those experienced by boys exert considerable influence at both the regional and the overall level. That is, not only are the numbers of countries exhibiting higher levels of female than male child mortality numerous but they also tend to include rather populous countries that drive down the average sex differentials at the regional and overall levels.

In terms of general patterns of excess mortality of one sex over the other, the appropriately weighted average sex differentials confirm the general observations made above with respect to the distribution of the sex differentials by region. With respect to infant mortality, male children tend to be subject to higher mortality than female children, though the excess male mortality recorded in Northern Africa and Western Asia, and especially in South-central Asia, is on the low side (surpassing equality by less than 10 per cent). With respect to child mortality, the average sex differentials indicate that female children are subject to higher risks of death than male children in Northern Africa and Western Asia, Eastern and South-eastern Asia, and South-central Asia. In the two other regions, although male children experience excess mortality, their disadvantage is not large. In terms of at least a 10 per cent excess in mortality, female children aged 1 to 4 are clearly disadvantaged only in Northern Africa and

Western Asia, and in South-central Asia. Those two regions can also be singled out as special in terms of appropriately weighted average sex differentials in under-five mortality since the latter indicate that excess female mortality prevails in South-central Asia among all children under the age of five, and that excess male mortality is very low in Northern Africa and Western Asia among the same group of children.

Although the present analysis of the available estimates at the regional level permits establishing the extent to which excess female mortality is present over large geographical areas, it is important to consider as well the country-level estimates to ascertain whether other patterns can be detected. In sub-Saharan Africa, out of the 28 countries with estimates available, 12 show excess female child mortality—Burkina Faso, Burundi, Cameroon, the Central African Republic, the Congo, Mali, Mauritius, Namibia, the Niger, Senegal, Togo and Zimbabwe. Child mortality among girls is at least 10 per cent higher than that among boys in half of those countries—Burkina Faso, Burundi, Cameroon, Namibia, the Niger and Togo. Although estimates for five of those six countries are derived from a single survey in each case, the fact that they show relatively large sex differentials in favour of boys makes it unlikely that the estimated excess female mortality may be produced by spurious random variation. For Cameroon, more than one source was used in the derivation of estimates, and consequently the estimated sex differential is likely to be more reliable. Though the sub-Saharan countries experiencing excess female mortality over ages 1 to 4 do not seem to conform to a specific pattern, they tend to cluster in Western Africa (Burkina Faso, Mali, the Niger, Senegal and Togo) and in Middle Africa (Cameroon, the Central African Republic and the Congo).

In Latin America and the Caribbean, 8 of the 23 countries with estimates available experienced excess female child mortality—Costa Rica, Ecuador, El Salvador, Guatemala, Haiti, Honduras, Mexico and Venezuela. Only in two of them, Guatemala and Haiti, did mortality among girls aged 1 to 4 exceed that of boys in the same age group by more than 10 per cent. Both of those countries are among the group experiencing the highest mortality levels in the region. In all other cases, the estimated excess female child mortality was moderate (about 5 per cent). Interestingly, most of the countries displaying such excess mortality are located in the Central American region.

In Eastern and South-eastern Asia, only 4 countries out of a total of 10 with estimates available showed excess female child mortality—China, the Philippines, Thailand and Viet Nam—and they varied considerably in the extent of the estimated excess. In both China and the Philippines, mortality among girls aged 1 to 4 exceeded that among boys by well over 10 per cent, whereas the excess in Thailand or Viet Nam was closer to 5 per cent.

As already noted, countries in Northern Africa and Western Asia have traditionally been considered to experience excess female child mortality. However, the estimates of sex differentials for countries in that region show that only Egypt, Oman, Syria and Turkey have female child mortality levels that exceed those of males by more than 10 per cent. In addition, out of the 14 countries in the region with data available, 4 did not show female child mortality levels exceeding those of males—Iraq, Israel, Kuwait and the Sudan.

South-central Asia has also been a region where excess female child mortality has been known to be common. According to the present estimates, all the seven countries of South-central Asia with data available showed higher mortality among girls aged 1 to 4 than among boys. Furthermore, in Bangladesh, India, Nepal and Pakistan, female child mortality exceeded that among males by over 10 per cent.

In conclusion, the comprehensive set of estimates presented in the present chapter confirms that the number of countries in which girls aged 1 to 4 are subjectto higher mortality risks than boys is large and comprises at least half of those with estimates available. Countries in regions that have been traditionally associated with higher mortality risks among girls than among boys were generally found to conform to that pattern. Thus, all the countries of South-central Asia included in the study and the majority of countries in Northern Africa and Western Asia were found to have higher levels of female child mortality than male child mortality. Similarly, China was found to experience relatively high excess female child mortality. In the rest of Eastern and South-eastern Asia, however, relatively few countries were found to experience excess female child mortality. In Latin America and the Caribbean, a pattern of moderate levels of excess female child mortality was detected in a number of Central American countries, including Mexico; in sub-Saharan Africa a number of countries, particularly in Western and Middle

Africa, were found to experience moderate to high levels of excess child mortality.

With respect to sex differentials in infant mortality, although only two countries—India and Jordan—displayed a level of female infant mortality higher than that of males, the existence of some degree of excess female mortality that reduces the "standard" or "expected" male disadvantage during the first year of life cannot be ruled out. There is, however, no agreed upon way of establishing a valid standard for all countries, and consequently the degree of excess female mortality cannot be properly ascertained. It is revealing, however, that in table 30 the appropriately weighted averages of the sex differentials for the regions most likely to experience some degree of excess female mortality in infancy—South-central Asia, and Northern Africa and Western Asia—were 102 and 109, respectively.

1. Sex differentials and level of mortality

An important question regarding sex differentials in mortality in childhood is whether they follow a specific pattern in relation to the level of mortality to which a population is subject. Would one expect, for instance, that sex differentials increase as overall mortality levels decline? In order to attempt to answer that question the estimated sex differentials in infant and child mortality have been related to the level of under-five mortality for both sexes combined. The estimates available for each of the 82 countries included in the previous analysis are used here with a small variant. Countries having estimates referring to the 1970s and the 1980s are entered twice, thus resulting in a total of 134 observations. Figure 12 shows a plot of the sex differentials in infant mortality against the level of under-five mortality for both sexes for all 134 cases taken together. The relation between the two variables is negative and significant, having a correlation coefficient of -0.46, suggesting that as the level of mortality declines the sex differential increases, that is, the tendency towards a male disadvantage rises. However, similar plots for each of the five regional groups shown in figures 13 to 17 reveal that the relationship between the sex differentials in infant mortality and the level of under-five mortality for both sexes is not as strong in Northern Africa and Western Asia, and in Eastern and South-eastern Asia as in the other three regions.

The different panels of figure 18 show similar plots for the sex differentials in child mortality against the

Figure 12. Ratio of male to female infant mortality, by level of under-five mortality for both sexes

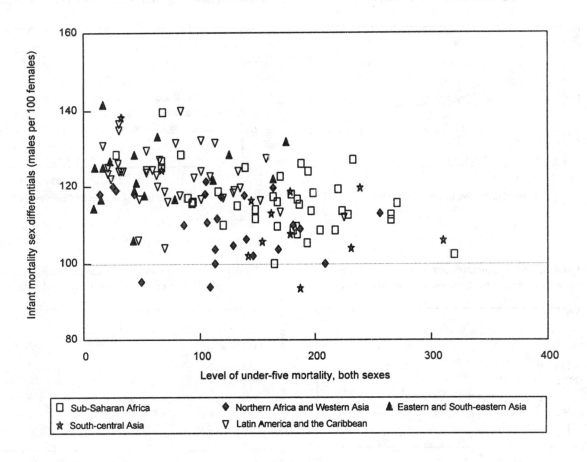

Source: Table 29.

under-five mortality level for both sexes. The relation between the two variables is negative and significant, although the correlation coefficient is only -0.25. Such a low correlation coefficient indicates a wide scatter of points around the regression line. It appears that a wide range of sex differentials can coexist with similar mortality levels, although the overall tendency is towards increasing sex differentials as overall levels of mortality decline. Consequently, a reduction of mortality is not *per se* a guarantee that the mortality levels of girls will fall faster than those of boys. The plots for each of the regions show that only in Northern Africa and Western Asia is the relationship between sex differentials in child mortality and the level of under-five mortality of both sexes strong and negative (figures 19-23). In Latin America, although the relationship is significant at the 5 per cent level there appears to be a lot of variation in

sex differentials for any given level of under-five mortality. In the other three regions, a relationship is virtually non-existent. It thus appears that whereas conditions leading to declines in overall levels of mortality depend on the particular socio-economic situation of each country, the conditions leading to high mortality among female children relative to that of male children depend on cultural and behavioural norms that favour one sex over the other, and that may tend to persist independently of changes in the socio-economic situation. It may be expected, however, that as the process of development advances, the cultural and behavioural norms underlying the existence of excess female child mortality may weaken. Since declining mortality, particularly at the younger ages, is a close correlate of development, reductions of mortality over the first years of life are likely to be associated with rising sex differentials in

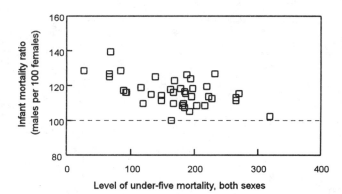

Figure 13. Infant mortality sex differentials, by level of under-five mortality: sub-Saharan Africa

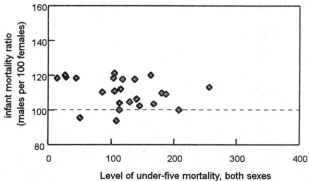

Figure 14. Infant mortality sex differentials, by level of under-five mortality: Northern Africa and Western Asia

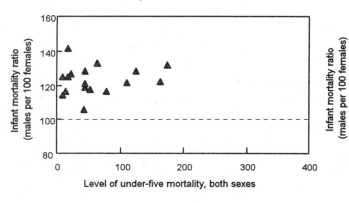

Figure 15. Infant mortality sex differentials, by level of under-five mortality: Eastern and South-eastern Asia

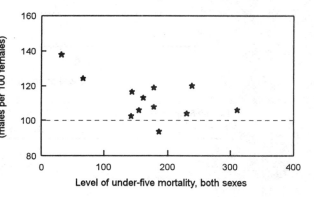

Figure 16. Infant mortality sex differentials, by level of under-five mortality: South-central Asia

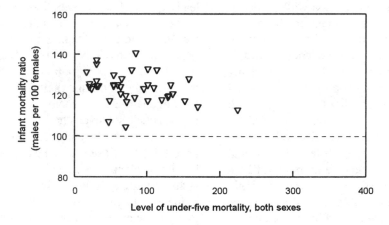

Figure 17. Infant mortality sex differentials, by level of under-five mortality: Latin America and the Caribbean

Figure 18. Ratio of male to female child mortality, by level of under-five mortality for both sexes

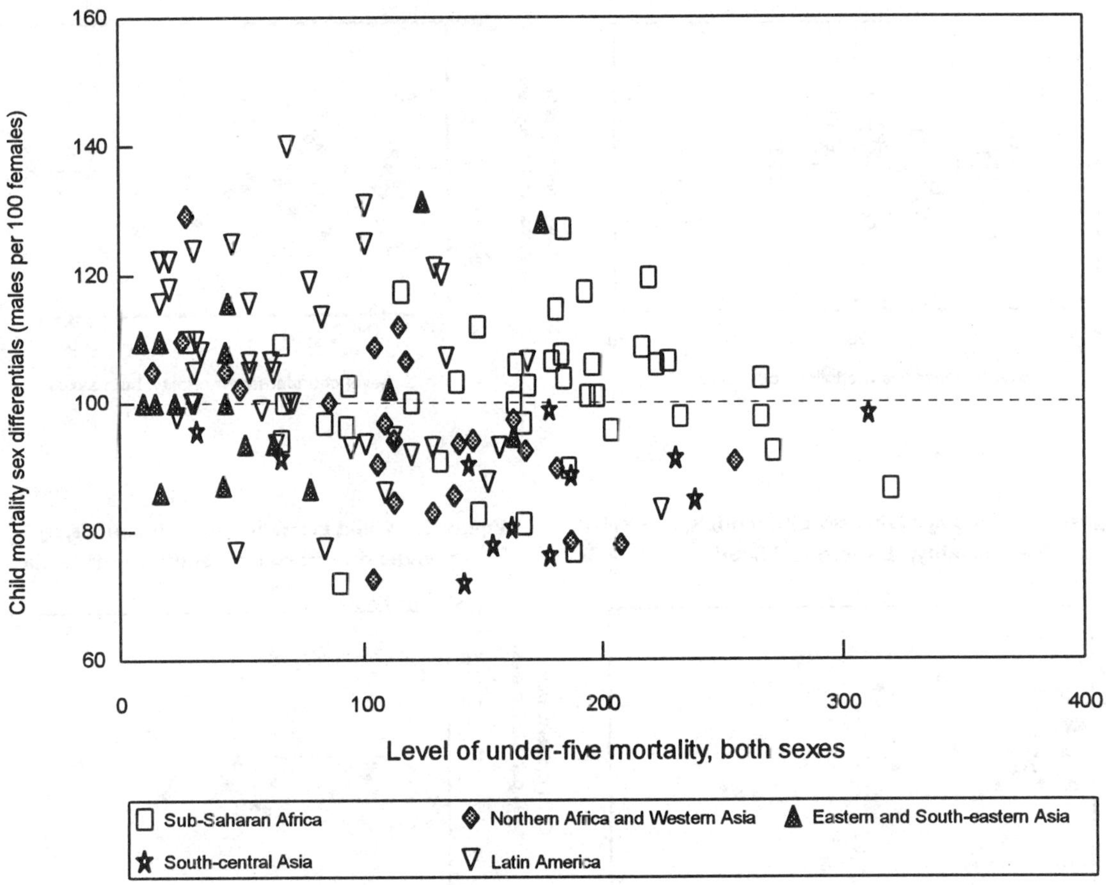

Source: Table 29.

child mortality, as experienced in Northern and Western Asia and to a lesser extent in Latin America. In that respect, South-central Asia represents a deviant case where declines in the level of under-five mortality of both sexes have not been accompanied by increases in the sex differentials of child mortality; if anything, the plight of girls in most countries of that region has worsened relative to that of boys.

The above evidence, though far from conclusive, does suggest that there is some relation between changes in mortality levels and the direction in which sex differentials in child mortality are likely to move. A more detailed assessment of country experiences is provided below by analysing trends in the sex differentials in

mortality in childhood for all those countries with data for two periods.

2. Trends in sex differentials in mortality in childhood

As already mentioned, for 52 countries the data available allow the estimation of sex differentials in infant, child and under-five mortality for two periods: before 1 January 1980 (the 1970s) and as of 1 January 1980 (the 1980s). At the regional level, trends in the sex differentials of mortality in childhood can be ascertained for 12 countries in sub-Saharan Africa; 10 in Northern Africa and Western Asia; 7 in Eastern and South-eastern Asia; 5 in South-central Asia; and 18 in

Figure 19. Child mortality sex differentials, by level of under-five mortality: sub-Saharan Africa

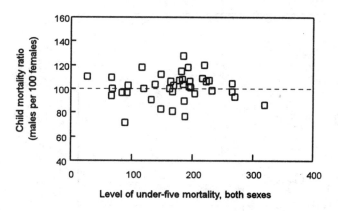

Figure 20. Child mortality sex differentials, by level of under-five mortality: Northern Africa and Western Asia

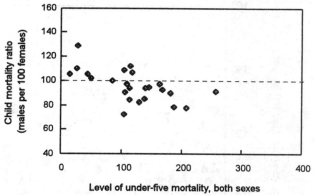

Figure 21. Child mortality sex differentials, by level of under-five mortality: Eastern and South-eastern Asia

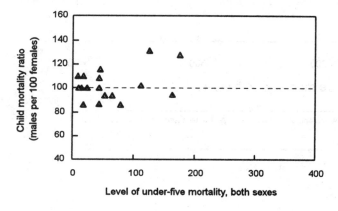

Figure 22. Child mortality sex differentials, by level of under-five mortality: South-central Asia

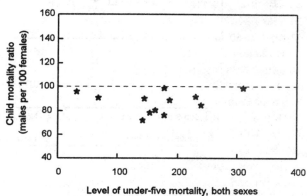

Figure 23. Child mortality sex differentials, by level of under-five mortality: Latin America and the Caribbean

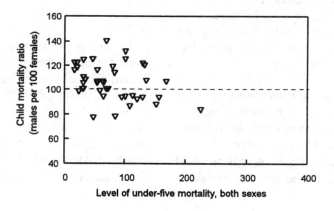

Latin America and the Caribbean. The 52 countries concerned accounted for 59 per cent of all births in developing countries in 1985. China was not included in that group because it lacked data relative to the 1970s.

In all 52 countries, the levels of mortality in childhood declined between the 1970s and the 1980s. Yet not all of them recorded an increase in the sex differentials of mortality in childhood. With respect to child mortality in particular, although in 31 of the 52 countries the sex differentials increased or remained unchanged (as they did in 5 countries), in 21 a decline was noticeable, including 9 in Latin America and the Caribbean; 5 in sub-Saharan Africa; 3 in South-central Asia; 2 in Eastern and South-eastern Asia and 2 in Northern Africa and Western Asia (see table 31). Declining sex differentials in child mortality imply that in relative terms, the risks of dying among girls did not decline as much as those of boys from one decade to the next. However, not all countries experiencing a decline in the sex differentials in child mortality can be characterized as having excess female child mortality over ages 1 to 4. In Latin America and the Caribbean, for instance, among the 9 countries experiencing a decline in the sex differentials in child mortality, only four (the Dominican Republic, Panama, Paraguay and Peru) saw their sex differentials decline from values above 100 in the 1970s to values below 100 in the 1980s. Among the rest, in four (Brazil, Colombia, Puerto Rico and Uruguay) the decline was from sex differentials that implied a male disadvantage in the 1970s to ones where the probability of survival for boys was still higher than that for girls. Latin America, as observed in the previous section, is one of the two regions in which a negative relationship between the level of mortality and sex differentials in child mortality was evident. Thus, the trends for the 9 countries that show declining sex differentials as mortality declines is puzzling. One possible explanation is that some of those countries (Panama, Paraguay, Puerto Rico and Uruguay) were characterized by very low levels of child mortality because small changes in the absolute levels of mortality of boys and girls result in large variations in the estimated sex differential.

Given that South-central Asia and Northern Africa and Western Asia are the regions in which excess female child mortality has been most evident, it is of interest to consider changes over time in those regions. Among the 5 countries of South-central Asia with trend data, all had sex differentials in child mortality below 100 in the 1970s, indicating the existence of excess female child mortality, and in 3 of the 5—Bangladesh, India and Nepal—the situation of girls relative to that of boys had worsened. Even among the two countries in which the situation of girls had improved—Pakistan and Sri Lanka—excess female child mortality was still evident in the 1980s. In contrast, in Northern Africa and Western Asia there was a clear trend towards the reduction of mortality risks among girls relative to those of boys and towards a disappearance of excess female child mortality. Thus, whereas among the 10 countries in the region with data on trends 8 showed sex differentials in child mortality that were 100 or lower in the 1970s, four of them had sex differentials of 100 or higher during the 1980s. In addition, among 7 countries the sex differentials had increased between the 1970s and the 1980s, although in Algeria, Egypt and Morocco excess female child mortality still prevailed during the most recent period. A notable exception to the general trend was Yemen, where the situation of girls had worsened between the two decades.

To ascertain the overall impact of changes in the sex differentials of childhood mortality at the regional level, the appropriately weighted average sex differentials were calculated for each period and are shown in table 32. With respect to infant mortality, the average sex differential increased at the overall level and for the two regions where excess female mortality was more common, namely, Northern Africa and Western Asia, and South-central Asia. In the other regions, the average sex differential in infant mortality tended to decline slightly or remained unchanged. At the overall level, the inclusion of India had a major effect; excluding India, the average sex differential declined slightly between the 1970s and the 1980s.

With respect to child mortality, the overall average sex differential declined from 93 male deaths per 100 female deaths in the 1970s to 88 in the 1980s, indicating an overall worsening of the situation of girls aged 1 to 4 with respect to their male counterparts. That worsening trend was mainly attributable to the situation in India since its exclusion resulted in an unvarying sex differential that, at 97 male deaths per 100 female deaths, nevertheless indicated the existence of some excess female mortality. At the regional level, average sex differentials increased in sub-Saharan Africa, Northern Africa and Western Asia, and Latin America and the Caribbean, suggesting changes consistent with a greater improvement in the survival chances of girls with

TABLE 31. TRENDS IN SEX DIFFERENTIALS, SELECTED COUNTRIES

Country or area	Infant mortality (males per 100 females)		Child mortality (males per 100 females)		Under-five mortality (males per 100 females)	
	1970s	1980s	1970s	1980s	1970s	1980s
Sub-Saharan Africa						
Cameroon	109	114	96	83	104	101
Congo	110	116	100	96	107	109
Côte D'Ivoire	124	119	101	118	114	119
Ghana	123	117	103	100	113	109
Kenya	112	116	112	103	111	111
Liberia	111	127	104	98	108	114
Mauritania	110	125	97	104	104	116
Mauritius	127	129	94	110	116	124
Nigeria	119	105	101	117	110	110
Rwanda	114	119	106	119	109	118
Senegal	116	117	93	104	105	110
United Republic of Tanzania	114	110	106	108	110	109
Northern Africa and Western Asia						
Algeria	104	104	93	94	100	100
Egypt	100	104	78	83	92	97
Israel	120	118	110	105	117	115
Jordan	94	95	97	102	95	96
Kuwait	118	119	105	129	115	124
Morocco	110	111	90	90	102	106
Sudan	120	117	97	107	109	113
Tunisia	106	110	94	100	101	107
Turkey	109	121	78	109	100	118
Yemen	113	118	91	85	103	107
Eastern and South-eastern Asia						
Hong Kong	125	114	110	110	127	125
Indonesia	132	122	128	102	128	113
Malaysia	129	127	108	107	120	119
Philippines	117	133	86	94	108	123
Republic of Korea	119	117	100	100	115	114
Singapore	142	125	86	100	127	122
Thailand	122	121	94	116	110	120
South-central Asia						
Bangladesh	120	119	85	76	103	101
India	94	102	89	72	92	93
Nepal	104	106	92	78	100	96
Pakistan	113	116	81	90	100	107
Sri Lanka	124	138	91	96	113	129
Latin America and the Caribbean						
Argentina	119	124	100	100	115	121
Brazil	132	131	125	119	128	129
Chile	118	124	113	122	118	121
Colombia	124	106	131	125	113	111
Costa Rica	127	125	94	118	120	128
Cuba	124	131	108	116	123	127
Dominican Republic	119	140	121	77	118	124

Table 31 (*continued*)

Country or area	Infant mortality (males per 100 females)		Child mortality (males per 100 females)		Under-five mortality (males per 100 females)	
	1970s	1980s	1970s	1980s	1970s	1980s
Ecuador	117	120	92	105	106	117
Guatemala	116	123	88	86	105	110
Haiti	112	127	83	93	101	114
Mexico	123	116	93	100	113	110
Panama	129	122	107	98	123	118
Paraguay	104	117	140	77	111	109
Peru	113	117	106	94	111	108
Puerto Rico	136	131	124	122	135	127
Trinidad and Tobago	124	135	105	105	120	130
Uruguay	124	124	116	110	120	125
Venezuela	124	126	99	100	119	122

Source: Table 29.

TABLE 32. AVERAGE AND MEDIAN SEX DIFFERENTIALS IN INFANT, CHILD AND
UNDER-FIVE MORTALITY, BY REGION, 1970S AND 1980S

	Number of countries	Median						Average					
		Infant mortality		Child mortality		Under-five mortality		Infant mortality		Child mortality		Under-five mortality	
		1970s	1980s	1970s	1980s	1970s	1980s	1970s	1980s	1970s	1980s	1970s	1980s
Total	52	118	119	100	101	111	114	107	110	93	88	102	102
Total (excluding India)	51							118	116	97	97	109	109
Region													
Sub-Saharan Africa	12	114	117	101	104	110	111	117	110	102	112	110	110
Northern Africa and Western Asia	10	109	114	93	101	102	107	107	112	85	93	99	106
Eastern and South-eastern Asia	7	125	122	100	102	120	120	127	124	116	101	122	115
South-central Asia	5	113	116	89	78	100	101	99	106	87	77	94	96
Latin America and the Caribbean	18	123	124	107	103	118	121	124	124	104	105	118	119

Sources: Table 29; and *United Nations database on mortality in childhood by sex: Africa,* database POP/1B/DB/95/2; *ibid., Latin America and the Caribbean,* database POP/1B/DB/96/1; *ibid., Asia,* database POP/1B/DB/96/2.

respect to those of boys. The opposite appears to have occurred in Eastern and South-eastern Asia and in South-central Asia, where the sex differentials declined from the 1970s to the 1980s. In South-central Asia in particular, the excess female child mortality that existed during the 1970s became accentuated during the 1980s, so that by then girls aged 1 to 4 were nearly 30 per cent more likely to die than boys of the same age.

Changes in the appropriately weighted average sex differentials in under-five mortality reflect the combined effects of changes in infant and child mortality, with the former dominating. At the overall level, average sex differentials remained constant; at the regional level, a noteworthy decline was registered in Eastern and South-

eastern Asia, and a moderate increase was noticeable in Northern Africa and Western Asia. For other regions, the average sex differentials in under-five mortality remained constant or increased slightly. Those trends help to confirm that the countries of Northern Africa and Western Asia having data for two different periods have made considerable strides in reducing the advantage in survivorship that boys have over girls. In South-central Asia, some improvement in the survivorship of girls with respect to boys has been achieved under age five, but it stems entirely from gains made over the first year of life. In Eastern and South-eastern Asia, the increases in survivorship of girls have failed to keep pace with those of boys, especially over the age range 1 to 4, but at the regional level excess female child mortality is not evident. In sub-Saharan Africa, there has been little change in the relative survivorship of boys and girls up to age five, but that has been the result of greater improvements in survivorship among girls over ages 1 to 4 and greater ones for boys before age one. Lastly, in Latin America and the Caribbean, regional sex differentials in all components of childhood mortality have changed only slightly during the two decades considered.

At the country level, the experiences of India and Jordan are worth highlighting since they were the only two countries to exhibit during the 1970s excess female mortality among infants (amounting to 6 per cent). By the 1980s, Jordan was the only country still exhibiting higher mortality among female infants than among males, whereas in India mortality among male infants had surpassed that among female infants by 2 per cent. In Eastern and South-eastern Asia, the case of Indonesia deserves attention since according to the estimates available the sex differentials in infant mortality in that country declined from 132 male deaths per 100 female deaths in the 1970s to 122 male deaths per 100 female deaths in the 1980s, and an even sharper decline was estimated with respect to child mortality, whose sex differentials dropped from 128 to 102 male deaths per 100 female deaths. Taken at face value, those estimates imply that both infant and child mortality among male children decreased more rapidly than infant and child mortality among females between the 1970s and the 1980s. However, the estimate for the 1970s was based on a single source—the Indonesian Fertility Survey—whose evaluation using reinterview techniques revealed the omission of dead children, and to a lesser extent, the reporting of dead girls as boys, errors that would result in an overestimate male mortality relative to that of girls (Macdonald and others, 1978). Given the large weight of Indonesia at the regional level, the trends that it appears to have experienced are largely responsible for the sharp decline in the average sex differential in child mortality in Eastern and South-eastern Asia between the 1970s and 1980s: from 116 to 101 male deaths per 100 female deaths (see table 32).

C. CONCLUSION

The present review of levels and trends in sex differentials of mortality in childhood has shown that the existence of excess female mortality among children aged 1 to 4 is far more widespread than generally thought. For the developing countries covered in the present study, our estimates imply that on average, male infant mortality was 8 per cent higher than that of females but female child mortality was 9 per cent higher than that of males. Excess female child mortality was found to exist in over half of the countries with estimates available, and those countries were found in all major regions. Thus, not only was it corroborated that China and the majority of countries of South-central Asia, Northern Africa and Western Asia experienced higher levels of female than male child mortality, but also a pattern of moderate levels of excess female child mortality was detected in a number of Central American countries, including Mexico, and moderate to high levels of excess female child mortality were detected in several countries of Western and Middle Africa.

In terms of infant mortality, only two countries—India and Jordan—displayed a level of female infant mortality higher than that of males, but in several other countries the estimated level of excess male mortality was on the low side and might indicate the existence of excess female mortality beyond the neonatal period. Thus, for South-central Asia as a whole the average sex differential of 102 male deaths in infancy per 100 female deaths is low. The weight of India in the regional average largely accounts for such a low value.

Both China and India are largely responsible for the excess female child mortality detected at the level of all developing countries combined. When those two countries are excluded, the average sex differential in child mortality approaches 100, indicating that there is almost equality in the probabilities of dying of girls and boys aged 1 to 4. However, as pointed out above the average still conceals significant differences among countries, with about half recording higher levels of child mortality among girls than among boys.

Data on trends available for 52 countries reveals that the survivorship chances of girls aged 1 to 4 have improved more rapidly than those of boys in 26 of the countries considered have improved less rapidly in 21 countries and have changed at the same rate in 5 countries. Of the 26 countries that registered an improvement in the situation of girls relative to that of boys, 13 passed from a situation in which excess female mortality prevailed in the 1970s to one in which excess male mortality was evident by the 1980s. In another 6 countries, mostly in Northern Africa and Western Asia, the mortality of girls remained higher than that of boys during the 1980s though mortality levels of both girls and boys declined. Among the 21 countries where the probability of survivorship for boys improved more rapidly than that of girls, 6 moved from excess male mortality in the 1970s to excess female mortality in the 1980s, and 6 countries—mostly in South-central Asia—saw a further deterioration of the situation of girls relative to that of boys. In the other 9 countries, excess male mortality declined between the 1970s and 1980s, but by the 1980s the mortality of boys was still equal to or higher than that of girls. In sum, the data on trends indicate that with the exception of some countries in South-central Asia, sex differentials in child mortality between males and females are narrowing over time. With regard to sex differentials in infant mortality, excess male mortality in infancy increased from an average of 7 per cent in the 1970s to 10 per cent in the 1980s for all countries combined.

The findings presented in the present chapter, therefore, provide a mixed message. They show that excess female child mortality is a widespread phenomenon, noticeable in a variety of countries whose level of economic development, social organization and cultural values defy a simple characterization. However, the findings also imply that with the exception of China and India, the overall effect on excess female child mortality in the countries where it exists is counterbalanced to a large extent by the excess mortality of male children aged 1 to 4 in other developing countries.

In conclusion, therefore, the situation regarding the existence of excess risks of death among girls in relation to those among boys is critical only in a few countries—though some of them, such as India, are particularly important because of their size. In the majority of countries in which excess female child mortality has been detected, the situation is less serious and more likely to respond to the normal forces of modernization, which involve the provision of adequate basic health-care services, more information about the care and nutrition of children, and incentives to treat equitably children of both sexes. Indeed, for several of the countries included in the present study, the evidence shows that impressive gains have been made in reducing the excess mortality risks to which girls are subject. Fostering the continuation of such trends is clearly important, but undoubtedly priority must be accorded to cases that

are characterized by cultural and societal norms that are detrimental to the status of women.

NOTES

[1]For details on the calculation of direct estimates of infant, child and under-five mortality from the Demographic and Health Surveys, see Sullivan and others, 1994.
[2]Data, sources and estimates are given in United Nations (1995), United Nations (1996a) and United Nations (1996b) for Africa, Latin America and Asia, respectively.
[3]Technically, if there are n observations, the median is the point that divides them into two groups of equal size, with half the observations falling above and half below the median. Similarly, the quartiles are the points dividing each of those halves in groups of equal size, so that a quarter of the observations fall above the upper quartile and a quarter below the lower quartile. The inter-quartile range, therefore, contains that half of the observations falling within the central part of the distribution.

REFERENCES

Bucht, Birgitta and M. A. El-Badry (1986). Reflections on recent levels and trends of fertility and mortality in Egypt. *Population Studies* (Cambridge), vol. 40, No. 1 (March), pp. 101-114.

Choe, M. K. (1985). On sex differentials in infant and child mortality in the Republic of Korea. East-West Population Institute. Unpublished manuscript.

Curtis, Sian L. (1995). *Assessment of the Quality of Data Used for Direct Estimation of Infant and Child Mortality in DHS-II Surveys*. Demographic and Health Surveys Occasional Papers, No. 3. Calverton, Maryland: Macro International.

D'Souza, Stan, and Lincoln Chen (1980). Sex differentials in mortality in rural Bangladesh. *Population and Development Review* (New York), vol. 6, No. 2, pp. 257-270.

Dyson, Tim (1987). Excess female mortality in India: uncertain evidence on a narrowing differential. In *Dynamics of Population and Family Welfare*, K. Srinivasan and S. Mukerji, eds. Bombay: Himalaya Publishing House.

Hill, Ken, and Abdo Yazbeck (1994). Trends in child mortality, 1960-1990: estimates for 84 developing countries. World Development Report 1993: Investing in Health, Background Paper, No. 6. Washington, D. C.

Hill, Ken, and Dawn M. Upchurch (1995). Gender differences in child health: evidence from the Demographic and Health Surveys. *Population and Development Review* (New York), vol. 21, No. 1 (March), pp. 127-151.

Macdonald, A. L., and others (1978). *An Assessment of the Reliability of the Indonesian Fertility Survey Data*. Scientific Reports, No. 3 (October). Voorburg and the Hague, the Netherlands: International Statistical Institute and World Fertility Survey.

Makinson, Carolyn (1986). Sex differentials in infant and child mortality in Egypt. Princeton University. Doctoral dissertation.

Nadarajah, T. (1985). The transition from higher female to higher male mortality in Sri Lanka. *Population and Development Review* (New York), vol. 9, No. 2, pp. 317-325.

Sullivan, Jeremiah, and others (1990). Assessment of the quality of data used for the direct estimation of infant and child mortality in the Demographic and Health Surveys. In *An Assessment of DHS-I Data Quality*. Methodological Reports, No. 1. Columbia, Maryland: Institute for Resource Development, Inc.

_____ (1994). Infant and child mortality. *Demographic and Health Surveys, Comparative Studies* (Columbia, Maryland), No. 15.

Tabutin, Dominique (1992). Excess female mortality in Northern Africa since 1965: a description. *Population: An English Selection* (Paris), vol. 4, pp. 187-208.

_____, and Michel Willems (1995). Excess female child mortality in the developing world during the 1970s and 1980s. *Population Bulletin of the United Nations*, No. 39 (United Nations publication, Sales No. E.95.XIII.17), pp. 45-78.

United Nations (1990). *Step-by-Step Guide to the Estimation of Child Mortality*. Sales No. E.89.XIII.9.

_____ (1995). United Nations database on mortality in childhood by sex: Africa. Database POP/1B/DB/95/2.

_____ (1996a). United Nations database on mortality in childhood by sex: Asia. Database POP/1B/DB/96/2.

_____ (1996b). United Nations database on mortality in childhood by sex: Latin America and the Caribbean. Database POP/1B/DB/96/1.

V. MALNUTRITION, MORBIDITY AND CHILD MORTALITY IN DEVELOPING COUNTRIES

*David L. Pelletier**

Malnutrition is common in developing countries and makes an important contribution to the burden of morbidity and mortality of infants and children. The United Nations reports that growth failure affects about one third of preschool children, and about 45 per cent of adult women are underweight because of either short stature or thinness (United Nations, 1992). In addition, about 190 million preschool children live in areas at risk of vitamin A deficiency, 211 million people are affected by goitre and 370 million women aged 15-49 are affected by anaemia. Those conditions are known to interact synergistically with infectious diseases (Scrimshaw, Taylor and Gordon, 1968), thereby exacerbating the incidence, duration and severity of morbidity.

Although the synergistic relation between malnutrition and disease is accepted in general terms, the implications for child mortality are not reflected in death reporting systems or in the policies and plans of Governments and international organizations. For instance, conventional methods for classifying cause of death focus on the proximate cause of death (infectious diseases), thereby ignoring the synergism between malnutrition and disease and concealing the contribution of malnutrition to mortality (World Bank, 1993). A second related example is the continued perception that mild-to-moderate malnutrition does not increase the risk of death (Bairagi, 1981; Ewbank and Gribble, 1993). That view also leads to an under-estimate of the contribution of malnutrition to mortality. A third example is the common tendency to equate malnutrition with inadequate food intake, so that the role of malnutrition in famine mortality is misunderstood and underestimated (De Waal, 1989). One purpose of the present chapter is to clarify the

nature of malnutrition itself and summarize recent evidence concerning its relation to child mortality. Another purpose is to investigate the extent to which sex differentials in nutritional status are related to sex differentials in child mortality, drawing upon community-based prospective studies and cross-national comparisons.

A. CONCEPTUAL AND METHODOLOGICAL CONSIDERATIONS

The nutritional status of an individual refers to the availability of energy and nutrients to the cells of the body relative to the individual's requirements. Malnutrition is a consequence of an imbalance in energy and/or nutrients at cellular level, including deficiencies and excesses. The terms nutritional status and malnutrition may be used in a global sense to refer to all nutrients considered simultaneously, or in a more limited sense to refer to specific nutrients. Thus, protein-energy malnutrition and iron deficiency represent specific and restricted forms of malnutrition.

The above-mentioned definitions have several important implications. First, they implicitly recognize the fact that an imbalance in energy and nutrients at cellular (and eventually individual) level can arise from inadequate nutrient intake and/or diseases, such as diarrhoea, measles, malaria and other parasitic infections. Such conditions can affect nutrient absorption, transport, storage and utilization. Thus, a vicious cycle can be established; infections impair nutrient intake and utilization and deficient intake impairs the ability of the body to resist and respond to infection. That cycle is well-established from clinical and biological research on individuals (e.g., Scrimshaw, Taylor and Gordon, 1968; Chandra, 1991), and has recently been confirmed at the population level, as described below.

*Associate Professor, Division of Nutritional Sciences, Cornell University.

Second, they concern the underlying causes of malnutrition. A large body of scientific evidence and applied experience pertaining to those underlying causes has been simplified by the United Nations Children's Fund (UNICEF) in 1990, which provided the foundation for the International Conference on Nutrition (1992). As shown in figure 24, those causes include the state of household food security, the adequacy of health services and health environment, and the adequacy of childcare (including infant and child-feeding). The causative role of childcare highlights the fact that malnutrition can arise even in the presence of household food security and adequate availability of health services. Conversely, as revealed by positive deviance studies,[1] good nutritional status can be maintained even in the face of food insecurity, poor sanitation and the associated conditions of poverty (Zeitlin, Ghassemi and Mansour, 1990). Those findings lead to the important overall conclusion that food, health and care, when considered individually, represent a necessary but not sufficient explanation for the existence of malnutrition in households and communities. The relative importance of each of those factors can and does vary across households and communities, although impaired nutritional status (as measured by weight-for-age, for instance) is a manifestation of the problem in all cases. Lastly, figure 24 shows that all three underlying causes are subject to the availability of and control over resources (including mother's time) as modified by political and economic forces.

Third, mortality among children can be seen as arising from the same causes as malnutrition itself as elaborated in figure 25 (Pelletier, 1994a), which emphasizes the interaction between disease and nutrient intake in the centre, as in figure 24, but is explicit about certain pathways leading to malnutrition and mortality. In particular, it distinguishes several types of childcare that are important for interpreting the literature on sex differentials in mortality. Specifically, it distinguishes the role of childcare and feeding as it relates to nutrient intake and disease from childcare as it relates to the treatment of illness. Studies from Bangladesh and India suggest that excess female mortality is caused by gender differentials in treatment of illness, rather than differences in food intake or health status in the home (Basu, 1989; Fauveau, Koenig and Wojtyniak, 1991). That is an important

conceptual distinction because it suggests that the effects of the malnutrition-morbidity synergism may be modified (i.e., ameliorated or exacerbated) by the timing, frequency and quality of health care sought during illness, all of which may vary according to the sex of the child, mother's education and other factors.

Fourth, biological indicators of nutritional status are intrinsically more meaningful in the present context than measurements of dietary intake because the former capture the combined effects of nutrient intake and disease on the nutritional status of the individual and reflect exposure over longer periods of time. Measurement of dietary intake is difficult over short periods of time and almost impossible over long periods of time. Moreover, although dietary intake is a contributor to nutritional status it is not a direct measure of status because it does not capture the effects of disease on the individual. The converse is that weight-for-age should not be interpreted simply as an indicator of food intake because that would ignore the synergism with infection. Lastly, weight-for-age is most useful as an indicator of current or recent nutritional status among young (aged less than 24 months) rather than older children (aged 24 months or over), because at older ages weight-for-age tends to reflect stunting (low height-for-age) that occurred earlier in the individual's life (Beaton and others, 1990).

B. MALNUTRITION AND CHILD MORTALITY

Bearing in mind the view of malnutrition presented above, the present section summarizes the results of a review of studies from developing countries on the relation between malnutrition and child mortality (Pelletier, 1994a). The overall review identified 28 community-based, prospective studies (all in Africa and Asia) that had measured anthropometric indicators of nutritional status at one point in time, and related that to the subsequent survival status of individual children. The focus in all cases was preschool children, usually defined as those aged 6-59 months, or a more narrow age band within that range. The present section describes the evidence concerning several related issues: (a) the impact of the malnutrition-morbidity synergism at the population level; (b) the

110

Figure 24. Causes of malnutrition and death

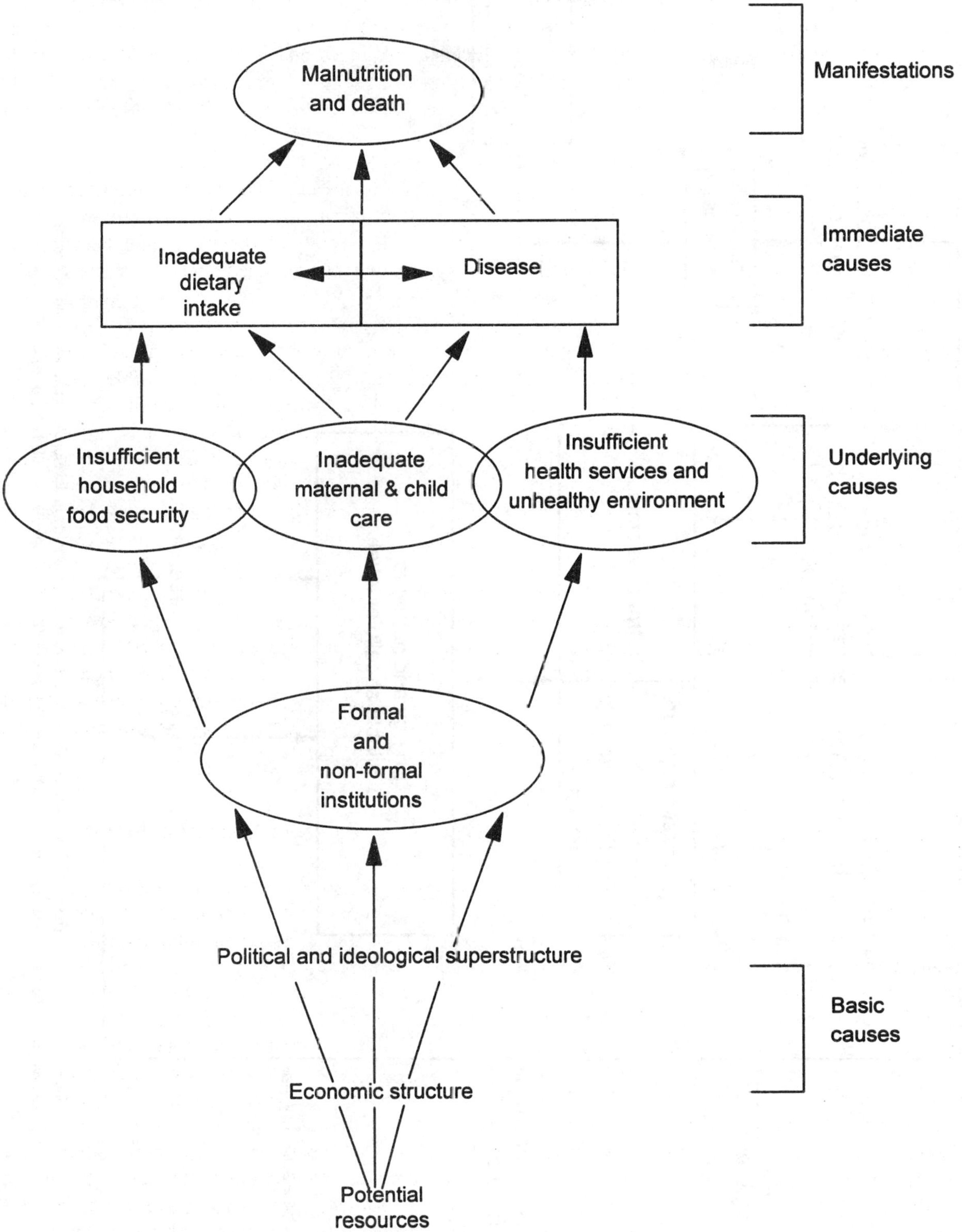

Source: *Strategy for Improved Nutrition of Children and Women in Developing Countries,* A UNICEF Policy Review (United Nations Children's Fund, 1990).

111

Figure 25. Behavioural determinants of child anthropometry and survival

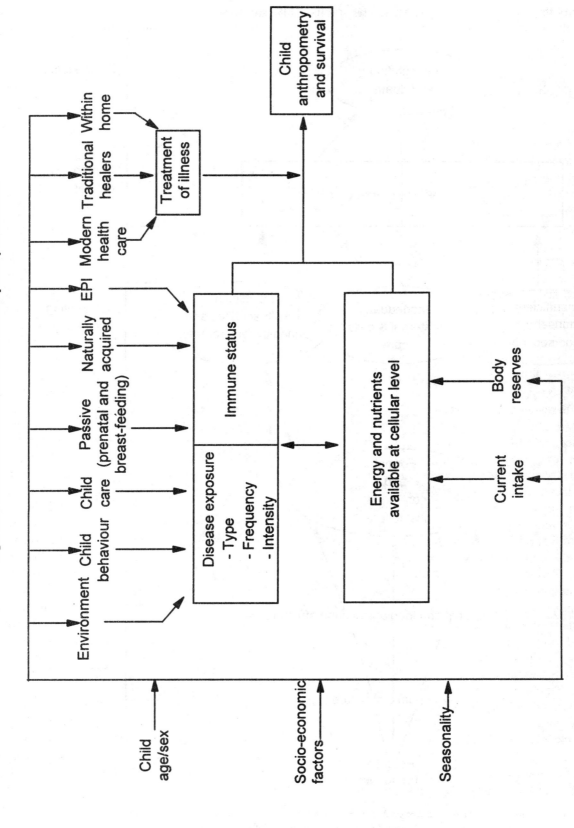

Source: D.L. Pelletier, "The relationship between child anthropometry and mortality in developing countries: implications for policy, programs and future research", *Journal of Nutrition Supplement* (Bethesda, Maryland), vol. 124, No. 10S.

possibility that those results are confounded by non-nutritional factors; (c) the quantitative contribution of malnutrition to child mortality; and (d) the impact of malnutrition on death due to different diseases.

1. Malnutrition-morbidity synergism at the population level

The overwhelming majority of studies show a significant association between anthropometric indicators and subsequent mortality.[2] Of particular relevance for present purposes is a subset of those studies shown in figure 26. The upper panel shows the relation between mortality of children and malnutrition in eight community-based studies that used comparable measures of nutritional status (i.e., weight-for-age as a percentage of median) and subsequent mortality[3] (within 6 and 24 months in various studies).[4] Compared with well-nourished children (i.e., weight-for-age > 80 per cent), it can be seen that mortality is slightly elevated among those with mild malnutrition (weight-for-age = 70-79 per cent), further elevated among those with moderate malnutrition (weight-for-age = 60-69 per cent) and greatly elevated among those with severe malnutrition (weight-for-age <60 per cent). Mortality rises more steeply as weight-for-age decreases, resulting in a characteristic exponential increase for seven of the eight studies.[5] When those data are modelled mathematically, mortality is found to have increased at a compounded rate of 5.9 per cent for each 1 percentage point decline in weight-for-age (Pelletier and others, 1994b). The compounding nature of that relation is what gives rise to the steepness of the slope at extremely low values of weight-for-age. Formal tests of the heterogeneity in slopes across studies, weighted for sample sizes underlying each data point, suggest that there are no statistically significant differences in the slope of mortality on weight-for-age between the different studies. That similarity is shown more clearly in the lower panel, which expresses mortality in logarithm units. Thus, it appears that the response of mortality to malnutrition is similar in all eight studies despite the differences in ecology, disease vectors, cultures, child-age ranges and absolute levels of mortality.

Those results are important for several reasons. First, they reveal remarkable consistency in the re-lation between malnutrition and mortality across populations. The accumulated evidence does not support the suggestion that the relation varies across populations (Bairagi, 1981; Ewbank and Gribble, 1993). Second, they show that mortality is elevated even among the mild-to-moderately malnourished (defined as those between 60 and 80 per cent of median weight-for-age), and that that link is also consistent across all or most populations.

Figure 26 also provides important confirmation that the long-recognized synergism between malnutrition and morbidity have potentiating (or multiplicative) effects at the population level. The mathematical confirmation of that synergism is provided elsewhere (Pelletier and others, 1993), but the phenomenon can be understood intuitively by comparing the results from Punjab, India and the United Republic of Tanzania shown in the upper panel of figure 26. With a baseline mortality rate of 2.8 deaths per 1,000 children per annum ("baseline" refers to the so-called well-nourished, with weight-for-age > 80 per cent), the Punjab study shows that an additional 34 deaths per 1,000 children per annum occurred among the severely malnourished; by contrast, in the United Republic of Tanzania, which has a baseline mortality rate of 23 per 1,000, there were an additional 189 deaths per 1,000 per annum among the severely malnourished. Thus, the absolute increase in deaths is about six times higher in the United Republic of Tanzania than in the Punjab (189 versus 34). That difference is exactly as predicted from the theory of synergism because populations with high exposure to disease are expected to have: (a) higher baseline mortality among the well-nourished; and (b) a stronger response to malnutrition. The parallelism in the lines shown in the lower panel shows that there is a consistent tendency for populations with high baseline mortality to experience a stronger response to malnutrition (in absolute numbers of deaths). Thus, it appears that the addition of malnutrition to a population with high disease exposure results in a multiplicative increase in mortality, rather than a simple additive increase.[6] Under an additive model, the United Republic of Tanzania would have experienced an increase of only about 34 deaths per 1,000 children per annum among the severely malnourished, identical to that seen in the Punjab.

Figure 26. Relationship between mortality among children and weight-for-age as a percentage of international median

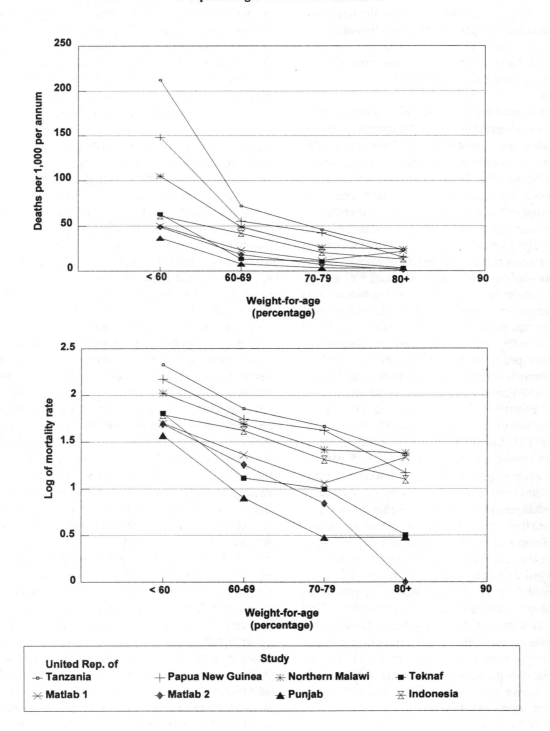

Source: D.L. Pelletier, "The relationship between child anthropometry and mortality in developing countries: implications for policy, programs and future research", *Journal of Nutrition Supplement* (Bethesda, Maryland), vol. 124, No. 10S.

2. The confounding hypothesis

Although the accumulated results of malnutrition-mortality relation are striking for their consistency, it can be hypothesized that that association is simply or largely due to statistical confounding. According to that hypothesis, malnutrition and mortality may co-occur in the same households simply because both are associated with poverty or low socio-economic status. It may be, for instance, that the malnutrition in those households is caused by poor nutrient intake and high disease exposure, whereas mortality may be caused by low immunization rates or inappropriate treatment of illness (figure 25). Another possibility is that low weight-for-age is a by-product of high disease exposure and is associated with mortality for that reason but actually plays no causal role in mortality. Several studies have examined the possibility of confounding, as described below, and all of them show that a significant association between malnutrition and mortality persists even after controlling for confounding through various statistical techniques.

The possibility of confounding by socio-economic status has been investigated in Bangladesh by Chen and others (1980), Cogill (1982) and Chowdhury (1988); in Tanzania by Yambi (1988); in Uganda by Vella and others (1994); and in Malawi by Pelletier and others (1994c). Chen, Chowdhury and Huffman (1980) and Chowdhury (1988) compared the relative risk[7] of mortality among the malnourished across different socio-economic strata defined by floor space, maternal height, maternal age and maternal education. A significant elevation in the relative risk was observed in all socio-economic strata, and surprisingly the relative risk is highest in the higher socio-economic groups. Using the same data set, Cogill (1982) applied multivariate discriminant analysis controlling for maternal age, parity, religion, education, number of cows, floor area and mother's height and weight. His results showed that each of the anthropometric indicators remains statistically significant even after controlling for those variables, and those indicators are 2.3 times (in the case of height-for-age) to 23 times (in the case of upper arm circumference) stronger predictors of mortality than any of the socio-economic indicators. Pelletier and others (1994c) and Yambi (1988) applied multivariate logistic regression to the studies from Malawi and the United Republic of Tanzania, respec-

tively, and showed that the effects of the anthropometric variables persist after controlling for socio-economic variables. Lastly, Pelletier and others (1994c) and Vella and others (1994) represent the only studies that tested for confounding among the mild-to-moderately malnourished separately from the severely malnourished. The study in Uganda (Vella and others, 1994) showed variation in relative risk estimates across socio-economic strata, relative to all strata combined, but found elevated relative risks for all four anthropometric indicators tested even among the mild-to-moderately malnourished. The Malawi study (Pelletier and others, 1994c) showed that one-year mortality remains significantly elevated among the mild-to-moderately malnourished when using weight-for-age among young children (<24 months), but not among older children or when using other indicators. Thus, the accumulated evidence suggests that the anthropometry-mortality relation cannot be attributed to socio-economic confounding.

As distinct from socio-economic confounding, four studies have examined the possibility that the weight-for-age-mortality association may simply reflect the weight-depressing effects of morbidity immediately preceding death. Kielmann and McCord (1978) tested this possibility in India by conducting an analysis in which the weight-for-age taken two months prior to death was used instead of the weight-for-age from the month immediately preceding death. They found that the weight-for-age-mortality association was equally strong in the two analyses. Briend and Bari (1989) used multivariate logistic regression to control for the presence of diarrhoea, respiratory infections, measles and oedema. The mortality odds ratio[8] was reduced from 14.7 (unadjusted) to 9.7 (adjusted), but the latter remained a strong and significant association. Briend and Bari (1989) and Yambi (1988) also tested that illness-induced, weight-loss hypothesis by testing for the effects of weight-for-age while controlling for the change in weight during the 1-2 months prior to death. Both studies found that weight-for-age is stronger than the change in weight-for-age as a predictor of death, and controlling for change in weight-for-age did not appreciably alter the relation. Thus, the literature does not support the hypothesis that the weight-for-age-mortality relation is simply a reflection of confounding by socio-economic factors or by the weight-depressing effects of immediately preceding illness.

115

3. *The quantitative contribution of malnutrition to mortality*

The results shown in figure 26 indicate that the absolute level of child mortality can be accurately modelled simply as a function of the baseline mortality (among those with weight-for-age > 80 per cent) and the percentage of children falling in each of the three grades of malnutrition below 80 per cent of the reference median. That observation has limited practical utility when stated in those terms, however, because most countries do not know the mortality level among those with weight-for-age > 80 per cent of median. Accordingly, it is not possible to estimate the contribution of malnutrition to child mortality in most populations. An alternative formulation can be derived from the fact that the relative risk of mortality at various grades of weight-for-age can be calculated from the data in figure 26. The relative risks are 8.4 for severe (weight-for-age < 60 per cent of reference median), 4.6 for moderate (weight-for-age 60-69 per cent of reference median) and 2.4 for mild (weight-for-age 70-79 per cent of reference median) malnutrition. The contribution of malnutrition to child mortality (through its potentiating effects on infectious disease) can then be calculated using the standard epidemiologic statistic of population attributable risk (PAR),[9] which simply combines the relative risk estimates with estimates of the prevalence of low weight-for-age in a given population. The methodology has been fully described and tested elsewhere (Pelletier and others, 1994b). The present subsection simply presents the results emerging from that approach, when applied to 53 countries for which suitable anthropometric data have been published (UNICEF, 1993).

Figure 27 (Pelletier and others, 1995) shows the percentage of child deaths among children aged 0-59 months due to the potentiating effects of malnutrition on disease in each of the 53 countries. The total population attributable risk is divided into the portion due to severe malnutrition (weight-for-age < 60 per cent) and that due to mild-to-moderate malnutrition (weight-for-age 60-79 per cent). Using the average for all 53 countries, the results indicate that 56 per cent of all child deaths are caused by the potentiating effects of malnutrition on disease, of which 83 per cent is due to mild-to-moderate malnutrition. The values for any given country vary in proportion to its prevalence of low weight-for-age. Among the countries shown here, the range for total population attributable risk is from about 15 per cent in Paraguay to about 85 per cent in India, indicating that from 15 to 85 per cent of deaths in those countries are caused by the potentiating effects of malnutrition on disease. The percentage of total population attributable risk that is due to mild-to-moderate malnutrition varies from 100 per cent among several countries in which severe malnutrition is absent to 68 per cent in India, where severe malnutrition is highly prevalent.

Those estimates are remarkably close to those arising from the Inter-American Investigation of Childhood Mortality over two decades ago (Puffer and Serrano, 1973). That study was based on community samples in Latin America and in selected countries in Northern America, and used clinical methods and verbal autopsies to ascertain cause of death. As in the present study, it reported that 54 per cent of child deaths (2-4 years) in Latin America had malnutrition as an underlying or associated cause, of which about 15 per cent was severe malnutrition. Among infants (0-11 months), about one fourth to one third of all deaths had malnutrition as an underlying or associated cause. The estimates for infants are lower than for children because a large proportion of neonatal deaths are due to congenital and obstetric complications. However, the Inter-American Investigation stressed the important role of maternal nutritional status as a cause of low birth weight and prematurity (which, in turn, are strong predictors of infant mortality), and the importance of inappropriate infant feeding practices as a contributor to post-neonatal deaths. Thus, the Inter-American Investigation, using a different methodology than the prospective studies shown in figure 26, confirms the quantitative estimates of malnutrition role during childhood (1-4 years), extends the analysis into the early infancy period not adequately covered in the studies shown in figure 26, and demonstrates that the results for Latin America are similar to those for Africa and Asia reflected in figure 26.

It is notable that the population attributable risk estimates shown in figure 27 and those of the Inter-American estimates are both far higher than those commonly found in health statistics from developing countries, which do not take account of the potentiating effects of malnutrition on infectious disease. By

Figure 27. Deaths of children under age 5 caused by the potentiating effects of severe and mild-to-moderate (MM) malnutrition on infectious diseases

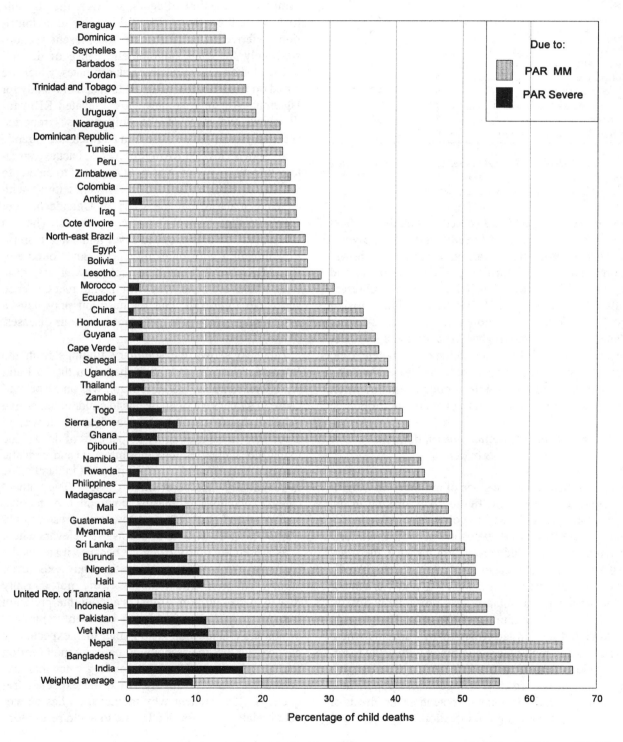

Percentage of child deaths

Source : D. L. Pelletier and others, *Bulletin of the World Health Organization* (Geneva), vol. 73, No. 4 (1995), pp. 443-448.

TABLE 33. GLOBAL BURDEN OF DISEASES IN
CHILDREN UNDER FIVE YEARS

Cause of death	Rank	Percentage of disability adjusted life-years lost
Respiratory	1	18.5
Perinatal	2	17.2
Diarrhoea	3	16.2
Childhood cluster[a]	4	10.7
Congenital	5	6.5
Malaria	6	4.7
Protein-energy malnutrition	7	2.4
Vitamin A	8	2.3
Iodine deficiency disorders	9	1.3

Source: World Bank, *World Development Report*, 1993 (New York, Oxford University Press, 1993).

[a]Including pertussis, polio, measles, tetanus.

way of example, table 33 (based on health statistics) shows the percentage of disability adjusted life-years (DALYs)[10] lost due to various causes. As shown, protein-energy malnutrition (PEM), vitamin A and iodine deficiency disorders (IDD) together represent only 6 per cent of DALYs lost. The estimate arising from the 53 countries shown in figure 27 is 56 per cent, roughly 10 times higher. That discrepancy arises because the latter estimate includes the potentiating impact of malnutrition on infectious diseases, and also includes the effects of mild-to-moderate malnutrition as well as clinically obvious, severe malnutrition.

4. *Effects of malnutrition on different causes of death*

The consistency in the slope of mortality on weight-for-age shown earlier in figure 26 is striking in the light of the differences in ecological circumstances and associated disease exposure, as well as cultural differences across study areas. For instance, the study in Papua New Guinea took place in the highlands, where acute respiratory infection was noted as a major cause of death and malaria was presumably absent; yet, it has a slope similar to those for Bangladesh, Malawi and the United Republic of Tanzania where diarrhoea and malaria are combined with acute respiratory infection as major diseases. The relative uniformity observed in the slope across populations suggests that malnutrition may potentiate the effects of many or all of the common infectious diseases.

Somewhat more direct confirmation of the present suggestion is provided by three of the prospective studies and the Inter-American Investigation. The three prospective studies collected verbal reports of symptoms at the time of death, and were thereby able to estimate the relative risk of death due to malnutrition (referred to as "RRm" in the present section) separately for each symptomatic cause of death.[11] Table 34 shows these relative risk estimates, which are based on two studies for Bangladesh and one study for Uganda. All three studies show elevated RRm for diarrhoea and measles, the only diseases reported separately in all three studies. In addition, the Uganda study shows elevated RRm for fever and acute respiratory infection. Fever is usually assumed to be due to malaria in clinical practice in African settings with endemic malaria, but the study in Uganda did not collect detailed clinical data to confirm this. The two Bangladesh studies grouped fever and acute respiratory infection with other infections, and found elevated RRm for that combined category. Thus, those three studies are consistent with the indirect evidence shown in figure 26, that malnutrition may have a potentiating effect on many or all infectious diseases.

Table 35 shows the summary findings from the Inter-American Investigation, based on the 13 Latin American samples.[12] Malnutrition was an associated cause in 47 per cent of all deaths to children under five years of age (excluding neonatal deaths). It was an associated cause in roughly 60 per cent of deaths due to diarrhoea, measles and other infective and parasitic diseases, compared to about 32 per cent in deaths due to respiratory disease or other causes. The "other" category includes neoplasms, congenital, metabolic, accidental and other lesser causes, and represents only a small proportion of total deaths. Its relevance here is as a pseudo-control category because it shows the frequency with which malnutrition may exist even among children whose deaths were not causally related to malnutrition. If that is a valid interpretation it suggests that the association between respiratory deaths and malnutrition is no higher than expected by chance, but that the association between malnutrition and all other infectious diseases is greater than expected by chance (roughly twice the expected frequency). It is unclear why malnutrition has an elevated relative risk for deaths due to acute respiratory

TABLE 34. RELATIVE RISK OF DEATH DUE TO MALNUTRITION,[a] BY CAUSE OF DEATH

Cause of death	Bangladesh (Matlab) Study 12-23 months Weight-for-age	Bangladesh (Matlab) Study[b] 6-36 months Wasting	SW Uganda 6-59 months Weight-for-age	SW Uganda 6-59 months Weight-for-height	SW Uganda 6-59 months Mid-upper-arm circumference	SW Uganda 6-59 months Height-for-age
Diarrhoea	3.7	16.8	7.1	3.8	7.5	1.4
Measles	2.3	4.2	4.6	8.6	4.9	1.2
Fever	-	-	7.3	3.4	8.2	4.7
ARI	-	-	1.9	1.9	9.4	2.3
Other infections	7.0	2.1	-	-	-	-
Accidents	1.2	-	-	-	-	-
Other	4.1	1.2	1.5	0.9	0.7	1.7
All causes	3.2	8.0	3.7	4.0	5.5	2.0

Source: D. L. Pelletier, "The relationship between child anthropometry and mortality in developing countries: implications for policy, programs and future research", Journal of Nutrition Supplement (Bethesda, Maryland), vol. 124, No. 10S.

[a]Malnutrition defined as follows:

Matlab (1a): weight-for-age < 65 per cent;

Matlab (20): Visible wasting (approximately arm circumference < 110 mm);

SW Uganda (17): weight-for-age < -2.5Z-scores;

Weight-for-height < -1.5Z-scores;

Mid-upper arm circumference < 12.5 mm;

Height-for-age < -3Z-scores.

[b]Defines malnutrition based on the presence/absence of visible wasting just prior to death and/or recent weight loss; differs from others, therefore, which used prospectively measured anthropometry to define malnutrition.

TABLE 35. MALNUTRITION AS AN ASSOCIATED CAUSE OF DEATH AMONG CHILDREN UNDER 5 YEARS OF AGE (EXCLUDING NEONATAL DEATHS), BY PROXIMATE CAUSE OF DEATH IN 13 LATIN AMERICAN PROJECTS COMBINED

Proximate cause	Total deaths	Malnutrition as an associated cause Number of deaths	Malnutrition as an associated cause Percentage
All causes	21 951	10 349	47.1
Infective and parasitic diseases	12 598	7 667	60.9
Diarrhoeal disease .	8 770	5 331	60.8
Measles	2 103	1 311	62.3
Other	1 725	1 025	59.4
Nutritional deficiency	1 163	-	-
Diseases of respiratory system	4 469	1 435	32.1
Other causes	3 721	1 247	33.5

Source: R. C. Puffer and C. V. Serrano, Patterns of Mortality in Childhood (Washington, D.C.: Pan American Health Organization, 1973).

infection in the Uganda study (table 34) but no elevation in the Latin American countries. One hypothesis is that the Latin American population may have had greater access to and utilization of curative care for acute respiratory infection than the Ugandan population covered in that study.

Lastly, a recent study in Zaire has challenged the notion that mild-to-moderate (subclinical) malnutrition is associated with elevated child mortality when weight-for-age is used to indicate malnutrition. The authors suggest that a major reason may be the uniformity with which malaria kills children regardless of nutritional status (Van Den Broeck, 1993). Van den Broeck and Eeckels (1994) have further suggested that weight-for-age may fail to identify some cases of protein-energy malnutrition, even some severe cases, which may flatten the slope of mortality on weight-for-age over the mild-to-moderate range of that indicator.

It is difficult to interpret the study in Zaire for two reasons. First, the authors note that it took place in an area that has been the target of an integrated health and development programme for the past 20 years. Accordingly, immunization levels are higher and the incidence of diarrhoea is lower than in most parts of Africa, and access to curative care is presumably greater. The authors suggest that these factors may help explain the absence of an overall effect of mild-to-moderate malnutrition on mortality in their study. If so, it may have limited generalizability to areas that do not share these characteristics.

Second, in contrast to the eight prospective studies included in figure 26, Van den Broeck and others (1993) excluded from the mild-to-moderate malnutrition sample any children showing clinical signs of malnutrition. Those signs included any muscle wasting (by inspection or palpation), with or without loss of subcutaneous fat, visible skeletal structures or hanging skin. Pitting oedema (a classic clinical sign of kwashiorkor) was also used to identify clinically malnourished children. The difficulty in interpretation arises from the fact that children with any of those signs were all considered severely malnourished but did not come exclusively from the category with weight-for-age < 60 per cent. Results published separately (Van Den Broeck, 1994) show that roughly 20 per cent of all children below 80 per cent of median weight-for-age showed those signs and were excluded from the analysis; that exclusion makes it impossible to compare that study with the other prospective studies included in figure 26.

In summary, the empirically observed consistency in the slope of mortality on weight-for-age suggests that malnutrition may potentiate the effects of many infectious diseases on mortality. That conclusion is supported by the results of three prospective studies that have analysed their data by cause of death. Results from the Inter-American Investigation (Puffer and Serrano, 1973) provide additional support for that thesis, but suggest that malnutrition may not potentiate the effects of acute respiratory infection. Results of a study in Zaire call into question whether malnutrition potentiates the effects of malaria. That question deserves further study, especially through case-control analysis of clinical data.

C. GENDER, MALNUTRITION AND CHILD MORTALITY

The previous subsections have addressed the fundamental character of malnutrition and its relation to child mortality. As shown, the nature of that relation is not widely appreciated. The present section builds upon the foregoing analysis, and focuses specifically on the question of whether sex differentials in nutritional status may play a role in sex differentials in mortality. That is a complex issue that requires consideration of the other chapters in the present volume in order to address it fully. Discussion is restricted to a conceptual analysis of the interrelations involved, analysis of prospective studies to glean some insights from that body of literature and analysis of a cross-national sample constructed for the present chapter.

1. *Conceptual model*

Figure 28 provides a conceptual framework for guiding the analysis of the interrelations between gender, nutritional status and mortality of children. For reasons cited in previous sections, it is impossible to conduct such an analysis without including child morbidity, owing to its synergistic relation with mortality. That is shown as a double-headed arrow in the centre to depict the vicious cycle between the two, as well as an oval that depicts the multiplicative or potentiating effects of those two factors on mortality. Child care and feeding are fundamental to morbidity and nutritional status and are shown explicitly, but some other underlying factors are treated as exogenous in the present framework, including household food security and the existence of health hazards in the environment. Use of health care in that context refers primarily to the use of curative care in order to uncouple the otherwise direct effects of the malnutrition-morbidity synergism on mortality. It has several dimensions, including the timing, frequency and quality of care sought and provided. As shown, the sex of the child may be conceptualized as one of the factors that determine the state of morbidity, childcare and feeding, nutritional status and use of health care.

For present purposes, it is important to re-emphasize that such an anthropometric index as children's weight-for-age reflects the combined effects of current and past childcare and feeding and morbidity. It does not reflect the adequacy of food intake alone, as is often mistakenly believed. Thus, in the analyses described below it is assumed that weight-for-age represents the nutritional status of the individual child or a population of children, and that any sex differentials in weight-for-age have been caused by gender-related differentials in child care, feeding or morbidity (the latter including incidence, duration and severity). It is further assumed that gender differentials in use of health care will manifest themselves in a flatter slope of mortality versus weight-for-age for the gender that

Figure 28. Main effects of gender on causes of mortality

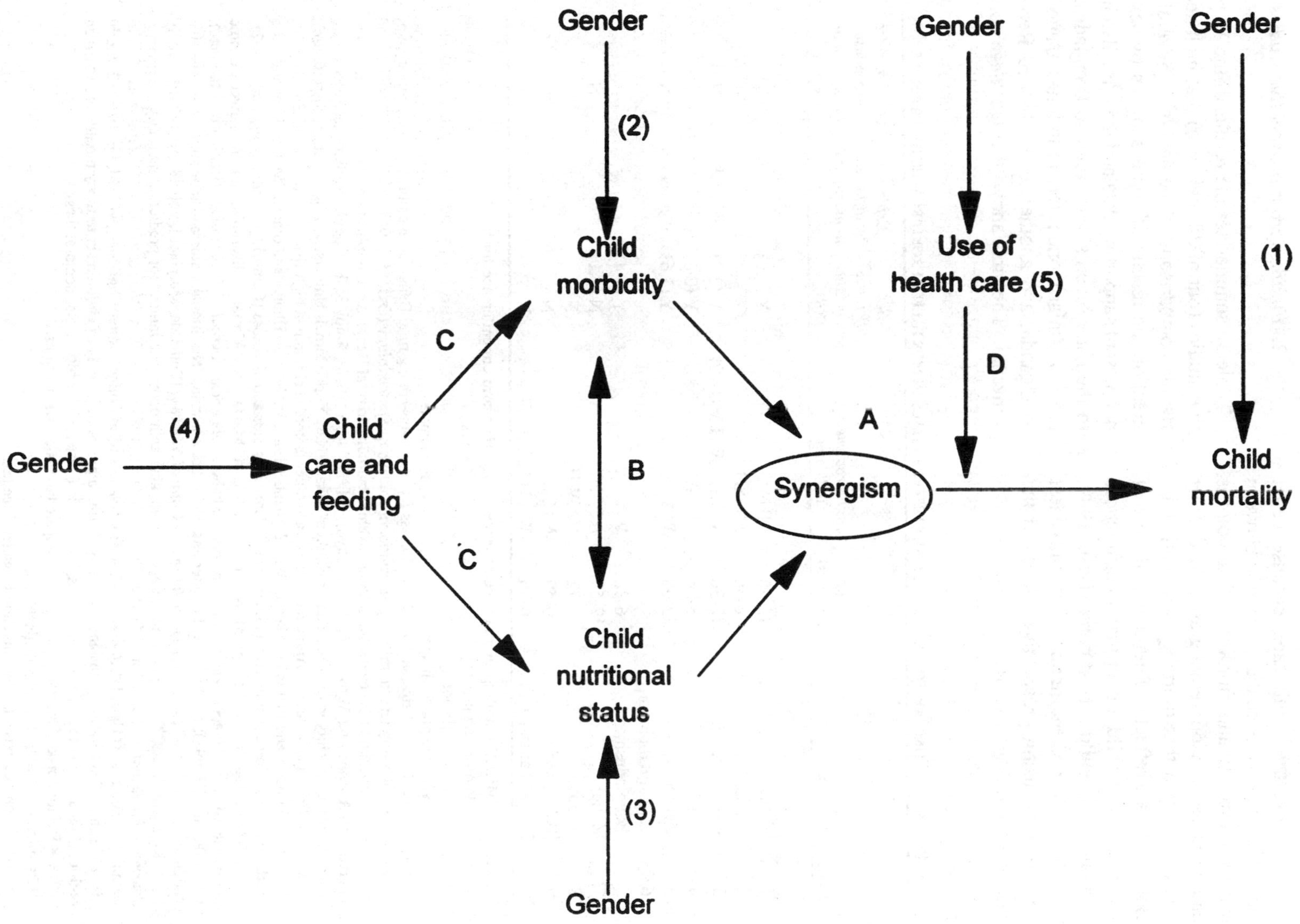

121

receives better quality health care, because better health care will tend to reduce the interaction between malnutrition, morbidity and mortality. That point is important because previous ethnographic and other studies have reported that mortality differentials by sex in Southern Asia reflect differentials in the use of health care by sex of child, rather than to differences in disease rates or in child care at home (Basu, 1989; Fauveau, 1991). The present framework permits a test of that hypothesis, using prospective studies of the anthropometry-mortality relation.

2. *Findings from prospective studies*

Table 36 summarizes the results of the 10 prospective studies (out of 28 reviewed) that included male-female comparisons in the analysis. Several studies mention the results of some analysis by sex but do not present supporting data and they are also included in the list. Seven studies refer to Bangladesh (most refer to Matlab), one refers to Indonesia, another one to Uganda; and another to the United Republic of Tanzania. The table shows the age range considered

TABLE 36. SUMMARY OF RESULTS ON SEX DIFFERENTIALS IN MORTALITY FROM PROSPECTIVE STUDIES

Study	Location	Age group (in months)	Anththropometric indicators	Sex difference in mortality (RR)[a]	Explained by difference in nutritional status	Sex difference in response to nutritional status
1	Matlab	12-15	MUAC	Y (1.8)	Y[b]	Y[c]
2	Matlab	6-36	MUAC	Y	..	Y[b] (F)
3	Matlab	12-36	WA,HA,WH,MUAC	Y (2.0)	N[d]	Y (F)
4	Matlab	3-36	MUAC	Y (2.6)	Y[e]	..
5	Matlab	2-60	WA	Y (1.6)	N	N
6	Sirjganj/Gopalpur, Bangladesh	6-36	WA	Y (1.4)	..	..
7	Matlab	12-59	AC/HT	N (1.1)	..	N
8	W. Java	0-72	HA,WH	N	..	..
9	SW Uganda	0-59	MUAC	N	..	..
10	Iringa, Tanzania	6-36	WA,HA,WH	N	..	..

Key: MUAC = mid-upper arm circumference   AC/HT = arm-circumference-for-height
WA = weight-for-age   Y = yes
HA = height-for-age   N = no
WH = wight-for-height   F = female

Sources: Study 1: V. Fauveau and others, "Excess female deaths among rural Bangladesh children: an examination of cause-specific mortality and morbidity", *International Journal of Epidemiology* (Oxford, 1991); Study 2: V. Fauveau and others, "The contribution of severe malnutrition to child mortality in rural Bangladesh: implications for targeting nutrition interventions", *Food and Nutrition Bulletin* (Tokyo), vol. 12, No. 3 (1990); Study 3: B. Cogill, "Ranking anthropometric indicators using mortality in rural Bangladesh children" (Ithaca, New York, Cornell University, 1982; doctoral dissertation); Study 4: A. Briend and others, "Arm circumference and other factors in children at high risk of death in rural Bangladesh", *The Lancet* (London, and Baltimore, Maryland) 26 September 1987; Study 5: A. Bhuiya and others, "Malnutrition and child mortality: are socio-economic factors important?", *Journal of Biosocial Sciences* (Cambridge, United Kingdom), vol. 21, pp. 357-364; Study 6: R. Bairagi, M. A. Koenig and K. A. Mazumder, "Mortality-discriminating and power of some nutritional, sociodemographic, and diarrheal and disease indices", *American Journal of Epidemiology* (Baltimore, Maryland), vol. 138, No. 5 (1993); Study 7: A. Sommer and M. S. Loewenstein, "Nutritional status and mortality: a prospective validation of the QUAC stick", *American Journal of Clinical Nutrition* (Bethesda, Maryland), vol. 28, pp. 287-292; Study 8: J. Katz and others, "The importance of age in evaluating anthropometric indices for predicting mortality", *American Journal of Epidemiology* (Baltimore, Maryland), vol. 130, No. 6 (1989); Study 9: V. Vela and others, "Determinants of child mortality in South-west Uganda", *Journal of Biosocial Sciences* (Cambridge, United Kingdom), vol. 24, pp. 103-112; Study 10: O. Yambi, "Nutritional status and the risk of death: a prospective study of children six to thirty months old in Iringa region, United Republic of Tanzania" (Ithaca, New York, Cornell University, 1988; doctoral thesis).
[a]RR = Relative risk of mortality for females compared to males, when reported.
[b]By inference, not by formal statistical tests.
[c]A sex difference exists but the direction is unclear (see text).
[d]Based on multivariate discriminant analysis that includes age, parity, religion, parental education and other SES variables.
[e]Based on multiple logistic regression, including MUAC breastfeeding and mortality symptoms.

in each study, along with the anthropometric indicators used.

Six studies on Bangladesh report that sex differences in mortality were detected in the sample studied. The relative risks expressed as the female mortality rate divided by the male mortality rate are shown in table 36 and range from 1.4 to 2.6. One of the studies (study 7) and all three studies on other countries—Western Java, South-western Uganda and Iringa, United Republic of Tanzania—(studies 8-10) reported no significant sex differences in mortality. Out of the six studies reporting sex differences in mortality, two did not indicate whether controls for sex differences in nutritional status accounted for the mortality difference (study 2, Matlab, Bangladesh; and study 6, Sirjganj Yopalpur, Bangladesh).[13] Two studies (studies 1 and 4, both on Matlab, Bangladesh) showed that the introduction of such controls could account for sex differences in mortality; and another two (studies 3 and 5, also on Matlab, Bangladesh) reported that sex differences persisted even after controlling for differences in nutritional status.

It is of interest to compare the last two sets of studies in terms of other characteristics displayed in table 36 in an attempt to determine why they produce divergent results. The two sets show no systematic differences in geographical area covered, the age ranges considered or the strength of the relative risk measured. However, the two studies that are supposed to have accounted for the sex differential in mortality (studies 1 and 4) used mid-upper arm circumference (MUAC), whereas the two studies that did not account for the sex differential in mortality used weight-for-age alone (study 5) or weight-for-age in combination with other anthropometric indices (study 3). That feature may be part of the explanation for the divergence in results because data provided in Cogill (1982) reveal that the sex differences in MUAC are considerably greater (t-statistic = 8.24) than the similar differences in weight-for-age (t = 2.61). In addition, MUAC is the strongest predictor of mortality when the child's age is not taken into account. Those two facts suggest that MUAC is a stronger control variable than weight-for-age. Unfortunately, the fact that MUAC is confounded by child's age (as a predictor of death) makes it difficult to interpret the results. Thus, the only useful conclusion that can be drawn is that the

two studies that control for weight-for-age were not able to account for the sex differential in mortality, suggesting that other systematic differences between the sexes may exist to account for the mortality differential.

Five of those studies (all on Bangladesh) reported results concerning sex differences in the slope of mortality plotted against anthropometric indicators of malnutrition. That reflects a greater interest in statistical interactions rather than statistical main effects, in that a statistically significant interaction indicates that the slope of mortality on nutritional status is greater for children of one sex. As noted earlier, theoretical considerations suggest that a weaker relation between mortality and malnutrition should exist within a group that is receiving better health care. Two studies (5 and 7) show no difference between the sexes but three of them (1-3) indicate that the mortality-malnutrition relation is weaker among males than females, suggesting that males receive better health care. The reasons for this inconsistency are unclear, but the balance of evidence supports the health care hypothesis emanating from previous work (Basu, 1989; Fauveau and others, 1991). It is uncertain whether similar processes are at work elsewhere because those relations have not been examined in other settings (8-10).

3. Findings from cross-national analysis

The analysis of cross-national data is another approach to examining the extent to which sex differentials in mortality can be accounted for by sex differentials in nutritional status. In order to address this question, results of World Fertility Surveys (WFS) and Demographic and Health Surveys (DHS) in 44 countries (summarized by Tabutin and Willems, 1995) were combined with results from nutrition surveys in 53 countries (as compiled by UNICEF, 1993). That compilation resulted in a data set containing 37 countries with data on sex-specific mortality (infants and children aged between 1 and 5 years, separately) and sex-specific prevalence of low weight-for-age (weight-for-age < -2 Z-scores in most cases) among children under five years of age. It was not possible to obtain sex-specific weight-for-age prevalences for infants (less than 1 year) and children (1-4 years) separately. The data set includes 13 countries from sub-Saharan Africa, 5 from Northern Africa or Western Asia, 8 from Asia and 11 from Latin America. Table 37 shows the descriptive statistics for the key variables in the total sample. It should be noted that the mean sex mortality ratio[14] is above 100 for infants (more males dying than females) and below 100 for children (more females than males dying). For infants, this is a fairly consistent result across all countries in all regions. For children, it is consistent in all regions except sub-Saharan Africa, where roughly half the countries included in the sample are above and half below 100 during childhood.

Figure 29 shows plots of infant and child mortality against the prevalence of low weight-for-age in the 37 countries. There is a moderate positive relation in both cases, with an R-square value of 0.214 for infants and 0.504 for children. Preliminary multiple regression analysis revealed that there are strong and significant main effects of region on infant and child mortality (as can be detected in figure 29); accordingly, these were controlled for through multiple regression analysis in order to assess the strength of the mortality-malnutrition relation (estimated by the slope of mortality on the prevalence of low weight-for-age) in those 37 countries. The results of those models for infant and child mortality in table 38 show that malnutrition has a strong association with infant and child mortality across those 37 countries, and the mortality rates for sub-Saharan Africa, Northern Africa, Western Asia and Latin America are all higher than those in Asia. Those models achieve remarkably high adjusted R-square values, with a value of 0.446 for infants and 0.714 for children, substantially higher

than values reported by Haaga and others (1985) in a similar analysis of 24 countries: they reported an R-squared value of 0.236 for children, and even that result was obtained only after omitting the Southern Asian countries because they did not seem to fit the overall pattern.

The purpose of the present analysis in the present context is to derive slope estimates for mortality on malnutrition in order to estimate the extent to which sex differences in mortality may be accounted for by sex differences in nutritional status across countries.[15] The resulting slopes shown in table 38 (1.74 for infants and 2.14 for children) were then used to predict what the mortality rate for females would be in each country if they had the same nutritional status as the males in that country, which involves applying the following formula to the 37 country data set:

INFANTS: $P_{mort(f)} = O_{mort(f)} + 1.74 \times [NS_m - NS_f]$

CHILDREN: $P_{mort(f)} = O_{mort(f)} + 2.14 \times [NS_m - NS_f]$

where:

$P_{mort(f)}$ refers to the predicted mortality of females; $O_{mort(f)}$ refers to the observed mortality of females; NS_m and NS_f refer to the prevalence of low weight-for-age for males and females, respectively, based on the data for all those under age 5.

The use of that approach implicitly assumes that the strength of the relation between malnutrition and mortality within a single country is similar to that seen

TABLE 37. INFANT AND CHILD MORTALITY AND LOW WEIGHT-FOR-AGE IN COUNTRIES USED IN CROSS-NATIONAL ANALYSIS

Variable	Males				Females				Sex ratio[a]			
	Mean	SD	Min	Max	Mean	SD	Min	Max	Mean	SD	Min	Max
Infant mortality[b]	84.4	35.1	29.0	161.0	72.6	31.3	25.0	126.0	118	16	85	160
Child mortality[c]	51.1	41.4	3.4	166.0	53.9	43.3	3.4	174.0	95	13	59	128
Low weight-for-age[d]	23.5	14.8	3.3	64.8	23.8	15.8	4.1	67.8	102	15	70	159

Source: Child Malnutrition: Progress Toward the Word Summit for Children Goal (United Nations Children's Fund, 1993); and Dominique Tabutin and Michel Willems, "Excess female child mortality in the developing world during the 1970s and 1980s", *Population Bulletin of the United Nations*, No. 39 (United Nations publication, Sales No. E.95.XIII.17), pp. 45-78.

[a]100 x males/females.
[b]Deaths per 1,000 per annum to 0-11-month olds.
[c]Deaths per 1,000 per annum to 12-59 month olds.
[d]Prevalence of weight-for-age < 80 per cent, children aged 0-59 months.

Figure 29. Relation between infant and child mortality and malnutrition prevalence in 37 developing countries

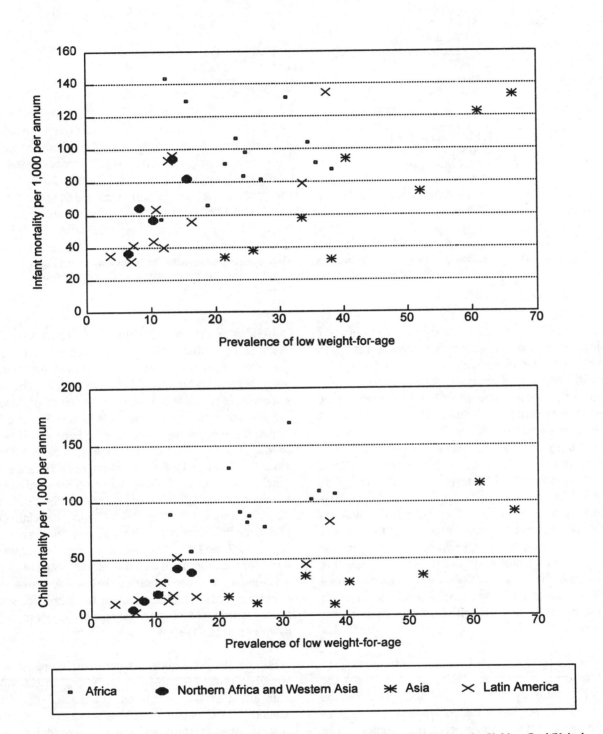

Sources: Based on data taken from *Child malnutrition: progress toward the World Summit for Children Goal* (United Nations Children's Fund, 1993); and Dominique Tabutin and Michel Willems, "Excess mortality among girl children in the world from the 1970s to the 1980s", *Population Bulletin of the United Nations*, No. 39 (United Nations publication, Sales No. E.95.XIII.17), pp. 45-78.

TABLE 38. MULTIPLE REGRESSION RESULTS FOR INFANT AND CHILD MORTALITY IN 37 COUNTRIES

Age group	Predictor variables	Coefficients	S.E.	T-value	Probability
Infants (less than 1 year)	Malnutrition	1.74	.39	4.47	.0001
	Africa	55.59	13.0	4.27	.0002
	Northern Africa and				
	Western Asia	48.56	18.62	2.61	.0137
	Latin America	39.44	15.62	2.52	.0167
	Constant	-0.61	18.7	-.033	.9742
	R² = 44.6 per cent				
Children (1-4)	Malnutrition	2.14	.36	5.96	.0000
	Africa	84.85	12.00	7.08	.0000
	Northern Africa and				
	Western Asia	48.15	17.14	2.81	.0084
	Latin America	43.36	14.38	3.02	.0050
	Constant	-47.43	17.17	-2.76	.0094
	R² = 71.4 per cent				

NOTE: A formal test for heterogeneity in malnutrition slopes accross regions is not statistically significant in either age group. ; omitted group for the regional dummy variables is Asia; "malnutrition" refers to the prevalence of low weight-for-age (< -2 Z-scores).

across countries, and that the slope is the same for males and females. The latter assumption was tested using this cross-national data set and found to hold at the national level of analysis. The assumption concerning the precise strength of the relation can be relaxed somewhat, if the objective of the present analysis is simply to observe the direction in which sex mortality ratios would change if males and females had the same nutritional status in each country. Then the only assumption is that the slope of mortality on malnutrition is positive in sign. In addition, it is necessary to bear in mind that the nutritional status variable being used here is based on all those under age 5 combined; that is an appropriate indicator for predicting child mortality, but its use for predicting infant mortality requires the assumption of a strong positive correlation between male-to-female ratios for infant malnutrition and child malnutrition across countries.

Figures 30 and 31 show the results of the analysis in graphic form. In each case (infants and children), the mortality ratio by sex is calculated based on the observed values (100 x males/females) and the predicted values (100 x males/predicted females). The observed and adjusted ratios are plotted in figures 30 and 31, arranged in ascending order within regions. In sub-Saharan Africa and Northern Africa/Western Asia, there is little difference between observed and predicted ratios, reflecting the similarity in nutritional status between boys and girls in that region. The one exception is Rwanda, where the prevalence of underweight among those under age 5 is almost 50 per cent higher for females, thereby causing a large adjustment in the ratio. In Asia, the adjustment causes little change in India and Pakistan (where sex differences in nutritional status of those under age 5 are minimal at the national level) but causes substantial increases in the ratio in some other countries. Thus, the relatively high male infant mortality in those countries (according to WFS and DHS data) would be even higher were it not for the more favoured nutritional status of male aged under 5 in those countries. In Latin America, the country-specific results are even more mixed, with some countries showing an increase in the sex mortality ratio and others showing a decrease.

The results for children shown in figure 31 are broadly similar for sub-Saharan Africa, in showing little effect of the adjustment procedure except in Rwanda. In Northern Africa/Western Asia, the unfavourable mortality of females would be even worse in Algeria and Jordan were it not for the slightly favoured nutritional status of girls in those countries.

126

Figure 30. Sex mortality ratios before and after equalization
of nutritional status (infants)

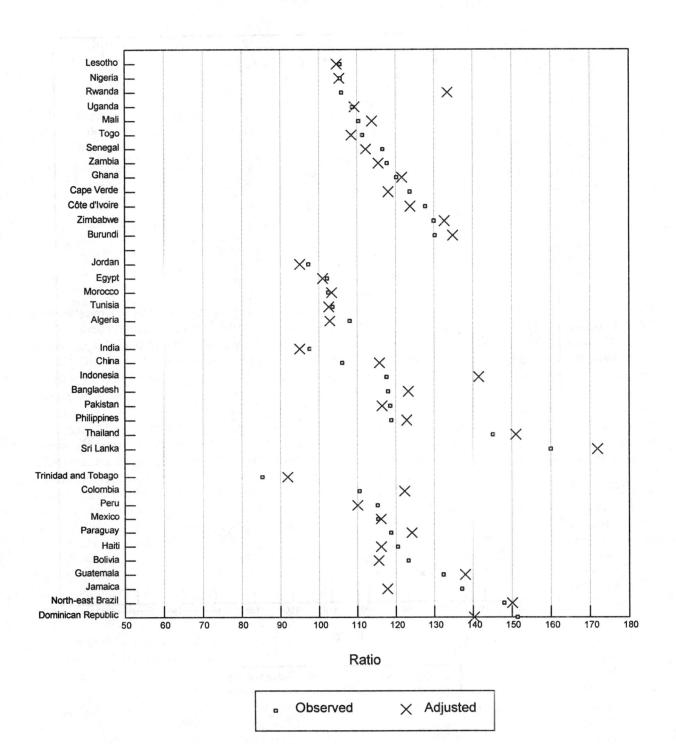

Ratio

Figure 31. Sex mortality ratios before and after equalization of nutritional status (children)

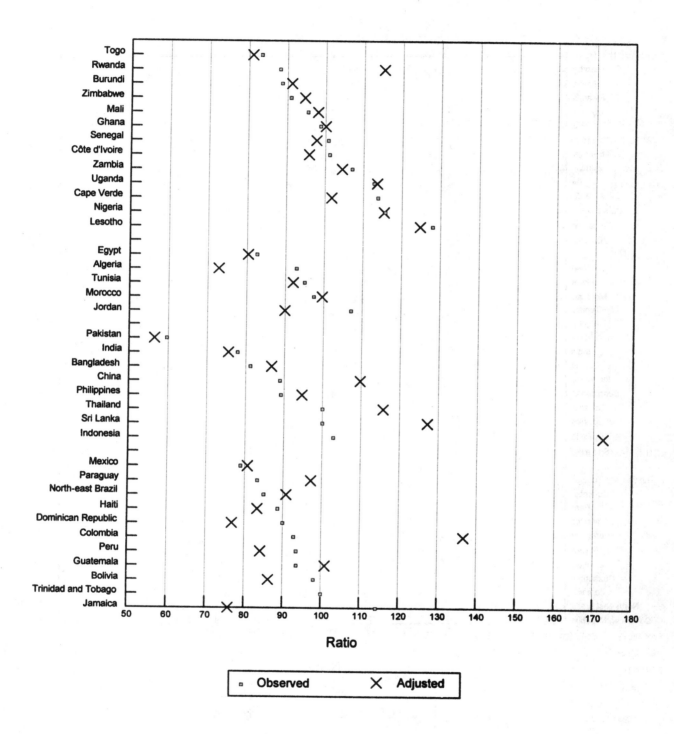

In most of the Asian countries (except Pakistan and India), the adjustment procedure results in an increase in the sex mortality ratio. Those increases are particularly large in Indonesia and Sri Lanka. In China, the current 10 per cent excess in female child deaths would be converted into a 10 per cent excess in male deaths if the two sexes had equal nutritional status. In Indonesia and Sri Lanka, the current parity in child mortality would be converted into an excess of male deaths if female nutritional status were raised to the current levels seen among males. The results for Latin America are again mixed; the current excess of female deaths in many countries would be made worse in about half those countries and better in the other half, but only in Peru would the changes be sufficient to cause an excess of male deaths. In other words, in most of the Latin American countries there are other factors at work (other than nutritional status) in explaining the excess female mortality among children.

D. DISCUSSION

1. *Malnutrition, morbidity and mortality*

The results on the fundamental relation between malnutrition and mortality have a number of implications for health policy and for interpreting mortality statistics and studies in developing countries. From a policy perspective, the population attributable risk estimates suggest that programmes directed at screening and treating only the severely malnourished would have the potential to prevent only about 17 per cent of malnutrition-related deaths (using the average figure for the 53 countries shown in figure 27). The remaining 83 per cent of malnutrition-related deaths are related to mild-to-moderate malnutrition. The analysis also shows that 56 per cent of all child deaths are caused by the potentiating effects of malnutrition on disease, which implies that only 10 per cent of all child deaths can be prevented by focusing only on the severely malnourished. Larger impacts could be achieved by pursuing policies and programmes that attempt to shift the entire distribution of nutritional status, thereby improving mild-to-moderate malnutrition, which accounts for most of the nutrition-related deaths. In addition, because of the multiplicative

effects arising from the synergism between malnutrition and morbidity, the largest impacts could be expected in populations with the highest exposure to disease and/or highest prevalence of malnutrition. It is important to stress that the nutritional improvement of populations is expected to reduce mortality from several diseases simultaneously, even if exposure to those diseases remains unchanged. That broad effect should be distinguished from a disease-focused approach that employs separate interventions to prevent or treat each disease. Clearly, it is desirable to improve nutritional status and to reduce disease exposure, but the multiple-disease impact of nutritional improvement should be taken into account when attempting to design the most cost-effective interventions in the face of resource constraints.

In addition to the above implications for policy, the results summarized here suggest that changes are warranted in the way planners and researchers compile and interpret statistics, and in the way they pose research questions. A common mistake is to equate nutrition with food (and malnutrition with lack of food), and to think of this as being a determinant of mortality that is somehow independent of and additive to health status. Another common mistake is to assume that severe malnutrition is the primary or only form of malnutrition that has consequences for mortality. One practical implication is that the tendency to divide total child mortality into the percentage due to various infectious diseases (the "pie chart approach") should no longer be considered a valid representation of reality. Such an approach cannot possibly incorporate the synergistic or potentiating role of malnutrition because malnutrition cannot be shown as an independent slice of the pie chart nor can it be left off the pie chart completely. The effect of malnutrition is to make the entire pie larger (i.e., multiply the number of deaths occurring to existing infectious diseases), although additional work is required to determine whether the slices making up individual infectious disease retain their relative proportions. Those practical aspects related to statistics and their presentation have important implications for policy because they have a strong influence on the allocation of resources to nutritional improvement versus disease-focused approaches.

2. *Malnutrition and sex differentials in mortality*

A number of studies have examined the possible reasons for sex differentials in infant and child mortality; they have been reviewed above. Many of them are based on ethnographic study of infant and child-care practices or small surveys of feeding, health-care practices and illness patterns. Those studies provide insights into some of the possible microbehavioural determinants of mortality differentials by sex but typically cannot link them directly to mortality. Another common approach involves the statistical analysis of household and national characteristics that predict mortality or mortality differentials. Studies of that type have the advantage of using mortality as the outcome variable rather than intermediate outcomes, such as feeding, health status and use of health care. However, most have not modelled the influence of nutritional status directly. The analyses described in the present chapter fall somewhere between those other two approaches; they include mortality as the outcome variable and nutritional status as a determinant, and they involve prospective studies at the individual level and cross-sectional analyses at the cross-national level. Thus, they add to the knowledge obtained from the other two broad approaches.

The cross-national analysis of sex differentials in nutritional status and mortality reveal the need for region-specific interpretation, and the discussion here is limited to children rather than infants (because information on nutritional status of infants was not available). In sub-Saharan Africa, countries vary from having a 20 per cent excess of female deaths to a 20 per cent excess of male deaths. That variation does not appear to be associated with sex differences in nutritional status because adjustment for nutritional status has little effect on the male-female mortality ratios. In Northern African and Western Asian countries, it appears that in two countries (Algeria and Jordan) the mortality bias against females would be much greater were it not for the fact that females have higher nutritional status than males. That result is consistent with a hypothesis of poorer health care for females but falls far short of proof. In India and Pakistan, it appears that the mortality bias against females has little to do with sex differences in nutritional status, at least at the national level of analysis

used here. In all the other Asian countries studied here, it appears that female mortality would be improved to a variable extent across countries if girls were to achieve the same nutritional status as boys. The results for Latin America do not appear to support any generalizations for that region.

Prospective studies of individual children do not have the same broad regional coverage as the cross-national studies but they are nonetheless revealing. They confirm that mortality is biased against females in Bangladesh but they do not reveal such bias in Indonesia, Uganda and the United Republic of Tanzania. The studies on Bangladesh provide mixed results concerning the question of whether the higher mortality among females can be accounted for by sex differences in nutritional status. Two studies indicate that that is so, but the other two indicate that a residual mortality differential persists even after controlling for the differences in nutritional status of males and females. The studies suggesting that nutritional status can explain the mortality differential by sex may be confounded by the use of simple arm circumference as an indicator of nutritional status, but the question requires further study.

The prospective studies have also been reviewed to confirm whether the higher mortality of females in Bangladesh may reflect differences in health care quite apart from any differences in nutritional status. Three of the five studies find a weaker association between nutritional status and mortality among males than among females, a pattern that strongly suggest that males receive higher quality health care. Those results confirm the findings of other studies that employed different methodologies.

The present results concerning sex differentials have additional importance because they further clarify the nature of the relation between malnutrition, morbidity and mortality. Specifically, they confirm that the mortality consequences of the powerful synergism between malnutrition and morbidity can be mitigated by access to health care (as seen among males in Bangladesh). They also reveal that the failure to address the synergism by either reducing exposure to disease or improving nutritional status places children in a high-risk situation for mortality when access to health care is limited (as seen among females in

Bangladesh). That feature has implications for the cost-effectiveness and sustainability of alternative approaches to reducing child mortality. Specifically, it suggests that cost-effectiveness calculations could be performed for various combinations of health care improvement, nutritional improvement and reductions in disease exposure to determine the most cost-effective strategy in the medium term. Such analysis would be extremely useful for policy planning. It should be recognized that curative care may mitigate child mortality, but that strategy is likely to be less sustainable (financially and politically) over the long term, and is likely to have negative effects on equity because of barriers in access to care.

NOTES

[1] Positive deviance studies attempt to identify characteristics of caretakers and their households that are associated with better-than-expected health and nutritional outcomes in their children, considering the poor socio-economic and environmental conditions in which they live.

[2] The only exceptions are two studies on Zaire: (*a*) the study of the Kasongo Project Team (1983), which appeared to grossly underenumerate deaths and did not have the quality of measurements seen in other studies; (*b*) a study (by Van Den Broeck and others (1993), which is described in section B.4.

[3] The age ranges at baseline for the various studies are as follows: United Republic of Tanzania (6-30 months); Papua New Guinea (6-30 months); Malawi (6-59 months); Teknaf (12-59 months); Matlab 1d (12-23 months); Matlab 4(12-59 months); India (12-36 months) and Indonesia (0-59 months).

[4] Weight-for-age refers to the weight of a child in relation to the expected weight of a same-sex, same-age child in a healthy, well-nourished population. Expected values, or reference values, have been published by the World Health Organization (1988). The child's weight is often expressed as percentage of the median value from the reference population. In the present paper, severe malnutrition refers to values less than 60 per cent of median, moderate malnutrition to values between 60 and 69 per cent of median, mild malnutrition to values between 70 and 79 per cent of median and "normal" to values at or above 80 per cent of median. Individual studies may employ somewhat different categories.

[5] One exception is the early study in Bangladesh by Chen, Chowdhury and Huffman (1980), which found mortality to be elevated only when weight-for-age is less than 65 per cent of the median. That result has not been confirmed in any other studies, including some from the same area of Bangladesh and some from other populations as shown in figure 26.

[6] Under a multiplicative model, the total death rate is a function of the product of malnutrition prevalence and disease exposure, whereas under an additive model total, death rate is a function of the sum of deaths due to malnutrition and deaths due to disease considered separately.

[7] Relative risk refers to the mortality rate among a given category of the malnourished relative to that among the well-nourished.

[8] Refering to the odds of death among the malnourished relative to the well-nourished.

[9] $PAR = P(RR-1)/(1+(P(RR-1)))$ where P = prevalence of malnutrition and RR = the relative risk of mortality among the malnourished.

[10] The World Bank (1993) defines DALYs as a measure of the global burden of disease. It combines the loss of life due to premature death with the loss of healthy life from disability. Among young children, as in the data contained in table 33, it primarily reflects premature mortality.

[11] In other words, $RRm = M(a)/m(a)$, where $M(a)$ is the mortality due to cause (a) among the malnourished and $m(a)$ is the mortality due to cause (a) among the well-nourished; that statistic is calculated separately for each cause of death and the results are shown in table 34.

[12] Samples drawn from Argentina, Bolivia, Brazil, Chile, Colombia, El Salvador, Jamaica and Mexico.

[13] Studies reviewed in the present section used either multiple discriminant analysis or multiple logistic regression analysis to examine the determinants of child mortality; these methods permit an assessment of the extent to which the sex differences in mortality (as observed in the simple bivariate analysis) persist after the other variables in the model are taken into account or "controlled for" in the analysis.

[14] Mortality rate among males divided by the mortality rate among females, multiplied by 100.

[15] An alternative approach would be based on the slope estimates derived from the prospective studies reviewed above. However, that would require sex-specific estimates of the prevalence of severe, moderate and mild malnutrition in each country, which do not exist. A more serious problem is that it would require knowledge of the "baseline mortality" (mortality among the well-nourished) in each country, if the interest is in predicting the absolute mortality rate as required here.

REFERENCES

Bairagi, R. (1981). On validity of some anthropometric indicators as predictors of mortality. *American Journal of Clinical Nutrition* (Bethesda, Maryland), vol. 34, pp. 2592-2594.

_____, M. A. Koenig and K. A. Mazumder (1993). Mortality-discriminating and power of some nutritional, sociodemographic, and diarrheal and disease indices. *American Journal of Epidemiology* (Baltimore, Maryland), vol. 138, No. 5, pp. 310-317.

Basu, A. M. (1989). Is discrimination in food really necessary for explaining sex differentials in childhood mortality. *Population Studies* (London), vol. 43, pp. 193-210.

Beaton, G., and others (1990). Appropriate uses of anthropometric indices in children. State-of-the-Art Series Nutrition Policy Discussion Paper, No. 7. New York: United Nations.

Bhuiya, A., B. Wojtyniak and R. Karim (1989). Malnutrition and child mortality: are socioeconomic factors important? *Journal of Biosocial Sciences* (Cambridge, United Kingdom), vol. 21, pp. 357-364.

Briend, A., B. Wojtyniak and M. G. M. Rowland (1987). Arm circumference and other factors in children at high risk of death in rural Bangladesh. *The Lancet* (London), 26 September.

Briend, A., and A. Bari (1989). Critical assessment of the use of growth monitoring for identifying high risk children in primary health-care programmes. *British Medical Journal* (London), vol. 298, pp. 1607-1611.

Chandra, R. K. (1991). Nutrition and immunity: lessons from the past and new insights into the future. *American Journal of Clinical Nutrition* (Bethesda, Maryland), vol. 53, No. 5, pp. 1087-1101.

Chen, L. C., A. K. M. A. Chowdhury and S. L. Huffman (1980). Anthropometric assessment of energy-protein malnutrition and subsequent risk of mortality among preschool aged children.

131

American Journal of Clinical Nutrition (Bethesda, Maryland), vol. 33, pp. 1836-1845.

Chowdhury, A. K. M. A. (1988). Child mortality in Bangladesh: food versus health care. *Food and Nutrition Bulletin* (Tokyo), vol. 10, No. 2, pp. 3-9.

Cogill, B. (1982). Ranking anthropometric indicators using mortality in rural Bangladesh children. Ithaca, New York: Cornell University. Master of Science Thesis.

De Waal, A. (1989). Famine mortality: a case study of Darfur, Sudan 1984-5. *Population Studies* (London), vol. 43, pp. 5-24.

Ewbank, D. C., and J. N. Gribble (1993). *Effects of Health Programs on Child Mortality in Sub-Saharan Africa*. Washington, D.C.: National Academy Press.

Fauveau, V., and others (1990). The contribution of severe malnutrition to child mortality in rural Bangladesh: implications for targeting nutritional interventions. *Food and Nutrition Bulletin* (Tokyo), vol. 12, No. 3, pp. 215-219.

_____, M. A. Koenig and B. Wojtyniak (1991). Excess female deaths among rural Bangladeshi children: an examination of cause-specific mortality and morbidity. *International Journal of Epidemiology* (Oxford), vol. 20, No. 3, pp. 729-735.

Haaga, J., and others (1985). An estimate of the prevalence of child malnutrition in developing countries. *World Health Statistics Quarterly* (Geneva), vol. 38, pp. 331-347.

Kasongo Project Team (1983). Anthropometric assessment of young children's nutritional status as an indicator of subsequent risk of dying. *Journal of Tropical Pediatrics* (Oxford), vol. 29, pp. 69-75.

Katz, J., and others (1989). The importance of age in evaluating anthropometric indices for predicting mortality. *American Journal of Epidemiology* (Baltimore, Maryland), vol. 130, No. 6, pp. 1219-1226.

Keilmann, A. A., and C. McCord (1978). Weight-for-age as an index of risk of death in children. *The Lancet* (London), No. 1, pp. 1247-1250.

Pelletier, D. L., E. A. Frongillo and J-P. Habicht (1993). Epidemiologic evidence for a potentiating effect of malnutrition on child mortality. *American Journal of Public Health* (Washington, D.C.), vol. 83, No. 8, pp. 1130-1133.

Pelletier, D. L. (1994a). The relationship between child anthropometry and mortality in developing countries: implications for policy, programs and future research. *Journal of Nutrition Supplement* (Bethesda, Maryland), vol. 124, No. 10S, pp. 2047S-2081S.

_____, and others (1994b). A methodology for estimating the contribution of malnutrition to child mortality in developing countries. *Journal of Nutrition Supplement* (Bethesda, Maryland), vol. 124, No. 10S, pp. 2082S-2105S.

_____ (1994c). Child anthropometry and mortality in Malawi: testing for effect modification by age and length of follow-up and confounding by socioeconomic factors. *Journal of Nutrition Supplement* (Bethesda, Maryland), vol. 124, No. 10S, pp. 2106S-2122S.

Puffer, R. C., and C. V. Serrano (1973). *Patterns of Mortality in Childhood*. Scientific Publication, No. 262. Washington, D.C.: Pan American Health Organization.

Scrimshaw, N. S., C. E. Taylor and J. E. Gordon (1968). *Interaction of Nutrition and Infection*. Monograph Series, No. 57. Geneva: World Health Organization.

Sommer, A., and M. S. Loewenstein (1975). Nutritional status and mortality: a prospective validation of the QUAC stick. *American Journal of Clinical Nutrition* (Bethesda, Maryland), vol. 28, pp. 287-292.

Tabutin, Dominique, and M. Willems (1995). Excess mortality among girl children in the world from the 1970s to the 1980s. *Population Bulletin of the United Nations*, No. 39 (United Nations publication, Sales No. E.95.XIII.17), pp. 45-78.

United Nations (1992). Second Report on the World Nutrition Situation: Global and Regional Results.

United Nations Children's Fund (1990). *Strategy for Improved Nutrition of Children and Women in Developing Countries*. A UNICEF Policy Review. New York.

_____ (1993). *Child Malnutrition: Progress Toward the World Summit for Children Goal*. New York.

Van Den Broeck, J., R. Eeckels and J. Uylsteke (1993). Influence of nutritional status on child mortality in rural Zaire. *Lancet* (London), No. 341, pp. 1491-1495.

Van Den Broeck, J. (1994). Assessment of child health and nutritional status in a rural tropical area. Leuven, Belgium. Doctoral dissertation.

_____, and R. Eeckels (1994). Effect of malnutrition on child mortality. *Lancet* (London), vol. 344, p. 273.

Vella, V., and others (1992). Determinants of child mortality in southwest Uganda. *Journal of Biosocial Science* (Cambridge, United Kingdom), vol. 24, pp. 103-112.

_____, and others (1994). Anthropometry as a predictor for mortality among Ugandan children, allowing for socio-economic variables. *European Journal of Clinical Nutrition* (Bethesda, Maryland), vol. 48, No. 3, p. 189.

World Bank (1993). *World Development Report, 1993: Investing in Health*. Oxford, United Kingdom; and New York: Oxford University Press.

World Health Organization (1983). *Measuring Changes in Nutritional Status: Guidelines for Assessing the Nutritional Impact of Supplementary Feeding Programmes for Vulnerable Groups*. Geneva.

Yambi, O. (1988). Nutritional status and the risk of death: a prospective study of children six to thirty months old in Iringa region, United Republic of Tanzania. Ithaca, New York: Cornell University. Doctoral thesis..

Zeitlin, M., H. Ghassemi and M. Mansour (1990). *Positive Deviance in Child Nutrition, with Emphasis on Psychosocial and Behavioral Aspects and Implications for Development*. Tokyo: United Nations University.

VI. SEX DIFFERENTIALS IN THE NUTRITIONAL STATUS OF YOUNG CHILDREN

A. Elisabeth Sommerfelt* and Fred Arnold*

Children's nutritional status is a reflection of their overall health. Children that have access to an adequate food supply and that are not burdened by disease reach their growth potential and are considered well-nourished. However, children in developing countries often do not receive an adequate food supply, especially during the critical first years of life. They are also exposed to repeated infectious illnesses that are often not managed properly. Poor nutritional intake in combination with repeated illness results in undernutrition. An examination of nutritional status is therefore crucial in order to gain an understanding of differentials in infant and child mortality since undernourished children are at a greater risk of dying than well-nourished children. Further discussion of the causes and consequences of poor nutritional status may be found in chapter V above.

Both feeding patterns and the treatment of disease may differ by the sex of the child, ultimately leading to poorer nutritional status for children of the sex that is less favoured. A strong preference for sons has been observed in many societies, particularly in countries of Northern Africa, Eastern Asia, Southern Asia and Western Asia (Williamson, 1976; Arnold, 1992, 1977). In some cases, son preference is manifested in discriminatory practices against female children (Ravindran, 1986). Discrimination against girls in the distribution of food has been noted in several countries (Chen, Huq and D'Souza, 1981; Miller, 1981; Roberts and others, 1981; Sebai and Reinke, 1981; Brown and others, 1982; Sabir and Ebrahim, 1984; Makinson, 1986; Das Gupta, 1987). There is substantial disagreement, however, on whether discrimination in feeding practices is a cause of excess female mortality in children (Ravindran, 1986; Waldron, 1987; Basu, 1989). Sex differences in

the prevalence of childhood diseases are generally insignificant where son preference is widespread (Hossain and Glass, 1988; Boerma and others, 1991; Arnold, 1992). However, a strong preference for sons may induce parents to provide better medical care for sons than for daughters when they become ill (Froozani, Malekafzali and Bahrini, 1980; Locoh, 1987; Khan and others, 1988; Jejeebhoy, 1991; Deolalikar and Vashishta, 1992). Unfortunately, most studies of children's nutritional status do not discuss the results separately for boys and girls. Among those that do, some report that there are no differences between males and females (Wolde-Gebriel and others, 1993; Chirmulay and Nisal, 1993; Rankins and others, 1993; Schoenbaum, Tulchinsky and Abed, 1995). A review comparing the percentage of children classified as underweight according to sex found that there was no consistent difference between boys and girls (Wardlaw, 1992). A few studies have found better nutritional status among girls than among boys, including one about Australian aboriginal children under age 2 (Gracey and others, 1992) and a meta-analysis of anthropometric studies in sub-Saharan Africa (Svedberg, 1990). But other studies have reported more undernutrition among girls than among boys (Visweswara Rao and Balakrishna, 1990; Rao and Kanade, 1992).

It has been suggested, however, that discrimination against girls in some countries may be focused on those with older sisters (Das Gupta, 1987). Since parents often want to have one daughter even in countries where son preference is strong, only girls that are considered to be in excess of parental wishes may suffer from relatively poor treatment. Sex differences in undernutrition may also vary by age of the children. In one of two subgroups in Malawi, Pelletier and Msukwa (1991) found a greater deterioration in the nutritional status of girls than that of boys as children grew older.

---
*Demographic and Health Surveys Program, Macro International, Calverton, Maryland.

The present chapter examines differences in nutritional status between boys and girls drawing upon recent data from the Demographic and Health Surveys (DHS) programme. Since many of the factors that lead to undernutrition are related to the behaviour of the child's mother or principal caretaker, sex differences in the nutritional status of children may emerge if either boys or girls are treated preferentially. For example, vaccination against measles prevents a disease that carries an increased risk of dying for children in developing countries. Those that do get measles and survive often exhibit a deterioration in nutritional status following infection. If the prevalence of measles vaccination is higher among boys than among girls, that factor may lead to sex differences in nutritional status.

Feeding practices also influence nutritional status. Feeding fluids or foods other than breast milk usually place young children at an increased risk of becoming undernourished. Liquids are often contaminated and they do not provide the nutrients required by the infant. The prevalence of bottle feeding also provides an indication of inappropriate feeding practices. The present study, however, does not examine either feeding practices or the incidence of childhood diseases as possible determinants of nutritional status and mortality risks. Instead, the aim is essentially descriptive, with a focus on assessing the nutritional status of boys and girls as measured by 41 cross-sectional surveys carried out as part of the DHS. Those surveys were conducted using comparable questionnaires, field procedures and data-processing operations. Moreover, the various measures of nutritional status on which the analysis is based were calculated using the same methodology so that direct cross-national comparisons can be made. Sections A and B describe the methods used by the surveys to measure nutritional status, and provide definitions of the indices and indicators used in the analysis; sections C and D present and discuss the empirical findings on differential undernutrition.

A. SOURCE OF DATA

The DHS programme, which is funded primarily by the United States Agency for International, assists developing countries in carrying out nationally representative surveys on health and demographic issues.

The surveys provide information for programme planners, policy makers and researchers. The first five-year phase, DHS-I, began in 1984; the second, DHS-II, in 1988; and the third, DHS-III, which is currently in progress, in 1992.

The surveys carried out under the DHS programme gather information necessary to estimate fertility levels, trends and desires, as well as infant and child mortality levels and trends. The surveys also include extensive sets of questions on contraceptive knowledge and use, and maternal and child health. The maternal and child health section records information on maternity care, childhood vaccinations, treatment of common childhood illnesses, breastfeeding and other feeding practices, and measurement of weight and height of children and mothers.

The DHS programme carries out nationally representative, cross-sectional household surveys, whose respondents are generally women aged 15-49, except in Brazil and Guatemala, where the upper age limit was 44. In most countries, all women in the relevant age group, regardless of marital status, were canvassed, but in Northern Africa and Asia only ever-married women were interviewed (except in the 1992 Morocco survey). Child health and nutrition information was obtained for all the respondent's children born after a specified date preceding the survey. In most DHS-I surveys, anthropometric measurements were obtained for children aged between 3 and 36 months at the time of the survey, whereas questions about breastfeeding and other feeding practices and child health were asked in reference to children under age 5. In DHS-II surveys, information on both nutrition and health was obtained for all children born during the five years preceding the survey. In DHS-III surveys, both nutrition and health information was obtained only for children born during the three years preceding the survey. Table 39 indicates the age group of children for whom anthropometric information was obtained in each of the surveys included in the present analysis.

For a small proportion of children in a population, anthropometric measures are not obtained in a typical DHS sample. Those omitted cases include children whose mothers were under 15 years of age or who were aged 50 years or more at the time of the survey; children whose mothers had died; and children living

134

TABLE 39. ANTHROPOMETRY IN DEMOGRAPHIC AND HEALTH SURVEYS

Country or area	Year of survey	Age group for anthropometric measurement (months)	Number of children aged 3-35 months[a]
Sub-Saharan Africa			
Burkina Faso	1992-1993	0 - 59	2 501
Burundi	1987	3 - 36	1 889
Cameroon	1991	0 - 59	1 455
Ghana	1988	3 - 36	1 795
	1993	3 - 35	1 687
Kenya	1993	0 - 59	2 736
Madagascar	1992	0 - 59	2 615
Malawi	1992	0 - 59	1 916
Mali	1987	3 - 36	909
Namibia	1992	0 - 59	1 572
Niger	1992	0 - 59	2 506
Ondo State, Nigeria	1986-1987	6 - 36	1 346
Nigeria	1990	0 - 59	3 266
Rwanda	1992	0 - 59	2 560
Senegal	1986	6 - 36	618
	1992-1993	0 - 59	2 327
United Rep. of Tanzania	1991-1992	0 - 59	3 826
Togo	1988	0 - 36	1 281
Uganda	1988-1989	0 - 59	2 327
Zambia	1992	0 - 60	3 041
Zimbabwe	1988-1989	3 - 60	1 496
Western Asia and Northern Africa			
Egypt	1988-1989	3 - 36	1 885
	1992	0 - 59	3 959
Jordan	1990	0 - 59	3 816
Morocco	1987	0 - 60	2 959
	1992	0 - 59	2 470
Tunisia	1988	3 - 36	1 970
Turkey	1993	0 - 59	1 756
Other Asia			
Pakistan	1990-1991	0 - 59	2 418
Sri Lanka	1987	3 - 36	1 962
Thailand	1987	3 - 36	1 808
Latin America and the Caribbean			
Bolivia	1989	3 - 36	2 512
	1993-1994	0 - 35	2 698
Brazil (north-east)	1986	0 - 60	571
Colombia	1986	3 - 36	1 307
Dominican Republic	1986	6 - 36	1 768
	1991	0 - 59	1 733
Guatemala	1987	3 - 36	2 207
Paraguay	1990	0 - 59	1 950
Peru	1991-1992	0 - 59	3 858
Trinidad and Tobago	1987	3 - 36	817

Source: Demographic and Health Surveys data.

[a]Number of children with acceptable height and weight measurements and complete information on year and month of birth; for Ondo state in Nigeria, Senegal (1986) and the Dominican Republic (1986), the age range is 6-35 months.

away from home. In DHS interviews, women are asked to provide information about their children even if those children are living away from them. Although the mothers interviewed may be able to provide information on antenatal and delivery care and on early childhood vaccinations for children that are not living with them, it is clearly not possible to measure the height and weight of those children. However, in most countries very few children live away from their mothers during the first few years of life, as was shown in an assessment of the data gathered in DHS-I surveys (Sommerfelt and Boerma, 1993). Consequently, no serious bias is expected from the lack of information on those children. Similarly the omission of children born to very young or very old mothers or to mothers that have died is likely to be minor in most settings.

During the first phase of the DHS programme, surveys were conducted in 29 developing countries, 19 of which included the measurement of height and weight of the young children of the women interviewed. During DHS-II, surveys were carried out in 22 countries, 18 of which included such measurements. For DHS-III, anthropometric data were available for only four surveys at the time of the present analysis. The study is therefore based on data from the 41 available surveys that gathered the relevant information. Six of those surveys are successive inquiries in the same country, typically with a five-year interval. It may also be noted that two surveys—in Ondo State, Nigeria, and north-eastern Brazil—were regional rather than national in coverage.

In training the interviewers responsible for the measurement of children, the guidelines contained in the United Nations manual *How to Weigh and Measure Children* (United Nations, 1986) were followed. A hanging spring-balance weighing scale was used to weigh the children in all DHS-I and a few DHS-II surveys. Most DHS-II surveys and all DHS-III surveys used a walk-on electronic scale, which is accurate to within 100 grams. Older children stood on that scale by themselves and younger children were held by their mother. The scale allowed a direct reading of the child's weight in both cases; no calculation was required by the person conducting the measurement. With respect to the measurement of height,

many of the DHS-I surveys used recumbent length for children up to age 36 months, although standing height is recommended for children aged two years or over. Because there is a systematic difference between recumbent and standing measurements, one centimetre was subtracted from the length of children aged 24 months or over that were measured lying down. The subtraction was done by computer during data processing, not during data collection in the field. The term "height" is used in the present chapter to refer to both standing height and recumbent length.

B. NUTRITIONAL STATUS INDICES AND INDICATORS OF UNDERNUTRITION

The terms "nutritional" and "anthropometric" status are used synonymously in the present chapter. Three different aspects of a child's nutritional status are considered: (*a*) height related to age (height-for-age); (*b*) weight related to age (weight-for-age); and (*c*) weight related to height (weight-for-height). Each measurement conveys somewhat different information about the child's nutritional status.

Because children's weight and height increase as they get older, those measurements need to be expressed in relation to the growth patterns of a reference population in order to allow for the proper comparison of the measurements of children at different ages. The World Health Organization (WHO) recommends that children's height and weight be related to age and that weight be related to height (WHO, 1986). Because in a well-nourished population boys are on average taller and heavier than girls of exactly the same age, the reference values differ for boys and girls, and consequently a child's sex needs to be taken into consideration when making comparisons with the reference population. WHO recommends that a child's weight and height be expressed in terms of the number of standard deviation units (SD) that a child's measurement (weight or height) deviates from the median value of the reference population for children of the same age and sex. Such standard deviation units are called "Z-scores". The distributions for the International Reference Population recommended for use by WHO have been developed by the United States Centers for Disease Control based on data from the United States National Center for

Health Statistics. In the case of weight-for-height, the weight is related to the median weight for a given height. In the International Reference Population, only a very small percentage of children (2.3 per cent) have a Z-score lower than -2 SD.

A child's nutritional status is expressed as his or her Z-score for each of the three anthropometric indices used: height-for-age; weight-for-age; and weight-for-height. At the population level, or for a subgroup of children, nutritional status is expressed by the children's mean Z-score.

The term "undernutrition" is used here to denote protein-energy malnutrition. Three indicators, "stunting", "wasting" and "underweight", are used to describe the extent of undernutrition in a population of children; each indicator corresponds to one of the three indices of nutritional status described above. Those indicators are defined as the percentage of children whose Z-score falls below a defined cut-off point, namely, -2 SD from the median of the International Reference Population.

A child whose height-for-age Z-score is below -2 SD from the reference population median is short for his or her age. The percentage of children whose height-for-age Z-scores fall into that category is an indicator of the extent of stunting, or linear growth retardation, in a population. Sometimes those children are referred to as stunted. It should be kept in mind that even a child whose Z-score is above the -2 SD cut-off point may be stunted, since a child with a height-for-age Z-score of -1 SD might have had a Z-score of +1 SD under optimal conditions. Linear growth retardation reflects long-term growth failure or chronic undernutrition. It results primarily from recurrent and chronic illnesses, especially when not treated properly, and from inadequate food intake. Diarrhoea, lower respiratory tract infection and measles are common illnesses that often contribute to the development or worsening of undernutrition among children in developing countries. Poor environmental sanitation and unsafe and inadequate water supplies place children at risk of gastrointestinal infections. Inadequate food intake in children can result from lack of access to food because of poverty or poor feeding practices. Undernutrition in turn places children at a greater risk of certain infections.

The weight-for-height index describes body mass in relation to height. A child with a weight-for-height Z-score below -2 SD is considered very thin, that is, the weight is low in relation to the child's height. The percentage of children in that category reflects the degree of wasting in a population. High levels of wasting are often the result of insufficient food intake in the recent past, and wasting is also commonly seen immediately following an illness episode, as for instance after diarrhoea. Seasonal changes in food supply may also result in changes in the wasting levels of a group of children. Since the fieldwork for a DHS inquiry typically spans a period of 4-5 months, DHS estimates may not reflect accurately the average level of wasting throughout the year in countries where seasonal variations in wasting are substantial.

A child whose weight-for-age is below -2 SD from the reference population median is underweight for his or her age. The weight-for-age index is a composite index, reflecting stunting or wasting or both. A child who is short is usually also underweight. A child who is very thin may similarly have a low weight-for-age even if he or she is not short. A child who is both very short and very thin will also have a low weight-for-age. Weight-for-age is often used for longitudinal growth monitoring of children.

An alternative to using the Z-score method to express the child's anthropometric status is the "percentage of median" approach, which has been used in earlier studies. In that method, a child's weight or height is expressed as a percentage of the median value of the reference population. For example, the median weight for boys aged 12 months is about 10 kilograms (kg). A boy of that same age weighing 8 kg is said to weigh 80 per cent of the median. For weight-for-age, mild undernutrition commonly refers to children whose weight is between 70 and 79 per cent of the median weight for their age, moderate undernutrition corresponds to 60-69 per cent and severe undernutrition refers to those whose weight is below 60 per cent of the median. Both the Z-score and the percentage of median approaches to the measurement of undernutrition allow comparison of groups of children of different ages.

A number of different measures are used in the present chapter to assess whether there are differences in the nutritional status of girls and boys. The commonly used indicators of levels of undernutrition (that is, the percentage of children that are stunted, wasted or underweight) are shown for the children included in the different surveys. Those indicators are the percentage of children with the relevant Z-scores below an arbitrary cut-off point (-2 SD). For almost all of the 41 surveys considered, the data available refer to children 3-35 months of age. The surveys of Senegal (1986), Ondo State in Nigeria and the Dominican Republic (1986) are the exceptions, since their anthropometric measurements include only children older than six months. For the 24 surveys that have weight and height measurements up to the fifth birthday (table 39), the indicators of undernutrition are also presented for all children under age 5.

To assess whether the levels of undernutrition differ for boys and girls, the differences between boys and girls in the percentages stunted, wasted or underweight were calculated. A negative difference implies that the percentage in a given undernourished category is higher among girls than among boys, and the reverse is true when the difference is positive.

Small differences in the estimated indicators of undernutrition between girls and boys in an individual country may not reflect real differences in nutritional status because of variability due to the sample design. In many cases, the measured sex differences can be attributed to sampling error. Table 40 shows illustrative sampling errors for the three anthropometric indicators for children 3-35 months of age in three countries with substantially different sample sizes and overall levels of undernutrition. The table shows the standard error of each estimate for male and female children and the related confidence intervals.

For example, in Egypt (1992), 29.1 per cent of girls 3-35 months of age are stunted. The standard error of the estimate is 1.4 per cent. That value implies that there is a 95 per cent probability that the actual percentage of girls of that age that are stunted is between 26.2 and 31.9 per cent. The standard errors of the estimates are lower in the case of wasting (0.5-1.3 per cent) than for the other two indicators (0.9-2.3 per cent). The confidence intervals shown in table 40 indicate that small differences between boys and girls in the level of undernutrition are not likely to be statistically significant.

TABLE 40. SAMPLING ERRORS FOR INDICATORS OF UNDERNUTRITION FOR CHILDREN AGED 3-35 MONTHS, BY SEX, EGYPT, MALAWI AND PAKISTAN

Country	Percentage under-nourished	Standard error	Confidence limits	
			R-2SE	R+2SE
Egypt (1992)				
Males				
Stunting	29.6	1.3	27.1	32.1
Underweight .	13.2	0.9	11.4	14.9
Wasting	4.3	0.5	3.3	5.3
Females				
Stunting	29.1	1.4	26.2	31.9
Underweight .	13.1	1.0	11.1	15.1
Wasting	4.1	0.6	3.0	5.2
Malawi				
Males				
Stunting	48.5	1.6	45.2	51.7
Underweight .	33.3	1.9	29.5	37.2
Wasting	8.2	1.0	6.1	10.3
Females				
Stunting	41.1	2.0	37.1	45.1
Underweight .	27.8	1.8	24.3	31.4
Wasting	6.1	0.9	4.3	8.0
Pakistan				
Males				
Stunting	46.8	2.3	42.3	51.4
Underweight .	40.8	2.1	36.6	45.0
Wasting	11.0	1.2	8.6	13.3
Females				
Stunting	45.3	2.2	40.8	49.7
Underweight .	37.9	2.0	33.9	42.0
Wasting	9.1	1.3	6.6	11.7

Source: Demographic and Health Surveys data.

Another indicator considered is the mean Z-score of children covered by each survey, which summarizes their overall nutritional status. In the reference population, the average Z-score is zero. A negative average Z-score means that the group of children being assessed has worse nutritional status than the reference population. As in the case of the indicators of undernutrition, the mean Z-scores are shown first for children 3-35 months of age, and then for all children under age 5, where available. The difference between the mean Z-scores of girls and boys is used to compare the nutritional status of the sexes. A negative difference once more indicates that the nutritional status of girls is worse than that of boys. Thus, if the mean height-for-age Z-score is -1.2 for girls and -1.0 for boys, the difference (-0.2) indicates that girls are on average shorter for their age than boys are in relation to the reference population.

Only children whose mothers reported their month and year of birth are included in the analysis. In addition, children for whom one or more of the anthropometric indices are highly improbable according to the guidelines provided by the Centers for Disease Control are excluded from the analysis on the assumption that those extremely improbable Z-scores were the result of errors in measurement in recording the results or in ascertaining the child's age. On average, for all countries 86 per cent of children 3-35 months of age are included in the anthropometric tables. More than half of the shortfall is due to children that were not weighed or measured. Most of the rest is due to lack of complete information on children's dates of birth. Fewer than 2 per cent of children were excluded because one or more of the anthropometric indices were highly improbable. There are only three surveys in which less than three-quarters of children are included in the tables: Mali (55 per cent), Pakistan (72 per cent) and Namibia (73 per cent).

C. General findings

Table 41 presents the percentage of children 3-35 months of age experiencing stunting, underweight or wasting for each of the 41 surveys. The data show that the prevalence of stunting and underweight tends to be considerably higher than that of wasting: whereas the median value for stunting is 30 per cent for boys and 29 per cent for girls, the corresponding value for wasting is 6 per cent for boys and 4 per cent for girls. Countries in sub-Saharan Africa generally display higher levels of stunting, underweight and wasting than countries in other regions. With regard to stunting, for instance, among the 21 surveys showing levels of at least 30 per cent among boys, 16 were carried out in sub-Saharan Africa. In the case of girls, 15 of the 21 surveys showing levels of stunting of at least 28.7 per cent were carried out in sub-Saharan Africa.

Although fewer surveys are available for other regions, those carried out in Southern Asia—Pakistan and Sri Lanka —also show high levels of undernutrition, whereas in Latin America only the survey for Guatemala shows high levels of both stunting and underweight.

Not only is the regional variation in the prevalence of undernutrition striking, but there are also indications of important variations over time. For those countries in which surveys were carried out at two different points in time, there appear to be changes in the levels of undernutrition, particularly wasting. In all cases, consecutive surveys carried out in the same country are sufficiently far apart in time that the children being measured belong to independent cohorts and might therefore have been subject to different period conditions affecting the general availability of food.[1]

1. *Stunting*

For children 3-35 months of age, the range in the percentage classified as stunted is similar for boys and girls (5-59 per cent for boys, and 5-57 per cent for girls). Thus, in every country considered, substantial proportions of boys and girls are shorter than their counterparts in the International Reference Population. The median values for stunting across all 41 surveys are 30 and 29 per cent for boys and girls, respectively (table 41). If stunting levels were about the same for boys and girls, one would expect about an equal number of positive and negative differences between the percentage of boys and girls classified as stunted. However, the left-hand box plot in figure 32 shows clearly that that is not the case. There are 35 surveys in which the difference in stunting levels between boys and girls is positive, indicating that boys are worse off than girls. Furthermore, in 11 of those surveys, the difference exceeds 4 percentage points, and 9 of them are in sub-Saharan Africa. In contrast, among the six surveys where girls appear to be less well-off than boys in terms of stunting, five were undertaken in countries in Northern Africa (Egypt, 1988; Morocco, 1992 and Tunisia), and in Southern and Western Asia (Sri Lanka and Jordan).

The mean height-for-age Z-scores reveal a similar pattern (table 42). Boys have lower mean scores than girls in 35 of the 41 surveys considered. Girls are worse off than boys in terms of height-for-age in only six surveys, mostly in countries of Northern Africa and Southern or Western Asia.

When all children under five years of age are considered, the median of the proportion classified as stunted among the 24 surveys with available data is 29 per

139

TABLE 41. UNDERNUTRITION AMONG CHILDREN UNDER 3 YEARS OF AGE: AMONG CHILDREN 3-35 MONTHS OF AGE, THE
PERCENTAGE WHO ARE CLASSIFIED AS STUNTED, UNDERWEIGHT AND WASTED

Country or area	Year of survey	Stunting: Percentage whose height-for-age Z-score is below -2 SD[a] from Reference Population Median			Underweight: Percentage whose weight-for-age Z-score is below -2 SD[a] from Reference Population Median			Wasting: Percentage whose weight-for-height Z-score is below -2 SD[a] from Reference Population Median		
		Males	Females	Difference: Males - females	Males	Females	Difference: Males - females	Males	Females	Difference: Males - females
Sub-Saharan Africa										
Burkina Faso	1992-1993	32.2	30.0	2.1	39.2	36.9	2.3	18.6	17.8	0.8
Burundi	1987	47.7	47.1	0.6	37.1	38.0	-0.9	6.2	5.1	1.2
Cameroon	1991	25.7	24.2	1.5	16.2	19.3	-3.1	4.7	3.7	0.9
Ghana	1988	30.0	28.8	1.2	30.1	30.4	-0.3	9.2	6.8	2.4
	1993	29.8	25.2	4.6	30.9	27.4	3.5	12.3	11.2	1.1
Kenya	1993	35.1	30.4	4.7	26.0	23.2	2.8	7.1	6.4	0.7
Madagascar	1992	55.2	49.7	5.5	43.7	40.3	3.4	6.5	5.8	0.7
Malawi	1992	48.5	41.1	7.4	33.3	27.8	5.5	8.2	6.1	2.1
Mali	1987	23.8	23.9	-0.1	29.8	31.4	-1.5	13.8	8.9	5.0
Namibia	1992	32.5	28.9	3.5	27.9	27.9	-0.0	9.4	9.1	0.2
Niger	1992	41.4	36.8	4.5	49.5	48.1	1.5	20.3	20.0	0.3
Ondo State, Nigeria	1986-1987	32.8	31.6	1.2	27.6	27.3	0.3	6.5	5.8	0.8
Nigeria	1990	39.6	38.5	1.2	38.8	36.7	2.1	13.2	9.2	4.0
Rwanda	1992	46.8	43.1	3.7	31.3	30.3	1.0	6.0	5.0	1.0
Senegal	1986	25.3	20.6	4.7	24.0	20.0	4.0	8.1	3.5	4.6
	1992-1993	25.3	21.1	4.2	25.6	21.6	4.0	12.4	9.4	2.9
United Rep. of Tanzania	1991-1992	43.7	39.8	3.9	31.9	30.2	1.7	8.1	6.0	2.1
Togo	1988	33.6	28.2	5.4	26.9	25.2	1.7	6.7	4.6	2.1
Uganda	1988-1989	46.3	41.4	4.8	25.6	24.6	1.0	2.2	2.3	-0.2
Zambia	1992	40.1	38.5	1.6	29.1	27.4	1.7	6.3	6.4	-0.1
Zimbabwe	1988-1989	31.0	28.7	2.3	13.6	11.7	1.8	1.5	0.9	0.6
Western Asia and Northern Africa										
Egypt	1988-1989	30.9	31.0	-0.1	13.8	12.9	0.9	1.4	0.8	0.7
	1992	29.6	29.1	0.5	13.2	13.1	0.0	4.3	4.1	0.2
Jordan	1990	16.2	17.2	-1.0	6.8	6.0	0.8	3.8	2.7	1.1
Morocco	1987	24.2	23.1	1.1	14.5	13.5	1.0	4.0	3.3	0.7
	1992	24.0	24.7	-0.7	11.5	10.4	1.1	3.3	2.0	1.4
Tunisia	1988	17.2	18.7	-1.5	10.5	10.0	0.5	3.8	2.2	1.6
Turkey	1993	16.7	16.3	0.4	10.8	10.2	0.6	4.4	2.8	1.5
Other Asia										
Pakistan	1990-1991	46.8	45.3	1.6	40.8	37.9	2.8	11.0	9.1	1.8
Sri Lanka	1987	26.0	28.7	-2.7	37.0	37.7	-0.7	11.6	11.5	0.1
Thailand	1987	21.9	21.1	0.8	25.3	25.4	-0.0	5.3	5.3	0.0
Latin America and the Caribbean										
Bolivia	1989	39.4	36.0	3.5	15.1	11.4	3.6	1.7	1.5	0.2
	1993-1994	28.2	28.1	0.1	16.1	15.2	0.9	5.5	3.1	2.3
Brazil (north-east)	1986	31.8	26.7	5.1	14.8	13.4	1.5	1.5	0.6	0.9
Colombia	1986	26.4	24.3	2.1	11.1	12.9	-1.8	1.4	1.2	0.2
Dominican Republic	1986	24.7	16.8	7.8	14.4	10.6	3.8	3.5	1.2	2.3
	1991	18.7	16.1	2.6	13.3	10.4	2.9	1.2	1.5	-0.3
Guatemala	1987	58.7	56.7	1.9	32.4	33.9	-1.4	1.1	1.5	-0.4
Paraguay	1990	16.7	14.7	2.0	4.2	5.0	-0.8	0.2	0.3	-0.2
Peru	1991-1992	29.3	26.8	2.4	12.9	11.1	1.8	2.3	1.9	0.4
Trinidad and Tobago	1987	5.0	4.5	0.5	6.0	6.9	-0.9	3.8	3.8	-0.0
Median value		30.0	28.7	-	25.5	23.2	-	5.5	4.1	-

Source: Demographic and Health Surveys data.
[a]Standard deviation.

140

TABLE 42. NUTRITIONAL STATUS OF CHILDREN UNDER 3 YEARS OF AGE: AMONG CHILDREN 3-35 MONTHS OF AGE, THE AVERAGE HEIGHT-FOR-AGE, WEIGHT-FOR-AGE, AND WEIGHT-FOR-HEIGHT Z-SCORE

Country or area	Year of survey	Average height-for-age Z-score			Average weight-for-age Z-score			Average weight-for-height Z-score		
		Males	Females	Differ-ence: Females - males	Males	Females	Differ-ence: Females - males	Males	Females	Differ-ence: Females - males
Sub-Saharan Africa										
Burkina Faso	1992-1993	-1.25	-1.17	0.08	-1.53	-1.44	0.09	-1.02	-0.92	0.10
Burundi	1987	-1.92	-1.80	0.12	-1.63	-1.59	0.05	-0.52	-0.51	0.02
Cameroon	1991	-1.12	-1.18	-0.06	-0.81	-0.85	-0.03	-0.16	-0.12	0.04
Ghana	1988	-1.33	-1.28	0.05	-1.39	-1.35	0.04	-0.73	-0.69	0.04
	1993	-1.27	-1.16	0.11	-1.36	-1.24	0.12	-0.75	-0.64	0.11
Kenya	1993	-1.43	-1.29	0.14	-1.11	-1.00	0.11	-0.30	-0.21	0.09
Madagascar	1992	-2.11	-1.97	0.14	-1.81	-1.65	0.16	-0.62	-0.50	0.12
Malawi	1992	-1.96	-1.69	0.27	-1.38	-1.16	0.22	-0.24	-0.10	0.14
Mali	1987	-1.11	-1.03	0.07	-1.42	-1.32	0.10	-0.92	-0.80	0.12
Namibia	1992	-1.36	-1.21	0.15	-1.21	-1.19	0.02	-0.42	-0.48	-0.06
Niger	1992	-1.65	-1.53	0.12	-1.86	-1.86	0.00	-1.08	-1.12	-0.04
Ondo State, Nigeria	1986-1987	-1.49	-1.39	0.11	-1.33	-1.33	-0.01	-0.52	-0.56	-0.05
Nigeria	1990	-1.57	-1.52	0.05	-1.52	-1.48	0.05	-0.69	-0.62	0.07
Rwanda	1992	-1.86	-1.73	0.13	-1.39	-1.32	0.07	-0.28	-0.25	0.03
Senegal	1986	-1.19	-1.15	0.04	-1.20	-1.01	0.19	-0.59	-0.33	0.26
	1992-1993	-1.07	-0.99	0.09	-1.12	-1.03	0.09	-0.58	-0.49	0.09
United Rep. of Tanzania	1991-1992	-1.79	-1.64	0.15	-1.39	-1.31	0.08	-0.33	-0.31	0.02
Togo	1988	-1.39	-1.31	0.08	-1.16	-1.08	0.08	-0.37	-0.30	0.07
Uganda	1988-1989	-1.88	-1.64	0.24	-1.24	-1.11	0.13	-0.08	-0.05	0.03
Zambia	1992	-1.70	-1.59	0.11	-1.29	-1.27	0.02	-0.30	-0.30	-0.00
Zimbabwe	1988-1989	-1.46	-1.32	0.13	-0.68	-0.67	0.01	0.30	0.23	-0.07
Western Asia and Northern Africa										
Egypt	1988-1989	-1.37	-1.39	-0.02	-0.72	-0.75	-0.03	0.18	0.19	0.01
	1992	-1.18	-1.15	0.03	-0.49	-0.46	0.02	0.30	0.36	0.06
Jordan	1990	-0.74	-0.77	-0.03	-0.35	-0.30	0.05	0.16	0.30	0.14
Morocco	1987	-1.07	-1.04	0.03	-0.70	-0.66	0.04	-0.03	0.02	0.05
	1992	-1.03	-1.04	-0.01	-0.42	-0.37	0.05	0.27	0.38	0.11
Tunisia	1988	-0.79	-0.82	-0.03	-0.59	-0.58	0.01	-0.09	-0.02	0.07
Turkey	1993	-0.67	-0.66	0.01	-0.49	-0.48	0.01	-0.08	-0.03	0.05
Other Asia										
Pakistan	1990-1991	-1.92	-1.81	0.11	-1.66	-1.55	0.12	-0.59	-0.48	0.10
Sri Lanka	1987	-1.35	-1.37	-0.02	-1.66	-1.62	0.04	-1.01	-0.95	0.06
Thailand	1987	-1.22	-1.14	0.08	-1.30	-1.23	0.07	-0.67	-0.62	0.05
Latin America and the Caribbean										
Bolivia	1989	-1.61	-1.53	0.08	-0.82	-0.72	0.11	0.21	0.33	0.12
	1993-1994	-1.23	-1.20	0.03	-0.83	-0.73	0.09	-0.08	0.06	0.14
Brazil (north-east)	1986	-1.33	-1.28	0.05	-0.68	-0.66	0.01	0.20	0.20	-0.00
Colombia	1986	-1.24	-1.22	0.02	-0.66	-0.62	0.05	0.10	0.18	0.09
Dominican Republic	1986	-0.97	-0.77	0.21	-0.68	-0.49	0.19	-0.07	0.05	0.12
	1991	-0.94	-0.77	0.17	-0.65	-0.50	0.14	-0.04	0.06	0.10
Guatemala	1987	-2.27	-2.26	0.01	-1.47	-1.47	0.01	-0.03	-0.01	0.02
Paraguay	1990	-0.88	-0.76	0.12	-0.27	-0.24	0.03	0.39	0.38	-0.01
Peru	1991-1992	-1.26	-1.20	0.06	-0.60	-0.51	0.09	0.23	0.34	0.11
Trinidad and Tobago	1987	-0.28	-0.23	0.05	-0.38	-0.47	-0.08	-0.20	-0.30	-0.10
Median value		-1.33	-1.22	-	-1.16	-1.03	-	-0.24	-0.21	-

Source: Demographic and Health Surveys data.

Country or area	Year of survey	Stunting: Percentage whose height-for-age Z-score is below -2 SD[a] from Reference Population Median			Underweight: Percentage whose weight-for-age Z-score is below -2 SD[a] from Reference Population Median			Wasting: Percentage whose weight-for-height Z-score is below -2 SD[a] from Reference Population Median		
		Males	Females	Difference: Males - females	Males	Females	Difference: Males - females	Males	Females	Difference: Males - females
Sub-Saharan Africa										
Burkina Faso	1992-1993 ...	34.5	32.1	2.4	33.2	32.2	1.0	13.2	13.2	-0.0
Cameroon	1991	27.3	24.6	2.7	13.8	16.5	-2.7	3.0	2.8	0.2
Kenya	1993	36.2	30.3	5.9	24.7	20.6	4.1	6.4	5.4	1.0
Madagascar	1992	56.2	51.9	4.3	41.7	40.1	1.6	5.0	4.3	0.7
Malawi	1992	51.6	46.9	4.7	28.7	26.5	2.2	6.0	4.9	1.1
Namibia	1992	30.3	26.7	3.6	26.8	25.6	1.3	8.7	8.5	0.3
Niger	1992	40.7	38.1	2.6	42.8	42.4	0.4	15.5	14.5	1.0
Nigeria	1990	43.0	42.4	0.6	35.2	35.4	-0.1	9.6	8.3	1.4
Rwanda	1992	50.0	47.4	2.6	29.0	29.8	-0.9	4.4	3.2	1.2
Senegal	1986	25.9	23.5	2.5	23.4	21.1	2.2	9.7	7.2	2.5
United Rep. of Tanzania	1991-1992 ...	44.5	42.0	2.4	28.9	29.1	-0.2	6.6	5.5	1.1
Uganda	1988-1989 ...	47.3	41.6	5.8	22.9	23.1	-0.3	1.9	1.9	-0.1
Zambia	1992	41.2	38.5	2.7	25.7	24.7	1.0	4.9	5.3	-0.4
Zimbabwe	1988-1989 ...	30.0	28.1	1.9	11.3	11.6	-0.2	1.3	1.2	0.1
Western Asia and Northern Africa										
Egypt	1992	26.1	25.8	0.4	9.7	10.1	-0.3	3.4	3.4	-0.1
Jordan	1990	16.2	15.5	0.7	6.6	6.2	0.4	3.7	2.5	1.2
Morocco	1987	25.3	24.6	0.7	12.1	12.1	-0.1	3.1	2.6	0.5
	1992	24.2	24.2	0.0	10.1	8.9	1.1	2.5	1.9	0.6
Turkey	1993	21.1	19.8	1.3	10.3	10.5	-0.2	3.3	2.5	0.8
Other Asia										
Pakistan	1990-1991 ...	50.4	48.7	1.7	40.6	39.8	0.8	10.2	8.2	2.0
Latin America and the Caribbean										
Brazil (north-east)	1986	32.3	26.6	5.7	12.6	12.9	-0.3	1.4	0.5	0.9
Dominican Republic	1991	17.5	15.4	2.1	11.1	9.5	1.6	1.4	1.5	-0.1
Paraguay	1990	14.3	13.5	0.8	3.2	4.1	-0.9	0.2	0.4	-0.2
Peru	1991-1992 ...	32.4	31.1	1.3	11.4	9.9	1.5	1.8	1.5	0.4
Median value		32.4	29.2	-	23.2	20.9	-	4.1	3.3	-

Source: Demographic and Health Surveys data.
[a]Standard deviation.

cent for girls and 32 per cent for boys, suggesting that girls tend to experience less stunting than boys (table 43). Furthermore, in 23 of the 24 surveys, the percentage of boys classified as stunted is higher than that of girls: that difference exceeds 4 percentage points in four African sites (Kenya, Madagascar, Malawi and Uganda) and in north-eastern Brazil. The mean height-for-age Z-scores reveal the same type of differentials and confirm that girls under five years of age are generally better off than boys in terms of height-for-age (table 44). Only in Turkey do girls appear to do slightly less well than boys in terms of the height they reach at each age.

2. Underweight

Information on the percentage of children classified as underweight shows differences by sex that are similar to those described above in the case of stunting (table 41), although the female advantage is less pronounced than for stunting (figure 32). In half of the surveys considered, at least 26 per cent of the boys

TABLE 44. NUTRITIONAL STATUS OF CHILDREN UNDER 5 YEARS OF AGE: AMONG CHILDREN 0-59 MONTHS OF AGE, THE AVERAGE HEIGHT-FOR-AGE, WEIGHT-FOR-AGE, AND WEIGHT-FOR-HEIGHT Z-SCORE

Country or area	Year of survey	Average height-for-age Z-score			Average weight-for-age Z-score			Average weight-for-height Z-score		
		Males	Females	Differ-ence: Females - males	Males	Females	Differ-ence: Females - males	Males	Females	Differ-ence: Females - males
Sub-Saharan Africa										
Burkina Faso	1992-1993 ...	-1.35	-1.24	0.11	-1.37	-1.32	0.05	-0.75	-0.72	0.03
Cameroon	1991	-1.22	-1.16	0.06	-0.76	-0.74	0.02	-0.01	-0.02	-0.01
Kenya	1993	-1.52	-1.33	0.20	-1.14	-0.99	0.15	-0.29	-0.19	0.10
Madagascar	1992	-2.17	-2.04	0.13	-1.73	-1.64	0.09	-0.53	-0.46	0.06
Malawi	1992	-2.03	-1.89	0.15	-1.25	-1.15	0.10	-0.03	0.02	0.05
Namibia	1992	-1.32	-1.16	0.17	-1.17	-1.12	0.05	-0.43	-0.46	-0.02
Niger	1992	-1.62	-1.56	0.06	-1.67	-1.68	-0.01	-0.90	-0.91	-0.02
Nigeria	1990	-1.72	-1.68	0.04	-1.46	-1.48	-0.02	-0.54	-0.55	-0.01
Rwanda	1992	-1.99	-1.88	0.11	-1.39	-1.31	0.08	-0.23	-0.17	0.05
Senegal	1992-1993 ...	-1.13	-1.08	0.05	-1.08	-1.04	0.04	-0.50	-0.44	0.06
United Rep. of Tanzania	1991-1992 ...	-1.80	-1.71	0.08	-1.31	-1.27	0.04	-0.26	-0.24	0.02
Uganda	1988-1989 ...	-1.90	-1.68	0.22	-1.17	-1.05	0.12	-0.01	0.02	0.03
Zambia	1992	-1.74	-1.61	0.13	-1.23	-1.18	0.06	-0.22	-0.20	0.01
Zimbabwe	1988-1989 ...	-1.44	-1.35	0.08	-0.73	-0.74	-0.00	0.21	0.16	-0.04
Western Asia and Northern Africa										
Egypt	1992	-1.07	-1.04	0.03	-0.33	-0.32	0.01	0.42	0.45	0.03
Jordan	1990	-0.78	-0.77	0.02	-0.41	-0.36	0.05	0.12	0.22	0.10
Morocco	1987	-1.15	-1.12	0.02	-0.72	-0.68	0.04	-0.01	0.05	0.06
	1992	-1.13	-1.11	0.02	-0.49	-0.40	0.09	0.26	0.38	0.11
Turkey	1993	-0.86	-0.87	-0.01	-0.56	-0.53	0.03	-0.04	0.04	0.08
Other Asia										
Pakistan	1990	-2.02	-1.95	0.07	-1.64	-1.56	0.08	-0.54	-0.45	0.09
Latin America and the Caribbean										
Brazil (north-east)	1986	-1.39	-1.23	0.16	-0.74	-0.67	0.07	0.16	0.16	-0.00
Dominican Republic	1991	-0.92	-0.76	0.16	-0.65	-0.52	0.13	-0.08	0.02	0.09
Paraguay	1990	-0.79	-0.69	0.10	-0.22	-0.21	0.02	0.38	0.36	-0.02
Peru	1991-1992 ...	-1.39	-1.34	0.05	-0.61	-0.53	0.08	0.32	0.41	0.09
Median value		-1.39	-1.29	-	-1.11	-1.02	-	-0.06	0.00	-

Source: Demographic and Health Surveys data

aged 3-35 months are classified as underweight, whereas the median for girls of the same age is 23 per cent. In 29 surveys, boys are underweight more often than girls. However, the advantage in favour of girls reaches 4 or more percentage points in only two populations: Malawi and Senegal (1986 and 1992-1993). In contrast, 10 surveys indicate that the per-centage of underweight girls is larger than that of underweight boys.

The mean weight-for-age Z-scores shown in table 42 corroborate the evidence in table 41 that girls aged 3-35 months are better off in terms of weight-for-age than boys of the same age. The differences between

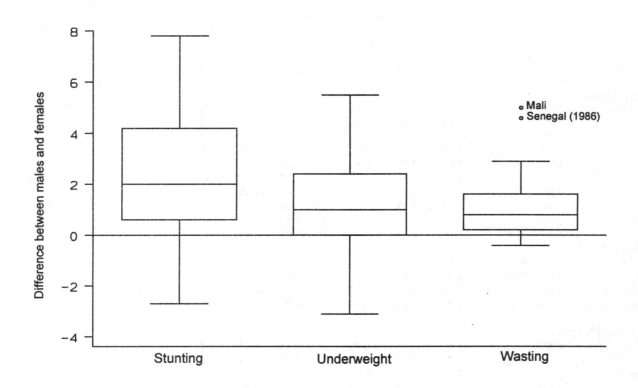

Figure 32. Difference between male and female undernutrition among children 3-35 months of age, who are classified as stunted, underweight and wasted

Source: Table 41.

the female and male Z-scores are positive for 37 of the 41 surveys considered. In only four populations (Cameroon, Egypt (1988-1989), Ondo State, Nigeria, and Trinidad and Tobago) do girls appear to be slightly worse off than boys.

With regard to children under five years of age, the differences between the percentages of boys and girls classified as underweight tend to be small. Among the 24 surveys with available data, 13 yielded positive and 11 negative differences (table 43). Although the sizes of the positive differences tend to be somewhat larger than those of the negative, the results suggest that the prevalence of low weight among children under five years of age is not substantially different between boys and girls. Differences with respect to mean weight-for-age Z-scores are also small although most tend to be positive, indicating that boys are somewhat worse off than girls in terms of weight-for-age (table 44).

Only in three countries, the Niger, Nigeria, and Zimbabwe, are girls slightly disadvantaged compared with boys.

3. Wasting

Differences in the percentage of boys and girls 3-35 months of age classified as wasted are largely positive. As was shown for stunting and underweight, girls tend to fare slightly better than boys in terms of weight-for-height in most countries (table 41). In only five surveys is there a negative difference between the percentage of boys and that of girls subject to wasting, and those differences are uniformly small (figure 32). A similar pattern prevails when considering the mean weight-for-height Z-scores, which are shown in table 42. In 33 of the 41 populations under study, girls are better off than boys in terms of their weight relative to their height.

144

For children under five years of age, differences in the proportions experiencing wasting are also small (table 43) and mostly positive (in 18 of the 24 surveys). In only five populations are girls more likely to experience wasting than boys. A pattern of differences favouring girls is generally corroborated by the mean weight-for-height Z-scores shown in table 44. The difference in the mean weight-for-height Z-scores of girls and boys is positive for 17 of the 24 surveys, although such differences are generally small.

D. UNDERNUTRITION AND NUTRITIONAL STATUS BY AGE OF CHILD

According to the data presented so far, boys are more likely to be undernourished than girls during both the first three and the first five years of life. It may be, however, that relative levels of undernutrition by sex change with children's age, particularly if boys and girls receive different health care or food. As children grow older, preferential treatment might become increasingly apparent. Hence, if girls were not treated as well as boys one would expect to see a deterioration in their relative nutritional status, as was found by Pelletier and Msukwa (1991) in Malawi. To assess that hypothesis, the data are examined by age group and sex. Children are divided into four age groups: under 12 months; 12-23 months; 24-35 months; and 36-59 months. An examination of the proportion of children classified as undernourished by age gives an indication of whether there are changes in patterns of undernutrition as children grow older. Tables 45, 46 and 47 present the proportions of children classified as stunted, underweight and wasted by sex and age group, and the results are summarized in figures 33, 34 and 35. The mean Z-scores for the three measures of nutritional status are not presented, but they reveal similar patterns of sex differences to those derived from the measures displayed in tables 45-47.

1. Children under 12 months of age

Among children under 12 months of age, 6-36 per cent of boys and 4-29 per cent of girls are classified as stunted (table 45). For half of the 41 surveys considered, at least 13.6 per cent of boys under 12 months of age and 11.2 per cent of girls are deemed to be stunted. High proportions of infants experiencing stunting are particularly common in sub-Saharan Africa and Southern Asia . The difference between the percentage of boys classified as stunted and that of girls is positive in 36 out of 41 surveys, suggesting that there is generally less stunting among girls than among boys under one year of age. That finding is further buttressed by the fact that the difference between the percentage of boys and that of girls considered stunted exceeds 4 percentage points in 13 of the 36 surveys with a positive difference. In contrast, in the five surveys where girls experience higher levels of stunting than boys—Bolivia (1993-1994); Colombia, Egypt (1992), Jordan and Tunisia—the largest difference observed is only 2 percentage points.

With respect to weight, differences in the percentage of boys and girls considered underweight also tend to be positive, and suggest that girls are less likely to be underweight than boys in infancy (table 46). However, among the 31 surveys where underweight levels are higher among boys than among girls, differences of 4 percentage points or more in favour of girls are found in only five surveys. In contrast, differences in favour of boys are recorded in 10 surveys but exceeded 2 percentage points only in Colombia and Paraguay.

In terms of wasting levels, the differences between boys and girls during the first year of life are smaller than those for stunting and underweight (table 47). But once again, most of the surveys considered show that levels of wasting are higher among boys than among girls (26 surveys out of 41). Among the remaining surveys, 14 indicate that a higher percentage of girls than of boys under the age of one are wasted but the differences are below 1 percentage point in most cases.

2. Children 12-23 months of age

With regard to stunting, only seven surveys show that girls between the exact ages of one and two years are more likely to experience stunting than boys of the same age group; however, the differences between the percentage of boys and girls experiencing stunting tend to be small, ranging from -0.3 to -2.9 percentage points (table 45). In contrast, among the 34 surveys that show a greater likelihood of stunting among boys aged 12-23 months than among girls, the differences

TABLE 45. STUNTING AMONG CHILDREN ACCORDING TO AGE: IN EACH AGE GROUP,
THE PERCENTAGE WHO WERE CLASSIFIED AS STUNTED

| | | Stunting: Percentage whose height-for-age Z-score is below -2 SD* from Reference Population Median | | | | | | | | | | | |
| | | Males | | | | Females | | | | Difference: Males - Females | | | |
Country or area	Year of survey	<12 months	12-23 months	24-35 months	36-59 months	<12 months	12-23 months	24-35 months	36-59 months	<12 months	12-23 months	24-35 months	36-59 months
Sub-Saharan Africa													
Burkina Faso	1992-1993	9.6	43.7	41.1	43.0	8.4	36.1	44.0	40.7	1.2	7.6	-3.0	2.3
Burundi	1987	32.5	47.8	60.6	-	29.1	50.7	58.1	-	3.4	-2.9	2.5	-
Cameroon	1991	10.1	35.0	28.4	33.8	6.9	27.6	36.0	30.3	3.1	7.5	-7.5	3.5
Ghana	1988	10.6	35.4	42.1	-	10.3	30.8	42.7	-	0.4	4.7	-0.5	-
	1993	8.2	37.1	40.8	-	7.2	30.5	36.9	-	1.0	6.6	3.9	-
Kenya	1993	16.1	47.3	36.2	39.9	12.5	34.0	40.4	32.9	3.6	13.3	-4.2	7.0
Madagascar	1992	28.7	66.1	61.5	66.0	23.6	60.1	61.8	61.8	5.1	6.0	-0.3	4.2
Malawi	1992	22.5	57.3	61.1	64.3	16.2	47.7	57.9	63.0	6.4	9.6	3.1	1.3
Mali	1987	15.3	29.7	32.1	-	10.2	32.5	34.3	-	5.2	-2.8	-2.2	-
Namibia	1992	19.1	41.4	33.4	29.8	18.1	33.8	32.3	25.1	1.0	7.6	1.1	4.7
Niger	1992	15.5	51.1	54.1	48.1	13.0	47.2	51.0	48.8	2.4	3.8	3.1	-0.7
Ondo State, Nigeria	1986-1987	12.0	34.1	44.8	-	9.8	29.9	49.6	-	2.3	4.2	-4.7	-
Nigeria	1990	18.9	46.2	52.0	55.0	15.7	42.8	54.6	53.4	3.2	3.5	-2.6	1.6
Rwanda	1992	25.8	58.4	49.7	59.9	17.9	51.6	51.3	59.3	7.9	6.9	-1.6	0.7
Senegal	1986	9.1	29.2	33.3	-	8.0	25.0	24.3	-	1.1	4.2	9.0	-
	1992-1993	12.3	28.2	33.8	29.9	6.8	27.2	29.0	30.6	5.5	1.0	4.8	-0.7
United Rep. of Tanzania	1991-1992	22.2	54.6	47.2	52.3	17.6	45.9	50.5	51.4	4.7	8.7	-3.2	0.9
Togo	1988	18.3	40.5	37.8	-	12.4	34.2	35.2	-	5.9	6.3	2.6	-
Uganda	1988-1989	23.0	56.8	52.5	55.2	19.7	49.2	51.9	47.0	3.3	7.5	0.7	8.1
Zambia	1992	17.4	48.1	50.8	48.9	14.1	47.9	48.2	44.4	3.3	0.3	2.7	4.5
Zimbabwe	1988-1989	18.0	35.7	36.5	28.5	16.2	30.1	36.3	27.1	1.8	5.6	0.1	1.4
Western Asia and Northern Africa													
Egypt	1988-1989	24.9	37.0	29.1	-	19.6	35.3	36.0	-	5.2	1.7	-6.9	-
	1992	13.1	38.7	30.2	23.8	13.5	39.2	28.5	23.6	-0.4	-0.4	1.7	0.2
Jordan	1990	8.4	22.9	13.9	17.7	10.8	22.3	15.7	14.0	-2.4	0.5	-1.8	3.7
Morocco	1987	10.9	30.5	28.1	29.6	9.3	29.5	31.0	29.7	1.6	1.0	-2.9	-0.1
	1992	10.0	28.5	29.7	26.3	6.5	29.7	31.4	26.0	3.5	-1.2	-1.7	0.3
Tunisia	1988	10.4	19.3	20.7	-	10.6	20.0	23.7	-	-0.2	-0.7	-3.1	-
Turkey	1993	7.3	20.1	21.9	28.6	5.7	18.7	22.7	26.6	1.6	1.4	-0.8	2.1
Other Asia													
Pakistan	1990	25.2	53.1	56.2	63.0	19.7	50.3	57.4	60.4	5.5	2.8	-1.1	2.5
Sri Lanka	1987	14.9	31.5	28.5	-	10.6	29.9	39.8	-	4.3	1.6	-11.3	-
Thailand	1987	13.0	22.6	27.6	-	9.4	23.7	26.6	-	3.6	-1.1	1.0	-
Latin America and the Caribbean													
Bolivia	1989	17.7	44.6	50.0	-	15.9	38.8	50.3	-	1.8	5.8	-0.4	-
	1993-1994	10.9	39.3	31.5	-	11.2	37.0	31.2	-	-0.3	2.4	0.3	-
Brazil (north-east)	1986	21.2	42.4	26.5	35.3	9.4	32.4	35.0	28.1	11.8	10.0	-8.5	7.2
Colombia	1986	13.6	25.1	37.7	-	14.9	24.6	30.5	-	-1.3	0.5	7.2	-
Dominican Republic	1986	12.1	26.1	29.9	-	7.9	17.8	21.0	-	4.2	8.4	9.0	-
	1991	13.6	25.7	13.0	16.7	11.9	16.3	17.9	15.8	1.7	9.3	-4.9	0.9
Guatemala	1987	35.5	70.8	66.6	-	29.3	68.1	68.5	-	6.1	2.7	-1.9	-
Paraguay	1990	8.8	25.4	12.2	11.9	8.2	22.7	11.9	12.7	0.6	2.7	0.3	-0.8
Peru	1991-1992	12.9	36.0	34.8	39.2	10.6	29.6	36.9	39.5	2.3	6.3	-2.1	-0.3
Trinidad and Tobago	1987	6.1	5.2	3.9	-	3.8	5.5	4.1	-	2.2	-0.3	-0.2	-
Median value		13.6	37.0	34.8	37.3	11.2	32.4	36.0	31.8	-	-	-	-

Source: Demographic and Health Surveys data.

NOTE: Height-for-age index expressed in terms of the number of standard deviation (SD) units from the median of the WHO/CDC/NCHS international reference population; children are classified as stunted if their height-for-age Z-score is below minus two (-2) SD from the median of the reference population.

* Standard deviation.

146

TABLE 46. UNDERWEIGHT AMONG CHILDREN ACCORDING TO AGE: IN EACH AGE GROUP,
THE PERCENTAGE WHO WERE CLASSIFIED AS UNDERWEIGHT

		Underweight: Percentage whose weight-for-age Z-score is below -2 SD[a] from Reference Population Median											
		Males				Females				Difference: Males - Females			
Country or area	Year of survey	<12 months	12-23 months	24-35 months	36-59 months	<12 months	12-23 months	24-35 months	36-59 months	<12 months	12-23 months	24-35 months	36-59 months
Sub-Saharan Africa													
Burkina Faso	1992-1993	17.3	52.6	41.9	28.5	15.3	47.4	43.2	29.4	2.0	5.3	-1.3	-0.8
Burundi	1987	23.2	42.5	44.3	-	23.9	44.1	43.6	-	-0.7	-1.7	0.6	-
Cameroon	1991	8.2	23.1	13.5	11.5	10.1	23.4	21.0	14.2	-1.9	-0.3	-7.5	-2.7
Ghana	1988	16.1	39.2	32.5	-	14.8	37.5	36.2	-	1.3	1.7	-3.7	-
	1993	14.8	37.4	36.1	-	12.6	31.2	35.9	-	2.2	6.2	0.2	-
Kenya	1993	12.8	34.6	25.9	24.3	9.8	28.0	28.0	18.9	3.0	6.6	-2.0	5.4
Madagascar	1992	22.3	54.1	46.0	44.5	18.7	50.7	45.9	45.2	3.6	3.4	0.1	-0.7
Malawi	1992	15.2	40.5	37.9	26.1	12.1	35.9	33.2	28.1	3.1	4.7	4.7	-2.0
Mali	1987	21.2	39.4	32.7	-	20.5	41.6	34.1	-	0.7	-2.2	-1.4	-
Namibia	1992	12.1	37.1	32.5	29.0	12.5	34.9	33.3	24.6	-0.4	2.2	-0.8	4.4
Niger	1992	20.6	65.8	54.9	39.1	21.8	63.8	57.2	40.3	-1.2	2.0	-2.3	-1.2
Ondo State, Nigeria	1986-1987	18.4	29.5	31.1	-	14.6	27.6	36.2	-	3.7	1.9	-5.0	-
Nigeria	1990	20.0	48.0	44.2	35.3	17.0	42.7	46.4	37.7	2.9	5.3	-2.2	-2.5
Rwanda	1992	17.0	41.6	30.4	28.0	16.6	36.3	32.5	32.3	0.4	5.3	-2.1	-4.2
Senegal	1986	3.9	30.6	31.0	-	5.3	26.6	22.4	-	-1.4	4.0	8.6	-
	1992-1993	10.4	33.1	29.3	23.3	8.0	27.7	27.2	23.7	2.4	5.4	2.1	-0.4
United Rep. of Tanzania	1991-1992	18.1	40.2	30.7	27.6	16.8	33.9	35.0	30.8	1.3	6.3	-4.3	-3.2
Togo	1988	15.8	35.3	25.2	-	11.6	31.6	29.6	-	4.2	3.8	-4.4	-
Uganda	1988-1989	14.2	34.5	22.7	21.3	12.6	28.7	29.4	23.6	1.6	5.8	-6.7	-2.4
Zambia	1992	12.1	37.9	34.4	22.3	10.5	33.8	33.9	23.4	1.5	4.0	0.5	-1.1
Zimbabwe	1988-1989	3.4	19.1	16.3	8.1	5.1	11.9	16.5	11.3	-1.7	7.2	-0.2	-3.2
Western Asia and Northern Africa													
Egypt	1988-1989	12.6	18.7	9.5	-	11.6	14.8	11.9	-	1.0	3.9	-2.4	-
	1992	8.2	15.2	13.1	6.2	7.9	17.1	12.1	6.9	0.3	-2.0	1.0	-0.8
Jordan	1990	3.6	8.6	6.9	6.9	4.5	5.9	6.7	6.9	-0.9	2.8	0.1	-0.0
Morocco	1987	7.2	17.6	16.0	9.8	6.0	17.9	15.9	11.5	1.2	-0.3	0.1	-1.6
	1992	5.5	13.4	13.5	8.9	5.3	11.3	11.9	8.0	0.2	2.1	1.5	1.0
Tunisia	1988	7.6	12.7	10.6	-	8.1	11.1	10.4	-	-0.4	1.6	0.2	-
Turkey	1993	5.9	13.0	12.0	10.4	5.6	10.0	13.3	12.0	0.3	3.0	-1.2	-1.6
Other Asia													
Pakistan	1990-1991	25.5	46.1	44.9	45.2	21.4	39.8	46.7	47.3	4.1	6.3	-1.7	-2.1
Sri Lanka	1987	18.7	45.8	41.5	-	13.3	38.3	53.8	-	5.4	7.6	-12.3	-
Thailand	1987	15.2	25.6	32.5	-	9.3	33.4	28.3	-	5.9	-7.7	4.2	-
Latin America and the Caribbean													
Bolivia	1989	6.7	23.6	11.0	-	6.5	13.8	13.1	-	0.2	9.8	-2.1	-
	1993-1994	8.7	21.3	15.8	-	6.2	19.7	17.4	-	2.5	1.6	-1.6	-
Brazil (north-east)	1986	9.7	23.7	8.8	10.2	6.8	13.0	17.5	13.6	2.9	10.8	-8.7	-3.4
Colombia	1986	5.1	13.0	13.4	-	9.0	14.2	14.2	-	-3.9	-1.2	-0.8	-
Dominican Republic	1986	9.0	15.0	16.6	-	4.9	10.4	14.0	-	4.0	4.6	2.6	-
	1991	8.7	17.4	10.3	8.9	5.5	10.1	14.1	9.1	3.2	7.3	-3.8	-0.1
Guatemala	1987	14.8	44.3	35.8	-	13.6	44.1	40.8	-	1.3	0.2	-5.0	-
Paraguay	1990	2.0	7.5	1.9	2.1	4.3	6.3	3.6	3.2	-2.2	1.2	-1.7	-1.1
Peru	1991-1992	6.0	17.8	12.8	10.5	4.1	14.0	13.3	9.4	2.0	3.8	-0.5	1.1
Trinidad and Tobago	1987	6.1	6.5	5.5	-	4.8	12.3	3.5	-	1.3	-5.9	2.0	-
Median value		12.1	30.6	25.9	21.8	10.1	27.7	28.0	21.2	-	-	-	-

Source: Demographic and Health Surveys data.

NOTE: Weight-for-age index expressed in terms of the number of standard deviation (SD) units from the median of the WHO/CDC/NCHS international reference population; children are classified as underweight if their weight-for-age Z-score is below minus two (-2) SD from the median of the reference population.

[a]Standard deviation.

147

TABLE 47. WASTING AMONG CHILDREN ACCORDING TO AGE: IN EACH AGE GROUP,
THE PERCENTAGE WHO WERE CLASSIFIED AS WASTED

| | | Wasting: Percentage whose weight-for-height Z-score is below -2 SD[a] from Reference Population Median | | | | | | | | | | | |
| | | Males | | | | Females | | | | Difference: Males - Females | | | |
Country or area	Year of survey	<12 months	12-23 months	24-35 months	36-59 months	<12 months	12-23 months	24-35 months	36-59 months	<12 months	12-23 months	24-35 months	36-59 months
Sub-Saharan Africa													
Burkina Faso	1992-1993	15.5	26.0	10.6	5.2	12.9	26.4	11.1	6.4	2.6	-0.4	-0.5	-1.2
Burundi	1987	3.3	10.8	4.7	-	3.4	9.9	2.1	-	-0.1	0.9	2.6	-
Cameroon	1991	1.8	8.6	1.7	0.7	2.3	5.8	2.1	1.6	-0.5	2.8	-0.4	-0.9
Ghana	1988	8.4	14.7	3.2	-	3.0	14.8	1.6	-	5.4	-0.1	1.6	-
	1993	11.5	17.4	6.1	-	8.1	16.8	8.0	-	3.4	0.6	-1.9	-
Kenya	1993	4.3	10.5	5.4	5.5	4.7	9.5	5.1	3.8	-0.3	0.9	0.3	1.7
Madagascar	1992	4.1	10.1	4.0	2.9	3.2	9.5	3.0	2.3	0.8	0.5	1.0	0.6
Malawi	1992	4.4	12.2	6.3	3.0	5.0	10.1	1.6	3.4	-0.6	2.1	4.7	-0.4
Mali	1987	10.3	20.8	10.2	-	5.4	16.1	3.6	-	4.8	4.7	6.6	-
Namibia	1992	5.9	13.0	8.5	7.9	6.0	12.2	8.2	7.8	-0.1	0.9	0.3	0.2
Niger	1992	13.4	31.0	11.5	8.9	10.1	35.3	14.5	6.0	3.4	-4.3	-3.1	3.0
Ondo State, Nigeria	1986-1987	2.5	10.5	4.1	-	5.5	6.3	5.4	-	-3.0	4.2	-1.2	-
Nigeria	1990	10.4	18.9	7.3	5.1	5.7	12.6	8.9	7.3	4.8	6.3	-1.5	-2.2
Rwanda	1992	6.5	8.4	3.6	1.2	6.3	6.3	2.2	0.3	0.2	2.1	1.5	0.9
Senegal	1986	3.9	10.4	8.0	-	0.0	7.0	1.9	-	3.9	3.4	6.2	-
	1992-1993	9.4	17.8	6.7	6.5	5.7	13.6	7.8	4.3	3.7	4.1	-1.1	2.2
United Rep. of Tanzania	1991-1992	5.3	11.0	6.6	4.2	3.5	8.6	5.0	4.9	1.8	2.4	1.6	-0.7
Togo	1988	2.5	11.6	5.0	-	2.4	8.0	2.6	-	0.1	3.6	2.4	-
Uganda	1988-1989	0.6	4.0	1.4	1.6	0.6	4.4	1.4	1.5	-0.1	-0.4	-0.0	0.2
Zambia	1992	3.3	10.6	4.4	2.7	4.5	9.3	5.3	3.5	-1.2	1.3	-0.9	-0.7
Zimbabwe	1988-1989	0.0	3.0	1.4	1.0	1.0	1.0	0.7	1.8	-1.0	2.0	0.6	-0.8
Western Asia and Northern Africa													
Egypt	1988-1989	2.6	1.9	0.0	-	0.5	1.3	0.4	-	2.1	0.6	-0.4	-
	1992	4.0	4.8	3.4	2.4	4.4	4.8	3.1	2.7	-0.4	0.0	0.3	-0.3
Jordan	1990	4.7	4.1	2.9	3.5	4.0	2.8	1.8	1.9	0.7	1.2	1.1	1.6
Morocco	1987	3.3	6.4	1.9	1.6	3.3	5.1	1.1	1.3	0.0	1.3	0.8	0.3
	1992	4.4	2.9	2.3	1.6	2.7	1.5	1.6	1.9	1.8	1.4	0.7	-0.3
Tunisia	1988	6.2	5.1	0.6	-	2.6	1.9	2.1	-	3.7	3.2	-1.5	-
Turkey	1993	4.0	5.0	3.6	2.0	1.0	5.0	2.1	2.4	3.0	-0.0	1.5	-0.3
Other Asia													
Pakistan	1990-1991	10.1	12.8	9.7	9.0	9.1	9.0	9.5	6.7	1.0	3.8	0.2	2.3
Sri Lanka	1987	4.0	20.1	8.8	-	1.3	18.5	11.3	-	2.7	1.6	-2.5	-
Thailand	1987	0.8	10.5	2.6	-	1.6	10.4	2.5	-	-0.7	0.2	0.1	-
Latin America and the Caribbean													
Bolivia	1989	10.8	2.9	0.9	-	2.4	1.2	1.2	-	-1.6	1.7	-0.3	-
	1993-1994	3.4	6.7	5.6	-	2.8	3.6	2.9	-	0.6	3.1	2.7	-
Brazil (north-east)	1986	2.7	2.5	0.0	0.9	0.0	1.9	0.0	0.4	2.7	0.7	0.0	0.4
Colombia	1986	1.9	0.9	1.7	-	1.8	1.6	0.4	-	0.1	-0.6	1.3	-
Dominican Republic	1986	5.8	4.4	1.3	-	0.8	1.4	1.3	-	5.0	3.1	0.1	-
	1991	1.4	1.5	0.4	1.7	0.5	0.9	3.1	1.6	0.8	0.7	-2.7	0.1
Guatemala	1987	0.3	2.3	0.5	-	0.9	3.3	0.3	-	-0.6	-0.9	0.3	-
Paraguay	1990	0.1	0.3	0.1	0.3	0.3	0.6	0.1	0.6	-0.1	-0.3	0.0	-0.2
Peru	1991-1992	2.0	3.2	1.6	1.2	0.8	2.9	1.7	1.0	1.2	0.3	-0.2	0.2
Trinidad and Tobago	1987	4.3	3.2	3.9	-	3.8	5.5	2.4	-	0.5	-2.3	1.6	-
Median value		4.0	8.6	3.6	2.6	3.0	6.3	2.2	2.4	-	-	-	-

Source: Demographic and Health Surveys data.
NOTE: Weight-for-height index expressed in terms of the number of standard deviation (SD) units from the median of the WHO/CDC/NCHS international reference population; children are classified as wasted if their weight-for-height Z-score is below minus two (-2) SD from the median of the reference population.
[a] Standard deviation.

between the sexes tend to be higher, ranging from 0.3 to 13.3 percentage points. Moreover, the differences exceed 4 percentage points in 20 cases mostly for surveys carried out in sub-Saharan Africa. Among the 21 surveys carried out in that region, 16 show an increase in the difference between the proportion of boys and that of girls suffering from stunting as age increases, suggesting that the weaker position of boys relative to girls in that regard worsens as they pass from the first to the second year of life. In Latin America and the Caribbean, similar trends are noticeable in most cases, with the exception of north-eastern Brazil, Guatemala, and Trinidad and Tobago. In Northern Africa and Asia, only one country—Jordan—shows a deterioration of the status of boys relative to girls with respect to stunting as they pass from the first to the second year of life.

In terms of weight, an examination of the differences by sex in the percentage of children aged 12-23 months classified as underweight shows similar differentials as those noted in the case of stunting. In half of the surveys, at least 31 per cent of the boys in their second year of life are underweight, whereas the equivalent figure is 28 per cent for girls (table 46). Eight of the 41 surveys indicate that the proportion underweight is higher among girls than among boys, whereas the reverse is true for the remaining 33 surveys. Among the latter, the difference in favour of girls is at least 4 percentage points in 18 cases. In contrast, among the eight surveys in which girls display higher percentages of underweight cases than boys, the difference exceeds 4 percentage points only in two countries: Thailand, and Trinidad and Tobago.

With regard to wasting, the percentage of boys aged 12-23 months that exhibit wasting exceeds 9 per cent in half of the surveys; the corresponding median for girls is 6 per cent (table 47). Wasting affects a smaller proportion of girls than boys in 31 of the 41 surveys, whereas the reverse is true in only eight cases. According to two surveys—Egypt (1992) and Turkey—the difference between boys and girls is virtually nil.

3. Children 24-35 months of age

The relative nutritional situation of boys and girls 24-35 months of age is considerably different from that of younger and older children (table 45). Con-

trary to the findings for younger children, stunting levels among girls exceed those among boys in more than half the surveys (24 out of 41). In 7 of the 24 surveys where there is more stunting among girls than among boys, the difference exceeds 4 percentage points (figure 33). Thus, by the third year of life there are signs that girls are more likely to experience stunting than boys.

Girls aged 24-35 months are also more likely to be underweight than boys in the same age group. In 26 of the 41 surveys, the percentage underweight among girls exceeds that among boys, and in 8 of those the difference is larger than 4 percentage points (table 46). Thus, for both stunting and underweight girls are more likely to be disadvantaged than boys in the third year of life.

With respect to wasting, the number of surveys showing that girls aged 24-35 months are subject to a greater likelihood of wasting than boys is larger than for younger children but does not constitute a majority (14 out of 41 surveys). In contrast, 24 surveys show that boys exhibit higher levels of wasting than girls. Thus, according to that measure the deterioration of the nutritional status of girls as they age is less clear.

4. Children 36-59 months of age

Only 24 surveys collected anthropometric data for children aged 36-59 months. The results available for that group of children are not consistent with the hypothesis that nutritional status among girls deteriorates relative to boys as age increases. With respect to stunting, there are 19 surveys in which stunting levels are higher for boys than for girls but only five surveys in which there is more stunting among girls. Furthermore, when the trend exhibited by the estimates related to children aged 1 year or over is considered, only the surveys for Malawi, the Niger and Paraguay show a consistent deterioration of the status of girls with respect to boys in terms of stunting levels.

The contrasting patterns between the estimates for children aged 24-35 months and those aged 36-59 months raise the issue of whether such contrasts may reflect the lack of information on older children for 15 surveys. However, that selectivity is not the cause of the different patterns detected. Even when the analysis for the three youngest age groups is restricted

Figure 33. Difference between males and females who were classified as stunted by age group

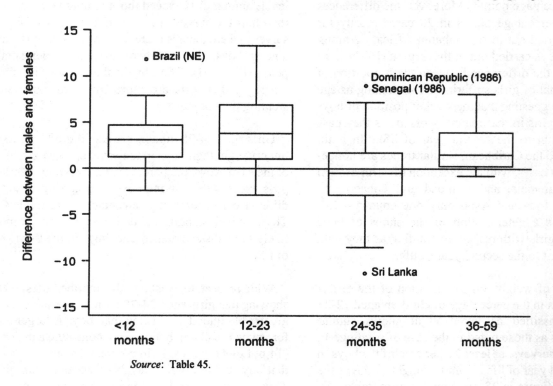

Source: Table 45.

Figure 34. Difference between males and females who were classified as underweight by age group

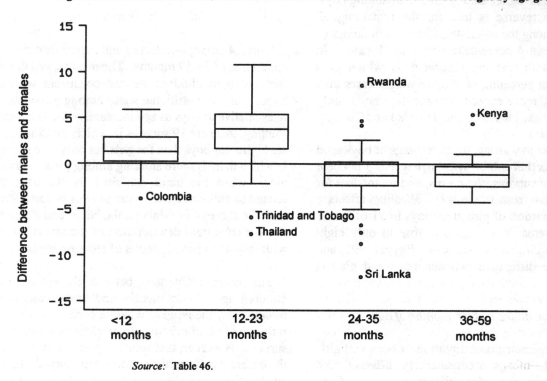

Source: Table 46.

150

Figure 35. Difference between males and females who were classified as wasted by age group

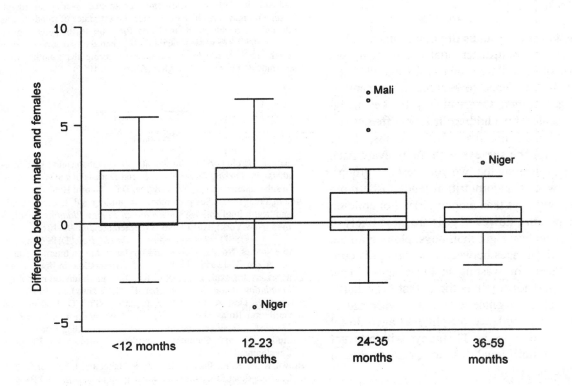

Source: Table 47.

entirely to the 24 surveys with full information, the conclusions are similar to those found for all 41 surveys.

In terms of low weight-for-age, the results are mixed. In 19 of the 24 surveys, the proportion of girls that are underweight is higher than that of boys (table 46). Data on mean weight-for-age Z-scores, however, indicate that the situation of girls aged 36-59 months is more favourable than that of boys in most countries (data not shown).

The data on wasting are shown in table 47. In 11 surveys, the proportion of girls aged 36-59 months that experience wasting is higher than that of boys, but the reverse holds in the remaining 13 surveys. The differences between boys and girls are small. An interesting finding is that with respect to wasting, nine surveys—mostly conducted in sub-Saharan

Africa—show a deterioration of the relative position of girls with respect to boys as they pass from age 1 to age 5.

E. Conclusion

Differences between boys and girls in nutritional status and levels of undernutrition have been analysed for 41 surveys conducted in 34 countries. All of the surveys recorded height and weight measurements of children 3-35 months of age, and 24 of them recorded such measurements for children under five years of age. An analysis of nutritional status by sex of children in those two age groups shows that there are relatively small differences between boys and girls in terms of the prevalence of stunting, underweight and wasting. If anything, the data suggest that girls are less likely to be undernourished than boys. Those

151

findings are corroborated by the mean Z-scores. Those findings are consistent with an earlier study based on a subset of the data presented here (Sommerfelt and Stewart, 1994).

Since the nutritional status of young infants is less likely to depend upon differential treatment by sex than that of older children, any unfavourable treatment of girls is expected to become more manifest as children grow older. Consequently, the key analyses were repeated for children in four different age groups: under 12 months; 12-23 months; 24-35 months; and, for the surveys with the relevant data, 36-59 months. Among the two youngest age groups, the data show that undernutrition tends to be more prevalent among boys than among girls. For children aged 24-35 months, however, girls are more likely to be stunted or underweight than boys, although there are no clear differences between boys and girls concerning the level of wasting at those ages. That tentative support for the hypothesis that the relative nutritional status of girls deteriorates with age is not confirmed by evidence for children aged 36-59 months. According to the 24 surveys with relevant data, only small nutritional differences exist between boys and girls in that higher age range.

Among the countries studied, nutritional problems overall are worse in sub-Saharan Africa and South-central Asia (Pakistan and Sri Lanka) than in Latin America, Western Asia or Northern Africa. Every DHS documents some degree of undernutrition relative to the international standard for the growth and development of well-nourished children. With respect to sex differences in nutritional status, however, there is not a single country in which the survey evidence suggests that girls are consistently at a nutritional disadvantage compared with boys. Therefore, despite evidence of discrimination against girls in feeding practices and medical treatment from small-scale studies in countries with a strong preference for sons, those types of discriminatory practices are evidently either not widespread or not sufficiently severe to show up in data on nutritional status at the national level among the 41 populations that form the basis for the present analysis.

NOTE

[1]Surveys were carried out in different seasons in two countries: Ghana and Morocco. There was partial overlap in the months of fieldwork in three countries and completed overlap in Egypt. Seasonality may have had some effect on estimates of trends but its influence is probably small. In Ghana, for example, the percentage of children that were wasted increased between the two surveys, even though the first survey was conducted during the months when undernutrition is generally higher (Alderman, 1990).

REFERENCES

Alderman, Harold (1990). Nutritional status in Ghana and its determinants. In *Working Paper No. 3*, Social Dimensions of Adjustment in sub-Saharan Africa. Washington, D.C.: World Bank.

Arnold, Fred (1992). Sex preference for children and its demographic and health implications. *International Family Planning Perspectives* (New York), vol. 18, No. 3 (September), pp. 93-101.

_____ (1997). *Gender preference for children*. DHS Comparative Studies, No. 25. Calverton Maryland: Macro International.

Basu, Alaka Malwade (1989). Is discrimination in food really necessary for explaining sex differentials in childhood mortality? *Population Studies* (London), vol. 43, No. 2 (July), pp. 193-210.

Boerma, J. Ties, A. Elisabeth Sommerfelt, Shea O. Rutstein and Guillermo Rojas (1991). *Childhood Morbidity and Treatment Patterns in Demographic and Health Surveys*. DHS Comparative Studies, No. 4. Columbia, Maryland: Institute for Resource Development.

Brown, K. H., R. E. Black, S. Becker, S. Nahar and J. Sawyer (1982). Consumption of foods and nutrients by weanlings in rural Bangladesh. *American Journal of Clinical Nutrition* (Bethesda, Maryland), vol. 36, No. 5 (November), pp. 878-889.

Chen, Lincoln C., Emdadul Huq and Stan D'Souza (1981). Sex bias in the family allocation of food and health care in rural Bangladesh. *Population and Development Review* (New York), vol. 7, No. 1 (March), pp. 55-70.

Chirmulay, D., and R. Nisal (1993). Nutritional status of tribal underfive children in Ahmadnagar District, Maharashtra in relation to weaning/feeding practices. *Indian Paediatrics* (New Delhi, India), vol. 30, No. 2 (February), pp. 215-222.

Das Gupta, Monica (1987). Selective discrimination against female children in rural Punjab. *Population and Development Review* (New York), vol. 13, No. 1 (March), pp. 77-100.

Deolalikar, Anil B., and Prem Vashishta (1992). The utilization of government and private health services in India. Report prepared under the Options Project. Washington, D.C.: The Futures Group.

Froozani, M. D., H. Malekafzali and B. Bahrini (1980). Growth of low income infants in the first year of life. *Journal of Tropical Pediatrics* (Oxford), vol. 26 No. 3 (June), pp. 96-98.

Gracey, M., H. Sullivan, V. Burke and D. Gracey (1992). Maternal and environmental factors associated with infections and undernutrition in young Australian aboriginal children. *Annals of Tropical Paediatrics* (Abingdon, United Kingdom), vol. 12, No. 1, pp. 111-119.

Hossain, M. M., and R. I. Glass (1988). Parental son preference in seeking medical care for children less than five years of age in a rural community in Bangladesh. *American Journal of Public Health* (Washington, D.C.), vol. 78, No. 10 (October), pp. 1349-1350

Jejeebhoy, Shireen J. (1991). Women's roles: health and reproductive behaviour. In *The Demographic Challenge: A Study of Four Large Indian States*, J. K. Satia and Shireen Jejeebhoy, eds. Bombay: Oxford University Press.

Khan, M. E., Richard Anker, S. K. Ghosh Dastidar and Sashi Bairathi (1988). Inequalities between men and women in nutrition and family welfare services: an in-depth enquiry in an Indian village. *Social Action* (New Delhi, India), vol. 38, pp. 398-417.

Locoh, Thérèse (1987). La répartition par sexe des enfants hospitalisés à Lomé (Togo). *Population* (Paris, France), vol. 42, No. 3 (May-June), pp. 549-557.

Makinson, Carolyn (1986). Sex differentials in infant and child mortality in Egypt. Princeton, New Jersey: Princeton University. Unpublished doctoral dissertation.

Miller, B. D. (1981). *The Endangered Sex: Neglect of Female Children in Rural North India*. Ithaca, New York: Cornell University Press.

Pelletier, David L., and L. A. Msukwa (1991). The use of national sample surveys for nuitritional surveillance: Lessons from Malawi's National Sample Survey of Agriculture. *Social Science and Medicine*, vol. 32, No. 8, pp. 887-898.

Rankins, J., N. R. Green, W. Tremper, M. Stacewitcz-Sapuntzakis, P. Bowen and M. Ndiaye (1993). Undernutrition and vitamin A deficiency in the Department of Linguère, Louga Region of Sénégal. *American Journal of Clinical Nutrition* (Bethesda, Maryland), vol. 58, No. 1 (July), pp. 91-97.

Rao, S., and A. N. Kanade (1992). Prolonged breastfeeding and malnutrition among rural Indian children below 3 years of age. *European Journal of Clinical Nutrition* (Basingstoke, United Kingdom), vol. 46, No. 3 (March), pp. 187-195.

Ravindran, S. (1986). Health implications of sex discrimination in childhood: a review paper and an annotated bibliography. Unpublished paper. World Health Organization/United Nations Children's Fund.

Roberts, A. B., P. Roberts, T. Tiva and K. Tulimanu (1981). Malnutrition and anaemia in Gilbertese preschool children: a case finding and epidemiological survey. *Journal of Tropical Pedictrics* (Oxford), vol. 27, No. 2 (April), pp. 78-82.

Sabir, N. I., and G. J. Ebrahim (1984). Are daughters more at risk than sons in some societies? *Journal of Tropical Pediatrics* (Oxford), vol. 30, No. 4 (August), pp. 237-239.

Schoenbaum, Michael, Theodore H. Tulchinsky and Yehia Abed (1995). Gender differences in nutritional status and feeding patterns among infants in the Gaza Strip. *American Journal of Public Health* (Washington, D.C.), vol. 85, No. 7 (July), pp. 965-969.

Sebai, Z. A., and W. A. Reinke (1981). Anthropometric measurements among pre-school children in Wadi Turaba, Saudi Arabia. *Journal of Tropical Pediatrics* (Oxford), vol. 27, pp. 150-154.

Sommerfelt, A. Elisabeth, and J. Ties Boerma (1993). Anthropometric status of young children in DHS surveys: An assessment of data quality. In *An Assessment of the Quality of the Health Data in DHS-I Surveys*. DHS Methodological Reports, No. 2. Calverton, Maryland: Macro International, Inc.

Sommerfelt, A. Elisabeth, and M Kathryn Stewart (1994). *Children's Nutritional Status*. DHS Comparative Studies, No. 12. Calverton, Maryland: Macro International.

Svedberg, P. (1990). Undernutrition in sub-Saharan Africa: Is there a gender bias? *Journal of Development Studies* (London, England), vol. 26, No. 3 (April), pp. 469-486.

United Nations (1986). *How to Weigh and Measure Children: Assessing the Nutritional Status of Young Children in Household Surveys*. Sales No. E.88.IV.2.

Visweswara Rao, K., and N. Balakrishna (1990). Discriminant function analysis: a case study of some socioeconomic constraints on child nutrition. *Indian Journal of Medical Research [B]* (New Delhi, India), vol. 92, pp. 66-71.

Waldron, Ingrid (1987). Patterns and causes of excess female mortality among children in developing countries. *World Health Statistics Quarterly* (Geneva), vol. 40, No. 3, pp. 194-210.

Wardlaw, Tessa (1992). *Child Malnutrition: Country Profiles*. New York: United Nations Children's Fund.

Williamson, Nancy E. (1976). *Sons and Daughters: A Cross-cultural Survey of Parental Preferences*. Beverly Hills, California: Sage Publications.

Wolde-Gebriel, Z., H. Gebru, T. Fisseha and C. E. West (1993). Severe vitamin A deficiency in a rural village in the Harare Region of Ethiopia. *European Journal of Clinical Nutrition* (Basingstoke, United Kingdom), vol. 47, No. 2 (February), pp. 104-114.

World Health Organization (1986). Use and interpretation of anthropometric indicators of nutritional status. *Bulletin of the World Health Organization* (Geneva), vol. 64, No. 6, pp. 929-941.

VII. CAN USE OF HEALTH CARE EXPLAIN SEX DIFFERENTIALS IN CHILD MORTALITY IN THE DEVELOPING WORLD?

Ian Timæus*, Katie Harris* and Francesca Fairbairn*

The present chapter examines differential use of preventive and curative health-care services by boys and girls. The focus is on children under the age of five years. The analysis is comparative in nature. It is based on the national surveys conducted by the Demographic and Health Surveys (DHS) programme during the past decade, supplemented by the National Family Health Survey (NFHS) of India.

The study of sex differentials in the use of child health services is an important topic in its own right. A right of access to facilities for the treatment of illness and rehabilitation of health is enshrined in the 1989 Convention on the Rights of the Child. In addition, modern health care can play a vital role in reducing susceptibility to disease and in improving the outcome of episodes of disease. If girls have more limited access to health care than boys, their health is likely to suffer.

Undoubtedly, the impact of service provision on child health varies between populations. It is likely to depend on the quality of the care provided, the accessibility of the services, the epidemiological environment within which they operate, and the social, cultural and economic characteristics of the population served. However, the potential efficacy of modern health technologies is not in doubt. Nevertheless, the relationship between sex differentials in service use and differential mortality is complex. Use of preventive and curative health care is only one of many factors affecting children's health. Thus, similar patterns of health care for boys and girls may coexist with differential health outcomes. Moreover, differential health service use may not be reflected directly in health. Its impact may be conditioned by the socialization of boys and girls into different patterns of behaviour or by how they are treated by their parents and other carers.

Excess female childhood mortality is particularly marked in South-central Asia, where it has been a major focus of research interest (Harriss, 1989). Field investigations into the factors responsible have shown that differential allocation of both food and health care is involved (Chen, Huq and D'Souza, 1981). However, recent research has emphasized the importance of health care (Das Gupta, 1987; Basu, 1989). It is argued that differentials in the use of curative health services are both larger and more widespread than those in food allocation, and that better health care is the main mechanism accounting for the more frequent survival of boys.

Limited uptake of preventive and curative care may reflect household and individual level constraints on demand. It may also stem from limited access to services, either because they are simply unavailable or because they are unaffordable or inappropriate. A study in Bangladesh reported lower rates of attendance at a free diarrhoeal disease clinic among girls aged less than 5 years than among boys, and found that that differential was related directly to the distance between the family's residence and the clinic (Rahaman and others, 1982). For distances of less than one mile, 90 per cent of diarrhoeal patients of both sexes were seen. At distances of one to two miles, the proportions fell to 70 per cent of boys and 45 per cent of girls, while at distances of two to three miles, 60 per cent of boys and only 35 per cent of girls were seen. Thus, in at least some populations sex differentials in service use are related inversely to service availability.

At the household level, the costs involved in obtaining care might have a differential impact on health-seeking behaviour for boys and girls. Ware (1981) states that in the Republic of Korea the introduction of a small fee for measles immunizations reduced the

*Centre for Population Studies, London School of Hygiene and Tropical Medicine.

proportion of girls receiving the vaccine more than the proportion of boys; with free immunization, there had been no differential. Economic considerations may also affect the uptake of curative services by sex. Sex differentials in service use may be expected to be larger for more costly types of treatment and for more expensive sources of care. Nevertheless, Chen, Huq and D'Souza (1981) found significant sex differentials in the use of a diarrhoea clinic in Matlab, a rural district in Bangladesh, although both the service and travel to and from the facility were free. They concluded that that pattern reflects the fact that the social, time and indirect costs involved in using the clinic remained considerable. Girls may receive different forms of treatment from boys rather than no treatment at all. In particular, a major advantage of traditional medicines over allopathic treatment can be their ready availability and low cost (Findley and Mbacke, 1993). A longitudinal study of 310 families in Bangladesh found that despite the marked differential by sex in the use of modern facilities, the proportions of boys and girls less than 12 years whose illness received some form of treatment were only slightly different (Koenig and d'Souza, 1986).

The present chapter does not attempt to model the impact of use of health services on child mortality by sex. Instead, the aim is to assess whether inequalities in patterns of health care are large and pervasive enough to be worth pursuing as an important part of the explanation of sex differentials in child mortality. Particular attention is paid to the investigation of three issues. First, the direction and size of sex differentials according to the overall level of service use in a country is assessed. Second, sex differentials in the use of more effective forms of service compared with all types of care are examined. Third, because culture and the status and autonomy of women may to have an important impact on sex differentials in service use, the pattern of differentials between regions of the world is examined.

Much of the literature on the differential use of health services according to sex, usually favouring males, uses terms such as discrimination and bias. Those terms imply an intention to give one child less or poorer health care than another on the grounds of their sex. Evidence from the present study and others shows that boys and girls are sometimes treated differently. Such statistical regularities clearly imply

the existence of social institutions and values that dispose mothers and other carers to act in ways that favour one sex or the other. They need not imply deliberate discrimination. Carers may never have conceptualized the matter in that way. Even if they have, such considerations may not be uppermost in their minds when they are deciding what to do to help a sick child. There is evidence from South-central Asia of deliberate neglect of children with older siblings of the same sex (Das Gupta, 1987; Muhuri and Preston, 1991). Such neglect may not be a widespread phenomenon. The poor have to decide what best to do for sick children, bearing in mind that the financial and other costs involved in seeking treatment often have an immediate adverse impact on other aspects of the family's welfare. The sex of the child may sway some such difficult decisions without that being apparent to the decision maker.

It is also important to recognize that perceptions of the cause of sickness and of the severity of illness influence the treatment of children. Gender may affect those perceptions and lead to sex differentials in the use of certain types and sources of treatment and in the timing of use (Santow, 1995). In Uttar Pradesh, Khan and others (1991) found that girls are treated less often than boys as families believe that they are inherently healthier. Issues of severity and duration of sickness interact. Girls in Uttar Pradesh are treated if their sickness persists. Perceived causes of illness also play a part in deciding which sources of treatment are used. For instance, a study in Gujarat shows that a quack doctor might be preferred to modern medicine if the cause of illness is perceived to be the evil eye (Visaria, 1988). Such diagnoses might be influenced by gender. Moreover, as Basu (1987), points out, a disinclination to take a girl to a doctor—especially a male doctor—may be the result of an over-protective attitude toward daughters rather than one of callousness towards their health. Thus, since the focus in the present chapter is on differences in patterns of parental behaviour and not on parents' intentions, the term discrimination is avoided. Similarly, while patterns of service use by boys and girls undoubtedly reflect the social construction of gender, the data are classified by children's biological sex.

The analysis uses data from 44 national surveys conducted by the DHS programme between 1986 and 1994 (table 48) and from the 1992-1993 NFHS of

TABLE 48. INFANT AND CHILD MORTALITY RATES, BY SEX, FOR THE 10-YEAR PERIOD
PRECEDING THE SURVEY (DHS, 1986-1993)

Region/DHS phase/country or area	Year	Infant mortality rate - $_1q_0$ (per 1,000 live births)		Child mortality rate - $_4q_1$ (per 1,000)	
		Males	Females	Males	Females
Eastern and Southern Africa					
I Botswana	1988	47.7	31.5	18.3	15.8
Burundi	1987	98.8	75.7	101.0	113.8
Kenya	1989	63.0	54.3	35.4	33.2
Uganda	1988/89	111.0	101.7	97.3	86.0
Zimbabwe	1988/89	64.9	49.7	30.2	32.5
II Madagascar	1992	103.2	101.8	85.4	81.9
Malawi	1992	141.0	130.4	125.9	114.4
Namibia	1992	66.6	56.5	29.7	34.3
Rwanda	1992	98.2	82.1	86.6	72.5
United Rep. of Tanzania	1991/92	103.7	95.1	63.2	57.1
Zambia	1992	106.2	90.3	91.3	85.1
Western Africa					
I Ghana	1988	88.8	54.3	78.3	79.4
Liberia	1986	168.0	136.0	89.0	93.0
Mali	1987	138.0	125.0	166.0	174.0
Ondo State, Nigeria	1986	59.0	53.0	58.0	51.0
Senegal	1989/90	98.0	83.6	131.0	129.7
Togo	1988	87.7	78.5	74.9	90.1
II Burkina Faso	1993	114.5	100.3	107.1	110.3
Cameroon	1991	86.4	74.6	63.6	74.8
Niger	1992	135.8	133.0	211.5	231.7
Nigeria	1990	93.7	89.1	117.6	101.5
Senegal	1992/93	83.4	68.7	95.5	79.5
Northern Africa and Western Asia					
I Egypt	1988	95.1	93.4	38.1	46.2
Morocco	1987	83.4	81.4	38.2	39.3
Tunisia .`................	1988	58.0	55.5	18.5	19.2
Sudan (Northern)	1989/90	83.4	70.6	62.2	63.1
II Egypt	1992	84.4	75.3	24.6	36.1
Jordan	1990	36.4	37.3	6.0	5.6
Morocco	1992	68.6	57.4	20.7	23.6
Yemen	1991/92	105.6	90.1	41.0	47.1
South-central and South-eastern Asia					
I Sri Lanka	1989	39.5	24.7	10.1	10.0
Thailand	1987	79.9	31.0	11.0	11.0
II India[a]	1993	88.6	83.9	29.4	42.0
Northern states		78.8	77.9	27.5	41.2
Southern states		72.7	62.0	18.8	23.0
Indonesia	1991	45.0	67.9	36.0	34.8
Pakistan	1990/91	102.1	85.5	22.0	36.5
III Bangladesh	1993/94	107.3	93.4	46.7	62.3
Latin America and the Caribbean					
I Bolivia	1989	105.5	85.5	50.7	51.1
Guatemala	1987	90.0	67.6	43.6	47.0
Mexico	1987	60.1	52.4	14.5	16.5
Peru	1986	83.2	74.8	36.4	41.0
Trinidad and Tobago	1987	28.8	33.5	3.4	3.4
II Colombia	1990	27.2	26.6	11.0	5.6
Dominican Republic	1991	53.3	35.1	17.5	20.4
Paraguay	1990	38.4	32.2	9.6	11.9
Peru	1991/92	68.0	59.0	29.0	31.0

Source: DHS-I, DHS-II and DHS-III country reports, NFHS national and state reports.
[a]The National Family Health Survey of India is not part of the DHS programme but used a similar questionnaire.

India, which adopted a design and questionnaire very similar to that used for DHS studies. Four countries are represented in the results twice because they participated and collected relevant data in both phase I and phase II of the DHS programme: Egypt, Morocco, Peru and Senegal. In addition, Ondo State in Nigeria is represented in phase I and the whole country in phase II. Results for northern India and southern India are presented separately, using a classification proposed by Dyson and Moore (1983) that reflects differences within India in the status and autonomy of women. Since state-level data were only available for 19 large states northern India is represented by Assam, Bihar, Delhi, Gujarat, Harayana, Himachal Pradesh, Jammu, Madhya Pradesh, Punjab, Rajasthan and Uttar Pradesh. Southern India comprises Andhra Pradesh, Gujarat, Karnataka, Kerala, Maharashtra, Orissa, Tamil Nadu and West Bengal. The all-India statistics incorporate data from the less populous states in northeast India but not from Kashmir.

The countries for which data are available are not a representative sample of all countries in the developing world. China has not participated in the DHS programme, and other parts of Eastern Asia are also under represented. In contrast, sub-Saharan African countries are heavily overrepresented. Most DHS surveys collected data from mothers on the immunization of children, on the recent prevalence of diarrhoea among children and on how that was treated. However, some DHS-I surveys in Latin America did not ask those questions. The core questionnaires also include questions about fever and cough. They have been used most often in sub-Saharan Africa and were also asked in India.

Interpretation of retrospective interview data on morbidity and service use is far from straightforward. Comparison across countries is obstructed by biased recall by respondents; the difficulty of translating questions about symptoms without modifying their meaning; and cultural variation in the salience of different symptoms (Assogba, Campbell and Hill, 1989). Although the focus of the present study on the comparison of results for boys and girls should avoid some of those problems, one influence on mothers' reports about the health of their children may be the sex of the child in question.

Most of the data presented here are culled from the first reports on the DHS and NFHS surveys or from other DHS publications. Few of those reports present confidence intervals for the estimates. For the present analysis, the significance of differences by sex has been calculated by assuming that the surveys used simple random sampling. They did not. Thus, the results will exaggerate the number of significant differences between the health care of boys and girls. Bearing that in mind, the overall pattern of the results is emphasized more than the findings for individual countries and aspects of health care.

The level of infant mortality varies greatly among the 41 countries (table 48). Based on data for the 10 years before the survey, the median infant mortality rate is 80 per 1,000 live births. In Colombia and Trinidad and Tobago, fewer than one in 30 children die before their first birthday, while in Liberia, nearly one child in six dies by age 1. The level of mortality after infancy is even more variable. Colombia, Jordan, and Trinidad and Tobago have the lowest levels of child mortality, with less than one child in a 100 dying between the age of one and five years. In contrast, child mortality remains high in most of tropical Africa: in the Niger, one in five children die between their first and fifth birthdays.

Sex differentials in infant and child mortality also vary greatly across the sample of countries analysed here. Only Jordan, Trinidad and Tobago, and half the northern Indian states have higher female than male mortality in infancy, but the excess mortality of boys is small in the three Northern African countries considered, Colombia, the Niger and the rest of Northern India. In contrast, mortality between the first and fifth birthdays is higher for girls than boys in the majority of the countries. Figure 36 summarizes regional patterns in the ratios of male to female child mortality in the form of box and whisker plots, which show the median, upper and lower quartile and extreme values of the ratios for countries within each region. In comparison with the historical experience of European countries, where girls usually had lower mortality than boys, the excess in girls' child mortality is even more marked (Hill and Upchurch, 1995). Most Northern African, Western and South-central Asian and Latin American countries, together with

Figure 36. Ratio of male to female childhood mortality (4q1), by region

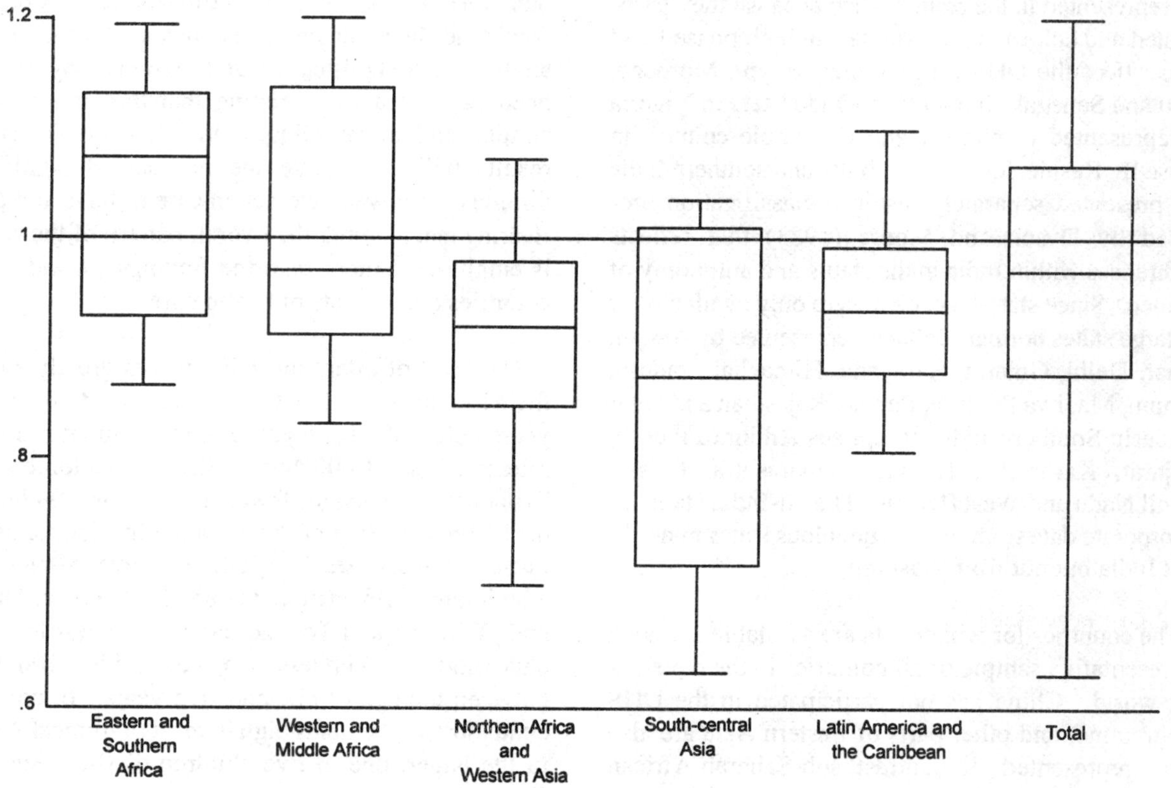

Sources: DHS-I, DHS-II and DHS-III country reports, NFHS national and state reports.

some sub-Saharan African countries, have higher female than male mortality. Higher mortality among boys is found in most of sub-Saharan Africa, Colombia, Indonesia, Jordan and Sri Lanka.

B. IMMUNIZATION

The present section investigates immunization coverage among boys and girls. The focus is on vaccines delivered to children by age 12-23 months as part of WHO's Expanded Programme on Immunization (EPI). Immunization against tuberculosis and measles and three doses of polio and DPT vaccines are recommended for all children by age one year.

The overall proportion of children aged 12-23 months who are fully vaccinated ranges from less than 20 per cent in Liberia and the Niger to almost 90 per cent in Botswana and Jordan. Many Eastern and Southern African countries have a high level of coverage, as do some countries in the Northern Africa, Western Asia, and Latin America and Caribbean regions. A similar mixture of countries has below 60 per cent coverage, with much of Western Africa and South-central Asia having particularly poor coverage.

One problem with those data is that in DHS-I surveys, information about specific vaccines was only collected for children whose vaccination status was recorded on health cards. In DHS-II surveys and the NFHS, such data were also collected for children whose vaccination status was recalled by mothers. The proportion of children with a health card varies from more than 85 per cent in Malawi and Rwanda to less than a quarter of that in Nigeria, with the median being about 58 per cent. Since the coverage of specific vaccines among children ever-vaccinated according to their mothers' report is 75-95 per cent of coverage among children with health cards (Boerma and others, 1990) comparisons cannot be made easily. Drop-out rates between the first and third doses of DPT and polio vaccines are also higher for children reported on only by mothers than for those with health cards.

In some countries, the probability of children possessing a health card varies by sex. In most of them the difference is small (ratios of 0.95-1.05). In Cameroon, however, girls are 10 per cent less likely than boys to have a card, while in Nigeria boys are 8 per cent less likely to have one. Figure 37 shows a

scatterplot of countries according to the sex ratio of children with at least one vaccination recorded on a health card and the sex ratio obtained from maternal recall only. The latter figures are estimated by subtracting the percentage with cards from the percentage who are ever-vaccinated recorded by both cards and recall. The upper-right quadrant contains countries where the sex ratio is greater than 1.0 for both sources of information, indicating a consistent male advantage in vaccination. The lower left quadrant contains cases where there is a consistent female advantage. The upper left and lower right quadrants denote countries where a gender advantage on one source is offset by a gender advantage in the opposite direction on the other

Figure 37. Ratio of the proportions of ever-vaccinated boys to girls aged 12-23 months, according to different reporting methods

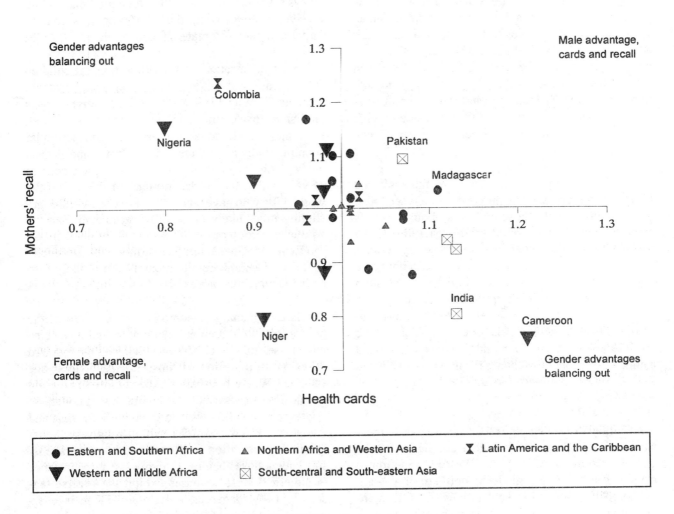

Sources: DHS-I, DHS-II and DHS-III country reports, NFHS national and state reports.

source. Only 26 per cent of the variability in sex differentials in the proportion of children ever-vaccinated by recall is explained by sex differences in card possession. The association is negative, meaning that if boys are more likely to possess cards (and thus also be vaccinated at least once), girls are more likely to be ever-vaccinated among those reported by maternal recall only. Thus, to some extent the probability of being ever-vaccinated is more equitable by sex than card possession suggests. Nevertheless, some countries are characterized by a male advantage in both forms of reporting (Madagascar, Pakistan, Rwanda) or by a female advantage in both (Niger, Paraguay, Senegal (1992-1993)).

Proportions ever-vaccinated

Many studies have examined whether immunization coverage differs for boys and girls. In general, significant sex differentials have not been found. Examples include studies in Lahore, Pakistan (Sabir and Ebrahim, 1984); Delhi, India (Basu, 1989); Senegal (Cantrelle and others, 1986; Barbieri, 1989) and Mali (Mbacke and LeGrand, 1991). In a few populations, girls are disadvantaged in terms of immunization. For example, less preventive health care for girls was found in a squatter settlement in Jordan (Teçke and Shorter, 1984).

Detailed findings are presented in table 49 and figure 38. On average, the proportion ever-vaccinated is about the same for boys and girls, though there is some variation by country. The sex ratio of the probability of being vaccinated does not vary systematically with immunization coverage but exhibits some regional patterning. In seven of the nine Western African countries, girls are appreciably more likely to have received at least one vaccine than boys. In contrast, more boys than girls have received a vaccine in all the Northern African and Asian countries, and significantly more boys than girls are ever-vaccinated in Bangladesh, Northern India and Pakistan, together with Madagascar.

A similar pattern emerges for the single-dose measles vaccine. Coverage is higher among boys than girls in Northern Africa, and Western and South-central Asia. In Bangladesh, northern India and Pakistan, together with Tunisia, significantly more boys than girls have received the vaccine. On the other

hand, measles immunization is more widespread among girls than boys in much of sub-Saharan Africa and Latin America and the girls' advantage is significant in two countries. Greater relative differentials by sex exist in countries with medium-to-low coverage.

Full immunization

Children need to receive all the EPI vaccinations recommended by WHO/UNICEF to protect them from childhood infections. For polio and DPT, three doses of each are needed before the vaccines are fully effective. Unfortunately, drop-out rates are often high. In urban areas of Mali, Mbacke and LeGrand (1991) found that sons were more likely than daughters to receive second and third doses of polio and DPT vaccine, although no significant difference existed for first doses or single-dose vaccines. According to their analysis, sex differentials in the likelihood that a child received a second or third dose of vaccine were even larger than those by maternal education.

Male-female ratios of the proportions of children fully immunized among those ever-vaccinated are presented in table 49. The dispersion of those ratios is similar to that of those for ever-vaccination. Both male and female advantage are found in particular countries. Only in northern India, Pakistan and Tunisia are boys significantly more likely to complete courses of vaccination than girls. In much of the rest of the world, girls who have received at least one vaccine are slightly more likely to be fully vaccinated than the equivalent group of boys. Moreover, in the Dominican Republic, Ghana, Kenya and the United Republic of Tanzania, girls are significantly more likely than boys to complete courses of vaccination.

It is enlightening to compare the sex ratio of the proportion of children receiving at least one vaccine with the sex ratio of children receiving all the required doses as a proportion of those having at least one vaccine. Where both ratios exceed unity, increasing female disadvantage exists in immunization coverage. That pattern is seen most clearly in northern India and Pakistan. A few countries exhibit relatively higher female immunization for first doses, but coverage by subsequent doses begins to favour boys, for instance in Nigeria. Most countries exhibit the reverse tendency. In Madagascar, a male advantage in ever-vaccination is offset in full vaccination, while in

Countries or areas according to overall percentage full immunized[a] in descending order	Year	Ever vaccinated[a]	Measles[b,c]	Completeness		
				Polio 3 as a proportion of those with Polio 1[b,c]	DPT3 as a proportion of those with DPT1[b,c]	Fully vaccinated[d] as a proportion of those ever vaccinated[b,c]
80-100 per cent						
Botswana	1988	1.00	1.02	1.01	1.04*	0.99
Malawi	1992	0.98	1.01	1.01	1.02	1.02
Rwanda	1992	1.02	1.00	0.99	0.99	0.98
Zimbabwe	1988/89	0.99	0.98	1.00	0.98	0.99
Tunisia	1988	0.99	1.06*	1.05*	1.05*	1.14**
Jordan	1990	0.99	1.00	1.00	1.00	1.00
Median		**0.99**	**1.01**	**1.00**	**1.01**	**1.00**
60-79 per cent						
Ondo State, Nigeria	1986	0.94	-	-	-	-
Kenya	1989	1.00	0.94*	1.00	1.00	0.92**
United Rep. of Tanzania	1991/92	1.00	1.00	0.94	0.96	0.94*
Zambia	1992	1.01	1.00	0.99	0.99	0.98
Morocco	1987	1.01	1.00	-	-	0.96
	1992	1.03	1.00	0.99	0.99	0.97
Egypt	1992	1.01	1.01	1.16	1.04	1.04
Colombia	1990	1.00	0.98	0.97	0.97	0.99
Median		**1.01**	**1.00**	**0.99**	**0.99**	**0.97**
40-59 per cent						
Ghana	1988	0.97	0.97	0.88*	0.96	0.84**
Senegal	1992/93	0.95	0.95	0.97	0.96	0.93
Sudan	1989/90	1.03	1.03	1.02	1.00	1.02
Uganda	1988/89	1.05	1.05	1.09	1.11	1.07
Namibia	1992	1.01	1.04	0.97	0.97	1.00
Madagascar	1992	1.09**	1.06	1.07	1.06	0.96
Yemen	1991/92	1.08	1.09	1.02	1.02	1.00
Bangladesh	1993/94	1.06**	1.11**	1.01	1.03	1.05
Indonesia	1991	1.02	0.98	1.00	1.01	0.99
Peru	1991/92	1.00	0.96	1.01	1.00	0.97
Median		**1.02**	**1.04**	**1.01**	**1.01**	**0.99**
20-39 per cent						
Nigeria	1990	0.94	0.98	1.08	1.07	1.15
Senegal	1989/90	0.95	-	-	-	-
Burkina Faso	1993	0.96	0.98	0.98	0.98	1.00
Cameroon	1991	1.03	1.08	1.03	1.00	1.04
Egypt	1988	-	1.03	1.03	1.03	-
India[e]	1993	1.07**	1.08**	1.00	1.01	1.01
Northern		1.09**	1.18**	1.02	1.04*	1.10**
Southern		1.02	1.00	0.99	1.00	0.96
Pakistan	1990/91	1.08*	1.18**	1.06	1.04	1.15*
Dominican Republic	1991	0.99	0.90*	0.95	0.97	0.77**
Paraguay	1990	0.97	0.92	0.93	0.99	0.86
Median		**0.98**	**1.01**	**1.01**	**1.01**	**1.01**
< 20 per cent						
Liberia	1986	1.00	0.99	1.10	1.08	1.02
Niger	1992	0.89	0.83	0.96	0.91	0.98
Median		**0.95**	**0.91**	**1.03**	**1.00**	**1.00**
Overall median		**1.00**	**1.00**	**1.00**	**1.00**	**0.99**

Sources: DHS-I, DHS-II and DHS-III Country Reports, NFHS National and State Reports.

NOTE: An asterisk (*) indicates that p < 0.05; two asterisks (**) indicate that p < 0.01.

[a] Recorded from health cards and maternal recall.

[b] DHS-I country reports; recorded from health cards only.

[c] DHS-II and DHS-III country reports; recorded from health cards and maternal recall.

[d] Fully-vaccinated children (those who have received BCG, measles, 3 doses of DPT and polio).

[e] National Family Health Survey.

Figure 38. Number of countries according to the direction of the sex differential in vaccination coverage, by region

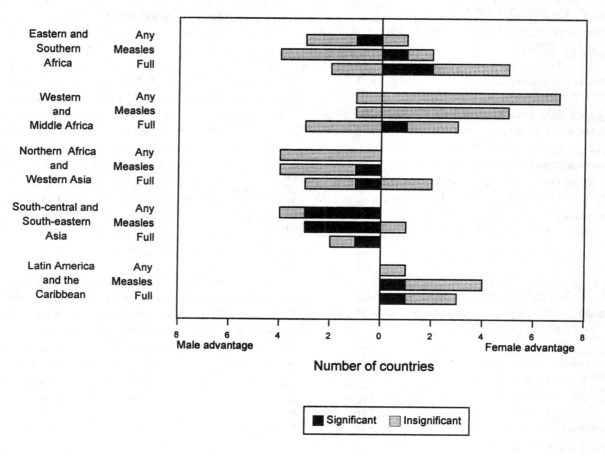

Sources: DHS-I, DHS-II and DHS-III country reports, NFHS national and state reports.

Ghana slightly higher levels of ever-vaccination among girls are compounded by much higher rates of continuation. Data on specific multiple-dose vaccines, namely DPT and polio, are also presented in table 49 and generally echo those patterns.

C. Morbidity

Many attempts to explain sex differentials in mortality by sex differentials in morbidity have either found few morbidity differentials or found morbidity patterns that could not explain the mortality differentials (Murray and Chen, 1992). Thus, the linkages between the severity and duration of infection, the medical treatment received, its timing and case-fatality rates by sex are clearly complex (Faveau, Koenig and Wojtyniak, 1991). Diarrhoeal disease, malaria and acute respiratory infections are leading causes of infant and child mortality in developing countries and the most frequently experienced illnesses (Boerma, Sommerfelt and Rutstein, 1991). Most of the surveys include questions on the symptoms and treatment of diarrhoea. Some, including the Indian NFHS, asked questions on fever and on cough or difficult breathing.

Questions about symptoms of disease were asked about living children less than five years of age in all the DHS surveys except that in Bangladesh, where the questions were asked about children aged less than three years. In the NFHS, the questions were asked about children aged less than four years. Mothers are asked whether their children have had diarrhoea in the previous 24 hours or in the two weeks before the survey. Most phase-I DHS surveys that collected data on the prevalence of fever or cough, with or without breathing difficulties, used a four-week reference period. Phase II surveys and the NFHS used a two-week reference period.

Those data have several limitations. First, recall biases are a problem: mothers might not be sure exactly when their child was ill. Underreporting of illness increases with the length of the recall period. Although there is no universal agreement on the ideal length of the recall period, for diarrhoea there is some consensus that reporting errors are inevitable if the reference period exceeds two days (Blum and Feachem, 1983; Alam, Fitzroy and Rahaman, 1989). Thus, underreporting of diarrhoea is likely with DHS data (Boerma, Sommerfelt and Rutstein, 1991). Although recall biases probably vary by country for the different symptoms, they are unlikely to affect male-female comparisons greatly.

A second problem is that the DHS questions about symptoms vary somewhat between countries and have evolved over time. Diarrhoea is usually defined only in the instructions for interviewers, and only phase II questionnaires probe about the severity of symptoms. Similarly, most DHS-I surveys asked whether children had suffered from cough or difficult breathing but others about difficult breathing only, while the DHS-II core and NFHS questionnaires include separate questions about each symptom. Such differences in the questionnaire obviously limit the cross-national comparability of the data. In addition, if the sex of the child affects the perceived severity of the condition, the data obtained about boys and girls will be affected differentially. Apparently lower female morbidity might result from a bias against reporting sickness among female children that is affected by the exact questions asked (Hill and Upchurch, 1994). Moreover, if girls are only classified as ill by mothers when they have more severe disease than boys, that difference could affect treatment patterns. Those considerations argue for caution in the interpretation of survey data on morbidity and its treatment.

As with mortality, great variations in levels of morbidity in children less than five years of age exist between countries and by symptom (table 50). Those differentials in the period prevalence of ill-health probably reflect differing interpretations of the questions and variation in the average duration of disease episodes, as well as variation in the incidence of new episodes of disease. Unfortunately, only a few of the surveys allow one to differentiate between the incidence and the duration of ill-health. The prevalence of reported diarrhoeal and fever morbidity both exhibit less variation between countries than cough prevalence. For cough, half the countries in the present study have relatively low morbidity, while the other half are spread out over a wide range from 17-57 per cent. Sub-Saharan African countries tend to report the highest levels of diarrhoea and fever, but many Western African countries report a rather low prevalence of cough or breathing difficulties.

For the statistics on the prevalence of ill-health a sex ratio above one represents male disadvantage, while sex ratios below one indicate female disadvantage. Thus, a pattern of lower female morbidity emerges for all three symptom groups (tables 51, 52 and 53). The results are summarized in the form of a box and whisker plot[1] in figure 39. Outliers, defined as countries with a ratio that falls more than one and a half times the inter-quartile range outside the inter-quartile range, are indicated separately. The excess morbidity of boys is most marked for diarrhoea, with many countries having ratios above 1.15, and is least clear

TABLE 50. MINIMUM, MAXIMUM AND MEDIAN VALUES OF THE PREVALENCE OF DIARRHOEA, FEVER AND COUGH

Prevalence (in last 2 weeks) percentage	Minimum	Maximum	Median
Diarrhoea	5.1 (Ondo State)	37.9 (Senegal, 1989/90)	18.2
Fever	3.9 (Botswana)	51.2 (Liberia)	33.6
Cough/difficult breathing	6.6 (Mali)	57 (Ecuador)	16.6

Sources: DHS-I, DHS-II and DHS-III country reports, NFHS national and state reports.

Countries or areas according to overall level of use of any curative treatment in descending order	Year	Diarrhoea prevalence in previous two weeks	Received any treatment as a proportion of those sick	As proportions of those treated				ORS and/or home solution and/or increased fluid intake
				Source		Type		
				Health facility/ provider	Traditional practitioner	Home solution	ORS packets	
80-100 per cent								
Zimbabwe	1988/89	1.08	1.00	1.01	0.80	-	-	0.95
Sri Lanka	1989	1.20	1.04	1.06	-	1.34	0.98	1.06
Kenya	1989	1.02	1.02	0.99	-	0.90	0.64**	0.81**
Ghana	1988	1.03	0.99	0.91	0.90	1.38	1.06	1.11
Uganda	1988/89	1.09	0.98	0.89	-	1.64	0.95	0.99
Ondo State, Nigeria	1986	-	1.04	0.76	-	1.42	0.00	1.22
United Rep. of Tanzania .	1991/92	0.98	0.98	0.94	-	0.83	0.97	1.00
Botswana	1988	1.01	1.02	0.94	-	1.27	1.02	1.09e
Thailand	1987	1.22*	1.02	1.05	-	0.76	0.87	0.85
Zambia	1992	1.14*	1.01	1.03	-	0.95	1.05	1.02
Mexico	1987	1.11	1.01	-	-	-	-	1.03
Malawi	1992	1.17*	1.02	1.17*	0.94	1.06	1.10	1.00
Bangladesh[a,b]	1993/94	0.92	0.98	0.96	1.15	0.64*	1.36**	1.15**
Namibia	1992	1.00	1.02	0.99	1.05	-	1.05	1.04
Togo	1988	1.01	1.03	0.88	0.85	1.10	0.96	0.98
India[c,d]	1993	1.05	1.04**	1.02	0.99	0.98	1.23**	1.03
Northern		1.15**	1.06**	0.98	1.03	0.89	1.28**	1.00
Southern		1.04	1.03	1.02	0.94	1.06	1.10	1.06
Median		**1.06**	**1.02**	**0.99**	**0.90**	**1.09**	**1.00**	**1.00**
60-79 per cent								
Trinidad and Tobago	1987	-	0.88	0.81	-	1.50	1.22	1.27*
Burkina Faso	1993	1.16**	0.99	0.83	0.98	1.22	0.96	1.08
Jordan	1990	1.05	1.04e	0.96	-	1.03	1.08	1.00
Indonesia	1991	1.07	1.01	1.00	0.94	-	1.08	1.01
Bolivia	1989	0.96	1.16**	0.96	-	1.11	0.89	0.98f
Rwanda	1992	1.02	1.02	0.99	1.01	0.76*	1.01	0.92
Peru[g]	1986	1.09	-	-	-	-	1.20	-
Peru	1991/92	1.06	1.06e	1.19**	0.84**	1.03	1.14	1.00
Paraguay	1990	0.92	1.04e	0.91	1.20	0.89	1.13	1.00
Egypt	1992	1.17**	0.99	1.09	-	1.48	1.14	0.97
Sudan	1989/90	1.05	0.97	1.03	-	0.79	1.02	0.96
Senegal	1989/90	1.05	1.10**	0.91	0.90	1.03	1.51	1.15
Cameroon	1991	1.18*	0.99e	0.94	1.62*	1.10	0.77	1.00
Mali	1987	1.08	1.00	1.33	1.06	0.82	1.53	1.25
Guatemala	1987	1.18*	0.91	1.19	-	0.94	1.41	1.30
Morocco	1992	1.10	1.00	0.93	-	1.71	1.13	1.00
Burundi	1987	0.96	0.93	1.05	-	1.24	0.96	1.01
Egypt[a]	1988	1.11*	1.04	1.01	-	-	1.14	1.14
Tunisia	1988	1.14*	0.99	1.29*	-	-	0.89	0.89
Madagascar	1992	1.21*	1.04e	0.90	1.04	1.15	1.16	1.00
Median		**1.09**	**1.00**	**0.99**	**1.01**	**1.07**	**1.13**	**1.00**
40-59 per cent								
Morocco	1987	1.08	1.07	1.07	-	1.09	0.95	0.96
Senegal	1992/93	1.19**	1.06e	0.97	1.00	0.93	0.93	1.00
Niger	1992	1.05	1.13*	0.86	1.05	1.03	1.04	1.04
Pakistan	1990/91	1.06	0.99e	-	0.76**	0.88	0.98	1.00
Colombia	1990	1.09	0.79*c	-	1.07	0.78	0.78**	0.98
Yemen . . . . : . . .	1991/92	1.05	1.13*	0.99	1.77	1.00	0.99	1.00
Median		**1.07**	**1.07**	**0.98**	**1.05**	**0.96**	**0.96**	**1.00**

164

TABLE 51 *(continued)*

Countries or areas according to overall level of use of any curative treatment in descending order	Year	Diarrhoea prevalence in previous two weeks	Received any treatment as a proportion of those sick	As proportions of those treated				
				Source		Type		
				Health facility/ provider	Traditional practitioner	Home solution	ORS packets	ORS and/or home solution and/or increased fluid intake
20-39 per cent								
Nigeria	1990	1.18**	0.92[a]	0.96	1.00	1.01	1.15	1.03[f]
Dominican Republic	1991	1.06	1.08[a]	0.98	-	0.91	1.02	1.00[f]
Median		1.02	1.00	0.97	1.00	0.96	1.15	1.01
Overall median		1.07	1.02	0.98	1.00	1.03	1.04	1.00

Sources: DHS-I, DHS-II and DHS-III country reports, NFHS national and state reports.

NOTE: An asterisk (*) indicates that $p < 0.05$; two asterisks (**) indicate that $p < 0.01$.

[a]Reference period for prevalence and treatment is 7 days.

[b]Children under 3 years.

[c]Children under 4 years.

[e]National Family Health Survey.

[e]Percentage treated is equal to 100 per cent minus percentage not treated, assumed to be "percentage not receiving ORT or increased fluids."

[f]Significance not tested as the "proportion" adds up to over 100 per cent since more than one treatment can be reported per child.

[g]Reference period for prevalence and treatment is 15 days.

for cough. The only loose regional pattern in the data is that unlike other regions, Eastern and Southern Africa do not exhibit clearly higher male morbidity from diarrhoea and fever. For all three symptom groups, the sex ratio of reported morbidity is unrelated to the level of reported morbidity.

Although apparently lower female morbidity may result from a bias in favour of reporting sickness of male children, other studies of sex differentials in morbidity have also found that female children under the age of five are generally healthier than males. For example, Chen, Huq and D'Souza (1981) found that in Matlab male incidence rates exceed those for females for a range of infectious diseases. A study by Levinson (1974) in rural India found that boys have higher infection and prevalence rates than girls.

D. TREATMENT

Most deaths from acute diarrhoea result from dehydration of the child, so the most effective treatment is oral rehydration therapy (ORT) in the form of manufactured oral rehydration solution (ORS) packets, home salt-sugar solutions or any increase in fluid intake. Upper respiratory tract infections are responsible for most of the non-fatal acute respiratory infections in young children. Lower respiratory tract infections, especially pneumonia, are a more important cause of death. Antibiotics are usually the most effective form of treatment. Attacks of malaria in young children with little or no immunity have a high case-fatality rate. Treatment with chloroquine or other drugs is very effective if the organism causing the disease is not resistant to the drug (Boerma, Sommerfelt and Rutstein, 1991). Other approaches to the treatment of those diseases, such as antibiotics for diarrhoea, cough syrup or traditional remedies, are unlikely to be as effective.

Studies in diverse parts of the world of populations with differing levels of health service provision and epidemiological and mortality profiles have found that girls receive less curative health care of any kind than boys. One review of that research is found in the annotated bibliography of Le Grand (1992). For example, in slums in Lahore, Pakistan, 27 per cent of sick girls compared with only 12 per cent of sick boys were not taken for any medical treatment (Sabir and Ebrahim, 1984). In rural Egypt, girls are less likely to receive medical care for diarrhoea than boys of the

TABLE 52. MALE-TO-FEMALE RATIOS OF FEVER MORBIDITY AND TREATMENT AMONG
CHILDREN AGED UNDER 5 YEARS

Countries or areas according to overall level of use of any curative treatment in descending order	Year	Fever prevalence in previous two weeks	Received any treatment as a proportion of those sick	As proportions of those treated			
				Source		Type	
				Health facility/ provider	Traditional practitioner	Anti-malarials	Antibiotics
80-100 per cent							
Paraguay	1990	0.99	0.99*	1.04	1.00	0.98	1.15
Nigeria	1990	1.05	1.00	1.12	1.41*	1.24**	1.23**
Ghana[a]	1988	1.06	0.98	0.97	1.07	0.95	0.79
Ondo State, Nigeria[a] ...	1986	1.00	1.00	1.11	-	1.09	-
Botswana[a]	1988	0.86	0.94	0.95	-	-	-
Colombia	1990	1.21**	1.02	1.11*	0.90	1.87	1.10
Togo	1988	1.02	1.03	0.97	1.05	0.99	1.01
Indonesia	1991	1.01	1.14**	0.96	0.65**	-	-
Uganda	1988/89	1.00	0.99	1.11*	-	1.00	1.88**
Senegal	1989/90	1.05	1.06**	0.97	0.87	0.88	1.00
Dominican Republic ..	1991	1.05	1.05*	0.97	1.33	-	1.01
Cameroon	1991	1.10	1.03	1.18	0.95	-	0.99
Malawi	1992	1.01	1.00	1.03	1.14	1.02	1.08
Pakistan	1990/91	1.01	1.03	1.03	1.40	0.86	0.90
Zambia	1992	1.02	1.00	1.00	1.01	1.04	0.99
Madagascar	1992	1.04	0.92**	1.15**	1.09	1.02	1.08
United Rep. of Tanzania	1991/92	0.98	1.01	0.96	0.75	0.89**	1.03
India[b,c]	1993	1.09**	1.05**	1.05**	0.83*	1.01	1.05
Northern		1.10**	1.07**	1.04**	1.03	1.10	1.03
Southern		1.05	1.03	1.06**	0.69**	0.88	1.04
Liberia[a]	1986	1.00	1.01	-	1.10	0.97	1.17
Median		**1.02**	**1.01**	**1.03**	**1.03**	**1.00**	**1.04**
60-79 per cent							
Namibia	1992	0.99	0.98	1.00	1.08	0.85	0.98
Burundi[a]	1987	1.04	1.07	0.98	-	1.04	0.89
Mali[a]	1987	1.11	0.94	4.35**	0.91	1.13	0.96
Burkina Faso	1993	1.08*	0.94*	1.09	1.01	1.20**	0.86
Senegal	1992/93	1.04	1.03	1.13*	0.85	1.02	0.93
Rwanda	1992	1.01	1.05	1.13*	0.98	1.34	0.93
Median		**1.04**	**1.01**	**1.11**	**0.98**	**1.09**	**0.93**
40-59 per cent							
Yemen	1991/92	1.03	1.09**	-	-	0.81	1.09
Morocco	1992	1.03	1.01	0.95	1.30	0.99	1.11
Niger	1992	1.00	1.11**	1.06	1.06	1.16*	0.89
Kenya[a]	1989	0.97	-	-	-	-	-
Median		**1.02**	**1.09**	**1.01**	**1.18**	**0.99**	**1.09**
Overall median		**1.03**	**1.01**	**1.04**	**1.01**	**1.01**	**1.01**

Sources: DHS-I, DHS-II and DHS-III country reports, NFHS national and state reports.
NOTE: An asterisk (*) indicates that $p < 0.05$; two asterisks (**) indicate that $p < 0.01$.
[a]Reference period for prevalence and treatment is 4 weeks, not 2 weeks.
[b]Children under 4 years.
[c]National Family Health Survey.

TABLE 53. MALE-TO-FEMALE RATIOS OF COUGH/DIFFICULT BREATHING MORBIDITY
AND TREATMENT AMONG CHILDREN AGED UNDER 5 YEARS

Countries or areas according to overall level of use of any curative treatment in descending order	Year	Cough/difficult breathing prevalence in previous two weeks	Received any treatment as a proportion of those sick	As proportions of those treated			
				Source		Type	
				Health facility/ provider	Traditional practitioner	Antibiotics	Cough syrup
80-100 per cent							
Paraguay	1990	1.17*	1.00	1.01	0.94	1.43*	1.01
Nigeria	1990	1.18	1.01	0.88	1.81*	1.03	0.96
Zimbabwe[a]	1988/89	1.09*	1.02	0.91	0.94	1.00	-
Ondo State, Nigeria[a]	1986	0.86	1.03	0.97	-	1.35	-
Indonesia	1991	1.03	1.01	1.06	1.02	-	-
Colombia	1990		1.07**	1.05	1.29	0.96	1.08
United Rep. of Tanzania	1991/92	1.13	0.99	1.02	0.64	0.89	0.90
Kenya[a]	1989	0.97	0.96*	0.94*	-	-	1.01
Botswana[a]	1988	1.03	1.02	0.99	-	-	-
Dominican Republic . . .	1991	0.97	1.01	1.03	1.14	1.07	0.96
Malawi	1992	0.95	0.96	0.97	1.22	0.87	0.93
Ghana[a]	1988	1.02	0.96	0.97	1.16	0.85	1.07
Zambia	1992	1.02	0.96	1.01	1.23	0.99	1.08
Uganda[a]	1988/89	1.01	1.00	1.00	-	1.00	1.00
Pakistan	1990/91	0.98	0.99	1.05	1.82	1.00	0.99
Cameroon	1991	1.03	1.07	1.14	0.82	1.04	1.07
Peru	1991/92	1.11*	1.01	1.04	-	1.17	0.97
Togo	1988	1.19	1.09	0.87	-	1.24	0.45*
Liberia[a]	1986	1.04	1.01	-	1.38*	0.68	0.92
Madagascar	1992	1.09	0.93*	0.95	1.30	1.05	0.98
India[b,c]	1993	1.20**	1.06**	1.09**	0.85	1.00	0.99
Northern		1.28**	1.07**	1.06**	1.15	0.93	0.99
Southern		1.15**	1.03	1.11**	0.70	1.00	1.05
Median		**1.04**	**1.01**	**1.01**	**1.15**	**1.00**	**0.99**
60-79 per cent							
Egypt	1992	1.16*	1.12**	0.96	1.34	1.31*	1.00
Burkina Faso	1993	1.03	0.96	1.00	1.02	0.98	0.90
Sudan	1989/90	1.02	1.08**	-	0.87	1.01	0.94
Namibia	1992	0.98	0.97	1.04	0.90	0.96	0.93
Rwanda	1992	0.99	1.03	1.08	1.01	1.24	0.99
Senegal	1992/93	1.13	0.99	1.05	0.84	0.96	0.98
Bangladesh[d]	1993/94	1.26	1.12*	1.06	-	-	-
Mali	1987	1.02	1.11	-	-	1.61	0.94
Niger	1992	0.97	1.06	1.36	0.92	1.08	0.81
Median		**1.02**	**1.06**	**1.05**	**0.92**	**1.05**	**0.97**
40-59 per cent							
Burundi[a]	1987	0.94	0.97	0.95	-	0.56	0.90
Morocco	1992	1.01	1.08	1.20	1.13	1.55	1.04
Yemen	1991/92	1.09*	1.05	1.00	4.76	1.01	0.97
Median		**1.01**	**1.02**	**1.00**	**2.94**	**1.01**	**0.97**
Overall median		**1.03**	**1.01**	**1.01**	**1.08**	**1.01**	**0.98**

Sources: DHS-I, DHS-II and DHS-III country reports, NFHS national and state reports.

NOTE: An asterisk (*) indicates that p < 0.05; two asterisks (**) indicate that p < 0.01.

[a]Reference period for prevalence and treatment is 4 weeks, not 2 weeks.

[b]Children under 4 years.

[c]National Family Health Survey.

[d]Children under 3 years.

167

**Figure 39. Ratio of the proportions of boys to girls aged less than 5 years
with diarrhoea, fever and cough, by region**

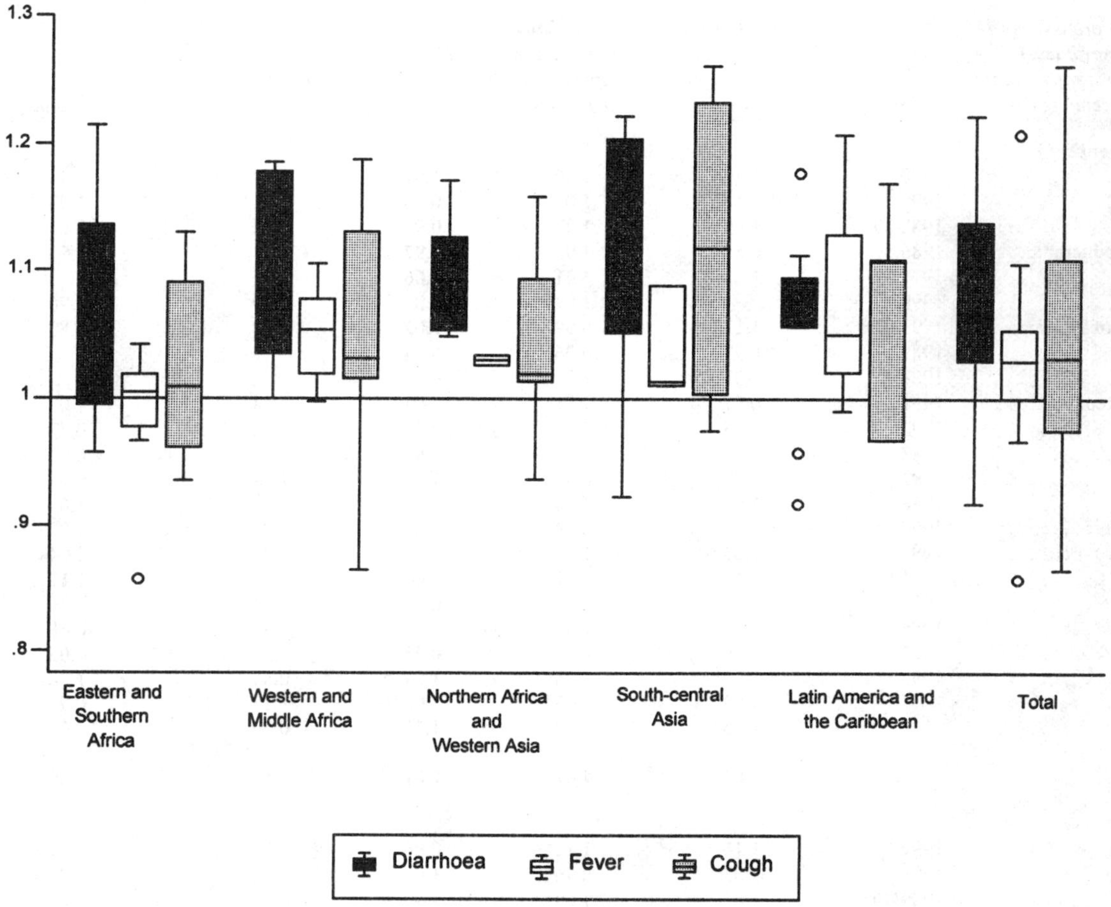

Sources: DHS-I, DHS-II and DHS-III country reports, NFHS national and state reports.

adequate health care than their male counterparts (Delgado, Valverde and Hurtado, 1986). DHS data from Senegal indicate that male children with diarrhoea and fever are more likely to receive treatment than girls (Barbieri, 1989).

A systematic examination was made of whether among those children who are sick there are sex differentials in being treated at all, and whether among those children who are sick and treated there are sex differentials in where treatment was obtained or the type of treatment received. The results are presented in tables 51, 52 and 53. The countries are ranked according to the overall level of treatment for the sexes combined, which varies greatly. The proportion of children under 5 years with diarrhoea who were treated varies from 31 per cent in the Dominican Republic to virtually 100 per cent in Zimbabwe. The overall level of treatment for fever is 53 per cent in the Niger but almost 100 per cent in Paraguay. For cough, it is 44 per cent in Yemen but almost 100 per cent in Paraguay and Nigeria. No clear regional variation in the amount of treatment is apparent for any of the symptom groups.

The sex ratios in the probability of being treated in any way vary only moderately. The widest range is for the treatment of diarrhoea, with ratios from 0.79 to 1.16. In countries where most children with diarrhoea receive treatment, differentials by sex tend to be small. One exception to that pattern is northern India, where levels of treatment are high but still favour boys. At intermediate levels of treatment (60-80 per cent), one finds both male-advantage and female-advantage countries. In countries where only a minority of children are treated, boys tend to be at an advantage. The pattern for treatment of fever is similar. Significantly more boys than girls were treated in six countries and significantly more girls in three. For cough, a significant sex differential in favour of girls is found in two countries but one in favour of boys in five countries.

Little consistency is detectable across the three symptom groups within individual countries. Only in India, the Niger, Togo and Yemen are boys more likely to be treated than girls for all three symptoms. In the Niger and Yemen, the differential is significant for two of the three symptoms and in India for all three. In addition, as Barbieri (1989) reported, boys with diarrhoea and fever in Senegal were significantly more likely to be treated than girls according to the survey in 1986. By the time of the 1992-1993 survey, however, those differentials had disappeared. No survey suggests that girls are treated more often than boys for all three symptoms. Despite the lack of consistency in the reports for particular countries, one regional pattern is apparent (figure 40). Eastern and Southern Africa is the only region of the world in which girls are as likely to receive treatment as boys for those symptoms of infectious disease. Elsewhere, particularly in Northern Africa and Western and South-central Asia, boys tend to be at an advantage.

E. SOURCE OF TREATMENT

In the present section, sex differentials in the propensity to use particular providers of curative health care are examined. If the quality of care obtained from different providers varies, that factor will have implications for child health. Thus, sex differentials in the source of treatment might help to explain sex differentials in mortality. However, that relationship is confounded by sex differentials in the timing of use of different providers and in the severity of the condition. For instance, girls might be taken to an effective provider only after their condition has deteriorated too far for treatment to save their lives. Unfortunately, data on the timing of the use of different health services were not collected in the DHS and NFHS surveys, so that issue cannot be investigated here.

Many studies have analysed sex differentials in the use of different health-care providers, though few consider the severity of illness or the timing of treatment. That large body of literature spans various sources of treatment and many regions. In Isfahan, Iran, male infants were taken to a public health centre more often than girls (Froozani, Malekafzali and Bahrini, 1980). In Lahore's slums, 58 per cent of ill boys were taken to a private practitioner, compared with only 37 per cent of ill girls (Sabir and Ebrahim, 1984). In Uttar Pradesh, northern India, boys were taken to city hospitals when warranted, while girls saw less qualified doctors (Khan and others, 1991). Girls in rural Egypt were less likely to receive any treatment outside the home than boys. If outside treatment was sought, girls were more likely to be taken to the public health unit, while boys were often taken to a private doctor (Makinson, 1985). Basu (1989) examined both the source and type of treatment in conjunction. Her study focused on two groups of children aged less than 12 years living in a resettlement slum in New Delhi; the parents of one group had emigrated from Uttar Pradesh and those of the other from Tamil Nadu. In addition to sex differences in both groups in the proportion of illnesses receiving no treatment, the northern Indian girls were more likely to receive non-professional treatment than the boys.

The counterpart of greater use of modern health services for treatment of sick children of one sex may be more use of home remedies and traditional healers for treatment of the other sex. In a rural district of Gujarat in northern India, 80 per cent of boys who died of diarrhoea, wasting or respiratory ailments had been taken to an urban centre for treatment but only 20 per cent of girls; 50 per cent of girls were taken to a local medical practitioner and 30 per cent were treated with home remedies alone (Visaria, 1988). A study of longitudinal data on the treatment of diarrhoeal disease from Matlab, Bangladesh, found that the treatment rate for boys aged less than five at the diarrhoea clinic was 66 per cent higher than that for

**Figure 40. Number of countries according to the direction of the sex
differential in the treatment of symptoms of disease, by region**

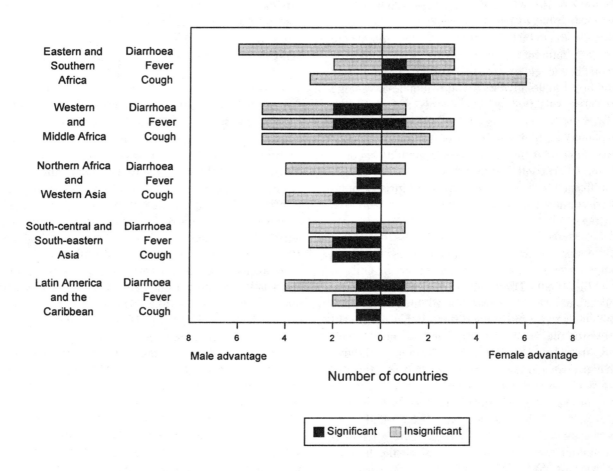

Sources: DHS-I, DHS-II and DHS-III country reports, NFHS national and state reports.

girls. Girls were treated more often using indigenous health systems than boys (Chen, Huq and D'Souza, 1981). Similarly, Bourne and Walker (1991) found that use of traditional remedies to treat girls equalled or exceeded their use to treat boys in six rural Bangladeshi villages.

In most DHS questionnaires and the NFHS, the information on use of modern health facilities and providers covers public and private health centres and clinics and pharmacies. The present section focuses on sex differentials in the use of such facilities since they usually provide more effective treatment. Because DHS definitions of the sources and types of treatment are not standard across all countries,

categories such as "other treatment" need to be interpreted carefully. Most of the questionnaires allow women to report on more than one source of treatment per episode of sickness in their child. Thus, if all the providers consulted are considered, it is possible for them to sum to more than 100 per cent. The relative sex ratios will only be affected if there is a sex differential in the number of different providers consulted.

The relative frequency with which different types of health-care provider are consulted for boys and girls is shown in tables 51, 52 and 53. The ratios are calculated as the percentage of boys receiving treatment from a particular source among boys who are both sick and treated, divided by the equivalent percentage of girls. Use of different types of provider varies by symptom and by region. For modern health facilities, it ranges among those sick and treated from 3 per cent in Mali to 95 per cent in the Dominican Republic for diarrhoea; from 4 per cent in Mali to 95 per cent in Botswana for fever; and from 22 per cent in the Niger to 90 per cent in Botswana for cough or difficulty in breathing. The proportion of treated children who are treated by traditional healers or with home remedies also varies very widely for diarrhoea but more narrowly for fever (up to 46 per cent in Mali) and cough or difficulty in breathing (up to 52 per cent in Burkina Faso). There is no consistent inverse relation between the use of modern health facilities and the use of traditional sources. Some sub-Saharan African countries, such as Madagascar, Nigeria, Rwanda and Senegal, combine frequent resort to traditional healers and home remedies with relatively high use of modern health facilities.

The relative frequency by sex with which children whose diarrhoea is treated are taken to a modern health facility ranges from a ratio in favour of girls of 0.76 to one in favour of boys of 1.33. For the treatment of fever and of cough the range is narrower, excepting an extreme ratio (4.35) for fever in Mali that reflects very low use of health facilities for the treatment of either sex. Among those children with fever who are treated, boys are significantly more likely to be taken to a modern service provider than girls in seven countries. For diarrhoea, boys are at a significant advantage in three countries. For cough or difficulty breathing, however, only in India is there evidence that boys are more likely than girls to be taken to a modern health facility.

Few consistent patterns exist in the ratio of boys to girls using modern health facilities across the three symptom groups. The only survey that detected a significant difference by sex in the use of modern health facilities for more than a single symptom was the very large one in India. Indian boys whose symptoms are treated are about 5 per cent more likely to be taken to a modern facility than sick girls who are treated. There is also little regional consistency when looking at health facility use for the individual symptom groups (figure 41). Boys are slightly more likely to be treated at a health facility in most parts of the world. However, all but one of the Western African surveys found that girls with diarrhoea who are treated

are more likely to be taken to a provider of modern services than boys who are treated. Equally, in most of the Western African surveys, boys whose fever is treated are more likely to be taken to a modern facility than girls whose fever is treated.

F. TYPE OF TREATMENT

The last three columns of table 51 and two columns of tables 52 and 53 present ratios of boys to girls who receive the most appropriate types of treatment for diarrhoea, fever and cough/respiratory difficulties as proportions of those treated in any way. Those data are summarized in figure 42. As Boerma, Sommerfelt and Rutstein (1991) note, there are limitations to those data. Mothers may not know what type of treatment was given to the child if it was administered outside the home and standardized definitions were not applied in every survey. However, it is unlikely that the impact of those problems varies by sex of the child, although mothers might tend to respond with the perceived best treatment for the preferred sex.

In most countries in the prsent study, ORS is used to treat less than 50 per cent of episodes of diarrhoea. In several Eastern and Southern Africa countries, together with Trinidad and Tobago, it is used more often. There is no clear pattern of differentials by sex. Use of ORS among children who are treated is significantly higher for boys than girls in Bangladesh, the Dominican Republic and northern India but significantly higher for girls in Colombia and Kenya. Moreover, no evidence exists that the sex ratio in ORS use is associated with that in the use of modern service providers. The use of home salt and sugar solutions or any increased intake of fluids also can help to prevent dehydration from diarrhoea. In most countries with a significant sex differential in ORS use, that contrast is offset by greater use of other forms of rehydration therapy to treat children of the opposite sex. Only in Bangladesh and Kenya are there significant differences by sex in the overall likelihood that the type of treatment used for childhood diarrhoea is appropriate.

Fewer observations exist for the treatment of fever by antimalarials or antibiotics. Overall levels of use vary from almost zero to about 57 per cent for antibiotics in Cameroon and 73 per cent for antimalarials in

171

Figure 41. Number of countries according to the direction of the sex differential in treatment at a facility among those treated, by region

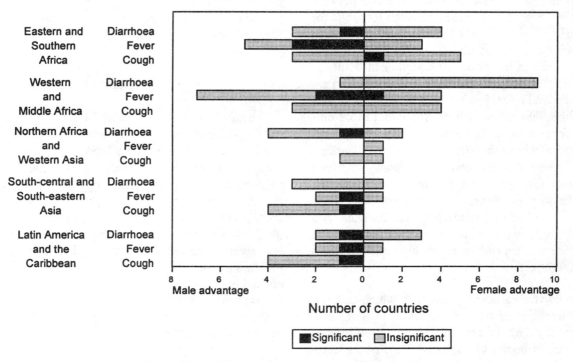

Sources: DHS-I, DHS-II and DHS-III country reports, NFHS national and state reports.

Figure 42. Number of countries according to the direction of the sex differential in effective treatment among those treated, by region

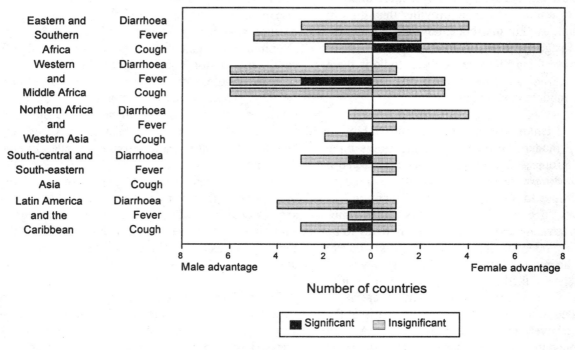

Sources : DHS-I, DHS-II and DHS-III country reports, NFHS national and state reports.

172

Liberia. There are modest differences by sex in the treatment of fever by antimalarials or antibiotics in most countries. They tend to favour boys. For both antimalarial and antibiotic use, a significant difference in either direction is associated with the equivalent differential in health facility use. The explanation is not only that those drugs are dispensed at clinics because that finding extends to several African populations where more children are given antimalarials or antibiotics than attend modern health facilities.

Use of antibiotics to treat children with coughs is uncommon; it exceeds 33 per cent only in Togo. Use of cough syrup is much more prevalent, ranging from just 7 per cent in Mali to 72 per cent in Peru (1991-1992). Two thirds of the countries in the present study record higher use of antibiotics by boys than girls among those treated. The differential is statistically significant only in Egypt (1992) and Paraguay. In most countries, girls who receive any treatment are more likely to receive cough syrup than boys. Only in one country (Togo), however, is there evidence that antibiotics and cough syrup are alternative treatments for cough that are used differentially for the two sexes.

As with other aspects of the use of curative care, there is little consistency across the three symptom groups in the appropriateness of patterns of treatment. In the Niger, boys who are treated receive more appropriate care than girls for all three types of symptom, while in the United Republic of Tanzania girls receive consistently more suitable forms of treatment. More generally, there seems to be a tendency for treatment of sick boys to be more appropriate than that of girls in Western and Middle Africa but for treatment of sick girls to be more appropriate than that of boys in Eastern and Southern Africa.

G. INDIAN STATES

The results presented already demonstrate that there are more marked sex differentials in the health care of children in Bangladesh, India and Pakistan than in most other regions of the world. Moreover, patterns of health care differ between northern and southern India. Figure 43 examines state-level differences across India in the health care of boys and girls in slightly more detail. The indicators are defined and derived in the same way as those for national populations.

Figure 43. Number of large Indian States according to the direction of the sex differential in use of preventive and curative health services, by region of India

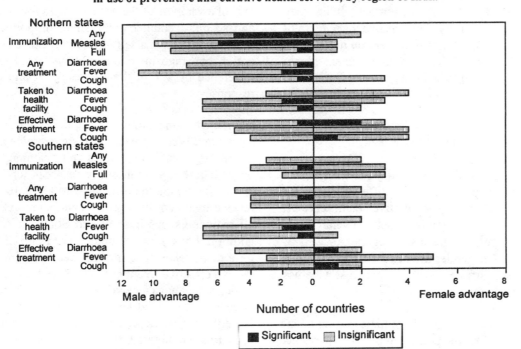

Sources: DHS-I, DHS-II and DHS-III country reports, NFHS national and state reports.

173

Immunization coverage is markedly higher among boys than girls throughout all of northern India except Assam. The differentials are largest and statistically significant in Bihar, Madhya Pradesh, Punjab, Rajasthan and Uttar Pradesh, where between 11 and 39 per cent more boys than girls have received both any vaccine and measles vaccine in particular. In Rajasthan and Uttar Pradesh, moreover, boys are about 15 per cent more likely than girls to complete courses of vaccination once they have received any vaccine. In southern India, in contrast, sex differentials in vaccination are small and insignificant, with the exception that boys are 11 per cent more likely than girls to have received measles vaccine in Kerala.

As in other parts of the world, mothers report more episodes of diarrhoea, fever and cough among their sons than their daughters in both northern and southern India. Sex differentials in whether those disease episodes had been treated in any way are smaller than those in immunization coverage in northern India, but except for cough still consistently favour boys. In southern India, there is no clear pattern in favour of either sex. For fever and cough, boys who receive treatment are more likely to be taken to a modern health care facility than girls in both northern and southern India. In southern India, girls who are treated are more likely than boys to be taken to traditional practitioners. In northern India, they tend to receive home remedies. Despite that pattern of consultations, the measures used here do not suggest that those sick boys who receive treatment obtain more appropriate care than those girls who are treated in either part of the country.

H. Discussion

The present study aims to identify the existence of and any regional patterns in sex differentials in the use of certain preventive and curative health services. Covariates of those differentials, such as overall levels of health service use, are also sought. As well as assessing whether gender affects use of any form of health care, sex differentials in effective service use are also investigated.

The investigation of sex differentials in immunization coverage divides the process into two components that are potentially affected by the sex of the child:

the probability of receiving any vaccinations, including a specific look at the single dose of measles vaccine, and the probability of acquiring effective immune status through receiving the full series of doses of EPI vaccines. Differentials by sex in immunization coverage and completeness are small in most parts of the world, and do not clearly favour either boys or girls. Within countries, differentials by sex of the child in the direction or extent of gender bias are seldom consistent between indicators (figure 38). South-central Asia is a striking exception to that generalization. In Bangladesh, northern India and Pakistan, boys are more likely to be ever-vaccinated than girls, are more likely to be vaccinated against measles and are more likely to complete courses of vaccination. Boys are also slightly more likely to receive vaccines than girls in Northern Africa and Western Asia. In other parts of the developing world, coverage tends to be slightly higher among girls.

Only the DHS survey in Yemen asked about reasons for not taking a child for immunization. The most frequent response was that the place of vaccination was far away (just over 30 per cent), followed by "other" (unspecified) reasons, lack of awareness of the need for immunization (14 per cent) and that the child was perceived to be too young (14 per cent). Other reasons, such as fear of vaccination, intention to go, lack of awareness of the need to return for other doses and so on, accounted for a small proportion of responses. Although a sex differential existed in vaccination coverage in favour of boys, there was little difference by sex in the frequency of any of those responses.

For the treatment of diarrhoea, fever and cough, the source and type of treatment were examined, as well as the "any treatment" versus "no treatment" dichotomy. There is a small but widespread tendency for boys with symptoms of disease to be more likely to receive treatment than girls. That pattern extends to all regions except Eastern and Southern Africa. In addition, boys who are treated are more likely than girls to be taken to a modern health facility and to receive effective treatment. In general, therefore, the evidence that boys receive better health care than girls is clearer for curative than preventive measures. Nevertheless, when the different indicators for a single country are compared, they often reveal inconsistent patterns. In most countries, boys' advantage is restricted to certain types of disease or of treatment. There is also little evidence that sex differentials in service use are associated with the overall level of service use other than because by definition, differentials must disappear as uptake becomes universal.

As with immunization coverage, most of the surveys did not include questions on reasons for not taking a sick child to a service provider or not using particular treatments. Even if such questions are asked, responses may be biased if mothers perceive the question as threatening and thus attempt to give a socially acceptable answer. The Yemen DHS (1991-1992) did include a question about untreated episodes of diarrhoea. The major reason given for not seeking medical assistance was lack of access to facilities (29 per cent). For 18 per cent of the children, mothers considered the child's illness to be mild, and for 7 per cent they were too busy to find time to seek treatment. For more than two in five children, "other" reasons are mentioned. There are no significant differences by sex of the child in the frequency with which mothers proffer those explanations.

The present comparative study reveals that differential health service use favouring boys is relatively rare. Clear evidence of systematically greater use of health services by boys than girls only exists in four of the countries for which data are available: Bangladesh, India, Pakistan and Yemen (tables 51, 52 and 53). In Cameroon, Egypt, the Niger and Tunisia, there is weaker evidence of the same pattern. All those countries except Tunisia are among the 14 of those that have conducted DHS surveys in which girls' mortality at ages one to four is more than 10 per cent higher than boys' mortality at the same ages. Equally,

in at least two countries parents make more use of preventive and curative services for their daughters than their sons. They are Ghana and Kenya; the United Republic of Tanzania may also fall into that category. Ghana and Kenya, however, are not among the nine countries in which male child mortality is at least 10 per cent higher than female child mortality, though the United Republic of Tanzania is. Thus, lower use of health care by girls than boys is associated with adverse mortality outcomes but not vice versa.

Examination of the whole sample of countries on which data are available, rather than just those for which there exists clear evidence of differential service use, also yields some evidence that differential child mortality by sex is associated with differential patterns of service use. Table 54 presents correlations between the sex differential in the child mortality rate ($_4q_1$) and sex differentials in ever-vaccination and ever-treatment and in full vaccination, treatment at a modern facility and effective treatment for those children who receive some care. For diarrhoea, ORS, home solutions and increased fluid intake are regarded as effective treatments. Antimalarials for fever and antibiotics for cough are also regarded as effective treatments, though they would not be appropriate for every disease episode. The outliers, Colombia and Mali for treatment of fever at a facility and Uganda for effective treatment of fever, are omitted from the analysis. The sex ratio in child mortality is associated inversely with the sex ratios of being treated or vaccinated at all. Only the associations between differential child mortality and differentials in the receipt of any vaccine and any treatment for cough are statistically significant. The associations between differential

TABLE 54. ASSOCIATIONS BETWEEN THE SEX DIFFERENTIAL IN CHILD MORTALITY ($_4q_1$)
AND SEX DIFFERENTIALS IN THE USE OF HEALTH SERVICES

Breakdown of treatment process	Vaccination	Curative		
		Diarrhoea	Fever	Cough
Received any treatment/ever vaccinated ...	r = -0.390*	r = -0.016	r = -0.216	r = -0.426*
Treated at health facility	..	r = -0.140	r = -0.187	r = -0.201
Effectively treated/fully vaccinated	r = -0.111	r = -0.060	r = -0.196	r = -0.117

NOTE: An asterisk (*) indicates that p < 0.05.

child mortality and measures of the sex differential in more effective use of health care and child mortality are also consistently negative. However, none of those associations distinguishing differential patterns of care among ever-vaccinated children and children receiving any form of treatment are statistically significant.

In-depth field studies in South-central Asia have yielded convincing evidence both that girls attend health-care facilities less often than boys and that that difference is implicated in excess female childhood mortality. The nationally representative survey data examined in the present study are consistent with that view. In Bangladesh, northern India and Pakistan, girls receive less preventive care than boys. In Bangladesh and northern India, they are also less likely to have their symptoms of disease treated at all or to receive appropriate care than boys. What the present comparative study emphasizes is that that finding cannot be generalized to other parts of the world. Although aggregate analyses that fail to control for confounding variables can mislead, differential health care is neither widespread nor important enough to explain excess female mortality in childhood in most of the developing world. According to the DHS surveys, higher child mortality among girls than boys is characteristic of much of the developing world. Since there is limited evidence outside South-central Asia of marked sex differentials in health service use other factors must account for excess mortality among girls in other regions.

The apparent contradiction between that conclusion and those of earlier research probably arises from a publication bias affecting investigations of the present topic. Studies of sex differentials in health care are less likely to be initiated or pursued to the point of publication in regions of the world where they are unimportant. Thus, they have tended to focus on South-central Asia, where excess female child mortality is particularly marked and girls often receive worse health care than boys.

The survey data on reported morbidity reinforce existing evidence that even in populations where girls' mortality is higher, the reported prevalence of disease is at least as high among boys. Objective anthropometric data collected by the DHS suggest the same conclusion (chapter VI above). Thus, the reason why

girls suffer higher mortality must be because they are less likely to recover from disease. Part of the explanation for the higher case fatality among girls may lie in more subtle aspects of health service use than are measured here. For example, parents' compliance with regimes of treatment may be more meticulous when they are caring for sick sons than when they are caring for daughters. In addition, wider aspects of the quality of child care within the home are probably relevant. It seems possible that subtle but pervasive differences in the way that parents interact with their sons and daughters are important. Thus, identifying particular aspects of behaviour that are of significance may be just as difficult as it has been to identify the mechanisms accounting for the impact of maternal education on child mortality (Cleland, 1990).

On occasion, boys receive worse health care than girls. That fact has been overlooked in the literature on sex differentials in mortality, largely because most studies of that subject have been conducted in societies where there is strong preference for sons. It seems unlikely that the instances of relative male disadvantage reflect deliberate discrimination by parents. Although that argument might be sustainable for some matrilineal populations in sub-Saharan Africa, the influence of gender on behaviour is probably more subtle. Equally, it seems likely that more complex processes than overt discrimination are also responsible for the mortality differential in at least some populations where it is girls that are disadvantaged.

Higher male service use in childhood is less pervasive than excess female mortality. Nevertheless, the health care received by boys and girls differs in countries with a range of levels of health service provision and epidemiological profiles. There is a long way to go before that potential source of inequalities in child health is eliminated. Plainly, the right of every child to facilities for the treatment of illness (UNICEF, 1990) is not being fulfilled.

NOTE

[1]Box plots indicate for a distribution, the location of the median (the horizontal line within the box) and the extremes of the distribution (the ends of the verticle lines extending beyond the central box or the individual points just above or below them if outliers exist).

Alam, N., H. Fitzroy and M. Rahaman (1989). Reporting errors in one-week diarrhoea recall surveys: experience from a prospective study in rural Bangladesh. *International Journal of Epidemiology* (Oxford), vol. 18, No. 3 (September), pp. 697-699.

Assogba, L., O. Campbell and A. Hill (1989). Advantages and limitations of large scale health interview surveys for the study of health and its determinants. In *The Health Transition: Methods and Measures*, J. Cleland and A. Hill, eds. Canberra: Australian National University.

Barbieri, M. (1989). The determinants of infant and child mortality in Senegal: an analysis of DHS data. Unpublished doctoral thesis, University of California at Berkeley.

Basu, A. (1987). Is discrimination in food really necessary for explaining sex differentials in childhood mortality? Paper presented at the British Society for Population Studies conference on health interventions and mortality change in developing countries, Sheffield, United Kingdom, 9-11 September.

_____ (1989). Is discrimination in food really necessary for explaining sex differentials in childhood mortality? *Population Studies* (London), vol. 43, No. 2 (July), pp. 193-210.

_____, and K. Basu (1991). Women's economic roles and child survival: the case of India. *Health Transition Review* (Canberra, Australia), vol. 1, No. 1 (April), pp. 83-103.

Bhuiya, A., and K. Streatfield (1991). Mothers' education and survival of female children in rural areas of Bangladesh. *Population Studies* (London), vol. 45, No. 2 (July), pp. 253-264.

Blum, D., and R. G. Feachem (1993). Measuring the impact of water supply and sanitation investments on diarrhoeal diseases: problems of methodology. *International Journal of Epidemiology* (Oxford), vol. 12, No. 3, pp. 357-365.

Boerma, J., A. Sommerfelt, S. Rutstein and G. Rojas (1990). *Immunization: Levels, Trends and Differentials*. DHS Comparative Studies, No 1. Columbia, Maryland: Institute for Resource Development.

Boerma, J., A. Sommerfelt and S. Rutstein (1991). *Childhood Morbidity and Treatment Patterns*. DHS Comparative Studies, No. 4. Columbia, Maryland: Institute for Resource Development.

Bourne, K., and G. Walker (1991). The differential effect of mothers' education on mortality of boys and girls in India. *Population Studies* (London), vol. 45, No. 2 (July), pp. 203-219.

Cantrelle, P., I. L. Diop, M. Garenne, M. Gueye and A. Sadio (1986). The profile of mortality and its determinants in Senegal 1960-1980. In United Nations, *Determinants of Mortality Change and Differentials in Developing Countries* (United Nations publication, Sales No. E.85.XIII.4).

Chen, L. C., E. Huq and S. D' Souza (1981). Sex bias in the family allocation of food and health care in rural Bangladesh. *Population and Development Review* (New York), vol. 7, No. 1 (March), pp. 55-70.

Cleland J. (1990). Maternal education and child survival: further evidence and explanations. In *What We Know about Health Transition*. J. Caldwell, S. Findley, P. Caldwell et al., eds. Canberra: Australian National University.

_____, and J. Van Ginneken (1989). Maternal schooling and childhood mortality. *Journal of Biosocial Science* (Cambridge, United Kingdom), vol. 10, Supplement, pp. 13-34.

Das Gupta, M. (1987). Selective discrimination against female children in rural Punjab, India. *Population and Development Review* (New York), vol. 13, No. 1 (March), pp. 77-100.

Delgado, H. L., V. Valverde and E. Hurtado (1986). Effect of health and nutrition interventions on infant and child mortality in rural Guatemala in the United Nations. In United Nations, *Determi-*

nants of Mortality Change and Differentials in Developing Countries (United Nations publication, Sales No. E.85.XIII.4).

Dyson, T., and M. Moore (1983). On kinship structure, female autonomy and demographic behaviour in India. *Population and Development Review* (New York), vol. 9, No. 1 (March), pp. 35-60.

Fauveau, V., M. A. Koenig and B. Wojtyniak (1991). Excess female deaths among rural Bangladeshi children: an examination of cause-specific mortality and morbidity. *International Journal of Epidemiology* (Oxford, United Kingdom), vol. 20, No. 3 (September), pp. 729-735.

Findley, S., and C. Mbacke (1993). Family, culture and community influences on maternal care-giving in rural Mali. Paper presented at the Twenty-second Population Conference of the International Union for the Scientific Study of Population, Montreal.

Froozani, M. D., H. Malekafzali and B. Bahrini (1980). Growth of a group of low income infants in the first year of life. *Journal of Tropical Paediatrics* (London), vol. 26, No. 3 (June), pp. 96-98.

Harriss, B. (1989). Differential female mortality and health care in South Asia. *Journal of Social Studies* (Dhaka), vol. 44 (April).

Hill, K., and D. M. Upchurch (1994). Gender differences in child health: evidence from the Demographic and Health Surveys. Paper presented at the annual meeting of the Population Association of America, Miami, 5-7 May.

Khan, M. E., R. Anker, S. K. G. Dastidar and S. Bairathi (1991). Inequalities between men and women in nutrition and family welfare services: an in depth enquiry in an Indian village. In *Selected Readings in the Cultural, Social and Behavioral Determinants of Health*, J. Caldwell and G. Santow, eds. Canberra: Australia National University.

Koenig, M., and S. D'Souza (1986). Sex differences in childhood mortality in rural Bangladesh. *Social Science and Medicine* (Elmsford, New York), vol. 22, No. 1, pp. 15-22.

LeGrand, T. (1992). Annotated Bibliography on Sex Differentials in Infant and Child Mortality in the Developing World. Document de travail, No. 22. Université de Montréal, Département de démographie.

Levinson, F. J. (1974). *Morinda: an Economic Analysis of Malnutrition among Young Children in Rural India*. Cambridge, Massachussetts: MIT/Cornell University Press.

Makinson, C. (1985). Age and sex differences in treatment of childhood diarrhoea episodes in rural Menoufia. Unpublished manuscript.

Mbacke, C., and T. LeGrand (1991). Differences de mortalité selon le sexe et utilisation des services de santé au Mali. In *Proceedings of the Demographic and Health Surveys World Conference, August 5-7 1991, Washington D.C.*, vol. III. Columbia, Maryland: Institute for Resource Development.

Muhuri, P. K., and S. H. Preston (1991). Effects of family composition on mortality differentials by sex among children in Matlab, Bangladesh. *Population and Development Review* (New York), vol. 17, No. 3 (September), pp. 415-434.

Murray, C. J. L., and L. C. Chen (1992). Understanding morbidity change. *Population and Development Review* (New York), vol. 18, No. 3 (September), pp. 481-503.

Premrajan, K. C., and D. K. Srinivasan (1991). Child health care: is there a gender difference? *Journal of Family Welfare* (Bombay, India), vol. 37, No. 4 (December), pp. 27-31.

Rahaman, M. M., K. M. S. Aziz, M. H. Munshi, Y. Patwari and M. Rahman (1982). A diarrhoea clinic in rural Bangladesh: influence of distance, age and sex on attendance and diarrhoeal mortality. *American Journal of Public Health* (Washington, D.C.), vol. 72, No. 10 (October), pp. 1124-1128.

Rutstein, S. (1984). *Infant and Child Mortality: Levels, Trends and Demographic Differentials*. WFS Comparative Studies, No. 43. International Statistical Institute.

Sabir, N. L., and G. J. Ebrahim (1984). Are daughters more at risk than sons in some societies? *Journal of Tropical Paediatrics* (London), vol. 30, No. 4 (August), pp. 237-239.

Santow, G. (1995). Social roles and physical health: the case of female disadvantage in poor countries. *Social Science and Medicine* (Elmsford, New York), vol. 40, No. 2 (January), pp. 147-161.

Tabutin, D., and M. Willems (1993). La surmortalité des petite filles dans le monde des annees 1970 aux années 1980. Paper presented at the Twenty-second Population Conference of the International Union for the Scientific Study of Population, Montreal.

Teçke, B., and F. Shorter (1984). Determinants of childhood mortality, a study of squatter settlements in Jordan. *Population and Development Review* (New York), vol. 10, Supplement, pp. 257-280.

UNICEF, Regional Office for the Middle East and North Africa. (1990). *Sex Differentials in Child Survival and Development*. Evaluation Series, No. 6.

Visaria, L. (1988). Sex differentials in nutritional status and survival during infancy and childhood: review of available evidence. Paper presented at the Conference on Women's Position and Demographic Change in the Course of Development, Asker, Norway, 15-18 June.

Waldron, I. (1987). Patterns and causes of excess female mortality among children in developing countries. *World Health Statistics Quarterly* (Geneva), vol. 40, No. 3, pp. 194-210.

Ware, H. (1981). *Women, Demography and Development*, Demography Teaching Notes, No. 3. Canberra: Australian National University.

World Bank (1993). *World Development Report 1993: Investing in Health*. New York: Oxford University Press.

VIII. THE EFFECT OF MATERNAL EDUCATION ON CHILD HEALTH AND SURVIVAL - DO GIRLS BENEFIT?

John Cleland* and Katie Harris*

The strong links between a woman's education, her reproductive behaviour and the survival of her children have been repeatedly demonstrated for the past 15 years. The advantages that appear to flow from chooling provide ample justification for policies designed to improve school enrolment and retention, particularly for females. In the policy debate, it is often assumed that daughters will benefit even more than sons from the exposure of their mother to schooling, thereby redressing a prevailing pro-son bias in parental care. The aim of the present chapter is to assess the validity of that assumption, using data from a wide range of developing countries.

First, evidence concerning the well established maternal education-child survival relationship and the possible mechanisms involved are briefly reviewed. That review is followed by an outline of existing hypotheses concerning the question of central interest: does the education of a mother bring about a relative shift in health and survival of her sons and daughters? The relevant literature is outlined. A description of the data and methods used in the present study, together with their limitations, follows. The most plausible pathways, differential nutrition and health-seeking behaviour, are then examined, by analysing data on health indicators from phase I Demographic and Health Surveys (DHS). Lastly, child mortality is analysed with the aim of ascertaining whether maternal education has a mediating effect on sex differentials.

A. BACKGROUND, HYPOTHESES AND EVIDENCE

Since the pioneering study in Nigeria by Caldwell (1979), a huge body of evidence has been assembled on the relationship between maternal schooling and child survival. Cross-national analyses of World Fertility Survey data (e.g., Hobcraft, McDonald and Rutstein, 1984) have been followed by similarly extensive investigations of DHS data (e.g., Bicego and Boerma, 1991). That comparative work has been complemented by a myriad of studies of single populations. In developing countries, the ubiquity and the strength of the statistical link, particularly for child rather than infant mortality, is in no doubt. However, there is less certainty and agreement about its underlying causes. Education is no mere proxy for income or wealth, but there are few convincing demonstrations, thus far, that exposure to primary schooling automatically enhances the knowledge, autonomy or power of women in ways that might impinge on child health. Similarly, the proximate pathways of influence have not been unambiguously identified. Better domestic hygiene is one possible pathway, but educational differentials in reported incidence or prevalence of diarrhoeal morbidity are usually modest and thus not strongly supportive of the thesis that educated mothers protect their children more effectively than less educated mothers from water or food-borne pathogens.

Evidence concerning curative care is somewhat more positive. Most investigations have found that maternal education is associated with an enhanced propensity to seek allopathic care for sick children. It is also probable but by no means proven that education encourages mothers to act more promptly when confronted by illness to extract a better quality of care from health services and staff and to comply more closely to recommendations. Here, then, is one plausible cluster of factors that offers at least a partial explanation for the powerful influence of mother's education on child survival. However, as can be seen from a recently published exchange on the subject, many factors may be involved and simple monocausal explanations are unlikely to prove adequate (Australian National University, Health Transition Centre, 1994).

---

*Center for Population Studies, London School of Hygiene and Tropical Medicine.

Interest among demographers and social scientists in differential valuation of sons and daughters has an even longer pedigree than interest in the education-child survival relationship. Evidence that sons may have a greater value in parental eyes than daughters can take many forms: the direct testimony of survey respondents concerning the desired sex of future offspring; inferences from reproductive behaviour itself; sex-selective infanticide and foeticide; and sex differentials in child survival and health. To summarize a huge literature in crude terms, son preference in one form or another has been found in much of Asia and Northern Africa but not to the same extent elsewhere.

There is much debate over whether son preference is a product of economic structures or sociocultural contexts and the extent to which it is expressed in forms of conscious discrimination. Das Gupta (1987) takes the view that cultural factors underlie differential treatment of males and females. Cultural factors are "translated into economic considerations" (p. 96), for instance, by denial of asset ownership rights and unfavourable household resource flows for women. Similarly, in rural Bangladesh the higher economic value of boys emanates from a complex set of cultural practices and institutional arrangements, such as purdah, dowries, early and patrilocal marriages (Koenig and D'Souza, 1986). In turn, boys' enhanced economic value perpetuates those sociocultural institutions by increasing women's dependency on men for economic and social security in risky and patriarchal environments (Cain, 1978; Koenig and D'Souza, 1986). Women therefore have a great incentive to bear sons and maintain them in good health (Pebley and Amin, 1991).

The finding that girls with older surviving sisters have increased mortality leads Das Gupta to the conclusion that intentional "selective discrimination" against girls exists, particularly higher order daughters. Conversely, Waldron (1987) concludes that parents generally do not engage in conscious discrimination between sons and daughters, but rather that sex discrimination is embodied in cultural beliefs; for example, girls may be seen as more hardy and there-fore in less need of health care.

Others argue that economic rationality underpins son preference. Gender inequality, with its associated health outcomes, is not uniform across time and space but tends to be heightened in specific contexts and for certain subgroups. Extreme economic pressure may force poor families to allocate limited resources in order to maximize chances of survival, and the criterion used for allocation may be gender. Again, that discrimination need not take the form of deliberate neglect of girls, but rather the preferential treatment of boys. The severe famine in Matlab, Bangladesh, in 1974 and 1975, provides evidence consistent with that interpretation: sex differentials in child mortality increased because girls received even less food and other care than usual relative to boys (Bairagi, 1986). Behrman's (1988) econometric analysis of intra-household nutrient allocation in rural India parallels that result. Behrman finds that pro-male bias in parental preferences is exacerbated by 5 per cent in the lean season; a combination of a response to differential expected labour market returns to nutrient investments in boys versus those in girls, and of a degree of tolerance to gender inequality.

It follows that son preference and sex differentials in mortality should be less evident in more favourable circumstances. That is the case in the study of Pebley and Amin (1991) on the impact of a public health intervention on sex differentials in child mortality in the Ludhiana District of the Punjab. The ratio of male to female child mortality rates declined in the villages that received nutritional supplements but remained constant in the control villages. That reduction in sex differentials was probably a consequence of the fact that family resource allocation systems were overridden by the project intervention rather than the result of any shift in attitudes.

However, the clearest evidence that sex differentials in mortality do not necessarily decline in more affluent settings also comes from the Punjab. Not only is the population of Punjab the wealthiest in India, it is the most biased against girls (Bourne and Walker, 1991; Das Gupta, 1987). Similarly, a study of two villages in West Bengal found a larger differential in nutritional status between boys and girls in the wealthier than in the other village (Sen and Sengupta, 1983). As Das Gupta (1987) emphasizes, "For India as a whole...scarcity of resources may at most accentuate the effects of sex bias within a given culture" (p. 96).

Those mixed findings of the association between socio-economic-cultural factors, son preference and sex differentials in mortality serve as a warning that any effects of maternal education on sex-biased attitudes and gendered behaviours may be complex and contingent upon whether the biases arise from intentional behaviour or from less deliberate predispositions. Two contrasting expectations are examined here.

The first expectation has three strands, all with the common theme that education is likely to reduce sex differentials in child mortality in settings where son preference exists. First, if son preference is seen predominantly as a reflection of patriarchal cultural values it might be expected that gender differentials will narrow as mothers become more educated. The rationale derives from the Nigerian research of Caldwell (1979) . Education can erode traditional sex-biased attitudes, encourage the development of more modern egalitarian views influenced by western values and thereby bring about a more equal allocation of resources between boys and girls. Caldwell asserts that education also affects the position of the woman in the family and in society. That improved status and self-esteem of the woman will also result in an increase in her perceived value of daughters, thereby reaffirming a more equitable division of resources by gender (Ware, 1984).

The second strand stems from the interpretation that son preference is an economically rational response to a situation of limited resources. It is still expected that sex differentials in health and mortality will narrow as mothers become more educated, but for different reasons than those advanced above. Educated women are likely to have greater resources available to them, associated to some extent with enhanced economic status. Furthermore, educated women might make better use of existing resources and gain improved health-related knowledge. One possible consequence is that even if underlying attitudes remain resistant to the experience of schooling, educated women are less likely than uneducated women to be forced into vital gender-biased decisions regarding the allocation of resources (Ware, 1984).

The third strand to the first type of expectation is that maternal education may decrease sex differentials in child mortality purely because of the changing cause-of-death structure that is associated with declining levels of mortality. In particular, accidents, which usually affect sons more than daughters, become more prominent as a cause of death when the impact of infectious diseases is lessened (Waldron, 1987). Thus, better educated groups with associated lower mortality from infectious diseases face risks of death that disadvantage boys rather than girls.

The competing expectation is that increased maternal education can actually inflate gender differentials in contexts where biases against daughters are intentional, whether for cultural or economic reasons. Even if the actual risks of death decrease for both boys and girls, boys benefit disproportionately. The main proponent of that argument is Das Gupta (1987), who proposes that educated mothers may deploy their enhanced skills as "producers" of child health in a selective manner that favours sons more than daughters.

There are two variants of that basic argument. First, if son preference has an intentional, cultural basis, as Das Gupta claims for the Punjab, discrimination against daughters will be closely related to family-building strategies; specifically, parents will be careful to restrict the number of daughters they have. More educated women want small family sizes but still wish to have one or two sons; those twin considerations create a pressure to have fewer surviving daughters. In other words, declining fertility associated with increased education exposes underlying attitudes. One solution, increasingly common in some Asian countries, is sex-selective abortion. The alternative is a relative neglect of higher order daughters, who experience excess mortality. The second variant assumes that son preference has a more economic but less deliberate basis. As Behrman's review in chapter X suggests, educated parents may be particularly sensitive to gendered market forces. They may act in an even more economically rational manner to the detriment of their daughters in contexts where boys bring the greatest economic returns to investment. The evidence for those two competing expectations is outlined below.

The most convincing evidence that education reduces sex differentials in child mortality is from northern India. Simmons and others (1982) found that the education of mothers improved the survival of daughters only, even after controlling for the age of mothers and health service access in Uttar Pradesh. Similar results were obtained from the 1981 Indian census data by Bourne and Walker (1991), who analysed the mortality tables of Indian states to determine whether mortality was different for boys and girls by region and age. They then classified the data by the educational level of the mother to assess the relative effects of education on sex-specific mortality. Their findings confirmed that maternal education has a clear effect on mortality that is greater for boys in infancy but more pronounced for girls thereafter, particularly in the northern states. The reduction in under-five mortality associated with a shift from no maternal education to matriculate but not graduate level was 77.4 per 1,000 for northern boys; for northern girls, the corresponding reduction was 95.9 per 1,000.

Tulasidhar (1993) also analysed the Indian census of 1981, this time defining education in terms of the number of years of schooling. He estimated mortality gradients (the decline in child mortality for an additional year of maternal education). Consistent with Bourne and Walker's findings, female under-five mortality rates fall more quickly in the entire country than those of males (a 20 per 1,000 decline for every year of additional education in the 1-7 years of education class, compared to 16.2 per 1,000). Furthermore, the steepest mortality-education gradients occur for girls in certain northern states. Even after controlling for female labour force participation, length of maternal schooling has a large and significant effect on female child mortality.

There is very little evidence to support the first expectation outside South-central Asia. One exception is an analysis of Egypt's World Fertility Survey. Mother's education was represented as a dichotomy: complete primary school or above versus incomplete primary or no schooling. Multivariate analysis indicated that daughters benefited significantly more than boys from the education of the mother (Ahmed, 1992). However, contrary results were obtained in Jordan, where Weinberger and Heligman (1987) found that boys benefited more than girls.

The second expectation is that increased education can actually exacerbate sex imbalances in mortality and other health outcomes. Supporting evidence comes from Basu's (1989) study of mortality and health care for Uttar Pradesh immigrants living in a Delhi slum. Mothers with some education were more likely than uneducated mothers to favour sons in terms of health care, and excess female mortality was correspondingly greater.

Further positive evidence comes from the Punjab (Das Gupta, 1987). Parity-specific sex differentials were found to be influenced by maternal education in that resurvey of the 11 villages in the Ludhiana District from the Khanna Study (Gordon and others, 1965). Uneducated women experienced markedly higher child mortality rates than women with one or more years of education, for all sons and for the first daughter. However, the mortality of girls born to mothers who already have one or more surviving daughters was similar among educated and uneducated mothers. An examination of sex ratios of food consumption, expenditure on children's clothing and medicine suggested that relative female disadvantage in medical care was the most important factor in accounting for the widening sex differentials in child mortality at higher birth orders. However, those data were not stratified by maternal education levels. Further, mortality rates during the first five years of life were based on fewer than 40 deaths that occurred over a period of 20 years, and statistical significance tests were not employed.

Results similar to those of Das Gupta are reported by Stanton and Clemens (1986). They failed to find any narrowing of the sex differential in childhood (under six years) mortality among families where the mother is educated, in their urban Bangladesh sample. The relative disadvantage of daughters worsened among better educated families because of a sharper mortality decline among boys. The authors conclude that female deaths are more resource-independent than boys, and that female deaths result from a "non-allocation of adequate family resources to the child" (p. 14).

Data from the Bangladesh Fertility Survey conducted in 1974 and 1975 also found the education of mothers to be associated with a relative deterioration in the welfare of girls. For mothers with an education above the primary level, female infants were three times as likely to die as boys; for mothers with no education, the ratio was 1.46. The ratios were lower, but in the same direction for the older age group of 2-10 year old children (Huda, 1980). However, the "above primary" category contained only 77 deaths and significance tests were not performed.

Bhuiya and others (1986) examined the relationship between child nutrition and socio-economic status for boys and girls using longitudinal data from Matlab district in rural Bangladesh. They found that the proportion of children classified as malnourished (less than 70 per cent of standard weight-for-age) declined with maternal education, but the decline was greater among boys. However, beyond the threshold of six or more years of education, the sex disparity in nutritional status narrowed considerably, though that result was based on few cases.

Further evidence for Bangladesh comes from a good study using a combination of longitudinal data (1982 to 1984) and a socio-economic household survey (1982). Bhuiya and Streatfield (1991) followed the 1982 birth cohort for 2 years in the Matlab district. A hazard model was used to investigate the relationship between household and individual socio-economic covariates and child mortality, thus taking account of the censoring of observations and also the rapid change of mortality risks from one age group to the next during childhood. A maximum-likelihood logit model analysis was carried out to ascertain the net effects of the independent variables (including maternal education, categorized as "no schooling", "1-5 years" and "6 or more years"), as well as their dependence on the sex of the children. Their results show that mothers' education had an unequal impact on the survival of boys and girls: both the female and male predicted risks of death between the ages of 6 and 36 months decreased with higher education of the mother, but the female one was always higher and decreased more slowly. Thus, sex ratios of mortality reflect an increasing relative female disadvantage. Bhuiya and Streatfield attempted to explain that phenomenon with the help of Mosley and Chen's (1984) model of proximate determinants of child survival and other research. Out of maternal characteristics, environmental contamination, injury, nutrient deficiency and personal illness control, the first two are unlikely to be conditioned by the sex of the child. Injury and accidents disadvantage boys more than girls. No evidence of sex differentials in preventive health measures, particularly immunization, was found for that study population. The authors were left with the suggestion that interactions between the mother's education and sex discrimination in curative health measures and feeding were responsible for the observed mortality inequalities. Increased education enabled mothers to become even more sensitive to illness in boys and effective in their care of them.

The results of several studies are neutral or ambiguous with regard to the two competing expectations concerning the influence of mother's education on sex differentials in mortality. Instead, they find that the influence of maternal education on the survival of boys and girls is equal or that it is conditioned by length of schooling. Weinberger and Heligman (1987) analysed World Fertility Survey data from six countries in South-central and Western Asia, and four countries in Eastern and South-eastern Asia, all of which are characterized by son preference to different extents. The South-central Asian countries showed consistent patterns; sex ratios of child mortality were lower for women with one to three years of education than for women with no education or with four to six years. Women with four to six years of education show higher sex ratios of mortality than those with fewer or no years. Thus, it appears that male children benefit disproportionately from initial increases in women's education, but girls benefit disproportionately as women pass the early primary years. No such pattern is seen for infant mortality among the South Asian countries, nor, at either age group, among the Eastern Asian countries. In the latter, sex ratios increase or decrease very erratically. Only Jordan provides significant findings, in favour of the second expectation (i.e., that education with exacerbate sex differentials) and only for infant mortality.

Muhuri and Preston (1991) found that sex differentials did not vary with the level of mothers' schooling in their Matlab study of longitudinal data linked to the 1982 Matlab census. Mothers' education does not interact with the sex of children to affect significantly their mortality, even when controlling for family composition. The authors expect that finding since they attribute much of the higher child mortality among poorly educated mothers to inadequate hygiene practices and to their lack of contact with modern health facilities. Both girls and boys should benefit equally from improvements that stem from maternal education.

To summarize, mixed conclusions have been reached concerning the mediating effects of maternal education on sex differentials in mortality and in their proximate determinants. Plausible results exist to support both the expectation that maternal education will reduce and its opposite—that it will inflate male-female differences in mortality. Unfortunately, evidence is largely restricted to South-central Asia, thereby inviting caution in extrapolating to other regions.

Perhaps the two competing expectations can be reconciled to a certain extent by combining several theories of how education influences child mortality, and by recognizing that more than one underlying reason for sex differentials may exist. Partin (n.d.) summarizes that possible reconciliation well, on finding that the sex gap in survival in Bangladesh was wider when the mother was moderately educated than when the mother was uneducated or highly educated: "those changes represent temporary adjustments to shifting circumstances and the differences will eventually converge" (p. 20). Partin accepts that education increases the availability and use of resources, but also realises that there may be a considerable time lag before sex-biased attitudes change in a society; only when those attitudes change will the original discriminating behaviour that favours males also change.

B. DATA AND METHODS

Data from the first phase of the DHS are analysed in the present chapter. Twenty-seven developing countries participated in that phase, and are listed in table 61. It should be noted that neither of the two countries (India and Bangladesh) that have furnished the bulk of evidence on sex differentials in mortality are represented. The majority of countries are in Central and South America or in Africa. Data from the birth history section provide the child mortality estimates, while the child health and child anthropometry sections furnish supplementary information on health indicators. Those child records were linked to the mother's characteristics, particularly her educational status. Comparable data on child mortality are available from all surveys, but coverage of health information is less complete; for instance, nine surveys did not collect anthropometric data.

1. *Mortality measures*

The indicator of child mortality used in the present chapter is the life-table measure, $_{54}q_6$, the probability of death between the age of six months and 5 years. That unconventional measure was chosen because the influence of maternal education on risks of death is known to be stronger in childhood than in early infancy, when biological determinants predominate (Waldron, 1987). Weaning rarely occurs before the age of six months, and that transition signals an increasing vulnerability of children to infection and malnutrition; thus, sex differentials in preventive or curative health measures will become more important following the introduction of breast milk supplements. Furthermore, data quality problems, such as birth displacement and age at death misreporting (especially heaping on 12 months), can have significant impacts on standard measures of infant and child mortality in DHS enquiries (Sullivan, Rutstein and Bicego, 1994). To minimize the effects of such errors, a mortality measure spanning 6 to 60 months of age is used. It represents the life-table probability of death between age 6 and 60 months per 1,000 children who were born in the 10 years prior to the surveys.

Sex differentials in child mortality are defined as of the ratio of male $_{54}q_6$ to female $_{54}q_6$. Thus, a ratio of greater than one is an indicator of male disadvantage, and a sex ratio less than one suggests female disadvantage. The Cox-Mantel test is used to assess the null hypothesis that there is no sex difference in mortality (see Namboodiri and Suchindran, 1987). The Cox-Mantel test statistic is normally distributed in large samples, with a mean of zero and variance of one. Age-standardized mortality risks are used (6-12 months, 12 months to 2 years, 2-4 years). Computational procedures are outlined below.

Firstly, the "expected numbers" of deaths are calculated among children of each sex under the assumption of no sex difference in mortality. That is done by distributing the number of deaths at each age interval in proportion to the numbers of males and females at risk at the beginning of that age interval. The Cox-Mantel test examines whether the observed number of deaths is significantly different from the expected number, for either males or females. The test statistic (C) is equal to the difference between the expected and observed number of deaths, divided by the square root of the variance of the difference. The equation for the variance includes a correction term for sampling from a finite population without replacement. Statistical tables for the normal distribution are used to assess the significance level of the resultant test statistic. Just two educational groups (none versus primary or higher) are used here in order that the sample size in each group may be large enough to justify the approximation to the normal distribution.

2. Health indicators

The review of evidence suggests that the two most likely mechanisms by which maternal education may interact with sex differentials in child survival are differential feeding practices (reflected in nutritional status and measured with anthropometric indices) and curative health care. The DHS collects children's anthropometric data and information on the case management of diarrhoea, fever and cough for recent morbidity episodes. Not all surveys, however, contain all the relevant questions, as discussed below.

Food intake is one of the major determinants of a child's health, and may be influenced by parental behaviour through intrafamilial food distribution practices. In turn, parental behaviour may be conditioned by educational status and the sex of the child. Since no direct data on food intake are available in the DHS anthropometric indices are used as a crude proxy. In fact, the growth of children is governed not only by food intake but also by incidence, duration and severity of infections (Bairagi, 1986; chapter V above).

Height-for-age is chosen as the indicator of nutritional status. Eighteen of the surveys collected those data (table 55) by measuring the height of surviving children in varying age ranges within the 0-60-month bracket. Such anthropometric data for children aged between 3 and 36 months are available in 16 surveys; an additional two surveys, Senegal and Dominican Republic, collected information for children aged 6-35 months. Height-for-age data provide a good indication of the overall health status of children. Since such measures taken for 3-35 month old children vary little from those among 4 and 5 year olds the narrower age range does not limit the comparison with the broader age ranges used for mortality and treatment indicators.

Differentials in that status, by sex and by maternal education, are measured by comparing the proportions of children who are stunted in any group. Stunting is defined as a height-for-age Z-score below -2 standard deviations from the median of the International Reference Population (WHO/CDC/NCHS), and reflects chronic malnutrition due to insufficient protein-energy intake and repeated morbidity.

Stunting is chosen in preference to wasting (low weight-for-age) since proportions stunted gives a larger numerator with which to analyse differentials. Furthermore, an indicator of long-term health status is desired to complement the information on recent morbidity and its treatment.

The second health indicator concerns mode of treatment of recent diarrhoeal episodes. Relevant morbidity information for a reference period of two weeks was elicited in most DHSs, while parallel questions on fever and respiratory disorders were less commonly included. Treatment rather than morbidity itself is the focus or attention, because of evidence that sex differentials are more likely for diarrhoeal case-fatality than for incidence (Fauveau, Koenig and Wojtyniak, 1991).

Effective treatment of an illness episode is crucial to the health of a child. It is the recovery rate from illness that is really of interest here, but there is no direct measure of that in the DHS. As an indirect proxy of the recovery rate, questions to mothers about their health-seeking behaviour for their sick child are used. Three indicators have been defined: proportions of sick children who are treated in any way; proportions taken to a modern health facility; and proportions treated with oral rehydration solution (ORS). The latter two indicators are assumed to be the most appropriate forms of case management for diarrhoea. They are also probably more sensitive to maternal education and children's sex than is "any treatment", since they require greater knowledge, greater time and monetary costs, and more complex decision-making.

Variations between surveys in the way in which questions on treatment are asked is a potential problem. Some surveys did not include a direct question on "any treatment"; they are excluded from the analysis of that particular variable. "Use of modern health facility" is elicited in a variety of ways; for instance, in

185

TABLE 55. NUMBER OF CHILDREN AGED 3-35 MONTHS, WHO ARE AT RISK OF STUNTING, BY MATERNAL EDUCATION

Region and country	No education		Primary education		Secondary and higher education	
	Males	Females	Males	Females	Males	Females
Eastern and Southern Africa						
Burundi	788	781	180	151	20	24
Uganda	460	535	612	635	86	90
Zimbabwe	139	135	470	493	140	161
Northern Africa						
Egypt	500	413	324	312	141	147
Morocco	1 319	1 338	150	147	92	76
Tunisia	552	552	391	349	72	90
Western Africa						
Ghana	400	357	485	510	43	46
Mali	389	368	93	77	5	4
Senegal	260	248	36	45	14	18
Togo	416	382	199	190	66	74
Southern and South-eastern Asia						
Sri Lanka	105	73	304	281	393	346
Thailand	77	74	746	711	84	86
Latin America and the Caribbean						
Bolivia	303	280	692	638	266	307
Brazil	55	57	197	203	39	23
Colombia	99	88	390	366	92	139
Dominican Republic	49	61	615	601	185	227
Guatemala	554	580	502	511	23	18
Trinidad and Tobago	3	3	195	218	199	209

Source: Demographic and Health Survey data tapes.

some surveys, a modern facility is equivalent to a hospital, while in others, it includes health clinics, private doctors and pharmacies. Definitions of the "modern health facility use" variable for each survey are contained in annex table A.2 below. It should be noted, however, that that inter-survey variability should not bias intra-survey estimates of differential treatment of boys and girls (Hill and Upchurch, 1994). The definition of "ORS use" is more precise, although the phrasing of questions on ORS and on home sugar-salt solutions (SSS) varies. For several surveys, the ORS use variable was constructed from responses to an open question on treatment types for diarrhoea. Other surveys asked specific questions on ORS use. Zimbabwe does not use ORS packets as national policy, so the SSS variable substitutes. However, as with place of treatment, those variations should not

have much impact on within-survey comparisons between boys and girls, or between maternal education groups.

Sex differentials in all the above health indicators are defined in the same way as mortality, namely in terms of male to female ratios of proportions stunted, and of proportions of children treated in specified ways. However, the interpretation of the ratios differs. Sex ratios of proportions stunted that are greater than one indicate male disadvantage: girls are less likely to be stunted than boys. Conversely, high sex ratios in proportions receiving treatment for diarrhoea indicate male advantage: boys are more likely to be treated (effectively) than girls. The Pearson Chi-square test is used to ascertain the statistical significance of those sex differentials.

3. Quality of data

The mortality analysis in the present chapter is highly sensitive to sex-selective omission of dead or surviving children. Displacement of dates of birth is less likely to bias results because of the use of a broad 10-year cohort of children. Dating errors in DHSs tend to be concentrated in years four to six prior to survey date. Similarly, misreporting of ages at death should not have serious consequences because the mortality measure ($_{54}q_6$) covers a wide age span. What, then, is the evidence for sex-selective omission in DHS enquiries?

One check for sex selective omissions is to analyse the sex ratios at birth for different time periods; they should fall in the range of 102 to 107 boys born for every 100 girls. For most surveys, that is the case for the period of zero to 10 years before the survey. In Botswana and Uganda, it is unusually low, suggesting some omission of male births. The reverse is true of Colombia, Indonesia and Sri Lanka (Arnold, 1990). There are two possible implications for interpretation of sex-specific mortality. First, if that differential coverage of male or female births is associated with differential reporting of deaths in childhood by sex, then underestimates in mortality of one sex will result in a misleading sex ratio of child mortality. Second, even if there is complete coverage of childhood deaths for both sexes, the underreporting of births for one sex will then result in an overestimation of mortality for that sex with its reduced denominator; again, the sex ratio of mortality will be misleading.

A related potential problem is sex-selective omission of dead children. Sullivan, Bicego and Rutstein (1990) checked the sex ratios of infant mortality rates of all DHS I surveys, and the sex ratio of their sub-intervals (neonatal and postneonatal periods) for those that had exceptionally high or low sex ratios of infant mortality. For Botswana, Sri Lanka and Thailand, very high infant mortality sex ratios were found (higher than the expected range of 1.16 to 1.30 from Regional Model Life Tables (Coale and Demeny, 1966)). High sex ratios for the neonatal period and more moderate values for the postneonatal period were found in Botswana and Sri Lanka, indicating that underreporting was likely of female infants who had died in those two surveys, but less likely in Thailand. For Morocco, Trinidad and Tobago, and Tunisia, the infant mortality sex ratios were 1.05 or lower, indicating possible omission of male deaths. However, the same check on Morocco and Tunisia revealed that for the neonatal period, male mortality exceeds female mortality as expected, but higher female relative to male mortality postneonatal mortality contributes to the very low IMR sex ratio. In Trinidad and Tobago, the evidence for omission of male deaths is stronger since female mortality exceeds male mortality in both subintervals (Sullivan, Bicego and Rutstein, 1990).

Because our measure of child mortality does not include the neonatal period but includes only the late post-neonatal period, that check for sex differentials in the reporting of births and early deaths implies overall fair quality of the data.

Hill and Upchurch (1994) combine the above two checks by comparing the sex ratios of neonatal mortality with sex ratios at birth across surveys, for births in the 60 months prior to interview. They suggest that an association of high proportion male at birth with high female neonatal advantage might imply systematic error. However, they find no signs of a positive association between the two. In general, it is possible to agree with Hill and Upchurch's view (1994, p. 7) that the data are of reasonably good quality, though there are country-specific anomalies that argue against overinterpretation of results for a particular country.

The DHS data on nutritional status and treatment are for surviving children only. Thus, sex differentials in those indicators could be distorted by selection effects. However, health status is a continuum with death at one extreme; when deaths are removed, the distribution of survivors (by sex and by mother's education) along that continuum should still reflect health status differentials in well-sampled cross-sectional surveys (Hill and Upchurch, 1994). Data quality issues pertaining to particular health indicators follow.

Height-for-age is an objective measure, independent of maternal perceptions (Hill and Upchurch, 1994). Thus, there is little if any possibility of reporting biases either by the sex of the child or by the mother's education. However, the extent of coverage of eligible children, the reliability of age reporting and the accuracy of measurement potentially can affect the interpretation of anthropometric findings.

The accuracy of birth dates is important for two reasons. First, the age of the child could be exaggerated to lie beyond the age boundary where child measurement is required, leading to missing anthropometric data for eligible children. That consideration is of most concern if selection effects operate. The proportion of children eligible for anthropometric measurement but who were not measured was similar across education categories in most surveys. In some, there was a slight increase among children of mothers with higher education, a feature that can usually be explained by higher fostering rates, as in Uganda and Zimbabwe (Sommerfelt and Boerma, 1993). That potential selection effect is unlikely to vary by the sex of the child. Systematic displacement of birth dates is also important because it leads to a misspecification of severe malnutrition, particularly for infants (Sommerfelt and Boerma, 1993). Such displacement was most pronounced in the African surveys, but it is unlikely that the latter bias will vary according to the sex of the child. Absolute levels of stunting may be estimated incorrectly from the surveys, but the sex ratios in the proportions stunted should not be affected.

Heaping of height measurements on the digits .0 and .5, due to inaccurate measuring, was common in the Dominican Republic, Egypt, Ghana, Guatemala, Morocco and Tunisia. That imprecision results in systematic undermeasurement since the design of the measuring board makes it impossible to read the scale beyond the child's height (Sommerfelt and Boerma, 1993). Again, however, errors of that type are unlikely to be affected by the sex of the child.

Unlike anthropometric measures, reported morbidity is a subjective indicator, open to differential reporting of sickness according to the sex of the child, and correlated potentially with mothers' education. It is possible that lower morbidity rates among girls result from mothers being less likely to report girls as sick than boys, given equivalent symptoms (Hill and Upchurch, 1994). It is difficult to identify such biases, especially since DHS data do not allow the distinction between incidence and duration of diarrhoea. It must be acknowledged that the analysis on treatment is vulnerable to sex-selective maternal reporting of morbidity. To the extent that minor episodes are more likely to be reported for boys than girls, or vice versa, interpretation of treatment is complicated because

perceived severity is bound to be one determinant of treatment.

Difficulties in interpreting specific reference periods can also lead to recall bias, and an under or over-reporting of diarrhoeal episodes. That also applies to questions on treatment; even though a two-week reference period is generally thought to give the best balance between the quality of information (best for current or very recent illness) and the representativeness of treatment information (good for recent, not current, episodes), reporting of diarrhoea prevalence may obscure the results on treatment practices (Boerma and Van Ginneken, 1993). Recall errors (underreporting and misinterpretation of recall period) are found to vary by educational characteristics in several countries: Bolivia, the Dominican Republic, Guatemala, Kenya, Sudan, Togo and Zimbabwe . Overreporting of current/recent diarrhoea (last 24 hours) among the less educated may reflect the difficulty of interpreting specific time periods, or may be genuine in that chronic diarrhoea might be more common among children of illiterate mothers. It is difficult to assess the extent of those data quality biases, which suggests that comparison of several different health indicators is the wisest way in which to assess whether differential reporting, by sex or education, is occurring.

4. Maternal education categories

The educational composition of samples in DHS-I enquiries varies hugely. In some countries, such as Mali, Morocco and Senegal, nearly 90 per cent of children born in the preceding 10 years had mothers with no exposure to formal schooling. In other countries, the corresponding figure is about 10 per cent (e.g., Colombia, Dominican Republic, Ecuador, Sri Lanka, Trinidad and Tobago, and Thailand). Those disparities give rise to two types of problem. First, it is clear that the social meaning of the educational attainment of an individual mother varies greatly across countries. Thus, lack of any schooling in some settings denotes no more than an identity with the vast majority of women. In other settings, lack of any education implies a position of severe disadvantage, even marginalization, compared to other women. It is also likely to be associated with relative poverty, a rural upbringing and an older age. Compounding that problem are cross-country variations in the educational system. Typically, primary school spans five or six grades, but in some countries it extends to eight or nine years. In a few countries, there is an additional tier (intermediate or middle school) lying between the primary and secondary levels.

In a large comparative analysis, there is no obvious way of evading difficulties of interpretation that stem from the diversity of national circumstances. Those difficulties are particularly severe when the focus of analytic attention is on cross-national differences. In the present study, however, the main interest lies in intracountry differences in the health and survival of boys and girls, within educational strata, and thus problems of interpretation are greatly reduced.

The other problem caused by the uneven educational composition of DHS-1 countries is of a more practical nature. In many surveys, the sex-specific numerators and denominators are very small at the upper end of the educational continuum. In a small number of countries, the same problem occurs at the lower end. Those distributional variations, coupled with the relatively small size of DHS samples, severely curtail the scope of the analysis. Ideally, a detailed examination of mortality and health-related sex ratios using rather fine educational categories is required to assess whether or not the mediating effect (if any) of maternal education on those ratios is linear or whether there is a threshold. However, consideration of the standard errors of estimates precluded such an option. Instead, a rather coarse classification of education into none, primary and secondary or high groups is used. In most analyses, that three-way split has to be further collapsed into a simple dichotomy: "none" versus "some" schooling. Furthermore, estimates based on very small denominations have been omitted. For instance, in the mortality analysis estimates based on groups where less than 250 unweighed births enter the-life table have been omitted.

C. FINDINGS

1. Nutritional status

Anthropometric measures were taken in only 18 of the 27 DHS-1 surveys. In all but two of those surveys,

data are available for children aged between 3 and 36 months. The two discrepant cases are the Dominican Republic and Senegal, where a lower boundary of six rather than three months was used. Table 55 shows the number of children available for the analysis. It is immediately clear that the numbers of boys and girls born to mothers in the secondary or higher schooling groups are too small to yield stable estimates in a number of surveys. Accordingly, primary and secondary school groups have been collapsed.

It will be recalled that the selected indicator of nutritional status was height-for-age. Children with a height-for-age Z-score below two standard deviations from the median of the International Reference Population were defined as stunted. As may be seen in the right hand panel of table 56, the percentage of children who were classified as stunted varies within a rather narrow range of 20-30 per cent for most countries. Levels are higher in Bolivia, Burundi Guatemala and Uganda, but markedly lower in Trinidad and Tobago. As expected, the educational status of the mother is strongly related to the probability of stunting in her children (figure 44). With only one exception, the proportion stunted declines monotonically, as educational status improves. The strength of the relationship, however, varies between countries. In some countries, such as Burundi, Ghana and Uganda, the transition from no schooling to primary schooling is associated with a marginal improvement only, but in other countries, there is a pronounced differential between those two categories. In nearly all cases, secondary or higher schooling brings about a further substantial improvement; the only clear exceptions here are Mali and Senegal.

Across all 18 countries, boys are slightly more likely to be stunted than girls. The overall sex ratio of stunting has a median value of 1.04 and a mean of 1.07. That slight female advantage is apparent in Central and South America, and sub-Saharan Africa but disappears in the five countries of Northern Africa and Asia. However, in only two of the 18 surveys is the sex differential in stunting statistically significant at the 5 per cent level. In the Dominican Republic, 24 per cent of boys aged 6-35 months are stunted, compared to 16.9 per cent of girls, giving a very high sex ratio of 1.40. In Uganda, the difference is in the same direction but the ratio (1.12) is modest by comparison.

TABLE 56. PERCENTAGE OF CHILDREN AGED 3-35 MONTHS WHO ARE STUNTED, BY SEX AND BY EDUCATION OF MOTHER

Region and country	No education			Primary and above			Total		
	Males	Females	Ratio	Males	Females	Ratio	Males	Females	Ratio
Eastern and Southern Africa									
Burundi	48.6	48.5	1.00	43.8	43.3	1.01	47.6	47.5	1.00
Uganda	48.9*	42.4*	1.15	43.6	39.6	1.10	45.7*	40.8*	1.12
Zimbabwe	36.0	38.5	0.94	29.5	26.4	1.12	30.7	28.4	1.08
Median	48.6	42.4	1.00	43.6	39.6	1.10	45.7	47.5	1.08
Mean	44.5	43.1	1.03	39.0	36.4	1.08	41.3	38.9	1.07
Northern Africa									
Egypt	35.4	33.6	1.05	24.9	27.6	0.90	30.0	30.3	0.99
Morocco	28.3	28.6	0.99	16.3	13.1	1.24	26.4	26.2	1.01
Tunisia	20.5	23.6	0.87	13.1	13.1	1.00	17.0	18.8	0.90
Median	28.3	2.6	0.99	16.3	13.1	1.00	26.4	26.2	0.99
Mean	28.1	28.6	0.97	18.1	17.9	1.05	24.5	25.1	0.97
Western Africa									
Ghana	33.8	30.8	1.10	27.3	28.8	0.95	30.0	29.6	1.01
Mali	24.4	25.3	0.96	20.8	19.8	1.05	23.6	24.3	0.97
Senegal[a]	28.5	22.6	1.26	11.8	12.5	0.94	26.0	20.7	1.26
Togo	34.4	31.9	1.08	32.1*	23.1*	1.39	33.5	28.3	1.18
Median	31.2	28.1	1.09	24.1	21.5	1.00	28.0	26.3	1.10
Mean	30.3	27.7	1.10	22.8	21.1	1.08	28.3	25.7	1.11
Southern and South-eastern Asia									
Sri Lanka	43.8	58.0	0.76	24.1	26.2	0.92	26.0	26.0	0.91
Thailand	30.9	29.0	1.07	21.6	21.5	1.00	22.3	22.3	1.01
Median	37.4	43.5	0.91	22.9	23.8	0.96	24.2	48.3	0.96
Mean	37.4	43.5	0.91	22.9	23.8	0.96	24.2	48.3	0.96
Latin America and the Caribbean									
Bolivia	47.2	42.5	1.11	36.8	33.8	1.09	39.2	35.7	1.10
Brazil	41.9	43.8	0.96	28.8	22.0	1.31	31.3	26.4	1.19
Colombia	34.1	35.6	0.96	24.4	22.9	1.07	25.8	24.8	1.04
Dominican Republic[a]	40.9	27.2	1.50	23.1*	16.2*	1.43	24.0*	16.9*	1.42
Guatemala	65.7	64.5	1.02	48.1	44.6	1.08	56.6	54.4	1.04
Trinidad and Tobago	..	..	..	5.0	4.4	1.14	4.9	4.6	1.07
Median	41.9	35.6	1.02	26.6	19.1	1.11	28.6	25.6	1.09
Mean	45.9	42.7	1.11	27.7	24.0	1.18	30.3	27.1	1.14
Overall median	34.9	33.5	1.02	24.7	23.0	1.07	28.2	27.4	1.04
Overall mean	37.8	36.8	1.05	26.4	24.4	1.10	34.3	28.1	1.07

Source: Demographic and Health Survey data tapes.

NOTES: Children are classified as stunted if their height-for-age z-score is below -2 SD from the median of the International Reference Population (WHO/CDC/NCHS); as asterisk (*) indicates that The differential between male and female proportions stunted is significant at 5 per cent level, using chi-square test.

[a] 6-35 months.

Figure 44. Proportions of children aged 3-35 months who are stunted, by education of mother

Proportions of children stunted by education (percentage)

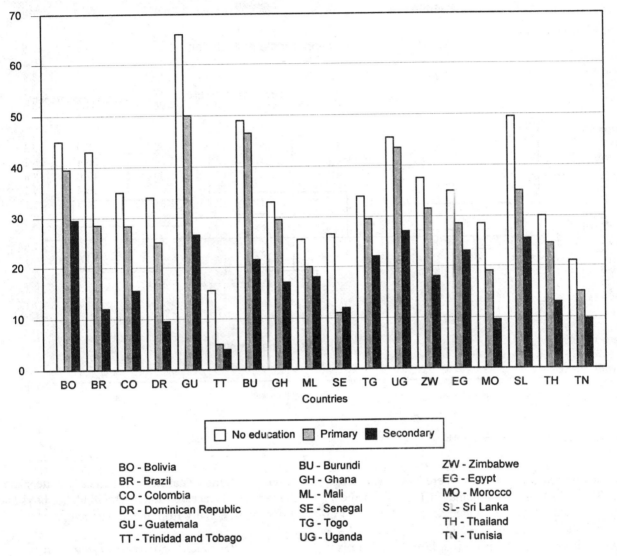

BO - Bolivia
BR - Brazil
CO - Colombia
DR - Dominican Republic
GU - Guatemala
TT - Trinidad and Tobago

BU - Burundi
GH - Ghana
ML - Mali
SE - Senegal
TG - Togo
UG - Uganda

ZW - Zimbabwe
EG - Egypt
MO - Morocco
SL - Sri Lanka
TH - Thailand
TN - Tunisia

Source: Demographic and Health Survey data tapes.

Levels of stunting are reassessed in the left and middle panels of table 56 for children of mothers with no schooling and with some schooling. An overview of results for all 18 surveys is provided in figure 45 in the form of box plots. It is evident that the slight female advantage observed for the whole sample is more pronounced among children with educated than uneducated mothers. For the educated group, the median sex ratio of stunting is 1.07 and the mean 1.10. The corresponding values for the no schooling group are closer to unity: 1.02 and 1.05, respectively.

That aggregate pattern of change masks an erratic picture at the country-specific or regional level. Within each region, there are instances where the stunting sex ratio is higher among the educated than

191

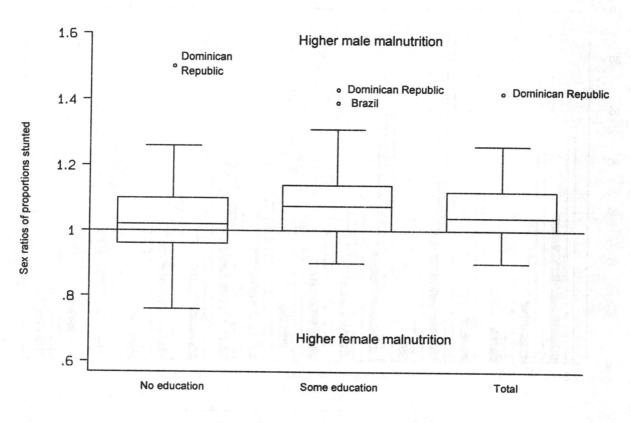

Figure 45. Sex differentials in proportion of children aged 3-35 months who are stunted, by education of mother, for all countries in sample according to different reporting methods

Source: Table 56.

the uneducated and instances where it is lower. Togo and Senegal illustrate that point. In Togo, the percentage of boys classified as stunted declines from 34.4 in the uneducated group to 32.1 for the educated - a modest improvement. For girls, however, there is a more pronounced decline in the prevalence of stunting from 31.9 to 23.1 per cent. Among the educated group the sex differential is high (1.39) and statistically significant. In neighbouring Senegal, in contrast, boys appear to benefit more from the presence of an educated mother. The sex ratio is .94 for the educated compared to 1.26 for the uneducated. Both because of the inconsistency in the differences between children of uneducated versus educated mothers and because very few of the stunting sex ratios shown in table 56 are statistically significant, there are no convincing grounds for concluding that maternal education mediates the relationship between the nutritional status

of boys and girls. That status is certainly better when the mother has received some schooling, but boys and girls benefit equally from that advantage.

2. Treatment of diarrhoeal morbidity

In 24 DHS- phase 1 surveys, mothers were asked about the incidence of diarrhoea in the past two weeks for each child under the age of five years. Slight deviations from that standard procedure are noted at the foot of table 57. The percentages of children for whom any episode of diarrhoea was reported (i.e., the two-week period prevalence) are shown in table 57. There is a wide range in reported morbidity, from 10 per cent or less in Botswana, Sri Lanka, and Trinidad and Tobago to nearly 40 per cent in El Salvador and several of the Western African surveys. In all but one country (Colombia), mothers are more likely to report

TABLE 57. REPORTED PREVALENCE OF DIARRHOEA IN THE TWO WEEKS PRIOR TO INTERVIEW
AMONG CHILDREN UNDER 5 YEARS OF AGE, BY SEX OF THE CHILD

Region and country	Males (percentage)	Females (percentage)	M:F sex ratio
Eastern and Southern Africa			
Botswana	10.0	9.8	1.02
Burundi	17.5	17.0	1.03
Kenya	12.8	12.8	1.00
Sudan	30.6	29.2	1.05
Uganda	25.3	23.1	1.10
Zimbabwe	20.5	19.1	1.07
Median	19.0	36.1	1.04
Mean	19.5	18.5	1.05
Northern Africa			
Egypt[a]	16.7*	15.1*	1.11*
Morocco	30.1	27.7	1.09
Tunisia	22.0*	19.2*	1.15*
Median	22.0	19.2	1.11
Mean	23.9	20.7	1.12
Western Africa			
Ghana	27.1	25.9	1.05
Liberia[b]	39.1	38.3	1.11
Mali	36.3	33.3	1.09
Senegal	39.2	36.8	1.07
Togo	29.9	29.2	1.02
Median	36.3	33.3	1.07
Mean	34.3	32.7	1.07
Southern and South-eastern Asia			
Indonesia	..	..	..
Sri Lanka	6.6	5.5	1.20
Thailand	17.2*	14.1*	1.22*
Median	11.9	9.8	1.21
Mean	11.9	9.8	1.21
Latin America and the Caribbean			
Bolivia[c]	28.6	27.5	1.04[d]
Brazil	17.2	16.6	1.04
Colombia	18.4	19.0	0.97
Dominican Republic	25.7	24.7	1.04
Ecuador[e]	..	..	..
El Salvador	37.9*	34.5*	1.10*
Guatemala	17.9*	15.3*	1.17*
Mexico	23.9	21.5	1.11
Peru[f]	33.5	30.6	1.09
Trinidad and Tobago	6.5	5.7	1.14
Median	23.9	21.50	1.09
Mean	23.3	21.71	1.08
Overall median	23.9	21.5	1.07
Overall mean	23.6	22.1	1.08

Source: Demographic and Health Survey data tapes.

NOTE: An asterisk (*) indicates that the differential between male and female diarrhoea prevalence is significant at 5 per cent level using the chi-square test.

[a]Reference period is 1 week.
[b]Reference period is 4 weeks.
[c]Survey asked "when was the last episode?" rather than the standard reference period.
[d]Male and female prevalences are the reverse of figures in DHS country report.
[e]Survey asked mothers about their last births only, rather than all surviving children under the age of five years.
[f]Reference period is 15 days.

diarrhoea among sons than among daughters. The sex differential, however, is only significant for three surveys (El Salvador, Thailand and Tunisia). Furthermore, it is difficult to attach a firm interpretation to those differences because they may arise not from any bio-medical divergence between boys and girls but from a greater sensitivity of mothers to minor illnesses of their sons than of their daughters.

Table 58 shows the denominators for the analysis of treatment of diarrhoea. When disaggregated by sex of child and educational status of the mother, the numbers of children for whom diarrhoea was reported become too small to sustain the deployment of three educational strata. Accordingly, the primary school group was combined with secondary and higher group for the main analysis of that topic.

TABLE 58. NUMBER OF CHILDREN UNDER 5 YEARS OF AGE, WHO ARE AT RISK OF DIARRHOEAL MORBIDITY, BY MATERNAL EDUCATION

Region and country	No education		Primary education		Secondary and higher education	
	Males	Females	Males	Females	Males	Females
Eastern and Southern Africa						
Botswana	428	484	745	797	288	254
Burundi	1 432	1 394	318	264	35	38
Kenya	791	936	1 808	1 788	611	580
Sudan	1702	1 729	893	827	441	385
Uganda	857	947	1 103	1 093	176	184
Zimbabwe	283	280	992	979	297	299
Northern Africa						
Egypt	2 133	2 000	1 278	1 221	507	498
Morocco	2 339	2 362	256	254	168	142
Tunisia	1 146	1 184	766	718	189	189
Western Africa						
Ghana	839	780	904	951	79	82
Liberia	1 469	1 424	426	399	298	304
Mali	1 227	1 191	194	202	15	12
Senegal	1 496	1 508	223	224	105	81
Togo	931	916	349	350	122	109
Southern and South-eastern Asia						
Sri Lanka	198	180	590	552	753	689
Thailand	172	159	1 401	1 318	149	152
Latin America and the Caribbean						
Bolivia	664	580	1 353	1 282	511	592
Brazil	218	196	1 128	1 112	226	181
Colombia	195	166	717	752	401	258
Dominican Republic	133	136	1 366	1 379	379	426
El Salvador	431	414	1 012	1 044	130	145
Guatemala	1 057	1 067	888	914	134	132
Mexico	376	405	1 596	1 566	628	574
Peru	248	227	661	628	443	438
Trinidad and Tobago	7	5	452	493	437	428

Source: Demographic and Health Survey data tapes.

The majority of sick children received some form of treatment. Figure 46 give the relevant results for both sexes combined within educational strata. In most surveys, the influence of maternal education is not pronounced. The obvious exceptions include Morocco and Tunisia, where sick children of uneducated mothers are much less likely to receive any treatment than other children, and Burundi, where it is the secondary school category that stands out from the primary and no schooling groups. Larger variations,

Figure 46. Percentage of children under 5 years of age with diarrhoea in the last two weeks, who received any treatment, by education of mother

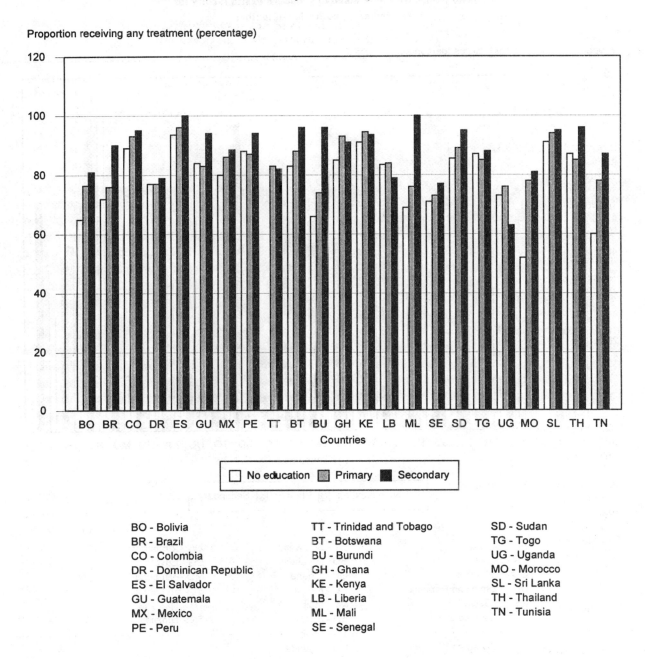

Proportion receiving any treatment (percentage)

BO - Bolivia	TT - Trinidad and Tobago	SD - Sudan
BR - Brazil	BT - Botswana	TG - Togo
CO - Colombia	BU - Burundi	UG - Uganda
DR - Dominican Republic	GH - Ghana	MO - Morocco
ES - El Salvador	KE - Kenya	SL - Sri Lanka
GU - Guatemala	LB - Liberia	TH - Thailand
MX - Mexico	ML - Mali	TN - Tunisia
PE - Peru	SE - Senegal	

Source: Demographic and Health Survey data tapes.

195

both between countries and between educational strata, are apparent when attention is restricted to treatment at a modern health facility (figure 47). Monotonic increases with education in the probability of taking a sick child to a health facility are observed in Bolivia, Colombia, El Salvador, Peru, Mali, Sudan, Tunisia and Uganda. In the remaining countries, differences are typically small and irregular.

Sex ratios in the three treatment variables are displayed in table 59. The overall impression is of little or no differentiation in the treatment of boys and girls.

Figure 47. Percentage of children under 5 years of age with diarrhoea in the last two weeks, who were taken to a modern health facility for treatment, by education of mother

Proportion using modern facilities (percentage)

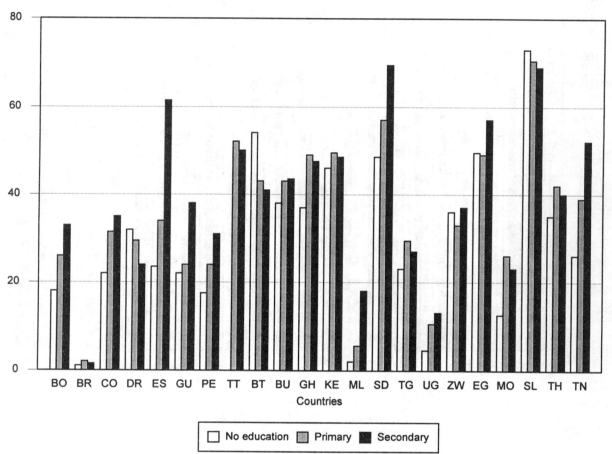

BO - Bolivia

BR - Brazil

CO - Colombia

DR - Dominican Republic

ES - El Salvador

GU - Guatemala

PE - Peru

TT - Trinidad and Tobago

BT - Botswana

BU - Burundi

GH - Ghana

KE - Kenya

ML - Mali

SD - Sudan

TG - Togo

UG - Uganda

ZW - Zimbabwe

EG - Egypt

MO - Morocco

SL - Sri Lanka

TH - Thailand

TN - Tunisia

Source: Demographic and Health Survey data tapes.

TABLE 59. SEX DIFFERENTIALS IN THE PROPORTION OF CHILDREN UNDER 5 YEARS OF AGE WITH DIARRHOEA IN THE LAST TWO WEEKS, WHO WERE GIVEN ANY TREATMENT, TAKEN TO A MODERN HEALTH FACILITY, AND WERE GIVEN ORS

Region and country	Any treatment M:F ratio	Modern health facility use M:F ratio	Given ORS M:F ratio
Eastern and Southern Africa			
Botswana	1.00	0.94	1.02
Burundi	0.93	0.99	0.91
Kenya	1.02	1.03	0.66*
Sudan	1.00	1.00	0.99
Uganda	1.01	1.02	0.91
Zimbabwe[a]	..	1.01	0.91
Median	1.00	1.00	0.91
Mean	0.99	1.00	0.90
Northern Africa			
Egypt	..	1.06	1.19*
Morocco	1.07	1.16	1.01
Tunisia	0.99	1.24*	..
Median	1.03	1.16	1.10
Mean	1.03	1.15	1.10
Western Africa			
Ghana	0.99	0.90	1.06
Liberia	0.99	..	0.93
Mali	1.80	1.39	1.53
Senegal	1.11*	..	1.25
Togo	1.03	0.90	0.97
Median	1.03	0.90	1.06
Mean	1.18	1.06	1.15
Southern and South-eastern Asia			
Indonesia	..	..	..
Sri Lanka	1.03	1.08	0.99
Thailand	1.02	1.07	0.89
Median	1.03	1.08	0.94
Mean	1.03	1.08	0.94
Latin America and the Caribbean			
Bolivia	1.01	1.06	0.85
Brazil	0.97	1.76	0.91
Colombia	1.00	0.97	1.16
Dominican Republic	0.94	0.81*	0.91
Ecuador	..	..	..
El Salvador	0.99	1.03	0.97
Guatemala	0.96	0.96	1.27
Mexico	1.02	..	1.05
Peru	1.01	1.17	1.29
Trinidad and Tobago	0.91	0.74	1.13
Median	0.97	1.00	1.05
Mean	0.98	1.06	1.06
Overall median	1.00	1.03	0.99
Overall mean	1.03	1.06	1.00

Source: Demographic and Health Survey data tapes.

NOTE: An asterisk (*) indicates that the differential between male and female diarrhoea prevalence is significant at 5 per cent level using the chi-square test.

[a]Survey questions did not include ORS use since national policy restricts ORS packet availability, but home sugar-salt solution use is presented here.

For all surveys, the mean sex ratios are 1.00, 1.03 and 0.99 for any treatment, modern health facility use and ORS treatment, respectively. Thus, for that large number of developing countries, it is fair to conclude that daughters fare as well as sons in terms of the treatment of diarrhoeal episodes. That broad conclusion remains valid at the regional level, with the possible exception of the three Arab States, where there is a suggestion of a pro-male bias in the resort to modern health facilities. In Egypt, there is a statistically significant difference in provision of ORS, and in Tunisia a significant difference in resort to a modern health facility. Only three other sex ratios attain statistical significance at the 5 per cent level; in the Dominican Republic and Kenya, a female advantage is apparent, while the reverse is true in Senegal.

Male-female disparities in treatment between educational strata are summarized in figure 48. In terms of treatment of any type, there is clearly no systematic difference between the children of mothers with no exposure to schooling and those with some exposure. In both groups, deviations from a sex ratio of unity tend to be small and symmetrical. For ORS use, dispersion is greater, but again the overall impression of symmetry is maintained for both educational categories. Thus, for two of the three dimensions of curative care there is no evidence of any general effect of maternal education on sex ratios in that group of countries. For the third treatment variable, however, the box plots suggests that education may mediate the reaction to diarrhoeal episodes among sons, compared to daughters. Among the uneducated category, there is a clear tilt towards male advantage in resort to a modern health facility; among the educated category, the impression of male advantage disappears to be replaced by a balance in the distribution of the treatment sex ratios.

Table 60 provides the detailed results. The comparison by mothers' eduction in use of a modern health facility can be made for 20 surveys. Of the 40 treatment sex ratios, only three are statistically significant at the five per cent level; in view of the large number of tests, little importance can be attached to those three cases. In terms of the general pattern, sex ratios are higher among the educated than the uneducated category in 10 countries, lower in nine and remain the same in one country. Clearly, there is no universal shift towards female advantage among educated

mothers. However, a different and intriguing picture emerges when attention is focused only on countries where sex ratios deviate from unity by more than 20 per cent. Among the uneducated stratum, there are seven such instances, all in the direction of male advantage. There is no obvious regional patterning. Three countries are from the Americas (Bolivia, Colombia, and El Salvador), two from Asia (Sri Lanka and Thailand) and two from Africa (Botswana and Tunisia). In six of those seven countries, that apparent male advantage disappears for children of educated mothers. The exception is Tunisia, where the treatment sex ratio drops only fractionally from 1.27 to 1.21.

There is a danger here of drawing inferences from a pattern that may have arisen by chance. Very few of those large sex ratios are statistically significant, nor can it be claimed that preferential treatment of sons by uneducated mothers is common among those 20 countries. Nevertheless, the results suggest that where such a pro-son bias does exist among the uneducated, it is likely to disappear among families where the mother has received some schooling.

3. Probability of death between the ages of 6 and 60 months

Thus far in the analysis, there has been only the faintest evidence that maternal education mediates sex differentials in health and health care. In the present subsection, the key outcome variable - the risk of death between 6 and 60 months - is examined. Unlike the analysis of stunting or response to diarrhoeal episodes, the relevant data are available for all 27 DHS-I enquiries, and because the reference period for the mortality analysis is a wide span of 10 years, the number of observations is greater than hitherto.

Figure 49 confirms that maternal education is strongly associated with child survival in that group of countries, as elsewhere. Monotonic declines in $_{54}q_6$ across the three educational categories are evident with only two exceptions (Liberia and Uganda), where the children of mothers with primary schooling register the highest mortality. In an additional two instances (Bolivia and Sudan), the difference between no schooling and primary schooling categories is small, but in all other countries primary schooling is associated with a marked improvement in survival chances

Figure 48. Sex differentials in any treatment, modern health facility use and ORS use for diarrhoea in children under 5 years of age, by education of mother, for all countries in sample

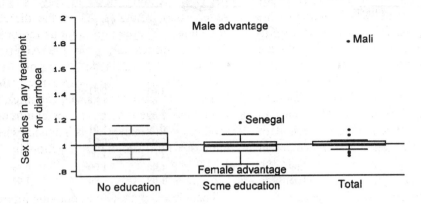

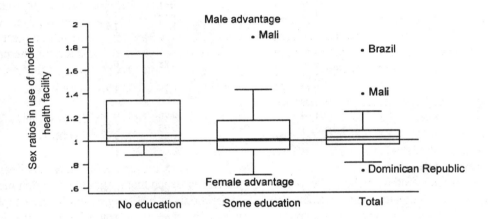

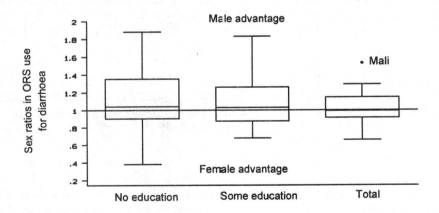

Sources: Tables 59 and 60.

TABLE 60. SEX DIFFERENTIALS IN THE PROPORTION OF CHILDREN UNDER 5 YEARS OF AGE WITH DIARRHOEA IN THE LAST TWO WEEKS, WHO WERE GIVEN ANY TREATMENT, WHO WERE TAKEN TO A MODERN HEALTH FACILITY, AND WHO WERE GIVEN ORS, BY EDUCATION OF MOTHER

(*M:F ratio*)

Region and country	Any treatment		Modern health facility use		Given ORS	
	None[a]	Some[a]	None[a]	Some[a]	None[a]	Some[a]
Eastern and Southern Africa						
Botswana	1.11	0.95	1.63*	0.71	1.45	0.87
Burundi	0.95	0.85	0.97	1.05	0.90	0.92
Kenya	1.10*	0.99	1.02	1.03	0.58	0.68*
Sudan	1.02	0.97	0.99	1.01	0.95	1.03
Uganda	1.09	0.96	0.92	0.97	1.35	0.69
Zimbabwe	..	..	1.00	1.00	1.02	0.89
Median	1.09	0.96	1.00	1.00	0.98	0.88
Mean	1.05	0.95	1.09	0.96	1.04	0.85
Northern Africa						
Egypt	..	..	1.00	1.08	1.04	1.40*
Morocco	1.07	1.08	1.15*	1.23	0.88	1.52
Tunisia	0.97	1.02	1.27	1.21	..	..
Median	1.02	1.05	1.15	1.21	0.96	1.46
Mean	1.02	1.05	1.14	1.17	0.96	1.46
Western Africa						
Ghana	0.93	1.04	0.88	0.92	1.01	1.11
Liberia	1.01	0.95	..	..	0.96	0.93
Mali	0.99	1.07	1.15	1.88	1.36	1.83
Senegal	1.09*	1.17	..	..	1.05	2.82
Togo	1.04	1.00	0.96	0.76	0.80	1.12
Median	1.01	1.04	0.96	0.92	1.01	1.12
Mean	1.01	1.05	1.00	1.19	1.03	1.56
Southern and South-eastern Asia						
Indonesia	..	..	..	..	..	..
Sri Lanka	1.15	1.01	1.61	0.99	1.43	0.87
Thailand	0.89	1.04	1.68	1.02	1.28	0.84
Median	1.02	1.02	1.65	1.00	1.36	0.86
Mean	1.02	1.02	1.65	1.00	1.36	0.86
Latin America and the Caribbean						
Bolivia	1.08	0.99	1.41	1.01	0.95	0.82*
Brazil	2.42	0.96	..	1.43	1.56	0.83
Colombia	1.14	0.97	1.74	0.88	1.88	1.08
Dominican Republic	0.96	0.94	0.88	0.81*	1.33	0.91
Ecuador	..	..	..	..	..	..
El Salvador	1.01	0.98	1.25	0.97	0.78	1.04
Guatemala	0.99	0.94	0.90	1.17	1.27	1.26
Mexico	0.96	1.02	..	..	0.38	1.38
Peru	0.95	1.02	1.07	1.17	1.30	1.27
Trinidad and Tobago	..	0.91	..	0.73	..	1.10
Median	1.00	0.97	1.16	0.99	1.28	1.08
Mean	1.19	0.97	1.21	1.02	1.18	1.08
Overall median	1.01	0.99	1.05	1.01	1.04	1.03
Overall mean	1.09	0.99	1.18	1.05	1.11	1.13

Source: Demographic and Health Survey data tapes.

NOTE: An asterisk (*) indicates that the differential between male and female diarrhoea prevalence is significant at 5 per cent level using the chi-square test.

[a] Education of mother.

200

Figure 49. Probability of death between 6 and 60 months, by education of mother

Levels of 54q6 (per 1,000) by education

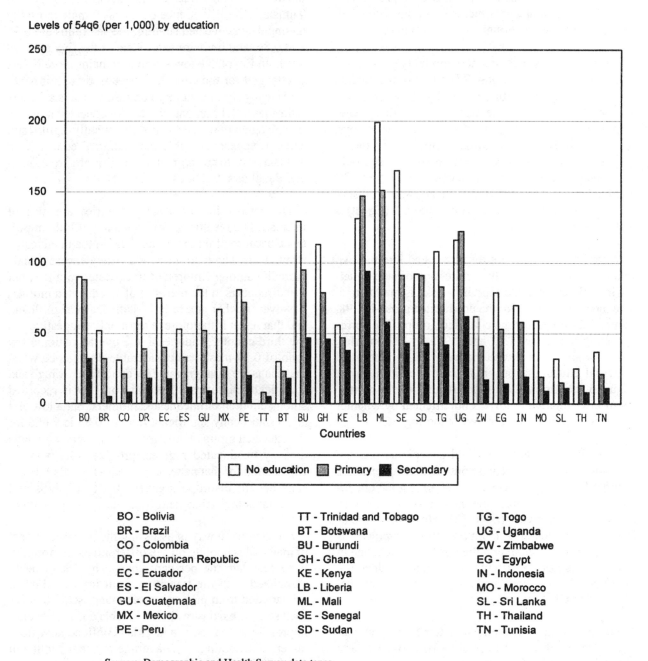

BO - Bolivia
BR - Brazil
CO - Colombia
DR - Dominican Republic
EC - Ecuador
ES - El Salvador
GU - Guatemala
MX - Mexico
PE - Peru

TT - Trinidad and Tobago
BT - Botswana
BU - Burundi
GH - Ghana
KE - Kenya
LB - Liberia
ML - Mali
SE - Senegal
SD - Sudan

TG - Togo
UG - Uganda
ZW - Zimbabwe
EG - Egypt
IN - Indonesia
MO - Morocco
SL - Sri Lanka
TH - Thailand
TN - Tunisia

Source: Demographic and Health Survey data tapes.

and there is a further drop in mortality among children of mothers with secondary or higher schooling.

Though the beneficial effect of schooling is universal, there still exist very large intercountry differences in child mortality within educational strata. For the no schooling stratum, the risks of death between 6 and 60 months ranges from 25 per 1,000 births in Thailand to 200 per 1,000 births in Mali. For children of mothers with primary schooling, the range is slightly narrower, from 17 per 1,000 births in Trinidad and Tobago to 152 in Mali. Those findings emphasise the point that

201

maternal schooling does not determine absolute levels of mortality. They also imply that large improvements in child survival are possible, even in the absence of changes in the educational status of women.

The preliminary assessment of mortality sex ratios is shown in table 61. For those 27 countries, the median sex ratio in the probability of dying between 6 and 60 months is 0.99 and the mean 0.97. Ratios greater than 1.10, indicating higher risks of death among boys, are found in Bolivia, Botswana, Brazil and Liberia. Excess female mortality, as indicated by a sex ratio less than 0.9, is apparent in five countries (Egypt, Sri Lanka, Togo, Trinidad and Tobago, and Tunisia). However, only one of those sex differentials (Egypt) is statistically significant.

When those results are disaggregated into the two main educational strata, the impression of near equality in male and female mortality risks is maintained. The median sex ratio for the uneducated group is 0.98, compared to 0.97 for the educated group. The corresponding means are 1.03 and 0.99. In 12 countries, the mortality sex ratio increases with improved maternal education, but in 13 countries it is lower. Figure 50 confirms that for those countries, the mortality of boys relative to girls is not affected by whether or not the mother has received schooling.

Does that generalization hold at regional and national levels? In Central and South America, sex ratios of mortality are appreciably higher among the uneducated than the educated; the median values are 1.15 and 0.95, respectively (table 62). However, none of the 18 estimates that comprise those averages is statistically significant, and the direction of change in sex ratios is not consistent. The evidence does not justify any claim about mediating effects of maternal schooling in that region.

Similarly, in sub-Saharan Africa there is no convincing evidence of a shift in relative risks of male and female mortality. The measures of central tendency for six countries of Eastern or Southern Africa and for five countries of Western Africa are very similar for both educational strata; and no single country result attains statistical significance.

The three countries of Northern Africa provide an interesting contrast. In Morocco, sex ratios are close to unity (1.04 and 0.96) for the children of both uneducated and educated mothers. In Egypt and Tunisia, there is evidence of excess female mortality among the uneducated stratum; the sex ratios are 0.75 and 0.86, and both are significant at the five per cent level. In Egypt, the low sex ratio remains more or less unchanged for the educated stratum, though it is not statistically significant. By contrast, in Tunisia the sex ratio rises to 1.17 among children of educated mothers, though again that result is not statistically significant. Thus, it appears possible that maternal education in Tunisia may foster a greater equality of care of sons and daughters, but not so in Egypt.

The results for the Asian countries are also of interest. The results for Sri Lanka are of little importance because of the small numbers in the uneducated stratum. In Thailand, there is a heavy excess female mortality among children of uneducated mothers, but that disappears in the presence of an educated mother; however, neither sex ratio is statistically significant, and that result is therefore at most only suggestive. In the third country, Indonesia, the overall national sex ratio of 0.94 masks a considerable divergence when the results are disaggregated by education. A high and statistically significant sex ratio of 1.29 is recorded among children of uneducated mothers, but a low and again statistically significant ratio of 0.83 is found for the educated group. Omission of daughters who have died by uneducated mothers provides one possible explanation for that pattern. It is equally possible that sons benefit disproportionately from the skills and other advantages that stem from maternal schooling.

An alternative way of assessing the possible impact of maternal schooling on sex differentials in mortality is to calculate the per cent change in risk of death associated with the transition from no schooling to primary and from primary to secondary schooling for each sex. The data are shown in table 63. The overall impression is that boys and girls benefit equally from maternal schooling. The average per cent decline in risks of death between 6 and 60 months associated with the first transition - from no schooling to primary schooling - is 30.2 for males and 29.1 for females. The corresponding figures for the primary to secondary transition is 51.6 and 54.4. There is thus no support here for the view that there might be an educational threshold beyond which daughters may benefit more than sons. Inspection of country -

TABLE 61. PROBABILITY OF DEATH BETWEEN 6 AND 60 MONTHS PER 1,000 LIVE BIRTHS, BY SEX

Region and country	Males	Females	Sex ratio
Eastern and Southern Africa			
Botswana	25.88	22.94	1.13
Burundi	119.57	122.39	0.98
Kenya	49.80	45.85	1.09
Sudan	78.83	79.46	0.99
Uganda	118.27	112.92	1.05
Zimbabwe	43.65	40.63	1.07
Median	64.32	62.66	1.09
Mean	72.67	70.70	1.11
Northern Africa			
Egypt	57.64*	68.06*	0.85*
Morocco	53.81	51.93	1.04
Tunisia	26.66	31.62	0.84
Median	33.81	51.93	0.91
Mean	46.04	50.54	0.94
Western Africa			
Ghana	96.15	92.91	1.03
Liberia	133.39	120.20	1.11
Mali	188.20	196.01	0.96
Senegal	150.17	150.78	1.00
Togo	91.98	105.21	0.87
Median	133.39	120.20	1.00
Mean	131.98	133.02	1.01
Southern and South-eastern Asia			
Indonesia	52.77	56.16	0.94
Sri Lanka	14.40	16.81	0.86
Thailand	13.77	14.09	0.98
Median	14.40	16.81	0.90
Mean	26.98	29.02	0.90
Latin America and the Caribbean			
Bolivia	86.91	72.70	1.20
Brazil	34.08	29.57	1.15
Colombia	20.95	19.30	1.09
Dominican Republic	35.83	37.70	0.95
Ecuador	38.64	37.30	1.04
El Salvador	35.90	37.99	0.95
Guatemala	68.24	62.93	1.08
Mexico	24.71	25.57	0.97
Peru	55.02	59.52	0.92
Trinidad and Tobago	5.13	9.66	0.53
Median	35.86	37.50	0.96
Mean	40.54	39.22	1.01
Overall median	52.77	51.93	0.99
Overall mean	63.75	63.71	0.97

Source: Demographic and Health Survey data tapes.

NOTE: An asterisk (*) indicates that the differential between male and female mortality ($_{54}q_6$) is significant at 5 per cent level using the Cox-Mantel test.

specific results reveals a number of erratic results, but there emerges no clear or interpretable pattern.

D. CONCLUSIONS

The aim of the present analysis was to assess whether maternal education brings about a relative shift in the health care, health status and survival of sons and daughters in developing countries. The raw material for the study came from recent nationally representative cross-sectional surveys, drawn mainly from Africa and Central and South America and conducted under the auspices of the Demographic and Health Surveys project.

In many policy discussions of gender, it is assumed that there exists a near-universal tendency for females to be disadvantaged compared to males. In the domains of education, employment and earnings, there is much evidence to support such assertions. Numerous studies in South-central Asia suggest that the female disadvantage also extends to health care and to survival in the childhood years. However, that analysis has provided little support for a thesis of widespread female disadvantage in health care or survival among those particular study populations. In general, girls were slightly less likely to be stunted than boys, were given similar treatment for recent diarrhoeal episodes, and were no more likely to die between the ages of 6 and 60 months than boys. The three countries of Northern Africa provide the only partial exception. In those three countries, the female advantage in terms of nutritional status disappears, girls are slightly less likely to receive effective treatment for diarrhoea, and in two of the three countries, their survival chances are lower.

That general equality makes it improbable that any strong mediating influences of mother's schooling on sex differentials in mortality or health would be found. Indeed, such was the case. In broad terms, equality between sons and daughters persisted both among children of uneducated and of educated mothers.

A few qualifications to those sweeping conclusions should be registered. In aggregate terms, the slight female advantage in terms of nutritional status is further increased among the children from educated homes. For curative health care, the evidence suggested that in a minority of countries, uneducated mothers may provide preferential treatment to sons but that that disparity disappears among the educated group. However, there was no pronounced regional pattern to that finding, and few of the sex differentials were statistically significant. The results are of sufficient interest to warrant further analysis on other countries and fresh data sets but are of themselves by no means conclusive.

As mentioned earlier, evidence of male advantage in matters of health, health care and survival was found with any level of consistency only for three countries of Northern Africa. Disaggregation of results for those three surveys by educational status leads to no firm conclusion regarding the mediating effects of education. Thus, the present analysis sheds no light on the contrary expectations outlined earlier, namely, that maternal education may reduce male advantage in health and survival or that it may exacerbate it.

Those somewhat negative results should be put into context. Included in the present analysis were none of the countries in which evidence of son preference is most pronounced and persistent. Very different results might have been obtained in those countries.

Figure 50. Sex differentials in child mortality risk ($_{54}q_6$), by education of mother, for all countries in sample

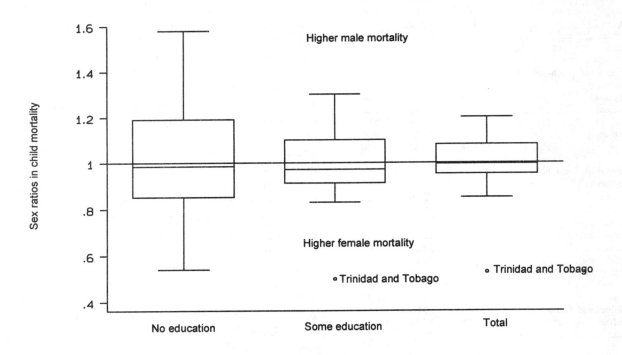

Sources: Tables 61 and 62.

Region and country	No education			Primary and above		
	Males	Females	Ratio	Males	Females	Ratio
Eastern and Southern Africa						
Botswana	35.23	23.02	1.58	20.67	22.81	0.91
Burundi	124.52	130.36	0.96	95.69	82.36	1.16
Kenya	59.65	51.16	1.17	44.10	42.74	1.03
Sudan	90.13	94.55	0.95	56.81	46.64	1.22
Uganda	110.35	120.03	0.92	123.26	106.65	1.16
Zimbabwe	72.37	54.03	1.34	35.73	36.57	0.98
Median	81.28	74.29	1.06	50.46	44.69	1.09
Mean	76.18	78.86	1.14	62.71	56.30	1.08
Northern Africa						
Egypt	72.32*	84.38*	0.86*	39.45	46.21	0.85
Morocco	59.92	57.37	1.04	14.54	15.12	0.96
Tunisia	29.89*	40.12*	0.75*	20.78	17.78	1.17
Median	59.92	57.37	0.86	20.78	17.78	0.96
Mean	54.04	60.62	0.88	24.92	26.37	1.00
Western Africa						
Ghana	119.03	106.81	1.11	72.31	77.47	0.93
Liberia	135.41	125.24	1.08	128.17	107.85	1.19
Mali	195.43	201.67	0.97	132.90	151.07	0.88
Senegal	163.54	163.76	1.00	75.96	76.03	1.00
Togo	97.57	117.4	0.83	77.63	70.39	1.10
Median	135.41	125.24	1.00	77.63	77.47	1.00
Mean	142.20	142.98	1.00	97.39	96.56	1.02
Southern and South-eastern Asia						
Indonesia	78.71*	61.07*	1.29*	44.97*	54.25*	0.83*
Sri Lanka	23.07	42.54	0.54	13.33	13.36	1.00
Thailand	21.52	29.27	0.74	12.68	13.17	0.96
Median	23.07	42.54	0.74	13.33	13.36	0.96
Mean	41.10	44.29	0.86	23.66	26.93	0.93
Central and South America						
Bolivia	99.11	78.69	1.26	65.47	69.89	0.94
Brazil	47.18	58.60	0.81	31.71	24.43	1.30
Colombia	36.99	40.61	0.91	16.45	16.95	0.97
Dominican Republic	72.02	51.25	1.41	32.84	36.81	0.89
Ecuador	87.10	60.58	1.44	31.63	33.61	0.94
El Salvador	49.82	58.49	0.85	29.62	29.88	0.99
Guatemala	86.85	75.33	1.15	46.35	48.50	0.96
Mexico	45.10	37.78	1.19	19.30	21.85	0.88
Peru	72.02	89.72	0.80	50.45	51.56	0.98
Trinidad and Tobago	..	..	..	4.95	9.87	0.50
Median	72.02	58.60	1.15	31.68	31.75	0.95
Mean	66.24	41.47	1.09	32.89	34.34	0.94
Overall median	72.35	60.83	0.98	39.45	42.74	0.97
Overall mean	80.19	78.99	1.03	49.55	49.03	0.99

Source: Demographic and Health Survey data tapes.

NOTE: An asterisk (*) indicates that the differential between male and female mortality ($_{54}q_6$) is significant at 5 per cent level, using the Cox-Mantel test.

TABLE 63. PERCENTAGE CHANGE IN PROBABILITY OF DEATH, BY SEX, FOR VARIOUS EDUCATIONAL TRANSITIONS
(Percentage)

Region and country	None to primary			Primary to secondary			None to some		
	Males	Females	Total	Males	Females	Total	Males	Females	Total
Eastern and Southern Africa									
Botswana	-40.02	+ 7.95	-20.54	- 8.14	-35.49	-22.60	-41.32	- 0.92	-25.26
Burundi	-18.37	-33.99	-26.66	-60.87	-38.00	-50.54	-23.16	-36.82	-30.37
Kenya	-20.96	-14.52	-17.91	-29.80	-10.59	-20.75	-26.07	-16.46	-21.89
Sudan	-35.21	-44.99	- 2.26	-10.61	-36.51	-52.55	-37.00	-50.67	-44.09
Uganda	+16.26	- 2.83	+ 6.69	-31.33	-67.10	-48.24	+11.7	-11.15	- 0.55
Zimbabwe	-43.31	-26.80	-36.03	-72.07	-43.74	-58.43	-50.63	-32.31	-42.68
Median	-27.50	-20.66	-19.20	-10.61	-36.51	-49.39	-24.62	-21.73	-27.82
Mean	-23.60	-19.20	-16.12	-30.39	-38.69	-42.19	-27.75	-24.72	-27.47
Northern Africa									
Egypt	-35.30	-29.14	-32.16	-61.89	-81.70	-72.68	-45.45	-45.23	-45.61
Morocco	-70.83	-65.57	-68.57	-44.68	-62.73	-53.75	-75.73	-73.64	-74.87
Tunisia	-20.94	-50.17	-37.92	-44.35	-45.57	-44.81	-30.49	-55.67	-45.17
Median	-35.30	-50.17	-37.92	-44.68	-62.73	-53.75	-45.45	-55.67	-45.61
Mean	-42.36	-48.29	-46.22	-50.31	-63.33	-57.08	-50.56	-58.18	-55.22
Western Africa									
Ghana	-37.24	-23.74	-31.38	-26.22	-55.64	-41.48	-39.25	27.47	-34.12
Liberia	+20.76	+ 2.06	+11.9	..	..	..	- 5.34	-13.89	- 9.42
Mali	-27.38	-19.80	-23.88	-61.99	-63.83	-62.50	-32.00	-25.09	-28.83
Senegal	-41.16	-48.13	-44.79	..	..	..	-53.55	-53.57	-53.71
Togo	-15.21	-27.25	-22.56	..	..	..	-20.43	-40.04	-30.35
Median	-27.38	-23.74	-23.88	-44.11	-59.74	-51.99	-32.00	-27.47	-30.35
Mean	-20.05	-23.37	-22.14	-44.11	-59.74	-51.99	-30.11	-32.01	-31.29
Southern and South-eastern Asia									
Indonesia	-35.07	+ 3.67	-18.06	-58.38	-74.66	-67.24	-42.87	-11.16	-29.45
Sri Lanka	-25.53	-68.74	-53.00	-36.15	+ 0.68	-20.48	-42.23	-68.60	-59.10
Thailand	-41.31	-55.01	-49.53	+ 3.33	-79.20	-44.81	-41.09	-55.01	-49.75
Median	-35.07	-55.01	-49.53	-36.15	-74.66	-44.81	-42.43	-55.01	-49.75
Mean	-33.97	-40.03	-40.20	-30.4	-51.06	-44.18	-42.06	-44.92	-46.10
Latin America and the Caribbean									
Bolivia	-18.21	+15.22	- 3.91	-56.93	-66.41	-61.90	-33.94	-11.18	-24.44
Brazil	-22.42	-51.26	-38.33	-82.84	-82.89	-82.96	-32.78	-58.31	-46.29
Colombia	-48.72	-46.76	-28.12	-43.38	-64.75	-58.40	-55.53	-58.26	-46.26
Dominican Republic	-50.46	-19.16	-37.16	-39.71	-59.33	-50.53	-54.40	-28.17	-43.48
Ecuador	-54.24	-37.59	-47.53	-65.13	-38.48	-53.22	-63.68	-44.53	-56.01
El Salvador	-32.62	-46.14	-39.44	-80.04	-39.43	-60.42	-40.34	-48.92	-44.68
Guatemala	-40.44	-27.23	-34.36	-77.31	-85.57	-81.56	-46.63	-35.62	-41.66
Mexico	-45.19	-29.38	-61.35	-88.71	-95.05	-91.64	-57.20	-42.15	-67.15
Peru	- 3.14	-17.30	-10.79	-70.01	-75.61	-72.85	-29.95	-42.53	-36.85
Trinidad and Tobago	..	..	..	-81.83	+13.19	-31.52	..	..	..
Median	-40.44	-29.38	-37.14	-73.5	-65.00	-61.30	-46.63	-43.53	-44.68
Mean	-35.05	-28.84	-33.44	-68.59	-59.43	-64.50	-46.05	-36.96	-40.68
Overall median	-35.14	-28.20	-32.16	-56.93	-59.33	-53.22	-40.72	-41.10	-43.72
Overall mean	-30.24	-29.10	-29.53	-51.59	-51.91	-54.41	-38.82	-37.98	-37.78

Source: Demographic and Health Survey data tapes.

Ahmed, K. (1992). Factors associated with sex differences in childhood mortality. *Studies in African and Asian Demography: CDC Annual Seminar 1991*. Research Monograph Series, No 21. Cairo: Cairo Demographic Centre.

Arnold, Fred (1990). Assessment of the quality of birth history data in the Demographic and Health Surveys. In *An Assessment of DHS-I Data Quality. DHS Methodological Reports, No. 1*. Maryland: Institute for Resource Development Inc.

Australian National University, Health Transition Centre (1994). *Health Transition Review* (Canberra), vol. 4, No. 2 (October).

Bairagi, R. (1986). Food crisis, nutrition and female children in rural Bangladesh. *Population and Development Review* (New York), vol. 12, No. 2 (June).

Basu, A. (1989). Is discrimination in food really necessary for explaining sex differentials in childhood mortality? *Population Studies* (London), vol. 43, No. 2 (July), pp. 193-210.

Behrman, J. R. (1988). Intra-household allocation of nutrients in rural India: are boys favoured? Do parents exhibit inequality aversion? *Oxford Economic Papers*, No. 40. Oxford: Oxford University Press, pp. 32-54.

Bhuiya, A. and others (1986). Socioeconomic differentials in child nutrition and morbidity in a rural area of Bangladesh. *Journal of Tropical Paediatrics* (London), vol. 32, pp. 17-23.

Bhuiya, A., and K. Streatfield (1991). Mothers' Education and survival of female children in a rural area of Bangladesh. *Population Studies* (London), vol. 45, No. 2 (July), pp. 253-264.

Bicego, G. T., and Boerma, J. T. (1991). *Maternal Education, Use of Health Services, and Child Survival: An Analysis of Data from the Bolivia DHS Survey*. DHS Working Papers, No. 1. Maryland.: Institute for Resource Development/Macro Systems Inc.

Boerma, J. T., and J. K. van Ginneken (1993). The quality of data on child morbidity and treatment in DHS-1 surveys. In *An Assessment of the Quality of Health Data in DHS-1 Surveys*. DHS Methodology Reports, No. 2. Maryland: Macro International, Inc.

Bourne, K., and G. Walker (1991). The differential effect of mothers' education on mortality of boys and girls in India. *Population Studies* (London), vol. 45, No. 2 (July), pp. 203-219.

Cain, M. T. (1978). The household life cycle and economic morbidity in rural Bangladesh. *Population and Development Review* (New York), vol. 4, No. 3 (September), pp. 421-438.

Caldwell, J. C. (1979). Education as a factor in mortality decline: an examination of Nigerian data. *Population Studies* (London), vol. 33, No. 3 (November), pp. 395-413.

Coale, A. J., and P. Demeny (1966). *Regional Model Life-tables and Stable Populations*. Princeton, New Jersey: Princeton University Press.

Das Gupta, M. (1987). Selective discrimination against female children in rural Punjab, India. *Population and Development Review* (New York), vol. 13, No. 1 (March), pp. 77-99.

Fauveau, V., M. Koenig and B. Wojtyniak (1991). Excess female death among rural Bangladeshi children: an examination of cause-specific mortality and morbidity. *International Journal of Epidemiology* (Oxford), vol. 20, No. 3 (September), pp. 729-735.

Gordon, J., and others (1965). Causes of death at different ages, by sex and by season in a rural population in the Punjab, 1957-1959. *Indian Journal of Medical Research*, vol. 53, No. 9, pp. 906-917.

Hill, K., and D. Upchurch (1994). Gender differences in child health: evidence from the Demographic and Health Surveys. Paper presented at the 1994 annual meeting of the Population Association of America, Miami. Revised.

Hobcraft, J., J. McDonald and S. O. Rutstein (1984). Socioeconomic factors in infant and child mortality: a cross-national comparison. *Population Studies* (London), vol. 38, No. 2 (July), pp. 193-223.

Huda, K. S. (1980). Differentials in child mortality in Bangladesh: an analysis of individual and community factors. New York: Cornell University. Unpublished doctoral dissertation.

Koenig, M., and S. D'Souza (1986). Sex differences in childhood mortality in rural Bangladesh. *Social Science and Medicine* (Elmsford, New York), vol. 22, No. 1, pp. 15-22.

Mosley, W. H., and L. C. Chen (1984). An analytical framework for the study of child survival in developing countries. *Population and Development Review* (New York), vol. 10, Supplement, pp. 25-45.

Muhuri, P. K., and S. H. Preston (1991). Effects of family composition on mortality differentials by sex among children in Matlab, Bangladesh. *Population and Development Review* (New York), vol. 17, No. 3 (September), pp. 143-169.

Namboodiri, K., and C. Suchindran (1987). *Life-Table Techniques and Their Applications*. London, Academic Press, Inc.

Partin, M. (n.d.). An investigation of mechanisms explaining excess female mortality during infancy and childhood in Bangladesh: evidence from the World Fertility Survey. CDE Working Paper, No. 90-25. University of Wisconsin: Center for Demography and Ecology.

Pebley, A., and S. Amin (1991). The impact of a public health intervention on sex differentials in childhood mortality in rural Punjab, India. *Health Transition Review* (Canberra), vol. 1, No. 2 (October), pp. 143-169.

Sen, A., and S. Sengupta (1983). Malnutrition of rural children and the sex bias. *Economic and Political Weekly* (Bombay), vol. 18, No. 2, pp. 855-864.

Simmons, G. B., C. Smucker, S. Bernstein and E. Jensen (1982). Post-neonatal mortality in rural India: implications of an economic model. *Demography* (Washington, D.C.), vol. 19, No. 3 (August), pp. 371-389.

Sommerfelt, E., and J. T. Boerma (1993). Anthropometric status of young children in DHS 1 surveys: an assessment of data quality. In *An Assessment of the Quality of Health Data in DHS-1 surveys*. DHS Methodological Reports, No. 2. Maryland: Macro International, Inc.

Stanton, B., and J. Clemens (1986). The influence of gender on determinants of urban child mortality in Bangladesh. Unpublished.

Sullivan, J., G. Bicego and S. Rutstein (1990). Assessment of the quality of data used for the direct estimation of infant and child mortality in the Demographic and Health Surveys. In *An Assessment of the Quality of Health Data in DHS-1 surveys*. DHS Methodological Reports, No. 1. Maryland: Macro International, Inc.

Sullivan, J. M., S. O. Rutstein and G. T. Bicego (1994). *Infant and Child Mortality*. DHS Comparative Studies, No. 15. Calverton, Maryland: Macro International, Inc.

Tukey, J. W. (1977). *Exploratory Data Analysis*. Reading, Massachusetts: Addison-Wesley Publishing Company.

Tulasidhar, V. B. (1993). Maternal education, female labour force participation and child mortality; evidence from the Indian censis. *Health Transition Review* (Canberra), vol. 3, No. 2, pp. 177-190.

Waldron, I. (1987). Patterns and causes of excess female mortality among children in developing countries. *World Health Statistics Quarterly* (Geneva), vol. 40, No. 3, pp. 194-210.

Ware, Helen (1984). Effects of maternal education, women's roles and child care on child mortality. *Population and Development Review* (New York), vol. 10, Supplement, pp. 191-214.

Weinberger, Marybeth, and L. Heligman (1987). Do social and economic variables differentially affect male and female child mortality? Paper presented at the 1987 annual meeting of the Population Association of America, Chicago, 30 April-2 May.

IX. SON PREFERENCE, FAMILY BUILDING PROCESS AND CHILD MORTALITY

Minja Kim Choe*, Ian Diamond**, Fiona Alison Steele**, and Seung Kwon Kim***

Parental preference for sons over daughters has been observed in countries with strong patrilineal family systems, such as those in Eastern Asia, South-Central Asia, and Northern Africa (Arnold, 1992; Arnold and Kuo, 1984; Arnold and Liu, 1986; Cleland, Verrall and Vaessen, 1983; Gadalla, McCarthy, and Campbell, 1985; Freedman and Coombs, 1974; Nag, 1991; Park, 1978, 1983; Williamson, 1976). In strong patrilineal systems, sons are thought to be valued for their potential roles in the economic and social support of the parents and for their role in the succession of the family line. Some religious beliefs and some social customs, such as dowry systems, are also believed to result in son preference (Nag, 1991). Many research studies suggest that parents in some societies consider their daughters less valuable than sons, and provide inferior care in terms of food allocation, prevention of disease and accidents, and care of sick children (Pebley and Amin, 1991; Chen, Huq and D'Souza, 1981; Das Gupta, 1987; Koenig and D'Souza, 1986; Muhuri and Preston, 1991; Phillips and others, 1987; Simmons and others, 1982). Chapter VII above also presents evidence of sex differences in preventive and curative care.

There is also a strong likelihood that the fertility behaviour and aspirations of couples in countries with strong son preference will be influenced by the current composition of their family. In particular, it is likely that childbearing will continue until there is a certain number of sons, and it is also likely that the loss of a son will be followed quickly by a new child. Infant and child mortality is known to be affected by family formation patterns, through birth spacing, birth order and the total number of surviving children in the family (Das Gupta, 1987; Hobcraft, McDonald and

Rutstein, 1985; Muhuri and Menken, 1993; Muhuri and Preston, 1991; Pebley and Stupp, 1986, Palloni and Milman, 1986; Retherford and others, 1989). Son preference is likely to result in family building behaviour that is detrimental to the survival of female children. For example, girls may experience increased mortality because they are more likely than boys to be followed by a younger sibling after a short interval. If women who have no sons continue to have children until a son is born, the average number of siblings will be larger for daughters than for sons (Park and Cho, 1995) which will result in a more competitive environment for daughters. That competitive environment can be especially disadvantageous to girls in families with limited resources, particularly in times of economic hardship (Choe and Razzaque, 1990; Razzaque and others, 1990).

The present chapter presents an assessment of whether son preference results in excess female child mortality indirectly through the family building process. A review of previous work will be followed by in-depth case studies, using recent data from Egypt, Bangladesh and the Republic of Korea, three countries that are characterized by a high level of son preference and excess female child mortality (Arnold, 1987; Arnold and Kuo, 1984; Choe, 1987; Park, 1955, 1978 and 1983; Park and Park, 1981; Makinson, 1986; Mankekar, 1987; Williamson, 1976). In Egypt and Bangladesh, fertility and mortality are relatively high, and economic and health-care conditions are poor. By contrast, in the Republic of Korea, fertility and mortality are low and economic and health care conditions are favourable. By studying the relationships between son preference, the family building process and child mortality in three countries in which son preference is common but the levels of fertility, mortality, and development are different, a better understanding may be gained of the mediating role of the family building process on differentials in child mortality in the context of demographic transition.

---
*Program on Population, East-West Center, Honolulu.
**Department of Social Statistics, University of Southampton.
***Korea Institute for Health and Social Affairs, Seoul.

A. THE CONSEQUENCES OF DIFFERENTIAL FERTILITY CAUSED BY SON PREFERENCE AND THEIR IMPLICATIONS ON CHILD SURVIVAL

There is considerable literature on the impact of son preference on fertility (e.g., Arnold, 1985, 1987; Arnold and Lui, 1986; Cleland, Verrall and Vaessen, 1983; Nag, 1991). In general, research has focused on the links between current family composition and desires for further children, the probability of having a further child and the use of birth control.

With regard to the study of sex-specific mortality, the most relevant feature of family formation is the observed probability of having another child (the parity progression ratio). A number of authors have shown that the likelihood of having an additional child is increased if a woman does not have a son (or in some societies has only one son). For example, figure 51 shows that in China the presence of a surviving son has a major impact on the probability of having an extra child. The key question to be addressed in the present chapter is whether that tendency to continue to have children until the desired number of sons is achieved can lead to an increase in the risk of death among daughters.

The most obvious consequence of a gender dimension to family formation behaviour is that a daughter is much more likely than a son to be followed by a younger sibling after a short interval. Studies on the determinants of child survival have identified the birth of a younger sibling within a short interval as an important risk factor for childhood mortality (Curtis, Diamond and McDonald, 1993; Hobcraft, McDonald and Rutstein, 1985; Pebley and Stupp, 1986; Palloni and Milman, 1986; Retherford and others, 1989; United Nations, 1994). Therefore, in son preferring societies girls may suffer a higher level of childhood mortality than boys partly because they are more likely to have a younger sibling born within a short interval.[1]

Family formation patterns may also affect sex differentials in infant and child mortality through sibling size and family composition. The effect of son preference on parity progression ratios implies that the mean number of siblings will be larger for female than for male children (Park and Cho, 1995). That difference means that on average daughters have to compete with more siblings for parental attention and resources than sons, which may have an adverse effect on female survival. At the family level, any parental discrimination against female children in the allocation of food and health care is more likely to be practised among those with a large number of children than among those with fewer children (Caldwell, Reddy and Caldwell, 1988; Chen, Huq and D'Souza, 1981; Das Gupta, 1987; Rahman and others, 1982). Discrimination against daughters seems to depend on the sex composition of other children in the family. In China, India and Bangladesh, for instance, excess female mortality is found to be more pronounced for girls who have elder sisters, perhaps because second or higher order daughters are less valued than first born daughters. (Choe, Hao and Wang, 1995; Das Gupta, 1987; Muhuri and Preston, 1991). Lastly, because girls are more likely to live in crowded households than boys they may be more exposed than boys to risks of death from infectious diseases.

Recently, techniques for identifying the sex of a foetus have become widely available. Most countries have laws to prevent their use purely for the purpose of sex identification (Choe and Han, 1994; Park and Cho, 1995; Zeng and others, 1993). However, some couples who are desperate to have sons and not to have additional daughters may use those techniques to identify and abort female foetuses. There is evidence that such practices have resulted in an abnormally high sex ratios at birth in China and the Republic of Korea (Park and Cho, 1995; Zeng and others, 1993). Because sex-selective abortion is more likely to be used at later parities, the sex ratio increases with birth order in those countries. The differential sex ratio by birth order may inflate female mortality relative to male mortality because risks of death tend to be higher for first born children than for later born children. Conversely, sex-selective abortion may act to reduce excess female mortality by lowering the numbers of unwelcome daughters that are born.

Eliminating the birth of unwanted daughters, however, is not likely to eradicate excess female mortality. Some of the excess female mortality may originate from gender-related differences in child rearing customs associated with deeply rooted cultural or religious beliefs, rather than from conscious discrimination by parents. Sons and daughters who are equally desired nevertheless may be treated differently because parents have different expectations and concerns based

Figure 51. The relationship between overall parity progression ratio and the effect of son preference measured by the relative risk: six provinces in China, 1977-1987

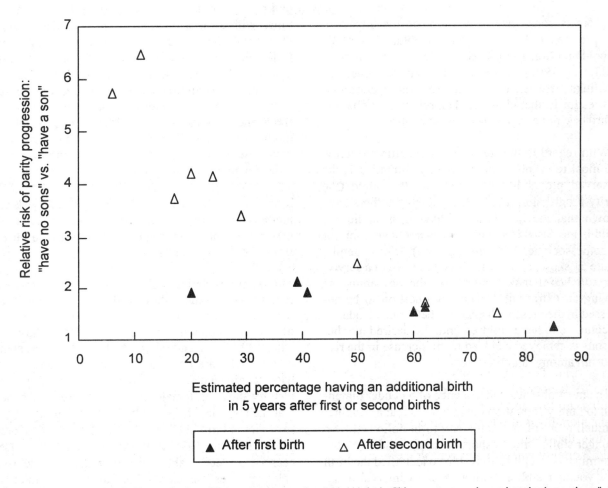

Source: M. K. Choe and others, "Progression to second and third births in China; patterns and covariates in six provinces", *International Family Planning Perspectives* (New York), vol. 18, No. 4 (December 1992), pp. 130-136, table 2 and 3.

on gender. For example, daughters may be taken to doctors less frequently than sons because parents do not think it desirable to expose their daughters in that way.

The present brief review reveals that family formation patterns may influence male-female differences in childhood mortality in many different and subtle ways. The rest of the chapter focuses on two pathways of influences: short birth intervals and family composition.

B. CASE STUDIES

The present section contains an examination of the interrelationships between son preference, the family building process and child mortality in detail, using recent large-scale demographic surveys in Egypt, Bangladesh and the Republic of Korea. Table 64 shows the levels of fertility, child mortality and differentials by women's education in those three countries. Egypt and Bangladesh are in the early stages of demographic transition, with moderately high levels of

TABLE 64. LEVELS AND DIFFERENTIALS OF FERTILITY AND CHILD MORTALITY IN
EGYPT, BANGLADESH, AND THE REPUBLIC OF KOREA

Country	Total fertility rate		Child mortality ($_4q_1$) (per 1,000)		
	Level (period)	Differential by mother's education	Level (period)	Differential by mother's education	Female to male ratio
Egypt	4.69 (1984-1988)	large	31 (1984-1988)	large	1.2
Bangladesh	4.83 (1987)	moderate	47 (1983 cohort)	large	1.3
Republic of Korea	1.56 (1987-1990)	very small	10 (1981-1985)	no information	1.1

Sources: Md. Najmul Huq and J. Cleland, *Bangladesh Fertility Survey 1989*, main report (Dhaka, National Institute of Population Research and Training, 1990), table 9.8, 9.10 and 10.4; Seung-Hyun Han and I.-S. Kim (1990), "Recent trends of infant death rates and their determinants in the Republic of Korea", *Korean Journal of Epidemiology* (Seoul), vol. 12, No. 1 (June 1990), pp. 57-81 (in Korean), tables A1.1 and A1.2; Sae-kwon Kong, A.-J. Cho, S.-K. Kim and S-H. Son, *Family Formation and Fertility Behaviour in the Republic of Korea: 1991 Fertility and Family Health Survey* (Seoul, Korea Institute for Health and Social Affairs, 1992; in Korean), table 9-1 and 9-7; Hussein Abdel-Aziz Sayed, M. Osmar, F. El-Zaraty and A. A. Way, *Egypt Demographic and Health Survey 1988* (Cairo, Egypt National Population Council, and Columbia , Maryland: Institute for Resource Development/Macro Systems, Inc., 1989), table 3.2, 8.3 and 8.8; S. N. Mitra, N. N. Ali, S. Islam and T. Saha, *Bangladesh Demographic and Health Survey, 1993-1994* (Dhaka, Bangladesh and Calverton, Maryland, National Institute of Population Research and Training, Mitra and Associates, and Macro International, Inc., 1994), table 7.3.

fertility and child mortality. In those countries, large educational differentials in fertility and mortality are also evident. The Republic of Korea is at an advanced stage of demographic transition. Levels of current fertility are low and vary little between educational strata; mortality is also low. It is interesting, however, to note that even in the late 1980s excess female child mortality was still apparent in the Republic of Korea.

When parents have a strong preference for sons, they may modify their family building behaviour according to whether or not they already have a son: families with surviving sons may be more likely to stop child-bearing than those without sons. When the level of child mortality is relatively high, families may want to have more than one son. In addition, families may like to have at least one daughter although their preference is for more sons than daughters. Those hypotheses are tested by estimating the effects of the sex of the youngest—or index—child and the sex composition of older surviving children on the probability of having another child, controlling for the survival status of the index child. In the discrete-time hazards model used in the present chapter, the time since index birth is divided into a series of time periods. The variable

indicating whether that child has survived varies according to whether the child was alive at the beginning of any of those time points. In addition, other demographic and socio-economic characteristics of the woman are controlled. The question is then asked: does the family building process explain some of the excess female child mortality? An answer to that question is sought by estimating the effects of family composition on sex-specific mortality, with and without controlling for the effect of the timing of the birth of the next child and other demographic and socio-economic variables.

The effects of family composition on parity progression and child mortality are estimated by hazard models. Gross effects of prior family composition on mortality of index children are estimated by a model that includes family composition, year of birth of child and age of child. Net effects of family composition are estimated by the model that includes birth of the next child within a short interval, and other demographic and socioeconomic variables. Comparison of gross and net effects provides an indication of the contribution of subsequent reproductive behaviour to the relative mortality of male and female index children.

1. Egypt

Egypt was identified as the country with strongest son preference among 25 countries covered by the first phase of the Demographic and Health Surveys, which included many countries in Africa and South America, but only two Asian countries: Sri Lanka and Thailand (Arnold, 1992). In recent years, fertility has declined moderately from a total fertility rate (TFR) of 5.3 in 1979 to 1980 to 4.4 in 1986 to 1988 (Sayed and others, 1989, table 3.4). The age pattern of fertility is broad, with a very high level of fertility up to ages 35 to 39. Infant and child mortality declined substantially during the 1970s and 1980s. Mortality under age 5, which was 203 per 1,000 births in 1974-1978, declined to 102 in 1984-1988 (Sayed and others, 1989, table 8.3). Both fertility and child mortality show wide geographic and socio-economic variations. The major causes of death for children between ages one and five are diarrhoea, respiratory infections and measles (Sayed and others, 1989, table 8.9).

The data come from the 1988 Egypt Demographic and Health Survey (Sayed and others, 1989) which obtained complete birth histories from a sample of 8,911 ever-married women aged 15-49. The sample is representative of the population of Egypt except for the frontier governorates, which comprise only around 2 per cent of the whole population.

The analysis of parity progression is limited to women who had their third, fourth or fifth birth in the 1979 to 1983 period, for the following reasons. The parity progression ratio to the third birth is nearly one in Egypt: more than 88 per cent of women who had their second child between 1979 and 1983 went on to have their third child within seven years. Thus, there is unlikely to be any effect of family composition on the probability of having a third birth. At parities six and higher, only a very small proportion have no son, and thus the scope of the analysis would be restricted. Although there is a high incidence of child-bearing until about age 40 in Egypt, the analysis would be seriously biased if it was extended further back than 1979 since the data would then be concentrated among younger women.

The results in table 65 show the estimated effects of family composition on the probability of having additional children in 2 years. The effects are estimated by discrete time hazard models, using succes-

sive twelve month periods after the birth of the index child as the unit of analysis. The parity progression ratios are high but vary according to the sex of the index child, as well as the sex composition of older surviving children.

Women whose index child is a son and who have older surviving children of both sexes record the lowest probability of having their next child within five years. Compared to that group, women whose last child is a daughter have a higher probability of another child and the probability is highest among women who have no surviving sons. Women whose index child is a son and whose older surviving children are also all sons also have a higher probability of having another child within 2 years. The differences in parity progression among women whose index child is a son are not statistically significant, however, except for the difference between women with all male children and those who have older surviving children of both sexes at parity three. The parity progressions from third, fourth and fifth births in the early 1980s clearly demonstrate strong son preference. To a lesser extent, those results also suggest that Egyptian women desire to have at least one daughter. Finally, the parity progression ratio among women whose index child died is much higher. If that child died during infancy, the ratio rises to over 90 per cent on average (not shown).

The next step is to estimate the effects of family composition on child mortality, with and without controlling for the effect of the birth of the next child. That estimation is achieved by fitting a discrete time hazards model for child mortality between ages two and five for children of birth orders three to nine who were born between 1979 and 1983. Successive twelve month periods from age two are used as the unit of analysis. Because the survey collected information on age at death of children in months before age two and in years after age two an analysis using smaller time periods is not possible. The effect of the birth of the next child is estimated by the inclusion of a time-dependent dummy variable, indicating whether or not the next child has been born before the beginning of the current analysis segment. That focus of attention on mortality from age two onwards reflects the fact that very few index children would experience the birth of another child before the age of 2 years.

The effects of family composition on mortality are shown in table 66 in terms of estimated probabilities of

TABLE 65. PROBABILITIES OF HAVING NEXT BIRTH WITHIN 2 YEARS BY INITIAL PARITY, SEX OF INDEX CHILD, AND SEX COMPOSITION OF OTHER SURVIVING CHILDREN IN EGYPT, FOR INDEX BIRTHS OCCURRING BETWEEN 1979 AND 1983

Initial parity	Sex of index child	Sex compositon of other surviving children	Percentage distribu- tion with parity	Probability of another birth	Relative risk[a]
3	Male	Male and female	18	0.327	1.000
		All female	18	0.338	1.034
		All male	17	0.418	1.278*
	Female	At least one male	32	0.412	1.260*
		All female	15	0.480	1.468*
4	Male	Male and female	35	0.179	1.000
		All female	9	0.215	1.201
		All male	11	0.225	1.257
	Female	At least one male	36	0.231	1.291*
		All female	10	0.259	1.447*
5	Male	Male and Female	40	0.179	1.000
		All female	5	0.260	1.453
		All male	5	0.216	1.207
	Female	At least one male	43	0.241	1.346*
		All female	6	0.284	1.587*

Source: Individual records from *1988 Egypt Demographic and Health Survey*.

NOTES: Probabilities are estimated by discrete hazard models controlling for year of last birth, number of surviving children, survival status of last child, maternal age, mother's residence, mother's childhood residence, mother's education, mother's religion, father's education and father's occupation; see annex table A.1 for details.

An asterisk (*) indicates that the difference between the relative risks or estimated probability is significant at the 5 per cent level.

[a]Relative to women whose index child is a son and who have at least one more surviving male child.

dying between ages 2 and 5. Three sets of estimates are shown. The estimates from model 1 show "gross effects". In addition to sex of child and sex composition of older siblings, this model includes year of birth to control for general trends in mortality, age of child to control for the age pattern of mortality and number of surviving children. Model 2 includes, in addition to the factors included in model 1, a time-dependent dummy variable, indicating whether the next child was born before the beginning of the current analysis segment. The estimates from model 2 show the effect of family composition, controlling for the effect of differential parity progression. In addition to all the factors included in model 2, model 3 includes other demographic and socioeconomic covariates of child mortality. Results from model 3 can be interpreted as the "net effects" of family composition on child mortality.

The estimates from the "gross effects" model show that, in general female children experience higher mortality than male children: overall, female child mortality is 31 per cent higher than male mortality.

The magnitude of the sex difference depends on the sex composition of older siblings. Female children who have older sisters experience much higher mortality than those who have no sisters. Although the differences in the estimated mortality are large, statistical tests show that only the difference between male with no brothers (lowest mortality) and female with both brothers and sisters (highest mortality) is significant at the 5 per cent level. The lack of statistical significance partly reflects the small numbers of deaths included in the analysis.

As shown in table 65, female children—especially those with no brothers—are more likely to be followed by a younger sibling within 24 months. Therefore, even if all children are treated equally girls may suffer higher mortality than boys just because they are more likely to be followed by a younger sibling after a short interval. Results from model 2 show the effect of the sex of the index child and the sex composition of older siblings on child mortality, controlling for the effect of the short following birth interval. The numbers in the column "no next birth in 2 years" are the estimated

TABLE 66. ESTIMATED RELATIVE RISKS OF PROBABILITIES OF DYING BETWEEN AGES 2 AND 5, BY SEX
OF THE INDEX CHILD AND SEX COMPOSITION OF OLDER SURVIVING SIBLINGS,
BIRTHS OF ORDER 3-9 BORN IN BETWEEN 1979 AND 1983, EGYPT

Sex of index child	Sex of other siblings	Percentage distribution	Model 1[a] (gross effects)	Model 2[b] (Intermediate)		Model 3[b] (net effects)	
				No next birth in 2 years	Next birth in 2 years	No next birth in 2 years	Next birth in 2 years
Male	All female	8.8	1.00	1.00	2.15*	1.00	1.82*
	Some male	42.1	2.93	2.93	6.31*	2.57	4.68*
Female	All male	9.6	1.94	1.86	3.99*	1.61	2.93*
	Male and female	30.9	3.89*	3.79*	8.15*	3.19	5.81*
	All female	8.6	3.23	3.00	6.45*	2.81	5.12*
Male	All	50.9	1.00	1.00	2.15*	1.00	1.82
Female	All	49.1	1.31	1.26	2.71*	1.23	2.23

Source: Individual records from *1988 Egypt Demographic and Health Survey*.

NOTES: Estimates are based on discrete hazard models. Model 1 includes sex, sex composition of older surviving siblings, year of birth and age. Model 2 includes the dummy variable, indicating whether next child was born within 24 months of interval in addition to the variables in model 1. Model 3 also includes the following demographic and socio-economic factors: number of surviving children, maternal age, mother's residence, mother's childhood residence, mother's education, mother's religion, father's education and father's occupation.

An asterisk (*) indicates that the difference between the relative risks is significant at the 5 per cent level.

[a]Relative to the group "Male with all female siblings".

[b]Relative to the group "Male with all female siblings and no next birth in 2 years".

relative risks of mortality between ages two and five for those children who are not followed by a subsequent birth in two years. Comparing those numbers with those in the model 1 column, it is clear that the effects of sex and sex composition are smaller when there is no subsequent birth within 2 years, confirming the hypothesis that part of the male-female difference in child mortality is due to differentials in parity progression. The statistical significance of the coefficients, however, did not change. The overall female excess mortality is reduced by 5 per cent (from 31 to 26). That result indicates that in Egypt, girls experience higher mortality than boys partly because they are more likely than boys to be followed within 2 years by a younger sibling. However, most of the excess female mortality is due to other factors. The results also suggest that girls who have older sisters experience particularly high risks of death between ages 2 and 5, perhaps because they are less valued than first-born daughters.

The "net effects" shown in the last two columns indicate that the effects of sex and family composition on child mortality are reduced further when the effects of other demographic and socio-economic covariates of child mortality are controlled. Statistical tests show that even the difference between the lowest and the highest mortality group is not significant at the 5 per cent level. The effect of parity progression is also reduced. Nevertheless, the effect of family composition on child mortality is still large, although not statistically significant, after controlling for the effect of the birth of the next child and other demographic and socioeconomic conditions. Thus, the results suggest that the survival of girls in Egypt depends in part of the sex composition of older siblings; specifically, girls who have older brothers but no sisters appear to fare better than girls with sisters.

Do parents discriminate against daughters in feeding and caring in Egypt? The evidence from the Demographic and Health Survey data is weak, at most. The nutritional status of children under age five does not show any sex differential (Sayed and others, 1989, tables 9-12, 9-13 and 9-14). Incidences of diarrhoea and respiratory infections are about the same for male and female children (Sayed and others, 1989, tables 9-7 and 9-10). However, there are some differences in the treatment of sick children. Among young children who suffered from recent diarrhoea or respiratory infections, male children are slightly more likely to have received treatment and the treatment is more likely to be from private physicians rather than from government clinics (Sayed, 1989, tables 9-8 and 9-10). Other studies have found sex differentials in children's immunization, feeding status, and in the incidence and treatment of disease in Egypt (Makinson, 1987; Mankekar, 1987). It is possible that that small amount of extra care provided to more valued male children results in their lower mortality. In chapter VI above, that possibility is examined in greater detail.

2. Bangladesh

Bangladesh is one of the most frequently studied countries with regard to excess female child mortality, owing to its high level of son preference and its excellent availability of information, including prospective data, with much detailed information on fertility, child mortality and child care. Those studies have shown that fertility behaviour depends on the sex combination of surviving children (Chowdhury and Bairagi, 1990; Rahman, Akbar and Phillips, 1990); daughters receive less food and health care than sons (Basu, 1989; Chen, Huq and D'Souza, 1981); and female children experience excess mortality during childhood (Koenig and D'Souza, 1986; Muhuri and Preston, 1991; Phillips and others, 1987; Razzaque and others, 1990). The interplay between son preference, family building and excess female child mortality, however, has not been examined in detail. In the present chapter, those relationships are assessed with data from the 1989 Bangladesh Fertility Survey (Huq and Cleland, 1990), which collected complete birth histories from a nationally representative sample of 12,096 ever-married women under age 50.

In recent years, fertility has declined substantially from a TFR of 6.8 in 1980 to 4.8 in 1987 (Huq and Cleland 1990, table 9.8), and has since continued to fall. Compared with Egypt, the fertility level was much higher in 1980 but it then declined more rapidly, resulting in a level only slightly higher than Egypt in 1987. The age pattern of fertility is broad, and compared with Egypt childbearing starts at an earlier age. Fertility differentials by geographic area and mother's education are large (Huq and Cleland, 1990, table 9.9 and 9.10). Mortality under age 5 declined moderately from 202 deaths per 1,000 live births for the 1979 birth cohort to 183 for the 1983 birth cohort (Huq and Cleland, 1990, table 10.4). Child immunization coverage has increased but was still low at the time of the 1989 survey: 19 per cent for measles and 19 per cent for the final dose of DPT. Immunization coverage varies between region and between urban and rural strata (Steele and others, 1996). Data from a later survey indicate that the level of child mortality also varies greatly by residence and the socio-economic conditions of the mother (Mitra and others, 1994, table 7.3).

Fertility rates and parity progression ratios were slightly higher in Bangladesh than in Egypt in the early 1980s. For example, among women who had their second births in the period 1979 to 1983 more than 92 per cent went on to have a third birth. The effects of family composition on parity progression for women with initial parities three to five are estimated with models similar to those used for Egypt. Table 67 shows estimated probabilities of having another child within 2 years, by the sex of the index child and the sex composition of the other surviving children. Women of initial parities three to five whose index child is a son and who have older surviving children of both sexes have the lowest probability of going on to have another child within 24 months. Compared with that group, women whose index child is a daughter are more likely to have another child within 2 years, and the probability is higher still for those who have no surviving sons. An interesting pattern, not observed in Egypt, is that women whose index child is a son and whose older surviving children are all daughters record a higher probability of having another child compared to women who have older surviving sons. One explanation is that women who produce a son after having a number of daughters tend to have additional children in the hope that the next child will also be a son. Any such tendency would not be surprising given the high level of both son preference and child mortality. Women with no surviving daughters have a higher probability of parity progression than women with surviving children of both sexes at parities three and four, a result that implies the desire for at least one daughter in Bangladesh. In summary, the family building process reflects a preference for two or more sons and at least one daughter.

TABLE 67. PROBABILITIES OF HAVING NEXT BIRTH WITHIN 2 YEARS BY INITIAL PARITY, SEX OF INDEX CHILD, AND SEX COMPOSITION OF OTHER SURVIVING CHILDREN IN BANGLADESH, FOR INDEX BIRTHS OCCURRING BETWEEN 1979 AND 1983

Initial parity	Sex of index child	Sex compositon of other surviving children	Percentage distribution with parity	Probability of another birth	Relative risk[a]
3	Male	Male and female	17	0.101	1.000
		All female	18	0.136	1.347*
		All male	18	0.119	1.178*
	Female	At least one male	30	0.140	1.139
		All female	15	0.171	1.693*
4	Male	Male and female	31	0.114	1.000
		All female	10	0.191	1.675*
		All male	10	0.150	1.316*
	Female	At least one male	36	0.133	1.167*
		All female	10	0.156	1.368*
5	Male	Male and female	35	0.116	1.000
		All female	5	0.243	2.095*
		All male	8	0.116	1.000
	Female	At least one male	44	0.150	1.293
		All female	7	0.198	1.707*

Source: Individual records from 1989 Bangladesh Fertility Survey.
NOTES: Probabilities are estimated by discrete hazard models controlling for year of last birth, number of surviving children, survival status of last child, maternal age, mother's residence, mother's childhood residence, mother's education, mother's religion, father's education, father's occupation, and mother's autonomy; see annex table A.3 for details.
An asterisk (*) indicates that the difference between the relative risks is significant at the 5 per cent level.
[a]Relative to women whose last child is a son and who have at least one more male surviving child.

Next, the effects of family composition and parity progression on child mortality are examined. Employing an analytic strategy similar to the one used for Egypt, estimations are made of the relative risks of dying between ages 2 and 5 for children of birth order three to nine who were born during the period 1979-1983. The results are shown in table 68. Overall, female children experience mortality that is more than 50 per cent higher than male counterparts, suggesting that there is greater excess female child mortality in Bangladesh than in Egypt. As in Egypt, male children who have no surviving older male siblings experience the lowest level of mortality. Compared with that group, female children—especially those who have older male siblings—experience higher mortality. The results from model 2 show that children who are followed within two years by the birth of next child experience higher childhood mortality, but the differentials in child mortality by sex and family composition do not change much when the effects of a short following birth interval are controlled. The absence of a mediating role of differential parity progression probably reflects the fact that birth intervals of less than 24 months are less common in Bangladesh than in Egypt (tables 65 and 67).

It is interesting to note that unlike the mortality of female children with male siblings, the level of mortality among female children who have no surviving male siblings is not significantly different from the lowest levels. In Bangladesh, the level of child mortality remains relatively high, and there are large differentials by geographic areas and by the socio-economic conditions of the families. It is likely that many families in Bangladesh have only limited resources, that can be used for child care, disease prevention and care of sick children. Families may have to make decisions about allocating scarce resources and it is possible that children who are more valued by parents receive better care and treatment than those who are valued less. Thus, it is likely that in families with children of both sexes male children would receive better care and experience lower mortality than daughters, especially if there is only one son. Girls in families with some surviving sons may suffer some discrimination because most of the limited resources

TABLE 68. RELATIVE RISKS OF CHILD MORTALITY, BY SEX AND SEX COMPOSITION OF SURVIVING SIBLINGS AT THE TIME OF BIRTH FOR CHILDREN OF BIRTH ORDER 3-9 BORN BETWEEN 1979 AND 1983, BANGLADESH

Sex of index child	Sex of other siblings	Percentage distribution	Model 1[a] (gross effects)	Model 2[b] (Intermediate)		Model 3[b] (net effects)	
				No next birth in 2 years	Next birth in 2 years	No next birth in 2 years	Next birth in 2 years
Male	All female	9.1	1.00	1.00	1.66*	1.00	1.52*
	Some male	40.9	1.36	1.37	2.26*	1.33	2.03*
Female	All male	10.3	2.24*	2.24*	3.70*	2.19*	3.34*
	Male and female ..	30.1	2.11*	2.08*	3.45*	2.05*	3.12*
	All female	9.6	1.47	1.44	2.38	1.42	2.16*
Male	All	50.0	1.00	1.00	1.66*	1.00	1.52*
Female	All	50.0	1.55*	1.53*	2.53*	1.53*	2.34*

Source: Individual records from *1989 Bangladesh Fertility Survey*.

NOTES: Estimates are based on discrete hazard models. Model 1 includes sex, sex composition of older surviving siblings, year of birth and age. Model 2 includes the dummy variable, indicating whether next child was born within 24 months of interval in addition to the variables in model 1. Model 3 also includes the following demographic and socio-economic factors: year of last birth, number of surviving children, maternal age, mother's residence, mother's childhood residence, mother's education, mother's religion, father's education and father's occupation.

An asterisk (*) indicates that the difference between the relative risks is significant at the 5 per cent level.

[a]Relative to the group "Male with all female siblings".

[b]Relative to the group "Male with all female siblings and no next birth in 2 years".

may be used for care of their brothers. On the other hand, if a daughter does not have a brother she does not have an advantaged competitor for limited resources and her mortality risk is not increased because of her sex.

3. The Republic of Korea

The third setting selected for analysis is the Republic of Korea. Since 1960, that country has experienced a rapid fertility decline. The estimated total fertility rate fell from 6.0 in 1960 (Coale, Cho and Goldman, 1980, table 1), to 2.1 in 1983 (Republic of Korea, National Bureau of Statistics, 1989), and has been below replacement level since 1984. The estimated rate for 1990 is 1.6 (Kong and others, 1992). At the same time, strong son preference has persisted (Arnold, 1985; Cho, Arnold and Kwon, 1982; Park and Cho, 1995). Surveys during the 1980s and 1990s document that although the preferred ideal family size dropped to two children, son preference persisted in a large segment of the population. For example, in a national survey conducted in 1991 41 per cent of women of

childbearing age gave a positive answer to the question, "Do you think it is necessary for a married couple to have a son (Kong and others, 1992, p. 128)?"

Concurrent with the fertility decline and accompanying socio-economic development, infant and childhood mortality also declined rapidly in the Republic of Korea. The infant mortality rate fell by more than 50 per cent and the child mortality rate declined by more than 70 per cent between 1970 and 1995 (Han and Kim, 1990). Throughout that period, infant mortality was higher for males than for females but the mortality sex ratio was much lower than the pattern found in other populations or expected from model life tables (Choe, 1987; Park and Park, 1981), suggesting that girls in the Republic of Korea suffer unusually high mortality relative to boys during infancy. Child mortality was higher for females than males. Clearly, girls in that country experience excess mortality at ages 1-4.

The data for the analysis come from the 1991 Family and Health Survey (Kong and others, 1992). The survey collected complete pregnancy histories from 7,462 ever married women age 15-49 years, together with the survival status of each child and the dates of deaths for those who had died. A slightly different analytic approach is used for the Republic of Korea than for Egypt or Bangladesh. The sample size is smaller, and the levels of fertility and mortality are much lower in the Republic of Korea than in the other two countries, which results in a small number of births and deaths to analyse. On the other hand, the age of children at death is collected in much more detail (number of days), and in the Republic of Korea the reporting of dates of events is considered to be very accurate (Coale, Cho and Goldman, 1980). Fertility is largely concentrated in the age range 20-34; since 1985, fertility after age 35 has been negligible (Kong and others, 1992, table 9-1). For family composition, a simple binary classification is used, indicating whether there are any surviving sons or not. With such a very low level of fertility, any further classification would be meaningless. The analysis of parity progression is extended to those women who had index births in the 10-year period 1975-1984, and to the progressions from first to third births. Analysis of child mortality is performed for those who were born in the 1971-1988 period. Month is used as the unit of analysis to take advantage of the accurate reporting of dates of events.

To examine the effects of changes in son preference in the context of a society experiencing considerable fertility decline, the parity progression ratios are analysed for two parity cohorts: 1975-1979 and 1980-1984. The parity cohorts are defined according to the year in which women gave birth to their first, second, third and fourth births. Table 69 shows the estimated probabilities of having a subsequent birth in the two years after the first, second, third, and fourth births by parity cohort for women classified by whether or not they have a surviving son.

Women whose one child was a daughter were more likely to have the second child than women whose child was a son. Although the differences are not large

TABLE 69. PROBABILITIES OF HAVING NEXT BIRTH WITHIN 5 YEARS, BY INITIAL PARITY, YEAR OF INDEX BIRTH AND WHETHER THE FAMILY HAS A SURVIVING SON IN REPUBLIC OF KOREA, BIRTHS OF INITIAL PARITY IN 1975-1984

Initial parity	Year of birth of index child	Presence of a surviving son	Percentage distribution	Probability of another birth	Relative risk[a]
1	1975-1979	Yes	54	0.88	1.00
		No	46	0.92	1.05*
	1980-1984	Yes	53	0.76	1.00
		No	47	0.82	1.08*
2	1975-1979	Yes	75	0.41	1.00
		No	25	0.78	1.90*
	1980-1984	Yes	76	0.12	1.00
		No	24	0.54	4.50*
3	1975-1979	Yes	89	0.22	1.00
		No	11	0.73	3.32*
	1980-1984	Yes	84	0.06	1.00
		No	16	0.48	8.00*

Source: Individual records from *1991 National Survey of Fertility and Family Health*.

NOTES: Probabilities are estimated by hazard models controlling for age at last birth, mother's education, residence, mother's childhood residence, and whether mother agrees with the idea that a couple "must have a son"; see annex table A.5 for details.

An asterisk (*) indicates that the difference between the relative risks is significant at the 5 per cent level.

[a]Relative to women who have a surviving son.

218

in magnitude, they are statistically significant. The parity progressions from second and third births declined much more drastically than the progression from the first birth. Clearly, those trends resulted in a rapidly declining level of fertility. The probability of having additional children among women with a surviving son differs from that among women with no surviving sons and the difference varies by parity cohort. In general, the difference is larger at higher parities than at lower parities, but for the more recent cohort the difference at lower parities increases as well. Thus, the situation in the Republic of Korea presents an interesting combination of a very low level of fertility and a persisting high level of son preference. The effect of son preference on the family building process actually increased as the level of fertility declined.

The next step is to estimate the effect of sex of the index child, short succeeding interval and other covariates on childhood mortality. Because of the low level of mortality, the number of children who died before age five is very small and complex hazards models cannot be estimated. Instead, a binary logistic model is used, with a dependent variable indicating whether the child survived to age five or not. Attention is focused on children who were born in the period 1971-1988 and whose birth orders are one through six. Table 70 shows that when other effects are not controlled, female mortality is 6 per cent less than male risks of death. When the effect of following birth interval is controlled the difference widens to 11 per cent, and when the effects of other demographic and socioeconomic factors are controlled female children record a mortality risk that is 12 per cent lower than the male risk. That last difference is closer to the expected difference between male and female child mortality in the absence of son preference. According to the United Nations estimates based on the death rates of more developed countries in the period 1950-1970, the median infant mortality was 18-21 per cent lower for females and the median death rate at ages 1-4 was 17-22 per cent lower for females (United Nations, 1982, table II.4).

If the next sibling is born within two years, there is a large and statistically significant increase in a child's probability of dying before age 5, the odds ratio being 2.46. Effects of all other factors are either statistically insignificant or small in magnitude. Thus, the data from the Republic of Korea demonstrate that girls experience higher than expected mortality, largely because they are more likely than boys to be followed by a younger sibling within 2 years. As overall levels of fertility and mortality have declined, socio-economic differentials in vital rates have attenuated. However, the relationship between family building behaviour and the sex of child plays an extremely important role in explaining the remaining differentials in child mortality. The elimination of son preference, as manifested by the link between the birth of a daughter and the rapid birth of another child, would therefore result in even further reduction in child mortality in the Republic of Korea.

TABLE 70. ODDS RATIOS OF UNDER-FIVE MORTALITY (BIRTH TO AGE 5), BY SEX, FOR CHILDREN OF BIRTH ORDERS 1 TO 5 BORN BETWEEN 1971 AND 1988, REPUBLIC OF KOREA

Sex of index child	Percentage distribution	Model 1[a] (gross effects)	Model 2[b] (Intermediate)		Model 3[b] (net effects)	
			No next birth in 2 years	Next birth in 2 years	No next birth in 2 years	Next birth in 2 years
Male	51.4	1.00	1.00	2.46[c]	1.00	2.46[c]
Female	48.6	0.94	0.89	2.18[c]	0.88	2.15[c]

Source: Individual records from 1991 National Survey of Fertility and Family Health.
NOTES: Estimates are based on logistic regression models. Model 1 includes sex and year of birth and age; model 2 includes, in addition to the variables in model 1, the dummy variable indicating whether the next child was born within 24 months; model 3 also includes the following demographic and socio-economic factors: maternal age, mother's residence, mother's education.
An asterisk (*) indicates that the difference between the relative risks is significant at the 5 per cent level.
[a]Relative to the group "Male".
[b]Relative to the group "Male and no next birth in 2 years".

C. Conclusions

The key issue addressed in the present chapter is the relationship between family building behaviour and sex differences in child mortality. In two of the three countries studied, girls experience higher child mortality than boys; while in the Republic of Korea, female mortality under age five, although lower than male mortality, is higher than expected. In Egypt and Bangladesh, where average family size remains large, the degree of excess female mortality depends on the sex composition of older siblings. In Egypt, only girls who have older surviving sisters experience appreciably higher mortality; but in Bangladesh, it is girls with older brothers who experience particularly high mortality. The results also show that overall excess female mortality is higher in Bangladesh than in Egypt.

The analysis also shows that when son preference is present, girls are more likely than boys to experience a family building environment with a high mortality risk. Girls are more likely to be followed after a short interval by a younger sibling. In each of the three countries examined, children who have a younger sibling born within 24 months experience significantly higher risks of mortality. Those findings suggest that girls suffer excess child mortality partly because of their parent's family building tendencies originating from son preference. There is some suggestion that the relative contribution of the family building process in explaining excess female mortality during childhood depends on the level of fertility and mortality. In Egypt and Bangladesh, where mortality levels are high, the family building process explains only a small proportion of excess female child mortality. In Bangladesh, where very short birth intervals are relative rare, the mediating role of parity progression in explaining excess female mortality is even weaker than in Egypt. In the Republic of Korea, however, the family building process explains much of the higher than expected level of female mortality. In the Republic of Korea, where mortality differentials are small and socio-economic conditions are good, parents are likely to be able to afford high quality child care, including the care of sick children, regardless of the sex of the child. But in Egypt and Bangladesh, parents have limited resources, insufficient to provide quality care to all children; accordingly, they may allocate resources favouring some children over others. In Bangladesh, girls with older brothers appear to be particularly vulnerable, while in Egypt the most vulnerable group is girls who have an older sister.

Note

[1] A short birth interval also increases the mortality risks of the child born after the interval. However, preceding birth interval length is unlikely to affect sex differentials in mortality because in general it cannot be influenced by the sex of the child following the interval.

References

Arnold, Fred (1985). Measuring the effect of sex preference on fertility: the case of Korea. *Demography* (Washington, D.C.), vol. 22, No. 2 (May), pp. 280-288.

_____ (1987). The effect of sex preference on fertility and family planning: empirical evidence. *Population Bulletin of the United Nations* (United Nations publication, Sales No. E.88.XIII.5), Nos. 23 and 24, pp. 44-55.

_____ (1992). Sex preference and its demographic and health implications. *International Family Planning Perspectives* (New York), vol. 18, No. 3 (September), pp. 93-101.

_____, and Eddie C. Y. Kuo (1984). The value of daughters and sons: a comparative study of the gender preferences of parents. *Journal of Comparative Family Studies* (Calgary), vol. 15, No. 2 (Summer), pp. 299-318.

Arnold, Fred, and Liu Z. (1986). Sex preference and fertility in China. *Population and Development Review* (New York), vol. 12, No. 2 (June), pp. 221-246.

Basu, Alaka M. (1989). Is discrimination in food really necessary for explaining sex differentials in childhood mortality? *Population Studies* (London), vol. 43, No. 2 (July), pp. 193-210.

Caldwell, J. C., P. H. Reddy and P. Caldwell (1988). *The Causes of Demographic Change: Experimental Research in South Asia.* Madison, Wisconsin: University of Wisconsin Press.

Chen, L. C., E. Huq and S. D'Souza (1981). Sex bias in the family allocation of food and health-care in rural Bangladesh. *Population and Development Review* (New York), vol. 7, No. 1 (March), pp. 55-70.

Cho, Lee-Jay, F. Arnold and T. H. Kwon (1982). *The Determinants of Fertility in the Republic of Korea.* Committee on Population and Demography Report, No. 14. Washington, D.C.: National Academy Press.

Choe, Minja Kim (1987). Sex differentials in infant and child mortality in Korea. *Social Biology* (Madison, Wisconsin), vol. 34, Nos. 1 and 2 (Spring-Summer), pp. 12-25.

_____, G. Fei, J. Wu, and R. Zhang (1992). Progression to second and third births in China: patterns and covariates in six provinces. *International Family Planning Perspectives* (New York), vol. 18, No. 4 (December), pp. 130-136.

Choe, Minja Kim, and S. H. Han (1994). Family size ideal and reproductive behavior in the Republic of Korea. Paper presented at an International Union for the Scientific Study of Population/International Research Center for Japanese Studies workshop on the theme "Abortion, infanticide and neglect in population history: Japan in Asian comparative oerspective", Kyoto, Japan, 20 and 21 October.

Choe, Minja Kim, H. S. Hao and F. Wang (1995). The effects of gender, birth order, and other correlates on child survival in China. *Social*

Biology (Madison, Wisconsin), vol. 42, Nos. 1 and 2 (Spring-Summer), pp. 50-64.

Choe, Minja Kim, and S. K. Kim (1995). *Son Preference and Family Building During Fertility Transition: Implications for Child Survival.* East-West Center Working Papers, Population Series, No. 77. Honolulu: East-West Center.

Choe, Minja Kim, and A. Razzaque (1990). Effect of famine on child survival in Matlab, Bangladesh. *Asia-Pacific Population Journal* (Bangkok), vol. 5, No. 2 (June), pp. 53-72.

Chowdhury, Mridul, and Rahdeshyam Bairagi (1990). Son preference and fertility in Bangladesh. *Population and Development Review* (New York), vol. 16, No. 4 (December), pp. 749-757.

Cleland, John, Jane Verrall and Martin Vaessen (1983). *Preference for Sex of Children and Their Influence on Reproductive Behavior.* World Fertility Survey Comparative Studies, No. 27. Voorburg, the Netherlands: International Statistical Institute.

Coale, Ansley, L.-J. Cho and N. Goldman (1980). *Estimates of Recent Trends in Fertility and Mortality in the Republic of Korea.* Committee on Population and Demography, report No. 1. Washington, D.C.: National Academy Press.

Curtis, Sian, L. I. Diamond and J. W. McDonald (1993). Birth interval and family effects on postneonatal mortality in Brazil. *Demography* (Washington, D.C.), vol. 30, No. 1 (February), pp. 33-43.

Das Gupta, Monica (1987). Selective discrimination against female children in rural Punjab, India. *Population and Development Review* (New York), vol. 13, No. 1 (March), pp. 77-100.

Freedman, Ronald, and L. C. Coombs (1974). *Cross-cultural comparison: data on two factors in fertility behavior.* New York: Population Council.

Gadalla, S., J. McCarthy, and O. Campbell (1985). How the number of living sons influence contraceptive use in Menoufia Governorate, Egypt. *Studies in Family Planning* (New York), vol. 16, No. 4 (December), pp. 164-169.

Han, Seung-Hyun, and I.-S. Kim (1990). Recent trends of infant death rates and their determinants in the Republic of Korea. *Korean Journal of Epidemiology* (Seoul), vol. 12, No. 1 (June), pp. 57-81. In Korean.

Hobcraft, J., J. W. McDonald and S. O. Rutstein (1985). Demographic determinants of infant and early childhood mortality: a comparative analysis. *Population Studies* (London), vol. 39, No. 3 (November), pp. 363-386.

Huq, Md. Najmul, and J. Cleland (1990). *Bangladesh Fertility Survey 1989,* main report. Dhaka: National Institute of Population Research and Training.

Kamal, Ghulam M., K. Streatfield and S. Rahman (1993). Cause of death among children in Bangladesh. In National Institute of Population Research and Training, *Secondary Analysis of the Bangladesh Fertility Survey, 1989.* Dhaka.

Koenig, Michael A., and S. D'Souza (1986). Sex differentials in childhood mortality in Bangladesh. *Social Science and Medicine* (Elmsford, New York), vol. 22, No. 1, pp. 15-22.

Kong, Sae-Kwon, A.-J. Cho, S.-K.-Kim and S.-H. Son (1992) *Family Formation and Fertility Behaviour in the Republic of Korea: 1991 Fertility and Family Health Survey.* Seoul: Korea Institute for Health and Social Affairs.

Makinson, Carolyn (1986). Sex differentials in infant and child mortality in Egypt. Princeton, New Jersey: Princeton University. Unpublished doctoral dissertation.

Mankekar, K. (1987). Sex differentials in infant and child mortality in Egypt. Paper presented at the annual meeting of the Population Association of America, Chicago.

Mitra, S. N., N. N. Ali, S. Islam, A. R. Cross and T. Saha (1994). *Bangladesh Demographic and Health Survey, 1993-1994.* Dhaka and Calverton, Maryland: National Institute of Population Research and Training, Mitra and Associates, and Macro International, Inc.

Muhuri, Pradip K. and J. A. Menken (1993). Child survival in rural Bangladesh: short subsequent birth interval and other circumstances of jeopardy. Paper presented at the annual meeting of the Population Association of America, Cincinnati, 1-3 April.

Muhuri, Pradip K., and S. H. Preston (1991). Effects of family composition on mortality differentials by sex among children in Matlab, Bangladesh. *Population and Development Review* (New York), vol. 17, No. 3 (September), pp. 415-434.

Nag, Moni (1991). Sex preference in Bangladesh, India and Pakistan, and its effect on fertility. *Demography India* (Delhi), vol. 20, No. 2 (December), pp. 163-185.

Palloni, A., and S. Milman (1986). Effects of inter-birth intervals and breastfeeding on infant and early childhood mortality. *Population Studies* (London), vol. 40, No. 2 (July), pp. 215-236.

Park, Chai Bin (1955). Statistical observations on the death rates and causes of death in the Republic of Korea. *Bulletin of the World Health Organization* (Geneva), vol. 13, pp. 69-108.

_____ (1978). The fourth Korean child: the effect of son preference on subsequent fertility. *Journal of Biosocial Science* (Cambridge, United Kingdom), vol. 10, No. 1, pp. 95-106.

_____ (1983). Preference for sons, family size, and sex ratio: an empirical study in the Republic of Korea. *Demography* (Washington, D.C.), vol. 20, No. 3 (August), pp. 333-352.

_____, and Nam-Hoon Cho (1995). Consequences of son preference in a low-fertility society: imbalance of the sex ratio at birth in the Republic of Korea. *Population and Development Review* (New York), vol. 21, No. 1 (March), pp. 59-84.

Park, Chai Bin, and B. T. Park (1981). *Infant mortality in the Republic of Korea.* Seoul: Korea Institute for Population and Health.

Pebley, Anne R., and Paul W. Stupp (1986). Reproductive patterns and child mortality in Guatemala. *Demography* (Washington, D.C.), vol. 24, No. 1 (February), pp. 43-60.

Pebley, Anne R., and Sajeda Amin (1991). The impact of a public-health intervention on sex differentials in childhood mortality in rural Punjab, India. *Health Transition Review* (Canberra), vol. 1, No. 2 (October), pp. 143-170.

Philips, James F., T. K. LeGrand, M. A. Koenig and J. Chakraborty (1987). The effect of a maternal and child health-family planning project on infant and child mortality in Matlab, Bangladesh. Paper presented at the annual meeting of the Population Association of America, Chicago.

Rahman, M. B., K.M. S. Aziz, M. H. Munshi, Y. Patwari and M. Rahman (1982). A diarrhea clinic in rural Bangladesh: influence of distance, age, and sex in attendance and diarrheal mortality. *American Journal of Public Health* (Washington, D.C.), vol. 72, pp. 1124-1128.

Rahman, Mizanur, J. Akbar and J. F. Phillips (1990). Sex composition and contraceptive use in Matlab, Bangladesh. Paper presented at the 1990 annual meeting of the Population Association of America, Toronto, 3-5 May.

Razzaque, Abdur, N. Alam, L. Wai and A. Foster (1990). Sustained effects of the 1974-1975 famine on infant and child mortality in a rural area in Bangladesh. *Population Studies* (London), vol. 44, pp. 145-154.

Republic of Korea, National Bureau of Statistics (1989). Outline and major results of the 1985 population and housing census in the Republic of Korea. Seoul.

Retherford, Robert D., M. K. Choe, S. Thapa and B. B. Gubhaju (1989). To what extent does breastfeeding explain birth-interval effects on early childhood mortality? *Demography* (Washington, D.C.), vol. 26, No. 3 (August), pp. 439-450.

Sayed, Hussein Abdel-Aziz, M. Osman, F. El-Zanaty and A. A. Way (1989). *Egypt Demographic and Health Survey 1988.* Cairo: Egypt National Population Council, and Columbia, Maryland: Institute for Resource Development/Macro Systems, Inc.

Simmons, George B., C. Smucker, S. Berstein and E. Jenson (1982). Post-neonatal mortality in rural India: implication of an economic model. *Demography* (Washington, D.C.), vol. 19, No. 3 (August), pp. 371-390.

Steele, Fiona, I. Diamond and S. Amin (1996). Immunization uptake in rural Bangladesh: a multilevel analysis. *Journal of the Royal Statistical Society* (London), Series A, vol. 159, pp. 289-299.

United Nations (1982). *Levels and Trends of Mortality Since 1950. A joint study by the United Nations and the World Health Organization.* New York: United Nations. ST/ESA/SER.A/74.

_____ (1994). *The Health Rationale for Family Planning: Timing of Births and Child Survival.* New York: United Nations. ST/ESA/SER.A/141.

Waldron, Ingrid (1987). Patterns and causes of excess female mortality among children in developing countries. *World Health Statistics Quarterly* (Geneva), vol. 40, No. 3, pp. 194-210.

_____ (1997). Sex differences in infant and early child mortality: major causes of death and possible biological causes. In the present volume, chap. III.

Williamson, Nancy E. (1976). *Sons or daughters: a cross-cultural survey of parental preferences.* Beverly Hills: Sage Publications.

Zeng, Yi, P. Tu, B. Gu, Y. Xu, B. Li, and Y. Li (1993). Causes and implications of recent increase in the reported sex ratio at birth in China. *Population and Development Review* (New York), vol. 19, No. 3 (June), pp. 283-302.

X. INTRA-HOUSEHOLD ALLOCATION OF RESOURCES: IS THERE A GENDER BIAS?

*Jere R. Behrman**

The present chapter considers evidence from developing countries on sex differentials in the intra-household allocations of goods and services to infants and children. That theme is closely related to the consideration of socio-economic factors that may underlie the sex differentials in causes of death, nutritional status, nutrition-morbidity-mortality linkages and health-care utilization, which have been considered in earlier chapters. Moreover, because of the widely perceived importance of maternal education in the intra-household allocation process, some of the concerns of the present chapter are relevant to those of chapter VIII above. The present chapter is distinguished from those chapters, however, by a focus on what happens within households.

A framework for analysing sex differences in intra-household allocations of goods and services that affect infant and child mortality is first discussed. Some such framework is essential for understanding the nature of and the determinants of sex differentials. In the framework presented in the present chapter, households are assumed to make choices, within the constraints that they face, that they perceive to be in their own interests. It is accepted that household choices may be severely constrained by cultural norms, traditions, markets and assets, and that there may be considerable uncertainty regarding future developments. But the assumption is made that within those actual and perceived constraints, households do not consciously choose alternatives that they expect to make them worse off rather than better off. That framework is used to illustrate some of the difficulties in interpreting empirical evidence on the present topic. One important point stemming from the present framework is that differences by sex in allocations of resources within the household or in outcomes determined within the household may exist for a number of reasons, not just because of gender discrimination in

the sense that there are preferences that favour children of one sex over the other. Sex differences in health or survival do not necessarily mean that there is gender discrimination within households. Females born in sub-Saharan Africa have higher life expectancies at birth than males born in the same region. That difference does not necessarily mean that there is gender discrimination in favour of females in households (or outside of households) in that region. Similarly, the fact that females born in much of Northern Africa and South-central Asia have lower life expectancies at birth than males born in those regions does not necessarily mean that there is gender discrimination against females in those regions. It is important for understanding behaviour and for policy purposes to attempt to understand the varied origins of the sex differences that are documented elsewhere in the present volume. It is not very useful for that understanding simply to equate all sex differences in health and survival with gender discrimination.

The analytical framework is then applied to a review of evidence on sex differentials in intra-household allocations that are relevant to infant and child mortality and related behaviours. A summary of what is known and what is not known regarding links between intra-household allocations and sex differentials in infant and child mortality is presented in the conclusion. Although there have been important gains in recent understanding, evidence about those links is still limited and possibilities of future advances in knowledge are considerable.

A. FRAMEWORK FOR ANALYSIS OF INTRA-HOUSEHOLD ALLOCATIONS AND SEX DIFFERENTIALS IN INFANT AND CHILD MORTALITY AND RELATED BEHAVIOURS

In the absence of experimental evidence, deductions about the impact of sex differences in intra-household

*William R. Kenan, Jr. Professor of Economics, University of Pennsylvania.

resource allocation on infant and child mortality rates have to be made from observing behaviour. Such behavioural data can lead to valid conclusions regarding associations between sex-specific mortality rates and observed variables, including those related to sex-specific intra-household allocations, but they generally cannot illuminate the underlying causes of sex differentials in infant and child mortality. The problem is that the data available for analysis are on outcomes (e.g., child mortality and intra-household allocations) that are the result of behavioural decisions taken in the light of a number of factors that are unobserved by researchers and policy makers (hereafter simply referred to as "unobserved" factors). Important among the unobserved factors are preferences of the key decision makers, their innate endowments and bargaining power, the genetic endowments of the infants and children, and a number of actual and expected prices related to the costs and benefits of different patterns of intra-household allocations of resources. Because many of those factors are not directly observed, it is usually difficult to identify their relative importance in causing the observed sex differences in outcomes. Such an understanding remains an important goal, because it is essential in order to predict future behaviour, including the likely impact of changes in policies or in markets.

To infer possible causal effects of intra-household resource allocation on sex differences in infant and child mortality rates, a framework must be used to analyse the existing behavioural data. That framework must include the critical unobserved factors in order to assess their effects. If critical unobserved factors are not accounted for in the analysis, the estimated impact of observed variables may be biased because the observed variables represent, in part, the unobserved variables. For example, assume that mothers are critical decision makers for intra-household resource allocations, that innately more capable mothers tend to make choices that increase the survival probabilities for daughters relative to those for sons, and that more capable mothers also are likely to be more schooled. Under those plausible assumptions, the estimated impact of mother's schooling includes in part the impact of her unobserved capabilities, and therefore is biased upwards unless maternal capabilities are controlled in the analysis. For another example, assume that expected rates of return to investing in child health differ by sex of the children but are not controlled in the

analysis. In that case, sex differences in intra-household resource allocations and in infant and child mortality rates may be attributed to gender discrimination in household preferences, though in fact they are due at least in part to gender differences in expected rates of return to human resource investments.

For such reasons, it is essential that the framework for analysing causality with behavioural data be laid out explicitly so as to clarify the assumptions on which the inferences of causality are based. It is not appropriate here to expand on the technical details of the leading models,[1] but it is important to present a simple framework for conceptualizing such issues, and then to note some implications for interpreting behavioural data.

1. A simple model of intra-household resource allocation related to sex differences in infant and child mortality rates

In the simplest model that has the essential features to illustrate the problems of empirical inference from behavioural data about intra-household resource allocation, households have an objective function that they maximize subject to production function constraints (in particular, for health/morbidity/mortality), a resource constraint, and market prices and available social services. Each of those components is discussed in turn below. There follows a discussion on how constrained maximization can lead to sex differences in intra-household resource allocations that may or may not be related to gender bias within the household or outside it. In subsection A.2, the two types of relations related to that framework are discussed.

Household objective function

The household objective function indicates how different combinations of outcomes affect the welfare of the household decision makers. The household objective function may depend directly and indirectly on child health, morbidity and mortality, as well as on other outcomes that reflect household decisions, such as parental consumption and time use and number of surviving children. The household objective function may depend directly on child health, morbidity and mortality, simply because parents (and any other household decision makers) care about the welfare of their children. How much they care may differ by the

224

sex (or birth order or other characteristics) of the children; a given health state may be valued differently for a daughter than for a son. There may be indirect dependence on child health, morbidity and mortality because household decision makers perceive that better health improves, for example, economic productivity, about which they have a concern either out of altruistic interest in their children's economic well-being or because they expect that they may benefit from transfers of monetary or time resources from their children. Again, they may weigh differentially the same expected economic productivity of sons versus daughters if their concern is altruistic. If their concern is to benefit, it would seem that money would be valued the same regardless of the sex of the child who provided it. However, other resources expected of children, such as help in old age, may be valued differentially depending on the sex of the child. Thus, all else being equal, sex differentials in child health, morbidity and mortality may have many different origins.

To clarify some critical characteristics of the household objective function it is useful to consider a simple household objective function defined over the expected lifetime earnings of two children, which in turn may reflect the health of the two children and thereby intra-household resource allocations of health-related goods and services. Figure 52 gives an illustration in which the household objective function depends on the expected earnings of a son (E^S, measured on the vertical axis) and the expected earnings of a daughter (E^D, measured on the horizontal axis). Of course, the welfare of the household decision makers also depends on many other outcomes, including the health of children and of the parents, but to keep the illustration simple, those other outcomes are considered to be fixed. Point A represents a combination of high expected earnings for the daughter and of low expected earnings for the son, which yields a welfare level W_1 for household decision makers. There are other combinations of expected earnings for those two children that yield the same welfare level W_1—such as at point B, where the expected earnings are the same for the two children, and at point C, where the expected earnings are higher for the son but lower for the daughter. All the points where the welfare level is the same can be connected by an "equal welfare" contour (similar to a contour line on a topographical map that gives locations with equal elevations). Along any equal-welfare line the expected earnings of one child must increase when the expected earnings of the other child decrease in order to keep the welfare of the household decision makers constant. Of course, household decision makers would prefer combinations of expected earnings that are higher over those that are lower. D represents such a combination of expected earnings that is higher for both the son and the daughter than at A, B, or C—which yields a higher level of welfare, say W_2. Through D, there is also an equal-welfare line or contour that represents all combinations of expected earnings that yield a welfare level of W_2, some with higher expected earnings for the daughter and lower expected earnings for the son than at D (e.g., E) and vice versa (e.g., F). Note that at any point on W_2 the expected earnings for at least one child—but not necessarily for both children—is higher than at any specific point on W_1 since more expected earnings for the children are valued positively. For example, at E on W_2 the expected earnings for the daughter are much higher than at C on W_1, but the expected earnings for the son are lower.

The equal-welfare lines illustrate the nature of the household objective function. Of particular interest are (a) the productivity-equity trade-off and (b) unequal concern—the latter including preference biases favouring sons.

The extent of curvature of the equal-welfare lines indicates preference trade-offs for changes in expected earnings of the daughter versus those of the son, and thus the productivity-equity tradeoff in preferences. If the equal-welfare line is linear, as illustrated by curve 1 in figure 53, the trade-off is constant, independently of whether the daughter has relatively low or relatively high expected earnings in comparison with the son; thus, the only concern about productivity is the sum of expected earnings of all children, regardless of the distribution of such earnings between the children. If the equal-welfare line is sharply curved, as for curve 2 in figure 53, the daughter would have to have considerable gains in expected earnings for a small reduction in expected earnings for the son (or vice versa) to keep welfare the same, because the distribution between the children affects welfare.

Whether or not the equal-welfare lines are symmetrical around the 45° line (i.e., the locus of equal earnings combinations for the two children) indicates whether

Figure 52. Household objection function--illustrative equal--welfare curves

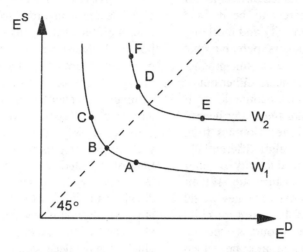

Figure 53. Curvature of equal-welfare curves: extremes for equity-productivity trade-off (curve 1--only productivity; curve 2--only equity)

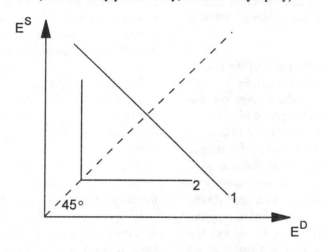

Figure 54. Symmetry of equal-welfare curves around 45° ray from origin: equal concern (curve 1) versus unequal concern favouring sons over daughters

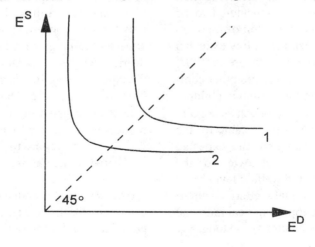

or not there is equal concern. If they are symmetrical, as illustrated by curve 1 in figure 54, they imply that household decision makers have equal concern in the sense that they weigh equal outcomes for the two children equally. Equal-welfare lines that are not symmetrical as in curve 2 in figure 54 imply that households weigh in their preferences a given expected earnings level more for one child than for the other. Curve 2 in figure 54 illustrates a case in which households weigh a given level of expected earnings for boys more that they value the identical level of expected earnings for girls.

The discussion of the household objective function and preferences to this point has not considered what determines the household objective function. The proximate determinants are the preferences and (perhaps implicit) bargaining strengths of various household members.[2] Casual observations suggest that implicit or explicit bargaining within the household determines intra-household resource allocations. That factor may be relevant for the present discussion if different household members have different preferences regarding outcomes for boys versus girls. For example, if mothers place greater weight than do fathers on the health and survival of daughters than of sons, the bargaining power of mothers versus fathers within the household may be important for analysing sex differences in intra-household resource allocations. It has been suggested that the bargaining power of women depends on their schooling; their monetary income; their formal or informal support networks; the attraction of alternative living arrangements outside of their marriages; social and legal provisions regarding child support from fathers; and effective legislation that protects their rights and access to former spouses' resources if there is marital dissolution. However, the importance of intra-household bargaining is very difficult to establish with non-experimental data.

Household production functions

Production functions specify technical (in part biological) relations that indicate how inputs (e.g., nutrients consumed, genetic endowments) produce outputs of interest (e.g., health, expected earnings). The most directly relevant production functions are those for child health. Health production functions show how health depends on a number of inputs, some of which reflect behavioural choices of the individual,

the household and the community, and some of which are given. Examples of individual inputs are the nutrients consumed by a child, curative health care directed towards that child—which Basu (1989) claims is particularly important for understanding sex differences in infant and child mortality rates—and the genetic endowments of that child. Examples of household inputs include the time and capabilities of child-care providers and the quality of household water supply. Examples of community inputs include health services and the general health environment. There are two critical points to note about those inputs. First, some reflect behavioural choices which, if not controlled in the analysis, may bias estimates of effects of inputs (see subsection A.2 below). Second, a number of the inputs into health production are not usually measured in social science or epidemiological studies—most notably, genetic endowments. Third, those health production functions may be related to sex differentials in intra-household allocations and in infant and child mortality rates. For example, there may be sex differences in endowments[3] so that the impact of a specified input affects differentially the health of males and females. Household and community behavioural decisions also may result in differential inputs by sex.

Other production functions may also be important. For example, human capital investments, such as education, may depend directly and indirectly on child health and morbidity—directly if better health improves learning in school, and indirectly if better health improves complementary pre-school and out-of-school learning. The relevant question for the present concern is whether the impact of health and morbidity on education differs by sex.

Also relevant are production functions that determine the impact of health on outcomes of interest, such as economic productivity. If there are gender differences in productivity that are affected by health, then there may be incentives for differences in investments in the health of males and females, and thus in intra-household resource allocation. For instance, males are sometimes characterized as having comparative advantages in agricultural and construction activities that involve physical strength, while females are often characterized as having comparative advantage in activities that involve stamina and manual dexterity. Any gender differences in occupational and task distributions may create incentives for sex differences in intra-household resource allocations by sex.

Household resource constraint

The resource constraint denotes that the total use of resources by the household cannot exceed the total value of resources over which the household has command. Resources include physical, financial and human resources (including time) and entitlement over transfers from or to other households through public transfer/tax systems or through private transfers. The value of each resource depends on its productivity or market rate of return. How much a household can obtain with a given level of resources depends on the prices that the household must pay for various items. Such prices include monetary and time components. Resource constraints may embody incentives for sex differences in intra-household resource allocation through a number of mechanisms:

(a) Prices for human resource investments may differ by gender, particularly if services related to such investments are segregated by gender. Even if prices for health-related services do not differ by gender, the existence of gender differences in the prices for other human resource related services, from which the expected gains depend on health, may induce sex differences in intra-household resource allocation. For example, gender differences in effective school prices (reflecting differential school availability or school quality) create incentives for sex differences in investments in infant and child health if learning in school depends in part on child health;

(b) Some resource uses may differ by gender, including dowries and bride prices in many societies. If such resource uses also depend directly or indirectly on long-term health, the existence of those differences in resource uses may induce sex differences in intra-household health resource allocation. For instance, if dowries are smaller for daughters with better health or with better education and long-run health affects education, there may be such incentives;[4]

(c) Returns to human resources may differ by gender, as noted above, because of gender differences in relations between productivity and long-term health or because of gender specialization in tasks or occupations;[5]

(d) Finally, the proportion of economic productivity generated by human resource investments over which the household decision makers have command may also differ by the sex of children. If, for example, adult sons stay in the family household and contribute to the common resources of that household but adult daughters move into their husbands' households and do not provide transfers to their parents, there may be greater incentive to invest in the long-run health of sons than of daughters.

Production possibility frontiers

The production function and resource constraints of a household can be combined into a production possibility frontier, given household assets and the prices that the household faces. Such a frontier gives the maximum production possible for one outcome given all other household production levels.

To illustrate, assume for simplicity that the production frontier is defined in terms of the expected earnings of two children, a daughter and a son, given the total resources that the household devotes to children, and the expected earnings of a child depend, *inter alia,* on that child's endowments and the health and other human resource investments in that child.[6] Graphically, the expected earnings of the daughter (E^D) can be measured along the horizontal axis and the expected earnings of the son (E^S) can be measured along the vertical axis, as in figure 55. Then, for any level of expected earnings for the daughter, the earnings production possibility frontier gives the maximum expected earnings for the son. If more resources are devoted to the daughter so that her expected earnings increase, the expected earnings of the son decreases because less resources are devoted to the son. The earnings production possibility frontier generally is elongated in one direction because the children have different earning endowments and may face different prices or availabilities of inputs.

Constrained maximization of the household objective function

Household decision makers are posited to behave as if they are trying to obtain as high a level of welfare as possible. They would prefer higher to lower welfare—that is, to be on W_2 rather than W_1 in figure 52. But the household production possibility frontier limits the choices available to the household, as in figure 55. The household decision makers can obtain the maximum level of welfare possible given the production and resource constraints if they make choices so that an equal-welfare line of the household objective function is just touching (or tangent to) the household production possibility frontier.[7] Figure 56 provides an illustration in which figure 52 is superimposed on figure 55. A level of welfare W_1 could be obtained by picking point C on the production possibility frontier, but a higher welfare level of W_2 could be obtained by moving to point D, where the equal-welfare curve W_2 is tangent to the production possibility frontier. That constrained maximization may mean that investments in children or outcomes for children differ systematically by sex for a number of reasons.

For example, assume that household decision makers have equal concern as in curve 1 in figures 54 and 56, and thus have preferences that favour neither sons nor daughters but have some productivity-equity trade-off in their preferences.[8] Consider a set of reasons why the earnings possibility frontier again is elongated in the direction of the son in most households, as illustrated in figures 55 and 56. An elongation may reflect that: (a) endowments associated with males, such as innate strength, are rewarded more in the labour market[9]; (b) investments in the health of sons have higher expected returns than investments in health of daughters because of a greater complementarity between male genetic endowments and such investments in the health production function; (c) discrimination against women in labour markets; (d) differences in costs of human resource investments in boys versus girls because human resource-related facilities such as single-sex schools, are more available for boys than for girls.

In all four of those cases, there is by assumption no gender bias in preference weights in the household objective function, but there are gender differences outside of the household that may or may not reflect a bias. Those extra-household factors result in sons having greater expected earnings than daughters. Under those circumstances, intra-household resource allocations of nutrients and other human resource investments will favour sons to the extent that households are predominantly concerned about productivity.

Conversely, if there is strong enough concern about equity intra-household resource allocations of nutrients and other human resource investment compensate by being more concentrated in daughters.

What happens if there is unequal concern favouring sons in the household objective function? That possibility is illustrated by curve 2 in figure 54 and by the equal-welfare curve in figure 57. More resources are shifted towards sons than they would have received had there been equal concern, which increases their expected earnings relative to those of females. In figure 57 the tangency is at G instead of at D, as in figure 56. However, unequal concern favouring sons does not guarantee that intra-household resource allocation leads to greater investments in sons than in daughters. If there is sufficient concern about equity rather than productivity (and the frontier is elongated in the direction of sons) or if marginal returns are sufficiently greater for human resource investments in daughters than in sons, greater resources are allocated to daughters than to sons.

Some conclusions regarding the difficulties in identifying gender biases in intra-household resource allocations follow: (a) sex differences in outcomes, such as health or earnings, do not necessarily mean that there are gender biases either within the household or outside of the household; (b) sex differences in outcomes do not necessarily mean that there are sex differences in intra-household resource allocations that favour the same sex. If household concerns about equity are strong enough, in fact, intra-household resource allocations compensate for the incentives created by factors outside of the household by allocating more to children of the sex with less favourable conditions outside of the household; (c) sex differences in conditions outside of the household may reflect discrimination in either markets (e.g., in labour markets) or in policies (e.g., provision of single-sex schools), and may also reflect not discrimination but simply sex differences in endowments or in health production functions that affect productivity; and (d) sex differences in intra-household resource allocations do not necessarily mean that there are gender biases within the household that favours the sex that receives the greater resources within the household.

Figure 55. Production possibility frontier for expected earnings of sons versus daughters

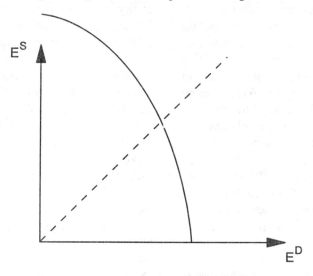

Figure 56. Constrained maximization of household objective function with equal concern between son's expected earnings and daughter's expected earnings

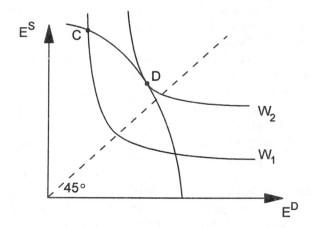

Figure 57. Constrained maximization of household objective function with unequal concern favouring son's expected earnings relative to daughter's expected earnings

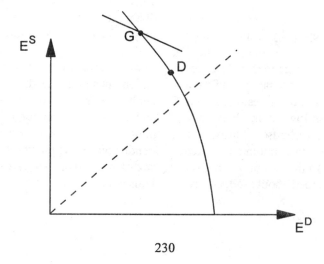

2. Implications for interpretation of behavioural data relating to intra-household resource allocation and sex differences in infant and child mortality rates

One basic implication of subsection A.1 above is that empirical data related to sex differences in intra-household resource allocations and infant and child mortality rates must be examined carefully within the context of behavioural decisions whose determinants may be imperfectly observed or not observed at all. The framework in subsection A.1 further suggests that there are two main types of relations that might be estimated from non-experimental social science data that might be informative regarding sex differences in intra-household resource allocations. First, there are "structural relations," such as the household objective function and the production functions in which a set of inputs, such as nutrients, health care, parental time and genetic endowments, produce an output, such as child health or expected earnings. The output produced by the household objective function (i.e., "welfare," "satisfaction"), however, is not easy to measure in an useful way that permits comparisons across households; such relations cannot therefore be estimated directly. In contrast, many data sets have information on indicators of outcomes of household production functions, such as child health, morbidity and mortality, and on indicators of inputs into those production functions, such as water quality, availability of health care, food, immunizations and characteristics of health-care providers (e.g., schooling of mothers). Estimates are often made with such outcomes as child health as the dependent variable and a number of inputs into the production of the outcome as independent variables. A major estimation problem is that some of those inputs reflect behavioural choices in the light of unobserved variables, such as child genetic endowments.

For example, if health-related inputs are allocated partly in response to children's genetic endowments that also in themselves have effects on child health, the estimated impact of the health-care inputs on child health will be biased because it will include not only the effect of the health-care inputs but also the effect of the correlated unobserved genetic endowments. Parents may reinforce genetic endowment differentials by allocating more resources to the child with greater endowments; conversely, parents may compensate for differences in genetic endowment by allocating more resources to the disadvantaged child. As a consequence, not even the direction of such a bias is obvious, and therefore the estimates cannot be interpreted as upper or lower bounds on the true values. To avoid such biases, the data on the inputs must be purged of their relation with unobserved genetic endowments (and any other unobserved child health production inputs with which they are correlated). Estimation techniques exist with which to obtain unbiased estimates. If, as in much of the literature, such techniques are not used (or not used well), the estimates obtained may be biased in an unknown direction.

Second, there are "reduced-form demand" relations that specify all of the variables that are determined by household behaviours (including health and mortality) as dependent on all the variables that are given or predetermined from the point of the view of the household—market prices, governmental policies, genetic endowments, environmental conditions and stock variables determined in the past. There is one set of such relations for each of the variables that are determined by household behaviours.

One important point about those relations is that all household behaviours depend in general on all of the same predetermined variables since the household makes all of its decisions based on all the constraints that it faces. That consideration means that child health depends not only on direct health production determinants, such as prices of health-related goods, but also on indirect determinants that affect any household behaviour. For example, the prices of adult clothing and of alcoholic beverages, entitlements for transfers, and, for farm households, the price of fertilizer, soil quality, water availability and the quantity of live stock, are among the predetermined variables that may affect child health, morbidity and mortality. Moreover, all of those effects may differ depending on children's sex for any of the reasons discussed in subsection A.1 above. It is an empirical question whether any of those given variables have significant or substantial effects on child health, and if so whether such effects differ by sex. Reduced-form demand relation estimates generally cannot distinguish estimated sex differences in these relations that are due to underlying preference from those due to price differences, unless (as is never the case) all the relevant prices are observed.

The estimation of reduced - form demand relations avoids the problems of unobserved influences on household choices that are encountered in the structural relations approach since only predetermined variables that are given (at least for the relevant time period) from the perspective of the household are included. But there may nevertheless be problems of omitted variable biases because all of the relevant predetermined variables, such as mothers' innate capabilities, are not observed.

There are other problems that limit an understanding of empirical values for both structural and reduced-form relations. A major set of problems are related to measurement errors, some of which have been addressed above for independent variables. In extreme cases, no direct indicators can be observed (e.g., genetic endowments). If such variables are fixed for outcomes for a given child, valid estimates of the other parameters can be obtained by purging the other variables of any correlation with the unobserved fixed variables. However, if the unobserved variables are household choice variables that enter in structural relations as independent factors, they complicate obtaining estimates of the impact of other choice variables because procedures that otherwise would purge the observed choice variables of any correlation with the disturbance also pick up the influence of the unobserved independent choice variable.

Another common problem is that critical variables are observed with measurement errors. If such measurement errors in independent variables are random, the well-known and intuitively plausible result is that they cause the estimated effects to be biased towards zero, the more so the greater the noise to signal ratio. Statistical procedures can be used (i.e. derivation of instrumental variables) to purge independent variables of such random measurement error. If measurement errors in dependent variables are random, they cause no bias in estimated coefficients (though they may cause misidentification of whether a particular child is above or below some interesting value, such as an adequate nutrition level). If measurement errors in either the dependent or independent variables are systematically related to other variables rather than random, purging their effects is much more problematic, but the failure to do so may jeopardize both description and analysis.[10]

B. EMPIRICAL EXPLORATIONS OF SEX DIFFERENTIALS IN INTRA-HOUSEHOLD ALLOCATION OF RESOURCES AS RELATED TO INFANT AND CHILD MORTALITY RATES

1. Structural estimates of intra-household nutrient allocations and gender biases

A small number of studies attempt to estimate structural parameters, that is, relations of the first type considered in subsection A.2 above, within the context of intra-household allocations of nutrients with explorations of possible gender biases within the household.

Reinforcement or compensation of endowments and gender preferences in intra-household allocations of nutrients in rural south India

As discussed in subsection A.1 above, two important attributes of household objective functions are: (*a*) productivity-equity tradeoffs; and (*b*) unequal concern. As also noted, estimation of such attributes is difficult, in part because household satisfaction or welfare levels are not observed. In Behrman (1988a and 1988b), estimates of those two attributes are presented with anthropometric measures of child health as the outcome[11] and nutrients as the inputs, for rural south India using the International Crops Research Institute for the Semi Arid Tropics panel data set on 240 households in six villages. The raw data do not indicate systematic sex or birth-order differences in nutrient intakes or anthropometric indicators of health (Ryan and others, 1984). But, as emphasized in subsection A.1 above, straightforward analysis does not always reveal whether there is gender bias in intra-household resource allocation. The general procedure adopted in those studies is to assume specific functional forms for the household objective function, in which the productivity-equity trade-off and unequal concern have specific parametric representations, and for the health production function, and then to derive expressions in terms of the objective function parameters and observed health and nutrient indicators from the conditions for constrained maximization. Those expressions are estimable with data on health (as represented by anthropometric measures) and nutrient allocations (as represented by 24-hour recall on individual consumption) within households. Since seasonal variations are strong in that region, separate estimates are made for the lean season, in which food is relatively scarce, and the surplus season, in which food is relatively abundant. The estimates suggest that there are significant differences between the seasons.[12] In the surplus season, there is significant compensation, with much greater concern about equity than in previous estimates for the United States (based on expected earnings as the outcome with schooling allocated, see Behrman, Pollak and Taubman, 1982 and 1986). In the lean season, there is substantial reinforcement (close to the pure productivity case and much higher than in the United States estimates). There is equal concern in the surplus season but unequal concern favouring sons and children of lower birth order in the lean season.[13] Those results suggest that during the surplus season, strong equity preferences and the equal concern result in fairly even distributions of nutrients across all children, despite higher labour market and agricultural productivity returns to males. But in the lean season, the strong productivity preference, reinforced by preference for males and for lower birth-order children, result in intra-household resource allocations that favour sons and leave daughters and higher birth-order children at considerable risk of mortality.[14]

The present study makes progress in estimating critical household objective function parameters by using particular functional forms for some of the central relations in the framework in subsection A.1 above and direct observations on individual nutrient and health data for at least two children in each household. However, the results concerning large seasonal differences in those parameters with gender and birth-order bias in the lean season must still be qualified because some important implications of the framework are not addressed. In particular, more extensive data that permit control for individual endowment differences among children are required to deal with those problems.[15]

Intra-household distributions of nutrients, health, work effort and endowments in rural Bangladesh

Pitt, Rosenzweig and Hassan (1990) develop and estimate a model that is consistent with the framework in section A above and that incorporates linkages among nutrition, labour-market productivity, health heterogeneity, and the intra-household distribution of food and work activities in a subsistence economy. Their approach explicitly integrates concerns about the productivity impact of health and nutrition in such societies and about sex variations in intra-household allocations. Their study is presented in some detail because it deals better than other studies with the problems discussed in section A, and thereby illustrates the difficulties in obtaining confident knowledge about gender bias in intra-household nutrient allocations.

A household is assumed to have individuals in a number of age and sex classes with the same health and wage production functions for all members of the household within the same class. The household objective function is defined over the health, food consumption and work effort of each individual (with positive effects of health and food consumption, and negative effects of work effort). Constraints on that maximization include (*a*) a budget constraint that posits that income from labour and other sources must be greater than or equal to expenditures on food and other consumption, and (*b*) production functions for health (positively dependent on nutrient intakes and endowments, and negatively dependent on energy expended) and wages (positively dependent on health and on energy expended[16]) for each class of individuals. The health endowments (i.e., that component of health influenced neither by nutrient intakes nor by work effort) are known to the household members but not observed by scientists.

The conditions for a constrained maximization indicate that the marginal cost of allocating nutrients to an individual is related negatively to the extent to which that person's health improves with more nutrition and the extent to which that person's wage increases with better health. Because different classes of individuals participate in different work and the wage effects of health vary across types of work, the marginal costs of food allocated to different classes of individuals may vary substantially. Within a class, the distribution of food and work effort across individuals depends on the distribution of endowments among those individuals. Compensation or reinforcement can be examined by investigating the impact of endowments on health, which includes the partial effects on health through both work effort and nutrient intakes.

To explore empirically whether there is compensation or reinforcement, estimates of the endowments first must be obtained. To do so, the health production function is estimated directly, and based on the parameter estimates and the actual nutrients consumed and work effort expended by each individual, endowments of individuals are calculated. There are two problems—related to general problems discussed in subsection A.2 above—that must be addressed in this "residual" endowment method. First, because endowments are not observed and because they influence household allocations, ordinary least squares estimates of the health production technology are not consistent. Accordingly, the authors use an instrumental variable technique to obtain consistent estimates of the health production function.[17] Second, the residually derived endowments are likely to be measured with systematic error because of random measurement error in the observed inputs into the health production function, such as individual nutrients, which carry over to cause errors in the estimated endowments that in turn causes biases in the estimated impact of the endowments on allocated variables. Those biases tend to make households appear more compensatory than they really are.[18] Therefore, they use statistical techniques to obtain consistent estimates.[19]

The data requirements for their study are considerable: observations on nutrient intakes, health outcomes, and work effort at the individual level; sufficient cross-sectional variation in exogenous instruments needed for consistent estimation of the health production function; and repeated observations on individuals to purge estimated endowments of measurement errors (Pitt, Rosenzweig and Hassan, 1990). The data source is the 1981-1982 Bangladesh Rural Nutrition Survey of 385 households in 15 villages, complemented by intra-household nutrient data available for about half of those households and longitudinal data on intra-household allocations available for a further subset. The authors use FAO/WHO classifications of the 14 occupations provided in the data as "very active" and "exceptionally active" to characterize higher than normal work effort. They also control for whether women were lactating or pregnant in the sample period to control for nutrient use that is unrelated to work.

Estimates of the health production function for weight-for-height suggest that the impact of calories is understated, and the signs of the coefficients of the work effort variables are wrong if there is no control for the choice aspect of inputs. The residual endowments obtained from the consistently estimated health production technology are used for the households with longitudinal data to obtain consistent estimates of the impact of individual endowments on individual nutrients intake. Those estimates suggest reinforcement in the sense that individuals with better endowments receive more nutrients; those effects are about 10 times larger for males than for females, which is consistent with their model, given that their data indicate that women do not participate in energy-intensive activities. Reinforcement is significant for males aged 12 years or older, and for both males and females in the 6-12 year age range; however, compensation may occur for those under six years of age of both sexes (though the standard errors are large); for females 12 years of age or older, the sign of the coefficient is positive but the magnitude is very small and the standard error very large.

Pitt, Rosenzweig and Hassan (1990) explore the impact of endowments on household income and on participating in an exceptionally active occupation (in the absence of data on individual wage rates or earnings). Their estimates suggest that there is a pecuniary return to health and effort, that adult males with better endowments are more likely to undertake exceptionally energy-intensive work, and that adult female health endowments are relatively unimportant (in comparison with those for adult males) in determining activity choices or household income. Finally, the net effect of a change in individuals' endowments on their own health is calculated from the estimated health production functions and the estimated endowment effects on the nutrient and work effort variables in those production functions. The elasticities of health with respect to endowments are 0.88 for adult males and 0.97 for adult females. Elasticities of less than one imply that Bangladesh households on balance exhibit compensatory rather than reinforcing behaviour with respect to adult health endowments; adult males are "taxed" to the benefit of other household members more than females. Therefore, what appears to be gender bias against adult females in the intra-household allocation of nutrients relative to "requirements" as conventionally measured, turns out to be bias against adult males when both the allocation of nutrients and the allocation of energy-intensive work effort are incorporated into the analysis.

Despite some limitations, that is the most thorough study available of intra-household allocations and gender, and is a model for emulation in a number of respects, including its wide perspective about what allocations are inter-linked, its care with regard to estimation issues, and its use of especially rich cross-sectional and panel data in a systematic and integrated manner. It also points to the considerable difficulties in identifying gender biases in intra-household allocations, and illustrates how incorrect inferences may be made in several respects if partial or less careful approaches are used.

2. Reduced-form demand relations, health and gender

As noted in subsection A.2 above, estimates of reduced-form demand relations may also give insights into determinants of sex differences in intra-household resource allocation related to health. But as also noted above, such estimates cannot usually identify whether the underlying causes of sex differences stem from the household objective function or from household production functions. Nevertheless, such reduced-form demand studies may reveal how households respond to factors that are given, such as labour market conditions, prices, the schooling of adult household members and social services. Even though the primary focus of the present chapter is on infants and children, sex differences in reduced-form demand relations for other age ranges are included below.

Male-female infant and child mortality differentials and labour markets in India

Using aggregate data, Basu and Basu (1991) report that among poor households in rural India in 1981, the probability of infant and child mortality increases with women's employment, but less so for daughters than for sons. They suggest that those associations reflect the fact that working mothers spend less time with their children (which raises infant and child mortality) but have more influence on intra-household resource allocation in ways that favour daughters relative to sons.[20] That interpretation is consistent with a simplified version of the framework in subsection A.1, but the authors do not control for behavioural choices nor for unobserved heterogeneities. Therefore, as they realize, their interpretations of associations are conjectural, with too many untested assumptions to make a confident leap from associations to causality.

Rosenzweig and Schultz (1982) analyse the determinants of male-female differentials in child survival rates in rural India, using both 1971 rural household and 1961 district level data. They have no observations on intra-household allocations, but they argue that the male-female survival differential depends upon the expected relative returns to male and female labour because those expectations influence parental investments in sons and daughters. That argument is consistent with the framework of subsection A.1 above, in which longer-term expected returns affect sex differences in intra-household resource allocation in infants and children, and thus sex differences in the health of children. The authors use predicted employment rates of current men and women as proxies for the economic returns to investing in boys and girls. In both the household and the district level samples, they find predicted female (but not male) employment rates to be a significant negative determinant of the male-female child survival differential. They interpret those results to imply that children who are expected to become more economically productive adults receive a greater share of family resources, and therefore have a greater propensity to survive than other children.

In a comment on the above-mentioned article, Folbre (1984) suggests that those results are consistent with the possibility that women with larger incomes have greater influence in intra-household allocations and tend to favour daughters relative to sons, an explanation similar to that of Basu and Basu. Such a possibility is also consistent with the framework in subsection A.1. But Rosenzweig and Schultz (1984) correctly respond by observing that the available data do not permit one to identify whether the underlying allocations reflect such a bargaining model versus responses to differential expected returns.

Morbidity demand relations
by gender in Indonesia

Pitt and Rosenzweig (1985) use data on 2,347 Indonesian farm households (from the 1978 Indonesian Socio-economic Survey) to estimate separate "illness demand" (ordered probit) functions for husbands and wives, and a fixed effect logit for the difference between the husband's illness and the wife's illness. The independent variables are the prices of 13 consumption goods (foods and non-foods); source of drinking water; availability of hospitals, family-planning clinics, public lavatories and clinics; land ownership; farm profits; and the age and education of the husband and wife. They find relatively few significant determinants of health,[21] but the fixed effects logit estimates suggest that there are some differences in the effects on men versus women. The presence of clinics and the price of vegetables, for example, significantly increase the health of women relative to that for men, while the opposite is the case for the price of fish. In that case, there is thus some evidence that the presence of health services in communities favours females more than males, as well as further evidence that households respond differentially for males than for females to some market prices.

Differential treatments of boys versus girls
in household expenditures in Côte d'Ivoire
and Thailand

Deaton (1989) uses household expenditure and demographic data to assess differential treatment of boys versus girls. The basic point of his approach is that for a given level of income, families with children spend less on adult goods (e.g., tobacco, alcohol, adult clothing and shoes, meals out, entertainment) in order to purchase children's goods. If household expenditures favour boys over girls, smaller expenditures on adult goods are made by families with boys than by families with girls. His examination of cross-sectional expenditure data reveals no evidence of statistically significant differentials favouring boys or girls in either Côte d'Ivoire or Thailand. However, his approach utilizes only surviving household members, and thus misses the effects of sex differences in previous infant and child mortality.

3. Tests of income pooling by gender
in demand relations

In subsection A.1 above it was noted that bargaining within households may influence allocation of resources. Furthermore, improvements in the bargaining position of women may favour daughters relative to sons. With non-experimental data, the relevance of bargaining is difficult to assess because the types of variables that usually are used to measure bargaining power also may be representing unobserved tastes and productivity.[22] There have been several recent studies, nevertheless, that purport to test whether male and female non-earned income can be pooled. Some observers have interpreted those estimates to be strong evidence in favour of household bargaining models over models with unified preferences (in the sense that all relevant household members have the same preferences or the preferences of one household member determine household decisions). Two of those studies on developing societies are summarized below.

Individual unearned income and Brazilian
child survival rates, anthropometric
measures and nutrient intakes

Thomas (1990) explores whether there are different effects of men's and women's unearned income on child survival rates, anthropometric measures and nutrient intakes for children using 1974/1975 *Estudo Nacional da Despesa Familiar* data for over 25,000 urban households in Brazil. Unearned income (not wages) is used, and parents' education is controlled in order to focus on the income effects alone, without the price and time-use preference effects that wages would entail. The estimates indicate a much larger effect on child survival and child anthropometric measures of women's unearned incomes than of men's. Moreover, unearned income of the mother has a greater impact on daughters than on sons, while the unearned income of the father has greater impact on sons. He also reports that the estimated effects of both women's and men's unearned incomes are positive but decline as incomes increase. The estimated impact of women's unearned incomes on nutrient intakes is about seven times of that for men's, for both calories and proteins. Thomas concludes that those results reject the unified prefer-

236

ence model of households often used for economic analysis,[23] and suggest that mothers' incomes are much more important in determining children's health than are fathers' incomes, but with the intergenerational gender links noted above.[24]

Cash income shares, consumption composition and child anthropometric indicators in Côte d'Ivoire

Haddad and Hoddinott (1994) use a sub-sample from a national household survey (the World Bank Living Standards Measurement Study) for the Côte D'Ivoire to estimate the relevance of income pooling. Since that survey does not identify non-labour earnings by individuals, they limit their analysis to a comparison of households with only adult males and households with only adult females. They then compare consumption shares and cash income effects on child anthropometric outcomes for those two types of households. They interpret their estimates to mean that increases in the share of cash income accruing to women significantly raise the budget shares of food and lower those of alcohol and cigarettes, and improve anthropometric outcomes for children (somewhat more for boys than for girls). They suggest that to the extent that such changes are regarded as desirable, the results provide additional reasons for policy measures to improve women's access to income-generating resources (pp. 23 and 24).

What do those studies mean with regard to the importance of bargaining versus price/tastes effects? There are a range of answers to that question. McElroy (1992, p. 12) interprets those and related studies to be part of the strong results favouring bargaining models. Thomas (1990) and Schultz (1990) claim that that evidence rejects one of the restrictions implied if households had unified preferences as defined above, but recognize explicitly that the evidence does not actually confirm the bargaining model. Udry (1995) provides related evidence of inefficient allocation of productive resources across land plots operated by different household members (men versus women) in Burkina Faso, which he interprets to reflect bargaining considerations.

The interpretation that those results reject the pooling assumption of the unified model is problematic. The ideal assessment would be to conduct an experiment in which extra income were distributed randomly to males and females, and then to observe whether the marginal propensities to use such income differed depending upon the sex of the recipient—in particular, for the present concern, whether daughters benefited differently than sons. Not surprisingly, none of those studies employ such an experimental method. Instead, Thomas uses individual "unearned" rather than earned income in order to abstract from price (i.e., opportunity cost of time) and taste effects that wages would represent. But is there any reason to think that unearned income is unrelated to wages, productivity and tastes? The answer depends in part on the sources of unearned income. In the data for Thomas' study, the sources of unearned incomes are largely pensions and social security, both of which are related to past wages, productivity and preferences regarding time use. Even earnings from assets may reflect past productivity and preferences if such assets were acquired out of past labour wages. Therefore, unearned income may in part represent productivity in labour market activities associated with household activities pertaining to health, nutrition, fertility and time allocations and/or preferences for time use. If so, those results do not necessarily mean that shifting income to women would have more positive effects on child health in general or on health of daughters than shifting equal income to men but simply that more productive women have more positive effects on their children's health. In fact, those results are consistent with the true effects involving income pooling, except that unearned income coefficient estimates are biased differentially by proxying for unobserved productivity endowments given gender specialization in household tasks. The Haddad and Hoddinott (1994) estimates have at least as great a problem in that respect since they use cash income that includes current labour income;[25] in addition, it is difficult to interpret what their results mean given their sample selection criterion for including only households with all adults of one sex.

4. Reduced-form demand relations for other related outcomes

Schooling and inter-generational transfers in the Philippines

Quisumbing (1993) examines schooling, land and non-land asset transfers from parents to children in

344 households in five rice villages in Central Luzon and Panay Island in the Philippines, using retrospective survey data. Unobserved family endowments are important, as suggested by the framework in subsection A.1 above. Families with different land constraints have significantly different patterns of schooling investments. For land-constrained households (but not those that bestow land), the estimates show that the eldest and the youngest daughters receive significantly less schooling, which may reflect unequal concern favouring sons and middle order daughters in the terminology of subsection A.1 above. Analysis of a sub-sample by combined land status with completed inheritance decisions, however, indicates that daughters are not disadvantaged in schooling, at least at the five per cent significance level, but receive significantly less land and total inheritance, with partial compensation through receiving greater non-land assets. Thus, those results for the sub-sample, with completed inheritance, suggest equal concern by gender with regard to human resources though unequal concern favouring males for land transfers and overall inheritances. All in all, if better health is sought in part because of its impact on learning in school, those estimates suggest little if any incentive to favour sons in the intra-household resource allocation of health-related resources because they will have greater subsequent returns from those health investments in schooling.

Infant and child morbidity and gender inequality in intra-household resource allocation of schooling in Indonesia

In most societies, there is gender specialization in the provision of home health care, with females providing most such care. Pitt and Rosenzweig (1990) develop and implement a method with data from Indonesia for estimating the effects of infant morbidity on the differential allocation of time of family members. They use a framework similar to that in subsection A.1 above, but with the health of various household members determined simultaneously. The contagious nature of some diseases is explicitly recognized, which complicates the estimation considerably, and indeed makes consistent estimation possible only with some strong assumptions. The data requirements for estimating such relations are substantial: information on child health, the activities of all household members and the prices of health-related goods, as well as a large sample size. The 1980 Indonesian Socio-economic Survey linked with other information on prices and health programmes has such data for 5,831 households. The estimates obtained indicate that in comparison with teenage sons, teenage daughters were significantly more likely to increase their participation in household care activities and to reduce their participation in market activities and at school in response to illness of infant siblings. Moreover, such estimates differ markedly from the estimates obtained if there was no control for the simultaneity of child health determination and time uses of household members. Thus, gender specialization in care for sick infants reduces the expected schooling of daughters, which reduces the incentives for investing in the health of female infants and children if one of the returns to such investments is subsequent schooling success.

C. CONCLUSIONS

Gender biases in intra-household resource allocation are thought by many to be very important in understanding sex differences in infant and child mortality rates. Intra-household allocations certainly appear to be important in determining child development as well as in the determination of time use, other human resource investments, and intra-generational and intergenerational transfers in developing countries. The nature of such allocations have important implications for equity, efficiency and the efficacy of policies.

Assessment of the influence of sex differences in intra-household resource allocation in infant and child mortality rates is severely limited by lack of relevant data. Many critical variables, often including the intra-household allocations themselves, are not observed in most data sets. Almost all of the data that are available, moreover, are observations on behaviours, which in part stem from unobserved variables, such as genetic endowments, unequal concern favouring sons (or daughters) and bargaining power. A simple framework for analysing intra-household resource allocation, such as that presented in section A above, points to the considerable difficulties in making simple inferences about sex differences in intra-household resource allocation related to infant and child mortality rates. That framework indicates, for example, that (*a*) sex differences in outcomes, such as health or mortality, may occur for a number of reasons other than gender biases in preferences of household members; (*b*) sex difference in such outcomes may occur even if there are neither gender biases in preferences underlying intra-household resource allocation nor in markets nor in policies; and (*c*) sex differences in intra-household resource allocation may favour girls even if there is gender bias in preferences of household decision makers that favour boys. Thus, simple observations about sex differences in intra-household resource allocation are not likely to be conclusive regarding either the importance of gender bias in households or what changes would alter sex differences in either intra-household resource allocation or in outcomes affected by households. Therefore, for better understanding, predictions and policy design, it is important to attempt to understand the sources of the sex differences that are documented elsewhere in the present volume. It is not likely to be productive, as is all too common, to define every difference by sex as discrimination. Although some studies in the large literature that describe sex differences in intra-household resource allocation are sensitive to the great difficulties in establishing causality (e.g., Koenig and D'Souza, 1986; Muhuri and Preston, 1991), many others are cavalier about those difficulties and unjustified in making the tremendous leap from observing associations to attributing causality.

Despite the huge difficulties in empirical measurement and conceptualization, there has been substantial progress in modelling intra-household allocations in ways that lead to testable propositions. That progress has been made by using better data, increasing the rigour of the relation between the modelling and the empirical estimation, and making assumptions that permit the circumvention of major data problems.

Most of the analytical modelling and most of the empirical work has been within a fairly simple framework, as outlined in subsection A.1 above. The best of those studies have elaborated on and tested hypotheses about the role of unobserved heterogenous endowments in intra-household allocations within the context of labour, product and marriage markets. Their results suggest that controlling for unobserved heterogeneity is indeed critical for understanding the nature of and the impact of intra-household allocations and how they relate to gender biases. Those studies have tended to deal with an ever-widening range of

issues in more integrated ways, with increasing sensitivity to estimation issues.

The substantive results from those studies include the following:

(*a*) When food is scarce in rural south India, intra-household resource allocation reflects a strong emphasis on productivity rather than equity; those are biases favouring male and lower-birth-order children, with a consequence that some of the most vulnerable children may be subject to large morbidity and mortality risks. When food is more available, there is much more concern about equity and there are no significant gender or birth-order preferences;

(*b*) In rural Bangladesh, nutrient allocations that appear to favour adult males in fact appear to be part of a "tax" on adult males in favour of other household members if energy-intensive uses are incorporated into the analysis;

(*c*) Sex differences in intra-household resource allocation related to childhood mortality rates respond significantly to sex differences in labour market opportunities in rural India. There remains some ambiguity whether the effect of labour market conditions operates through expected returns to human resource investments or through time use and resource command of mothers;

(*d*) Whether mothers or fathers receive income is associated with sex differences in intra-household resource allocation in Brazil, as well as adult-children differences in intra-household resource allocation. However, interpretation of that association in terms of prices, preferences and bargaining power is not easy;

(*e*) Gender specialization in household tasks, such as care for sick infants, reduces daughters' expected schooling in Indonesia, which may induce less investment in their health.

The number of systematic studies within the framework outlined in section A above is very small. Moreover, on some topics their results differ—e.g., whether more mother's income or schooling is associated with more resources going to daughters (Thomas, 1990, on Brazil) or to sons (Haddad and Hoddinott,

1994, on Côte d'Ivoire) or whether care of sick infants reduces daughters' schooling (Quisumbing, 1994, on the Philippines versus Pitt and Rosenzweig, 1985, on Indonesia). There is no clear indication whether those differences reflect differences in reality or differences in approaches. Furthermore, even the best studies are characterized by untested assumptions, unobserved variables and other problems, such as uncertainty and imperfect information.

So, although progress has been considerable in the systematic socio-economic analysis of sex differences in intra-household resource allocation that relate to childhood mortality rates in developing countries, there remains considerable potential for making advances in that area. The most useful advances will probably be those in which theoretical modelling, special data and appropriate statistical analyses are carefully integrated.

NOTES

[1]For such elaboration see Behrman (1994 and 1996). For related considerations, see Deaton (1995) and Strauss and Thomas (1995).

[2]Underlying the preferences of individual household members are likely be cultural norms and traditions that may change over time, but are assumed to be given for the present illustration of how households allocate resources at a point of time. Usually cultural norms and traditions are thought to change relatively slowly, so the working assumption here that the resulting individual preferences and the household objective function based on such preferences are fixed to illustrate intrahouse-hold allocations is not likely to be too misleading. But it should be noted that there is considerable debate among social scientists about what determines cultural norms and individual preferences (and their interactions).

[3]It often is claimed, for example, that there is excess male mortality during the first year of life because of the genetically lower resistance of boys during the neonatal or longer periods (see for example, chaps. II and III above; Gbenyon and Locoh, 1992; and Pebley and Amin, 1991).

[4]Rao (1993), for example, reports that dowries in rural south India are less for more educated and healthier (as indicated by anthropometric measures) women, though the estimated effects are imprecise.

[5]Boserup (1970) and Svedberg (1990), for example, conjecture that indicators of health, morbidity and mortality favouring females in sub-Saharan Africa in comparison with those favouring males in South Asia reflect in part the gender division of labour. Women produce food crops in sub-Saharan Africa, where there is relative labour scarcity and land abundance. Together with polygamy, such factors lead to women being desired in those marriage markets so that positive bride prices are the norm. In contrast, daughters are a financial burden to their parents in South Asia, because of the predominance of monogamy and the dowry system, in conjunction with land scarcity and labour abundance.

[6]To make this illustration as simple as possible, it is assumed here that the household decides first how much resources to devote to their two children, and then decides how to allocate those resource between the two children. The example thus ignores important questions, such as how the household decides how many children to have or how to divide overall household resources between the adults and children. But the basic points made below would hold with a more complicated set of assumptions that incorporated those decisions.

[7]There is an assumption here that household decision makers cannot simply maximize the total expected earnings of all the children and then enforce redistribution among the children to obtain the desired equity.

[8]In one limiting case in which there is only concern about equity (in which case the preference contours are L-shaped) so that no value is placed on expected earnings of any child that exceed the expected earnings for the child in the family with the lowest expected earnings, constrained maximization leads to equal expected earnings for all children.

[9]However, it is far from clear whether endowments are systematically better for males than for females. With regard to health, in fact, the dominant conjecture is the opposite (e.g., Kane, 1991): if males tend to be less well endowed, then sons rather than daughters tend to benefit from greater emphasis on equity.

[10]To illustrate regarding pure description, Courtwright (1990) argues that patterns in estimated female to male child mortality rates that have been interpreted to reflect considerable female neglect in parts of the nineteenth century United States in fact reflect failure to correct census and other data for differential sex patterns in migration.

[11]Health is the outcome in that it fulfills the role of expected earnings in the discussion of subsection A.1; health may still be of interest in itself or because it has an impact on expected productivity.

[12]The seasonal differences in the estimates do not necessarily mean that preferences change across seasons. Instead, the relevant region over which preferences determine behavior may change because the resource constraint may change across seasons (e.g., be much more limiting in the lean season).

[13]Those results are robust, moreover, when the specification is augmented by including in the household objective function the estimated impact of nutrients on labour market productivity, as estimated from the experience of current adults (under the assumptions that labour markets are quite stable in that part of India, and that there are high correlations between child age-standardized anthropometric indicators and those that the children will have when they are adults).

[14]Studies on other parts of South Asia (e.g., Das Gupta, 1987, on the Punjab; Muhuri and Preston, 1991, on Bangladesh) document an interaction between high birth order or having older sisters on female infant and child mortality.

[15]Behrman, Rosenzweig and Taubman (1994 and 1996) show how data on identical and fraternal twins can be used to control for unobserved endowments and to estimate the impact of individual endowments on intra-household resource allocations with minimal assumptions. They present estimates for the United States that show that households allocate investments in years and resource-intensity of schooling so as to reinforce endowments (i.e., with emphasis on productivity relative to equity) for both males and females.

[16]Work time is assumed to be the same for all individuals because there are no data on time allocations, and because casual observations suggest that there is very little leisure in the sample area.

[17]They use instrumental variable procedures with food prices, labour-market variables reflecting labour demand, and exogenous components of income as instruments, under the assumption that such variables determine resource allocations but do not directly affect health status, given food and activity levels (Pitt, Rosenzweig and Hassan, p. 1145).

[18]Pitt, Rosenzweig and Hassan (1990) show that if the true impact of such endowments on nutrients is positive, the estimated impact will be downward biased. But if the true impact is negative, the classical measurement error bias is towards zero (and therefore positive), while the bias due to the correlation of the estimated endowment with the measurement error in nutrients is negative, so the overall effect is indeterminate.

[19]More specifically, to obtain consistent estimates they use instrumental variables in the form of estimated health endowments for weight-for-height, mid-arm circumference, and skinfold thickness from other survey rounds than the one for which the allocation estimate is being made under the assumption that the period-specific measurement errors are not correlated across time periods.

[20]Blau, Guilkey and Popkin (1996) explore the first part of that conjecture. They estimate health production functions using data from a longitudinal household survey in 1983-86 for a sample of over 3,000 children in Cebu, the Philippines, in 1983-1986. They note that simple associations of women's work with child anthropometrics are in some cases negative, which would seem to be consistent with that conjecture. But when they adopt specifications that are consistent with the framework in subsection A.1 above with women's work reflecting behavioural choices in the presence of and in part in response to unobserved endowments, they find that there is no significant effect of mothers' work on child health directly through the production function, and that mothers with higher wages tend to have healthier children despite the fact that they are less likely to breastfeed as long as do non-workers. That is an interesting illustration of the possibility that incorporating behavior into the analysis, as in the framework in subsection A.1 above, can change substantially our understanding of causal effects from those that might be deduced from simple associations in the data.

[21]Pitt and Rosenzweig (1990) attribute the lack of precise estimates to measurement problems: illness was reported by the sick themselves (or by the household head or spouse) and hence subject to differences in sensitivity to symptoms and in propensities to report them, and was recorded over a period of only one week.

[22]Some studies (e.g., Basu, 1989; Das Gupta, 1990) interpret variables, such as reported decision-making power regarding cooking, where births took place (i.e., maternal family home, paternal family home, hospital, clinic) and time use (i.e., time in paid employment) as measures of women's autonomy in mortality and related relations. That interpretation of such behavioural variables seems problematic within the framework of subsection A.1 above, since those variables also respond to all of the observed and unobserved prices, policies and assets that the household faces.

[23]Though he notes that ratios of income effects are not significantly different from each other, which is consistent with the common preference model if income is measured with error, as well as consistent with differential intra-household preferences that are homogenous in the relative preference weights that mothers and fathers have for health outcomes.

[24]In a more recent paper, Thomas (1993) further explores the income pooling possibility with the same data, by investigating whether non-labour income or total income can be pooled across men and women in estimates of the determinants of income shares. He finds that income under the control of women is associated with a larger increase in the share of the household budget devoted to human capital investments (i.e., health, education and household services) but less devoted to food consumption.

[25]They recognize that there may be a simultaneity problem and use a set of instruments for income (e.g., demographic variables, location variables, indicators of the nature of consumer durables and housing, schooling variables, land variables). However they do not present persuasive evidence that these instruments are independent of the disturbance terms (which may include unobserved productivity and taste factors).

REFERENCES

Ainsworth, Martha (1992). *Economic Aspects of Child Fostering in Côte D'Ivoire*. Living Standards Measurement Study Working Paper No. 92. Washington, D.C.: World Bank.

Arnold, Fred (1992). Sex preferences and its demographic and health implications. *International Family Planning Perspectives* (New York), vol. 18, No. 3 (September), pp. 93-101.

Basu, Alaka Malwade (1989). Is discrimination in food really necessary for explaining sex differentials in childhood mortality. *Population Studies* (London), No. 43, pp. 193-210.

_____, and Kaushik Basu (1991). Women's economic roles and child survival: the case of India. *Health Transition Review* (Canberra), vol. 1, No. 1, pp. 83-103.

Becker, Gary (1991). *A Treatise on the Family*. Cambridge, Massachusetts: Harvard University Press.

Behrman, Jere R. (1988a). Nutrition, health, birth order and seasonality: intrahousehold allocation in rural India. *Journal of Development Economics* (Amsterdam), vol. 28, No. 1 (February), pp. 43-63.

_____ (1988b). Intrahousehold allocation of nutrients in rural India: are boys favoured? Do parents exhibit inequality aversion? *Oxford Economic Papers* (Oxford), vol. 40, No. 1 (March), pp. 32-54.

_____ (1992). Intrahousehold allocation of nutrients and gender effects: a survey of structural and reduced-form estimates. In *Nutrition and Poverty*, Siddig R. Osmani, ed. Oxford: Clarendon Press.

_____ (1994). Intrafamily distribution in developing countries. *Pakistan Development Review* (Islamabad), vol. 33, No. 3 (Autumn), pp. 253-296.

_____ (1996). Intrafamily distribution. In *Handbook of Population and Family Economics*, Mark R. Rosenzweig and Oded Stark, eds. Amsterdam: North-Holland Publishing Company.

_____, and Anil B. Deolalikar (1990). The intra-household demand for nutrients in rural South India: individual estimates, fixed effects and permanent income. *Journal of Human Resources* (Madison, Wisconsin), vol. 25, No. 4 (Fall), pp. 665-696.

Behrman, Jere R., and Victor Lavy (1994a). Dynamic decision rules for child growth in rural India and the Philippines: catching up or staying behind? Philadelphia: University of Pennsylvania. Mimeograph.

_____ (1994b). *Child Health and Schooling Achievement: Association, Causality, and Household Allocations*. World Bank Living Standards Measurement Study Paper, No. 104. Washington, D.C.: World Bank.

Behrman, Jere R., Robert A. Pollak and Paul Taubman (1982). Parental preferences and provision for progeny. *Journal of Political Economy* (Chicago), vol 90, No. 1 (February), pp. 52-73. Reprinted in Behrman, Pollak and Taubman (1995). *From Parent to Child: Inequality and Immobility in the United States*. Chicago: University of Chicago Press.

_____ (1986). Do parents favour boys? *International Economic Review* (Osaka, Japan), vol. 27, No. 1 (February), pp. 31-52. Reprinted in Behrman, Pollak and Taubman (1995). *From Parent to Child: Inequality and Immobility in the United States*. Chicago: University of Chicago Press.

_____ (1995). *From Parent to Child: Inequality and Immobility in the United States*. Chicago: University of Chicago Press.

Behrman, Jere R., Mark R. Rosenzweig and Paul Taubman (1994). Endowments and the allocation of schooling in the family and in the marriage market: the twins experiment. *Journal of Political Economy* (Chicago), vol. 102, No. 6 (December), pp. 1131-1174.

_____ (1996). College choice and wages: estimates using data on female twins. *Review of Economics and Statistics* (Amsterdam), forthcoming.

Behrman, Jere R., and Paul Taubman (1986). Birth order, schooling and earnings. *Journal of Labor Economics* (Chicago), vol. 4, No. 4 (July), part 2, pp. S121-S145.

Bhuiya, Abbas, and Kim Streatfield (1991). Mothers' education and survival of female children in a rural area of Bangladesh. *Population Studies* (London), vol. 45, No.2 (July), pp. 253-264.

Blau, David M., David K. Guilkey and Barry M. Popkin (1996). Infant health and the labor supply of mothers. *Journal of Human Resources* (Madison, Wisconsin), vol. 31, No. 1 (Winter), pp. 90-139.

Boserup, E. (1970). *Women's Role in Economic Development.* Wiltshire, United Kingdom: Grower.

Bourne, Katherine L., and George M. Walker, Jr. (1991). The differential effect of mothers' education on mortality of boys and girls in India. *Population Studies* (London), vol. 45, No. 2 (July), pp. 203-219.

Courtwright, David T. (1990). The neglect of female children and childhood sex ratios in nineteenth-century America: a review of the evidence. *Journal of Family History* (Greenwich, Connecticut), vol. 15, No. 3, pp. 313-323.

Das Gupta, Monica (1987). Selective discrimination against female children in rural Punjab, India. *Population and Development Review* (New York), vol. 13, No. 1, pp. 77-100.

_____ (1990). Death clustering, mothers' education and the determinants of child mortality in rural Punjab, India. *Population Studies* (London), vol. 44, No. 3 (November), pp. 489-505.

Deaton, Angus (1989). Looking for boy-girl discrimination in household expenditure data. *World Bank Economic Review* (Washington, D.C.), vol. 3, No. 1 (January), pp. 1-15.

_____ (1995). Data and econometric tools for development analysis. In *Handbook in Development Economics*, vol. 3A, Jere R. Behrman and T. N. Srinivasan, eds. Amsterdam: North-Holland Publishing Co.

Folbre, Nancy (1984). Market opportunities, genetic endowments, and intrafamily resource distribution of resources: comment. *American Economic Review* (Nashville), vol. 74, pp. 518-520.

_____ (1986). Cleaning house: new perspectives on households and economic development. *Journal of Development Economics* (Amsterdam), vol. 22, No. 1 (June), pp. 5-40.

Gbenyon, Kuakuvi, and Therese Locoh (1992). Mortality differences in childhood by sex in sub-Saharan Africa. In *Mortality and Society in Sub-Saharan Africa*, Etienne van de Walle, Gilles Pison and Mpembele Sala-Diakanda, eds. Oxford: Clarendon Press.

Haddad, Lawrence, and John Hoddinott (1994). Women's income and boy-girl anthropometric status in the Cote d'Ivoire. *World Development* (Boston), vol. 22, No. 4 (April), pp. 543-554.

_____, and Harold Alderman, eds. (1993). *Intrahousehold Resource Allocation in Developing Countries: Methods, Models, and Policy.* Washington, D.C: International Food Policy Research Institute.

Horton, Susan (1988). Birth order and child nutritional status: evidence on the intrahousehold allocation of resources in the Philippines. *Economic Development and Cultural Change* (Chicago), vol. 36, No. 2 (January), pp. 341-354.

Kane, Penny (1991). *Women's Health: From Womb to Tomb.* New York: St. Martin's Press.

King, E. M., and R. E. Evenson (1983). Time allocation and home production in Philippine rural households. In *Women and Poverty in the Third World*, M. Buvinic, M. Lycette and W. P. McGreavy, eds. Baltimore: The Johns Hopkins University Press.

Koenig, Michael A. and Stan D'Souza (1986). Sex differences in childhood mortality in rural Bangladesh. *Social Science and Medicine* (Elmsford, New York), vol. 22, No. 1, pp. 15-22.

McElroy, M. (1992). The policy implications of family bargaining and marriage markets. Durham, North Carolina: Duke University. Mimeograph.

Muhuri, Pradip K., and Samuel H. Preston (1991). Mortality differentials by sex in Bangladesh. *Population and Development Review* (New York), vol. 17, No. 3 (September), pp. 415-434.

Pebley, Anne R., and Sajeda Amin (1991). The impact of a public-health intervention on sex differntials in childhood mortality in rural Punjab, India. *Health Transition Review* (Canberra), vol. 1, No. 3, pp. 143-169.

Pitt, Mark M., and Mark R. Rosenzweig (1985). Health and nutrient consumption across and within farm households. *Review of Economics and Statistics* (Amsterdam), vol. 67, No. 2 (May), pp. 212-223.

_____ (1990). Estimating the behavioural consequences of health in a family context: the intrafamily incidence of infant illness in Indonesia. *International Economic Review* (Osaka), vol. 31, No. 4 (November), pp. 969-989.

_____, and M. N. Hassan (1990). Productivity, health and inequality in the intrahousehold distribution of food in low-income countries. *American Economic Review* (Nashville), vol. 80, No. 5 (December), pp. 1139-1156.

Pollak, Robert A. (1985). A transaction cost approach to families and households.*Journal of Economic Literature* (Nashville, Tennessee), vol. 23 (June), pp. 581-608. Reprinted in Behrman, Pollak and Taubman (1995). *From Parent to Child: Inequality and Immobility in the United States.* Chicago: University of Chicago Press.

Psacharopoulos, G. (1988). Education and development: a review. *The World Bank Research Observer* (Washington, D.C.), vol. 3, No. 1 (January), pp. 99-116.

Quisumbing, Agnes R. (1994). Intergenerational transfers in Philippine rice villages: gender differences in traditional inheritance customs. *Journal of Development Economics* (Amsterdam), vol. 43, No. 2 (April), pp. 167-196.

Rao, Vijayendra (1993). The rising price of husbands: a hedonic analysis of dowry increases in rural India. *Journal of Political Economy* (Chicago), vol. 4, No. 101 (August), pp. 666-677.

Rosenzweig, M., and T. P. Schultz (1982). Market opportunities, genetic endowments, and intrafamily resource distribution: child survival in rural India. *American Economic Review* (Nashville), vol. 72, pp. 803-815.

_____ (1984). Market opportunities, genetic endowments, and intrafamily resource distribution of resources: reply. *American Economic Review* (Nashville), vol. 74, pp. 521-522.

Rosenzweig, M., and Kenneth J. Wolpin (1988). Heterogeneity, intrafamily distribution, and child health. *Journal of Human Resources* (Madison, Wisconsin), vol. 23, No. 4 (Fall), pp. 437-461.

Ryan, J. G., and others (1984). *The Determinants of Individual Diets and Nutritional Status in Six Villages of Southern India.* Pantachara, Andhra Pradesh, India: International Crops Research Institute for the Semi-Arid Tropics.

Schultz, T. P. (1990). Testing the neoclassical model of family labor supply and fertility. *Journal of Human Resources* (Madison, Wisconsin), vol. 25, pp. 599-634.

Strauss, John, and Duncan Thomas (1995). Human resources: empirical modelling of household and family decisions. In *Handbook of Development Economics*, vol. III, Jere R. Behrman and T. N. Srinivasan, eds. Amsterdam: North-Holland Publishing Company.

Svedberg, Peter (1990). Undernutrition in sub-Saharan Africa: is there a gender bias? *Journal of Development Studies* (London), vol. 26, No. 3 (April), pp. 469-486.

Thomas, Duncan (1990). Intra-household resource allocation: an inferential approach. *Journal of Human Resources* (Madison, Wisconsin), vol. 25, pp. 635-664.

_____ (1993). The distribution of income and expenditure within the household. *Annales d'économie et de statistiques* (Paris, Institut national de la statistique et des études économiques), vol. 29, pp. 109-136.

Udry, Christopher (1995). Gender, agricultural production and the theory of the household. Evanston, Illinois: Northwestern University. Mimeograph.

242

ANNEX TABLES

TABLE A.1. TIME SERIES OF THE PROBABILITY OF DYING FOR AGE GROUPS, 0-1, 1-4 AND 5-14, AND MALE TO FEMALE RATIOS OF SUCH PROBABILITIES FOR 24 COUNTRIES OR AREAS

Australia

| Period | Probability of dying (per 1,000) | | | | | | Male/female ratio (percentage) | | |
| | Less than 1 | | 1-4 years | | 5-14 years | | | | |
	Male	Female	Male	Female	Male	Female	0-1 year	1-4 year	5-14
1901-1910	95.1	79.5	32.1	30.0	20.5	18.7	119.6	107.0	109.9
1911	73.8	59.3	25.6	23.8	18.8	17.2	124.5	107.5	109.8
1921	70.4	55.8	27.9	24.0	18.4	15.8	126.3	116.1	116.4

Sources: For 1901-1910, based on communications with J. Pollard; for 1911 and 1921, S. Preston, N. Keyfitz and R. Schoen, *Causes of Death: Life-Tables for National Populations* (New York, Seminar Press, 1972).

Austria

| Period | Probability of dying (per 1,000) | | | | | | Male/female ratio (percentage) | | |
| | Less than 1 | | 1-4 years | | 5-14 years | | | | |
	Male	Female	Male	Female	Male	Female	0-1 year	1-4 year	5-14
1868-1871	297.7	250.1	136.8	131.8	62.3	62.1	119.1	103.9	100.3
1879-1882	274.1	229.0	149.6	143.1	72.8	77.2	119.7	104.5	94.2
1889-1892	266.8	227.3	126.2	119.2	51.7	59.0	117.4	105.9	87.6
1899-1902	230.4	193.1	90.6	90.4	39.3	44.1	119.3	100.2	88.9
1909-1912	205.9	171.6	70.0	69.4	33.1	36.6	120.0	100.8	90.5
1926-1930	136.2	108.1	34.1	31.4	20.3	19.8	126.0	108.6	102.5

Source: Osterreichisten Statistichen Zentralamt, *Entwicklung der Sterblichkeit in der Republik Osterreich* and *Geschichte und Ergebnisse der Zentralen amtlichen Statistik in Osterreich, 1829-1879* (Vienna, 1960 and 1979).

Belgium

| Period | Probability of dying (per 1,000) | | | | | | Male/female ratio (percentage) | | |
| | Less than 1 | | 1-4 years | | 5-14 years | | | | |
	Male	Female	Male	Female	Male	Female	0-1 year	1-4 year	5-14
1881-1890	167.0	141.0	96.6	94.7	38.7	42.6	118.4	102.0	90.8
1891-1900	169.0	142.0	82.2	78.4	33.7	35.7	119.0	104.9	94.5
1893-1997	182.5	149.0	83.8	80.0	34.1	36.0	122.5	104.8	94.9
1898-1902	178.9	150.9	75.0	69.6	30.0	32.8	118.6	107.8	91.4
1908-1912	162.2	132.6	62.3	60.4	27.3	26.7	122.3	103.2	102.5
1920-1924	121.2	96.2	42.8	37.0	20.0	20.5	125.9	115.7	97.5
1928-1932	109.1	84.9	32.3	28.1	19.6	18.4	128.5	114.7	106.7

Sources: Life-tables for 1881-1890 and 1891-1900 by J.M.J. Leclerc, cited in Robert J. André and J. Pereira-Roque, *La démographie de la Belgique au XIXe siècle* (Brussels, Editions de l'Université de Bruxelles, 1974); for other periods, based on life-tables by D. Veys, *Cohort Survival in Belgium in the Past 150 Years* (Leuven, Belgium, Sociological Research Institute, 1983).

245

TABLE A.1 (*continued*)

Canada

| Period | Probability of dying (per 1,000) | | | | | | Male/female ratio (percentage) | | |
| | Less than 1 | | 1-4 years | | 5-14 years | | | | |
	Male	Female	Male	Female	Male	Female	0-1 year	1-4 year	5-14
1831	185.7	162.4	135.0	135.8	59.0	65.7	114.4	99.4	89.8
1841	187.0	164.0	129.7	129.9	54.8	58.9	114.1	99.8	93.0
1851	186.6	163.6	126.1	126.0	52.7	55.9	114.0	100.1	94.2
1861	189.2	166.4	125.4	125.1	51.1	53.5	113.7	100.3	95.4
1871	175.9	153.5	114.6	113.8	49.5	52.1	114.6	100.6	95.1
1881	164.6	143.0	101.1	99.6	45.0	46.3	115.1	101.5	97.1
1891	165.1	143.6	99.4	97.8	43.6	46.4	115.0	101.6	94.0
1901	144.2	124.0	78.8	76.4	37.2	36.8	116.3	103.0	101.0
1911	121.9	103.3	58.8	56.1	30.4	29.0	117.9	104.9	104.8
1921	93.0	76.7	38.7	36.1	23.9	22.1	121.2	107.3	108.1
1931	79.6	65.1	28.9	26.5	19.1	16.9	122.3	109.3	113.5

Source: R. Bourbeau and J. Légaré, *Evolution de la mortalité au Canada et au Québec, 1831-1931* (Montreal, Presses de l'Université de Montréal, 1982).

Czech Republic

| Period | Probability of dying (per 1,000) | | | | | | Male/female ratio (percentage) | | |
| | Less than 1 | | 1-4 years | | 5-14 years | | | | |
	Male	Female	Male	Female	Male	Female	0-1 year	1-4 year	5-14
1869-1870	265.0	265.0	143.1	135.7	50.2	51.6	-	105.4	97.2
1880-1881	264.0	264.0	155.7	150.4	61.5	63.9	-	103.5	96.3
1890-1891	265.0	265.0	152.1	145.1	56.8	63.4	-	104.8	89.6
1900-1901	225.0	225.0	98.1	98.1	36.8	44.0	-	100.0	83.6
1910-1911	191.0	191.0	70.4	69.3	30.5	35.4	-	101.6	86.3
1920-1922	186.0	152.0	42.6	39.9	25.3	25.5	122.4	106.8	99.3
1929-1932	129.9	107.2	29.7	26.2	22.3	21.9	121.2	113.4	101.9

Sources: *Statistika a demografie* (Prague, Czechoslovak Academy of Sciences Press, 1959; *Demograficka prirucka* (Prague, Federal Statistical Office, 1982).

TABLE A.1 (*continued*)

Denmark

| | Probability of dying (per 1,000) | | | | | | Male/female ratio (percentage) | | |
| | Less than 1 | | 1-4 years | | 5-14 years | | | | |
Period	Male	Female	Male	Female	Male	Female	0-1 year	1-4 year	5-14
1840-1849	155.3	132.4	95.7	93.1	63.4	70.4	117.3	102.7	90.0
1850-1859	147.8	124.1	99.4	98.1	72.3	76.8	119.1	101.3	94.1
1860-1869	145.4	123.7	102.2	101.1	77.9	83.8	117.5	101.0	93.0
1870-1879	148.3	127.5	81.0	80.0	60.9	67.5	116.3	101.3	90.3
1880-1889	149.0	124.9	75.0	73.6	56.4	64.3	119.3	101.9	87.8
1890-1900	148.6	122.3	62.7	61.5	45.0	51.6	121.5	101.9	87.2
1901-1905	130.7	104.1	37.2	35.8	26.8	28.9	125.5	104.0	92.8
1906-1910	120.7	97.7	30.8	29.6	20.5	22.1	123.5	103.9	92.8
1911-1915	111.2	88.8	27.9	25.3	18.5	19.2	125.3	110.3	96.2
1916-1920	102.5	80.9	30.2	28.6	21.1	22.5	126.7	105.9	93.7
1921-1925	93.6	72.4	21.7	18.9	14.5	13.6	129.4	114.6	106.0
1926-1930	91.3	71.1	19.0	16.5	12.6	10.7	128.4	114.8	117.2

Source: Life-tables for Denmark (undated).

Finland

| | Probability of dying (per 1,000) | | | | | | Male/female ratio (percentage) | | |
| | Less than 1 | | 1-4 years | | 5-14 years | | | | |
Period	Male	Female	Male	Female	Male	Female	0-1 year	1-4 year	5-14
1871-1875	172.2	150.7	129.9	125.7	67.5	65.1	114.3	103.4	103.6
1876-1880	158.3	136.0	137.2	132.0	73.9	75.8	116.4	104.0	97.5
1881-1885	153.0	132.2	140.2	132.1	80.9	79.1	115.8	106.1	102.3
1886-1890	139.9	118.1	112.1	106.6	61.2	61.8	118.4	105.2	99.0
1891-1895	139.9	119.2	122.8	116.1	72.0	72.2	117.3	105.8	99.7
1896-1900	134.0	114.8	103.3	94.8	60.8	64.8	116.7	109.0	93.8
1901-1905	127.5	108.2	100.3	94.6	64.1	70.5	117.8	106.0	90.8
1906-1910	114.9	97.6	87.9	84.0	56.7	63.8	117.8	104.7	88.9
1911-1915	108.1	90.6	70.8	68.7	45.7	51.5	119.4	103.0	88.8
1916-1920	111.3	95.2	90.4	87.7	61.1	64.4	116.9	103.1	95.0
1921-1925	94.4	79.4	52.0	48.5	34.1	36.5	118.9	107.2	93.5
1926-1930	88.1	72.93	41.66	38.71	31.8	31.8	120.8	107.6	100.0

Source: A. Strömmer, *The Demographic Transition in Finland* (Tornio, Finland, 1969).

France

| | Probability of dying (per 1,000) | | | | | | Male/female ratio (percentage) | | |
| | Less than 1 | | 1-4 years | | 5-14 years | | | | |
Period	Male	Female	Male	Female	Male	Female	0-1 year	1-4 year	5-14
1740-1749	317.0	275.0	253.0	253.0	155.5	147.0	115.3	100.0	105.7
1750-1759	291.0	263.0	236.0	242.0	123.4	119.0	110.6	97.5	103.7
1760-1769	307.0	256.0	255.0	235.0	118.6	124.5	119.9	108.5	95.3
1770-1779	292.0	254.0	239.0	233.0	125.1	122.5	115.0	102.6	102.1
1780-1789	291.0	265.0	234.0	243.0	124.6	123.6	109.8	96.3	100.8
1806-1810	203.4	176.9	148.1	149.4	85.6	84.5	115.0	99.1	101.3
1810-1814	202.0	174.4	142.1	141.5	86.8	86.3	115.8	100.5	100.6
1815-1819	196.6	168.8	140.5	139.9	82.2	84.8	116.5	100.4	96.9
1820-1824	201.4	172.8	140.7	139.5	81.1	83.9	116.5	100.8	96.6
1825-1829	200.6	172.9	145.8	145.3	83.6	87.4	116.0	100.3	95.6
1830-1834	199.2	169.3	147.8	146.8	85.4	90.4	117.7	100.7	94.5
1835-1839	180.0	155.7	132.8	131.4	71.6	77.4	115.6	101.1	92.6
1840-1844	170.3	147.8	131.1	128.7	71.9	78.9	115.2	101.9	91.2
1845-1849	172.5	149.6	132.0	130.7	72.2	78.4	115.3	101.0	92.0
1850-1854	172.0	146.7	128.5	126.4	69.1	74.7	117.3	101.6	92.5
1855-1859	198.5	169.5	140.5	140.6	77.1	83.1	117.1	99.9	92.7
1860-1864	185.0	157.1	121.2	123.6	58.5	64.6	117.8	98.1	90.5
1865-1869	191.4	164.7	122.9	122.4	57.6	62.4	116.2	100.4	92.3
1870-1874	199.8	171.3	130.9	125.9	67.4	72.4	116.6	103.9	93.1
1875-1879	177.6	149.7	103.4	103.5	49.1	53.2	118.6	99.9	92.2
1880-1884	184.8	155.6	106.3	103.3	51.5	57.4	118.8	102.9	89.8
1885-1889	176.5	148.2	104.1	99.0	45.8	51.7	119.0	105.1	88.6
1890-1894	184.8	153.4	95.9	92.4	41.8	47.1	120.5	103.8	88.8
1895-1899	177.6	147.9	76.3	73.5	35.7	39.8	120.1	103.7	89.8
1900-1904	161.0	135.3	66.7	64.0	35.6	39.2	119.0	104.2	90.7
1905-1909	146.9	121.8	58.3	55.8	30.2	33.9	120.6	104.4	89.1
1910-1914	135.2	112.1	53.8	52.4	26.7	30.1	120.7	102.7	88.7
1915-1919	145.5	120.7	62.8	60.5	34.4	38.9	120.6	103.9	88.4
1920-1924	113.6	91.7	39.8	37.8	22.7	24.5	123.9	105.4	92.6
1925-1929	105.4	84.1	37.9	35.4	21.0	22.2	125.3	106.9	94.5

Sources: Y. Blayo, "La mortalité en France de 1740 à 1829", *Population* (Paris), vol. 30 (1975), pp. 123-142, for estimates referring to 1740-1789; other estimates by the authors based on life-tables in France Mesle and Jacques Vallin, "Reconstitution des tables annuelles de mortalité pour la France au XIXe siècle", *Population* (Paris), vol. 44, No. 6 (1989), pp. 1122-1158.

Greece

| | Probability of dying (per 1,000) | | | | | | Male/female ratio (percentage) | | |
| | Less than 1 | | 1-4 years | | 5-14 years | | | | |
Period	Male	Female	Male	Female	Male	Female	0-1 year	1-4 year	5-14
1928	98.2	96.9	113.8	114.8	44.6	45.9	101.4	99.1	97.1

Source: S. Preston, N. Keyfitz and R. Schoen, *Causes of Death, Life-Tables for National Populations* (New York, Seminar Press, 1972).

Hungary

| Period | Probability of dying (per 1,000) | | | | | | Male/female ratio (percentage) | | |
| | Less than 1 | | 1-4 years | | 5-14 years | | 0-1 year | 1-4 year | 5-14 |
	Male	Female	Male	Female	Male	Female			
1900-1901	249.1	196.6	132.4	131.3	73.4	81.0	126.7	100.8	90.7
1910-1911	215.4	184.5	121.1	120.8	65.4	72.0	116.7	100.3	90.9
1920-1921	207.2	177.4	105.3	102.0	57.5	60.3	116.8	103.2	95.3
1930-1931	179.1	141.5	50.3	49.1	28.6	30.6	126.5	102.6	93.5

Source: Hungary, Central Statistical Office, *Magyararszag Halandasagi Tablai*, 1900-1968 (Budapest, 1971 and 1972).

Ireland

| Period | Probability of dying (per 1,000) | | | | | | Male/female ratio (percentage) | | |
| | Less than 1 | | 1-4 years | | 5-14 years | | 0-1 year | 1-4 year | 5-14 |
	Male	Female	Male	Female	Male	Female			
1864-1870	-	-	168.7	153.8	41.8	44.1	-	109.7	94.7
1871-1880	-	-	180.9	165.6	40.7	45.1	-	109.2	90.2
1881-1890	-	-	166.5	151.0	36.6	42.6	-	110.3	86.0
1891-1900	-	-	171.7	154.1	32.8	39.5	-	111.4	83.1
1901-1910	-	-	159.6	142.2	29.3	36.3	-	112.2	80.8
1911-1920	-	-	143.0	126.4	28.6	34.3	-	113.1	83.5
1920-1929	-	-	113.5	98.7	21.9	24.6	-	115.0	88.9
1930	-	-	105.4	86.1	21.2	21.8	-	122.5	97.5

Source: Ireland, Central Statistics Office, *Annual Report* (Cork, 1930); probabilities for age group 0-1 by sex are not available.

Italy

| Period | Probability of dying (per 1,000) | | | | | | Male/female ratio (percentage) | | |
| | Less than 1 | | 1-4 years | | 5-14 years | | 0-1 year | 1-4 year | 5-14 |
	Male	Female	Male	Female	Male	Female			
1887	214.7	193.0	209.7	209.1	80.1	89.4	111.2	100.3	89.6
1895	200.9	176.6	171.8	172.6	60.2	66.3	113.8	99.5	90.8
1900	174.7	154.6	154.2	151.6	54.1	55.3	113.0	101.7	97.8
1910	162.0	145.2	129.2	126.4	53.9	54.8	111.6	102.2	98.4
1920	157.0	143.8	133.9	134.7	59.0	59.4	109.2	99.4	99.3
1930	128.4	113.2	73.7	72.2	26.1	25.2	113.4	102.1	103.6

Source: G. Caselli and V. Egidi, "A new insight into morbidity and mortality transition in Italy, *Genus* (Rome), Nos. 3 and 4 (1991), pp. 1-29.

TABLE A.1. (*continued*)

Japan

Period	Probability of dying (per 1,000)						Male/female ratio (percentage)		
	Less than 1		1-4 years		5-14 years				
	Male	Female	Male	Female	Male	Female	0-1 year	1-4 year	5-14
1883-1888	253.2	209.5	135.9	132.8	56.0	67.9	120.9	102.3	82.4
1891-1898	149.0	133.8	104.2	99.2	54.7	55.0	111.3	105.0	99.6
1899-1903	156.9	140.9	88.1	88.1	42.7	48.1	111.3	100.0	88.8
1909-1913	160.5	145.0	89.8	89.8	40.8	50.4	110.7	100.0	81.0
1921-1925	162.0	144.0	98.2	99.2	41.0	50.0	112.5	99.0	82.0
1926-1930	140.1	124.1	87.6	88.1	35.1	41.9	112.9	99.4	83.9

Sources: Japan, Ministry of Health and Welfare, Statistics and Information Department, *The Life-Tables* (Tokyo, 1987); and S. Takahashi, "An attempt to estimate vital statistics in Meiji period based on Honseki population date", *Kokumin Keizai Zasshi* (Kobe, Japan), vol. 163, No. 5 (1993), pp. 39-58, for 1883-1888.

New Zealand (non-Maori only)

Period	Probability of dying (per 1,000)						Male/female ratio (percentage)		
	Less than 1		1-4 years		5-14 years				
	Male	Female	Male	Female	Male	Female	0-1 year	1-4 year	5-14
1876	109.0	96.0	49.0	49.0	32.7	32.7	113.5	100.0	100.0
1881	99.0	83.0	43.0	41.0	31.8	29.8	119.3	104.9	106.7
1886	98.0	81.0	39.0	37.0	28.8	26.8	121.0	105.4	107.4
1891	97.0	77.0	35.0	33.0	24.8	22.9	126.0	106.1	108.6
1896	88.0	72.0	27.0	19.9	17.9	122.2	112.5	111.1	
1901	83.0	69.0	26.0	24.0	19.9	17.9	120.3	108.3	111.1
1906	78.0	62.0	23.0	22.0	17.9	16.9	125.8	104.5	105.9

Source: Ian Pool, "Changing patterns of sex differentials in survival: an examination of data for Maoris and non-Maoris in New Zealand", in *Sex Differentials in Mortality, Trends, Determinants and Consequences*, Alan D. Lopez and Lado Ruzicka, eds. (Canberra, Australian National University, 1983).

Norway

Period	Probability of dying (per 1,000)						Male/female ratio (percentage)		
	Less than 1		1-4 years		5-14 years				
	Male	Female	Male	Female	Male	Female	0-1 year	1-4 year	5-14
1910	74.8	61.3	30.9	28.7	30.5	33.1	121.9	107.9	92.0
1920	64.7	50.3	26.5	24.0	29.8	28.4	128.7	110.5	104.9
1930	50.3	40.6	16.6	13.6	17.5	12.3	124.0	122.7	141.8

Source: S. Preston, N. Keyfitz and R. Schoen, *Causes of Death, Life-Tables for National Populations* (New York, Seminar Press, 1972).

The Netherlands

Period	Less than 1		1-4 years		5-14 years		Male/female ratio (percentage)		
	Male	Female	Male	Female	Male	Female	0-1 year	1-4 year	5-14
1850-1854	223.7	192.1	129.2	127.0	61.2	66.6	116.4	101.8	91.9
1855-1859	249.2	214.0	158.6	157.1	81.2	84.0	116.4	101.0	96.6
1860-1864	232.6	198.6	144.0	144.3	75.9	79.5	117.2	99.8	95.4
1865-1869	245.1	209.0	137.0	134.5	74.8	75.9	117.3	101.9	98.5
1870-1874	255.4	215.5	137.0	134.8	71.5	72.2	118.5	101.6	99.1
1875-1879	241.8	201.8	112.3	109.1	50.6	51.9	119.8	102.9	97.4
1880-1884	232.5	192.7	111.0	108.1	47.5	48.8	120.6	102.7	97.4
1885-1889	213.5	177.6	105.8	102.5	46.2	47.8	120.2	103.2	96.8
1890-1894	203.4	168.6	92.6	89.4	39.0	41.5	120.7	103.5	94.0
1895-1899	188.1	156.6	72.2	69.8	31.0	32.2	120.1	103.5	96.3
1900-1904	173.9	144.7	70.9	65.7	30.3	31.3	120.2	107.8	97.0
1905-1909	146.2	121.7	57.6	52.8	25.2	25.4	120.2	109.1	99.3
1910-1914	126.6	105.9	47.0	44.6	21.6	21.2	119.5	105.3	101.9
1920-1924	87.5	69.1	32.2	28.9	16.6	15.9	126.5	111.5	104.7
1925-1929	65.9	50.3	28.0	24.0	16.3	14.1	131.1	116.5	115.2

Source: Diskette issued by the Netherlands Interdisciplinary Demographic Institute, 1994.

Portugal

	Less than 1		1-4 years		5-14 years		Male/female ratio (percentage)		
	Male	Female	Male	Female	Male	Female	0-1 year	1-4 year	5-14
1920	259.3	219.3	170.0	166.1	62.9	60.5	118.3	102.3	104.0
1930	195.6	165.5	90.2	87.4	25.6	25.4	118.2	103.2	100.8

Source: S. Preston, N. Keyfitz and R. Schoen, *Causes of Death, Life-Tables for National Populations* (New York, Seminar Press, 1972).

Quebec

Period	Less than 1		1-4 years		5-14 years		Male/female ratio (percentage)		
	Male	Female	Male	Female	Male	Female	0-1 year	1-4 year	5-14
1831	192.5	169.5	137.0	137.0	57.5	62.1	113.6	100.0	92.5
1841	191.8	169.0	133.0	134.0	54.9	58.9	113.5	99.3	93.1
1851	191.0	168.0	129.0	129.0	52.7	57.4	113.7	100.0	91.8
1861	189.5	168.0	125.0	125.1	50.3	53.2	112.8	99.9	94.6
1871	189.0	167.0	123.0	123.5	49.4	51.5	113.2	99.6	96.0
1881	173.8	151.5	111.0	120.0	48.5	50.6	114.7	92.5	96.0
1891	164.8	142.8	103.0	102.0	46.4	48.6	115.4	101.0	95.5
1901	155.0	134.0	91.5	89.0	41.9	42.8	115.7	102.8	97.7
1911	130.0	110.5	70.4	68.0	36.7	37.0	117.6	103.5	99.2
1921	109.0	91.6	51.8	49.7	29.6	28.7	119.0	104.2	102.8
1931	84.8	69.9	35.4	36.0	23.7	22.4	121.3	98.5	105.7

Source: R. Bourbeau and J. Légaré, *Evolution de la mortalité au Canada et au Québec, 1831-1931* (Montreal, Presses de l'Université de Montréal, 1982).

Russia

| | Probability of dying (per 1,000) | | | | | | Male/female ratio (percentage) | | |
| | Less than 1 | | 1-4 years | | 5-14 years | | | | |
Period	Male	Female	Male	Female	Male	Female	0-1 year	1-4 year	5-14
1874-1883	327.2	283.3	245.9	228.1	108.7	98.8	115.5	107.8	110.0
1896-1897	302.9	265.1	202.4	196.8	83.7	84.3	114.2	102.9	99.3
1907-1910	275.6	243.1	186.7	179.2	77.6	77.1	113.4	104.2	100.5
1926-1927	221.3	191.2	133.0	125.0	47.7	44.8	115.8	106.3	106.4

Source: Former USSR, Département de l'économie et des statistiques du Gosplan, *Mortalité et durée de la vie de la population de l'URSS, tables de mortalité* (Moscow, 1930); there are certain differences in the territory covered over the four dates.

Spain

| | Probability of dying (per 1,000) | | | | | | Male/female ratio (percentage) | | |
| | Less than 1 | | 1-4 years | | 5-14 years | | | | |
Period	Male	Female	Male	Female	Male	Female	0-1 year	1-4 year	5-14
1930	149.7	129.7	93.4	90.0	31.1	30.5	115.5	103.8	102.0

Source: S. Preston, N. Keyfitz and R. Schoen, *Causes of Death, Life-Tables for National Populations* (New York, Seminar Press, 1972).

Sweden

| | Probability of dying (per 1,000) | | | | | | Male/female ratio (percentage) | | |
| | Less than 1 | | 1-4 years | | 5-14 years | | | | |
Period	Male	Female	Male	Female	Male	Female	0-1 year	1-4 year	5-14
1751-1760	214.0	194.0	146.1	140.0	93.2	87.8	110.3	104.4	106.2
1761-1770	226.0	206.0	149.6	144.8	97.0	91.1	109.7	103.3	106.4
1771-1780	211.0	192.0	173.7	167.1	121.5	108.3	109.9	104.0	112.2
1781-1790	209.0	190.0	160.3	154.2	107.0	98.5	110.0	104.0	108.6
1791-1800	207.0	184.0	133.7	127.1	76.7	72.4	112.5	105.2	106.0
1801-1810	211.0	185.0	141.6	133.0	96.0	88.1	114.1	106.4	109.0
1811-1820	196.0	170.0	133.8	125.0	75.8	71.2	115.3	107.0	106.4
1821-1830	179.0	155.0	104.2	97.3	60.2	57.0	115.5	107.2	105.7
1831-1840	179.0	154.0	98.1	91.4	61.1	56.9	116.2	107.3	107.4
1841-1850	165.0	141.0	94.7	87.0	61.8	56.7	117.0	108.8	109.0
1851-1860	157.0	134.0	116.4	107.5	82.3	75.6	117.2	108.3	108.8
1861-1870	149.0	128.0	117.1	110.9	67.0	63.3	116.4	105.6	105.8
1871-1880	140.0	119.0	98.2	93.9	61.5	61.3	117.6	104.6	100.3
1881-1890	120.0	101.0	86.0	82.5	57.0	57.4	118.8	104.2	99.3
1891-1900	111.0	92.0	67.1	64.5	45.7	47.7	120.7	104.1	95.9
1901-1910	93.0	76.0	47.0	44.7	34.3	36.7	122.4	105.3	93.4
1911-1920	77.0	62.0	36.4	34.7	31.1	32.2	124.2	105.0	96.4
1921-1930	66.0	51.0	22.3	19.7	18.8	18.8	129.4	113.2	99.7

Source: Sweden, National Central Bureau of Statistics, *Historical Statistics of Sweden*, part 1, *Population, 1720-1967* (Stockholm, 1969).

Switzerland

| Period | Probability of dying (per 1,000) | | | | | | Male/female ratio (percentage) | | |
| | Less than 1 | | 1-4 years | | 5-14 years | | | | |
	Male	Female	Male	Female	Male	Female	0-1 year	1-4 year	5-14
1876-1880	204.2	171.9	81.6	82.0	49.8	51.8	118.8	99.5	96.2
1881-1888	182.0	151.6	70.3	69.9	40.2	42.7	120.0	100.6	94.3
1889-1900	165.0	135.8	58.3	56.0	35.1	36.7	121.5	104.1	95.5
1901-1910	138.4	112.6	42.8	41.6	25.9	27.8	122.9	103.1	92.9
1910-1911	128.3	104.3	38.5	37.5	25.2	26.6	123.1	102.6	95.0
1920-1921	90.5	70.2	31.6	30.4	25.2	24.8	129.0	103.9	101.7
1921-1930	66.7	52.5	21.2	19.4	17.5	16.0	127.1	109.2	109.5
1929-1932	56.2	44.1	17.7	16.5	16.5	14.8	127.4	106.8	111.9

Source: Switzerland, Bureau fédéral de statistique, *Tables de mortalité de la population suisse, 1876-1932*, Contributions à la statistique suisse, 4e fascicule (Berne, 1935).

England and Wales

| Period | Probability of dying (per 1,000) | | | | | | Male/female ratio (percentage) | | |
| | Less than 1 | | 1-4 years | | 5-14 years | | | | |
	Male	Female	Male	Female	Male	Female	0-1 year	1-4 year	5-14
1841-1845	162	133	-	-	33.1	33.6	121.8	-	98.6
1846-1850	172	142	-	-	36.2	36.2	121.1	-	100.0
1850-1855	172	141	-	-	34.1	33.6	122.0	-	101.4
1856-1860	166	137	-	-	31.5	32.2	121.2	-	97.8
1861-1865	166	136	136.8	133.0	32.2	31.9	122.1	102.8	100.7
1866-1870	170	142	133.7	130.7	29.8	28.6	119.7	102.3	104.2
1871-1875	167	138	115.3	111.5	27.2	26.0	121.0	103.4	104.6
1876-1880	159	130	121.5	115.3	23.8	23.1	122.3	105.4	103.1
1881-1885	152	125	104.5	99.2	22.4	22.1	121.6	105.3	101.1
1886-1890	159	131	102.4	96.7	19.0	19.2	121.4	105.8	98.7
1891-1895	165	135	96.0	92.1	17.5	18.0	122.2	104.2	97.3
1896-1900	170	141	91.4	87.1	15.8	16.3	120.6	104.9	97.0
1901-1905	151	124	76.6	73.4	14.3	14.8	121.8	104.5	96.7
1906-1910	129	105	67.9	64.2	13.1	13.6	122.9	105.7	96.4
1911-1915	121	97	64.2	60.5	13.4	13.6	124.7	106.1	98.2
1916-1920	101	79	57.5	55.3	15.3	15.8	127.8	104.0	96.9
1921-1925	86	66	41.3	37.9	10.7	10.2	130.3	109.0	104.8
1926-1930	77	59	35.2	31.8	10.2	9.4	130.5	110.9	107.8

Source: United Kingdom of Great Britain and Northern Ireland, Office of Population Censuses and Surveys, *Mortality Statistics, 1841-1990*, Series DH1 (London, 1992).

United States

| Period | Probability of dying (per 1,000) | | | | | | Male/female ratio (percentage) | | |
| | Less than 1 | | 1-4 years | | 5-14 years | | | | |
	Male	Female	Male	Female	Male	Female	0-1 year	1-4 year	5-14
1900	146.0	119.7	79.8	75.3	37.3	37.6	121.9	106.1	99.2
1910	120.1	98.3	57.8	53.7	29.7	28.1	122.2	107.6	105.6
1920	85.9	67.7	40.4	37.6	27.5	24.3	126.9	107.3	113.1
1930	65.0	51.8	23.8	20.9	18.8	15.2	125.4	113.8	123.7

Source: J. Faber and A. H. Wade, *Life-Tables for the United States: 1900-2050*, Actuarial Study, No. 89 (Washington, D. C., United States Department of Health and Human Services, 1983).

TABLE A.2. DEFINITION OF "MODERN HEALTH FACILITY USE" VARIABLE BY DHS

Region and country	H	PUH	PRH	HC	PUHC	CL	PRCL	PHD	D	PRD	O
Eastern and Southern Africa											
Botswana		X			X	X	X			X	
Burundi	X			X				X			
Kenya	X					X				X	
Sudan	X					X		X		X	
Uganda		X	X		X		X			X	u
Zimbabwe										X	z
Northern Africa											
Egypt								X		X	e
Morocco		X		X				X		X	m
Tunisia	X			X				X	X		
Western Africa											
Ghana	X					X				X	
Togo											t
Southern and South-eastern Asia											
Sri Lanka		X				X				X	
Thailand	X					X				X	
Central and South America											
Bolivia		X	X	X				X	X		
Brazil	X					X				X	
Colombia	X					X				X	
Dominican Republic		X	X				X				
El Salvador								X	X		s
Guatemala		X	X	X			X	X			
Peru	X					X				X	
Trinidad and Tobago	X					X				X	

Key:
H	hospital	PRCL	private clinic	u	fieldworker
PUH	public hospital	PHD	pharmacy/dispensary	z	health facility
PRH	private hospital	D	doctor	t	health facility
HC	health centre	PRD	private doctor	e	government health service
PUHC	public health centre	O	other modern facility/provider	m	first aid post
CL	clinic	s	nurse/midwife/first aid post		

254

TABLE A.3. ESTIMATED EFFECTS OF SEX COMPOSITION OF SURVIVING CHILDREN AND OTHER COVARIATES ON PARITY PROGRESSION: EGYPT, WOMEN WHO GAVE BIRTHS OF INITIAL PARITY IN 1979-1983

Covariates	3rd to 4th	4th to 5th	5th to 6th
Sex composition of surviving children (reference: last is M, have other M and F)			
Last is M, all others are F	0.04763	0.22200	0.45907
Last is M, all others are M	0.36176*	0.27943	0.22633
Last is F, have other M	0.34054*	0.30864*	0.36062*
Last is F, all others are F	0.58806*	0.45912*	0.57259*
Death of index child (reference: no death)			
1st year after death of index child	0.30018	1.37809*	0.75516
2nd year after death of index child	1.71199*	1.42276*	0.81036*
3rd year after death of index child	1.07874*	0.91927*	0.51038
4th year after death of index child	0.43047	0.95171	0.43535
5th year after death of index child	0.53348	0.88628	1.12891*
Last is M, all others are F, last child died	0.25973	-0.69150	-0.62874
Last is M, all others are M, last child died	-0.94110*	-0.43421	0.34713
Last is F, have other M, last child died	-0.31957	-0.89647	-0.38256
Last is F, all others are F, last child died	-1.19909*	-0.44879	-0.15072
Maternal age at last birth	-0.06037*	-0.06292*	-0.08261*
Mother's childhood residence (reference: urban governorate)			
Village	-0.32743*	-0.67146*	-0.34303
Town	-0.38976*	-0.65246*	-0.25574
Mother's residence (reference: urban governorate)			
Lower Egypt, urban	-0.13149	-0.01436	-0.01454
Lower Egypt, rural	-0.00332	0.09528	0.54725*
Upper Egypt, urban	0.19077	0.49704*	0.79254*
Upper Egypt, rural	0.14864	0.30224	0.65254*
Religion is Christianity	0.00171	-0.16260	-0.05725
Mother had more than primary education	-0.45881*	-0.53959	0.11763
Father had more than primary education	-0.12917	-0.15873	-0.09482
Father's occupation (reference: self employed agriculture)			
Agriculture, employed	-0.04048	-0.10076	0.15660
White collar or skilled	-0.18471	0.09534	0.01028
Unskilled	-0.13536	-0.06897	0.14084
Time since birth of index child (reference: 1st year)			
2nd year	1.26036*	1.99822*	1.62023*
3rd year	1.24722*	2.62664*	2.17174*
4th year	1.12312*	2.44327*	2.19259*
5th year	0.36815	2.09180*	1.96461*
6th year	0.17750	1.91470*	1.25593*
7th year	0.00000	1.56367*	0.70705
Constant	-0.38506	-1.81101*	-1.29551*

Source: Individual records from *1988 Egypt Demographic and Health Survey*.
NOTES: Effects are estimated by discrete hazard models; women with multiple births excluded from analysis.
An asterisk (*) indicates p < 0.05.

TABLE A.4. ESTIMATED EFFECTS OF SEX COMPOSITION OF SURVIVING CHILDREN AND OTHER COVARIATES ON CHILD MORTALITY (AGES 2-5): EGYPT, CHILDREN OF BIRTH ORDER 3-9 BORN IN 1979-1983

Covariates	Gross effects model	Intermediate model	Net effects model
Sex composition of surviving children (reference: last is M, all others are F)			
Last is M, some other M	1.08088	1.08499	0.94979
Last is F, all others are M	0.66857	0.62271	0.47677
Last is F, some other F	1.37431*	1.34546*	1.16986
Last is F, all others are F	1.18557	1.10711	1.04146
Next child is born with interval < 24 months		0.77996*	0.60681*
Family experienced previous child death (reference: none)			
One			0.48818
More than one			0.13605
Total number of surviving children			0.02014
Maternal age			-0.00264
Mother's childhood residence (reference: urban governorate)			
Rural			-0.51190
Town			0.15038
Mother's residence (reference: urban governorate)			
Lower Egypt, urban			0.55469
Lower Egypt, rural			1.37000
Upper Egypt, urban			0.89467
Upper Egypt, rural			1.58160*
Mother's religion is Christianity			0.24007
Mother had more than primary education			0.36844
Father had more than primary education			-1.25019
Father's occupation (reference: self employed agriculture)			
Agriculture, employed			-0.04931
White collar or skilled			-0.09875
Unskilled			0.22334
Year of birth	-0.03618	-0.02908	-0.02107
Age (four is used as reference)			
Two	2.09349*	2.09284*	2.09064*
Three	0.91436	0.91352	0.91325
Constant	-4.51801	-5.32627	-7.09934

Source: Individual records from *1988 Egypt Demographic and Health Survey*.
NOTES: Effects estimated by discrete hazard models; multiple births excluded from analysis.
An asterisk (*) indicates that p < 0.05.

TABLE A.5. ESTIMATED EFFECTS OF SEX COMPOSITION OF SURVIVING CHILDREN AND OTHER COVARIATES ON PARITY PROGRESSION: BANGLADESH, WOMEN WHO GAVE BIRTHS OF INITIAL PARITY IN 1979-1983

Covariates	3rd to 4th	4th to 5th	5th to 6th
Sex composition of surviving children			
(reference: last is M, have other M and F)			
Last is M, all others are F	0.34044*	0.60356*	0.88896*
Last is M, all others are M	0.18306	0.31613*	-0.00317
Last is F, have other M	0.37095*	0.17655	0.29054*
Last is F, all others are F	0.61162*	0.35580*	0.62811*
Death of index child (reference: no death)			
1st year after death of index child	1.55343*	1.50001*	1.00859*
2nd year after death of index child	1.48810*	1.68599*	1.30295*
3rd year after death of index child	0.88687*	0.86384*	0.58006*
4th year after death of index child	0.07142	0.47276	0.45793
5th year after death of index child	-0.50285	0.91131	0.08279
Last is M, all others are F, last child died	0.11594	-0.46636	-0.78459
Last is M, all others are M, last child died	-0.70459*	-0.30717	-0.27199
Last is F, have other M, last child died	-0.40736	-0.46368	-0.32545
Last is F, all others are F, last child died	-0.32379	-0.27285	-0.71524
Maternal age at last birth	-0.09142*	-0.11394*	-0.09855*
Mother's childhood residence (reference: city)			
Village	0.37874	0.07326	0.52719
Town	0.15752	-0.18756	0.32987
Mother's residence (reference: city)			
Rural	-0.09072	0.29512	0.26998
Urban	0.03232	0.02287	0.12438
Division (reference: Chittagong)			
Dhaka	-0.41558*	-0.45608*	-0.15680
Khulna	-0.48057*	-0.57707*	-0.52301*
Rajshahi	-0.46283*	-0.45917*	-0.28453*
Religion is Muslim	-0.11983	-0.33421*	-0.22124
Mother's education (reference: none)			
Lower primary education	-0.08521	0.03327	-0.25287
Upper primary or more education	-0.28629*	-0.24074	-0.40512
Father's education (reference: none)			
Primary education	0.12376	-0.08728	-0.02815
Secondary education	0.82141	-0.47603	-0.40538
More than secondary education	-0.94222	0.07877	0.18015
Father's occupation (reference: business/service/sales)			
Agriculture/fishing/domestic	0.01598	-0.05428	-0.07198
Others	-0.14960	0.11637	-0.14441
Mother has low level of independence	0.34499*	0.06759	0.51708*
Time since birth of index child (reference: 1st year)			
2nd year	3.53556*	3.32996*	3.09327*
3rd year	5.09329*	4.72851*	4.45862*
4th year	5.21266*	4.63709*	4.40179*
5th year	4.32201*	3.68651*	3.31180*
6th year	3.79394*	2.91557*	2.59187*
7th year	3.49779*	2.23674*	2.40234*
Constant	-3.72552*	-2.26067*	-3.12776*

Source: Individual records from *1988 Egypt Demographic and Health Survey*.
NOTES: Effects estimated by discrete hazard models; women with multiple births excluded from analysis.
An asterisk (*) indicates that $p < 0.05$.

TABLE A.6. ESTIMATED EFFECTS OF SEX COMPOSITION OF SURVIVING CHILDREN AND OTHER COVARIATES ON CHILD MORTALITY (AGES 2-5): BANGLADESH, CHILDREN OF BIRTH ORDER 3-9 BORN IN 1979-1983

Covariates	Gross effects model	Intermediate model	Net effects model
Sex composition of surviving children (reference: last is M, all others are F)			
Last is M, some other M	0.31407	0.31793	0.29250
Last is F, all others are M	0.82780*	0.82414*	0.80281*
Last is F, some other F	0.76444*	0.75018*	0.73156*
Last is F, all others are F	0.39319	0.39319	0.35549
Next child is born with interval < 24 months		0.51992*	0.43172*
Family experienced previous child death (reference: none)			
One			-0.20576
More than one			-0.14704
Total number of surviving children			0.04960
Maternal age			-0.03149
Mother's residence (reference: city)			
Rural			-0.08690
Town			-0.00031
Division (reference: Chittagong)			
Dhaka			-0.28836
Khulna			-0.24277
Rajshahi			-0.34681
Mother's religion is Muslim			0.44078
Mother's education (reference: none)			
Lower primary education			-0.18409
Upper primary or more education			-0.66054*
Father's education (reference: none or primary)			
Secondary education			-0.19695
More than secondary education			-0.87197
Father's occupation (business/service/sages is used as reference)			
Agriculture/fishing/domestic			0.25459
Others			0.19619
Year of birth	-0.0671	-0.06955	-0.06910
Age (4 is used as reference)			
Two	1.56691*	1.56528*	1.56160*
Three	1.33993*	1.33968*	1.33928*
Constant	-0.63318	-0.51938	0.12964

Source: Individual records from *1989 Bangladesh Fertility Survey.*
NOTES: Effects estimated by discrete hazard models; multiple births excluded from analysis.
An asterisk (*) indicates that p < 0.05.

TABLE A.7. ESTIMATED EFFECTS OF SEX COMPOSITION OF SURVIVING CHILDREN AND OTHER COVARIATES ON PARITY PROGRESSION: REPUBLIC OF KOREA, WOMEN WHO GAVE BIRTHS OF INITIAL PARITY IN 1975-1984

Year of last birth	Covariates	1st to 2nd	2nd to 3rd	3rd to 4th
1975-1979	Have a surviving son	-0.1665*	-1.0737*	-1.6351*
	Maternal age at last birth	-0.0329*	-0.0544*	-0.0432
	Years of education	0.0154	-0.0411*	-0.0190
	Mother's residence (reference: rural)			
	Metropolitan	-0.0185	-0.3417*	-0.5590*
	Other urban	-0.0272	-0.1275	-0.3041
	Mother's childhood residence (reference: rural)			
	Metro	-0.1214	-0.3212*	-0.1208
	Other urban	-0.0272	-0.1777	-0.0742
	Does not agree with "must have a son" .	-0.2336*	-0.4198*	-0.5238*
1975-1979	Have a surviving son	-0.2063*	-1.7871*	-2.2863*
	Maternal age at last birth	-0.0458*	0.0027	-0.0710
	Years of education	0.0138	-0.0747*	-0.1194*
	Mother's residence (reference: rural)			
	Metropolitan	-0.1817*	-0.4589*	-0.3352
	Other urban	-0.0931	-0.3126*	-0.2354
	Mother's childhood residence (reference: rural)			
	Metropolitan	-0.1765*	-0.3810*	-0.6777
	Other urban	-0.0723	0.0361	-0.1552
	Does not agree with "must have a son" .	-0.3446*	-0.7004*	-0.6023*

Source: Individual records from *1991 National Survey of Fertility and Family Health*.

NOTES: Effects estimated by hazard models; women with multiple births and women whose index child died excluded from analysis.

An asterisk (*) indicates that $p < 0.05$.

TABLE A.8. ESTIMATED EFFECTS OF SEX AND OTHER COVARIATES ON CHILD MORTALITY (BIRTH TO
AGE 5): REPUBLIC OF KOREA, CHILDREN OF BIRTH ORDER 1-6 BORN IN 1971-1988

Covariates	Gross effects model	Intermediate model	Net effects model
Sex is male	0.06495	0.12269	0.13428
Next child is born with interval < 24 months		0.91625*	0.91325*
Number of surviving children			0.17533
Maternal age			-0.09278*
Mother's residence (reference: rural)			
Metropolitan			-0.52857*
Other urban			-0.31371
Mother's years of education			-0.07688*
Year of birth	-0.08253*	-0.07690*	-0.04797*
Constant	2.33304	1.59742	2.29417

Source: Individual records from *1991 National Survey of Fertility and Family Health*.
NOTES: Multiple births excluded from analysis.
An asterisk (*) indicates that $p < 0.05$.

Litho in United Nations, New York
15797—July 1998—6,825
ISBN 92-1-151325-1

United Nations publication
Sales No. E.98.XIII.13
ST/ESA/SER.A/155